ROUTLEDGE LIBRARY EDITIONS: WYNDHAM LEWIS

Volume 2

THE LETTERS OF WYNDHAM LEWIS

THE LETTERS OF WYNDHAM LEWIS

Edited by
W. K. ROSE

LONDON AND NEW YORK

First published in 1963 by Methuen & Co. Ltd

This edition first published in 2022
by Routledge

4 Park Square, Milton Park, Abingdon, Oxon OX14 4RN

and by Routledge
605 Third Avenue, New York, NY 10017

Routledge is an imprint of the Taylor & Francis Group, an informa business

© Text 1962 Mrs Wyndham Lewis
© Editorial Matter 1962 W. K. Rose

All rights reserved. No part of this book may be reprinted or reproduced or utilised in any form or by any electronic, mechanical, or other means, now known or hereafter invented, including photocopying and recording, or in any information storage or retrieval system, without permission in writing from the publishers.

Trademark notice: Product or corporate names may be trademarks or registered trademarks, and are used only for identification and explanation without intent to infringe.

British Library Cataloguing in Publication Data
A catalogue record for this book is available from the British Library

ISBN: 978-1-03-205725-5 (Set)
ISBN: 978-1-00-322366-5 (Set) (ebk)
ISBN: 978-1-03-211886-4 (Volume 2) (hbk)
ISBN: 978-1-03-211892-5 (Volume 2) (pbk)
ISBN: 978-1-00-322204-0 (Volume 2) (ebk)

DOI: 10.4324/9781003222040

Publisher's Note
The publisher has gone to great lengths to ensure the quality of this reprint but points out that some imperfections in the original copies may be apparent.

Disclaimer
The publisher has made every effort to trace copyright holders and would welcome correspondence from those they have been unable to trace.

Mr. Wyndham Lewis as a Tyro, ca. 1920

THE LETTERS OF
WYNDHAM LEWIS

―

EDITED BY
W. K. ROSE

METHUEN & CO LTD
36 Essex Street London WC2

First published 1963
Text © 1962 Mrs Wyndham Lewis
Editorial Matter © 1962 W. K. Rose
Printed in Great Britain by
Western Printing Services Ltd, Bristol
Catalogue No 2/6435/1

Contents

PREFACE   *page* xvii

NOTES ON EDITING   xxv

ACKNOWLEDGEMENTS   xxix

Part I: 1890–1910 Youth and the World of *Tarr*

1890–1900
1. To his Grandmother Stuart, 3
2. To his Mother, 4
3. To his Mother, 4
4. To his Mother, 5
5. To his Mother, 5

1900–1910
6. To his Mother, 6
7. To his Mother, 8
8. To his Mother, 9
9. To his Mother, 10
10. To his Mother, 11
11. To his Mother, 11
12. To his Mother, 12
13. To his Mother, 13
14. To his Mother, 15
15. To his Mother, 16
16. To his Mother, 17
17. To his Mother, 18
18. To his Mother, 19
19. To his Mother, 20
20. To his Mother, 20
21. To his Mother, 21
22. To his Mother, 22
23. To his Mother, 23
24. To his Mother, 24
25. To his Mother, 25
26. To his Mother, 25
27. To his Mother, 26
28. To his Mother, 28
29. To his Mother, 29
30. To his Mother, 30
31. To his Mother, 30
32. To his Mother, 31
33. To his Mother, 32
34. To his Mother, 34
35. To his Mother, 35
36. To his Mother, 36
37. To his Mother, 37
38. To his Mother, 37
39. To his Mother, 38
40. To his Mother, 38
41. To T. Sturge Moore, 39

Part II: 1910–1920 Blasting and Bombardiering

1909–1910
42. To J. B. Pinker, 43
43. To J. B. Pinker, 44
44. To J. B. Pinker, 44

1910
44A. To Augustus John?, 44

1913
45. To Cuthbert Hamilton, 46
46. To Roger Fry, 46
47. The "Round Robin," 47
48. To Clive Bell, 50
49. To P. G. Konody, 52
50. To Clive Bell, 53
51. To Mrs. Percy Harris, 53

1914
52. To the Editor of *The New Age*, 54
53. To the Editor of *The New Age*, 56
54. To the Editor of *The New Age*, 58
55. To Frederick Etchells, 60
56. To Alick Schepeler, 61
57. To the Editor of *The Observer*, 62
58. To Beatrice Hastings, 63
59. To Augustus John, 64

1915
60. To Ezra Pound, 66
61. To Ezra Pound, 68
62. To Alick Schepeler, 68
63. To Kate Lechmere, 69
64. To Augustus John, 70
65. To Augustus John, 72
66. To Mary Borden Turner, 73

1916
67. To Captain Guy Baker, 74
68. To T. Sturge Moore, 75
69. To Harriet Shaw Weaver, 76
70. To his Mother, 78
71. To his Mother, 78
72. To Ezra Pound, 79
73. To his Mother, 81
74. To his Mother, 81
75. To his Mother, 82
76. To his Mother, 83
77. To Ezra Pound, 83
78. To Violet Hunt, 84
79. To Ezra Pound, 85
80. To his Mother, 85

1917
81. To John Quinn, 86
82. To T. Sturge Moore, 87
83. To his Mother, 88
84. To Alick Schepeler, 89
85. To Ezra Pound, 90
86. To Helen Saunders, 91
87. To Alick Schepeler, 91
88. To Ezra Pound, 92
89. To Ezra Pound, 93
90. To Harriet Shaw Weaver, 95
91. To Ezra Pound, 96

1918
92. To Ezra Pound, 97
93. To T. Sturge Moore, 98

94. T. Sturge Moore to Wyndham Lewis, 99
95. To T. Sturge Moore, 100
96. To Rupert Hart-Davis, 101
97. To Herbert Read, 101

1919

98. To Herbert Read, 102
99. To John Quinn, 103
100. To John Rodker, 105
101. To John Rodker, 105
102. To John Rodker, 106
103. To Paul Nash, 107

104. Paul Nash to Wyndham Lewis, 108
105. To Paul Nash, 109
106. To John Quinn, 109
107. To Paul Nash, 113
108. To E. McKnight Kauffer, 115
109. To E. McKnight Kauffer, 115

1920

110. To the Editor of *The Athenaeum*, 116
111. To John Quinn, 119

Part III: 1921-1939 "The Enemy"

1921

112. To Agnes Bedford, 124
113. To John Rodker, 124
114. To Harriet Shaw Weaver, 126
115. To Robert McAlmon, 127
116. To Robert McAlmon, 128
117. To Agnes Bedford, 130

1922

118. To James Joyce, 131
119. To Herbert Read, 131
120. To Robert McAlmon, 132

1923

121. To Osbert Sitwell, 133
122. To T. S. Eliot, 134
123. To T. S. Eliot, 135
124. To T. S. Eliot, 136
125. To T. S. Eliot, 137
126. To T. S. Eliot, 137
127. To R. Cobden-Sanderson, 138

1924

128. To T. S. Eliot, 139
129. To T. S. Eliot, 139
130. To T. S. Eliot, 140
131. To T. S. Eliot, 140
132. To T. S. Eliot, 141
133. To Mrs. Edward Wadsworth, 142
134. To Richard Wyndham, 142
135. To Richard Wyndham, 143
136. To Mrs. O. R. Drey, 145
137. To Richard Wyndham, 146

1925

138. To T. S. Eliot, 147
139. To T. S. Eliot, 149
140. T. S. Eliot to Wyndham Lewis, 150
141. To T. S. Eliot, 152
142. To Charles Whibley, 154

143. To Robert McAlmon, 155
144. To Robert McAlmon, 156
145. To Robert McAlmon, 157
146. To Agnes Bedford, 157
147. To Ezra Pound, 158
148. To Robert McAlmon, 160
149. To Robert McAlmon, 161
150. To O. R. Drey, 162
151. To O. R. Drey, 163
152. To O. R. Drey, 163

1926

153. To T. S. Eliot, 164
154. To Miss I. P. Fassett, 165
155. To Robert McAlmon, 165
156. To Robert McAlmon, 166
157. To C. H. Prentice, 167

1927

158. To the Editor of the *Evening Standard*, 168
159. To C. H. Prentice, 169
160. To T. S. Eliot, 170
161. To John Middleton Murry, 170
162. To Herbert Read, 171
163. To Herbert Read, 172
164. To the Rev. M. C. D'Arcy, S.J., 173
165. To C. H. Prentice, 174

1928

166. To C. H. Prentice, 175
167. To C. H. Prentice, 176
168. To C. H. Prentice, 177
169. To David Garnett, 178
170. To H. G. Wells, 180
171. To W. B. Yeats, 181
172. To W. B. Yeats, 182
173. To A. J. A. Symons, 185

174. To C. H. Prentice, 185
175. To a Tax Inspector, 186

1929

176. To A. J. A. Symons, 187
177. To C. H. Prentice, 187
178. To A. J. A. Symons, 188
179. To Richard Aldington, 188

1930

180. To Richard Aldington, 190
181. Circular Letter from The Arthur Press, 191
182. To A. J. A. Symons, 192
183. To A. J. A. Symons, 193
184. To Augustus John, 193
185. Augustus John to Wyndham Lewis, 194
186. To C. H. Prentice, 195
187. Circular Letter from The Arthur Press, 196
188. To Shane Leslie, 197

1931

189. To C. H. Prentice, 198
190. To the Editor of *Time and Tide*, 199
190. To Naomi Mitchison, 201
190. To C. H. Prentice, 203
190. To Naomi Mitchison, 203

1932

194. To A. J. A. Symons, 204
195. To Roy Campbell, 205
196. To the Editor of *Time and Tide*, 207
197. To Mrs. Winifred Henderson, 209

198. To Desmond Harmsworth, 210
199. To Naomi Mitchison, 211

1933
200. To A. J. A. Symons, 211
201. To Sydney Schiff, 212
202. To Naomi Mitchison, 213
203. To the Editor of *New Britain*, 214
204. To Hugh Gordon Porteus, 215

1934
205. To Naomi Mitchison, 216
206. To Sir Nicholas Waterhouse, 217
207. To Richard Aldington, 217
208. To A. J. A. Symons, 218
209. To Sir Nicholas Waterhouse, 218
210. To Roy Campbell, 219
211. To Desmond Flower, 220
212. To Denys Kilham Roberts, 221
213. To Hugh Gordon Porteus, 222
214. To the Editor of *The Spectator*, 222
215. To the Editor of *The Times Literary Supplement*, 225
216. To Herbert Read, 227
217. To John Grey Murray, 229
218. To the Editor of *The New Statesman and Nation*, 229
219. To the Editor of *The Times Literary Supplement*, 231
220. To Naomi Mitchison, 232

1935
221. To Richard Aldington, 233
222. To Richard Aldington, 234

1936
223. To the Editor of *The Observer*, 235
224. To the Rev. M. C. D'Arcy, S.J., 236
225. To Sir Nicholas Waterhouse, 237
226. To Mrs. Roy Campbell, 238
227. To Oliver Brown, 238
228. To Roy Campbell, 239
229. To G. Wren Howard, 240
230. To Desmond Flower, 242

1937
231. To Oliver Brown, 242
232. To Lovat Dickson, 244
233. To William Gaunt, 245
234. To the Editor of *Twentieth Century Verse*, 245
235. To Douglas Jerrold, 248
236. To P. Van der Kruik, 249

1938
237. T. S. Eliot to Wyndham Lewis, 251
238. To the Editor of the *Daily Telegraph*, 251
239. To the Editor of *The Times*, 253

240. To the Editor of *The Times*, 255
241. To the Editor of *The Times*, 257
242. To Naomi Mitchison, 258
243. To Sir William Rothenstein, 258
244. To R. A. Scott-James, 259

1939

245. To Lord Carlow, 261
246. To Lord Carlow, 262
247. To P. Van der Kruik, 262

Part IV: 1939-1945 Self Condemned

1939

248. To T. J. Honeyman, 263
249. To T. J. Honeyman, 265
250. To Charles D. Abbott, 267
251. To Terence W. L. MacDermot, 268
252. To Mrs. John Rothenstein, 269

1940

253. To Geoffrey Stone, 270
254. To the Editor of *The New Republic*, 271
255. To Charles D. Abbott, 272
256. To Leonard Amster, 273
257. To Geoffrey Stone, 275
258. To James Johnson Sweeney, 276
259. To Terence W. L. MacDermot, 277
260. To Geoffrey Stone, 278
261. To John Slocum, 279
262. To Geoffrey Stone, 281
263. To Geoffrey Stone, 282
264. To Geoffrey Stone, 283

1941

265. To Henry T. Volkening, 284

266. To Geoffrey Stone, 285
267. To Augustus John, 285
268. To Robert Hale, 286
269. To Lorne Pierce, 288
270. To Lorne Pierce, 289
271. To Lorne Pierce, 290
272. To Lorne Pierce, 291
273. To T. Sturge Moore, 291
274. To Lorne Pierce, 293
275. To Robert Hale, 295
276. To Geoffrey Stone, 297
277. To Geoffrey Stone, 297
278. To Naomi Mitchison, 298
279. To Frank Morley, 299
280. To Archibald MacLeish, 302
281. To John Crowe Ransom, 303
282. To Lorne Pierce, 304
283. To Robert Hale, 305
284. To Mrs. Thomas W. Lamont, 307
285. To Leonard W. Brockington, 308
286. To Edmund Wilson, 309
287. To J. M. Dent & Son, Ltd. 310

1942
288. To Geoffrey Stone, 311
289. To R. D. Jameson, 312
290. To Sir Nicholas Waterhouse, 312
291. To Lady Waterhouse, 314
292. To R. D. Jameson, 317
293. To Mrs. Thomas W. Lamont, 317
294. To Leonard W. Brockington, 319
295. To Theodore Spencer, 320
296. To Theodore Spencer, 322
297. To Eric Kennington, 323
298. To Sir Nicholas Waterhouse, 326
299. To Naomi Mitchison, 327
300. To Louis MacNeice, 331
301. To H. G. Wells, 332
302. To David Kahma, 335
303. To Sir Nicholas Waterhouse, 336
304. To James Johnson Sweeney, 337
305. To John Burgess, 337
306. To Augustus John, 338
307. To John Rothenstein, 339
308. To James Johnson Sweeney, 341

1943
309. To Henry Moore, 342
310. To Naomi Mitchison, 344
311. To Lord Carlow, 347
312. To Theodore Spencer, 347
313. To the Rev. J. Stanley Murphy, 348
314. To Eric Kennington, 350
315. To the Rev. J. Stanley Murphy, 352

316. To Naomi Mitchison, 353
317. To Malcolm MacDonald, 356
318. To John Burgess, 357
319. To Malcolm MacDonald, 358
320. To Malcolm MacDonald, 359
321. To Felix Giovanelli, 361
322. To Naomi Mitchison, 361
323. To John Rothenstein, 363
324. To John Burgess, 364
325. To Charles Nagel, 365
326. To Marshall McLuhan, 366
327. To Edgar Preston Richardson, 367
328. To Marshall McLuhan, 369
329. To John Burgess, 370
330. To Felix Giovanelli, 371
331. To Marshall McLuhan, 372
332. To Marshall McLuhan, 373

1944
333. To Mrs. Roy Campbell, 374
334. To Felix Giovanelli, 375
335. To Felix Giovanelli, 375
336. To T. S. Eliot, 377
337. To Pauline Bondy, 377
338. To Gerty T. Cori, 378
339. To Dwight Macdonald, 379
340. To James Johnson Sweeney, 379

1945
341. To T. S. Eliot, 380

342. To Allen Tate, 381
343. To Allen Tate, 382
344. To Augustus John, 383
345. To Allen Tate, 384

Part V: 1945–1956 The Writer and the Absolute

1945
346. To Lady Waterhouse, 389
347. To Sir Nicholas Waterhouse, 389
348. To Allan Gwynne-Jones, 390
349. To Naomi Mitchison, 391
350. To Augustus John, 392

1946
351. To Allen Tate, 393
352. To T. S. Eliot, 394
353. To Ezra Pound, 394
354. To Allen Tate, 395
355. To Ezra Pound, 397
356. To Augustus John, 398
357. To Augustus John, 399
358. To Augustus John, 401
359. To Geoffrey Grigson, 401

1947
360. To Dwight Macdonald, 402
361. To Ezra Pound, 403
362. To Michael Ayrton, 405
363. To James Thrall Soby, 406
364. To Naomi Mitchison, 407
365. To Felix Giovanelli, 408
366. To Mrs. K. H. Webb, 410
367. To Allen Tate, 410
368. To David Kahma, 411
369. To James Thrall Soby, 412
370. To Mrs. Ezra Pound, 413

371. To the Editor of *The Times Literary Supplement*, 415
372. To Mrs. Ezra Pound, 416
373. To David Kahma, 417
374. To David Kahma, 418
375. To Mrs. Ezra Pound, 420
376. To William Gaunt, 420
377. To James Thrall Soby, 421
378. To David Kahma, 422
379. To Felix Giovanelli, 423

1948
380. To Ezra Pound, 424
381. To David Kahma, 425
382. To Geoffrey Stone, 427
383. To Herbert Read, 428
384. To David Kahma, 429
385. To Alan Pryce-Jones, 430
386. To Felix Giovanelli, 431
387. To David Kahma, 434
388. To Ezra Pound, 436
389. To Mrs. Ezra Pound, 437
390. To David Kahma, 438
391. To Ezra Pound, 440
392. To David Kahma, 442
393. To David Kahma, 442
394. To Geoffrey Stone, 445
395. To the Editor of *The Listener*, 447
396. To David Kahma, 448
397. To the Editor of *The Listener*, 450
398. To Geoffrey Stone, 451

399. To the Editor of *The Listener*, 452
400. To Ezra Pound, 453
401. To David Kahma, 454
402. To Augustus John, 455
403. To Kenneth Allott, 456
404. To Geoffrey Stone, 457
405. To Geoffrey Stone, 458
406. To David Low, 459
407. To Keidrych Rhys, 459
408. To David Kahma, 460
409. To D. D. Paige, 461
410. To Felix Giovanelli, 463
411. To Felix Giovanelli, 464
412. To the Rev. Willis Feast, 465
413. To D. D. Paige, 466
414. To Edgar Preston Richardson, 469
415. To David Kahma, 470
416. To D. D. Paige, 471
417. To T. S. Eliot, 473
418. To D. D. Paige, 473
419. To Geoffrey Stone, 474
420. To Felix Giovanelli, 475
421. To David Kahma, 476
422. To Archibald MacLeish, 477

1949

423. To D. D. Paige, 478
424. To Julian Symons, 479
425. To Felix Giovanelli, 479
426. To Augustus John, 480
427. To Gene Nash, 482
428. To David Kahma, 483
429. To James Thrall Soby, 485
430. To J. E. Palmer, 486
431. To Theodore Weiss, 488

432. To the Rev. Willis Feast, 490
433. To the Editor of *Partisan Review*, 491
434. To Hugh Kenner, 493
435. To T. W. Earp, 493
436. To David Kahma, 494
437. To T. S. Eliot, 495
438. To David Kahma, 495
439. To John Rothenstein, 496
440. To Felix Giovanelli, 496
441. To David Kahma, 497
442. To Alfred Barr, Jr., 500
443. To Felix Giovanelli, 500
444. To David Kahma, 501
445. To a London Photographer, 502
446. To Charles Handley-Read, 503
447. To Charles Handley-Read, 504
448. To David Kahma, 505
449. To W. K. Rose, 509
450. To the Rev. Henry Swabey, 509
451. To David Kahma, 510
452. To David Kahma, 513
453. To Augustus John, 513
454. To David Kahma, 515

1950

455. To J. E. Palmer, 516
456. To Sir Nicholas Waterhouse, 517
457. To Ezra Pound, 517
458. To T. S. Eliot, 518
459. T. S. Eliot to Wyndham Lewis, 519
460. To Meyrick Booth, 519
461. To David Kahma, 521

462. To Roy Campbell, 522
463. To Helen Saunders, 522
464. To T. S. Eliot, 523
465. To Sir Nicholas Waterhouse, 524
466. To Meyrick Booth, 525
467. To Herbert Read, 527
468. To J. Alan White, 528
469. To the Editor of *The Listener*, 529
470. To Meyrick Booth, 530
471. To the Editor of *The Listener*, 531
472. To James Laughlin, 532

1951

473. To the Editor of *The Listener*, 532
474. To the Editor of *The Listener*, 533
475. To David Kahma, 534
476. To I. A. Richards, 535
477. To Naomi Mitchison, 536
478. To J. R. Ackerley, 537
479. To Cynthia Thompson, 537
480. To Miss Vanner, 538
481. To Julian Symons, 538
482. To Stephen Spender, 539
483. To D. G. Bridson, 540
484. To Augustus John, 540
485. To David Kahma, 541
486. To Roy Campbell, 542
487. To Sir Louis Fergusson, 543
488. To David Kahma, 544
489. To Mrs. Ezra Pound, 544
490. To D. G. Bridson, 545
491. To I. A. Richards, 546

1952

492. To I. A. Richards, 547
493. To Sir Nicholas Waterhouse, 547
494. To Ezra Pound, 548
495. To David Kahma, 549

1953

496. To Henry Regnery, 549
497. To Stuart Gilbert, 550
498. To T. S. Eliot, 551
499. To Hugh Kenner, 552
500. To T. S. Eliot, 553

1954

501. To Marshall McLuhan, 554
502. To T. S. Eliot, 555
503. To Hugh Kenner, 556
504. To T. S. Eliot, 556
505. To Mrs. Amor Liber, 558
506. To Ezra Pound, 558

1955

507. To J. Alan White, 559
508. To J. Alan White, 559
509. To Sir Nicholas Waterhouse, 560
510. To Ruthven Todd, 560
511. To Frederick Morgan, 561
512. To Hugh Kenner, 562
513. To Russell Kirk, 563
514. To T. S. Eliot, 563

1956

515. To Ezra Pound, 564
516. To Hugh Kenner, 564
517. To Ezra Pound, 565
518. To Michael Ayrton, 566
519. To a London Editor, 567

Illustrations

Mr. Wyndham Lewis as a Tyro, ça. 1920   *frontispiece*
By courtesy of Sir Edward Beddington-Behrens

1. Percy W. Lewis, ca. 1888   *facing page* 1
2. Percy W. Lewis, ca. 1893   4
3. Letter written by Lewis at the age of twelve   5
4. Anne Stuart Lewis   8
5. Lewis at twenty, by Augustus John   9
6. Self-Portrait, ca. 1913   48
7. Lewis in uniform, ca. 1916   80
8. 1920 drawing of Ezra Pound   116
   Cover design for *The Tyro No. 2*, 1922   *page* 125
9. At the summer residence of Mr. and Mrs. Sydney Schiff, ca. 1921   *facing page* 132
10. Lewis in Venice, 1922 (from a snapshot by Miss Nancy Cunard)   133
    Letter from A. J. A. Symons, ca. 1928   *page* 184
11. New Year's Card to David Garnett   *facing page* 188
12. Jacket design for *The Apes of God*, 1930   189
13. Portrait drawing of the Artist's Wife, 1936   240
14. T. S. Eliot pointing to the 1938 portrait of himself (Photograph taken in Durban in 1954)   253
    By courtesy of *the* Natal Mercury
15. Draft of a letter to Sir William Rothenstein, 1942   328
16. Wyndham Lewis at 29 Notting Hill Gate in 1951   544
    Photograph by Douglas Glass

All illustrations not otherwise acknowledged are by courtesy of Mrs. Wyndham Lewis.

Preface

THIS IS NOT the moment or the occasion to "place" Wyndham Lewis. The subject of this book is his letters, not his artistic achievement; and we are too close in time to his controversial career to see it clearly and in perspective. This much it is safe to say: Lewis was one of the most dynamic figures in British art and letters in the first half of this century. One can claim also with a degree of assurance that he left behind numbers of drawings and a few paintings of genuine distinction. His literary work is, I think, even more impressive. Bearing everywhere the stamp of his individuality and powerful intelligence, it includes pieces of fiction and criticism charged with what seems enduring vitality. One can cite a story such as "Cantleman's Spring-mate," essays in *Time and Western Man* and *Men Without Art*, two or three novels: *The Revenge for Love* and *Self Condemned*, perhaps *Tarr*.

If the letters do not invite one to assess Lewis as a creator, they do certainly provoke comment on him as a figure and as a human being: what he stood for, how he acted, who he was. For one thing, we learn from this collection – as we do from his painting, his books, and his journalism – that he took a lively part in the major artistic revolution of our time. Looking back on it, this movement seems to have stood above all for values of form and intellect. We see it coming to a head in the years before World War I and exploding in the 1920's. We see it clearly – indeed, it saw itself – as in reaction to the flabbiness, the bourgeois coziness, the hollow idealism that dominated the arts at the turn of the century. What Braque, Kandinsky, and the rest were doing on the Continent, Lewis was attempting on the less fertile soil of England. Art is form, these new artists said; it requires cerebration and refinement; it must be wrenched from the control of the middle class and the academy and restored to its rightful eminence and exclusiveness.

Literarily, Lewis was on better ground. The verbal arts have always found Britain's climate more hospitable than have the visual. And there occurred at this moment in London an unusually propitious meeting of talents. Ezra Pound, T. S. Eliot, James Joyce (on the Continent but closely allied), T. E. Hulme, Wyndham Lewis: these writers, the best of the avant-garde, saw each other constantly and felt very much in agreement. Lewis called them "The Men of 1914," and but for them we might still be wrestling with the legacy of Chesterton and Barrie, of Gosse and Masefield. Thanks to their declaration of independence – which Lewis helped to draft – English and American writers felt a new pride of craft, greater freedom of expression, and stronger obligations to truth and intelligence. Forty years later we have not come to the end of their impact, any more than Browning was free of Wordsworth and Coleridge.

Lewis did not go on being consciously revolutionary all his life. (For one thing, the new order, *his* new order, very soon established itself.) Like other leaders of the movement, he followed his own lines of development while remaining faithful to most of the attitudes and values of the cause. One of the crucial lines for him, as for Pound, was the political. The revolutionary artist cannot go far before he comes face to face with society; and if the artist is activist (Pound and Lewis as opposed to Eliot and Joyce), society will become politics. Given the premises of the movement – its idea of the aristocracy of art, its hatred of the market-place – it was natural that its originators should lean towards the Right rather than the Left. One need think only of the Byzantine elegance of Yeats's late poems, of Joyce's non-committal naturalism and the bestial Sweeney. Unlike Pound, Lewis felt impelled to change his position when he discovered it to be in conflict with his patriotic and humanitarian instincts. By the end of World War II, he had in fact swung almost to another extreme, at least as far as nationalism was concerned. But the damage to his reputation had been done and it took the pathos of blindness to regain for him a measure of the respect he merited. Now that he is dead and we do not have to feel sorry for him any more, Lewis is again politically suspect among liberals of the intelligentsia. The letters, by affording a longer and closer view, should help to call attention to the complexity of his political development and thereby reduce to size one sensational fragment of it.

Of greater significance, I think, is the fact that we see in Lewis's correspondence the personal validity of his causes. He was so suited to create and expound the new art that one wonders if perhaps he didn't make it all up. (One wonders about the other revolutionaries too. Did Eliot and Joyce, just because they were half-romantic in temper, get more value from the new style than did Lewis, who subscribed to it whole-heartedly?) Let us take two of Lewis's favourite theses: the separation of body and mind and the conflict between the artist-intellectual and the rest of society. The Cartesian notion belongs clearly to the cluster of ideas around the revolution's advocacy of intellect; the artist-*vs.*-society idea was, as I have noted, one of the movement's main themes. The letters show that both were for Lewis not only ideas but deeply rooted attitudes, and that as such they existed long before the new art came into being and they endured long after the tumult was over.

In *The Magic Mountain* Thomas Mann has his humanist mouthpiece say: "'Did you know that the great Plotinus is said to have made the remark that he was ashamed to have a body?'" Herr Settembrini cites this in support of his humanistic idea that "'within the antithesis of body and mind, the body is the evil, the devilish principle, for the body is nature, and nature . . . is evil, mystical and evil.'" He adjures the young Hans Castorp to *despise* the body "'in so far as it sets itself up as the principle of gravity and inertia, when it obstructs the movement toward light . . . in so far as it represents the principle of disease and death, in so far as its specific essence is the essence of perversity, of decay, sensuality, and shame.'" Anyone familiar with Lewis's heroes from his earliest Breton automatons to René Harding of *Self Condemned* (1954), unwilling victim of his own sensuality, will know how to apply Settembrini to Lewis. It has remained for the letters to reveal how natural, or indigenous, the dichotomy was for him. When he is just past twenty we find him giving a little illness a life of its own. He commiserates with his rheumy mother because at the end of winter "there are so few places for a cold to go, that when it finds itself well treated it's apt to stop; I'm sure you spoil it, and make too much fuss with it." Mann's idea that matter independent of mind is "evil" has, because Lewis's genius was essentially comic, become a joke – which does not mean of course that it is less seriously held. It remained a joke, albeit a grim one, when the laugh boomeranged a half-century later. By 1951

Lewis's vision had deteriorated to the point where he was virtually sightless. Forced to renounce his position as art critic for *The Listener*, he composed a valedictory to which his view of the body as nuisance gives an almost unbearable poignancy. One hears the same note in a letter to an admirer who had read the piece: "I am so glad I succeed in making you laugh in unison with me. For it is of course idiotically funny suddenly to be deprived of one's main prop, the EYE."

The point that the men of 1914 made about the artist and society had little to do, I think, with the romantic idea of alienation that gained ground in the 1920's and that flourishes today in certain quarters. It was, rather, an assertion of values, of the superiority of intellect and creativity and their rightful place at the top of the heap. Early on, Lewis erected the figure of the Crowdmaster, and after World War I he developed brilliantly his thesis of the Lion and the Fox, the lion of genius *vs.* the little foxes that eat the grapes. But, again, in the letters we see the attitude forming long before it became a programme and holding to the bitter end. Little Percy Lewis wrote home from school, "Jones is not a bad fellow, but a deuce of a fool. Thorpe sextus is an ass too."

The stance is held through this entire volume. One can call it arrogance, immodesty; but there is no doubt that it found its *raison d'être* in an era. Characterising the common tastes of "the old avant-garde," Dwight Macdonald has recently written that these consisted of "a shared respect for certain standards and an agreement that living art often runs counter to generally accepted ideas."

> It was an elite community, a rather snobbish one, but anyone could join who cared enough about such odd things. Its significance was that it simply refused to compete in the established cultural market places. It made a desperate effort to fence off some area within which the serious artist could still function, to erect again the barriers between the *cognoscenti* and the *ignoscenti* that had been breached by the rise of Masscult. (*Masscult and Midcult*.)

This is what Lewis meant when he declared himself a member of the "Party of Genius," when he wrote in *Blast*, "The moment a man feels or realizes himself as an artist, he ceases to belong to any milieu or time. . . . The Man in the Street and the Gentleman are equally ignored." It is what he *felt* when he addressed his mother from training camp in 1916: "And I don't want to get killed for Mr. Lloyd George, or Mr. Asquith, or for any community except for that elusive but excellent one to which I belong."

Leaving aside questions of literary history, if we ask what the letters tell us about Lewis the man, the answer is "everything." Or at least as much as we shall ever know about this extraordinary human being. Lewis seems not to have kept a journal. If he had, it is unlikely, given his view of life, that it would have been confessional. And it is fair to ask whether a person's letters, when assembled in number, are not anyway as helpful a key to his identity as his diary. In letters we see the writer focused in the mirrors of his correspondents as in a fun-house. Each new mirror gives a new image, a different distortion. At the same time, the writer's distinguishing features (assuming he has some) – his moustache or his red necktie – will always be discernible. The composite at the end may be confusing but it may also be as *true* as the diarist's vision of himself standing naked before a cheval glass in the obscurity of his locked room.

I believe this to be the case even when the letters are not notably intimate or reflective. Lewis's are on occasion – for instance, when as a young man he is writing home to his mother – but more often they are *about something* and written with a definite purpose. Thus he has little to do with what is called "epistolary art." Which is what he meant when he said in an open letter of 1938, "I never write a letter," and went on: "This must be a short letter. You did not expect it to be written in the periods of Gibbon, did you, or in the style of the Authorized Version?" Instead, one gets immediacy, the everyday tone of Lewis's voice – grainy, insistent, sometimes garbled, by turns strident and chuckling, always unaffected. Even when he tries to sound "official," full of serious business, the note will sneak in, deflating the rodomontade of formal communication.

The purposive nature of so many of these letters and the fact that they were often written in heat make them illustrative in another way too. For if they have the effect of belying the joyful, friendly side of Lewis which made him a delightful companion, they do enable us to understand what an energetic and aggressive man he was. At their most violent, the letters give a glimpse of the writer at the mercy of his passion. Thus Wyndham Lewis is revealed in an aspect which our experience normally restricts to persons intimately known.

Another effect of Lewis's functional view of letter-writing is that it gives this collection a quite direct historical interest. Not only do we see Macdonald's "old avant-garde" as represented by Lewis, we catch the reflexion of an entire cultural milieu over a span of sixty years. Except when he was soldiering in World War I and stuck in Canada in World War II, Lewis was in the thick of things and writing to others who were similarly placed about something of immediate concern to himself and often to the artistic community. A glance at the list of correspondents will indicate the remarkable range and eminence of his contacts. Not only did Lewis have to do with most of the important figures of his world, but his relations with some – Augustus John, Ezra Pound, T. S. Eliot – threaded through the whole of his adult life.

To return to the man Wyndham Lewis, as he emerges from this volume: I think the letters tell better than any single book of his what distinguished him. Here we see, with all his imperfections on, the exceptional person – exceptional in his vitality, in his gifts of intellect and imagination, in his individuality. The qualities are so notable that one need not even try to ignore the imperfections.

Chief among these, by far I feel, was Lewis's persecution mania. Covering such a long period, the letters provide a definitive history of the rise and fall of the affliction. They do not, I think, make a reader more charitable towards it; at times its destructiveness is all too apparent. Thanks to its broad and detailed view, the collection does, nevertheless, offer support to the truism that those who believe themselves sinned against often are. Better, the disorder makes for a kind of subplot. We observe the seeding of it (abandonment by father, etc.), watch it develop till it becomes a trait of character. Then towards the end, noting the subject's suffering in his American exile and his physical trials, we see the trouble subside. Lewis *vieux* is not less discriminating or satirical than he ever was, but he is less at the mercy of anger and bitterness, more in tune with the good spirits and humanity that were instinctive to him.

It goes without saying that feelings of persecution entered Lewis's attitudes, coloured his character. They did not, I believe, support the whole structure of his individuality nor even touch parts of it. To say in what that individuality consisted is as difficult and chancy as it would be with any original human being. There is a distinguishing bumptiousness about Lewis. He presents an image by turns lowering and hearty, but always energized. One sees him leading a company to the brink of a volcano and then, seeming as surprised as they to be there, burst out laughing. At the same time there are sympathy, urbanity (a mental, not social, sophistication), impatience with cant; and over all, a feeling of the wonder and fatality of the world such as most great men have had. No small sample can show the whole Wyndham Lewis. But I think of a letter of 1907 wherein he gives a comic account of what must have been a disturbing imbroglio in Paris. A crippled American friend jealously flourishes a revolver against the appearance of a known rival. Young Lewis tries to calm him. "The man arrived, was shot, and I was arrested." That is Wyndham Lewis. Writing to an American in 1941 he wants to give a sense of the unreality of Toronto in war-time. He felt it the other day "when a tank moved down the street and as it was abreast a group of people, myself among them, waiting to cross the road, it let fly at a range of fifteen feet with a quite sizeable little cannon it had hidden in its flank. Its red flash darted at us, there was a deafening roar, the tank stopped and rocked." Then "the monster rumbled on, firing as it went at shoppers. No one took the slightest notice." The personality that these sentences bespeak has placed its thumbprint on every page of this collection. It is a feature of Lewis's power that through all his changes of mind, of place, of fortune, of physical condition (and distorted by the multitudinous reflexions of his correspondents), he remained so vitally himself.

The letters express in full measure Lewis's vitality, as in their robust, idiomatic language they give notice of his literary gifts. Human energy radiates from him in awesome quantities. One feels it especially in the way he is always committing himself. Reading Lewis's letters is like reading Shaw's prefaces. There are few new ideas but thousands of fresh opinions. Lewis had hardly digested a fact before he was taking a position on it – whether it was a political issue or a horse race or a new painter. And if his chief cause was Number One, he had enough gusto to devote himself to an interminable succession of others: human and ideological, selfish and generous, material and aesthetic. It is this unflagging awareness and this impulse towards engagement that, I believe, most distinguish Wyndham Lewis's letters (as they do the letters of Pound and D. H. Lawrence). Such qualities go far towards producing an indelible image in a house of mirrors.

W. K. ROSE
Poughkeepsie, New York

Notes on Editing

THE chief problem in making this book has been that of selection. Three or four times the number of letters included were available. No one criterion operated of course in determining inclusions and exclusions, but after a time a kind of sliding scale of values emerged. According to this, liveliness took first priority, topical interest second, and biographical informativeness third. Usually at least two of the three were found together; if a letter held only topical *or* biographical interest it was, except in rare cases, dropped. Some letters, in themselves perhaps less interesting than ones that were omitted, were included for the sake of the coherence or shape of the collection.

Deletion has been an important aspect of the problem of selection. Clearly, the shorter the letters the greater the number of them that could be fitted into a book of manageable size. After much deliberation, it seemed the best policy to pursue a fairly ruthless course of deletion. Purists will find this practice inexcusable. If asked to read all the deleted passages, they might feel more tolerant. Because Lewis's letters were communicative acts and not exercises in style or form, the gold is all mixed in with the dross. In a letter to a publisher, striking observations on the current scene might follow three pages of notes for proof revisions. An itemized appreciation of a CARE parcel might lead to a passage of personal revelation. It seemed best to leave in enough dross to give the flavour and the look of Lewis's letters, and to exclude the rest in order to allow as much room as possible for gold. In many cases the dross was simply repeated material. For example, when Lewis was writing from America to friends at home, he would often go over the same series of events in several letters; yet these letters will also contain dissimilar paragraphs quite worth printing. Finally, in this respect, it ought to be said that very little material was excised because it was scandalous.

To avoid complexities, three dots (. . .) have been used to indicate deletions of whatever length. A fourth dot indicates a period. In the rare places where Lewis himself used dots, these have been reproduced without spaces (...). A short line (———) indicates the omission of a proper name. Names have been omitted where they might cause embarrassment or invite libel action.

An unusual feature of the book is that many letters have been taken from holograph drafts or typed carbons rather than from the posted copies. Where this is so, a dagger (†) has been placed after the name of the recipient. The reason for not always using posted copies is that in many cases it would have been impossible or impracticable. And comparison with posted copies has revealed that Lewis was usually careful to correct and emend carbons or originals to correspond with the sent versions of letters. Lewis left among his papers vast numbers of drafts and carbons of letters, as well as some posted copies which had, for one reason or another, come back to him. This mass of material (now in The Cornell University Library) was made available in the preliminary stages of the editor's work, and thus it became the core of the book.

Lewis was an inaccurate speller and an eccentric punctuator. In typed letters, however, it is not always possible to tell whether an error or inconsistency is his or the typist's. Therefore I have felt some leeway in regularising details. The idea has been to preserve enough of Lewis's individual way of doing things so that he will come through as himself (as he, in his letters to Pound's editor, insisted Pound should come through). Thus, for example, his custom of omitting apostrophes in possessives has been honoured in the printed text.

Lewis's handwriting was highly personal and at some periods of his life nearly illegible. (I do not refer to his writing after his blindness, which can be read only by those who were working with him.) Fortunately, Mrs. Lewis, who typed for her husband for many years, has been able to decipher most obscurities. Where reading proved impossible, the difficulty is indicated so: [words].

The presence of brackets around the sender's address or the date indicates that the information has been supplied by the editor. To save space, the sender's address has been abbreviated to one line after its first use. Lewis, of course, normally signed his letters. He didn't normally sign the copies he kept: hence the letters without a signature in this book.

In annotating, no attempt has been made to point out every sentence in the letters that relates to something in Lewis's published writing. The notes are meant chiefly to supply a context and to prevent mystification.

Acknowledgements

For the loan of letters, and in many cases helpful information regarding them, I am deeply indebted to the following persons: Professor Charles D. Abbott, Michael Ayrton, Miss Iris Barry, F. N. Beaufort-Palmer (for letters to Alick Schepeler), Miss Agnes Bedford, D. G. Bridson, Mrs. Roy Campbell, Messrs. Chatto and Windus (for letters to C. H. Prentice), the Reverend M. C. D'Arcy, S.J.; O. R. Drey and the late Mrs. Drey, Desmond Flower, David Garnett, William Gaunt, Mr. and Mrs. Felix Giovanelli, Charles Handley-Read, Lord Harmsworth, Rupert Hart-Davis, David Kahma, Hugh Kenner, Mrs. Naomi Mitchison, Miss Riette Sturge Moore and Mrs. Ursula Bridge (for letters to T. Sturge Moore), the Reverend J. Stanley Murphy, Professor Norman Holmes Pearson (for letters to Robert McAlmon), Hugh Gordon Porteus, Mr. and Mrs. Ezra Pound, Sir Herbert Read, Mrs. John Rodker, Geoffrey Stone, James Johnson Sweeney, Miss Harriet Shaw Weaver, J. Alan White. For the loan of letters, for interviews, and especially for permission to print certain letters of his to Lewis I am especially grateful to T. S. Eliot.

I am also indebted to the following libraries for the use of letters: The Lockwood Memorial Library of the University of Buffalo (for letters to A. J. A. Symons and inscriptions to Lord Carlow), the University of Illinois Library (for letters to H. G. Wells), the John Quinn Collection and the Berg Collection of The New York Public Library (for letters to John Quinn and J. B. Pinker), The Pierpont Morgan Library (for letters to E. McKnight Kauffer). I wish to thank the City Art Gallery, Manchester, for reproducing their drawing of Ezra Pound.

I am grateful to the late Augustus John, O.M., Miss Riette Sturge Moore, the late Mrs. Paul Nash, and Julian Symons, for permission to print letters to Lewis from Mr. John, T. Sturge Moore, Paul Nash, and A. J. A. Symons.

A great many persons have contributed to my knowledge of Lewis and especially of his correspondence. Others have helped to lead me to the acquisition of letters. Knowing, and regretting, that this roster is incomplete, I am nevertheless pleased to list the following names: Walter Allen, Leonard Amster, Mrs. R. Kirk Askew, Clive Bell, Sir Arthur Bliss, Mrs. Neville Braybrooke, Leonard W. Brockington, the Marchioness of Cholmondely, Miss Nancy Cunard, Duncan Grant, Allan Gwynne-Jones, the late Augustus John, O.M., Lord Kennet of the Dene, N. C. Kittermaster (Librarian, Rugby School), Thomas S. Lamont, Miss Kate Lechmere, Professor Harry Levin, Dwight Macdonald, Archibald MacLeish, Philip Mairet, John Palmer, Dr. Lorne Pierce, Omar S. Pound, I. A. Richards, Sir John Rothenstein, Miss Helen Saunders, the late Mrs. Violet Schiff, the late R. A. Scott-James, John J. Slocum, Lady Spears (Mary Borden Turner), the Reverend Henry Swabey, Mr. and Mrs. Otto Theis, R. M. Thorp, Henry Volkening, Dame Rebecca West, Miss Antonia White, R. H. Wilenski, Edmund Wilson, Mrs. Violet Wyndham.

For assistance in research and preparation of the text, I wish to thank Professors Pamela Askew, Charles Burkhart, Elizabeth Adams Daniels, and James Early; Miss Heather Gieves, Mrs. Robert Greacen (Patricia Hutchins), Miss Susan Knox, Mrs. Arthur Mizener, and Grayson Trapnell. I am also indebted to Martin Butlin and his staff at the library of The Tate Gallery, the staff of the Poetry Room at The Lockwood Memorial Library, and the staff of The Rare Book Room of The Cornell University Library; The British Museum, the library of The Victoria and Albert Museum, The Yale University Library, and The New York Public Library. The excellent bibliographies in Geoffrey Wagner's *Wyndham Lewis* must be mentioned here too.

The greater part of this book has been composed on the premises of the Vassar College Library. I have appreciated very much the cheerful co-operation of its staff. The names of all those who have shown interest and kindness would make a list of cumbersome length. I shall single out only the invaluable Reta Ridings.

The final draft of this book was typed in its entirety by Miss Eleanor Rogers. Her skill and good nature have earned my lasting gratitude.

There must always be someone "without whom this book...." The services of Miss Agnes Bedford have been such as to merit her being considered a co-editor. Her devotion to this work and her readiness to enjoy it have made a large task pleasurable as well as possible.

W. K. ROSE
Poughkeepsie, New York

1. Percy W. Lewis, ca. 1888

PART I. 1890–1910

Youth and the World of *Tarr*

Percy Wyndham Lewis was born November 18th, 1882, on his father's yacht, the "Wanda," then tied up at Amherst, Nova Scotia. His father, Charles E. Lewis, belonged to a well-to-do upstate New York family which had settled in the town of Nunda in Livingston County. He attended West Point for a year and then, in 1862, joined the 1st New York Dragoons and went off to fight with General Sheridan. But after the Civil War, while others of his family prospered as lawyers and merchants, Charles Lewis seems to have been without a career, leading instead the life of transatlantic sportsman and dilettante. Writing was among his avocations. He had several accounts of his war experience privately printed and was more successful with two books of belles-lettres. He was evidently still dependent on family income when he married Anne Stuart, an English girl of Scotch-Irish descent, and they produced two children, the first of whom died in infancy.

During the early years of their marriage, Charles and Anne Lewis lived on both sides of the Atlantic. Then around 1893 the couple separated, and mother and son began to make a life together in a succession of London suburbs. During Percy's school years, Charles saw his son occasionally, corresponded with him, and contributed financially to his support. Later, as the boy became a young man, their contacts – and the cheques – dwindled. The elder Lewis lived through World War I, but it is doubtful that he and his son met more than a few times after 1900.

Mrs. Lewis, as the letters show, bore almost alone the burden of Percy's upbringing and later of his support. Besides the boy, there were in her ménage, for a time, his grandmother, and for a long period, a servant named Tompkins. The little family moved about a good deal, eventually settling in London (Highgate and Hampstead) and after in the suburb of Ealing. At first they could depend – though uneasily – on help from "C.E.L." and his family. Later, to make ends meet, Mrs. Lewis, a woman of artistic interests, engaged in small business ventures. Thus, to the time of her death in 1920, she managed to maintain her household, as well as to help her son during school and after.

Percy was educated in a series of private schools, sometimes as boarder, sometimes as day pupil. He seems never to have stayed long at one school and not to have distinguished himself at any. This career culminated at Rugby, where his place was twenty-sixth in a class of twenty-six and which he left when he was sixteen.

Not until he attended the Slade School of Art (1898–1901) were Lewis's talents noted and did he begin to cut a figure. There, in the reign of Brown, Tonks, and Steer, he made his mark as a draughtsman – and as a budding writer (he was known as "Lewis the poet"). In the latter capacity he fell in, about this time, with a group of older men variously occupied at the British Museum. Among them T. Sturge Moore, R. A. Streatfield, and Laurence Binyon were impressed by the young artist's intellectual power; their advice and encouragement gave the impetus to his literary growth that had been lacking before. On the painting side, Lewis's chief friend among his elders seems to have been William Rothenstein.

Not long after leaving the Slade, Lewis went to the Continent, where he was to spend most of the next eight years. He stayed for short periods in Holland, in Munich, in Madrid; he spent summers in Brittany, travelled in Spain, and returned now and then to London. But from 1902 to 1909 he was mostly in Paris – drawing and painting, attending occasional lectures, and having his fill of the pre-war vie de bohême. Contemporaries recall him as a romantic figure in Montparnasse and the Quartier Latin, caped in black with a large black hat, carrying slim, soft-leather-bound books of poetry, their coloured silk markers fluttering. This was the world he was to memorialise in Tarr, and there are glints of Percy W. Lewis – café intellectual, spendthrift Don Juan, aspirant to Parnassus – in several of the book's male characters.

Bertha Lunken, of the same novel, is most likely Lewis's own Ida, in caricature. As the letters tell, Lewis took up casually enough with Ida, an attractive German girl living in Paris; but the relationship soon became complicated. What had begun as a lark ended – after *progressing through many places and seasons – as a searing emotional experience for both. Lewis's association with Augustus John was of a brighter texture. The two men had known one another in London; in Paris between 1903 and 1908 they were much together. There were frictions: Lewis, poor and uncelebrated, could not always support the company of his older friend, already an established artist and prince of bohemia. But there was for both men the pleasure of lively intercourse, and for Lewis – as he developed his own style in drawing and writing – the delight of John's admiration.*

Through these years of trial Mrs. Lewis stood by in England offering constant devotion and financial aid. Her tolerance of her son's vagaries, her susceptibility to his importuning bespeak the typical fond mother. Her continuing faith in his talent and her insight into his temperament were more remarkable. They explain the candour, and perhaps the affection, we find in the letters this unusual youth wrote to her.

1. *To his Grandmother Stuart* [ca. 1890]

   Ravenstone

dear Grannie
 I send my
love to Mother
and you and I
will be glad
when you come
  [p. 2]
home How do you
like Bournemouth?
and how do you
like the rumbling
of the sea? I hoPe
you are quite
well Mrs Char
  [p. 3]
-lwood sends
two kisses to mother

and you. Mrs.
Grummer sends
love . Good
bye from
your loving little
 [p. 4]
Grandson
    PERCY

2. *To his Mother*   County School, Bedford.[1]
                                                          [1894]
My dear Mother.

    I hope you are quite well. I am having a very good time indeed. I am in the third form, I hope I shall soon be in the fourth. I got an exit to go in the town yesterday and fooled about the whole afternoon, while Marshall secundus and Madame Mildred (Waldram) went up the river in a boat (Farrar wont let me, I can't swim). Marshall is a nice chap, but a deuce of a prig. Waldram is all right. Micaule or Butcher is head prefect. He is not the oldest chap in the school only being about 18. Jones is not a bad fellow, but a deuce of a fool. Thorpe sextus is an ass too. Mansell Jones is a fine fellow. So's Boby Clarke, a chap of about sixteen, I work with. I say, there are a lot of big fellows in our form. It is nearly eleven, and I must say (the fellows will talk) Goodbye.

                                       Your very loving son,
                                                             P. LEWIS

. . .

3. *To his Mother*   Castle Hill School, Ealing W.
                                                              18th January 1895.
My dear Mother.

    I arrived here safely, at 8 o'clock on Wednesday evening. I am getting on very well with my wood-carving. Mr. Morgan has

---

[1] Bedford County School changed its name to Elstow school in 1907; it closed in 1916. L. entered in September 1894 but was gone by January 1895.

2. Percy W. Lewis, ca. 1893

CASTLE HILL SCHOOL, EALING. W.

18th January 1895.

My dear Mother.

I arrived here safely, at 8 o'clock on Wednesday evening. I am getting on very well with my woodcarving

3. Letter written by Lewis at the age of twelve

given me permission to practice in the playground shed. Hoping you are quite well, and with much love,

> I remain,
>> Your loving son,
>>> PERCY W. LEWIS

4. *To his Mother*   Rugby School,
G. Stallard Esq.[1]
[March 1897]

My dear mother. Please excuse pencil. I have no ink, except a little at the bottom of my ink well. I shall get some this afternoon. I am awfully sorry I did not write before, but I have had very busy times. Football has stopped, and brookjumping has begun. If you dont mind I wont write quite so often now, as I have lots of things to do. Will write every 5 days. If I dont write, it "*wont be my fault*". You must come to the Sports, wont you, eh? I have got in a fairly high running set. I have "played for the house" 2 or 3 times (4) this term in footer. We have lectures here sometimes instead of drawing.

Nansen[2] came the other day I suppose you saw the proceedings in the papers. I was there. Will write again soon. Excuse not writing before.—

Have not yet had any news from Pops. Hope I shall soon. Will send you the letter and money directly it comes.

> I remain,
>> Your loving son,
>>> P. W. LEWIS

I borrowed ink to address envelope.

5. *To his Mother*   Rugby School
[ca. 1898]

My dear Mother.

I am awfully sorry I did not write before. My hands have been full. I [?] house has been in continual excitement. First a fellow

---

[1] L. was in Stallard's house, now known as Tudor House.
[2] Nansen visited Rugby March 3rd, 1897, and lectured on his expedition to the North Pole.

got a "sixth licking" (stripes from every sixth in the house,) the second that has taken place since the founding of the house. A sixth (form boy) has been bunked (expelled) for stealing out of the shop in the town. The heats for the sports have been run and many other things. The "sports" come off Friday and Saturday of this week, lasting two days. Do come! I'll show you round the museums, gallery, etc. and you can see me lose the 100 yards again.

Will write again soon.
I enclose a letter from C. E. L. and 'ooff.
I remain, Your loving son, with much love to you and Gran,

PERCY LEWIS

6. *To his Mother* 92 Calle Mayor Tercero. c/o Mrs. Briggs.
[Madrid][1]
[1902?]

Chere Maman. . . . I've been in bed for a day or so with a bad cold (which apparently met me at the station 10 days ago) and have been feeling rather exhausted on account of it; had a sore throat and cough for the last few days, which have happily departed. Doctor, (friend of Miss Briggs,) chanced to visit her yesterday, while she was talking to me: he said he thought I'd had a little ulcer in throat, gone now. Everyone in Madrid, Queen included with a chamberlain or two, have ulcerated throats and colds. It's not very cold here, but for the last two days it's been very grey and rainy. I don't think I shall stay in Madrid in December or January or February.

Gore and I have got a Studio for which we pay about 4/6 a week each: we bought some things for it, which we can sell again for a half I suppose when we leave.

For an English pound one gets 33 pesetas: 33 or more or less – varies.

We paid 15 pesetas for a good coke stove.
    8 pesetas for the pipe.
    5 pesetas for two chairs.
    3 or 4 pesetas for a sort of table.

[1] L. was travelling and working in Spain with his friend the artist Spencer Gore (1878–1914).

1½ pesetas for a deal box.
30 pesetas for a carpet (all floors are stone here;)

I think that was very cheap furnishing. We wanted to know about models etc. and wanted to get a studio and not waste time, so Mrs. Briggs said she knew of a man that would help us: he's been as quick as a Spaniard could be and got us settled in our studio, bought our furniture cheap, and got us any amount of models, and been very helpful: we'll have to pay him about 50 pesetas between us I expect, to be generous.

Models are cheap here: three pesetas for three hours: so if we spend 3 pesetas each day we'll have no lack of work: we go to bed at 10 and get up at 8 without the least variety, and spend no money outside, as there's nothing worth spending it on! . . .

Sunday

Since writing the above several days have elapsed. . . .

I'm feeling rather ill again today, and think I have caught a fresh cold, (a slight one:) I still have the old one: Gore's not well, either.

I suppose I must stay here another month, and see the run of the Studio out, but dare not longer. I think Madrid in the really winter time (for them) must be an extremely dangerous place, and one's life would be crowded with precautions and not worth living . . . . The Prado is a very wonderful place: we got shown yesterday the room of Goya drawings:

We also visited an artist, (ridiculous person) and to do so hired a conveyance: I've never had a more exciting twenty minutes than that cab drive: we had our side-step smashed by a carriage, and stopped the traffic several times, quarrelled with everybody; were turned out of main street for frightening a mule-team and using bad language: dived into dark narrow lane, and finding large cart facing us, turned round, having first driven on to pavement, and nearly into shop-window: we reached the artist at last, and found him, as I said, a ridiculous person.

I rather think that I should like to go to Italy soon,[1] before returning to England . . . .

With love etc.
I am,
PERCY W. LEWIS

[1] L. did not get to Italy till many years later.

7. *To his Mother*   41 Rue Denfert Rochereau.
chez Madame Picnot
Paris.
[ca. 1903]

Chère Maman. I've got here safely enough, in my usual state; I got the 2.20 from London, but the cabman insisted on having 6/2. At first I went to a cabman in the rank, and he asked 5/–; so I left him as a blageur; but it appears that it is without the 4 mile radius, and it is 1/– a mile. . . .

But please write me letters chez Schelfhout each week as I want to hear from you; if you dont write nice letters to me as well, I wont write any news to you.

I am very pleased with Paris, more than formerly, – and intend to stay my two months: but I dont think that I shall stay chez Schelfhout any longer than I can help: two or three weeks: I arrived in Paris with 12 francs: the people at the Bureau de Change having cheated me of a shilling or two: and the porter and cabman (3 francs) being paid, I spent the rest in getting a dinner, and giving Lou Lou some coffee and bread, which he sorely needed, and the luxury of a cigarette: I have now 1 franc 3 pence.

The Schelfhouts have no people staying with them and look all of them ill and unshaved; still.

Two spaniards are coming *perhaps* on the first of January; none of the Schelfhouts have got any work: so it isn't lively: They pawned something this morning, I suppose to get my dinner with: I borrowed a franc or two, and cant pay back now, as they would suspect that I knew of their pawnings. . . .

On my way to the Cooks Agency, I visited Walter; and he, having just returned from Paris, was in a position to give advice, he said that restaurants like Roche[1] were very numerous in Paris, but cheaper; and that studios were very cheap; – I think that the best and cheapest way of living, and, as he said, the *only way* in Paris, is that; I should suppose for long a pension here would be as bad as one in London: or nearly as bad as living at home. – But I dont see for the moment how I can leave a destitute family, who look on me as a godsend: Well, when I have looked about a bit, and got to know people, I will report to you.

[1] A London restaurant popular with artists and writers.

4. Anne Stuart Lewis

5. Lewis at twenty, by Augustus John

I have a letter from Walter to Miss Bruce[1] who knows heaps of people, and may be very useful. . . .

I am yours
P. W. LEWIS

8. *To his Mother* [Paris]
[ca. 1903]

Chère Maman. . . .

The old man told me a Balzac-like story of his visit to M. Faure[2] the singer and his old master a week or so ago; how he had not seen him for thirty years, and at first did not recognise him: the coldness of his reception (he could hardly have expected anything else,) and, how, after recounting his misfortunes and asking for help, which of course had no effect, he said in despair, "Well, to tell you the truth we have nothing to eat; can you lend me 5 francs?" M. Faure threw up his hands and said "C'est impossible, monsieur;" it was told me alternatively with great wit and with tears in his eyes – but I'm afraid you or I would have done the same as M. Faure? – A precedent is a bad thing. Speaking of precedents, even between those nearly related, I think we might get something out of C. E. L. by a vigorous letter: or anyway, a Good one to Uncle Alb:[3] I dont suggest this as a thing I am very particular about . . . .

I met Gatty,[4] who was at the Slade: he has a studio here, a very good one; and has models more or less in abundance; he only has £3 a week; the Studios here I have discovered are extremely cheap; you can get a studio here for £28 a year that would be £50 or £60 in London. Italian models here are very cheap, – you can often arrange with them for a napoleon a week: – the french models a franc an hour; – eating for me would be about the same as London; if one likes, one can live much cheaper, I suppose Walter is not so particular as I am. – The concierge in Paris

---

[1] Kathleen Bruce (1878–1947) studied sculpture in Paris from 1901 to 1903. Later she exhibited as Kathleen Scott, having married the explorer Scott in 1908. In 1922, nine years after Scott's death, she married Edward Hilton Young, later Baron Kennet, of the Dene.

[2] Probably J.-B. Faure (1830–1914).

[3] Albert Lewis, brother of C. E.

[4] David Ivor Vaughan Gatty (d. 1947) was at the Slade 1899–1903.

appears to be a most tyrannous person, and would object, even if the landlord didn't, to a room being used as a studio . . . .

I visited Miss Bruce, – alone in a room without any light but the fire, which happily hid my embarrassment: – I shall probably see her again soon: she plied me with tea, and I cross-examined her about the likelihood of getting a studio and a Mistress, and the price of cigarettes: – an extremely agreeable young person, but hardly enough clothes on for the time of the year . . . .

Give Tom[1] [?] any affectionate epithet that you can remember that I was in the habit of using –

> I am your devoted piccaninnie
> PIERCE-EYE THE LEWIS

9. *To his Mother* [Paris]
[ca. 1903]

Chere Maman. . . .

Now Miss Bruce has kindly found me a studio next to her own; I dont much relish that aspect of it, but it is cheap, already furnished, and light enough, – and, more important, to be let only for a month or two, and not a year. – It is very difficult here, except in the case of a chance let, like this, – to get a studio for less than a year . . . .

I'm installing myself there today, and begin a series of paintings and drawings of the Creation of the World:[2] I have been busy trying drawings (caricatures) for the Paris papers, which certainly seem very successful in themselves, but the french joke is the difficulty: I may send you some to give to an agent in London.

At this studio there is a femme de menage that does your room any morning for trente centimes: that, four times a week would be 1/– which is cheap also. . . .

There is a magnificent concierge here, – enfin, an epical concierge, and Mrs. Schelfhout has terrible tussles with her, "Je m'en fiche" – "Et moi, je m'en fiche, madame" – "vieille sale tête," – "bête", and so on. – There is a law here that when furniture (hired furniture) enters a house, the concierge has to

---

[1] Tompkins, the family retainer.
[2] L. showed a picture titled "Creation" at the exhibition of the Allied Artists' Association at the Albert Hall in July 1912 and at the Brighton Exhibition in 1913.

sign a paper; this particular concierge refuses to (since the Schelfhouts so far have bestowed no pourboire upon her) – also she has taken to keeping my letters, that is ended now, I think. . . .

I am sending you a little picture of Poverty leaving the house of the Schelfhouts. I shall also include a caricature of the concierge.

I am your devoted child,
PERCY W. LEWIS

10. *To his Mother*   41 Rue Dufret Rodnerer. [?]
[Paris]
[ca. 1903]

Chere Maman. . . .

. . . I went to the Messe de minuit 3 days ago with Miss Bruce, a french painter, a Member of Parliament, and an Irish girl: we had supper after at the Frenchman's studio, and under the stress of champagne the Member of Parliament told me the most ludicrous stories, and I went to bed in a very good humour. – . . . I'm working very hard, and trying to make my stay here fruitful. – I am rather worried because I dont know whether I am being watched or whether I am becoming a monomaniac, – I suppose the latter. . . .

I am,
Yours ever,
P. W. LEWIS

11. *To his Mother*   90 Rue d'Assas.
[Paris]
[ca. 1904]

Chere Maman.

. . . – I wrote asking you for some shirts; if you haven't yet dispatched them, could you make up in one packet the shirts and the book of John's torn-up drawings, – the album, you know, with the drawings I found and stuck together: also place among them the separate drawing of an old man's head that John did at Lullworth and gave to me; – but only send the drawings if you think it's quite safe, as I shouldn't like to lose them: Make a very firm package. – I suppose they would not be regarded as works of art, even if the Customs discovered them among the shirts – il doit mystifier les pauvres gens. I lapse into french of course quite by mistake. . . . I went to see Miss John[1] a couple of days ago, and she tells me John is going to camp on Dartmoor, with a numerous retinue, or a formidable staff, – or a not inconsiderable suite, – or any polite phrase that occurs to you that might include his patriarchal menage. – Before I forget it, I have a curious sombre tint between two teeth, and a young lady tells me if I dont go to a dentist that they will decay; it is the two centre teeth, and where they join there is a little sort of semicircle of black, [sketch of teeth] not black but grey. What shall be done about it? . . .

A most damnable deluge, making the atmosphere extremely damp, has stopped me from working from the nude today, as my stove isn't in order, and the studio is not a warm one: so I have nothing to thank the weather for, today. – Will write in a day or so: take care of your cold, s'il fait mauvais tempts; with love.

Yours ever,
PERCY W. L.

12. *To his Mother* [Paris]
[ca. 1904]

Chere Maman. . . . On the way to Dieppe shall I stay at Rouen for a night? I dont think however that I want to see Rouen so much as all that. – It was very very good of you to send me the money, and I quite realise your warnings, and feel myself that I have a veritable campaign in the autumn, – all the more need for a pleasant healthy summer; I'm only sorry that you must stay there the whole time; but p'raps you can come over to Dieppe for a bit. . . .

. . . I'm going seriously to *work out* say 10 or 20 compositions for Milton, so that I shall have something, as a basis to show to a serious publisher: – I hope to do several paintings sufficiently good to hook a dealer, – but anyhow, I'm sure that my campaign will succeed in one way or another.

One thing, – for heavens sake dont worry about yourself and become melancholy, – although you have reason enough, with your son and other things, – and if anything bothers you write

---

[1] The painter Gwen John (1876–1939), sister of Augustus.

and tell me. I think at your age you must know that whatever life one leads one has assez des chagrins, and all modes of life are almost equally wearing, morally; – and as far as the physical fatigue goes, you must face it intelligently and do just as little as ever you can, – or rather as little fatiguing things as possible, and then work is really rather a relief than not. – Its really much better than giving music lessons, or running a boarding house or teaching languages, – to be in trade of any sort. – I'm sure you must be lonely; – but then that is better than having unsympathetic companions, – and when I get back we can manage something to make the time pleasanter.

Send by saturday morning if you possibly can, and if you get this in time. With love

I am yours ever
PERCY W. LEWIS

P.S. the little girl didn't turn up again, so I couldn't do the drawing for Eva, – I'm afraid most of my drawings are too serious or not serious enough. I heard from John yesterday; he is at Dartmoor.

13. *To his Mother* [Postmarked "Haarlem, 7 Oct. 1904".]
send letters to Poste Restante.
Chere Maman.

Next Wednesday or Thursday my month's up here, and home I come: I have given up copying Hals, and that was the only thing to keep me here: I've done lots of work; and if I can get in 2 or 3 weeks work before the "New English"[1] in London I shall be very glad.

There is alas, a definite reason for my returning: there is a girl here, the daughter of the house, that is very attractive: she's very stupid, uninteresting and not in the least exciting for me; but being exiled from the "fair," I have taken certain opportunities to bestow a kiss upon her blanched brow, and may perhaps have stroked her bosom; but of course I have done nothing more and didn't intend to, as there are too many difficulties and objections in such a case: Well, the mama and papa seem to have noticed these mild attentions. – As I told you not to send my letters here you can imagine that I didn't put very much trust in my hostess:

[1] L. showed one picture – "Study of a Girl's Head" – at the New English Art Club exhibition of 1904.

the old man, as far as that goes, is very entertaining, but I don't expect he's much better than the woman. Well, lately, papa has asked a great many questions about you, (I had mentioned the fact that I had a mother,) and Mama informed me a week ago that "of course the furniture would go to her dear little Lesbie," at which I scream with laughter, for its the sort of remark Mama's make in Dickens' books, but I thought were too sophisticated to do so in actual life. Papa also, when he's posing for me, talks about marriage etc., also I hear the family having loud disputes very often (one an hour ago; and when I enquired jestingly, was told casually that the subject was marriage-contracts etc.). I think that I am often the subject of these disputes: – also, which is very unpleasant, the people here talk about me in a disagreeable way in the next room, and so on. Now, no power on earth can force you to marry; and I'm sure no power would force me: but people might say you'd trifled with their daughter, and make things unpleasant: henceforth I will no more implant kisses on her blanched brow or stroke her bosom – no: but I had better leave on Wednesday, I think: an air of conspiracy in a house is one of the most unpleasant things imaginable, if you are the object of it.

If you will send me a letter here on monday, *with nothing much inside*, I will say to the people that I had heard something from home, and had better go back to London on Wednesday: giving them still to understand, more or less as I already have done, that it is quite unlikely I will return later, in a month or so: I don't want them to think I'm going for any reason to found "en famille" [?] here, or they might become unpleasant. – You might write another letter to Poste Restante telling me what you think. I really have a most absurd dread of the very thought of marriage: I feel like packing up and flying to the British Consul for protection.

There is of course no cause whatever for alarm; but when unpleasantness sets in, like the winter winds, I, the swallow, flee away.

I think also that a week or so in London, to work [with?] Will Rothenstein,[1] and do a drawing, a pastel, of that Italian woman, would be as well. . . .

---

[1] L. was at the Slade when he first met William Rothenstein (1872–1945). They remained friends throughout their lives. See William Rothenstein, *Men and Memories*, Vol. II (London, 1932).

As it is they ask continually why you dont write to me, and I cant exactly say I get letters at Poste Restante.... This woman kept a large pension at Zandfurt [Zandvoort] for eight years, so she really must be pretty knowing: her name was Picknut and her family came from Rochester – near to Dickens: her father was a physician at Bruxelles; ever heard the name?

Well, it's nothing to get excited about; but one cant be too careful in these things.
Write immediately ....
au revoir
I am yours ever
P. W. LEWIS

P.S. Remember me to Tomkins and Mrs. Castell: you can give Mrs. Castell anything short of my love that would be "convenable". I am now very cautious. Write immediately.

Later
I dont know whether second thoughts are best: several hours of living more have brought the thought into my head that I perhaps might stay here another two weeks with comparative safety as I do not see what possible thing the people could do to annoy me, – beyond the beastly hinting the whole time that I might marry their daughter: and I may exaggerate that: I tell them incessantly that I have no money. Still, write and tell me what you think.... I suppose its rather awkward, in a foreign country if people try and bully you, – I know absolutely nothing you see of this place: still, probably its all imaginary, and they only think they might insinuate their daughter into my affections, thinking I have enough money to live on. You probably understand these tricks better than I: write and give your opinion. P. W. L.

14. *To his Mother* 59 Grafton Street, London.
[ca. 1904]

Chere Maman. I have resolved, by hook or by crook, to go to Hamburg tomorrow (Wednesday) at 8 o'clock in the evening from Liverpool Street: I shall take my little hand-bag only.

I have got £1 from Maclean: he was extraordinarily impressed, and I asked him £1 for a drawing with the idea of borrowing the rest.... I think he will be a "buyer" some day: he was extremely interested, and in fact took the bait. I am on such excellent terms with John, that I dont want to slacken them by a loan....

.... — Maclean was in every way a success; he thought very few people could do a drawing like the one he got; he was amazed at the prodigious numbers of drawings that passed beneath his eyes, and in fact left me a sure capture for some future occasion....

Yours
PERCY W. L.

15. *To his Mother*   19 [rue] Mouton-Duvernet [Paris]
[ca. 1904]

Chere Maman.

You mustn't think I'm intoxicated, but I really forget how old I am, – I couldn't remember yesterday, and it worried me rather: am I 22 years or 23 years old; please let me know by return of post; seriously I actually do forget. —— I'm sorry your cold cant drag itself away from you; but I can quite understand it, – towards the end of the season, the winter, there are so few places for a cold to go to, that when it finds itself well treated it's apt to stop; I'm sure you spoil it, and make much too much fuss with it. Will you write and tell me exactly what I have or have not to do as regards a packet of dirty clothes? Must I declare them dirty? that you would recognise to be a farce, if you saw them: must I count them and leave the number at the office. If I can merely do them up in brown paper, have them weighed, and post them, – then I'll send them. – Can you send me a little packet of books, that I want to lend to Miss Bruce? ... I wanted –

Porphyrion by Lawrence Binyon.[1]
Sonnettes by S. Butler.[2]
The Vinedresser by Sturge Moore.[3]

[1] Laurence Binyon, *Porphyrion and other poems* (London, 1898).
[2] This is undoubtedly Butler's *Seven Sonnets and a Psalm of Montreal*, edited by R. A. Streatfield and privately printed in Cambridge in 1904.
[3] T. Sturge Moore, *The Vinedresser and other poems* (London, 1899). It was Moore's first volume of poetry.

The Vinedresser is a very little bright green book; Butler's sonnettes, there are only six sonnettes, is a little paper book of six pages Streatfield[1] gave me, – it's not a book of course, – you could slip it inside the leaves of Porphyrion; – Porphyrion is an ordinary sized orange coloured book.

Well, ça marche: I'm working hard and my bowels are open, – though I dont suggest any connection between two such independently amusing facts.

16. *To his Mother*   Paris.
[February 1905]

Chere Maman. . . .

. . . I am going to a conference tonight to help get Gorki out of prison, whereat Anatole France is going to speak:[2] I've seen a lot of remarkable things, but one can hardly recount them all; I've been for example to Russian dances, – am going to one on Saturday, by the way, – and I have also entered Maxim's without the expense of a sou: however, – I have just sent a note to John: tell me about the "Whistler" show[3] and the French impressionists,[4] if you have read about it in the papers: I dont want to miss them if possible. – Also could you manage to abstract Will's book and Streatfield's from the Hampstead flat: *El Ombú*[5] and Absalom?[6] – I will write tomorrow some time.

                                I am yours, ever,
                                        P. W. LEWIS

[1] R. A. Streatfield (1866–1919) was Assistant in the Department of Printed Books at the British Museum and a noted music critic; he was Samuel Butler's executor.

[2] Early in February, France participated in several meetings in Paris protesting the troubles in St. Petersburg.

[3] A Whistler Memorial Exhibition opened February 22nd, 1905, at the New Gallery, London.

[4] In January 1905, a large exhibition of French Impressionists, organised by Durand Ruel, opened at the Grafton Gallery.

[5] W. H. Hudson, *El Ombú (and other tales)* (London, 1902).

[6] T. Sturge Moore, *Absalom, a Chronicle Play in Three Acts* (London, 1903).

17. *To his Mother* [Paris]
[ca. 1905]

My dear old lady. I'm very very sorry to hear that you're not better; but then you couldn't have planned a surer way of keeping your 'grippe' than going away for a week: the change of air, for the moment always makes you feel worse.... I expect it is a sort of mild, nervous collapse, the sort of thing I get, – only as you're older it lasts a bit longer: and living as you do it's apt to depress you more, as you haven't anything to excite you out of it. Still ça passe; if not, which seems hardly probable, I should go in another two or three weeks to Dieppe for a fortnight or so; I might spend some time with you there, – or something of that sort: but I expect when the choppy april weather is over the Spring will chase your rheum away. You must let me know how you feel always, as I can help you much better than Tom I'm sure. – I'm working away, and succeeding also to live pleasantly enough. I'm afraid I must stay here another six weeks or so, as I do want to bring something substantial home with me, – that is if you can keep things going for the moment.... I'm afraid Reynolds[1] has fallen into the clutches of Lord Henry Somerset,[2] in Florence; may it only be one of these wicked histories. – My drawing has improved a great deal in Paris, and my ideas are taking a certain shape, that is shapeliness, which I hope will be for the best. I am engaged in a very extraordinary love affair; the German lady[3] – the which by the way, I had slighted somewhat – came round to see me one day and to my unquenchable amazement asked me to kiss her, and threw herself into my arms and kissed me with unabated vigour for three hours: well, I'm very glad, since – ça marche: it saves me a lot of trouble and expense to have a very beautiful and nicely bred mistress: and also I think there is no likelihood of complications – if there were I could easily go away

---

[1] Victor Reynolds had been a fellow student at the Slade. About the time of this letter, he wrote to L. from Genoa, noting that the police of Florence "keep a close eye" on the English colony. This, he goes on, "is headed in the social scale by no less a priest of 'The Vice' than Lord Henry Somerset himself." Reynolds was killed in action in 1916, leaving a widow.

[2] Lord Henry Somerset (1849–1932), second son of the eighth Duke of Beaufort.

[3] Presumably Ida. This is L.'s first reference to her.

– but in this case I think all is for the best. – Well, let me know how you get on on your return to London: dont let silly old Tom bother you. . . .

You must tell me when I'm to begin my letter to the old man: – good luck and better health,

Yours ever,

PERCY W. LEWIS

18. *To his Mother* [Paris]
Wednesday. [1905]

Chere maman. . . . I had a miserable headache for 3 days, I suppose a bilious one, the after effects of my being shaken up crossing the Channel, without being sick. For the last few days I have been blessed with an extremely bad cold in the throat and head, and a feeling of general weakness, and have done no work, which is worse today, my cold is very bad, and I shall buy some sort of medicine. There's nothing to be anxious about – apart from the accidents accompanying a bad cold and a cold wind; – but it is rather miserable to be unable to work. I shall probably come back to London in about 3 weeks, and hope to be able to work soon.

The Whistler show is coming on here,[1] so that if by any chance I am here on the 1st May, I shall see it. I hope your cold is better, but I suppose you're rather like me – and the rest of the world for that matter, for Gatty is grimly idle, and he has influenza, – that is that you get gloomy under the weakening effects of a cold.

I naturally have no news, without the four walls of this "rheum" which is my present prison. I dont know which I dislike most, a bilious headache or a weakening cold. I see the Bruce occasionally: I met Carlo Lotti [?] chez elle the other day, – a most ridiculous personage, but a friend and admirer of Horne,[2] and very well known at Florence. My German lady seems inclined to quarrel with me about Mrs. Hawes, and I really dont very much mind: tant pis – pour elle.

I hope to make a proposition of marriage to my norwegian lady before I return to London, though for the moment ça ne marche

[1] The Whistler Memorial Exhibition organised in London opened at the Ecole de Beaux Arts on May 10th, 1905.
[2] Perhaps the architect and art historian H. P. Horne (1864–1916).

pas. – You mustn't think from my gossip that my ills are imaginary; – naturally the days, and especially that part spent at the restaurants, are not entirely a blank. – I can at least assure you of this – that given reasonably good health, and a roof above me I shall always work, though rightly or successfully always is in the hands of fate. . . .

Yours ever,
PERCY W. LEWIS

19. *To his Mother* [Paris]
[ca. April 1905]

Chere Maman.

I got the money the other day, saturday, in good time, for which relief, much thanks:

I think I shall stay in this studio another week or so, and shall stay in Paris for the time being: I want to try a throw or two here with the dealers. – I went, rather against my will, last night to a Russian Ball, and am in consequence rather tired today; but I am working quite regularly now. –

A youth called Clarence of Norwood[1] and Rugby, has turned up like my evil spirit: – I've not seen him, but Miss Bruce – he seems to be a friend of hers – told me of him! Did you know any people called George at Ravenstone? I suspect them of having been there, and have an intense dislike for them consequently. (George is the name.) . . .

I shall wait here anyway for the Whistler show, and try and profit by it. . . .

I am,
Yours ever,
PERCY W. LEWIS

20. *To his Mother* Paris
[1905]

Chere Maman.

Of all the infamous things ever brought to my knowledge, I think the law in France permitting old beggars to sing in the courts, beneath one's window (for alms) is the most pitiably and intolerably bad piece of misgovernment of a state, really and

[1] L. had lived with his mother in this London suburb.

truly, apart from the fact of my being, – obviously and because of my vocation, – a nervous person, – apart from that, they are a constant and insufferable nuisance, producing, as they do, the most awful travesties of song that sadden one to the heart (many of them old men of eighty and others) the most ear-splitting noise. . . .

I am yours ever,
P. W. LEWIS

21. *To his Mother* Noordwijk [Holland]
[Postmarked "30 Sept. 1905".]

Ma chère petite Mère. . . .

When I return to London, in addition to the necessity of being, I will be, in any case, perfectly content, with a large room at the top of a house, where I can eat sleep and work, when I'm not eating sleeping or working elsewhere, and may this room be near the museum, and editing offices, as I dont want to make a journey across London, as one has to if the room be in Notting Hill, say. . . . Pray god the old man sends, as a model constantly with me, as the Kleiner is, shows the necessity of that artist's material.

If Tom prophesys (cant spell it) your decease, or has morbid fancies of that sort, make her take a strong dose of Codliver Oil; – I'm afraid you dont know how to treat morbidness, – I'm sure you dont know how to treat Tom.

Let me know if the flat, aided by the coquettry of Tom, has managed to let itself.

How are your affairs proceeding, il faut agir avec precautions, toujours, no splashing about.

If I manage to scrape a little money together, we might run over to Brussels, and spend the Christmas there: that might freshen you up a bit.

I'm afraid no New English triumphs this autumn: I shall probably have a drawing to send, but that wont do me much good: my triumphs must be subterranean – that is to say not on the gaudy surface of the exhibitions, but rather amongst friends and dealers or 'sich' like. . . .

una stretta di mano,
Yours ever,
PERCY

22. *To his Mother*   Villa Cato. Nordvyk am Zee
[1905]

Chere Maman. So [?] we installed Villa Cato, with a studio for me, large bedroom, and a little eating room with a magnificent prospect of the surging sea, the bijou white bathing machines and all the attractions sought by the town-weary toiler.

I got with a throb of gratitude and satisfaction the £2 the other day: I made a journey to Leiden to change them, (the postal orders), but all the money changers were closed, so they are not changed yet, and I had to borrow from my German garden. . . . send orders again saturday, by saturday morning if you can, as the German back-yard is hard-up, though always willing to lend.

My German allotment and I entered the Kurhaus last night to drink a cup of coffee; we looked at all the papers, wander'd over the building (late Gothic, or dutch chic) and in fact spent a very pleasant evening; there were a great many people also employing their time pleasantly, but a grotesque and wholly unexampled lack of domestics, – in fact we didnt so much as smell the kitchen the whole evening, and finding no one to address our remarks to, anent the coffee, we absconded with a belly-ache, – caused in my case by the quality of the cigars affected by my neighbour in the billiard-room, and in that of my german accomplice by hearing a dutch family employing the German language, – and in so doing, she assures me, accomplishing a feat I had imagined impossible, that is, making it more barbarous than it is already. . . .

. . . I am working very well, though I have the ghost of a headache, and am not altogether in splendid health, – but I expect that that's the change of air, and the extraordinary hours of feeding prevalent in this country. . . .

. . . Kleiner sits for me every morning for 2 hours; I am in clover as far as models go. Good luck and keep well and don't bother yourself or let Tom bother you.

                                             P. L.

23. *To his Mother*   Nordvyk on Zee.
[1905]

Chere Maman. Forgive me for not writing during the week: I've had three bad headaches, and when I've not been occupied with them, I've been busy working, and each evening have felt very tired and lazy.... I am very sorry you cant get away for a couple of weeks; though I confess ... I was extraordinarily "put about" to know what to do; as I didn't think your innocent little plan of "not understanding our relations, or domestic arrangements" would go very well, or make the Kleiner less uncomfortable: and since I didn't want to drive her away, – and for one very substantial reason, – she poses for me regularly, and I reap a rich harvest: – I certainly couldn't have such a model in London for less than 15/– a week for the number of hours. ...

I am glad that your cold and other ailments have forsaken you, though take care of yourself cold and damp days. I think the episode of the Harlot who ineffectually attempted to set up Her red lantern at 16 Canfield Gardens,[1] and introduce her clientele to those bourgeois precincts not devoid of amusements, though extremely trying for your nerves, necessary as it is to let the flat. Let me know of course, if you have a bite, or (might we hope it!) land a two pounder, – or two guineas. I hope that Tom, like all children of unrighteousness, flourishes abundantly.

I am doing some excellent work; and really this time, – following up my good start of the last months at Paris, begin to see my way to some Parnassus: though my road, like all those of art and high living, is uncertain and rocky enough: Let us pray together that there will be some commercial aspect at the turn of the hill.

I think my little lady is going away in two weeks, and I will depart with her: will that suit? Since the port closes here shortly – la, there the Kleiner cometh with her batch of barbarous german letters, to various guttural friends and relations.

Good luck with the flat and yourself.

                                  Yours ever,
                                     PERCY W. L.

P.S. In your capacity of mama, listen; why am I bilious (it was biliousness at Dieppe) why have I headaches, – I didn't have such

---

[1] Mrs. Lewis's residence in Hampstead at this time.

things once, not so long ago: and now although my headache has departed, why have I paid a diarrhetic visit to the W.C.? Praps a lack of exercise and the difference of air. . . .

I left a painting in the drawing room, Pembroke Mansions:[1] although it may not strike you, it has a certain worth, I want to take care of it.

24. *To his Mother* [Munich]
[1906]

Chere Maman.

Me voici,[2] and not a particularly happy 'me'. – I thought there was a douane at Rotterdam, as there wasn't my bag stayed at the Hook: – they telegraphed from Rotterdam, and the customs said they'd send it: in three hours time I was at the station to await it: it however was Sunday, and so it didn't come, and as I didn't like the prospect of a day in Rotterdam and the baggage man assured me he would send it on by petite vitesses, I continued my journey. At this point my weakness got the better of me, and I went to see Ida, intending to stay two hours; – my bag however only arrived, despite all my efforts, in three days. The only effect of my visit to Ida had on me was to make me sadder. – I dont think as things are I could marry that girl, and it's awful for one reason and another, – my doubt of myself amongst them, to have to gain time as it were. But I suppose all will arrange itself. . . .

. . . I go to an evening class and pay sixpence a time, but I find, that without friends, it's necessary to go to cafes and that's expensive. The pension's cheap, the eating is not so good, when cheap as in Paris, although one can feed cheaply enough. – Musique, however, is cheap enough, – 3d a ticket. I met that austrian man (Paris, and London – I told you, the pension Imans at Paris) and he is a little useful: – and I have an acquaintance or two in the night-class, – voilà tout. I intend to find a room, and eat in restaurants, – the austrian is going to show me a cheap one. . . . Love and wishes for luck.

PERCY W. L.

[1] Block of flats in Canfield Gardens.
[2] L. went to Munich early in 1906. While there, he studied at the Akademie Heimann.

25. *To his Mother* [Munich]
[Postcard.] [Postmarked "3 Feb. 1906".]

Carnival lasts till the month of March. There is still a month of it. I have made several acquaintances and am invited to the Bal Paré next week, Wednesday. I should like to go: it only costs 2 marks 50: but one must wear fancy dress, or "frac." I have in my drawer at home a virgin coat, opera hat, cloak etc. which would really be in these days of great use, and would spare me considerable expense for a costume: also, during the next month, perhaps three times I might want to go again to the Bal Paré, with a sweet companion [?]!

Find out how much it will cost to send me the black clothes, crush hat and then the silk waistcoat, – I may never have the chance to wear them again, perhaps, and if it costs less than fancy dress, send them at once. There are also balls where the men wear "frac" only and no fancy dress.

You must not think, because I am going to the bal paré that I am leading a debauched life – on the contrary . . . .

[Translated from the French.]

26. *To his Mother* [Munich]
[February 1906]

Chere Maman. . . . Don't forget to seal the letters with wax – buy a stick. If I don't write you letters, it's because of the uncertainty still of my mind, and that I don't know what to write . . . . I shouldn't think pops was in England; if he is money could be extracted in an interview or otherwise. It's a pity one cant get information at the bureau of police as one can abroad, as to a person's whereabouts. I think that you should not neglect to pay your visit to the American Embassy, – but still, if you think its not worthwhile. – O, before I forget, I want to impress upon you, so that you may impress upon Tom or whoever it may be, – never to destroy a single *written* paper of mine, – as at any moment I might want to hunt up an old poem of mine and not be able to find it: *this is really a serious injunction, as one cant* rewrite them, and often forgets them: – And the book with the brown paper cover, my play, cherish it above all things. –

I gave some drawings to Ida, – some of the best; I think that was as well. – I draw every evening still in an Abende Akte, evening classe, and have I think found an extremely cheap studio . . . .

. . . About Ida, I am in an impasse – a moral cul de sac. God knows what to do: I dont however look towards marriage as a solution, and suppose that with infinite pain I shall drift away, and other interests eventually help me to forget the strongest and most unfortunate attachment I'm ever likely to have. – She sent me a hamper a week ago, and a wire yesterday; I'm going however to put an end gradually to any *absolute* hopes of marriage she may have. – I haven't written to you much chiefly because I was very occupied with all this and until I could say something definitely, it seemed better not to write much. *Do* write to her, however. – I dont like Munchen as well as Paris, but that may be associations: no, as a town, naturally Paris is infinitely better to live in, and has a thousand times more charm; still, Munchen doesn't lack certain qualities; and this colossal carnival gives it a quite extraordinary quality. – I was glad to hear good news of the business: you know the utility of shops, and I wish you luck with this one: – if you find you've made a mistake, however, dont be afraid to own it, or be discouraged. . . .

27. *To his Mother* 85 Amalien Strs. Stephanie.
[Munich]
[February 1906]

Chere Maman. I have at last found a studio: it is 20 marcs a month . . . . I think that eating in a restaurant will be a gain in the matter of food, and cost no more; there is always veal for dinner here, and that doesn't agree with me very well; – and 3 times out of 4 the meat, if other than veal is dry and without nourishment and soaked in gravy, – also a beastly vegetable predominates, which haunts my shoulders. . . .

. . . I find to my inexpressible delight that IBSEN inhabited the room in front of mine in the pensione for 6 weeks; – I feel this a good omen, among so many bad ones! – *Oh, dont forget to write to Ida*; you must do that and ought to have done it long ago, – it would have been much more convenient too: – she'd have the right to call you an egoist, – like me, – though I suppose she must know that you're terribly busy. – I am having again german lessons from a young lady: I dont enjoy them very much, and have in fact very little interest left in young ladies in general, and only a real desire to meet some day a woman that I can take seriously, and that will help me to forget Ida: I suffer very much about all this, and spend many hours of great despondence; I dont see any prospect of this feeling passing, and must resign myself to it, and go on with my life, in spite of it, and not wait for it to depart in idleness and misery: – 'praps work cures best. – On the other hand I see no prospect of my ever being able to live with Ida, that would be another form of suffering, with many disadvantages to boot. However, 'praps the time even yet has not come for me to be able definitely to say anything.

I have in Munich just as many friends as I need, and no more; – I should prefer to have *one* serious friend, but praps its best, most intimately speaking, to be alone. Ida has done another rather embarrassing thing, she wrote to Lilly, – the gal that gives her the money, – telling about her prospective marriage, and is now given the money for another 2 years – 3 years more, in all: – it's really rather a temptation to marry her, even for this mess of potage. – But I think with this money you give me for the moment, and what I must earn in the near future, whatever it may be, I should be freer and happier for the moment, and infinitely freer afterwards. – Tell me how the shop makes its debut: when I feel more at my ease in my atelier, I will do you the three posters; – one of them might be useful for the shop. I think I told you they're doing the symphonies of Beethoven here just now in the Kaimsaal;[1] – students nights it costs only 30 pfennigs – you can get here in a restaurant a good lunch for 70 pfennigs . . . . So you see living is cheap enough, and one's spiritual existence is also sustained au bon marché:

– I've not been very assiduous with my German, but can talk a bit. . . .

PERCY

[1] Later known as the Tonhalle.

28. *To his Mother* [Munich]
[March 1906]

Chere Maman.... The Carnival ended yesterday: I temporarily enjoyed myself excessively, and was a great success: several women asked me to accompany them without my having so much as looked at them: a magnificent Parisienne cocotte called me, and caressed me under the nose of her entreteneur for a considerable time: I made a crowd of acquaintances, and have any number of appointments: – one very pretty little woman that I had been confetting the whole night, just after the interrement of the Carnival rushed up to me and embraced me and I'm going to meet her next Tuesday: I think she is the most hopeful of my acquaintances, since she was most particularly struck with me and I with her: – she told all my friends that I "pleased her from every point of view," and that I had the coldest mouth she had ever met with: and that she would take french lessons with me. And apart from all my female conquests I must mention a band of young artists that called me and insisted on standing me drinks, because I had a head like a portrait of "Lenbach",[1] which was a doubtful compliment. So I have grown extremely vain though none the less unhappy. I should like to write you more about the carnival, but I expect I shall see you before long, and will tell you all about it then: It is an incredible thing, the Munich Carnival; one ought to have plenty of money, naturellement, – but can enjoy oneself without also.... I bought a "passe-partout", 5 marcs, for the Luitpold Café, an enormous place where everyone goes before and after and during the Balls, and which is really the centre of the carnival: there are always thousands of people there, and one walks from one salle to another, and needn't drink at all, unless one wants to. I spent the last night with several young officers, who spoke french very well, and were more agreeable than the average student....

... I found, as I told you, a perfect studio, – in price, in everything. – I said at the time it was too good to be true: the day before I was to move into it, the occupant arrived chez-moi, at

[1] Franz von Lenbach (1836–1904) was one of Munich's most celebrated painters. His portrait of the explorer Nansen, whom L. had heard at Rugby, resembles some pictures of L. at this period. See Adolf Rosenberg, *Lenbach* (Bielefeld and Leipzig, 1905).

8 o'clock in the morning to say that I couldn't have it . . . . After this blow my energy really deserted me: I felt it was really too bad of Fortune to play with me in this fashion, and despair of ever getting settled in this ill-omened city. . . .

I distracted myself sometimes during the Carnival, but when I am alone again and face to face with the old question, more than ever I can neither forget Ida, nor can I marry her.

I am convinced that my suspicions are well-founded – the more I think of her conduct with me, and the more I hear of german women, the more sure I am: but that, unfortunately in no way helps me: a general sort of hopeless feeling settles down upon me, and I can see no reasonable or sane issue. – I think 'praps if she told me I might suffer less, but one day or another, everything seems for the worst. – Whilst I have energy, and if all this doesn't affect my health too much, I have the great resource of work: pleasure is none.

During the Carnival night I had palpitation of the heart for half an hour, and felt ill: I think half an hour is rather a long time: – but I had not eaten a very good dinner, and then for 4 hours I took the most violent exercise in a crowded and stuffy place; – and also I judged from my "belching" propensities that it was due somewhat to indigestion, as well as fatigue. I don't suppose it's necessary to see a doctor: I shall be very careful now the Carnival's over.

I shall come back to England as soon as I see any prospect of having the money to come back with . . . .

29. *To his Mother* [Paris]
[ca. 1906–7]

Chere Maman. . . .

Well, so long as you give me enough to keep me in food, etc: and pay for the stove, etc., it's all I can expect: Its frightfully cold here: I dont know how to keep warm. – I have joined an evening-class, and draw every evening from the nude, in the day I draw in my room.

I shall be infinitely thankful if I can get a little money for models, I must try a dealer or two soon.

I am going to spend Christmas day chez John. There is no Messe de Minuit this year in Paris or I should have gone to St. Sulpice.

I have a beautiful room overlooking the cemetery of Montparnasse; there are many handsome tombs, and wonderful rows of cypress trees; I wish I could have room and studio as well. . . .

au revoire,
bonne chance,
PERCY

. . .

30. *To his Mother* [Paris]
[Final page of a letter.] [January 1907]

I think that the Governor of Jamaica will get into trouble, dont you: Still, he was quite right: I was glad to see that the Toronto Star said that Admiral Davies "exhibited a considerable amount of Bounce."[1] Do you know that word?
 – Oh just as I should counsel you to take care of yourself, not to catch cold, so I should counsel you not to catch cockney; dont forget, little mother: – disinfect Tom's mouth, so that the H's or the cavity where an H ought to be, does not get as far as you. – I am getting a beautiful french accent: I'm at last getting hold of the idioms. – Au revoir; – will write again soon.

Yours ever
PERCY W. L.

31. *To his Mother* [Paris]
[Final page of a letter.] [ca. 1907]

The weather is excessively disgusting here: it is very cold and damp. I'm sure that the earth's late distressing colic[2] must have something to do with this state of things.

---

[1] This refers to a press sensation arising from the earthquake at Kingston on January 14th, 1907. Rear-Admiral C. H. Davies, U.S.N., brought an American detachment to the aid of the island on January 16th. Questions of jurisdiction then arose between Davies and the British Governor, Sir Alexander Swettenham. Soon the situation had become a *cause* in Whitehall and in the British and Canadian newspapers. See Ian Malcolm, *The "White Flag" in Jamaica* (1907).

[2] Perhaps the Kingston earthquake.

John has moved, as I think I told you, to the Avenue d'Orléans with his families; he has an apartement, garden and studio all together, parterre. The elder of his children, that I hadn't seen for some time, are becoming excessively interesting personalities: but their conversation, although sparkling, is slightly disgusting to a person of a pure mind, – which is the more distressing since it be so edifying to the more urgent exigencies of the intellect. – They called me a "smutty thing" and a "booby" because I insisted that a lion could climb up a beanstalk, – nay, *had* done so, in my presence! – and one of the first wife's children has contracted the indelicate habit of spitting at one of the second wife's children while having his bath: – by the way, Miss MacNeil is producing another infant.

John is taking a studio in Montmartre, where he thinks of installing two women he has found in England: and I think John will end by building a city, and being worshipped as sole man therein, – the deity of Masculinity. . . .

John's father saw the other day in a paper, a description of John's personal appearance, as "not at all that of a Welshman, but rather a Hungarian or a Gypsy", and wrote to John a reproving letter: – John has now ordered a complete typical Welsh outfit, and will be more extraordinary than ever for the populace astounded.

I am arranging for a cheaper means of living in little things, such as making my own cafe and milk for the dejeuner etc: – Ida is here, and warily I renew my relations with her: I haven't the least intention to get married . . . .

                                                         Love   W. LEWIS

32. *To his Mother*   Hotel de la Haute Loire.
                                              Boulevard Raspail.
                                                          [Paris]
                                                          [ca. 1907]

Chère Maman.

En voici impoten! – Ida, for some mystical reason, has to go to Germany on Sunday. She is abusing me for not having any money to give her . . . .

. . . you must send my rug with the washing, – I forgot it – I had to forget something, you know. . . . a few little things I can get from Ida for the moment, although I want eventually to be independent of this amiable lady even down to a spoon . . . .

To show how changed I am, Everett,[1] who met me in the street yesterday, talked to me for 10 minutes and left me without recognising me! I met him again today, he'd seen Gore the night before and Gore had told him that he had seen me – it is 4 years since I saw Everett . . . .

Good Luck.
Yours ever
PERCY W. L.

33. *To his Mother*   16 Rue de la Grd. Chaumière.
[Paris]
[ca. 1907]

Chère Maman. . . .

I am at last installed. I work hard and will have plenty done in 3 or 4 months if I can go on as I have commenced.

I have roughly the following plan of campaign: it is much better to set oneself a definite task, one is more likely to do something useful.

I will do a dozen extremely careful heads in pen and ink, – to which I may add an etching or two: with these I might at once get some portraits to do since they will be extremely good. – Then I'm going to do 2 or 3 series of "illustrations" – say twenty or thirty drawings – 5 or 6 finished in your sense of the word, to always have ready to show: additionally I will have a portfolio of various studies, nude, heads etc: – to back up "the sets". – This will take me all my time till May or April: – I will then along with these do as much painting as ever I can, but set myself no task, as yet merely studying: I must so to speak go into training in that matter, and will as soon as possible take up a picture, but it would be useless to do that at once: – still, we'll see how that goes in a month or so.

I'm convinced that success in art is only a matter of common sense with a matter of disposing of one's work, and a certain amount of discipline in the doing of it; if for 3 or 4 months I apply myself regularly to doing what I have set out to do, I ought to make a beginning somehow and somewhere before the summer: –

[1] Henry Everett (b. 1876) was at the Slade with L.

roughly what I'm doing, it may not sound very much, but is a most sound programme: – the dozen heads in ink are a most important item, as I have done one or two that please extremely, in popular quarters. – The painting will go all right: of course there's a great deal of grind and one has to be very hard on oneself – reject inefficient work, slovenly work etc. – never work in a tired fashion etc. The beer and skittles are not so far away, I hope however. –

Ida is back, I dont know if I told you: I dont like her at all and avoid her as much as possible: it naturally is a cause of great annoyance, her presence, but then if I hadn't that I should have another. – I couldn't, quite simply call my soul my own if I were married to her: as since, I dont by any means like her as well as I did, and wish to call my soul very much my own – and even shouldn't mind calling other peoples also, if they were so disposed, – I think marriage dwindles steadfastly: – my affair with her has "lowered my temperature" in the matter of good spirits, gaiety a good many degrees; generally speaking I feel a little bit heavier hearted all round, but marrying her would be no solution of this, quite the contrary: – I regret this change of temperature, as it makes life rather boring when one's not working, and I have very few distractions: – still I'm far from being desperate, Heaven be praised.

My studio is excellent: the light, everything, is about as I wanted it. – I have bought a wonderful new hat which makes me look ever so much more handsome. I'm going to buy a fur collar as soon as I can see one cheap for this next winter: like this: a long one, that buttons onto the coat. I let my hair down underneath the hat: the effect is astonishing. [2 sketches of himself in hat.]

I suppose, as you say, it's difficult to extract money, even one's due, from our fellow beings especially at Christmas time. – I didn't certainly think that the Parent over the Water would respond to my amiable letter: he's an old rip. – I dreamt of a fire the other night. Mrs. John tells me it's the luckiest thing in the world: praps he's posting me £50 in this minute: however if I wont have anything to do with bad omens, I cant feel aggrieved if good ones dont come true.

I should like to see you on sunday, as ever, but I expect I shall spend time enough in London in the course of my life, and also I hope that my exile will be fruitful. Come over if you can soon: we would dine at the Boeuf à la Mode, and see the Nouveauté piece . . . .

Yours ever,
PERCY W. L.

. . .

34. *To his Mother*   [Paris]
                                                                           [ca. 1907]

Chere Maman. . . .

. . . I have a request to make you. That yank at the hotel shot a man while I was with him the other day, and as his life is threatened more than ever, and hardly dare show himself, he is sighing after "nice peaceful England": I want you to get the "Lady", and look for a cottage in a pretty place, not far from London, that is to be let immediately; also not too dear, as he is going to take a man with him to look after him: I think I told you he's a cripple, he had rheumatic fever a couple of years ago, and his legs shrivelled up. – I was going out to tea the other day, when I found him in the court of the hotel, flourishing a revolver and saying that if a certain individual so much as showed his nose again, he'd shoot him. I did all I could to pacify him, and even stayed with him an hour to this end, but all to no purpose. – The man arrived, was shot, and I was arrested: however, finding I had no firearms, and perceiving the Yank's mistress with a revolver in her hand, they arrested her, and carried her off to the police-station: – however, finding at last they'd got the wrong one, they released her, and now the Yank is going to be tried in a week or two: – nothing will happen, as the man he shot had been following him about wherever he went for the past month, and had threatened his life continually: – so you can imagine the little cottage, covered with honeysuckle, with the dear little black cat and the good natured countrymen of old England recommended themselves to this poor Yank's imagination. Well, try and find that for him: it isn't of any importance, but if you notice an advertisement in the "Lady" or another paper let me know.

Oh, so it's the £40 interest that bothers Ida: she says she's very hard up, and I can quite believe it: I dont see her very often: that is to say I see her every couple of days or so, but our interviews are not always too cordial: I think I may go a step farther than my august father, and say there are "too many bitches in this *world*"; I've had a lesson in the matter of women, such as I shant forget in a hurry. . . .

. . . I'm sorry to bother always about that little green book, I always forget, and always need it more or less. – Please send me . . . Lawrence Binyon's *Odes*,[1] a pale coloured pinkish book; *Porphyrion* by the same author. *The Vinedresser* (the little green book) by *Sturge Moore*, and *Absalom*, a green book, first cousin to the other, but a little bigger. . . .

Yours ever,
P. W. L.

35. *To his Mother* [Paris]
[ca. 1907]

Chere Maman. . . .

. . . I am rather out of sorts for the moment, – my belly raising certain difficulties, and rejecting sulkily certain dainties that I would thrust upon it. – I shall however drop a pill into it tonight, and have done with this "boudeur" [?], – "sans manège"! – I am working assiduously, and may all go for the best.

I have at once an adherent and a model: – I showed some drawings to Everett the other day: he said they were a million times better than he had ever imagined they could be, as good as John etc. etc.: – and that, since he had seen my drawings he would sit as often as I liked. – I'm not sure I want him to sit as often as all that; still every little helps.

We spent a musical evening yesterday in the bosom of the family – in the bosom of the seraglio I should say: – there was a quartette: Violin, Accordion, Guitar and Flute: – an amazing combination, and they played Bach, such as I have seldom heard him render'd.

John has taken a vast room off the Boul St. Germain, in an old hotel belonging to the famous Rohan family: – he is however returning to London today to finish a portrait. – Mrs. John and the bonne will have their babies about the same time, I expect. – I suppose beneath John's roof is the highest average of procreation in France. . . .

[1] Laurence Binyon, *Odes* (London, 1901).

... I've not seen Ida for a day or so, and wish from the bottom of my heart that she were in the bottom of the sea; it reached a climax the other day when in one gigantic effort she seemed to have wished to fuse all her most disagreeable qualities into one. – I suppose every human creature has these possibilities of nastiness, and malevolent propensities, but they are of little use to one once they have manifested them: – happily I have a tender feeling in another direction, which may ripen into covetousness: then farewell ... german ....

36. *To his Mother* [Paris]
[ca. 1907]

Mrs. John[1] died about 4 or 5 days ago, and on saturday I was at her funeral; she was cremated, and buried at Père la Chaise, in Montmartre.

John has been drunk for the last three days, so I cant tell you if he's glad or sorry: I think he's sorry, though.

Miss McNeil has taken up her position in the vacant chair, in the vacant bed: the queen is dead, live the queen!

Mrs. John had a baby, and six days afterwards was dead, – of peritonitis and a heap of other things: one of her former 'accouchements' had apparently something to do with it, and then she was rather delicate.

Mrs. Nettleship[2] was over here, but I do not know what's become of her: I suppose she's gone back again.

McEvoy[3] the painter came over for the day – that is to say he intended to go back the same night, but he apparently, owing to inebriety, has not done so – he got so drunk in the early evening of the day of the funeral, and has been consistently imbibing ever since, that he will lose his return ticket if he doesn't pull himself up within a day or so.

John has a very disagreeable set of people round him just now, and the average morality, taste, sensibility or whatever one calls

---

[1] Augustus John's first wife, Ida. They had been married in 1900.

[2] Mrs. Jack Nettleship, mother of Ida John.

[3] Ambrose McEvoy (1878–1927) was one of John's closest friends. He had come to Paris in the emergency of Mrs. John's illness. See William Rothenstein, *Men and Memories* (New York, 1932), p. 90.

it of the average English medical student who has read Nietzsche prevails among these persons.

I took no part in this Roman programme. I take no merit to myself, – I didn't feel gay, only: and then there is my incapacity to drink. . . .

Yours ever, PERCY W. L.

37. *To his Mother* [Paris]
[ca. 1907]

Chere Maman. . . .

I've not a notion why Ida wants to see you, but will ask her tomorrow. She has some beastly friends here, that make her an even less satisfactory person than when she only has herself to depend on. I dont see her very often, that is I see her every day or so, and get abused if I don't go to see her, but my visits are short and always disagreeable; I dont remember having spent an agreeable half hour with her for many a month. I dont know whether she imagines that that is the way to make oneself liked: I dont suppose she does, as this idea would be too original for her; I suppose she's so nervous that she doesn't know what to do with herself, and that "scenes", quarrels, are the only means of letting off steam – nice for me, isn't it?

I'm pretty well, and working hard: I have no news in particular. If I could sell a drawing or something, I'd devote it to getting you over to Paris for a week or so. I wish there were some means of your having a holiday every month: – pray god I make some money soon. . . .

Yours ever,
PERCY W. L.

38. *To his Mother* [Paris]
[ca. 1907]

Chere Maman. . . .

What have you decided to do about your holiday. I dont think Ida need assist at it; even if you come to Paris you needn't see her the whole time. – I've come to that stage at which I positively hate the sight of her, and I think we would amuse ourselves better without her. Still as, in any relations except her love relations, she's amiable enough, you could see her once or twice. I think Paris is better than any other place to spend your holidays in, as it's more distracting, and in the event of bad weather, it is more easily faced.

Well, write me at once about the money.

Yours ever,
PERCY W. L.

39. *To his Mother* [Paris]
[ca. 1907]

Chere Maman. . . .

About the heritage. . . . Did they say why they wanted you to "resign a right?"[1] . . . Still, it is unnecessary to offend the people over there, since I might want to go and see them some day: though I dont know whether their hospitality would be worth all that: – and are you sure that it mightn't fetch more! – My relations are dishonest people: all they say must be taken with a grain of salt. – However, en effet, there's nothing to be done, than to give 'em the money. I cant think why the Old Rip should likewise resign his right . . . .

Yours ever,
PERCY W. L.

40. *To his Mother* St. Honorine des Perthes.
Mch Blaizot.
[France]
[ca. 1908]

Chère Maman. I cant do a stroke, not a stroke of work here. – If I stay here it will be time lost utterly. – What to do? I dont know.

It's a very enervating climate, I can hardly lift up my arm for quite half the day: All John's family are ill also, – more or less. Now this summer I *must* do something or hang myself: – so I must go somewhere else, not too far. . . .

As an example of how I feel, it is as much as I can do to write this letter to you! . . .

[1] C. E. Lewis's New York state family was trying to secure Mrs. Lewis's signature on a legal document involving family inheritance.

I want also to do some painting very badly, and cant do so near John: – I think I may go to Honfleur or Dieppe, and get a cheap room. Also, although cheap, I am starved chez John, and it would offend them if I went elsewhere, or if I said they did not eat enough for me. As to money; I went to Bayeux the other day, and, at Ida's request visited her near Flers: this cost me a little. I have no money left. . . .

. . . I dont think it's necessary to tell you that I'm off my head, – that goes without saying.

There is this also, it is not fantastic on my part, – it is an *extremely* depressing place – more so than Devonshire, I should think, – and I need a more or less bracing place: and, more, in my present state of mind, it is doubly depressing. Also, I had thought to write chiefly: I feel that if I were left alone, I could both write and paint just now: but near John I can never paint, since his artistic personality is just too strong, and he much more developed, naturally, and this frustrates any effort. . . .

You see, I've had a good deal of worries, one after another lately, – all my own fault: – I am always rather bilious the first week or so at the seaside, and this is an unhealthy place: – so one cant exactly wonder at my state.

Well, do what you can; and, I will promise, if this happens again, to choose the alternative of drowning myself, – or rather, of "lumping it." . . .

PERCY

41. *To T. Sturge Moore* [Paris]
[Unfinished; probably not sent.] [ca. 1909]

Dear Moore. I had forgotten that such a thing as the English Review[1] existed and have been living the life of a young student with just enough to live on, and who can work selon son gré, for the last few weeks. But now I find that I have come to the end of my tether; I must hurry back to London in a day or two, and plunge "dans les affaires de nouveau." I hope Hueffer will keep

[1] Ford Madox Hueffer (later Ford) founded *The English Review* in 1908. L.'s first published work, "The 'Pole,'" appeared in the May 1909 issue of the magazine. L. never became a member of the staff or a regular contributor, as Hueffer seems to have proposed.

to his promise of taking me on as a regular hand. Troublesome as the monthly article would be, it would be nothing compared to the uncertainties of other work.

I am bringing some spaniards over with me; one to buy six suits of clothes, – another to have his pimples cured; – a third is coming because he dare not let the man with the pimples out of his sight, as he is his only means of support, – having lived with him and on him for several years now; he is very jealous of his benefactor's pimples, and when the latter grows despondent, or broods on some vague plan of curing once and for all his disfigurement, he who is his shadow sees ruin staring him in the face. I will bring my troupe to the Vienna[1] one of these days.

[1] A café near the British Museum, and meeting-place for the Sturge Moore–Streatfield group.

PART II. 1910–1920

Blasting and Bombardiering

Not long after resettling in London, Lewis began to emerge from the obscurity of his desultory life abroad. In 1909 his first stories appeared in English Review; *in 1911 he showed his work in the first exhibition of the Camden Town Group. During the following decade, and despite the interruption of war, he became well-known as a visual artist, a writer, and a leading "art politician" (as he called it) of the avant-garde. By 1920 he had spearheaded a movement, published a first novel of recognised distinction, and had a one-man show in London.*

Lewis owed his remarkable bourgeoning to a confluence of circumstances: a sudden and continuing access of vitality that rendered his talents productive; good fortune in meeting and attracting people who shared his interests; an atmosphere that favoured novelty and allowed for it economically. About 1910 his drawing and painting began to reveal the hard, formal yet energetic style that became his signature. During this period of growth, under cubist-futurist influences, he produced drawings, paintings, and decorations which made him stand out among "revolutionary" artists in London. At the same time he was writing stories, essays, propaganda, and finally Tarr. *These combined to show him as an innovator in letters ranking with Pound, Eliot, and Joyce.*

As a personality in the world of art and letters, Lewis quickly attracted cohorts and admirers. That he was secretive and temperamental only made him more glamorous to those who recognised his gifts and felt the force of his energy. Sturge Moore and Augustus John survived from the days of obscurity. To them were added Ford Madox Hueffer and Violet Hunt, whose entertainments at South Lodge before the war drew, besides Edwardian notables, the entire avant-garde of London. Through Hueffer came Ezra Pound. The friendship began with Pound acting as an ally in artistic revolt and a promoter of Lewis's career; he sold Lewis to Harriet Shaw Weaver, to The Little Review, *to John Quinn. It became as years passed one of the most influential relationships in Lewis's life. His association with T. E. Hulme, perhaps the chief theoriser of the avant-garde, was briefer; but its potency is revealed in the work of both men, as well as in Lewis's reminiscences of Hulme in* Blasting and Bombardiering. *Finally, there were the many women in London who favoured the arts and patronised them – Olivia Shakespear, the Countess of Drogheda, Mary Borden Turner, Mme Strindberg, Lady Cunard, Kate Lechmere, to name a few.*

All these connexions helped of course to promote the art politician. During this period Lewis's political career, aside from appearances in print and on platforms, can be described as a series of affiliations. First came the Camden Town Group, then the London Group and concurrently Roger Fry's Omega Workshops, then Marinetti and Futurism. By 1914 *he was strong enough to lead his own movement. The name, "Vorticism," was Pound's; but Lewis – with his Rebel Art Centre and his sensational review,* Blast *– was the driving force. The aim of the movement, not unlike that of Futurism, was to create a vital response to the new look and feel of the time. Verbally imagistic and visually abstract, the Vorticists approached, nevertheless, a distinctive amalgam – features of which were the dominance of intellect, hostility to the genteel, and the idea of a still centre. The war ended Vorticism, though not its influence. With the armistice Lewis was organising again. This time it was X Group.*

In the perspective of history much of this activity strikes one as unimportant. Two of the episodes had, however, a permanent effect on Lewis. His angry rupture with Roger Fry confirmed in him a lifelong opposition to the Bloomsbury group and what it signified for him: art as the province of the socially and financially established, dilettantism, the effete versus the vital. His casual connexion with Marinetti taught him techniques of propaganda – brash statement, aggressive mien – that gradually became integrated in his public personality.

During most of the war Lewis was either a soldier in training camps in England or a War Artist. He did, though, spend some months in heavy fighting at the front. This experience too made a lasting mark: Lewis became an enemy of war. Thus, it was partly his view of Hitler as a "man of peace" that led him to sympathise with Nazism in the early thirties. And it was largely his opposition to atomic combat that led him to a vision of Cosmic Man after World War II.

Lewis was evidently at work on Tarr *after his return to London. At the same time, to help maintain himself, he produced a pot-boiler. This he sent to J. B. Pinker, the well-known literary agent.*

42. *To J. B. Pinker*   14.B. Whiteheads Grove, Chelsea.
[ca. 1909–10]

Dear Mr. Pinker,

Here is the novel I told you about.[1] – When you have looked through it will you let me know what can be done with it. It was done to get if possible a little money so that I could complete comme il faut my other novel.[2] As the only thing of which there is question as far as this book is concerned is money-making, should you think the first chapter too long, as I suppose first impressions on the reader's mind are important; – or should anything else strike you, will you let me know?

The titles of the chapters are chosen as vulgarly effective: – suppose that is right? But perhaps I am going too quickly, and my miserable pot-boiler has not even any money value. – But if you decide that it *has*, is it in any way suitable for serial publication? If this were the case, and you thought of sending it to a Newspaper, certain disagreeable remarks about newspaper-reporters would have to be removed, and replaced by agreeable ones. As to the title of the book, again, it is merely a question of which would be the most vulgarly striking. I thought of "the three Mrs. Dekes", but this is inadequate. – I am going to choose myself a name and will send it you tomorrow: also a better title for the book if I can find one. – I hope it will have success with you, as I hope later it may with some publisher.

You will let me know as soon as possible your opinion?

Yours faithfully,
P. WYNDHAM LEWIS

[1] A few years ago Charles Handley-Read discovered the typescript of this novel in a London junkshop. It bears corrections in the writing of L. and of his mother. The typescript, never published, is now in the Lewis Collection at Cornell University Library.   [2] Doubtless *Tarr*.

43. *To J. B. Pinker*   Chelsea.
[ca. 1909–10]

Dear Mr. Pinker. I hope you got my MSS. this morning. *James Sed* is the name I will take for this book to disguise its origin. "Khan and Company"[1] would be a good title, I think: or "A will happily revised" perhaps.

                                     Yours faithfully,
                                          P. WYNDHAM LEWIS

44. *To J. B. Pinker*   Chelsea.
[ca. 1909–10]

Dear Mr. Pinker. When I came to your office the other day I took my MSS. away as you had told me it was not marketable. I shall not trouble any more about it, I think; and it is a lesson showing the futility of pot-boiling for me. . . .

                                     Yours faithfully,
                                          P. WYNDHAM LEWIS

44A. *To Augustus John?*†   [London?]
[Fragment of a letter.]   [1910]

. . . just struck me that I am speaking with an immodesty almost Gascon; overlook this fault. It is a sort of humility I assume with you. Even entre copains this sans gêne and humility is inadmissable. There have been two literary events lately: an admirable book by Sturge Moore on Flaubert:[2] – you are wrong not to like Sturge Moore, he's a very fine fellow, and not to be confounded with Ricketts.[3] Then John Masefield has just published a play on the Tragedy of Pompey the Great.[4] He makes Pompey a sort of Tolstoyan or neo-Christian hero. Its very good and also a good sign; theres no Shaw Barker nonsense about it. I'm making a poem

[1] This title appears on the typescript.
[2] T. Sturge Moore, *Art and Life* (London, [1910]).
[3] The painter, printer, and stage designer Charles Ricketts (1866–1931). Moore was closely associated with him.
[4] John Masefield, *The Tragedy of Pompey the Great* (London, 1910).

about a Breton Town; the name is fabulous.[1] I send it you as a very small insignificant present merely. I hope the big present I shall be able to make you soon will be a book of verse. I'm going to do nothing but poetry now this novel's finished.[2] My weakness and vices are quite patent to me, and I live with them with alternate irritation and bonhomie that I suppose everybody else bestows on similar anomalies chez lui. I believe with a Calvinistic uncompromisingness that one cannot be too hard on the stupidities of one's neighbours; and I thank you quite unaffectedly for having knocked a good deal of nonsense out of [me?], and am only sorry that I was not able (owing to my tender years and extravagant susceptibilities) to have rendered you a similar service. Among Baudelaire's titles to wisdom, as well as his deliverance of the poet from being the 'inspired' person of laurels and fine frenzies, is his clairvoyant treatment of the Man. – The benevolence and rayonnement that is the sign and beauty of a fine nature shines on faults without hiding them. Criticism being only valuable when it is disinterested, when one of the parties, between whom there is friction, pretends to impartiality, superiority, as with Lamb,[3] the harm he may do is more to be redouted than it would otherwise be. I have no objection to people being saints. I naturally object to their being saints at my expense.

P. W. L.

In 1913 Lewis, along with several other artists – among them Cuthbert Hamilton – made decorations and did scenic designs for the Cabaret Theatre Club, off Regent Street. This modernist night-club, known also as the Cave of the Golden Calf, was the brainchild of Strindberg's second wife, Freda. Like many who worked with her, Lewis had his troubles with the temperamental Mme Strindberg.[4]

[1] A draft of the poem is in the Lewis Collection at Cornell.
[2] Presumably a version of *Tarr*.
[3] Henry Lamb, R.A. (b. 1883), was a friend of John.
[4] Augustus John writes entertainingly of Mme Strindberg in *Chiaroscuro* (London, 1952). Osbert Sitwell describes an evening at her club in *Great Morning* (Boston, 1947), pp. 229–30. See also Violet Hunt, *I Have This to Say* (New York, 1926), p. 267; Edgar Jepson, *Memoirs of an Edwardian* (London, 1937), p. 155; and Lewis, *Rude Assignment* (London [1950]), pp. 124–5.

45. *To Cuthbert Hamilton*†¹ Paris.
[Draft of a letter.] [1913]

Dear Hamilton. I have come over here for a couple of days to transact a little piece of business. I shall be back on Thursday or Friday at latest.

I was concerned the other day at your ruffled state during the shadow-picture bustle. I hope that beastly Cabaret, that has been the cause of so many ridiculous vexations to me, is not going to add lessening of our good camaraderie to the number of its senseless misdeeds. See that it doesn't, for Heaven's sake.

I must still try and get something out of it; I am so hard up, and it serves to fill up the necessary gaps financially. I feel that you may have misunderstood my silence when the Strindberg broke loose about the black screens. – I assure you I was far more exasperated, if anything, than you were, and only held back for that reason, that I knew I should say too much: or rather only did so on the strict promise made to myself that if she repeated it I would clear out and leave her "en panne".

Lewis was invited by Roger Fry (1866–1934) to join the Omega Workshops in July 1913, when Fry organised his venture in decoration and design. The following letter indicates that within a month or two their relations were strained.

46. *To Roger Fry*† 142 Brecknock Road. Studio I.
Islington N.
[August–September 1913]

Dear Fry. Your answer yesterday I confess puzzled me. – "I forgot to ask if you have anything to send": – whereas all other contributors to Grafton were asked merely if their paintings or drawings then in Gallery should be sent on to Liverpool.² The implication is obvious.

¹ Cuthbert Hamilton (b. 1884) had been at the Slade with L. Later he followed L. through the break with the Omega Workshops, the establishment of the Rebel Art Centre, and the formation of the Vorticist Group.
² L. had shown a painting and several drawings in Fry's Second Post-Impressionist Exhibition at the Grafton Galleries in October 1912.

I am animated by most cordial sentiments as regards yourself and your activities. But to continue in an atmosphere of special criticism and ill-will, if such exist, would have manifest disadvantages, as well as being distasteful, to me.

You cannot say, I think, that I bemoan my financial situation to my acquaintances and colleagues. Yet it is the worse. Otherwise I should exhibit less interest in such slights as the one I am writing about. – An attitude of denigrement on your part, or absence of cordiality your initial action as regards me implied, might hurt my stomach as well as my vanity.

I wish you could give me, quite roughly, my bearings; and perhaps there is some unguessable reason for the incident I am directly writing of, that would alter its significance somewhat?

Yours very sincerely,
WYNDHAM LEWIS

Lewis broke completely with Fry in October 1913. The immediate cause of trouble was an Ideal Home Exhibition for which Lewis and his friend Spencer Gore were invited to participate in the decorating of a room. Before the invitation reached Lewis, Fry – through negligence or ill-will – appropriated the commission for the Omega. When Lewis discovered what had happened, he walked out, accompanied by his fellow artists Edward Wadsworth, Frederick Etchells, and Hamilton. A lawyer was consulted, and to publicise their protest, the dissidents sent to the press and to friends of the Omega a celebrated "Round Robin." The stir created by this document, composed by Lewis, focussed public attention on the group of rebellious young artists of whom Lewis was the leader.[1]

47. *The "Round Robin"* Brecknock Road, N.
[October 1913]

Dear Sir,

Understanding that you are interested in the Omega Workshops, we beg to lay before you the following discreditable facts.

---

[1] An extensive account of L. and the Omega appears in John Rothenstein, *Modern English Painters: Lewis to Moore* (London, 1956), pp. 26–27. The Bloomsbury side of the controversy is presented in Virginia Woolf, *Roger Fry* (New York, 1940), pp. 190–4. L.'s own entertaining account is in *Rude Assignment*, pp. 123–4.

(1) That the Direction of the Omega Workshops secured the decoration of the "Post-Impressionist" room at the Ideal Home Exhibition by a shabby trick, and at the expense of one of their members – Mr. Wyndham Lewis, and an outside artist – Mr. Spencer Gore. The facts are as follows.

Mr. Spencer Gore was approached last July by the Agent of the Daily Mail, and, in an interview at Carmelite House was invited, in conjunction with Mr. Wyndham Lewis and Mr. Roger Fry, to do a room for the Ideal Home Exhibition. It was the idea of those who recommended these artists to the Daily Mail authorities that a room should be decorated on the lines of their joint decorations in the Cabaret Theatre Club: Mr. Fry, as head of the Omega Workshops, should supply the Furniture.

Mr. Gore was asked to arrange a meeting between the Agent of the Daily Mail and his colleagues. Immediately on leaving Carmelite House, he went to the Omega Workshops, there seeing a director of the company and leaving word to the above effect; neither Mr. Fry nor Mr. Lewis being there at the time. Mr. Lewis, then working at the Omega Workshops, would, he naturally thought, be at once communicated with. After that Mr. Gore heard nothing further of the matter.

Not only was this visit not mentioned to Mr. Lewis, but the Direction at the Omega Workshops appropriated the commission, with the results at present visible to anyone visiting Olympia. As an example of the detailed working of this sordid game the following manoeuvre may be cited. When it was announced in the Workshop that the Ideal Home room had been secured by the "Omega", and it came to apportioning the work, Mr. Lewis was told by Mr. Roger Fry that no decorations of any sort were to be placed on the walls, and was asked if he would carve a mantelpiece. Shortly after this, Mr. Lewis went away on his holidays, and on his return in September, found large mural decorations, destined for the Olympia Exhibition, around the walls of the workroom.

(2) A second unpleasant fact is the suppression of information in order to prevent a member from exhibiting in a Show of Pictures *not* organised by the Direction of the Omega. Mr. Rutter, the Curator of the Leeds Art Gallery,[1] in organising a Post-

[1] Frank Rutter (1876–1937), art critic and editor, was Curator of Leeds Art Gallery from 1912 to 1917.

6. Self-Portrait, ca. 1913

Impressionist Exhibition in Bond Street,[1] wrote to Mr. Fry some weeks ago. In this letter he asked for Mr. Etchells'[2] address, wanting some of his work for the Exhibition. He was given to understand that Mr. Etchells had no pictures ready and would have none till 1914. This statement of Mr. Fry's was not only unauthorised but untrue. It is curious that a letter from Mr. Rutter to Mr. Lewis on the same subject, and addressed to the Omega Workshops, should never have reached him.[3]

This mean and ludicrous policy of restraining artists might, perhaps, be justified if the Direction at all fulfilled its function of impresario, but its own Shows are badly organised, unfairly managed, closed to much good work for petty and personal reasons, and flooded with the work of well-intentioned friends of the Direction.

More incidents of the above nature could be alleged, but these two can be taken as diagnostics of the general tone of the place.

As to its tendencies in Art, they alone would be sufficient to make it very difficult for any vigorous art-instinct to long remain under that roof. The Idol is still Prettiness, with its mid-Victorian languish of the neck, and its skin is "greenery-yallery", despite the Post-What-Not fashionableness of its draperies. This family party of strayed and Dissenting Aesthetes, however, were compelled to call in as much modern talent as they could find, to do the rough and masculine work without which they knew their efforts would not rise above the level of a pleasant tea-party, or command more attention.

The reiterated assurances of generosity of dealing and care for art, cleverly used to stimulate outside interest, have then, we think, been conspicuously absent in the interior working of the Omega Workshops. This enterprise seemed to promise, in the opportunities afforded it by support from the most intellectual quarters, emancipation from the middleman-shark. But a new

[1] Rutter's Post-Impressionist Exhibition opened at the Doré Gallery in October 1913.

[2] Frederick Etchells (b. 1886) had been associated with L. in various exhibitions of the new art. He went with him into the Rebel Art Centre and Vorticism. After World War I, Etchells gave up painting for architecture.

[3] On October 2nd Rutter wrote to L. saying he had already written to him at Fitzroy Street asking him to send two or three paintings to the exhibition. See next letter.

form of fish in the troubled waters of Art has been revealed in the meantime, the Pecksniff-shark, a timid but voracious journalistic monster, unscrupulous, smooth-tongued and, owing chiefly to its weakness, mischievous.

No longer willing to form part of this unfortunate institution, we the undersigned have given up our work there.

    FREDERICK ETCHELLS WYNDHAM LEWIS
    C. HAMILTON   E. WADSWORTH.[1]

At the same time Lewis wrote to Clive Bell (b. 1881), who, though not directly involved in the Omega fracas, was already closely associated with Fry.

48. *To Clive Bell*†   Brecknock Studios.
[Probably not sent.]   [October 1913]

Dear Bell. May I place before you, as one considerably interested in the Fitzroy Square business, a few facts that cannot be made pretty (as most things in Heaven and Earth can) by Mr. Roger Fry? I have severed my connection with the Fitzroy Sq. place, on the discovery, following on several others, of a piece of pitiable chicanery, worthy, in its inception and execution, of a bastard of Pecksniff by some half-cracked scullery-maid.

The people getting up the Ideal Home Exhibition asked Spencer Gore, in an interview they had with him, to arrange with me to do the decoration for a room at Olympia, the idea coming from knowledge of my work in that direction at the Cabaret Club. They also wanted Fry to cooperate, in his capacity of Proprietor (or whatever he is) of the Omega Workshops.

Gore came to Fitzroy Square and left this message with a presumably responsible and honourable individual found on the spot, neither Fry or myself being there at the time.

When a day or two later I appeared there to work, Fry came up and told me that the 'Omega' had been commissioned to do a

---

[1] Edward Wadsworth (1889–1949) met L. at the Omega and became closely associated with him in L.'s subsequent undertakings. During the 1920's the friendship ended (see Part III), as did their artistic kinship.

room at Earl's Court,¹ that everybody was going to put in extra time etc. He omitted absolutely any mention of the fact that the invitation had anything to do with me, and until a few days ago I had imagined it was a matter purely concerning the Omega Workshops. When it came to the question of who should do what, Fry suggested I should undertake the mantlepiece carving. When I asked what was going to happen on the walls, he replied 'Nothing at all, [just?] a few irregular spaces of colours. No decorations; he had concluded 'this would be better'. When I came back from France, I find large decorative panels for the walls all over the place, now figuring at the Earl's Court Exhibition, I believe. – Then the other day I met Gore, and it all came out.

You will hardly expect me to be amused at these tricks and contrivances, or wish to remain longer in the vicinity of a bad shit.

You no doubt will have heard of Roger Fry's manèges [?] as regards the Doré Gallery exhibition. My part of that is merely that a letter sent by Frank Rutter to Fitzroy Square never reached me. When I tackled Fry on the subject yesterday, he denied that my name had ever been mentioned. I then saw Gore again, and he affirms that the facts of the case are as I have told them above. From any point of view Gore's evidence is preferable, as he has no interest in the matter. No doubt Fry entered at once into communication with the Daily Mail people as the "Omega Workshop" only, I being one of his "workmen" as he would say if necessary. And I can quite believe that all further negotiations were carried in that name.

You must excuse me for having expressed myself with certain heat and precision. These facts are easily verifiable: and not for any irreparable harm done, bien entendu, but from the disgustingly mean nature of his behaviour, you will see that no case can be made out for moderation.

With such mischievous and weak-minded folk.... [Draft ends here.]

P. G. Konody (1872–1934) was at this time art critic for the Daily Mail, *which sponsored the Ideal Home Exhibition. Having recommended Lewis for a part in the "Post-Impressionist" room, he was eager to get to the facts of the controversy that ensued.*

¹ A confusion; L. means Olympia.

49. *To P. G. Konody*†　　　　　　　　　　　　Brecknock Road. N.
[October 1913]

Dear Mr. Konody. I have just seen Gore, and he bears out every word, naturally, of what we have written, with the one exception that he says that he did not go to Carmelite House, but to the *offices of the Ideal Home Exhibition*, which are, he believes, in Fleet Street. He is at present looking for the letter from the Secretary of the Ideal Home Exhibition asking him to make an appointment with "their Agent", as he wrote.

What we say in the circular letter, and what is perfectly easy to prove, is that *Gore first* got in touch with the Daily Mail, was asked to do this room, went to Fitzroy Square after seeing the Ideal Home Agent, and left his message with Duncan Grant, a director of the Omega Workshops and a friend of Fry's. – From that moment nothing further was heard of the matter. – Fry's defense does *not deny that he got Gore's message*, but says, with much specious rigmarole, that somehow or other when he got in touch with Ideal Home People, the commission became exclusively his. That is exactly what we say.

It would be absurd for the Daily Mail People to say that Gore had never seen their representative. Gore has little interest in the matter, and he is not a man whose word could be doubted.

If the Omega people made this lying defence it would be more damaging to them than the original facts were. You can be sure that they will not, as indeed Clive Bell says they "do not think of doing." – 6 Cambrian Road, Richmond, is Gore's address should you wish to communicate with him. I must thank you very much for the trouble you have taken in this affair, as I was grateful for your original kindness in recommending [me], with Gore, to decorate the room.

　　　　　　　　　　　　　　　　　Yours sincerely,
　　　　　　　　　　　　　　　　　WYNDHAM LEWIS

Please excuse this untidy letter. W.L.

50. *To Clive Bell*† [London]
[October 1913]

Dear Bell. You will by this time no doubt have received the round letter signed by me among others. – One more fact may now be added.

A letter sent by Rutter 10 days ago to Fitzroy Square about a Bond Street Show never reached me. Yesterday I got it in a letter from Fry, opened, with explanation, incidentally, that he had read it, before noticing it was meant for me!

There is no fact in the round letter that can be disputed. Fry's only explanation of the Ideal Home Exhibition business is that, although he received Gore's message, that when he got in touch with the Daily Mail man the commission somehow or other became wholly his, and Gore's name and mine somehow or other disappeared. Exactly. That is what the round letter says.

Fry is a bad egg, [word], and I for one wish no longer to remain in his neighbourhood. He has some vulgar nasty, mean crookedness in his nature, that has left a trail of particular unsavouriness in his life.

I hope this rather rough episode will not have entirely alienated you. Anyhow, I thought I would send you a personal word on my side of the matter.

Yrs,

WYNDHAM LEWIS

51. *To Mrs. Percy Harris*†[1] [London]
[November 1913?]

Dear Mrs. Harris. I was sorry you did not come to the Cabaret Club last night, as Marinetti[2] declaimed some peculiarly blood-

---

[1] L. knew Mrs. Percy Harris, wife of the Deputy Chairman of the London County Council, as an art patron and friend of Hueffer. He was planning to do some decorations for her house in Sloane Street.

[2] F. T. Marinetti (1878–1944), the Futurist leader, was often in London from 1912 to 1914. He lectured at the Doré Gallery on November 20th, 1913, and again several times during 1914. L. describes his platform style in *Blasting and Bombardiering* (London, 1932), pp. 36–7. There is also a vivid account in Sir Jacob Epstein's autobiography, *Let There Be Sculpture* (New York, 1940), pp. 52–3.

thirsty concoctions with great dramatic force. – He is lecturing at the Doré Galleries at 8.45 on Thursday evening next. He will not, there, enter into direct rivalry with the Grand Guignol, I imagine; but will no doubt be worth hearing.

I enclose you a handbill of the affair.

Yours sincerely,
W. LEWIS

On December 18th, 1913, The New Age printed a highly unfavourable review by its art critic, Anthony M. Ludovici, of an exhibition of sculpture by Jacob Epstein. The following week T. E. Hulme, Epstein's friend and advocate, took Ludovici to task in a letter titled "Mr. Epstein and his critics." On January 1st, 1914, appeared Ludovici's "An Open Letter to My Friends," defending himself against Hulme's accusations and ranging himself on Hulme's side – that is, in favour of the classic virtues. Lewis entered the controversy the following week; Ludovici replied to this letter in the issue of January 15th.

52. *To the Editor of "The New Age," January 8th, 1914*

EPSTEIN AND HIS CRITICS, OR NIETZSCHE AND HIS FRIEND

Sir, – Mr. Ludovici, scuttling away, took up so much of the road, spread himself so self-obliviously in your last number, that it was difficult to avoid him if one read the paper.

Cannot this cowardly and shifty individual even stick to his words? His impudent journalism, where he describes Mr. Epstein as a "minor personality of no importance" was chiefly responsible for Mr. Hulme's indignation. Now, chastised as he deserves – or rather does not, since to say the least he was not worth so much ink or space – he would escape further trouble by beginning to talk innocently of *all* artists as "minor personalities". He does not say directly: "But, Mr. Epstein, *all* artists are minor personalities." He introduces into his discourse this statement, Mr. Epstein apparently being meant to think: "Oh, so all artists are minor personalities; come come I needn't mind so much!" In this way our rather frightened little friend thinks he may escape with his skin from the awkward corner in which he finds himself.

He eventually has the word "minor" on the brain – which is natural, I daresay. In the first sentence of his reply he gives an explanation of his use of the epithet: "and, indeed, in comparison with, the man who produces, the critic enjoys but a *minor* and notoriously less dignified position." This minor and less dignified position is, perhaps, unpleasant, and induces such people as Mr. Ludovici to find satisfaction in passing on to the "man who produces" this rankling adjective. Perhaps Mr. Ludovici made his first appearance hedged about with inverteds and "as Nietzsche saids." That present, in any event, dispenses with them. Yet "Artists are the most sensitive men in a community" and following sentences surely might be fenced off from the contamination of his balderdash by a few commas at least.

He is obviously a fool it is worth no one's while to notice. But he suddenly threatens to engulf the entire superficies of one of the only good papers in the country with his jibberish, wildly and vacantly, inflated, like some queer insect, in terror when attacked. May I use this occasion as a great admirer of *The New Age*, to hope that for those "most sensitive men" (Nietzsche) some less ridiculous go-between may be found. His dismal shoddy rubbish is not even amusingly ridiculous. It is the grimmest pig-wash vouchsafed at present to a public fed on husks.

WYNDHAM LEWIS

In his letter of December 25th, Hulme had said that Ludovici should be dealt with physically but that he was too small to attack. On January 22nd Mr. Arthur Rose wrote to The New Age *suggesting that he employ a pugilist of Jack Johnson's size to present Ludovici's case. Then Hulme, he says, could feel free to take him on. Mr. Rose offers his "large and secluded garden" for the fight and predicts total defeat for Hulme. He ends by deploring Hulme's prize-fighting approach to aesthetics.*

53. To the Editor of "The New Age," February 12th, 1914

MR. ARTHUR ROSE'S OFFER

Sir, – I am sure all your readers will see the appropriateness of a Rose possessing "a large and secluded garden." But the rose would be merely misunderstanding the intentions of Nature in putting it forward as a place where your correspondents should settle their differences.

Settlements according to avoirdupois would, we all have felt, be arbitrary. But Mr. Hulme must have meant rather the half-pony-power of the spirit, than the weight of the physical machine, of the traducer of Flenites.

We are here on unsubstantial ground. Mr. Rose unconsciously brings a sensational illumination. Jack Johnson has been mentioned. At once the real protagonists are plainly visible, and Mr. Rose's suggestion might have terrible results for his overman protégé. For, in defence of those savage effigies we see even huger forms than that of the Illinois champion rearing themselves from the depths of Virgin Forests. Instead of fun and gain, religious fury spurs their pugilistic proportions.

The Savage against the Superman! That is the piquant situation invented by hospitable and garrulous Mr. Rose (to drop the metaphorical style of referring to him).

The Zambesi, however, is far away. Meanwhile, might not Jack Johnson, despite himself, and more formidable than ever before, be found in the Rose garden taking his stand on the side opposite to that your correspondent supposes, in defence of secular gods?

WYNDHAM LEWIS

The history of Lewis's association with London art factions begins in 1911, when he participated in the first exhibition of the Camden Town Group at the Carfax Gallery. His affiliation with the Camden Town painters was personal rather than stylistic – his friends Spencer Gore and Harold Gilman[1] *figuring among the*

---

[1] Harold Gilman (1876–1919) had also been at the Slade with L. After his death, L. and Louis F. Fergusson produced a memorial volume in his honour: *Harold Gilman: An Appreciation* (London, 1919).

chief organisers of the venture. When it became clear that Sickert's was to be the guiding spirit of the group, Lewis found his membership definitely uncongenial. He admired Sickert's work but could hardly subscribe to the pissarroesque principles he saw it as representing. Finally in 1913 *Camden Town merged into the newly formed London Group, and Lewis got a chance to assert his direction. In the larger London Group, the post-Impressionist element – including such artists as Epstein, Etchells, David Bomberg, C. R. W. Nevinson, Wadsworth – played a stronger role. It was Gore of Camden Town who chose the pictures for the first exhibition of the London Group, held in Brighton in December* 1913, *but now Lewis wrote one of the forewords to the catalogue.*[1] *Sickert spoke at the opening, putting himself on the side of catholicity and experiment. Yet, as his biographer says, he felt at this time little sympathy for the new art.*[2] *The rift widened and of course soon reached the press. In an article titled "On Swiftness" in* The New Age *of March 26th,* 1914, *Sickert lashed out against the English Cubists. Among his indictments was this: ". . . while the faces of the persons suggested are frequently nil, non-representation is forgotten when it comes to the sexual organs. Witness Mr. Wyndham Lewis's 'Creation,' exhibited at Brighton, Mr. Gaudier-Brzeska's drawing in last week's* New Age, *and several of Mr. Epstein's later drawings." Lewis was not the man to ignore such an attack.*[3]

[1] John Rothenstein calls this a "comprehensive exhibition" of the Camden Town Group. See *Modern English Painters: Sickert to Smith* (London, 1952), p. 201.

[2] See Robert Emmons, *The Life and Opinions of Walter Richard Sickert* (London, 1941), pp. 147–52. The author points out that Sickert later modified his harshness to the extent of resigning from the Royal Academy in defence of Epstein!

[3] Sickert struck back at L. in *The New Age* of June 25th, where he accuses the cubists of becoming professional refusés, "the type of the *douanier* Rousseau." Only, "Our Nevinsons, Wyndham Lewises, Phelan Gibbses, etc., are not custom-house officers, but more or less clever and superannuated art-students trying to paint like custom-house officers."

54. To the Editor of "The New Age," April 2nd, 1914

MODERN ART

Sir, – I will, with your leave, deal with two attacks made on me last week, one in the guise of morals, was it, or taste, the other, criticism.

Mr. Sickert's latest little game, played on we poor innocent artists, is to get a fireman's helmet and razor-strop, and so disguised as a policeman of Bedford burlesque,[1] to set out towards us, his chuckles propelling him somewhat like the jerks of a motor-cycle. Arrived in our neighbourhood, he gathers a little crowd, mixes us a little with it, and would then Koepenick us all, shepherd-like, towards that prison where Oscar Wilde lay for two years, struck down by the bourgeoisie. We have been amused at his antics; but at this point we withdraw.

Mr. Walter Sickert, for twenty or thirty years, was the scandal of the neighbourhood (as a painter) and he was very proud of it. His bedroom realism, cynical and boyish playfulness with Mrs. Grundy, his French "legerté" (as he would write), all marked him out as the Bohemian plague-spot on clean English life – part, indeed, of that larger Yellow Plague-spot edited by Arthur Symons.[2] But now he has survived his sins, and has sunk into the bandit's mellow and peaceful maturity. He sits at his open front door and invents little squibs and contrivances to discomfort the young brigands he hears tales of, and of whose exploits he is rather jealous.

"If we can fasten pornography on to them, on top of their aesthetic enormities, we shall have them on toast. They'll be nabbed – every man-jack of them, and soon be under lock and key." So he gets hold of the Brighton catalogue. There he finds the very thing!

In a preface I wrote for that catalogue I spoke in detail of the work of several of the more important artists. Among them was Jacob Epstein. Now, there is only one thing to say about his work: first, that it is good, and, secondly, no man could avoid placing foremost, in considering it, the heroic pre-occupation with Human

---

[1] The Old Bedford was one of Sickert's favourite subjects.

[2] L. refers to the close links between the New English Art Club and *The Yellow Book*.

Birth.[1] No other artist showing in that exhibition has, to my knowledge, ever exhibited works in which this especial artistic impulse was inordinately present. "Cubism," as a matter of fact, would tend quite in the contrary direction, as it is a movement largely occupied in banishing extraneous or literary stimulus, concentrating on forms and colours for their own sake; essentially inhuman and pure. But I consider that Mr. Epstein's work has such merit that, whatever your prejudice, or personal bias, it can be praised.

The choosing of this passage, therefore, was a trick merely; Mr. Sickert's description of my painting "Creation" a deliberate misstatement and invention. I have always found pornography extremely boring and regarded it as the hallmark of the second-rate. As for Phallic aesthetics, I have no quarrel with them, only I don't happen to participate myself, that is all: though much preferring the naked and clean thing to the boudoir suggestiveness and Yellow Book Gallicisms.

We all admire Mr. Sickert's go, sense of fun, etc., very much. But I thought I would state publicly, for those who might have been taken in or mystified by the proceedings in last week's NEW AGE, that it was not a *real* policeman (not even a cinematograph company at work) but only a genial malefactor, not from Koepenick this time, but from Camden Town.

In my article on a more general subject I will add a word on Mr. Hulme's views of the London Group.

WYNDHAM LEWIS

Lewis and Miss Kate Lechmere, his backer, established the Rebel Art Centre in the spring of 1914.[2] *The idea was that Lewis and his Vorticist cohorts – among them, Henri Gaudier-Brzeska, Pound, Wadsworth, Nevinson, and Etchells – should give classes, lectures, and exhibitions at the house which Miss Lechmere took in Great*

---

[1] Sickert quotes from L.'s foreword: "Hung in this room as well are three drawings by Jacob Epstein, the only great sculptor at present working in England. He finds in the machinery of procreation a dynamo to work the deep atavism of his spirit."

[2] Violet Hunt evokes the Rebel Art Centre and L.'s world at this time in *I Have This To Say*, pp. 211–16. Her version of L.'s background is, however, compounded of error.

Ormond Street. But by autumn the Centre was closed; war had come, and Lewis was not in any case suited to serve long as the director of such a venture.

55. *To Frederick Etchells*   Rebel Art Centre.
                           38 Gt. Ormond Street, Queen's Square, W.C.
                                                      [April–May 1914]

Dear Etchells.[1]

I am sending you some Prospectuses of *Art School* and *Art Centre*. I should be immensely obliged if you could do the following things. Ask the *American Artist's Chairman* [?] in the *Boul. Montparnasse* if he will stick up copies of Prospectus on his walls. Also, and more important, ask the [words] shop in the Rue de Grande Chaumière (It is called Dolores or something) if they would do so. – Also the American artshop in the Boul. Raspail. – Anywhere else you know of. . . .

In two weeks Blast will *positively* appear.[2] I will then send you copies promised. – Before that time I may send in a few subscription forms and notices.

How are you getting on? The general hum-drum of life of the little cliques continues here. Marinetti still lectures. Balla is a good painter, you know. Bomberg[3] has cut his beard, wears a bowler hat, and lives in Lamb's Conduit Street. The —— Bookshop doves have flown to their cote at Rye, bill and coo there, and besmirch the Spring sunshine. . . .

                         Donne-moi de tes nouvelles.
                                       W. LEWIS

P.S. La vie de Charles Blanchard (by Charles-Louis Philippe)[4] is worth reading, though quite French. – If you want to see the Derain picture of a seated woman, go to Kahnweiler's. It is like an extremely good Henry Lamb. – There are good Picassos there too.

[1] Etchells was in Paris at this time.
[2] *Blast No. 1* appeared in June 1914.
[3] David Bomberg (1890–1957) exhibited with the Vorticist group in 1915.
[4] Charles-Louis Philippe, *Charles Blanchard* (Paris, 1913).

56. *To Alick Schepeler*[1] Café Royal.
[ca. May 1914]

Dear Alic. . . .

As to *Blast*, subject of your letter, please get in any subscribers or buyers you can. Two to three weeks will see it set up and ready to produce.

It is an awful business to get it out. I am not a business man, despite John[2] twitting and my (alas!) undeniable political activity. Hence the delays in getting the paper out.

Well, à bientot.

Yours ever
WYNDHAM LEWIS

Lewis and his friends showed interest in Futurism from the time Marinetti began to campaign for it in London. But although they mixed openly with the Italian and his followers – Marinetti was asked to lecture at the Rebel Art Centre – they did not, except for C. R. W. Nevinson, declare their allegiance to the movement. On June 7th, 1914, there appeared in The Observer *a Futurist Manifesto, citing Lewis and other Vorticists as "the great Futurist painters or pioneers and advance forces of vital English Art." The Manifesto was signed by Marinetti and C. R. W. Nevinson and addressed from the Rebel Art Centre. As the following letter indicates, Lewis lost no time in dissociating his group from Marinetti's rival cause.*[3]

[1] Alick Schepeler, a friend of Lewis and other artists and writers, worked for the *Illustrated London News*.

[2] Probably Augustus John.

[3] The exchange between Nevinson and L. appeared in the *New Weekly* as well. In the *New Weekly* of June 20th, and *The Observer* of the 21st, Nevinson wrote disclaiming any intent to implicate the Rebel Art people as followers of Marinetti. He had written directly to L. in the same vein on June 13th. For an account of the whole incident, see John Rothenstein, *Modern English Painters: Lewis to Moore* (New York, 1956), pp. 130–5.

57. To the Editor of "The Observer," June 14th, 1914

FUTURISM

Dear Sir,

To read or hear the praises of oneself or one's friends is always pleasant. There are forms of praise, however, which are so compounded with innuendo as to be most embarrassing. One may find oneself, for instance, so praised as to make it appear that one's opinions coincide with those of the person who praises, in which case one finds oneself in the difficult position of disclaiming the laudation or of even slightly resenting it.

There are certain artists in England who do not belong to the Royal Academy nor to any of the passéist groups, and who do not on that account agree with the futurism of Sig. Marinetti. An assumption of such agreement either by Sig. Marinetti or by his followers is an impertinence.

We, the undersigned, whose ideals were mentioned or implied, or who might by the opinion of others be implicated, beg to dissociate ourselves from the "futurist" manifesto which appeared in the pages of the 'Observer' of Sunday, June 7th.

> SIGNED: – Richard Aldington,[1] David Bomberg, Frederick Etchells, Ezra Pound, Edward Wadsworth, Lawrence Atkinson,[2] Gaudier Brzeska,[3] Cuthbert Hamilton, William Roberts,[4] Wyndham Lewis.

P.S. The Direction of the Rebel Art Centre wishes to state that

---

[1] Richard Aldington (b. 1892) came to know L. through Pound and through their various connexions with *The Egoist* and *The New Age*. He also signed the Manifesto of "the Great London Vortex" which appeared in *Blast No. 1*.

[2] Lawrence Atkinson (1873–1931), another signer of the *Blast* Manifesto, exhibited with the Vorticists in 1915.

[3] The remarkable French sculptor Henri Gaudier-Brzeska (1891–1915) came to L. through Pound. He was active in the Rebel Art Centre, contributed to *Blast*, and exhibited with the Vorticists before his death at the front on June 5th, 1915. See *Blasting and Bombardiering*.

[4] William Roberts (b. 1895) met L. at the Omega; for the next several years they were close allies, Roberts joining in all of L'.s projects of the period.

the use of their address by Sig. Marinetti and Mr. Nevinson[1] was unauthorised.

Rebel Art Centre
June 8th

(In reference to the above Mr. Bomberg asks us to say that he signed the letter not as a member of the Rebel Art Centre ((being unconnected with that group)), but independently. – Editor. Observer.)

58. *To Beatrice Hastings*†[2] 4 Percy Street, W.C.
[ca. 1914]

Dear Mrs. Hastings. I have never been so commiserated with. If you go on in this way you will make me quite sorry for myself. – You even lyrically advise *all* young artists to go on boozing and wasting rather than get to work, and have to affront the poor, obscure and pimply tongues of some refuse corner of the disgusting Art-World! Vous êtes bizarre, quand même, vous savez!

Seriously, get rid of this hautise of the Hulme [?]–Kibbelwhite [?] combination.[3] They are pretty boring folk: Epstein is the only individual in that little set who does anything or has any personality. And he is not fool enough to go too far, as far as I am concerned.

Let us talk of something more interesting.

Yours WYNDHAM LEWIS

[1] C. R. W. Nevinson (1889–1946) had been casually associated with L. in art-propaganda activities for a year or so. Together they organised a welcoming dinner for Marinetti in the autumn of 1913, and Nevinson allied himself with the Rebel Art Centre at the time of its establishment. He was invited to exhibit as "Nevinson (Futurist)" at the Vorticist show in 1915.

[2] Beatrice Hastings was a friend of A. R. Orage of *The New Age* and a sub-editor of the paper, to which she contributed regularly. In her irate pamphlet *The Old "New Age," Orage – and Others* (London, 1936), she claims credit for having brought Pound and his friends to the paper.

[3] L. evidently refers to the group that gathered round T. E. Hulme at the house of Mrs. Kibblewhite in Frith Street.

59. *To Augustus John*† [London]
[1914?]

Dear John. I dont move in those circles – voire artistic and high mondaine – where news of your doings circulates as naturally as blood. But should I meet any isolated individual imbued with the degenerate philosophies – those awkward systems – that seek to prove you have abandoned the Lane's House job,[1] I shall know how to settle him.

What you tell me of your designs on the Town of London is very welcome: smite it hip and thigh! I should not be sorry if you made an end of it once and for all, artistically. Let it be an authentic earthquake!!! – a really prodigious and elemental disturbance. (For old acquaintance sake you could warn me in time and I would remove to Paris). – But I am always regretting that I was not born in a volcanic land; in the matter of art anyhow: the sort of place where the aesthetic structures have a slight shake-up every day and are periodically swallowed up altogether. Whats the good of being an island, if you are not a *volcanic* island? ... There is a difference between hedonism (as this word is habitually used) and retaining pleasure in one's curriculum. I think in the new diagram that men are busy drawing; with "les éclairs de la tête" and all the anatomy of dreams we call the soul, – in its old familiar place, half-way down the figure, what world would be, indeed, poetic, without the rooster and his dunghill, – planked in the midst of the story of Christ?

But I think that the body has been eloquently enough praised in the last century by men who did nothing else, without bête reactions, and surtout without letting the ever accursed dilletantes make it smell for us, let us keep that joyful engine, charger of what not, under us. That it was the rich and noisy material of my essay on exercise signifies nothing more in my case. If I continue my tub-thumping in the New Age my next article will be directed at one of the bêtest [?], and most sickening phases of a dirty

[1] Sir Hugh Lane (1875–1915) had taken a house in Cheyne Walk and asked John to decorate a room in it. According to John, there were too many people coming round while he was working, and he took his panels away. Later he and Sir Hugh settled their differences and it was decided to continue the project. Before this could be done, however, Sir Hugh went down on the *Lusitania*.

modern journalistic spiritual and intellectual "paresse": – I refer to the Henley Dodd business.¹ I might devote two or three [word], even, to scourging the "banal" nakedness of various "Return to Nature", shits. I hear that MacEvoy, the playwright, when he arrives at a house, however many vacant beds there may be in it, insists on sleeping on the floor, his head on the saddle of the large charger on which he is always (apparently) to be seen. Shall we allow these tiresome little enthusiasms to be petted a year or so longer, or shall I at once "taper dessus"?² . . .

I have just finished an "analytic" novel about a German student (again working over material a year old).³ The language is not travaillé: any beauty it may possess depending on the justness of the psychology, – as is the case in the Russian novels, I suppose. I think it is a great thing to have ready to one's hand a good many forms, – novel, jaunty or vernacular essay, story like Verlaine's etc; – si on a quoi les remplir: – if a man has any considerable "trop plein", *valuable dross* it should not be lost because it is no longer, in our enlightened age, to remain with the rarest metal. This coarse rich mass will never be absent when the vein is rich. It has just struck me that I am speaking . . . .

[Rest of copy missing.]

*Lewis and Ezra Pound first met in 1909 or 1910, not long after Pound's arrival in London and Lewis's return from the Continent.*⁴ *By 1912 or 1913 they had become closely associated in advancing new art and new writing. Pound, having given Vorticism its name, became one of its chief publicists. He was, as well, the most active*

¹ The painter and etcher Francis Dodd, R.A. (1874–1949), was known for his scenes of suburban life. He painted the poet W. E. Henley shortly before Henley's death in 1903. About the same time John was Professor of Fine Arts at Liverpool and was friendly with Dodd. It may be "Henley Dodd" was an epithet coined by John.

² Charles McEvoy (1879–1929) was writing plays in the new naturalistic vein. In his reply, John wrote: "I think I would leave McEvoy's uncomfortable little habit alone. He is one of the most richly ridiculous people I know – and I am full of gratitude to him for his drollery."

³ *Tarr*.

⁴ In his memoir of Pound, L. writes vividly of their early friendship. See Peter Russell, ed., *An Examination of Ezra Pound* (New York, [1950]), pp. 257–66. See also *Blasting and Bombardiering* (pp. 277–81) for L.'s account of his first meeting with Pound at the Vienna Café.

supporter of Lewis's entire creative output.[1] *He sold Lewis's writing to* The Egoist *and* The Little Review *and his pictures to the American collector John Quinn. While Lewis was in the army, Pound acted as his agent and general manager in London. The association persisted until Pound left London in 1921. Thereafter the two men necessarily saw less of one another. But in spite of periodic lapses and occasional misunderstandings, they stayed friends and mutual admirers until Lewis's death.*

60. *To Ezra Pound* 18 Fitzroy Street
Fitzroy Square, W.C.
[January 1915?]

Dear Pound. Many thanks for your excellent piece on Binyon and the Sea Serpent.[2]

I think by the way of *Blessing* the Vienna Cafe.[3]

Can you give me Coburn's address.[4] Arbuthnot[5] has a malicious photograph of me in an article in *Leaders of Modern Movement*. There I figure with Poynter,[6] Sargent, Jacob and John. Poynter, they say, is the leader of a "movement that is almost extinct." It is full of wit. But for Arbuthnot's behaviour I know no parallel in the history of art. I must at once see Coburn. I feel Arbuthnot must be fought against.

Eliot has sent me Bullshit and the Ballad for Big Louise. They are excellent bits of scholarly ribaldry. I am trying to print them

---

[1] See D. D. Paige, ed., *The Letters of Ezra Pound* (New York, 1950), *passim*.

[2] Probably Section III, titled "Lawrence Binyon," of Pound's "Chronicles" in *Blast No. 2* (July 1915), p. 86. Reprinted in *Pavannes and Divagations* (New York, 1958), pp. 148–50.

[3] The Vienna Café does not appear in the list of people and things blessed in *Blast No. 2*.

[4] Alvin Langdon Coburn. This American photographer had been a member of Stieglitz's Photo-Secession group. He was associated with Pound and Lewis in Vorticist experiments in photography.

[5] Malcolm Arbuthnot was a well-known Bond Street photographer of the time.

[6] Sir Edward Poynter, Bart. (1836–1919), best known for his Whistlerian genre painting, was President of the Royal Academy from 1896 to 1918.

in *Blast*;[1] but stick to my naif determination to have no "words ending in -Uck, -Unt, and -Ugger."

I am doing a power of painting. If I get my head blown off when I am pottering about Flanders, I shall have left something. . . . I have a piece of news. The excellent Mrs. Turner is going to take a large studio or hall near Park Lane and there house my squadron of paintings, until after the war a large building is constructed for them in the rear of her own house. She will pay the rent, furnish it, and I suppose supply a page boy or secretary: also a stage for Theatrical Performances, Lectures etc.[2] En voila une bonne nouvelle! I hear that your article on the Vortex came out sooner than was expected.[3] Wadsworth is giving it me tomorrow. I have not seen it yet. Anything to be Blessed or Blasted where you are (except Yeats)?[4]

Blast should be under way this week. I will notify you of the start.

My compliments to Mrs. Pound. I hope she is drawing.[5] My respects to your host.

Yrs
WYNDHAM LEWIS

[1] No such poems appeared in *Blast*.

[2] L. became friendly with Mrs. Turner – later Lady Spears, and better known as the novelist Mary Borden – not long before World War I. In *Blasting and Bombardiering* (pp. 60-3), he describes a pre-war visit, with Hueffer and Violet Hunt, to her place in Berwickshire. The project referred to here was abandoned.

[3] Pound's article, "Vorticism," appeared in the *Fortnightly Review* of September 1914.

[4] Pound was presumably staying at the time with Yeats at Coleman's Hatch in Sussex.

[5] Pound had a few months before married Dorothy Shakespear, the daughter of Yeats's friend Olivia Shakespear, mentioned earlier as an admirer and patron of Lewis's work. The young Mrs. Pound was herself an artist; there are designs by her in *Blast No. 2*.

61. *To Ezra Pound* 18 Fitzroy Street.
[1915]

Dear Pound. . . .

I am sending you tomorrow a copy of *Timon*[1] for Quinn.[2]

Thank you for Eliot poem.[3] It is very respectable intelligent verse, as you say, and I found —— a most poisonous little bugger on Saturday, repellently hoarse (this may be a form of jealousy) and with abominable teeth, not to mention his manner. I am sure you cant say anything too bad about him. He told me he had written a lot of filthy sexual verse, which, if he sends it, I shall hang in the W.C. He described it as Verlainesque, damn his shifty little eyes. Well, well.

Sturge Moore turned up, and we had Bomberg to entertain us, on Saturday.

Is Mrs. Pound still busy in the Vortex?

Blast will not be delayed many hours now.

Yrs

W. LEWIS

62. *To Alick Schepeler* 18 Fitzroy Street.
[Postmarked "June 24, 1915."]

My dear Alick. . . .

You caused me this morning to almost alter all my arrangements: for the pink nightgown on sunday (though I dont believe you've got one) captured my sense, over-susceptible as you know. But I kept my head, and the result is that I regret to say that I shall *be away* on Sunday next. I am going to the country again tomorrow (partly to the Hueffers') and could not, save by extreme dislocation of arrangements, get back in time for the pink night dress.

Perhaps when you can once more move,[4] and are no longer

[1] *Timon of Athens*, a folio of drawings by L. published by the Cube Press in 1914.

[2] In March 1915, in what was evidently his first letter to John Quinn (1870–1925), Pound began to stimulate the interest of the American collector in L.'s work. The sending of *Timon* was probably an initial step in the successful campaign to get Quinn to buy L.'s pictures.

[3] Presumably one of Eliot's poems – "Preludes" and "Rhapsody of a Windy Night" – which appeared in *Blast No. 2*.

[4] Miss Schepeler had been seriously ill.

wrapt round with the odour of disinfectants, I may yet hope to have a glimpse of that garment? . . .

Can I procure you any books?

Yours ever
WYNDHAM LEWIS

In addition to supporting the Rebel Art Centre, Kate Lechmere had put up one hundred pounds towards the publication of Blast *No. 1. When in July* 1915 *a second* Blast *appeared, Miss Lechmere assumed that Lewis was solvent and attempted to recover her original loan.*

63. *To Kate Lechmere*† [London]
[Perhaps not sent.] [Summer 1915]

Dear Miss Lechmere . . .

Your solicitor explained his letter to me and your new claim by the fact of the reappearance of Blast: "certain moneys" supposedly would "be coming to me."

Far from this being the case, the next 2 or 3 numbers of *Blast* will be engaged in paying off the cost of the first number. I am not getting a halfpenny. . . .

Your solicitor offered to return the works you have of mine, and which you accepted in lieu of anything outstanding between us: I don't know legally whether things accepted in this way can be handed back at will, and a money obligation revived! But I do know that a time like the present is not a time to try to do so. For you know that the War has stopped Art dead. I have no money at all. I am shortly going to the Front, and am meantime desperately struggling to get my immediate affairs in order. . . .

The best arrangement I can offer you is this. I am willing, once the Printer has righted his account, for you to take out of *Blast* the amount we agree on as due to you, in the event of my consenting to take the pictures back and revive the debt. . . .

Yrs etc.
WYNDHAM LEWIS

64. *To Augustus John*† [London]
[Summer 1915]

Dear John. Your letter received this morning.¹ After your clear display (in front of a lady) the other night, I looked up my article in Blast. I there found I had said that I had a mental feud with you, for "I resented your stage-gypsies emptying their properties over your splendid painter's gift." The fact that I open that terrible and 'unjust' attack by admitting to a 'mental feud' rather mitigates its wickedness, it seems to me. – In the same article, along with tilting at your boring Borrovian cult of the Gitane, I pay homage to the substantial talents God has endowed you with.

Had you chosen a time when neither you nor I were accompanied and overheard, I should have supplemented my remarks in the articles as follows. – I consider you had, pour commencer, as much talent as a man may comfortably possess. The time you dropped into was a rather stagnant time just after the full blast of Victorianism – surely one of the most hideous periods ever recorded. You began by shipwrecking yourself on all sorts of romantic reefs. Among other things you consumed a good deal of Verlainesque liquor. Whether a craft is still sea-worthy after such buccaneering I dont know. But lately you have not, to put it mildly, advanced in your work. That you will enter the history books, you know, of course! Blast is a history book, too. You will not be a legendary and immaculate hero, but a figure of controversy, nevertheless. What have you to grumble about? c'est mieux ainsi. – Now, to accuse me, as you did the other night, of initiating an attack on you in 'your' present state is absurd. When I think of you the work I look to is the magnificent series of paintings, drawings, etchings you led off with, and the equals

---

¹ John had written to L. apologising for an intemperate response to L.'s criticism of his work in *Blast No. 2*. There, in an article titled "History of the Largest Independent Society in England," L. calls John "a great artist," but finds him lacking in control and prematurely exhausted – "an institution like Madame Tussaud's." He credits John with bringing some exotic subject-matter to English painting; at the same time he sees the gypsy cult as rather hothouse and *fin de siècle*. (See *Blast No. 2*, pp. 80–1.) In his letter of apology John wrote: "Your thrusts at me in 'Blast' were salutary and well deserved – [?] as to the question of their exact justice – any stick will do to rouse a lazy horse or whore and the heavier the better."

of which you latterly have not exhibited. I should like only to have had those to speak of, while complaining of the manner in which your gypsy-minded contemporaries fitted you out for the pilgrimage of life, and the ridiculous properties they often slipped onto the models in your masterpieces.

As you said the other evening, I could not harm you particularly even if I would. But you may take it from me that I did not write that article with that intention: I will own to having used you as a particularly picturesque argument; and perhaps I should have remembered my early acquaintance with you and your brilliant energy at that time, and refrained, since this 'journalism', as you obviously call it, is a thing of very slight importance to me.

Now for the personal matter. – The other night I walked into the trap that you set: for had you not presented such a generous and engaging front, but allowed your true sentiments to transpire from a distance, I should have remained on my own ground. – It was natural that some years ago when I no longer agreed with you or shared your illusions you should find some abusive tag to describe my dissent. Malignant was the one you chose. A Machiavellian figure was evoked. But I may here attest that I have never found you wanting in cunning yourself, although not a good judge of it, or the absence of it, in others. – My own naiveté, when you were accusing me of 'deepness' – or darkness – was super-human. – You displayed, I think, some strategy the other night, and 'being very drunk' is an euphemism.[1]

The thought of scrapping with you causes me a feeling of shame, referrable to our long intimacy and my position at first of a cadet. – But I do not like the names you found for me in the presence of your woman-friend. I had two reasons for not stopping you the other night. – But these reasons are local, and my more general fastidiousness [and?] fancy has limitations.

Unless you want your head broken you had better take my word for it that this is so, and not attribute my gentleness the other night to lack of spirit. – When I say, 'want your head broken' I feel I am dropping into a florid lingo, perhaps, result of infection. Let me say, that, being active and fairly strong, I will try and injure your head. Anyhow, we will not meet again in any friendly way,

[1] John's letter: "I must apologise for being so stupid yesterday. I must have been positively drunk to assume so ridiculously truculent an attitude upon such slender grounds."

if you do not mind. – There are some folk I actively dislike and am disgusted by. I entertain no sentiments of that sort towards you: I never did nor ever shall, as you probably divine, despite 'quatch' about malevolence.

Yourse sincerely,
W. LEWIS[1]

65. *To Augustus John*† [London]
[Probably not sent.][2] [1915?]

Dear John. I have received your letter. Whether I am worth insulting or not (you cast up your hands at the mere idea, and invoke the Deity) I shall find, in convenient time, means of enlightening those who try it on as to how it affects me.

I dont hold you responsible for the lack of sympathy many of your young or rich friends have exhibited at times towards me. That is of course a quite independent and personal lack expected and even encouraged by me. Nor do I identify you with the hostility, however loftily it may veil and deny itself, persisting in Harry Lamb and his friends. Lamb is quite astute. In allying himself to snobbish intellectual society he not only follows his bent (which you yourself described in the 'past' as priggish) but gains the many advantages similar to the Touring Club badge, shown at a wayside hotel. We all of us are apt to forget the measure of an individual when he appears as the mandatory of the taste, wisdom or influence of a Society. Yet you will agree with me that individual invention and not the refined custom of a community is the better thing. Take the judgements on [word] or actions of this eye of Custom and Education, or of any finished mandatory of it, – take any single instance and compare it with the richer, subtler and more humane judgement of your own mind! Every man who can, remains independent of Society,

[1] What seems to be John's reply to this letter begins: "Percy Windham Lewis: Renouncing the illusions I have nourished (with my heart's blood) for years, and amongst them (bien entendu) that of my own sagacity and permitting myself that linguistic license, if not that stylistic and caligraphic obscurity which serve you, at the same time for protection and adornment, I briefly confess, your note, once deciphered...."

[2] It seems likely that this letter was intended to continue the controversy of which the preceding letter forms part.

however much he may use it. He never uses its jargon, seeks support for its manners, or allows any doubt to subsist as to whether the words he utters come from him or from it.

I have personally no political axe to grind, do not yearn for honours; I feel sure that what I can do will be sufficiently good to bring me in food until decay sets in. This being the case, old fellow .... [Draft ends here.]

The first, and only, Vorticist Exhibition opened at the Doré Gallery in May 1915. *Besides Lewis, avowed Vorticists showing were Jessie Dismorr, Etchells, Gaudier, Roberts, Helen Saunders, and Wadsworth. A few outsiders, such as Bomberg and Nevinson, were also invited.*

66. *To Mary Borden Turner*† [London]
[Summer 1915]

Dear Miss Turner. In your last letter you seemed to feel that my communication was of an unusual character. You also said that you could do me a good turn if you *liked*. I concluded that you meant to say by this that because the poor artist (imaginary melodramatic figure) asked the rich woman (howls from the Gallery) for the settlement of an obligation a little forcibly in his 15th letter or wire, that the plutocrat would spitefully withold thenceforth etc. etc.

Now, I know the rich woman well enough to be sure that she is not capable of that spite. Bad tempered or thoughtless letters are not fortunately a person's character.

The business of this letter is nothing to do with money I may preface. It is:

1. To ask you if the largest of the paintings I am sending to your solicitors (as Doré show now being at an end) can be sent, carefully packed, to New York. Quinn has bought a few things of mine, and is seeing if a one-man show can be arranged.[1]

2. I must join the Army. I have as little reason to be shot at once and *without a hearsay* as any artist in Europe, but have

[1] In the autumn of 1916, Quinn's Vorticist show, featuring L.'s work, finally came on at the Penguin Club in New York.

certain accomplishments (such as an unusual mastery of French) that might be of more use to pen-polyglot alliés than my trusty right arm, which, I flatter myself, is rather a creative than a destructive limb.=Can you be of any use to me? 2. Are you willing to be of any use to me?

I understand that interpreters get shot *at once*: that 80 per cent already lie dead. A 2nd lieut.'s commission in the infantry is a death warrant more or less. A private soldier stands doubtless the best chance of surviving, but I should find the ennuis & fatigues of that intolerable. I should therefore, if it came to choosing, take the Infantry sub's job & get shot at once.=There are these things I know of, although there are doubtless many I don't know of that seem places of advantage.

  1. The Army Service Corps (commission)
  2. The Howitzer Brigade (commission)
  3. The secret service.

In any case, I have now told you my present ambitions. . . .

                   Yrs W. LEWIS

During the war years Lewis's closest comrade – and one of his chief patrons – was Captain Guy Baker. The two met in 1914 and were much together until Baker's death in the 'flu epidemic that followed the armistice. The engaging "professional soldier" is vividly evoked in Blasting and Bombardiering. *Baker bequeathed his collection of Lewis's drawings to the Victoria and Albert Museum.*

67. *To Captain Guy Baker*†   18 Fitzroy Street.
                     4th January 1916.
Dear Baker,

In your letter the other day you referred to a painting "for which you had not yet paid." Therefore I put the following before you.

I have written an extremely good book, a novel called "Tarr". I spent £15 on the typing and re-typing of it. The idiot Lane[1] says it is "too strong a book" for the present time. To my amazement I find it is difficult to place it. Disarray in all my calculations! –

    [1] John Lane, who had published *Blast*.

Now. I *must* get it out by hook or by crook. I will vouch that there is nothing in it that the Police could get a prosecution on. I vouch also that a thousand people in London would read it, eventually many more. I know it is a sound book.

Are you hard up? If you are not hard up, and if you cared to do it, would you as a speculation part-publish my book? That is to say, I could find a small Publisher who would *print* it and bring it out. . . .[1]

If you get my letter, let me know about this soon, if you will. I am on the threshold of my military career, and have to settle this business, for money reasons, before I can enlist. . . .

Yours
WYNDHAM LEWIS

68. *To T. Sturge Moore* 18 Fitzroy St.
Jan. 4. 1916.

Dear Moore,

I am trying another publisher=I like him too; I like all the publishers I have had dealings with so far. But this one seems to me to answer the most fastidious requirements. He is *so* nice that he will probably fling my book out into the street, and send his office boy out to besmirch it afterwards!

As to Yeats:=Pound suggested that he should take a section of my book down to the country with him, and read it to Yeats, with a view to subsequent action in the direction of the *Fund*.= I did not fall in with this suggestion, as I knew Yeats would not like the book, and also that he can hardly approve of me? You see of course what I mean.[2]

Well, I shall persevere. I must: for too much depends on my

[1] This project was evidently abandoned. *Tarr* was first published as a book in England by The Egoist Ltd. in June 1918.

[2] Moore had written to L. on January 2nd, saying: "How are the publishers treating your Ms. Yeats refuses to back an application to the Royal Literary Fund and it seems very difficult without influence to get your case put forward in the right way. You have published so little." Pound, evidently unaware of this exchange, wrote in March to L.: "Perhaps old Stg. Moore could do something with the Royal Lit. Fund." The idea presumably was to get money from the Royal Literary Fund for the publication of *Tarr*. At this time Yeats knew L.'s painting but perhaps not his writing.

novel not to do so. Meantime, if I can possibly get my belongings stored *etc.* by then, I shall enlist next week, as a preliminary step.[1] I will let you know how I get on with my book.

Yours ever,
WYNDHAM LEWIS

At Pound's urging, Harriet Shaw Weaver, then co-editor of The Egoist, *accepted* Tarr *for serial publication in January* 1916. *The first instalment of the novel appeared in the April number, the series running till November* 1917.

69. *To Harriet Shaw Weaver*   18 Fitzroy Street.
[March 1916]

Dear Miss Weaver. Thank you for your letter. Your giving me frankly your opinion is of course just what I want. The criticism you made I made myself to a friend of mine about those first chapters.[2] I make Tarr too much my mouthpiece in his analysis of Humour etc:=Only what you say does not apply to the fourth chapter, of Part. I., in which there are, I think, no opinions, only an analysis of character and action. And you will find, in the rest of the book, that the story and the business of the story is stuck to almost entirely.=In the rest of the book the "opinions" of the principal English character do not exceed the proportion that not only may be allowed, but, to be real, is necessary in describing a person like Frederick Tarr.

You must really consider the first three chapters as a sort of preface. But I will admit that Tarr has just a trifle too many of my ideas to be wholly himself, as I conceived him.

But as I say, you struck the worse part for that.
I thought you would probably find the tone of the book too heartless, bitter and material. But, if the book has a moral, it is that it describes a man's revolt or reaction against his reason.

[1] L. did not actually get into uniform until March.
[2] In her letter accepting the manuscript, Miss Weaver wrote: "The characters appear to me mechanical automatons, wound up in order to spout forth opinions, instead of breathing with life."

As regards the serializing of it: as I told you – but more so – the money is an urgent necessity for me: I think your offer extremely fair,[1] and if it is endorsed by Miss Marsden[2] (I believe you wrote that that would have to happen?) I would, as soon as I can get hold of it, do the necessary cutting.=Why all Publishers should keep their readers in the country I cannot conceive. But so it is: and my MSS: at present has to be got back from some distant valley, which it must be jarring with its insistence on the harshness and humour of life.=Should the Publisher I have left it with like the book very much, perhaps some arrangement could be come to with him as regards the publishing of the book after it has finished as a serial.=But I will tell you within three or four days what he says, and, should Miss Marsden agree, I could proceed with the shortening of 2nd 3rd & 4th parts.[3]

Yours sincerely
WYNDHAM LEWIS

Lewis was unwell during much of the first year of the war and thus in no condition to attest. His health regained, he made several abortive attempts to place himself in some desirable branch of the service. Finally he gave up and volunteered in March 1916. He spent the rest of the year in a succession of English artillery camps, first as a Gunner and then, having achieved the rank of non-commissioned officer, as a Bombardier. His transfer to the front was many times postponed because of his repeated, though not always wholehearted, efforts to gain admission to the Cadet Artillery School at Exeter. Towards the end of 1916 he was finally accepted as an officer's candidate, and he received his commission just before Christmas. His departure from England continued to be delayed, however. It was not till the end of May that Lewis, now a subaltern in a Siege Battery, left for France.

[1] Miss Weaver offered fifty pounds for the serial rights.
[2] Dora Marsden was at this time co-editor of *The Egoist* with Miss Weaver.
[3] Miss Weaver suggested shortening for serial publication.

70. *To his Mother*   Dover.
[Postmarked "25 March 1916."]

Chere Maman. . . .

I shall be here 2 or 3 weeks, it seems. Then some Garrison or Fort for gun-training. I am Gunner Lewis. My bed is in a hut, and is abominable. There is no food. I am now in the Town getting a good meal. – I dont think that my training here will be very hard. Probably the gun part, later, will be harder. But by that time I shall be used to it. . . .

                                                Yrs.
                                             W. LEWIS

71. *To his Mother*   Gunner W. Lewis.
                                                           71050. R.G.A.
                                                           Hut 20.
                                                           Fort Bayonne,
                                                           Dover.
                                                         [April 2nd, 1916.]

Chere Maman. . . .

Nothing new to record of my life here. Same drill. – There is one feature of it however, that I have found trying: i.e. their extreme solicitude for our lives when air-raids happen. For three nights now, I have spent 3 and 4 hours out of the 7 sleeping on a stone floor in the Fort, with my coat for my pillow. When the hooting goes in the town warning the district of a coming raid, we are bustled off to the security of the Fort.

Otherwise, things pass with regularity and not unpleasantly. I had better make a rough will here, which you could produce if anything should happen to me.

                                               April 2nd. 1916. . . .

I hereby bequeath to Mrs. Anne Stuart Lewis, my mother, any property or money left by me at my death. (This includes my drawings, pictures, and Mss.)

                               Signed. PERCY WYNDHAM LEWIS.

This form is premature, most probably. But it is just as well to be on the safe side. . . .

72. *To Ezra Pound*

THE SALVATION ARMY
RECREATION AND READING ROOM
For His Majesty's Troops

Gunner W. Lewis.
71050. Hut 61.
R.G.A. Menstham Training Unit.
Weymouth. Dorset.
[Postmarked "April 12, 1916."]

Dear Pound. I have got shifted in here, and lost my leave. Heaven knows when I shall get any leave now. They wont let me go to town about my teeth: and if I get a week end, it will only be noon Saturday to midnight Sunday. Then I shall have to wait *20 weeks* before getting any more leave: or rather, as most likely we shall be off with a Siege Battery in a couple of months, my next leave after my *first* leave (supposing I get that) will be my two days before going abroad. – These are now War Office regulations, applying to all camps and people, and it is difficult to get round them.

This being so, what is to be done about the pictures? – We will suppose I induce the Sergeant-Major to let me up next week-end (Sunday rather.) – That will leave no time except to move from my flat. Now, the Kermesse is in its primitive state:[1] as it stands it was praised by Roger Fry in 'the Nation',[2] John wrote 'thanking me' for it etc. But even for a wall painting it is too uncouth and its unfinished state would not recommend it to the very discriminating, *with which ideal audience we must always suppose we are dealing*.

Now, the problem as regards the Quinn money appears to me as simple as A.B.C. – You hold a number of my drawings. – Eventually (as soon as I get up to town) you will, if you accept the responsibility and are willing to store them, hold all that I have completed and arranged with a view to immediate exhibition.

[1] John Quinn had contracted to buy L.'s painting "Kermesse" for £150. He was sending the sum in instalments to Pound, who was acting as intermediary. The painting went to Quinn as per arrangement and was in his collection at his death.

[2] L. may mean Clive Bell, who praised "Kermesse" in *The Nation* on October 25th, 1913. The picture was then on view in Frank Rutter's "Post-Impressionist and Futurist Exhibition."

You also could have within your grasp the Kermesse *as it is*.

Should I come through the War safe and sound, I can, and undoubtedly shall, paint a hundred Kermesses, finishing Quinn's to begin with. Quinn does not mind waiting 12 months before entering into possession of an important picture, I imagine, *if he has guarantees*. Well then, should all go well, Quinn has nothing to fear: I will do him another Kermesse, and throw it in, to celebrate Peace. (This is without prejudice.) On the other hand, should I get killed or smashed up so that I cant paint any more Kermesses, he can have 1. The Kermesse as it is. or 2. As many more drawings as would, by their combined price, cover the money he had paid out. – The drawings are good ones: you could recommend this without qualms of conscience.

My provisions with reference to any accident to myself in this way are aimed at putting into the hands of my mother any pence that could be scraped together to help. Therefore when I say I intend to put good prices on the drawings you must not accuse me of fancy-pricing my things, – I have always priced my drawings and things remarkably low. But I know that little lot of drawings will bear looking into and count for something with what is being done nowadays. And if they sell at all they can sell well: (this excepting three already reserved for Quinn.)

Please digest this letter, the facts contained therein, and their reference to the £70 you hold for the Kermesse. I may add I have about £1 in my Bank, and I find soldiering costs about 30/– a week, with occasional additional sums for odds and ends. – It will be cheaper a little later on. It is cheaper already. – I have been put into an N.C.O. class, and pass an Examination in a month for my stripe. – I shall be here 1 month, I expect. – I have seen the Colonel, who was very aimiable and discussed the Independents etc. and I may get a commission. That would mean 6 weeks or 2 months at Cadet School I expect. But the likelihood of the commission I shall know about later. – Do not under any circumstances speak to Mr. Masterman, by the way.[1] – How are you getting on?

Yours ever
W. LEWIS

[1] C. F. G. Masterman (1873–1927) was at the time Director of Wellington House (Propaganda Department). L. is referring no doubt to some plan of Pound's to get him a commission or transfer. See his letter to Violet Hunt, p. 84.

7. Lewis in uniform, ca. 1916

73. *To his Mother*   Weymouth.
                                                                                       June 22/16.

Chere Maman. . . .
As regards money, I am afraid I haven't got the sum you mention in the Bank. I have written to Pound, asking him when he thinks I shall get some more from Quinn. . . . Meantime I'm wondering what I shall do myself. I have neither good or bad news: just worry and uncertainty. The great mistake I made was to attest. I should have waited and said "Commission or nothing." Had I realised what I was in for I should certainly have done that. . . .

                                          Love to all
                                                        Yrs.
                                                            W. L.

P.S. No confidences, however, in letters. They often go astray here.

74. *To his Mother*   Weymouth.
                                                                       183 Siege Battery
                                                                       Menstham Camp
                                                                       Friday. 4.8.16.

Chere Maman. We are leaving here on Wednesday next for Horsham. We shall probably stop there for $2\frac{1}{2}$ weeks, then to Lydd for 2 or 3 weeks. From there we go somewhere to mobilize, as it is called. That takes a week, then France. This is subject to extension . . . . But they are in a hurry, I think, to get Batteries out, now.

I have come to no decision about my commission. The R.G.A. is not quite so "safe as church" as Miss Asquith (or Mrs Bonham Carter, rather)[1] would have it, it seems. A man just back with shell-shock tells me that over a space of 6 months his battery (a "heavy") lost 5 officers killed, and the sixth wounded, arm amputated. The loss amongst officers in the Artillery seems higher than in the ranks, as in other arms. And I dont want to get killed for Mr. Lloyd George, or Mr. Asquith, or for any commmunity except that elusive but excellent one to which I belong. It is really difficult to know what to do about it. I shall probably be made full

[1] Helen Violet Asquith, eldest daughter of the Prime Minister, was married to Maurice Bonham-Carter in 1915.

Bombardier soon, and get consequently 19/- a week, better than nothing. The N.C.O.'s in the Battery, if they stop with us, are not such bad sorts. I am not sure that I shouldn't be better off to stick where I am. – On the other hand, a commission in the hands of a skilful person has possibilities. . . .

Love to you and family,
Yrs
W. LEWIS

P.S. Remember in writing that letters may be examined. We are in tents, so you put no hut number.

75. *To his Mother*
R.A. Mess.
Roffey Camp.
Horsham.
[August 1916?]

Dear Mama. . . .

Nothing new to record here. Full complement of officers, except O.C. All dull dogs: it is a pity I couldn't get into a Battery with a rather more amusing lot. Tant pis.

General F. Marshall French came down yesterday. I was disclosed laying down a D.D. Platform. He shook my hand and thanked me. Next Sunday I am Orderly Officer, so I shall not be able to get away.

. . . – Evan Morgan[1] was to visit Pound on Sunday last, and was expected to loosen his purse strings. But as I have not heard from Pound, I presume he has not done so. – I am writing a story for an American paper.[2] Pound is placing it. A bientot and best wishes for all.

Yrs.
W. L.

[1] The Hon. Evan Morgan (1893–1949), eldest son of Baron Tredegar. He was at this time active as a painter and a writer. He succeeded to the barony in 1934.

[2] Presumably "Cantleman's Spring-Mate," which appeared in *The Little Review* in October 1917.

76. *To his Mother* Horsham.
[August 1916?]

Chere Maman. . . . I think all things considered I shall apply as soon as possible for a commission. But I am afraid that the authorities will avail themselves of the shortness of the time between now and my departure abroad to let the matter drop. We shall see.

I have heard from Pound. Quinn has forwarded another small sum of money, the lot, now I think, and is seemingly going to purchase more.[1] I could pass on 10 shortly: but only if you could pass it gradually back again. . . . Be *most guarded* in anything you write. Leave financial, family and other discussions till we meet. . . .

Love. Yours ever.

W. L.

77. *To Ezra Pound* Bdr. W. Lewis. 71050.
Hut 60. – Wood Town.
183 Siege Battery.
(C. Sub-Section.)
Lydd. Kent.
[Postmarked "August 20, 1916."]

Dear Pound. . . . – We stop here 3 or 4 weeks, going through a firing course. I may add that occasionally first blood is drawn at this so called "live" camp. But it is chiefly signallers that are killed.

. . . – I was very glad to hear that Quinn now has matured his judgement: and that there are prospects of a further sale over there. I hope we may arrange for a small show in London this autumn: but England is a bloody and abominable place to be anything but a fool in.

I am progressing favourably in my military exercises, I think. I might even put in successfully for a commission. But we have

---

[1] Pound wrote to L. in July, saying that Quinn had sent another £25 and that "He expects to make an offer for certain other works 'ten or twelve or possibly 15.'"

no commanding officer as yet: and it would be no good applying to the . . . Sub, who is at present in his place.

We are attached to the F. Brigade, which is in Egypt. So I expect the Balkans or Asia Minor is where we shall eventually find ourselves.

I am writing a book called "The Bombardier": only in my head, of course. – I have received a letter from my naval colleague at Mudros, who is surrounded by warships and volcanoes he tells me.[1] Such propinquity, and the seclusion of this island office, should in the end produce a furtive woodcut or two, painted in "romantic" reds.

Are you being very active? . . .

Thank you for news – Hueffer's shell shock etc.[2] Do you ever hear of Mrs. Turner?

Yours ever
WYNDHAM LEWIS

Prior to the war, Lewis was, as has been mentioned, often a guest at South Lodge, the house of Violet Hunt and Ford Madox Hueffer. In 1913 he had painted decorations for one of their rooms. At the time of this letter Violet Hunt was helping him in his application for a commission.

78. *To Violet Hunt*   Lydd. Kent.
[ca. August 1916]

Dear Mrs. Hueffer. . . .

If Masterman signs the paper he will send it back to you. Would you be so extremely kind as to forward it to Binyon,[3] to whom I am writing? – His address in telephone book. – He will return it to me, and I will then get the Education part signed. This will all take time, and my O.C. asked me this morning if I had got it filled in. I must not delay the filling of it up too long.

[1] Edward Wadsworth served as Intelligence Officer in the Royal Naval Volunteer Reserve in the eastern Mediterranean from 1915 to 1917.

[2] Pound wrote to L.: "Met Hueffer's brother-in-law on the plaisaunce. He said a shell had burst near our friend and that he had had a nervous breakdown . . . ." *The Letters of Ezra Pound* (New York, 1950), p. 86.

[3] Laurence Binyon (1869–1943) was at this time an Assistant Keeper in the British Museum.

I shall probably be up next week end, and hope we may have dinner together chez Stulik.¹

           Yours ever
             WYNDHAM LEWIS

79. *To Ezra Pound*   Lydd. Kent.
               [ca. August 1916]

Dear Pound. . . .

Give Quinn time, and he is all right.² The slow-starters are not the worst in the long run, etc. The news generally is very good; and I am particularly glad that Bobby is going to get something. I hope the show will be a success. Edward's peasant-mania about pence has no doubt not been seen as a charming, almost graceful weakness, but as a stunted and disagreeable sign.

Bobby is jogging round France with an ammunition column, leading a pleasant caravan-like life. – I will send you his address tomorrow, and Etchells' if I can find it.

           Yours ever
             WYNDHAM LEWIS

80. *To his Mother*   Bde. W. Lewis. 71050.
             East Weare Battery.
             Portland. Dorset.
                [1916]

Chere Maman. We are still here. – They are forming another Siege Battery next week. We may be for that. But everything is uncertain as yet, as far as I know.

. . . The Naval defeat (as I suppose it was) has caused great excitement here. – We have all sorts of odd jobs to do about the

---

¹ Stulik was proprietor of the Eiffel Tower Restaurant. "Percy Street is a short street off the Tottenham Court Road – it would be called Soho by a careless guide. It is principally noted for Stulik. There are other people in it, but he's the one who counts." *Blasting and Bombardiering*, p. 90.

² This no doubt refers to Quinn's plans for his Vorticist Show in New York. Hence L.'s mention of his cohorts – "Bobby" Roberts, Edward Wadsworth, Etchells – and of financial considerations.

fort: unloading shells, carting planks about etc. I am down in Weymouth for the evening.

I find it difficult to work in my spare time, as I have no objective. There is only the old stuff to go over; and Williams, the sergeant who coaches me a bit, seems to experience the same boredom, in the absence of a definite object to work for. – I learn that Nunn the Examiner who diddled me out of my marks, has a nephew in France who is trying to get a commision without success. That may account for something.

Love to family.
Yrs. W. L.

81. *To John Quinn*† R.A. Mess,
Hut Town,
Lydd, Kent.
January 24, 1917.

Dear Mr. Quinn,

I am sorry that I had to trouble you the other day via Ezra Pound. Everything at present is a little uneven and urgent in my affairs.

I should have written to you some weeks ago had I not had either three "stables" a day, or ten hours of lectures and notes. However, now let me say how much I appreciate your action in buying my drawings, and all the kindness and interest you have shown in my work and my friends'. You may believe also that this is quite genuine, and that, apart from pleasant financial results, I see what it means for a man to be angel enough to find himself invariably on the side of the angels. Your support is at once a privilege and of incalculable use to the few artists with whom I am associated here: let me speak for them.

As to the work you know of mine, a good deal was a preparation only. But the problems of art as I see them are pretty clearly stated there. The enervating warmth, immobility and flatness of Eastern art do not seem proper to our surroundings and traditions. Yet their steady power of fundamental vision and impeccable taste are a model for us. The Bee in the Bonnet about Modernity, again, seems to me an imbecility. But sections of our present life are more edifying than the very obvious manners of Rossetti's Grail World – or even Blake's Hell World, though that is not obvious. The French painters today are all Nature Mortes, Dialectics and Delicacies. But Picasso is adorably resourceful; and there are dozens of small, exact, intelligent streams of light.

I have heard little of the New York show, except for accounts from one or two people lately over there.

I am going to the Front in anything from two to six weeks: the above address is only for a fortnight. Once more then, my sincere thanks for all you have done.

Yours,
P. WYNDHAM LEWIS

82. *To T. Sturge Moore*   Cosham.
23/5/17.

My dear Moore,

I have intended on several occasions lately to pay you a visit before going away, but have been deflected when I turned my steps your way by a variety of idle things.=I am leaving for France tomorrow (the 24th). I am going as a subaltern in a Siege Battery of 6 inch guns.=I got through my exams all right, and got my commission just before Christmas. The difficulty I had during nine months in issuing from the ranks was perhaps in my interest: as otherwise I should have been at the front a long time ago. I expect as it is, however, that I shall be there a precious long time.=I shall try later on for some job in which my Spanish would serve me. They asked for officers who could speak Spanish some time ago. I thought it better to apply later on from the front.=I have a great deal of time for work, or have had so far; and yet it is very difficult to do any.=Will you give me some news of Mrs. Moore and yourself? Are you doing anything new?

My novel, which I called "Tarr" in the end, is probably going to be published soon as a book in New York.[1] I will send you a copy. Pound, as you perhaps have heard, is starting a Review called the Little Review in New York,[2] in which he is publishing stories and things of mine.

---

[1] *Tarr* was published in New York by Alfred A. Knopf in July 1918 – *i.e.*, concurrently with its appearance in England.

[2] *The Little Review* was founded in Chicago by Margaret Anderson and later moved to New York. Pound became its London editor in 1917.

I envy you your quiet seclusion!=I will send you my address in France. My best wishes to your wife and yourself.

> Yours ever,
> P. WYNDHAM LEWIS

Lewis was at the front, or near it, from the beginning of June 1917 till near the end of the year. Although relatively shortlived, this time in France and Flanders was characteristically active. The Battery Officer, as the letters tell, knew days and nights of heavy fire and gas attacks. Early on he contracted trench-fever and spent time in hospital and in a convalescent home near Dieppe. Then he was back at the front with all its vicissitudes, physical and psychological. The whole experience is narrated with vivid humour in Blasting and Bombardiering.

83. *To his Mother* [France]
6/6/17.

Chere Maman. I am now in the firing line with a new battery. We were sent up without guns, and split up into small detachments and sent round as reinforcements. . . . I am writing you this note in my dugout, surrounded by a continuous din from all quarters. Guns of all descriptions blaze away day and night. I am with 6" 26 cwt guns; the ones we did practice shots with. They have had casualties this week. But it is the same with all these 26 cwt Batteries. During busy times like this it is unavoidable. But you need not be unduly anxious. *Many* more people are wounded than killed. One of the officers of the Battery the day before yesterday got seventeen wounds: but all of them together did not amount to a mortal wound, or a permanently serious one. – Anyway it is all pure chance. – I cannot tell you what part of the line I am in. But it is one of the busiest parts for the moment. – We left our base some days ago, so I expect any answer you may have sent to my letter from that place will not reach me for a day or two. It will probably be loitering about en route. Did you get Pound's letter to me, which I enclosed? – I will send you regularly 2 or 3 times a week a field post card letter. If you do not hear for some days, however, do not be anxious. It will probably only mean that I have missed a post; or that the letter has been delayed in the post.

It is extremely difficult to write a letter with the Censor's restrictions hanging over one's head. Almost any description of conditions here might be interpreted as news to a possible enemy. As to how it affects me, and is likely to: I am not in the least afraid nor even have I felt any excitement in the face of this novel experience; my pulse has so far not beat any quicker, though we had shrapnel within 50 yards of us today, and the whole business is strange and abnormal enough. This does not mean if a shell comes straight for me I shall not be passably moved, I suppose. – What I expect will eventually happen, will be that the lack of sleep and bad food (chiefly tinned) will break down my vitality, if I am not otherwise damaged. They say they have gas shells every night scarcely with any exception. This necessitates sitting sometimes for two hours or more with gas-masks, and makes regular sleep out of the question. – Well, that is my news for the present. My love to you and family. . . .

Yours. W. L.

84. *To Alick Schepeler* No. 8 (Michelham) Convalescent Home
c/o A.P.O. S8. B.E.F. France
24/7/17

My dear Alick. Many thanks for your aimiable and diverting letter. I was glad to hear that Albert Rothenstein has the Military Cross, *as well* as the Legion of Honour.[1] He must have been hustling the Hun as the Hun was never hustled before. Bravo Albert!—You give me no news of the indomitable Mr. C.R.W.N.[2] . . .—Why the King has elected to assume the patronymic of your versatile friend Charles Windsor I cannot see.[3] But it must be an event not without gratifying repercussions in that distinguished

---

[1] Albert Rothenstein, later Rutherston (1881–1953), had been at the Slade with L. and was at this time serving in Palestine.

[2] C. R. W. Nevinson.

[3] On June 20th, 1917, the royal house officially proclaimed the change of its name to the House of Windsor. Charles Windsor was a Polish friend of Miss Schepeler.

young Polish gentleman's soul. On the continent in days to come he will be supposed to be, by prostrated hôteliers, a scion of our Royal House travelling incognito! What luck the dear boy has. = Dear Alick, do not read the first two of my contributions to the Little Review.[1] They are unfinished lucubrations that Pound sent off without authorization.

I shall be here about 2 weeks more I expect. My disease is oozing out of me in the rays of the sun. You would enjoy yourself here, Alick! There are hosts of convalescent officers of all shapes and sizes, ranks and rentes. They would come shivering out of the water and fling themselves on the sands at your feet: you would fling pebbles at them and howl with hearty laughter. Then you would go to the American bar and have a Bronx or two, and be taken home in a cab by the nicest.

Bien à vous, Alick.

W. L.

85. *To Ezra Pound* [France]
[August 1917]

My dear Pound. I am back now with my old Battery. I have come to a tedious spot. It is really extremely bad. The parapet of one of our guns was smashed last night. We were shelled and gassed all night. I had my respirator on for two solid hours. There is only one bright side to the picture: a good concrete dugout.

I hope Miss S.[2] has shown you my revised Petrograd Letters.[3] Also the drawings I sent over you may care to have a look at. Le Feu[4] contains good things: have you read it? I got a lot of books during my stay in the delightful back areas. I am now not so far from the part where I did my Timon drawings one summer. . . .

Yrs
W. L.

[1] "Imaginary Letters" I and II, which appeared in the May and June numbers of *The Little Review*.

[2] The Vorticist painter Helen Saunders (b. 1885). She was closely associated with L. at this period.

[3] Some of the "Imaginary Letters" for *The Little Review*.

[4] Henri Barbusse, *Le Feu* (Paris, 1916). It was one of the first realistic accounts of the war.

86. *To Helen Saunders* [France]
[ca. August 1917]

Dear Miss S. . . . In the more or less illusory security of the concrete dugout (shortly full, however, of three different kinds of gas) it is not too unpleasant to listen to the absurd enemy smashing the parapets of your guns just outside. When you are not in that mortared stronghold, things are less pleasant. Yesterday I had quite a half dozen splinters within a yard or two of me. It is in fact, my dear Miss S., I know you will be interested to hear, a bad place. I admit to being rather glad myself. I have got many good books. *Le Feu* is worth reading. . . . Give me any news available.

Yrs.

W. L.

87. *To Alick Schepeler* France.
September [8th,] 1917

My dear Alec. Thank you for your last letter. I shall shortly be expecting another one. You must remember that I depend entirely on you for news of the Great World; and I am sure that much water must have flowed under that bridge at the bottom of Oakley Street[1] since you last sent me a greeting.=Gilman's elopement,[2] for instance, I got at second hand from Miss S: a garbled version of the delighted father's telegram: and palpably the wrong suburb as their Gretna Green. All this is very trying for a man fighting battles in which he does not take the faintest interest, and forced to listen from morning till night, (when it is not happily drowned by the truly admirable and African sound of the guns) to the strains of "The End of a Perfect Day" and "Give me your *Sym*-pathy!" Should I ever in after life meet the man who composed that song, I shall – the mere thought of what I shall probably do makes my flesh creep, Alec.=At present, Alec, I am living in a sort of archipelego – you know what an archipelego is? – Circular holes full of water somewhat [word] and certainly [word] in a certain amount of land. I live on the land. You doubtless know the story of the famously tactless French President who,

[1] Albert Bridge.   [2] Harold Gilman.

on one occasion, was told that he must go to a district of France boiling with discontent, sedition and rheumatism on account of a lot of gratuitous floods, not properly provided against by the government. He arrived in the most tried commune, and standing on a raft, gazed in amazement at the flood. The people looked at him, at their flood, and back at him. He noticed this, and felt the moment had come to say something tactful. So he said "Que d'eau! Que d'eau! Que d'eau!"=This is not at all a bad story to tell, if you know two or three more like it.

Well, there's a lot of water here.=Give me the news, then, Alick, and news of yourself. But news of yourself is inextricably mingled with that of the great world; n'est-ce pas, ma chère? Best wishes.

Yrs

W. L.

88. *To Ezra Pound* France.
Sept. 1917.

Dear Pound. We have been suddenly plucked up from our position in the North, and have since journeyed many a mile. So the climax of *that* story has, I expect permanently, been skipped or missed. I will tell you some day, when we meet what that *was*. Before going to our new position (a bad one, they say) we are billeted for 4 days in a pleasant country.

I think I told you we had a new C.O. He comes from Hull, from its Slums undoubtedly, and its Sunday Schools. The proud Naval man to whom we were attached would hardly speak to him, and wondered once more at the ways of the Army, in giving such unspeakable foolish and dismal [word] a Battery. – Bad as are the things I have been witness of, I have never seen as bad a case. I am now absolutely sardine-packed with the quintessence of the prosperous slums of a Protestant country. – Two of these charming boys today have been to a neighbouring bourg to buy a *few pictures to decorate our dugout*, – the one in which we shall have to live probably through this warlike winter. Yesterday, when for the third time this individual had attempted to prevent my having a square meal in a restaurant, there being nothing to do, I said to him; "I am in your Battery, not in your Sunday School." He considers, apparently, that a meal in a restaurant and the accompanying half bottle of wine is a treat for little children, indulgently provided by a kind O.C. every 3 weeks. – He drummed with his fingers for some minutes after my remark, and blushed as – one of Edward's[1] uncles blushes. – He stoops, is going bald, and has a hanging crimson underlip.

Excuse me for harrowing you with this picture of war. But I am very full of it at present.

Otherwise nothing further to report. Happily this awful situation has its interludes and entreactes: which if I weren't so damnably near to my chief colleague at the present moment, and if it were not for acrobatics, required to avoid giving information of use to the enemy, I might more profitably tell you about: – a weak-minded and hoary old Area Commandant, who, when he hears wheels, tumbles out of his office and regulates traffic like a Policeman: the inhabitants of these farms etc. The beauty of these farms, by Christ! – But I shall forget the ugliness as soon as I turn my back on it, and it helps me to forget it communicating it to you (excuse me, once more) whereas the excellent thrills, and the scene and the humour, are a possession, undoubtedly. (Sentimentalized into an importance out of all proportion with what they are.)

Remember me to Mrs. Pound.

Yrs
W. L.

89. *To Ezra Pound* France
September 1917.

Dear Pound. . . .

I am very glad that you can print Bland without chopping his backside off. I hope that the five short sentences contain nothing of the spiritual importance of a rump.[2] I hope for the best.

It is at present an hour [in the line when?] the vitality is not high, and I have had much work and little sleep lately. I have to sit up here because some officer must be awake, and *conscious* in the Battery. I am taking this opportunity of writing a few letters, but so far they have not said quite what I wanted to say. – My

---

[1] Edward Wadsworth.

[2] William Bland Burn was L.'s persona in the "Imaginary Letters." Pound, as European Editor of *The Little Review*, presumably had mentioned the need for some cutting.

domestic troubles in the Battery have in one sense diminished. For some reason my C.O. is not unfavourably disposed towards me. On the other hand an open rupture has occurred with my most active colleague. We sit dead opposite each other in the Mess, and henceforth do not exchange conversation or extend to each other the usual courtesies. – The Battery position is ten thousand times less shelled than the Nieuport position.[1] To counterbalance this (very much) we have to do a lot of forward observation. Ainsi, I was F.O.O. (forward ob officer) of the Group three days ago, and on that occasion had the extreme gratification of seeing, in the midst of our barrage, a large Bosche fly into the air as it seemed a few feet beneath me. From the ridge where I was observing things I looked down into the German front line as you might into Church Street.[2] I was, as a matter of fact, 400 yards behind our line, and 600, I suppose, from the Bosche. We were shelled steadily for three and two hours respectively, and I eventually left with my party of signallers through a 5.9. barrage. The journey to this particular O.P. is long (2 hours walk or more) and shelled for half that distance, especially at night. You meet plenty of dead men. I stumbled onto one (or two) with his head blown off so that his neck, level with the collar of his tunic, reminded you of sheep in butchers shops, or a French salon painting of a Moroccan headsman. He was a scot, and had been killed a few hours before. Every track and road is spasmodically infested with shells. Two officers in the following evening were wounded, one very badly, in performing my trick, – the famous dive through the barrage round this notorious O.P. So you see – . The O.P. amuses me. I volunteered for the F.O.O. job as an opportunity of leaving the Battery for a bit. But lack of sleep, military competition, and such human society as I find here m'excède, exceeds me; is more than even I bargained for "when I first put this uniform on."[3] In a few months I shall see about Intelligence, Camouflage, or something.[4] – Another thing I notice is this: that when I was registering a Battery on a church the other day as

[1] According to L., half-way between Ostend and Dunkerque. See *Blasting and Bombardiering*, p. 145.
[2] Church Street, Kensington, where Pound lived.   [3] Song in *Patience*.
[4] For over a year Pound had been urging L. to try to remove himself from the perils of active combat: *e.g.*, ". . . you should not be allowed to spill your gore in heathen and furrin places." See *The Letters of Ezra Pound*.

F.O.O. I was glad that it was a presumably empty ruin that I was guiding the burst upon. I am truly not sanguinary except when confronted by an imbecile: not, thank God, from lack of stomach. Too much sense. Alas, too much sense.

Farewell. Rappelez-moi a nos amis.

Yrs
W. L.

90. *To Harriet Shaw Weaver* France.
29/9/17.

My dear Miss Weaver. I dont know if Pound has infected you, as he has most of my friends and acquaintances, with the belief that I am in another Battery to the one I am really in. He appears to have dreamed a dream one night, and to have awoken convinced that I was deceiving him as to the real number of my Battery.= I have not seen an Egoist lately, and thought, anyway, that this might account for it. 330. Siege Battery, B.E.F. France is my address, in case – . You may have heard of the sale of Tarr? Quinn has cabled Pound to that effect; that Tarr is disposed of to New York Publisher it was sent to: I forget his name.[1] This is good news. But I have been thinking: is Tarr complete? Is there not a page missing somewhere? If there is, and you remember which & where it is, will you be so good as to send me the two numbers of the Egoist *preceding*, & the two *succeeding* this hiatas . . . . – I have a recollection that it has something to do with the character Butcher.[2]

Tarr will shortly be finishing in the Egoist, I expect. I wish once more to express my appreciation of your action in serializing Tarr, and the generous terms on which you did it, at a time when the money was very useful to me.

Do you still [?] dinner in Compton Street? Or have Wilenski's[3] battalions rendered your reunion unrecognisable and useless?

Yours etc
P. WYNDHAM LEWIS

[1] Pound had sent *Tarr* to Knopf on August 20th.
[2] In her reply Miss Weaver explained the omissions, these having occurred in the September 1916 and May 1917 instalments.
[3] The artist and art critic R. H. Wilenski (b. 1887) was a lifelong friend of L.

91. *To Ezra Pound* France.
Oct. 1917.

Dear Pound. I again dined the other night with Orpen.[1] R.A. (Major) (Royal Academy, not Royal Artillery) – also with a youth in the Intelligence, De Trafford or de Travers;[2] – only remaining son of Sir Humphrey de Trafford.[3] This youth told me that Gen. Sir John Charteris[4] is the head of the Intelligence department at the War Office. When I last heard of him (if it is the same man) he was a Major in charge of the department of Flight. Tonks is a friend of his, and gave Bob[5] a letter to him at the time Bob wished to enter the Flying Service. As he knows Tonks, he doubtless likes Art. (I am not suggesting you should send him Inferior Religions.[6] Art was my word, and I was thinking of avenues of approach.)

There are many Intelligence jobs I am quite competent to do, but forget that for goodness sake, if you move, should you be able to.

MacEvoy threatened to come out here as a Major, and peep through the periscope at the Mist from Boulogne. But Diana Manners put her foot down.[7]

No Little Review this month yet. – Did you have time to look at my revised Letters. They are what the first should have been.

Yrs

W. L.

Late in 1917 *Lewis's mother became ill and he returned to England on leave. It was then, according to the account in* Blasting and Bombardiering, *that Captain Guy Baker suggested that Lewis*

[1] Sir William Orpen (1878–1931), who was at the Slade with L., had become an official war artist in April 1917.

[2] Probably Captain Sir Humphrey Edmund De Trafford, 4th Bt.

[3] Sir Humphrey De Trafford (1862–1929), 3rd Bt.

[4] Brigadier-General Sir John Charteris.

[5] William Roberts.

[6] L.'s essay on humour which appeared in *The Little Review*, September 1917. Reprinted in *The Wild Body* (London, 1927).

[7] Ambrose McEvoy was at this time attached to the Royal Naval Division. He was a friend of Lady Diana Manners and had done several portraits of her.

apply for a place in Lord Beaverbrook's "Canadian War Memorials" scheme. A fund to provide pictures for the new Parliament building in Ottawa had been organised by Beaverbrook, under the auspices of the Canadian War Records Office, in October 1917. Lewis's application was accepted, thereby releasing him from the Royal Artillery. On December 30th, 1917, he was ordered to proceed to France as a war artist. He spent some time at the front making sketches for paintings and then returned to London to work on these. Later in 1918 he fell victim to the flu epidemic and was therefore not demobilised till early in 1919

92. *To Ezra Pound*   War Records Office,
                                     Headquarters Canadian Corps.
                                     B.E.F., France.
                                     16/1/18

Dear Pound. Enough as you say, of coxcombs.[1] But where you say that many of those paintings might have been done by the wise old cock itself, I must demur. – The Cock would paint pieces of interest to other Cocks. And in going round the exhibition I noticed no signs of interest down below, any more than up above! Miss S. writes me that your medievalities are very fine.[2] If they are all as good as the one I read, you are on the point of producing an important book, even if the Contemp. Mentality will not be me. I am contending here with unfavourable conditions, chiefly bad weather and scarcity of cars. All the same, I shall soon have enough to go on with.

Bobby writes me that he has practically got the Canadian job![3] That is Watkins (Records Office) has written him asking if he is willing to do the painting on spec: if not found suitable, no £250 but expenses paid. This since "their advisor" cannot guarantee his not doing a "Cubist picture" or something of that rot. He naturally accepts, with amertume, on any terms.

[1] This passage may refer in part to Augustus John. In a note written later L. says that Pound had referred to John as a "coxcomb."
[2] Probably the poems in "Langue d'Oc."
[3] William Roberts was applying for a place in the Beaverbrook scheme. L. had been helping him in his effort to be accepted.

I enclose the passages from Montaigne I want stuck at the front of Tarr.[1] – Should you ever be my executor, allow no one to publish any *poems* of mine. I looked through them the other day, and I should be very sorry to see any of them published.

I expect in a week I shall be coming back.

Yours ever.
W. L.

93. *To T. Sturge Moore* 1 Hatfield House,
Grt. Titchfield Street, W.1.
Wednesday Aug. 14th/18.

Dear Moore,

I return you the MSS. of your story, which I liked immensely.[2] I had intended to bring it back myself one day: but, harassed as I am, and full of boring worries, I do not take myself about very much, and thought I would wait till a happier moment. Meantime I send you on my book, Tarr.=Do, some day, if you are down in London, look me up here. . . . I am frequently here at tea-time: but dull, dull: hypochondriacal and even vicious. Lest however this account of myself should prevent you from coming, I may add that I have accesses of vitality, and to see you would give me so much pleasure that I would undoubtedly belie myself. My affairs, I may add, go to all appearance well. Remember me to your wife, please.

Yours ever,
P. WYNDHAM LEWIS

P.S. I enjoyed the Blind Thamyris as much as I did the poem. I liked its language, movement and pictures – sunlit storm outside the cave, centaur in the pool, scene with the rank and file centaurs, better than the implied character of the young gentleman god who had come to rough it with the half-horse and acquire wisdom. That, if you will allow me, I will talk about at our next meeting a little more.=Have you written anything in prose of the poilucentaurs, grouped round some celebrated centaur, with a greater profusion of pictures of their life?

[1] See the English edition of *Tarr*.
[2] "Blind Thamyris," *Danae, Aforetime, Blind Thamyris* (London, 1920.)

Your earlier poems cover a good deal in that way of course.=
How goes Iscariot?[1]

a bientôt,

W. L.

94. *T. Sturge Moore to Wyndham Lewis* London.
[September 1918]

Dear Lewis. We are back and I expect you are also by now. I have immensely enjoyed your book Tarr – far more than any book I have read at all comparable to it for many years. It is full of lights and reflections that are captivating and just. It is a true creation and will doubtless remain a landmark and monument. Of course I have some (unnecessary from your point of view) reservations to make especially about Tarr as opposed to Kreisler; I never see Tarr as I do the German and I find a difficulty in swallowing some of your artificially prepared talk about him. I wish he had either been more frankly you or more wholly distinct from his creator. However I am looking forward to reading it aloud with my wife, and a second perusal may correct some of my mistrust which is very likely due to prejudice in some measure. The duel and Kreisler are colossal: a really big thing in a field where success is very rare.

On receiving the copy you sent me I wrote at once to the Times Lit Supplement begging to be allowed to review it, only to find that it had been done weeks before in a number that the little girl who brings our papers had left at another house and never succeeded in making them disgorge. I hope it was well done as I should have liked to sound the loud clarion for you. I find the style wonderfully restrained and usually concise and clear. There are lots of charmingly appropriate images. I hope it has a real success. I rather regret the preface and epilogue; they will distract reflection from the book itself to the doctrine it will be supposed to illustrate, which is far from being so sound or certain a thing. They are like a rope anchoring it to Pound's Little World, whereas it might sail the blue quite unattached with advantage.

I am glad you like Thamyris (and see you pay me back in my

[1] *Judas* (London, 1923). Moore began work on this long poem in 1910.

own coin by demurring over the character of my Tarr),[1] and shall be glad to talk him over with you.

Could you come to supper at 7.30 on Monday next? Hoping that you are well and productive,

Yours ever
T. S. MOORE

P.S. Please let us know if you can come by return, and if you cant propose another day. Pray bring some more poems to read us with you.

95. *To T. Sturge Moore*   Grt. Titchfield Street, W.1
Sunday Sept. 22nd 1918

Dear Moore,

Thank you for your letter: I am glad to hear that my book wears well with you: for I have been talking about it so long, and showing you pieces of it, that I feared, when it eventually arrived completed, you might fix it with a satiated eye. Any satisfaction of achievement that may accrue to it, you must share with me: for it was in conversations with you that I found confirmation and help for my writing. = As to what you say of my English hero: anyone else's Tarr or Thamyris must, I think, always be demurred about. You and I don't quarrel: but should Tarr and *Thamyris meet in some Crab-Tree Club, they would growl and bristle at once. How is that? – All I can suppose is that I am really Tarr's hero, and you are the Centaur Hermit, what was his name? I should have got on quite well with him: so would Tarr for that matter. *(You must substitute for Thamyris the name of the Centaur's pupil.) However we must speak further of our puppets tomorrow night, Monday: when I am looking forward to seeing you and Mrs. Moore again.

Yours ever,
W. LEWIS

[1] Thamyris is also a kind of spokesman for his author.

96. *To Rupert Hart-Davis*[1] Grt. Titchfield St. W.1.
[ca. 1918]

Thank you for the cigarettes, Rupert, duly handed to me by your mother yesterday.=I am afraid that you must have been disappointed about the cigarette cards: for some time now that pastime has become extinct, for they no longer stick pictures in the cigarette packets. Here is one, however, that I have just found from a box of State Express cigarettes. I sometimes buy a considerable variety of cheap brands; and should I find any cards still lingering among them I will forward them to you.

WYNDHAM LEWIS

Lewis and Sir Herbert Read (b. 1893) first met in 1917 when Read was on leave in London. At the time Read and Frank Rutter were projecting the review Art and Letters, *and they urged Lewis to contribute. He complied by giving them a story, "The War Baby" (Winter number, 1918–19); a drawing; and a cover design, before* Art and Letters *vanished in 1920. Another of Read's proposals was that Lewis should decorate a book of his poems which Cyril Beaumont was to publish at his new Beaumont Press. This project fell through, but Read and Lewis continued to associate in artistic and literary ventures in the 1920's. By the 1930's patently divergent points of view in the arts and politics had made collaboration more difficult.*

97. *To Herbert Read* [London]
17.12.18

My dear Read. I should like to do the drawings you require for your book: 8 or 10 small decorations? The horror of the subject would not dismay me. But I should want Beaumont to give me at least £10[2] . . . . Were it for you, I would gladly do them for

[1] Sybil Hart-Davis, mother of the author and publisher Rupert Hart-Davis, was a close friend of L. at this time. She was the sister of Alfred Duff Cooper.
[2] The book was probably *Naked Warriors*, published by *Art and Letters* in 1919. Cyril Beaumont (b. 1891) is now chiefly known for his work on the ballet.

nothing. The fact that I had drawings in the book would insure a certain number of sales amongst people who for the moment, you might not reach. . . .

I am very very busy. Rutter may have told you that the War-Baby has appeared on earth, and is to be cradled in your Review – without having his balls cut off; or rather Kunt treated for appearance before a bestial public. I am getting a drawing down to him by Wednesday (for reproduction in Jan number of Review.)

On looking at my Canadian painting today I came to the conclusion that Konody had succeeded in making me paint one of the dullest good pictures on earth.[1] I have just done another painting in an afternoon which is at least 17 times as alive. What a nightmare this wicked war has been! . . .

Yours
W. LEWIS

98. *To Herbert Read* 1ᵃ Gloucester Walk. Kensington. W.8. [February 1919]

Dear Read. . . . For the last week or so I have been infernally busy with my show.[2] . . . I too am sorry that the book with the designs did not come off. But people like —— arouse all my worst passions. . . . You will do far better by bringing it out yourself: if you want a *stamp* or design such as Art and Letters has for its cover, I should be delighted to do it free of charge.

I am so glad to hear that you are getting demobilized & going to take up your quarters in London. Also the Ministry of Labour sounds a lively post at present.[3]

The Rutter-Nevinson correspondence should certainly be printed

[1] P. G. Konody was Art Adviser to the Beaverbrook scheme and was responsible for L.'s appointment to it. The painting is presumably *A Canadian Gun Pit*, now in the National Gallery of Canada at Ottawa.

[2] L.'s first one-man exhibition, "Guns," opened at the Goupil Gallery in February.

[3] It was actually the Treasury that Read joined. He was Assistant Principal from 1919 to 1922.

in Art and Letters.[1] Osbert[2] suggests that Nevinson should be informed of this and be given a chance of adding to it. I dont think that would be necessary: the point of the printing would be that the naked and unadorned little —— that our triste contemporary is, should be displayed, without any adornment or concealment. – Not that if you gave him three years to conceal himself in he could do it! He fortunately for all of us possesses neither the art nor the sense! . . .

Yours
WYNDHAM LEWIS

99. *To John Quinn*　　　　　　　　　　Kensington. W.8.
　　　　　　　　　　　　　　　　　　　　Feb. 7th. 1919.

My dear Quinn. . . . The show has opened, and this is what I have done. I got Pound to come round the show with me, & we marked independently on our catalogues the things that you would be likeliest to want. On comparing notes, we had come to the same conclusions, except in 2 or 3 cases.

Since a cable had not arrived by the opening day, I did what I told you I thought of doing under those circumstances. I required eleven of the best drawings for you. . . . In a few days time I will also send a batch of photographs of the eleven drawings set aside.[3] I am sending you in another envelope the cuttings to hand from the Press. . . . The show has been extremely well received by almost everybody, & I hope great things from this success in the coming year. It was very important to have the show at this time, & as you will see I got together a good number of things for it. Politically, the show has this result. As you know, in England one is up against the least imaginative and the most self-satisfied public in the world. They suppose that an artist is entirely occupied with *them*. They are accustomed to get *exactly* what they want. They have not the haziest conception of a man as an artist, with different, in most cases opposite, standards to their own. Yet they

---

[1] No such correspondence appeared in the review.

[2] Osbert Sitwell (b. 1892). He was a friend of C. R. W. Nevinson and at this time literary editor of *Art and Letters*.

[3] Quinn wrote to L. saying that he was reluctant to buy from photographs; but he did in the end buy a number of items from this show.

have a certain fairness, much more than the French; & if they ever become aware of that anomaly, they make [?] something that might pass in a crowd for an effort of conscience. The continental public, less fundamentally self-complacent, less unimaginative, respects this remote phenomenon more, but is less fair. The Englishman accepts the poet or the artist as he accepts a "native" in a colony, as different & therefore inferior, & proceeds unruffled with his British life, & in most cases treats the native [?] better, & quite inhumanly.

Keeping in mind the *fairness* that does exist somewhere in this [?] monster's makeup, it is clear that if you can convince him you are not hoaxing or spoofing, but that you are *honest*, he will be more tractable than the more partial & vehement Latin public has ever proved itself at first: though the Latin public is always in reality more interested, hence its violence, & [enables?] France [1 or 2 words] to uphold its position as the chief civilized place. Well, with a show like this, that does, in the things exhibited, have a subject-matter postulated, & therefore necessitates a more representative treatment, you have your opportunity with the smaller public here, & that portion of the larger public most liable to the pains and perils of reflection. I put in a half dozen drawings from life done of the figures in my Canadian picture. They are archi- [?] exact, as exact as a [word]. *It will be more difficult henceforth in the set politics of London* for certain gentlemen to assert that myself or my companions are "spoofers" & so on. I feel that I should have rendered all concerned a service had I done this earlier. For the public's eye first struck a canvas of mine when I was already experimenting beyond the zone of that eye's comprehension or special knowledge of the subject. The show in other ways is, I think, a thoroughly sound one, & has satisfied sticklers for experiment, even, like Pound. At the same time it has won over a number of people. Every day fresh things are being sold. . . .

                 Yrs

                 W. LEWIS

100. *To John Rodker*[1]   20[a]. Campden Hill Gardens.
Notting Hill Gate.
Sunday June 1st. [1919]

Dear Rodker. By next Tuesday (June 3rd) I shall have gathered enough drawings here to make a choice. Could you come round some time in the evening? ... – I hope that by Tuesday I shall have more to tell you of my plan for an art-paper. ...

Thank you so much for the Gaudier portfolio which Wadsworth handed on.[2] It is very successful; Top-hole, in fact, as the Prince of Wales said at the Beaver Hut.[3]

         Yrs,

         WYNDHAM LEWIS

101. *To John Rodker*   20 A Camp. Hill Grdns.
21st July 1919

Dear Rodker. ...

I will guarantee to get the 15 drawings ready for you by Aug 3rd. But I want to see you again soon if possible; and I should be glad if you could manage to get to my studio. The things are here ....

Have you dreamt of a perfect civilization, that would really suit you: so adjusting matter & society as to eliminate every emetic sight and makeshift person?[4] I do hope you have: or will before Aug 3rd!

         Yrs WYNDHAM LEWIS

[1] John Rodker (1894–1955) was among the young poets whom Pound encouraged at the time of World War I. When, at the end of the war, Rodker set up his Ovid Press, he undertook to publish a portfolio of L.'s drawings. The portfolio, *Fifteen Drawings*, appeared in 1919.

[2] *Twenty Drawings from the Note-books of H. Gaudier-Brzeska* (Ovid Press, 1919).

[3] Canadian Army Centre in London.

[4] L. addressed himself to this question in *The Caliph's Design. Architects! Where is Your Vortex?*, which The Egoist Ltd. published in October 1919. Rodker constructed his world of the future in a comic piece, "Mr. Segando in the Fifth Cataclysm," which appeared in *The Tyro No. 1* (April 1920). See next letter.

102. *To John Rodker* 20ᵃ Campden Hill Gardens. W.8.
Aug. 21st. 1919.

My dear Rodker. Thank you very much for the MSS: which is exquisite. I have been away for a week or so, & have only just got it. When we meet you will tell me what device you had for slightly adapting it.=I did not really want a satire on Effort. English good-breeding too sharply juxtaposed (or if you like my psychological pastiche of the effortless pair that you have got as a half-tone for the Portfolio) to Kalak [?], Memphis or probably Mexico, with their sublime demonstrations of human effrontery and absurd gusto, is to be deprecated when the time is so short! But come some day soon if you can: I should like to talk about that with you. And I hope to have your drawings ready early next week.

            Yrs

              WYNDHAM LEWIS

Although he preferred public scope for exercising himself in invective, Lewis could – out of pique or amusement or both – blast away privately as well. A notable example is an exchange between him and Paul Nash (1889–1946). The two artists had known one another since Omega days, but they had never been close friends nor co-partners in any movement. Then in the spring of 1919, Lewis wrote to Nash, saying he wanted to buy a design made, in Nash's words, "for some indifferent satires published at the Poetry Bookshop." Something about Lewis's request for this drawing of a human pyramid annoyed Nash. He replied twice, the second letter beginning; "My dear Lewis, I am always pleased to hear from you. Much as I admire your work as a whole, most particularly do I regard you as a great wit. You, above all men I meet, never fail to amuse me. That is why I like you. Of course I know you are a great artist . . . ." The exchange – only a part of which is included – evidently raged on for weeks and resulted in a permanently disrupted relationship.[1]

[1] Sir John Rothenstein recounts what seems to be an aftermath of this affair, although he is vague as to date and subject of the correspondence. See *Modern English Painters: Lewis to Moore*, pp. 42–3.

103. *To Paul Nash*† [London]
[August 1919]

My dear Nash

The delay in answering your first letter was owing principally, if not entirely, to a difficulty I found in couching my reply in such a form as could not possibly be interpreted as an offense. And my acute desire to possess the original of the beautiful design that was the Object of my first letter, in quickening my punctilio, has, I fear, made me remiss.

Now, my difficulty has only been increased by the receipt of your second letter. For in your letter of a few days ago you again put forward the suggestion with certain dismay. I once had dinner with you, some time ago: and I (may I confess it?) I feel after my references of almost unbridled admiration to your pyramid I can allow myself this frankness: – yet, will you understand? Should you *not* do so, where will be the very valuable testimonial you have given me as a Wit? And surely, being yourself in such a gentlemanly, frank, a trifle bluff, but humourous manner, a fine old type of the fruity flowering of this quality, this is not a thing any man would willingly see recalled or cancelled. But your second letter leaves me no alternative. I must speak. Well then: on that former and solitary occasion, I was so *frozen* with what showed every indication of being the most horrible form of boredom, and which, nevertheless, I know, seeing from whom this apparently devastating emanation was proceeding, could not be that, but must be (baffling though) the *reverse* of that: and that I consequently must, the entire time, be finding myself amused, effervesced, Volponeized; *that*, as a result of all this inevitable confusion and perplexity, (and I *swear* that, actually in *result* it left me precisely in the state in which I should expect to find myself after supping with a heavy, witless, mean, dreary, trivially vain, sententious, mournful *dolt*) when I received your unexpected invitation to a repetition of this perplexing and ponderous affair, I racked my brain for some means by which I might at once (a) secure the lovely design I wanted: and (b) evade, in order to gain my end (a), this peculiar encounter.

As regards an exchange of works, which you suggest, I again am baffled.[1] I am conscious that, should I toil from now till

[1] Nash had written: "... perhaps you would rather exchange one of your lesser drawings (I suppose the best of us do lesser drawings) for one of my important ones."

Xmas, I could not produce anything that I should dare to place in the scales against such a piece of aesthetic ordnance as your human pyramid. Therefore I must take refuge in the simple arrangement of offering you what my small means will allow – a trifling sum, but every penny of it weighted with admiration of your accomplishments – somewhere between the silver Crown, and its burnished copper counterpart!

Yours etc,

104. *Paul Nash to Wyndham Lewis*   9 Fitzroy St.
Aug 21 1919

My dear Lewis You need have been under no apprehension that I should misunderstand your delay in answering my letter. Altho' I recognise you as a man of wit I realise it is *not* of the spontaneous order. There is nothing of the Whistler about you. That method of yours – accumulative, parenthetical, monumental, one might say, – in fact your passion for pyramids – is all opposed to brevity and the rapier thrust. You, like the mills of God, grind slow, and I might add, grind exceeding small. I was able to realise this – with you, I was sure, it was only a matter of time.

I confess I am astonished by some of the things you eventually say, for while I am as much at a loss as you appear to be, to account for your strange feelings after dinner; I am more at a loss to explain how you should so far forget your *pose* as to express them in such a laborious and boorish fashion, exposing to my astonished understanding the indication of a nature so calculating, petty; malicious and uncivilised, in short so strangely sub-human, as to realise almost the popular estimate of your character; an estimate in which, hitherto, I have steadfastly refused to believe. Nor am I yet persuaded to accept it, for then I should be ignoring the fact of your highly sensitive, somewhat excitable temperament. No: I believe you to be a vain, extremely thin-skinned gentleman 'touched on the raw.' And that, my dear Lewis, is the long and short of it. So let us cry 'quits' over this entertaining but rather long-winded correspondence. And let your [word missing] to this letter be of such a polite and friendly character as I might have expected from you before the fount of all your varied inspiration *sat down* with such unexpected suddenness upon that 'hapilly-humanized' pyramid.

With kind regards
Yours etc
PAUL NASH

105. *To Paul Nash*†   20a Campden Hill Gdns W.8
                              August 25th [1919]

My dear Nash,

I am distressed to find that all my labour has been in vain. Also that I should have driven such a dignified gentleman into the lamentable lapse of a series of tu quoques. But I might have known that would happen! I sprinkle myself with a few ashes. Muffled and buried in parentheses and pomposities, in which I attempted to speak to you in your own tone, yet it seems that some harsh words of mine (not *meant* harshly, dear Nash) have pierced the wads that cover what you imply is your pretty thick hide. So be it. Had I that butterfly touch that (and naturally enough indeed) you appear to prize so highly, I could perhaps rescue, even yet, the super-human pyramid that I engaged in this dreary desert to acquire. But in your last communication not a word could I find of the lovely design that has been my objective all along. I must therefore leave you for the present to ruminate on the "uncivilized" means that some folk take to come by what they want (especially pyramids:) and how back-biting, shittishness and every mean practice is the speciality of your "sub-human" and bestial enemies, (whom Yaveh confound!)

You will hear from me again soon. We must allow the erupting pyramid a few weeks in which to cool!

Yours etc.
WYNDHAM LEWIS

106. *To John Quinn*   London, W.8.
                                    3rd September, 1919

My dear Quinn,

You must excuse me for the long delay in answering your letter. This is the reason: On receiving your letter I wrote a reply.

But, unfortunately, at the time two of the drawings you mentioned were not available.[1] They were in Paris at the Musée de Guerre. . . . So I waited for these cursed French-Salon bureaucrats to send back the things to Marchant,[2] and they have taken all this time to do it. A lively correspondence has taken place between Goupil's and the Frenchmen. At last a gush of apologies came from a higher official, followed at a respectful distance by the things. I did not think it was much use sending them over there, as I imagined that the machinery of official art in France was in even more conservative hands than it is here. . . .

I am glad that all has turned out for the best as regards the war show. I sold a good many things, and to new buyers: but your adherence naturally impresses Marchant, puts money in his pocket, and makes the thing from his point of view a real success. This is important to me. I should not have minded your not liking the war things, except in so far as it affected me materially, because they are an episode in my life. They were done under conditions unfavourable to art production. But, I can say quite seriously that I think some of the things on their way to you are as good things as will be done of the war from the English side, and are worth having.

. . . I should pass them without squinting, if the Next World were a place where men were judged by their merit as artists, and I were getting my works together to face my judges. And I usually know what I'm doing without that being in my case, I think, a demerit. . . .

As to my activities this autumn, I am bringing out in three weeks (by the end of September, I hope) a sixty-page pamphlet dealing with the art position generally.[3] I will write you more about this when I send it to you. Roughly, it is a consideration of how an abstract design of direction and masses can be applied to a street or a city. It is an appeal to the better type of artist to take more interest in and more part in the general life of the world, if only in the interest of his own shop, and to attempt to change the form-content of civilized life. The artist labouring in his

---

[1] Quinn wrote on June 16th to say that the photographs of things from L.'s "Guns" exhibition had arrived and that he wanted seven or eight of the pictures.
[2] William Marchant, director of the Goupil Gallery.
[3] *The Caliph's Design.*

studio, the absolute schism between him and life, is displayed: and I consider how this is affecting painting and is likely to affect its further progress. That is, more or less, what it is about. But, as I say, I will write you again, soon, about that.

Then, I am bringing out another volume of *Blast* (about November I expect).[1] This will be, one half, the matter of my pamphlet: these theories illustrated by fifteen or twenty designs by Roberts, Etchells, Wadsworth, Turnbull,[2] Dismorr[3] and myself; the other half consisting of less specific matter: a story by myself, a long, new poem by Eliot, and some other things. Pound has vanished into France and is in a mist of recuperation and romance. I have not heard from him, so I don't expect he will take part in this, although he may.

Another task is my big, eleven-foot canvas, for the Imperial Government, which I must finish sometime this autumn.[4] And there is the completion of my designs for Rodker's portfolio of fifteen drawings (this I am on at present). Another (this is a very great secret!) is a set of designs I am doing for a Rowlandson ballet, which I hope Diaghilief will take. A young musician named Walton is doing the music.[5] He is believed in by a good many people and I am sure is a man of parts, or boy rather. He is 17 or 18; though I have heard none of his music and should not know what it was like if I had. The ballet deals with the adventures of Dr. Syntax, Rowlandson's illustrations for which you have no doubt seen.[6] This I shall follow (whether accepted or not) by a Sea Ballet: scene at Deptford, sailors, chanties (1780), etc. I will send you photographs of these designs which will give you an idea of the scope and character of this little enterprise of mine (or rather of Sitwells, as Walton is a friend of theirs, and it was they who started this scheme).

I have, next, formed a group of ten painters: Etchells, Roberts, Wadsworth, Kauffer, Dismorr, Dobson (a sculptor), three others

[1] The volume never appeared.
[2] John Turnbull, who had done pictures of air battles which L. admired.
[3] Jessie Dismorr (1885–1939) had signed the Vorticist Manifesto and contributed to *Blast No. 2*. Later she contributed to L.'s second *Tyro*.
[4] The canvas, *A Battery Shelled*, is in the Imperial War Museum.
[5] This project with William Walton was never carried out.
[6] Dr. Syntax was the subject of three volumes produced by Rowlandson and his collaborator William Combe between 1812 and 1821.

and myself. We are holding a first exhibition at the Maddox Galleries, I think, in November.¹

The above artists are, furthermore, taking a shop or office, where it is proposed to sell objects made by them, paintings and drawings, to a certain extent, and especially to have a business address from which the poster, cinematograph and other industries can be approached.²

I am having a show of my own drawings and paintings, some hundred, either in December or February. I will give you details of that as it comes along.³ I will send you shortly photographs of two paintings, showing what I have been at for the last few months.

If you add to these things a half-dozen articles or stories for the English Review, *Art and Letters*, a Hindu magazine, etc., also a lecture (the subject-matter of my pamphlet) at the Westminster Hall on October 28th⁴ (Eliot is giving one on Poetry for the same people a week or so later), and my labours on the Arts League of Service, you will see that I shall be fairly busy! But you will also have to remember that I have just re-written several of my early stories and essays, and am looking for a publisher for that book under the title of "Inferior Religions" or "A Soldier of Humour."⁵

I think that this is about all my news up to date.

There is a French show here at present (held at Heal's, Tottenham Court Road). It has been got up by Sitwells, and brought over by a dealer called Zborovsky. It contains three excellent Modiglianis (too much Cezanne but very able); a very nice, but slight, Matisse; a lot of stormy, Constable-like Vlamincks; a few interesting things by Kisling, Survage (do you know him? – a very sweetly-coloured, fantastic brand of cubism, but quite beautiful), and Archipenko. Except for the Vlamincks and Modiglianis, and these Survages, the show is not an important one. Only one small, early, Picasso. The show has had some success, in spite of the time chosen to hold it. Arnold Bennett has come out as one interested in modern art, and bought a Modigliani, a Kisling and a Vlaminck.

¹ L. refers to X Group. See letters to Kauffer.
² This aspect of the venture was evidently dropped.
³ The show did not transpire till April 1921, when it went on at the Leicester Galleries as "Tyros and Portraits."
⁴ L.'s lecture was titled "Modern Tendencies in Art."
⁵ The volume finally appeared in 1927 as *The Wild Body: A Soldier of Humour and Other Stories.*

I am glad my "Gun-pit" pleased you. I find it difficult to conceive of a more dreary and desperate collection of Pseudo-pictures than Ottawa will shortly possess in that Canadian War Memorial show.[1] As you say, the war might have been going on in another planet, for all the interest paid to it by most of the artists employed. But, until you get other standards in life, and a general shuffling of energies, you cannot hope for anything but such spectacles. You cannot have Egypt or Sung without paying for it and without good luck.

I am sending two copies of this letter, one expressed. I shall do this in the case of my letters to America for a year. I am sure that the Atlantic is full of mines, mutinous crews, icebergs, whales and storms; and that all postal services are incompetent and malignant.

My best wishes to you, excuses for being a nuisance, and thanks for your last letter and the decision as regards the eight drawings.

Yours sincerely,
P. WYNDHAM LEWIS

107. *To Paul Nash*†   20a Campden Hill Gardens, W8
Sept. 11th 1919.

My dear Nash,

I have just got your last valuable letter.

I am *so* glad, you are working hard![2] (Dont overdo it, though!) But I am sorry that my notes affect your work in any way, and am naturally surprised to learn of the difficulty experienced by you in writing those easy and graceful replies. I can hardly credit this. The air of suave and very gentleman-like negligence, so noticeable in them cannot be a pretence: not *entirely* the traditional naif arm of the trickster cornered. Are you sure that you are not a little neurasthenic about it?

---

[1] Quinn reported having been to an exhibition of the Canadian War Memorial pictures at the Anderson Galleries. He complimented L. on the realism and harsh vigour of his *A Canadian Gun-pit*; the rest "might be called paintings of 'moving picture war in Algiers, staged by David Belasco'."

[2] After another exchange of missives, Nash wrote on September 7th saying he had a good deal of work to do and suggesting they call a halt to the correspondence.

As to your referring me to your Agents, Messrs. Brown![1] Ha! Ha! Ha! You *are* the soul of playfulness, arent you!

Of course, Sunday "depresses" our little gentleman![2] Of course it does, then! "Sundays always depress me!" That was in your best style; *so* clever, and shows *such* a hypersensitive nature! But (uneasy though: I become solicitous once more) are you *sure* that you are not working a little too hard? Is it not perhaps a little *too* oversensitive?

(You know the well-nigh preponderating role that *teeth* play in the health? Are you quite sure that your teeth are all right. It's true they *look* all right, but appearances are deceptive, as you would remark!)

Goodbye for the present,

Yours:

WYNDHAM LEWIS

The history of Lewis's group affiliations ends with the forming of the short-lived X Group. At the urging of E. McKnight Kauffer and other pre-war associates, Lewis agreed to the reconstituting in post-war London of what was essentially the Vorticist Group. So X Group was launched. It managed an exhibition at Heal's Mansard Gallery in March 1920, *Lewis writing the preface to the catalogue. But the organisation lacked any vital force and, after differences between Lewis and some of the other members, it soon disintegrated.*[3]

[1] Nash said he couldn't unfortunately part with the drawing at L.'s price. "Should you wish to bargain let me refer you to my agents Messrs Brown & Phillips...."

[2] In closing, Nash wrote: "Forgive me if this letter sounds peevish, it is Sunday and Sundays depress me.

Yours wearily."

[3] See *Blasting and Bombardiering*, p. 211. The American artist E. McKnight Kauffer (1890–1954) had settled in London in 1914 and exhibited with the London Group in 1916. After the dissolution of X Group, he devoted himself almost entirely to the posters and book illustrations that made him famous.

108. *To E. McKnight Kauffer*   Campden Hill. W.8.
[September? 1919]

Dear Kauffer. I am sorry that you had no luck with the Maddox Galleries. I am also sorry that it looks as though your enterprise would not thrive for the moment. But surely if a strong group were formed, a way would be found to arrange premises for an Exhibition? – Why not proceed with the forming of the group: making a group on such lines that the usual discord and contradiction of character and aim did not weaken it, and I think the assumption is strong that some dealer would undertake to shelter its works at the agreed periods: or the Group itself with £2 subscriptions might otherwise launch itself and rent a gallery. The present London Group is a bad working collection of individuals, and will not improve. I think if you got Ginner,[1] myself and half a dozen other people together (Roberts, Turnbull, Hamilton, Dismorr, and so forth, any people you specially favour [?]) something definite might be done. Or shall I do that? I should like to see you soon. I will write further this week.

Yrs. W. L.

109. *To E. McKnight Kauffer*   [London]
[1919?]

Dear Kauffer. Roberts told me on Sunday that at the London Group Meeting Fry was very excited [?] in his mind about X Group getting their show in before the London Group. Also, that he advocated at once getting in touch with Heal, and preventing this happening. I therefore resolved today to see Heal. . . .
Ginner and myself saw Heal. It happens that the London Group have definitely chosen May: and that (Easter coming April 2nd to 6th.) we had better open on March 26th. Since Heal has the Gallery occupied up to March 6th: there is no chance of the London Group getting in before our show. . . .

I hope I shall see you soon.
Yrs.
W. L.

[1] L. had been associated with Charles Ginner (1878–1952) in the Camden Town and London Groups.

In an article titled "Wilcoxism" in The Athenaeum *of March 5th, 1920, Clive Bell blasted the exhibition of Imperial War Pictures – especially the section by "advanced" artists – at Burlington House. He was annoyed both by the inferiority of the work – "mere 'arty' anecdote" – and by the air of self-congratulation accompanying the show. Compared with the French, the best English painter was second-class, he said. Yet these artists' friends were so foolish as to compare them to Leonardo – R. H. Wilenski having done so in writing about Lewis.[1] The attack, loftily contemptuous, runs on for several columns. Lewis came forward quickly, for the question was not simply one of personal affront. It involved as well two of his firmest convictions: the right of English art to an open view, unprejudiced by foreign affinities, and the baneful influence of the Fry-Bloomsbury faction.*

110. *To the Editor of "The Athenaeum," March 12, 1920*

20a, Campden Hill Gardens

MR. CLIVE BELL AND "WILCOXISM"

Sir, – Since so much of Mr. Bell's "querulous hostility" (*Athenaeum*, March 5, p. 311)[2] appears to come in my direction, you will perhaps allow me the publicity of your correspondence columns to pay him a compliment he has more or less deserved; that is, to examine his pronouncements.

First of all, Mr. Bell is discovered confronting the "Imperial Painters at Burlington House"; and the whole warlike array of painters marshalled there by this mighty Empire is the monster

---

[1] Bell closes by conjuring his readers to admire "the admirable though somewhat negative qualities in the work of Mr. Lewis ... without forgetting that in the Salon d'Automne or the Salon des Indépendants a picture by him would neither merit nor obtain from the most generous critic more than a passing word of perfunctory encouragement" (p. 312). The coinage "Wilcoxism" was derived from Mrs. Wilcox, author of *The Worlds and I*. Bell compares her illusions as to the greatness of her literary friends to the enthusiasm of critics like Wilenski.

[2] Bell begins his article by protesting that on returning from France he found himself "forced immediately into an attitude of querulous hostility" by the self-applause accompanying this exhibition.

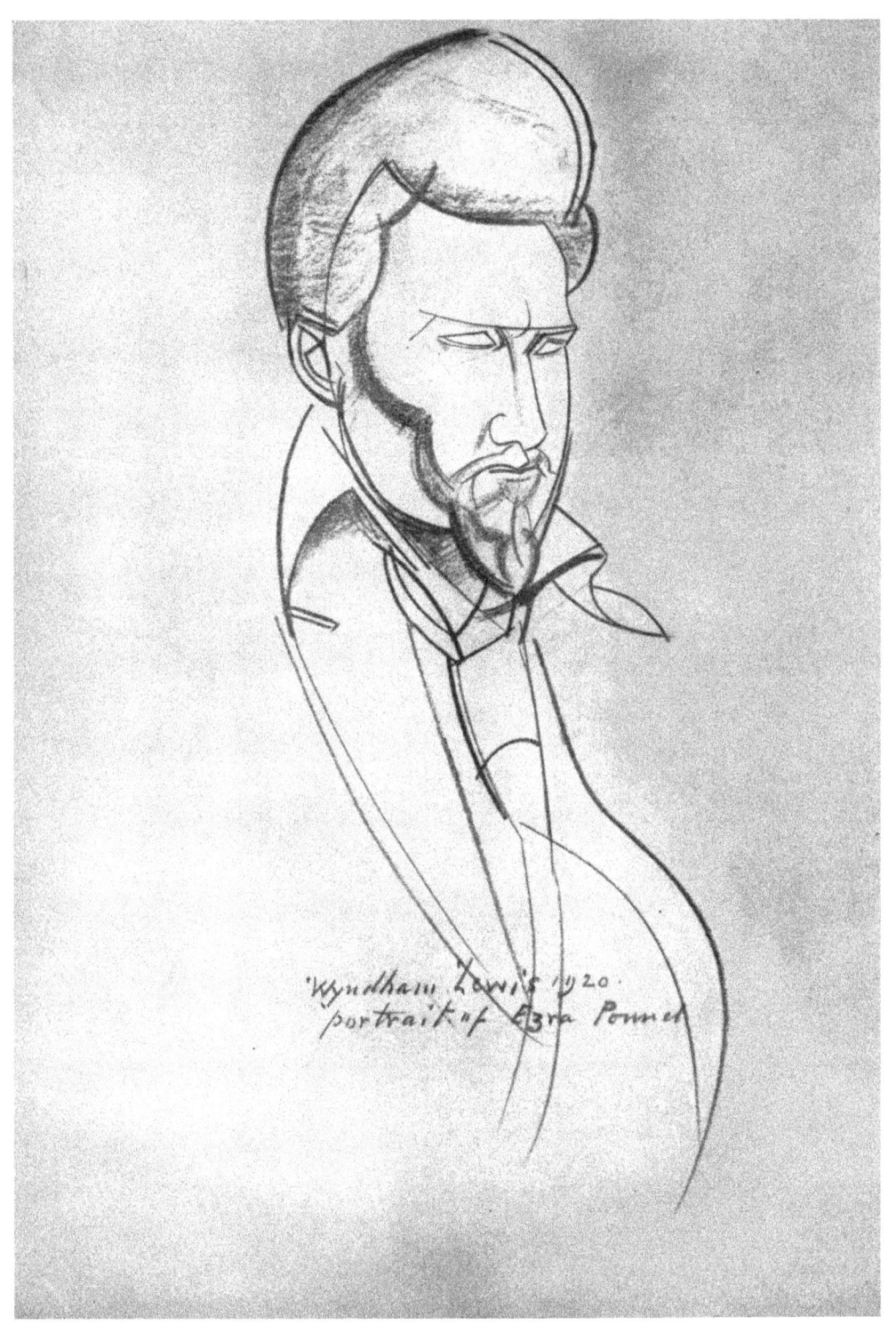

8. 1920 drawing of Ezra Pound

before which he abusively struts. He is concerned for the honour of his country. The military character of the spectacle is alone sufficient to vex and disturb him; and, of course, he had no hand in marshalling it – not even that of the non-com, barking at its heels.

But Mr. Bell knows as well as anybody else that this vast display does not represent the serious painting being done in England, any more than a promiscuous exhibition of the same extent and nature in Paris would represent that of France. Furthermore, had Derain, Matisse, Vlaminck and those painters of his choice working in Paris been employed by a similar authority in France, they would have been unlikely to produce work at all comparable to the best of their independent and unconditioned work.

It must be admitted at once, however, that beneath his parade of dishonesty and effrontery, Mr. Bell is really a sincere, if hallucinated, soul. For he regards Paris with something of the awestruck glee and relish of a provincial urchin at the sight of a Cockney guttersnipe. Is there anything that almost any artist with a little prestige in Paris might not tell him that he would not swallow unhesitatingly? He is almost, you might say deliberately, the comic "Anglais" of French caricature. He is a grinning, effusive and rather servile Islander, out on his adventures among French Intelligences. Besides, when you consider the five long years he has been exiled from France it is no wonder that he should give proof of an almost ecstatic contentment at being able at last to get there again.

As regards the details of his concoction, "Wilcoxism": to write one week that his friend Mr. Grant is greater than William Blake or Hogarth,[1] and to object the next to your contributor R. H. W. asserting that "Mr. Lewis possesses certain affinities with Leonardo," is just a dull essay in impudence. R. H. W. does not, as far as I can find, say that "Mr. Lewis was a match for Leonardo"; so Mr. Bell has, "not unnaturally," indulged in a little dishonest shuffling of words.

To write, "Mrs. Wilcox has no reason to suppose that her friends were not the greatest writers alive," is to challenge the reflection which must come to anyone's mind that, if ever it were so, Pot is calling the Kettle black; and calling it black with

[1] See "Duncan Grant," *The Athenaeum*, February 6th, 1920, pp. 182–83.

the full consciousness that those conversant with the tenderly sympathetic attitude of Mr. Bell and his friends to each other would say either, "What charming effrontery on the part of Mr. Bell!" or "Mr. Bell is overreaching himself!" according to their attitude of mind with respect to that gentleman.

But already a method is apparent, directing Mr. Bell's utterances. Any offence Mr. Bell indulges in this week we must expect to be accused of by him during the course of the following week. Any vice of mind that is essentially Mr. Bell's you can wager he will attribute to you at the first opportunity, with many a sly shake of the finger, and splutter of the mouth.

So when he writes, "To talk of modern English painting as though it were the rival of French painting is silly," it is a silliness that Mr. Bell would be far more likely to be guilty of than anyone else. With his "French colts 7 lb. below English" and "English normally a stone below French," and all the rest of his Winstonian sporting parallels,[1] does he not show himself, indeed, very apt at such stupidities, only the other way on! For Intellectual champions are of more individual growth than physical ones. There are always a few good artists in every country. A country can have a monopoly of general taste, as it can of general athletic efficiency, for a time; but hardly of individual triumphs of the intellect. Supposing a Brazilian of genius or a talented Turk see the light; must he settle in Paris in order to take his place beside an ineffable Four, who, alas! (Mr. Bell "bravely recognizes the disagreeable truth") are even more compelling than Mr. Duncan Grant![2]

But Mr. Bell mixes Empire with Art, and Art with Sport, in his excitable nature. And moth-like he returns without cease to the *Ville Lumière*. But has it never occurred to Mr. Bell that, to undertake such a comparatively comfortable task as that of critic of Art, a *permanent* residence in Paris may be essential? Or is Mr. Bell's calibre as a critic to be reckoned only as minus avoirdupois? However this may be, on his eternal "return from Paris" his flunkeyism puffs itself out more and more, until it has made him one of the most ridiculous figures we possess.

---

[1] Bell constructs an analogy between the seven-pound inferiority of French horses to English and the one-stone inferiority of English painters to French.

[2] Bell says he is "not yet prepared to class" Duncan Grant with Matisse, Picasso, Derain and Bonnard.

At least in this little matter of the comic Mr. Bell's unfortunate provincial native land is not a stone, nor yet 7 lb., behind her seductive and so "artistic" neighbour, France. This should be some consolation to Mr. Bell's distressed patriotism.[1]

Yours faithfully,
WYNDHAM LEWIS

111. *To John Quinn*   37 Redcliffe Road, Fulham Road,
London.
June 14, 1920.

Dear Quinn,

The reason that I have delayed this letter so long has been because, principally, I have been put out of action for several months by my mother's death, and the subsequent business worries. Her death was a loss and misery to me: that would not have held up my work, rather the contrary. But it has entailed a good deal of practical and business activity.

I have not your letter by me now, but I remember several points – a very great poussée towards Henri Matisse, among others. I am with you in that respect, but not so exclusively as your remarks indicate that you feel. As a student of the absolute use of oil paint, I don't think that Picasso compares unfavourably with him. Matisse's use of that medium appears to me, if anything, too monotonously summary and thin: rather an *adequate* than a positive quantity. As to your repeated statement, in your letters to me and to Marchant, of your preference for French painters (over English painters), I am wholly of your opinion. It is *almost* a physical impossibility for a young painter here (in England) not to be slowly but surely spoilt and broken. For one person here interested in modern painting (or, more, modern thought and life), there are a hundred in Paris, Milan, Berlin, Moscow: but let us say Paris, only, for that we know about. *Therefore*, as talent does not vary very much from country to country (facility, perhaps, "artisticness", but *not* talent), it is inevitable that any ten English painters should be less good than

---

[1] Bell's angry reply to this letter appeared in *The Athenaeum* of March 19th. L. struck back briefly the following week and suggested that the controversy not be pursued.

any ten French painters, because the conditions are ten times worse here than in France.

There is only one way of meeting this state of affairs, which it would be unwise to regard as anything but permanent. That is, to supplement exhibiting here very largely with exhibitions and practice abroad; and generally for the painter living mainly here to regard himself as a European first, and to paint and think for that wider audience.

As to your remarks about my work: By writing and publishing a novel and some stories, and adding criticism of art to that, I have been aware all along that I ran the risk of creating a misunderstanding about my painting: that I left a flank open to my enemies (whenever a man wishes to get at me over here he invariably starts by praising "Tarr"); also I know that it would be a temptation to me to neglect my painting for this other activity. But I know myself that, as things have worked out, no leakage of energy of that sort has occurred. What has occurred is that: (A) In the three years before the War, during which I started my work as a painter, I had to waste 50 per cent. of my time in propaganda and similar activities. (B) The whole War-time was sheer loss of time, big war-paintings included. Hence, I should be the last person to claim for my finished work anything more than a character of essay, and unfulfilment. I will ask you in five years' time, when I am forty years old, to have another look. These coming few years should be my first years of *complete* work.

I feel this is an egotistic letter: but when you hear *from* me you want to hear *about* me, don't you? I am sending over to the *Dial* this week, in which I understand that you are interested.[1]

Are you, as you had expected, visiting England this summer? If so I shall hope to see you. . . .

With best wishes,

Yours,
WYNDHAM LEWIS

[1] L.'s article "Paris Versus the World" appeared in *The Dial* of July 1921.

PART III. 1921–1939

"The Enemy"

The twenty years between the two wars were the most fruitful of Lewis's life. Between 1920 *and* 1939 *he wrote twenty-three books, revised three more, and edited and wrote most of two reviews* (The Tyro *and* The Enemy) *and one pamphlet. The accomplishment becomes more remarkable when one considers the significance of this work. The three vast critiques of mass mind and its modern diseases* – The Art of Being Ruled, The Lion and the Fox, *and* Time and Western Man – *formed the foundation of all Lewis's future criticism and provided a stimulus for many of the younger artists and intellectuals in Britain.* The Childermass, The Apes of God, *and* The Revenge for Love *mark, for most readers, the apex of their author's creative achievement. Add to this his most incisive volume of literary criticism* (Men Without Art), *a brilliant collection of essays on aesthetics* (Wyndham Lewis the Artist), *his only book of poetry, his ebullient autobiography, and such provocative essays in social psychology as* Pale-face *and* The Doom of Youth, *and one gets some notion of the talent and energy operative in Lewis during these years.*

His work as a visual artist was more sporadic, but here too the period was Lewis's most productive. The large number of drawings accomplished between 1920 *and* 1922 *show the draughtsman at the peak of his powers. Almost all of his best-known paintings date from a second spell of creativity, the five years between* 1933 *and* 1938. *The celebrated portraits of Edith Sitwell, Pound, and T. S. Eliot are of this time, as are* The Surrender of Barcelona, The Armada, *and* La Suerte.

Yet Lewis was neither healthy nor prosperous in this epoch. For about five years during the 1930*'s he was almost constantly unwell and often seriously ill, having several times to undergo surgery.*

Having no steady employment, he had usually to get what living he could from free-lance journalism and publishers' advances, with occasional help from portrait commissions. Now and then a patron appeared, but cultural largesse was no longer the custom in post-war London society.

Nor was Lewis any longer the public person he had been in the days of Blast. *He continued to move in "high Bohemia" in the early 1920's, but gradually he found himself circulating less, devoting his time more and more to his own work. The days of group affiliations and group wars were also past.*

Since a part of Lewis flourished in the limelight, it is not surprising that he should have worked out a solution to the dilemma created by this growing singleness and privacy. A public image appeared in his writing and drawing and began to lead a dual life with the private person. Wyndham Lewis left the stage to "Mr. Wyndham Lewis," The Tyro, The Enemy. The personae themselves were given a variety of masks: at times one was confronted with a jocose, toothy fellow roaring at man's fatuousness (see illustrations); this might change abruptly to an angry, mind-scourging Savonarola. Elsewhere, as the letters demonstrate, the human being – certain aspects of whom were magnified in the public projections – carried on his highly self-protective personal life.

The privacy of the off-stage Lewis is most strikingly revealed in his marriage in 1929 to G. Anne Hoskyns, an attractive young woman of Cornish descent who had been an art student. The couple were privately wed at a register office in London. For the next several years, during which Mrs. Lewis served her husband often as a model as well as a devoted wife, the marriage was kept a secret from all but a few friends.

Yet while the public figure, The Enemy, was inscribed in bold letters, noli me tangere, *the man went on being the sociable, usually affable person he always was. The letters indicate a growing talent for friendship – with patrons like Richard Wyndham and Sir Nicholas Waterhouse; with his publisher, C. H. Prentice; with fellow writers such as Roy Campbell, A. J. A. Symons, Richard Aldington, and Naomi Mitchison – most significant of all, with T. S. Eliot. Begun earlier, Lewis's association with Eliot became in this period as influential in his creative life as his friendship with John and Pound. His relationship with Joyce was briefer – being confined to the 1920's – but clearly momentous.*

At the same time, Lewis was settling into his public part of outsider and making the most of it. In a very few years he became known as the most inventive and outspoken gadfly on the English intellectual scene. An idea or kind of art had only to be popular, to be accepted, it seemed, to provoke a barrage from the Lewis gun (as he liked to call it). First, the premises of modern man, as The Enemy saw them, were laid bare: the sacrifice of mentality to emotion, of the solid and spatial to the nebulous and the fluent. The entire legacy of the Romantic Movement was brought before the firing squad of his prose. As the liberal left gained sway among artists and intellectuals, Mr. Wyndham Lewis committed himself more and more to the right. Partly aware of the harm he was doing himself, he went so far as to state the case for Hitler, and to insist on the wickedness of Communism almost up to the beginning of the war.

In the arts, and especially literature, The Enemy laid waste on all sides. Hardly an author of note escaped his attack at some time between the two wars. Not just the sham artist figures of The Apes of God, *but the most serious artists and writers, such as Picasso and Joyce, were found guilty of participating in the general decay. Nor were Lewis's victims confined to such hostile camps as those of the élite (the Sitwells and Virginia Woolf), of the "romantics" (Gertrude Stein and D. H. Lawrence), of the left-wing (transition group). His closest allies, Pound and Eliot, had their turn as targets.*

All these public explosions naturally had their consequences. Lewis found he could not always place his work suitably; occasionally on the appearance of a new book of his, something like a press boycott seemed to be shaping up. Even more maddening for him were the restrictions imposed by the tight British libel laws. Whether voiced in fiction or in critical essays, The Enemy's criticism was never discreet. Suits and threats of suits plagued him and his publishers. Between 1932 and 1936, Lewis had three books withdrawn either just before or after publication. He could not find a publisher at once bold enough and generous enough to undertake The Apes of God *and so had to bring out the gigantic satire first under his own imprint. This history of bans came to an appropriate climax just before the second World War, when his first portrait of T. S. Eliot was rejected – though not on grounds of libel – by the Royal Academy. As the letters show, Lewis met the rebuff with the relish of an old campaigner.*

112. *To Agnes Bedford*[1] 2 Alma Studios, Stratford Rd, W.8.
14.4.21.

Dear Miss Bedford. Thank you for your note. I was glad to hear that you liked the show. I expect that, with the exception of the drawings, or most of them, it was not easy to like.[2] I am sending you a copy of my paper, The Tyro, and thank you for your subscription.[3] Please, if you can, sell some copies to any folks who would not in an ordinary way hear about it. I have had an initial trouble or hitch with my publishing: the place from which it was supposed to be published I discovered, to my extreme astonishment, was locked up, and the staff away in Egypt. But I am making other arrangements. In a few days it should be obtainable at the principal booksellers. The Bomb Shop, Charing X Rd, meantime has it on sale. – The Strike will interfere. I hope it will be short.[4] I propose to draw Pounds table again before very long.[5] Will you come to tea with me?

Yours sincerely,
WYNDHAM LEWIS

113. *To John Rodker* Stratford Road. W.8.
14/4/21

Dear Rodker. Here is a copy of the Tyro, my long announced publication. – You told me when you gave me your article, that I might do what I liked with it. I availed myself of that, cut out

---

[1] Agnes Bedford, a musician with strong artistic interests, met L. through Pound, whom she was helping with his music. They became friends, seeing one another often during the Twenties. On the Lewises' return to England at the end of World War II, L. and Miss Bedford met again. Their friendship re-established, she remained a devoted ally till his death.

[2] The exhibition *Tyros and Portraits*, held at the Leicester Galleries in April 1921.

[3] The first number of *The Tyro* came out in April 1921. The second and last number appeared in 1922.

[4] The coal-miners had struck on March 31st. On the day of this letter a general strike was to have been called in sympathy. The government achieved a last-minute settlement with the other unions, but the miners stayed out for twelve weeks more before they reached an agreement.

[5] Pound had given a triangular table to Miss Bedford. L. intended to make some sketches of it for a picture he was doing.

Cover design for *The Tyro No. 2*, 1922

the part at the end, and wherever Mr. Wells' name occurred accompanied by deliberate irony I substituted the name of Segando. I hope that this slight alteration will meet with your approval.¹ . . .

Yours
WYNDHAM LEWIS

114. *To Harriet Shaw Weaver*   Kensington. W.8.
26/7/21.

Dear Miss Weaver. . . . It was too late to do anything, of course, before September. I hope then to get out another and more interesting number of the Tyro, with some more adequate financial backing.² Wadsworth appears very willing to help. If he does, that will simplify matters.

I had some half tone [?] blocks done for the next Tyro number (one of my painting, Praxitella.)³ A few weeks after I had received the blocks and a few prints, the Sun Engraving Comp. summonsed me in the County Court. I saw their lawyers; they explained that it was a big Company, and that therefore the business was run with less forethought or trouble than it otherwise would be. This may account for it.

In any case, you will see by the enclosed letter how I have arranged things. Would it be troubling you very much to send them (or me) a cheque for £7. 8. 0. out of the small Tyro fund?

The above may well be my address in a week or so. I think that I may have disposed of this place. If that turns out satisfactorily, I should store my things next week, make August a holiday, and return to London and settle in a studio in September. . . .

Thank you for the batch of Ulysses notices. Miss Beach did *not* forward me any, as she was asked to do by Joyce.⁴

¹ Thus the title of the article became "Mr. Segando in the Fifth Cataclysm."

² *The Tyro* was published by The Egoist Ltd., of which Miss Weaver was head. L. received financial support in the venture from his friend Sydney Schiff (1869?–1944), who wrote as Stephen Hudson.

³ The painting was originally owned by Edward Wadsworth. It is now in the City Art Gallery, Leeds.

⁴ L. refers no doubt to the prospectuses for *Ulysses* which Sylvia Beach sent out from Shakespeare & Company in Paris. The novel did not appear till February 1922.

I hope you have a pleasant holiday.

Yrs very sincerely
WYNDHAM LEWIS

Robert McAlmon (1896–1956), the American expatriate writer and publisher, sought out Lewis soon after his arrival in London in 1921. McAlmon had just married Winifred "Bryher," daughter of the millionaire Sir John Ellerman, and he was full of projects. Lewis was attracted to McAlmon as a convivial companion and possible patron. They became friends and continued to see one another, very congenially, in London and Paris for the next six years. They reciprocated as well in advancing each other's career – Lewis publishing McAlmon in The Tyro *No. 1; McAlmon getting work for Lewis (through the Ellermans) and later, laying plans for Lewis's books.*[1] *But with McAlmon's failure to pursue these plans and the resultant attack on him in* Time *and* Western Man *(see "The Revolutionary Simpleton"), the intimacy was strained and the friendship gradually faded.*[2]

115. *To Robert McAlmon*   Lee Studio, Adam and Eve Mews,
Kensington, W.8.
Oct. 14. 21.

Dear Macalmon. Studio-moving: hideous trouble. At present better, and installed as above. Your account of rooms [?] you have sounds as though you [word] resources of information and help in Berlin that were denied to me. If I come there again I will certainly find out DEN ZELTEN, and dwell there.

My plans at present are circumscribed by money considerations. I am extremely hard up. Once having established myself here, I shall not be able to stir until I have accumulated a bit. – I shall probably go over to Paris about Nov 20 (perhaps before) for a few

---

[1] In a private note, written many years later, McAlmon denied ever having given Lewis assurances that he would publish his work.

[2] For their own accounts, see *Blasting and Bombardiering*, p. 230, and McAlmon's *Being Geniuses Together* (London, 1938), *passim*.

days. As to Berlin, I hope to get there again in the early Spring: but it is very uncertain.

When you next find yourself back here come and see me. I was very vexed at having missed you in Berlin by a few hours. I would [word] have stayed there a few days longer.
Ivan Puni
Trabenerstrasse. 25.
Grünewald.
and his wife Bogoslewskaya, [?] are two people I met at 'Waldens'[1] tea. Puni is a young Russian painter (ex-Communist, lately arrived from Petrograd) with lovely dark wife, also painter, who will ogle you till you are sick (not probably of love). I think you might go and see them, since they know everybody. Remind them of the English painter they met at Waldens. Another, but more compromising [?] person to visit is Alex. Archipenko.[2]
Atelier.
Kaiserdamm. 4.
He is well-known Paris-Russian sculptor getting worse every day. (Walden has a nasty thing of his you may have seen.)

Let me know how you get on, and what you are going to do next.

Yrs
WYNDHAM LEWIS

P.S. I have sent off a note to Puni for you.
[on side of letter] Tell Mina Loy[3] to visit me if she comes to London. She cant make any money here: but I will tell her what galleries to visit.

116. *To Robert McAlmon* Kensington W.8.
Nov. 16. 21 [?]

Dear Bob. Thank you for photos. I am very glad to have the big one of yourself. (I wish I could get a drawing from them for my

---

[1] Most likely Herwarth Walden (b. 1878), composer and writer. He was the author of several volumes of art criticism and editor of *Der Sturm*.
[2] Alexander Archipenko (b. 1887), now residing in the United States.
[3] Expatriate American artist and poet.

series.¹ But I think I must wait till we next come together which will be soon, I expect, as drawings from photos are not good). The Giotto p.c. beautiful. Gozzoli interests me only as a colour-user.

I was going to telegraph you Rodkers address when I got your letter. Rodker I suppose has to be careful of the susceptibilities of his ped. patrons. As a woman objects to hearing her charms too grossly labelled, so I suppose there are certain brutalities where the ped. is concerned etc. . . .

The photo of self shall be sent to [word] B. Today I have got the colour [?] drawings to the Sketch at last: and am proceeding with more. Nancy² is going to Paris next Wed. or Thurs. and I may go over with her for a week or so, and do a few people there, look for a good studio, and see if a man Pound speaks of wanting portrait is any good.

The Little Rev. are at length bringing out my [?] number.³ Give me news of all and send me story when you have a copy done.⁴ What are your movements for New Year?

Yours

W. L.

[1] Presumably the series of drawings of society people L. was doing, thanks to the Ellermans' influence, for *The Sketch*. Only a part of the series actually appeared. *The Sketch* said it was forced to discontinue printing the pictures because of the objections of its readers to L.'s style.

[2] Nancy Cunard, the writer and publisher and well-known figure in post-war Paris. L. had first known her mother, Maud, Lady Cunard, during the war, when he attended Lady Cunard's literary and artistic gatherings in London.

[3] Pound wrote to L. in April:

"Am taking up the *Little Review* again, as a quarterly, each number to have about twenty reprods of *one* artist, replacing Soirées de Paris.

"Start off with twenty Brancusi's to get a new note.

"You have had since 1917 to turn in some illustrations for *L.R.*, but perhaps the prospect of a full Lewis number will lure you." (*The Letters of Ezra Pound*, p. 166.)

The Lewis number never appeared, however.

[4] Evidently L. intended to publish the story in the second *Tyro*. Nothing came of this.

117. *To Agnes Bedford*   16a Craven Rd. Paddington.
[1921]

Dear Miss Bedford. Glad to hear from you. . . . Was it you who stimulated Pound to the purchase of a BASSOON?[1] And if so, do you think that is an action justified by the facts of existence, as you understand them? . . .

                                                            Yrs
                                                      W. LEWIS

Lewis and James Joyce met first in the summer of 1920 or 1921 when Lewis was in Paris with T. S. Eliot, the latter having been commissioned by Pound to deliver a parcel to Joyce.[2] Despite their touchy sensibilities, the two artists got on well, and Lewis continued to spend time with Joyce on his frequent visits to Paris during the succeeding years. Then, in 1927, Time and Western Man appeared, with its long, very sharp critique of Ulysses. Joyce felt the attack, extending as it did from the novel to himself. Thus a coolness set in, and though they never broke openly, the two men were never again so friendly as they had been.[3]

[1] Miss Bedford had been in Paris in August 1921 helping Pound with his opera *Villon*. After her departure, feeling unable to cope with a keyboard instrument, he purchased a bassoon. L. found him struggling with the instrument when he visited Paris later in the year.

[2] L. in his superb account of this event (*Blasting and Bombardiering*, pp. 270–6) places it in the summer of 1920. But although all the details of the occasion are, according to T. S. Eliot, perfectly remembered, it is possible that L. misdated by a year. In a letter of June 24th, 1921, to Harriet Shaw Weaver, Joyce indicates that he and L. have recently had their first meeting. See *Letters of James Joyce*, edited by Stuart Gilbert (New York, 1957), pp. 165–7.

[3] In his biography of Joyce, Richard Ellman gives a good account of the effect on Joyce – including reprisal in *Finnegans Wake* – of L.'s criticism. (See *James Joyce* (New York, 1959), pp. 607–9, 618, 626.) Miss Weaver has, in an interview, corroborated his facts. L. gives his retrospective view of the incident in *Rude Assignment*, p. 55.

118. *To James Joyce*

The Tyro
A Review of the Arts of Painting,
Sculpture and Design
Edited by Wyndham Lewis.

Publishers:
The Egoist Press,
2, Robert Street,
Adelphi,
London.

[January 1922?]

Dear Joyce. Pound tells me that it is your kind intention to have me sent a copy of Ulysses. I am therefore writing to thank you, but to prevent your having that done, as someone has just promised me a copy; she possessing two, for some reason. – I should have subscribed myself some time back, but have been very hard up.

I was sorry not to see you on my two days visit to Paris, but had not much time, & I expect you are very busy. Also I expect to be coming to stay for a month or two shortly.

Miss Beachs, & Pounds account of the success of your first edition is good news.[1] I hope [word] will rapidly follow with further editions, & that [the?] affair will be a triumphant success on the practical side.

With every good wish,

Your devoted friend,
WYNDHAM LEWIS

119. *To Herbert Read*   Adam and Eve Mews. W.8.
March 10/22

Dear Read. Thank you for letter: and I am very glad Tyro pleases you. (The "essay" you mention is rather mutilated, to get it in, and the general scheme of the essay is wider than may appear in

---

[1] L. refers to the subscription sales. See Sylvia Beach, *Shakespeare and Company* (New York, 1959), pp. 45–86.

its present printed form. It is a book, over which I propose to take my time.)[1] . . .

Your offer of Hulme mss. very welcome. If the notes are at all coherent, I should like very much to have them full in Tyro.[2]

Yours
WYNDHAM LEWIS

120. *To Robert McAlmon* Casa Maniella[?]
[Venice][3]
Saturday [October 1922]

Dear Bob. Yesterday I got a good drawing of M.'s sister:[4] also 2 good starts of Nancy.[5] Today Ruby is coming.[6] Tomorrow I shall finish Nancy and tackle M. Lady C.[7] can be dealt with following day (Monday) and a few more pictures [word?]. Then I shld. be ready to start off. The weather is wretched; and my proposed packet of sketches of house, ornaments, canals, etc. must I am afraid be postponed.[8]

Rod.[9] has sold a drawing to Jealoux[10] for a good price. Nancy buys Mondino, and I can float off so.

You say your wife arrives Monday. If it were *certain* you were

[1] Doubtless the "Essay on the Objective of Plastic Art in Our Time," which appeared in *Tyro*, No. 2. This significant statement of L.'s aesthetic was never expanded into a book; it did reappear in *Wyndham Lewis: The Artist, from 'Blast' to Burlington House* (London, 1939).

[2] Read had evidently offered either one of the collections of Hulme's notes that he compiled for *Speculations* (1924) or the "Notes on Language and Style," which he left out of *Speculations* and published in *The Criterion* of July 1925. The third number of *Tyro* indicated by L. never came out.

[3] L. was staying in Venice as a guest of Nancy Cunard.

[4] "M." is Mondino del Robilan, a friend of Nancy Cunard.

[5] A drawing by L. of Nancy Cunard in Venice is in the collection of the British Council.

[6] Ruby Peto, niece of the Duchess of Rutland and cousin of Lady Diana Manners (Cooper).

[7] Presumably Lady Cunard.

[8] So far as is known, L. completed only one of these sketches. It was inscribed to his friend Richard Wyndham.

[9] John Rodker.

[10] Edmond Jealoux, French writer and sinophile.

9. At the summer residence of Mr. and Mrs. Sydney Schiff, ca. 1921. Lewis is on the left, T. S. Eliot on the right. Seated in the centre is Lady Tosti, widow of the composer. Kneeling in front is Mrs. Violet Wyndham, daughter of Ada Leverson and niece of Mrs. Schiff

10. Lewis in Venice, 1922. (*From a snapshot by Miss Nancy Cunard*)

stopping, and that I could get a further drawing of you, and one of your wife, I would come Florence Tues. morning or Monday night. I should of course like to see Florence. . . .

Yrs
W. L.

Among the art and society figures whom Lewis saw during the war were Osbert Sitwell and his brother Sacheverell (b. 1897). By the end of war the acquaintance had become a friendship. Both Sitwells admired Lewis's gifts and enjoyed his brilliant discourse, and Lewis on his side appreciated the acclaim of these younger writers and was amused by the company of "High Bohemians" that gathered round them. He made drawings of the brothers and began his painting of their sister at this time.[1] The three men met often during the 1920's, Edith Sitwell (b. 1887) joining them on occasion. Then in 1930 The Apes of God *appeared, with the Sitwells figuring prominently among the models for Lewis's satire. The congenial, if somewhat ill-assorted, relationship became at once a public feud, repercussions of which have not yet ceased.*[2]

121. *To Osbert Sitwell*†   Kensington W.8.
June 14. 23.

Dear Sitwell. I enjoyed Facade, and think it was an improvement on the first performance.[3] When we meet I will tell you. I was too late for your party (same day) but perhaps that was as well, as I hear all my old chums were there disporting themselves.

If that is equally convenient for you, let us begin the portrait

---

[1] The Portrait of Edith Sitwell, now in the Tate Gallery, was not completed until 1935.

[2] Sir Osbert Sitwell writes acidly of an early meeting with L. in *Laughter in the Next Room* (London, 1949), pp. 30–2. L. describes entertainingly his relations with the family in *Blasting and Bombardiering*, pp. 96–8.

[3] The Edith Sitwell–William Walton entertainment, *Façade*, was first performed on January 24th, 1922, at Osbert's house in Carlyle Square. The first public performance, referred to here, occurred on June 12th, 1923, at the Aeolian Hall. The audience responded violently, according to Sir Osbert. See *Laughter in the Next Room*, pp. 182–95.

of you and Sach next week. Today I have two other troublesome things to attend to. . . .

All the best
Yrs W. L.

Lewis places his first meeting with T. S. Eliot between the summers of 1914 and 1915. Pound, already the friend of both, brought the two together in his flat and promoted further association.[1] *Eliot admired Lewis's talents from the first; Lewis found he could share in part, anyway, Pound's high estimate of the younger American. More important, each seems to have taken pleasure in the other's company. Thus by the end of the war a friendship had developed. Lewis and Eliot took holidays together in France; they saw much of one another in London. On the professional side, their co-operation had begun with the publication of Eliot in* Blast No. 2. *It continued with Eliot's appearances in* The Tyro *and Lewis's in* The Criterion. *It persisted in various forms of mutual support – including the two portraits of Eliot*[2] *– till Lewis's death. There were, as the letters show, quarrels and periods of coolness; at one point Lewis, as he had with Joyce and Pound, launched a lengthy critical attack.*[3] *But Eliot's loyalty seems never to have been seriously shaken. At the end of this volume we find him reading copy for his blind old friend's last major work,* The Human Age.

122. *To T. S. Eliot* Kensington. W.8.
[September? 1923]

Dear Eliot. Have been hanging on – and have not written – because undecided about a title for fragment. But I suppose the one I first thought of is all right

---

[1] L. gives his first impressions of Eliot in *Blasting and Bombardiering* (pp. 283–5) and again, most brilliantly, in "Early London Environment" in *T. S. Eliot: A Symposium* (Chicago, 1949).
[2] The first portrait, which was rejected by the Royal Academy, was painted in 1938 and is now in the Durban Municipal Art Gallery, South Africa. The second, painted in 1949 just before L. lost his sight, is in Magdalene College, Cambridge.
[3] See *Men without Art* (London, 1934).

Mr. Zagreus and the Split-Man.[1]

My first batch of short essays have taken longer than I expected. In a day or two I will send you one however. That will not be the one for Criterion, as I want between now and March to bring out this set as a small book, as I told you.[2] But it will be one of those I propose sending to Crown Shields.[3] . . .

Thank you very much for the Waste Land.[4] Rereading it was a great pleasure. I am sure you shld develop what you have started there: and I am inclined to think that for the moment you should be busy with a new structure of that sort. You have got all your material lying about: and in a year or two might not be so convenient as now. This not meaning I squint at EELDROP:[5] but perhaps the play should not [?] come next. It is a matter of time. – I tender this advice putting myself in your shoes, and conscious that that operation is apt to be inelegant.

In any case, good wishes!

Yrs

W. L.

123. *To T. S. Eliot*　　　　　　　　　　　　　Lee Studio.
[October? 1923]

Dear Eliot. During the last few days it has been difficult to write a letter. I am writing you this between a sitting and a tea-visit. –

[1] From the beginning of his editorship of *The Criterion* in October 1922, Eliot urged L. to contribute. It was almost a year, however, before L. sent in the fragment of *The Apes of God* referred to here. On receiving it, Eliot wrote to the author: "I think this will be a great book – don't let anything interfere with it." The piece appeared as "Mr. Zagreus and the Split-Man" in the February 1924 number.

[2] The "small book" never appeared. These essays grew and merged into the long critical books which L. produced during the next four years.

[3] Probably Frank Crowninshield (1872–1947), then editor of *Vanity Fair*.

[4] Presumably Eliot had sent L. a copy of the first English edition of the poem, published by the Hogarth Press in September 1923.

[5] Two instalments of Eliot's prose work "Eeldrop and Appleplex" had appeared in *The Little Review* in 1917. Replying to this letter, Eliot wrote: "I understand you encourage me to go on with the Sweeney play. . . . Eeldrop was only intended as a fill up or an occasional release of otherwise useless cerebration."

I have had to leave my long books to get the essays well-started. You can depend on the Zagreus Mss. and can have it at a week's notice anytime. In the ordinary way as things are at present I should be sending it you in 2 or 3 weeks. Before that I should be glad if you would look at the first draught of a few essays. If that is all right we can leave it at that, and as soon as possible I will communicate.

I have seen Bell's article. The tone of it is so clearly personal, that I should think you could take their printing it as an indication of the attitude of the Nation to you. I should withdraw any articles you have given them, or cancel any arrangement to write for them.[1]

I hope soon to hear that you are getting the play done.[2] Why dont you stop writing articles for a bit and do nothing but work of your own?

Nothing further from Pound.

Yrs
W. L.

124. *To T. S. Eliot* 61 Palace Gardens Terrace.
Kensington. W.8.
[October? 1923]

Dear Eliot. Thank you very much for the Criterion. Your article is superb.[3] It is like a stone in the middle of a lot of shit. I've not had time to read the rest of the number yet. – My little treatise "The Man of the World" has taken longer even to get on its legs

---

[1] Clive Bell's review of *The Waste Land* appeared under the title "T. S. Eliot" in *The Nation and Athenaeum* for September 22nd, 1923, pp. 772–3. Bell, claiming to have introduced Eliot to the English élite, lamented that the "immense hopes" engendered by "Prufrock" had not been fulfilled. He scored Eliot for borrowing (a result of his lack of imagination) and compared him to Landor. Eliot wrote to L. on September 26th, asking if he had seen the article and saying that it was the "sort of thing one can only receive in silence." Except for two reviews already submitted, he did not contribute to *The Nation* again until December 1926.

[2] Sweeney. See preceding letter.

[3] Perhaps "The Function of Criticism," which appeared in *The Criterion* for October 1923.

than I had expected.¹ I work incessantly at it. I am never in bed before 2, or often later; and for the present dine alone to get it done. This week I really think I shall be able to. And Zagreus will follow shortly.

Yrs W. L.

125. *To T. S. Eliot*   61 Pal. Gard. Terrace. W.8.
[November 1923?]

My dear Eliot. The article will turn up in a day or two. A little word with regard our meeting the other night: I thought afterwards that, as I am rather shy with you, I may not have made my meaning clear about *Criterion*. As I understand with your paper that you are almost in the position I was in with the *Tyro* and *Blast* I will give you anything I have for nothing, as you did me, and am anxious to be of use to you: for I know that every failure of an exceptional attempt like yours with the Criterion means that the chance of establishing some sort of critical standard here is diminished. If I got desperately hard up I would always borrow a fiver from the paper or something like that. This anyhow can apply to odd articles.

Yrs

W. L.

126. *To T. S. Eliot*   Kensington. W.8.
[November 1923?]

Dear Eliot. Letter from Pound saying Hueffer and he starting paper.² No answer of course to that. So natural. The articles have taken much longer than I anticipated.³ I hope by saturday to get

¹ "The Man of the World" was L.'s title for a prose work – philosophical, critical, and narrative – in which he planned to make a comprehensive statement of his views. When the project had proliferated beyond manageable bounds, he broke up the material and incorporated it into such books as *The Art of Being Ruled*, *Time and Western Man*, and *The Childermass*.

² *The Transatlantic Review*, edited by Ford Madox Ford, first appeared in January 1924. Pound, then living in Paris, was a contributor.

³ Eliot had written that *The Criterion* wished to bring out the book of essays L. was planning.

them typed and send you. If I do, hope I can see you beginning of the week. Sorry for delay: but am working like nigger (up last night till 5 a.m.). Soon as possible get them round. . . .

Yours W. L.

127. *To R. Cobden-Sanderson*[1]   [London]
13/12/23

Dear Mr. Cobden-Sanderson,

Here is the galley of Mr. Zagreus, with corrections. 1. There are a good many minor corrections. For example in the first few lines you have queried CALVITY. But that is the word I want, and it is important to me that that should not be altered.[2] Some other queries, on the other hand I have found useful.

2. As regards the use of the word BUGGER, this is an ugly word that is however, I regret to say, often used, and perhaps sometimes justifiably. Still you don't want me to use it.[3] In consequence *I have rehandled that passage.* Over the deleted passage I have stuck a typescript alternative passage . . . *I should very much like you to substitute this.* If it costs you a little to alter put down the portion of it you think fair to me and I will pay you for it. . . .

Yours very truly
WYNDHAM LEWIS

[1] R. Cobden-Sanderson, son of T. J. Cobden-Sanderson (1840–1922), was publisher of *The Criterion* from its inception to the end of 1925. Beginning in 1926 the review became *The New Criterion*, published by Faber & Gwyer.

[2] As published the sentence reads: "The nails softly guided the cold hair . . . smoothing so as to cloak a slight calvity in the centre." "Mr. Zagreus and the Split-Man," *The Criterion*, February 1924, p. 124.

[3] On December 31st, Eliot wrote to L. saying that the words in question were queried by the printer, not by Cobden-Sanderson. He is glad, however, to have them removed, for "in a book a writer can and ought to say anything he likes." But in a periodical "an editor is not justified in risking offending harmless and otherwise desirable readers."

128. *To T. S. Eliot* 61 Palace Gardens Terrace, W.8.
Feb. 5. 24.

Dear Eliot. . . .

Should you be at May Sinclair's[1] on Thursday I will give you the Mss then: or if you are not there will post it. . . .

"The Apes of God" would be the title of the fragment of the book I shall be sending you in a week or so.[2] Please conscientiously keep to yourself anything that as friend and contributor to your paper I communicate to you of my literary plans.

Yours

W. L.

129. *To T. S. Eliot* 61 Palace Gardens Terrace, W.8.
[February 1924]

Dear Eliot. Since I've seen you, there is no need to detail the circumstances connected with the leaving of the Mss. with you. – It is a section (roughly 50 pages) of a book Man of the World: and it is left with you as a security; so that, should the Apes of God by any mischance not turn up by March 10, you have something in hand you could use (corresponding number of pages to Zagreus).

I want you to look at it, as it will give you an idea of the situation of my book. But I will send you a few more sections to cast a little more light on this. I want your opinion of it as a – what, a colleague, not in your official capacity. I am sure this would be of great use to me.

I need not tell you that it is still rough. For instance, to establish the full relationship of the monad to God (in the Leibnizian sense) I shall require at least three or four pages. And I wish to give a small chart of the vicissitudes of the ego, through Kant down to the "Critical realists".[3]

[1] The novelist May Sinclair (1865?–1946), a friend of Eliot, was helpful to writers in the modern movement.

[2] This second fragment – an "Encyclical" in which the term "Apes of God" is elucidated – appeared as "The Apes of God" in *The Criterion* for April 1924. As was often the case, L. was behindhand with his copy; Eliot wrote to him on March 13th: "Zagreus is a masterpiece. Want Apes at once."

[3] The sections referred to here, and in the following letter, seem all to have been incorporated into *Time and Western Man*.

But I will give you a few more explanations when we meet.

Yrs
W. L.

130. *To T. S. Eliot* 61 Palace Gardens Studios. W.8.
[ca. March 1924]

Dear Eliot.

Here is a little more as promised. As you are so good as to say that you will read *all* the Mss. I have given you, you had better read what I am sending you *first*. It will give you a better idea of what my objects have been from the start.

. . . (The blank pages represent a piece about Kant which I have not given you, as it is only a recapitulation of some of his theories. . . . I aim at a more or less popular audience of course.)

B. of Part I. deals with evolution, the usual teleology of the biologist, (his interpretation of Form) and the evolution of "forms" over into civilised life. . . .

After Part II comes (with all the resources of inductive vividness at my command) a part burrowing, on more personal lines, into the "problem of knowledge" and so forth.

When I see you I can give you any further explanation.

Yours
W. L.

131. *To T. S. Eliot* Kensington. W.8.
[March 1924]

Dear Eliot. Many thanks for letter, and I am very glad you like Apes, especially in the way you describe. It is very encouraging.[1] I must send you a note (2 or 3 lines) to accompany this extract. Lord Osmund's party is of considerable length; and as it will appear in the Criterion is only taken up to the arrival of Zagreus.[2]

[1] On receipt of the fragment titled "The Apes of God," Eliot wrote to L.: "You have surpassed yourself and everything. It is worthwhile running the Criterion just to publish these. It is so immense I have no words for it."

[2] In the finished version of *The Apes of God*, "Lord Osmund's Lenten Party" became the last and longest section. It never appeared in *The Criterion*.

As to the hosts surname, you will give me your best advice when we meet.¹ . . .

Yours
W. L.

132. *To T. S. Eliot* [London]
[ca. March 1924]

Dear Eliot. Here is the MSS. *Mrs. Farnhams tea-party*² may seem to you outside, but it introduces Boleyn (Dan Bull): and it shows specimens of my "unproductive apes."

In *Lord Osmunds Lenten party* the name Stillwell (if too suggestive of certain people) could be anything you like. — "Bloomsbury" (only recurring once) could be deleted.³

Let me know.

Yrs
W. L.

P.S. I even think that in any case another name, for the purposes of this extract, had better be given to Lord Osmund.

In the autumn of 1923 a little group of Lewis's friends and admirers set up a fund to provide him with a small monthly allowance. Among the subscribers were Mr. and Mrs. Edward Wadsworth, Mr. and Mrs. O. R. Drey (the painter Anne Estelle Rice), and the painter and writer Richard Wyndham. Their idea was to enable Lewis to carry on his work free from constant financial worries. But the difficulties inherent in the situation soon manifested themselves. By April 1924 Lewis was at odds with the Wadsworths.

[1] The surname in the book is Finnian Shaw.
[2] In the book the episode became "Pamela Farnham's Tea-Party." It did not appear in *The Criterion*.
[3] "Bloomsbury" was kept in the book.

133. *To Mrs. Edward Wadsworth*† [London]
[May 1st, 1924]

Dear Fanny.¹ There is no good indulging in humbug: and no letter I could write you under the circumstances would be pleasant reading. I am taking the £13 (the fund has been "reducing") you sent me this morning² because I am so hard up that if the devil himself offered me anything from a half crown upwards I should have to accept it: and having got so far with my writing, I cannot jeopardize this last week or so by being squeamish. . . .

To be quite plain with you, I dont wish to take it for a moment longer than I can help. When we were discussing the fund before it started . . . You may remember how much I desired some other less personal arrangement. Well, nothing has transpired to alter my feelings or misgivings on that head. But if your idea is a disinterested one to help not a person so much as a thing, art or whatever you like to call it, then there is nothing to prevent you or anybody else interested in doing what could have been done all along: namely buy some of my accumulated stock, or commission me to produce something of a stated sort. . . . As the few people involved all possess and are interested in my work, I should have had the sense from the start to make some such arrangement. . . .

But as regards the fund in its present form I cannot any longer accept it. If you sent it on June 1st and I were still penniless I should I suppose again have to take it. But your natural delicacy will suggest to you that situations of that sort should be avoided.

134. *To Richard Wyndham*†³ [London]
[ca. May 1924]
Dear Dick. . . .

As I was in constant touch with you, the Wadsworths and Dreys, the "fund" could obviously have come spontaneously by the

¹ Mrs. Wadsworth, an accomplished violinist, was born Fanny Eveleigh.
² On April 30th Mrs. Wadsworth sent L. a cheque for thirteen pounds. In her accompanying letter she asked him "to put aside all personal quarrels or misunderstandings and keep to your part of the agreement by continuing to receive what has been subscribed."
³ L. met Major Guy Richard Charles Wyndham (1896–1948) while visiting Venice in October 1922. They seem to have formed almost at once a kind of master-disciple relationship. "Dick" Wyndham emulated

buying of work . . . . I displayed my bad business intelligence – and also social tact – by ever accepting it.

Yesterday when you received my letter announcing my intention of winding that up, following the telegram episode, you write to me in unmeasured terms of abuse, as though my action were the action of some unscrupulous rascal attempting to cut a dash, (although at the same time a "genius", as so many rascals are) and engaged in the most cynical manoeuvres. Why? . . .

What people do whose "money" you offend is to "make you suffer" for the lèse-argent of which you have been guilty. You have not at least participated in anything like that: but you have jibed at me in a very unfriendly way. I think that you are made of finer and more delicate material than your present allies: dont allow the graceful and aimiable qualities that are natural to you to be consumed in the conventional passions and instincts with which (at present at fever heat no doubt) you are in touch. Let *something* remain "un peu sur la montagne." – Meantime I am at your disposal any evening . . . .

Yrs.
W. L.

135. *To Richard Wyndham*† [London]
[ca. May 1924]

My dear Dick. First your letter:[1] Your "open diplomacy" (though if "open" it ceases thank god to be "diplomacy" – which is a game for fools that leads nowhere) is much more to my taste than anything else you could devise.[2] It makes it much easier for me,

L. in drawing and writing; L. found in the attractive young man a pleasant companion. (See *Blasting and Bombardiering*, pp. 236–7.) Before long Wyndham had become a patron, buying L.'s pictures in quantity and then joining with the Wadsworths and Dreys in the fund. The trouble over the fund did not seriously disrupt the friendship – as it did with L. and the Wadsworths. But after the publication of *The Apes of God*, in which Wyndham recognised himself as another model for the satire, there was little further contact between the two.

[1] Wyndham wrote to tell L. that despite the rift with the Wadsworths, he (Wyndham) hoped to remain friendly with both sides.

[2] In his letter Wyndham said: "As a believer in open diplomacy and as you have sent me a copy of your letter to Fanny, I propose sending the Wadsworths a copy of this."

and disposes of the sensation of blind-mans-buff which is such an uncanny characteristic of the life of the cautious herd. Your letter returns constantly to one idea, and I wish I were able to enlighten you on that point. *Money* spoils many things, for it seems to most people who possess it so much more important than their poor humble selves, that they cannot believe, or trust their judgement to believe, that it does not overshadow them: and where their personality is called upon to compete with it (as is I suppose always the case with a wealthy person) they feel that it will master them forever. – So, when a man is rich, he is apt to become that dreary abstraction "the rich man": and not only love, but life, flies out of the window. To be any similar *abstraction* is a dreary thing, with the same penalties. I have not however treated you like that, or any other *abstraction*, but as a living person: and I should naturally prefer to be treated in the same way myself. "Great man" for example is an abstract notion, by which great vitality is described: and it is as often used *against* a person, paradoxical as that may sound, as *for* him. For being too "great" is rather like being very much too tall: and people are apt to make that tag an excuse for a lot![1]

To come down from these speculative heights, however, you say you wonder if I should be your friend if you were penniless. I daresay I should find it easier to be your friend if that were so, because at least one cause of mistrust would be removed on your side. I can only say that I dont think you would find me different. But let us put it in another way and suppose *I* were rich, and you poor: what would happen then? Suppose I had helped you when you needed it: you would regard that as natural, you would not like me any better or any less: it would, surely, be just the same. When a liking exists, and common interests, money *should* be – though of course I know it very seldom is – taken as a matter of course. If I do not therefore appear over grateful in an obvious and demonstrative way for your help, you should not misunderstand it. If you like a person, and accept him as a true artist, from that moment conventions can be dispensed with. I should only be surprised if you *didn't* help me. That sounds a

[1] Wyndham wrote: "I sometimes wonder whether; if you were not such a great artist, I should still have the same admiration for you as a man. As I also wonder whether you, in the event of me being penniless, would still include me in your extremely exclusive set of friends."

bald statement, but if you look at it properly it is a compliment to you.

The ——s look on money very differently to you: they feel they *depend* on it much more: and they never so much as question their being able to compete with their great ally. They therefore naturally resent any disrespect shown to *money*, taking it almost to themselves: just as, if you sniffed at ——'s car, he would feel *himself* lesé. The "power" it gives them (and what a disgusting thing *fictitious* power is) is probably their dearest possession. . . .

As to your jibe about my qualifying by my actions, for a position of favour with the "chosen people" and so forth, I'm afraid (if you refer to the good sense of values and astuteness of the jew) that I should never recommend myself to him by the conduct of my practical affairs, in which I am afraid I shall never excel. . . .[1]

. . . People act as correctives to each other, dont they? I have no desire to be your mentor – heaven preserve me from such a responsibility. But I still may be a healthy check in a few little ways. In any case, get your mind clear of inflammatory elements, and we will meet.

Yrs etc.

W. L.

136. *To Mrs. O. R. Drey*[2]   Kensington. W8.
[December 9th, 1924.]

Dear Ann. "Life," as you say, is "frightful": but is there any necessity to make it still more alarming? You ask me to come to your house to be *poisoned* and apparently *burnt*. I dont think that I will do that just yet. When you return I shall be through with my present work, and I hope will be living under slightly less repellent conditions – we shall both, in short, be rather less frightening than

---

[1] Wyndham wrote: "Sometimes you inspire me into a feeling that I am dealing with a very lovable and very great genius – sometimes (though still recognising the genius) I feel I am being duped by an adventurer, with a mind that would be greatly appreciated by the 'chosen race.'"

[2] Mrs. Drey (d. 1959) had known L. early in the century, when both were painting in Paris. After her marriage, she and her husband, who contributed to *Blast*, became patrons as well as friends.

we have been lately. La vie not being then so "frightful," we shall be able to foregather in comparative comfort. – In any case it is evidently at present out of the question. . . .

Yrs
W. L.

137. *To Richard Wyndham*†   Kensington. W.8.
[1924?]

Dear Dick.

(1) If you are worried, I have had far more cause for worry than you.[1]

(2) As an honest painter you should cast your mind back, and remember that the occasion in question was not the first time I had hastened to a 6.15 to 6.50, or 6 to 7 cocktails rendezvous and found you not at home.

(3) I have had many disputes in my life with people who were never my friends, but I have relinquished (as I have possessed) few friendships.

(4) For helping me so simply and generously to do my book (Man of the World) I shall be your debtor always.

(5) But if you were inconsiderate I should always tell you so.

(6) I hate "management" among friends: "managing" people should be left to women.

(7) You know as well as I do that the trick you impute to me would appear from the outside to originate from you, not me. I am sure this is not the case. So let us drop the "trick" theory altogether.

(8) As you are very busy and worried, there is no object in making appointments that it is irksome for you to keep.

(9) When you are free of your embarrassments and have plenty of time, let me know and we will have a glass of gin.

(10) But there is no hurry at all about this.

(11) If I were the kind of person who "used" other people, as you accuse me of doing, nothing would ever offend me.

---

[1] Wyndham had missed an appointment with L. and received, in consequence, a letter generally dressing him down. Wyndham replied to this, pleading his many worries as excuse for his negligence. He also accused L. of using the small incident as a pretext for breaking off relations.

(12) If you decide to avail yourself of No. 9 eventually, give a little consideration first to these remarks, it would not be amiss to do so in any case.

(13) I hope you will get successfully through your bothers, and be able to go on with your work.

Yrs
W. L.

138. *To T. S. Eliot* [London]
[January 1925]

Dear Eliot. As regards The Perfect Action:[1] first of all the length: we computed you may remember that it came to seventeen thousand. You said . . . that that was very long, but that you would try and manage it. I dare say, however, that it is twenty thousand. . . . Now as to the thing itself: it consists of two unequal parts, the first and shortest worked round Elliot Smith's account of egyptian origins of art, and the second round Miss Jane Harrison's *ritual and art*. I should say that (if 20000 is the length of the whole article) the first part (Egypt) would work out at about four or five thousand; which would make the second (Greece) about fifteen thousand.

The only thing to do with it, if the whole were not going to be printed, would be to use only the Miss Harrison part. (The Elliot Smith part, by itself, I do not wish printed.) . . . Otherwise we must consider that as a failure.

I am publishing in a couple of months now, I hope, my book: which is a big one and in addition one such as will not often be written (even by me).[2] I think a bigger extract from it would help both of us, each (in this case) in his different way. But you

---

[1] An earlier title of "The Dithyrambic Spectator," L.'s polemic on the origins of art. Eliot wrote to L. on December 2nd, saying he had just learned "The Perfect Action" was 20,000 words. He asked if *The Criterion* could use it in parts.

[2] L. may have still been contemplating *The Man of the World* and planning to make "The Perfect Action" part of it. His next book was actually *The Art of Being Ruled*, which came out in March 1926, but did not include "The Perfect Action." The essay first appeared in book form in 1931 as part of *The Diabolical Principle and the Dithyrambic Spectator*.

must please yourself about that, as I hope you will always know that you are *privileged* to do where I am concerned. What pleases you will please me – so long as I know that its you I am pleasing. I have quarrelled with almost everybody in order to get the money and time to write this and other books: and I have really worked very hard. My gesture, at the moment, may seem a foolish one (people are angry, and in consequence laugh): but there is an old saying, he laughs best who laughs last.

I have no doubt at all with regard to the success of what I have done: which I care very little about, but which will help me to live and to do *more* work.

Later on I hope to write constantly for different papers: but since I have adopted my present programme of work on these books (and that only, first) I naturally have had no convenient sized occasional essays or articles handy: and the constant writing of them would have so seriously interfered (in addition to other interruptions) with my main track that I should never have got it done if I had not excluded them. That is why I have had nothing but fragments of books to offer you, of course. But as these fragments have consequently [been] work conceived on a different scale it would in most cases do me more harm than good to print a 5.000 word fragment. When a longish argument is involved, as in the case of the Perfect Action, it cannot be easily reduced .... One of the things I have wished to see you about was this: you remember we discussed the publishing by Criterion of *Archie*?[1] I may, in order to get ready money, have to sell that outright to somebody if I can. Would you mind that? I should have no difficulty a little later on in giving you a substitute volume of the same quality.

Yours ever.
W. L.

[1] "Archie" was never published; it became part of *Joint*, a narrative work left incomplete by L.

139. *To T. S. Eliot* 61. Palace Gardens Terrace. W.8.
Jan 30/25

Dear Eliot.[1]

You advertized my article as appearing in the forthcoming number of the Criterion but Miss Fassett[2] tells me you do not intend printing it after all. . . . I hope the following statement will simplify matters. (1) The Perfect Action is no longer available for publication in the Criterion. I have just sold it to another paper.[3] (2) You have still various fragments of mine, such as the Lenten Party. These fragments are no longer at your disposal for publication in the Criterion.

I do not wish under any circumstances any of these odds and ends (belonging to *groups* of which you have used portions) either to appear, or to be announced as about to appear or as likely at some future date to appear in the Criterion. (3) Should any of these fragments find their way into other hands than yours before they appear in book-form, I shall regard it as a treachery rather than a harmless trick, or as the inadvertence of a harassed man.

This simplification will not I hope seem unfriendly to you. I have no wish to be unfriendly, but am anxious to avoid any further ambiguities.

. . . As to the other work you ask for, as I have already said I have nothing of the length you desire, and as I think you will agree with me it is by no means easy to make such an extract as shall be intelligible and not diminish the subsequent effect of the book.

Yours
WYNDHAM LEWIS

[1] In reply to the preceding letter of L., Eliot stated the difficulty of publishing such a long piece as "The Perfect Action" in *The Criterion*. At the same time he reaffirmed his support of L.'s work and his desire to print him.

[2] Miss I. P. Fassett was secretary to T. S. Eliot and a frequent contributor to *The Criterion*.

[3] The essay appeared as "The Dithyrambic Spectator: An Essay on the Origins and Survivals of Art" in *The Calendar of Modern Letters* for April and May 1925. L. had already contributed to the January *Criterion* reviews of books by G. Elliott Smith and W. H. R. Rivers which went into the material of the essay.

140. *T. S. Eliot to Wyndham Lewis* 9, Clarence Gate Gardens,
Regent's Park, N.W.1.
31st January, 1925.

Wyndham Lewis Esqre.,
61, Palace Gardens Terrace,
W.8.

Dear Lewis,

I have your letter dated the 30th January. You are certainly entitled to some explanation of the advertisement in question, and the tone of your letter seems to call for a clear statement of my attitude in this matter. The notice of "*The Perfect Action*" was to have been followed by a letter to you which was unfortunately prevented by my illness; from which, as a matter of fact, I have not yet recovered. The point is this. You will remember that I have repeatedly expressed my desire that there should be a contribution of some kind from you in every number of THE CRITERION; that is to say a chronicle and also a review (whenever any books appeared which you wished to review) in every number and a leading essay or piece of fiction as well in two numbers out of four. This is more than I care to take from any other contributor. Apart from the benefits of this regularity to the review and the benefits (upon which you will of course put your own valuation) to yourself, I had always in mind the benefit to us collectively. That is to say, there are as you are quite well aware a number of people who would be glad to see and to instrument any possible separation or disagreement between us for their own purposes. Such separation, or even the report of it, would I believe be harmful not only to ourselves but to the public good. The last number unfortunately contained nothing from you except a book review, which, although a valuable piece of writing and given the first place among the reviews, was not in my mind sufficient to keep the association before the public mind. I therefore advertised the contribution from you for the next number and gave it the name which I had. . . . I am quite well aware that you wish to devote the whole of your attention to the preparation of your books. I think that you ought to be convinced by this time that I have wished to do everything in my power to assist in the speedy completion and publication of your principal book. . . . Everyone has his own methods of work and no one is entitled to say that another person's methods of work are mistaken. But I have felt very strongly that it would be in your own interest to concentrate on one book at a time and not plan eight or ten books at once, and I have endeavoured to intimate this. On the other hand you are certainly entitled to respect, and you certainly have mine, for making every sacrifice to devote yourself to your main work and not disperse your activity. But the dispersing in one direction seems to me possibly as unwise as a dispersal in another would be. And I cannot help feeling that it is possible, with organisation, for a man who is not engaged in any outside business merely for his livelihood to write a book and at the same time do a certain amount of current journalism without damage to his work and with advantage to his pocket. . . . I have also assured you that, so far as the means of the paper permitted, you should receive better terms of payment than other contributors. Under present conditions even the ordinary rates are only made possible by my taking no salary or other remuneration for running the magazine. I only mention this fact because my friends seem sometimes to ignore it.

Please do not think that I am pressing upon you, in the manner of one of our friends whose name I need not mention, a reminder of supposed services. I consider that anything I do is equalised by any support which you give to THE CRITERION. Furthermore I am not an individual but an instrument, and anything I do is in the interest of art and literature and civilisation, and is not a matter for personal compensation. But in the circumstances I cannot help feeling that your letter expressed an unjustified suspiciousness . . . .

You say that your letter is not intended to be unfriendly and mine is certainly not so intended. If you are unable to do any work for THE CRITERION for an indefinite period, it will be very much to my disappointment and regret.[1] . . .

Yours,
T. S. ELIOT

. . .

TSE/IPF

[1] L. evidently replied unsatisfactorily to this letter. For on February 2nd, Eliot wrote: "I had certainly supposed that you were in contact with certain persons who would be pleased to find that you were no longer a contributor to 'The Criterion.' The tone of your two letters strongly suggests a definite grudge which you have not disclaimed."

141. *To T. S. Eliot*† [London]
[March 1925]

Dear Eliot. Please take this letter as a good proof of my desire to stop you. Since before Christmas you have been guilty where I am concerned of a series of actions each of which, had I done the same to you, would have made you very indignant. For example, had you been writing for me a Poetry Chronicle for a paper I was running, and had I put a long poem into my paper by some writer you thought very little of, and who was notoriously unfriendly to you, would not you have asked me what was the use of your Poetry Chronicle?[1] Or, suppose you had left your employment and started to make your living as a writer, that you were about to be turned out of your place for rent, having just been served with a writ for possession. The rest of the analogy you can put in for yourself: I know that, had you told me, I would not have left you without a letter, even had I been unable to help.[2] . . .

Either you, or some person or persons who are able to influence you (with even the most strong-minded such a contingency must be reckoned on) appear from some time before Christmas to have decided to treat me in such a way as to make my estrangement a foregone conclusion. In the letter you wrote me last you said I did not recite the series of events that I have since specified more or less for you: though why you should have wished me to talk over things that you must have been quite conscious of yourself it is difficult to understand.

I am not in possession of the reasons that make you, or the people able to influence you, wish to bring about this rupture, so I am not able to say if those reasons justify it. You must therefore excuse me if I regard this series of small but rather offensive events as unreasonable.

I have said to you already that letters are a very unsatisfactory way of dealing with matters of this sort; the abbreviation required makes it easy to misunderstand them. So it would have been far better had you arranged to see me. But in this instance I will

---

[1] L. refers perhaps to an article by Clive Bell, "Prolegomena to a Study of Nineteenth Century Painting," which appeared in the January *Criterion*. An Art Chronicle by L. had appeared in the preceding number.
[2] L. refers to an episode late in 1924 when he was in financial straits.

persevere. Yesterday Monro[1] said that in selling something to a paper called the Calendar I was associating myself with a rival venture to yours or his.[2] I mention this for two reasons. First in my letter to you (one in which I charged you not to make use of things of mine you held before consulting me as to whether they were appearing elsewhere or not) I said then that my article was sold to another paper. Actually I had not sold it but wished to make my statement sufficiently forcible to make you take some notice of it. At that time I had already received three letters from the Calendar which I had not answered (the last one forwarded via Schiff Cambridge Sq.). The terms they offered were very good ones: but as I had nothing available I had not replied to them. Under another title I then (after my letter to you) offered them the Perfect Action, but the difficulty of the length again presented itself. According to their rate of payment I should have received seventy pounds for it in the form I offered it to you. I had (and still have) three writs out against me and had weekly to find money somehow to get along. Under these circumstances I eventually agreed to arrange it for them in two portions. I cut out passages that gave it its first title – the Perfect Action. For these fragments I received on the receipt of the MSS. forty pounds. This sum at that moment I could have got in no other way.

These facts I hope you will keep to yourself. In conversation with Munro I am naturally unable to go into these details.

Under any circumstances, and quite independently of any reasons I had to be sore as a result of your behaviour, I should have had to have sold something at such a time, but normally I should have informed you of my intention.

My second reason for referring to this is the following. I dont consider that a paper like the Calendar will harm your paper. But if you on your side thought it would, that might be used in the service of this notion of yours – however acquired: (namely the notion that it would not be a bad thing to terminate your association with me). The Calendar had already Lawrence, Huxley and

---

[1] Harold Monro (1879–1932), poet, critic, and publicist, was at this time editor of *The Monthly Chapbook*.

[2] *The Calendar of Modern Letters* ran from March 1925 to July 1927, edited by Edgell Rickword, Douglas Garman, and Bertram Higgins. It published some of D. H. Lawrence's best work, as well as poems by Hart Crane and John Crowe Ransom.

so on as its contributors, with Joyce benevolently in the background. I think that, unless the editors have a great deal of personal merit themselves, that these well-known names will limit the nature of their enterprise, rather than confer it with any special character, which you are so eminently able to give yours.[1] . . .

The idea of this letter is, by throwing a final ray of light on to your uncivil purpose, to make you examine it a little more closely than you have done. For ten years now we have been vaguely associated, and have been a certain support to one another. It is not I admit much to weigh in the scale against passionate intrigue. But it is still those passionate, muddy and hot factors of action against which we, in different ways, pretend to stand. You will not by a few well-chosen words, dispel the impression I have received in consequence of your behaviour to me at a very critical and distracting moment of my life. But I shall bear you no grudge and should always be prepared to support you as far as I was able. If however you do not reply to this letter in a reasonable time, or arrange a meeting with me, then I shall conclude that the devil has you by the heel, and there will be no necessity for me to tell you where to go for you will be there already, as I see it.

This letter is of course private. It will not help me for people in general to know the straits I am in, and I rely on you not to advertize it. I did not go to your office on Wednesday as arranged with your secretary because, having a great deal of a very harassing nature to occupy me, I forgot my appointment, for which I am very sorry, and have written a note to Miss Fassett to that effect.

142. *To Charles Whibley*†[2] [London]
[ca. March 1925]

Dear Mr. Whibley. Eliot told me some time ago that he had shown you an Mss of mine and that you have very kindly said that you

[1] In a letter of March 23rd, Eliot says that it wouldn't have occurred to him that L.'s dealings with the *Calendar* "required any justification on your part."

[2] Charles Whibley (1859–1930), critic and editor, was an influential person in conservative literary circles in London. For many years he conducted a monthly column in *Blackwood's Magazine* and was at the time of this letter a reader for Macmillan. See T. S. Eliot, *Charles Whibley: A Memoir* (English Association Pamphlet No. 84) (London, 1931).

would introduce me to Macmillans with a view to getting it published.¹ . . .

The Mss I have given to Macmillans is a book of about a hundred thousand words, which I have called *The Politics of the Personality*.² It is part of the same system as the fragment you saw. The fragment you saw forms part of a second volume of about the same length, which I have called *The Politics of Philistia*.³ This I am holding: should Macmillans accept my *Politics of the Personality* I shall submit the other book to them, and suggest their publishing it as soon afterwards as possible.

Whereas The Politics of Philistia – of which you read a part – deals more with politics, the book I have now handed to them (*The Politics of the Personality*) is based largely on the evidence, for my general argument, of philosophy and science. It traces the systematic crushing of the notion of the Subject in favour of the propaganda of collectivism: and aims at showing philosophy obediently harnessed to physics and psychology, circumscribed to a fashionable and purely political role. That is very vaguely what it is about.

. . . I wish also to express the very great pleasure it gave me to hear from Eliot that you had liked the part of it you had seen.

Yours sincerely

143. *To Robert McAlmon*   Kensington W.8.
April 1. 25.

Dear McAlmon. The remodelling of certain passages in the book you have agreed to publish⁴ – and which, as I have not found a

¹ A piece of *The Man of the World*.
² By this time L. had begun to break the larger work down into its components. *The Politics of the Personality* became *Time and Western Man*. None of these volumes was published by Macmillan.
³ This became *The Art of Being Ruled*, published in 1926 by Chatto and Windus.
⁴ L. and McAlmon had had conversations and correspondence with regard to McAlmon's bringing out, at his Contact Publishing Co. in Paris, one of the volumes stemming from *The Man of the World*. On the day of writing, L. received from McAlmon a cheque for £30 as an advance towards publication. In his later disavowal of intent, McAlmon wrote that he knew L. was hard up and meant the money simply as a present.

final title for it yet, we will call *The Politics of the Primitive*[1] – will take rather longer than I thought. It is important, if it is to be first book out, that I should not spare any trouble over perfecting it. Yet of course there is no time to lose, and I shall confine myself to the remodelling of the passages where I felt, for a book of that length, there was an excess of quotations.

I am anxious however to settle the business side of the arrangement.... I agree to hand you over the book (... of roughly 70,000 words length, divided in 3 parts, named respectively the Cliché-Personality, the Patria Potestas and Primitive Communism) in two weeks time.... When we meet you will be able perhaps to give me a hint or two about the agreement, if you have already had experience of them in connection with Mountains Press.[2]

Yours etc.
WYNDHAM LEWIS

144. *To Robert McAlmon* Kensington W.8.
[ca. 1925]

Dear Bob. Your letter just to hand. I hope to see you soon, then I shall be able to make plainer to you than is possible in a letter my views affecting your request for a contribution to Mountains.[3] I do not want to make part of such an assembly as you suggest, of people however eminent or the reverse, however "modern" or "ancient": although as you know (I hope) my great personal liking for you would make me throw over my principles sooner than most things. When we meet I shall have no difficulty in showing you that my refusal in no way touches you. – I am very anxious that the friendship we struck up some years ago should

[1] Evidently another title for *The Art of Being Ruled*.
[2] The Three Mountains Press, founded by William Bird (b. 1889) as a hand press. Although a separate venture, Bird's press set up some books for McAlmon, with the result that McAlmon began to disregard distinctions and bring out almost all his books with the imprint "Contact Editions – Three Mountains Press."
[3] L. most likely refers to the anthology, *Contact Collection of Contemporary Writers*, which McAlmon published in 1925. Among the contributors were Ford Madox Ford, Joyce, Pound, Edith Sitwell, and Gertrude Stein.

not be affected by anything. I had a drink with old [name?] in London when she was here. Remember with her, for example, that as an information bureau she is very corrupt and unreliable. And dont let this refusal of mine about the little piece of writing influence your mind in any way. . . .

Yours ever
W.L.

145. *To Robert McAlmon*   61 P. G. Terrace. W.8.
[April 1925]

Dear Bob.
In case I forget to bring it, I am sending you an article in *G.K.'s Weekly* (April 4/25) this weeks, about Joyce.[1] Dont tell him it was I who drew your attention to it, but I expect he would like to read it. . . .

Yrs
W.L.

146. *To Agnes Bedford*   Hotel de Fribourg,
Rue de Trevise, 46.
Paris (9ᵉ)
12 April. [1925]

Dear Agg. . . . – We got in at 11-30 (leaving at three) and the only room I could find was a sumptuous one with a bath, at 60 francs, which, after a little delay, I took. I made every conceivable use and misuse of the many luxurious appointments of my suite. Now I am in a room of moderate price. Easter appears to be here, as elsewhere, a three-day holiday: but running to the café's and so forth is quite agreable, in spite of that. It may mean that I shall not see anyone till late on Tuesday, as my only way of communicating with prospective clients is by way of a shop, which will be closed. Offices also will be closed, of course. So for two days I shall be able to do little business. I came over on the boat with Sir T. Beecham and Lady Cunard. Sir T. stood me several drinks, and sketched the history of music for the last two hundred years. Without consulting you, it is impossible for me to decide whether

---

[1] Bernard Gilbert, "The Tragedy of James Joyce," pp. 36–9.

what he said was right or wrong. He also referred to the articles in the Daily Mail,[1] and said he had been daily expecting a terrible outbreak, the results of which, in the law courts, would put the Dennistoun case in the shade.[2] – Lady C said she had been wondering who that "wild looking fellow" was. I had had my shoes blacked before entering the train, had on my latest coat and three guinea hat, also gloves. This lack of discrimination on her part embittered what was otherwise an agreable chat. There was a dense fog in the channel, and both the ships and lighthouses, as well as the coastguard stations and services on the jetties and in the ports were firing guns and exploding large crackers the whole time. The ship hooted so loudly meanwhile that conversation was very difficult: so by the time Sir T. was able to go on I had usually forgotten what he had started by saying. I shall not perhaps be able to give you a very coherent account of his very brilliant exposé of the musical situation. His face, however, during the periods when he was unable to speak, was very expressive. He remarked that the din reminded him of Stravinskys latest compositions. – The sun is shining in a very brilliant way here, and all the people and conveyances look very cheap and shabby compared to the luxury of London. . . .

Yrs
W.

147. *To Ezra Pound*   61. Palace Gardens Terrace. W.8.
June 11/25.

Dear E.P. I do not want a "Lewis number" or anything of that sort in This Quarter or *anywhere* else, at this moment.[3] My reasons are my own affair, although I indicated them as much as

[1] Perhaps a series of articles, "At the Sign of the Blue Moon," by D. B. Wyndham Lewis which had been running in the *Daily Mail*. L. made a point of disowning his "namesake," and Beecham may have been teasing him on this score.

[2] The case involving Lt.-Col. Ian Onslow Dennistoun and his former wife, Dorothy, had been the scandal of London for some weeks.

[3] On June 6th Pound wrote to L. from Rapallo, telling him of his campaign for an "art supplement" devoted to L. in *This Quarter*. The first number (Spring 1925) of the review, edited by Ernest J. Walsh and Ethel Moorhead, had been dedicated to Pound.

was necessary. *Have I said this to you or not?* You insist on disregarding what I write to you, is not that so?

Please note the following: because in the glorious days of Marinetti, Nevinson, machinery, Wadsworth Wormwood Scrubs[1] and Wyoming, we were associated to some extent in publicity campaigns, that does not give you a mandate to interfere when you think fit, with or without my consent, with my career. If you launch at me and try and force on me a scheme which I regard as malapropos and which is liable to embarrass me, you will not find me so docile as Eliot.

If you are offended with me because my note written to you in Sicily had not what Macalmon calls "abondon", and are disposed to be troublesome in consequence, then I am sorry that my letter had not more zip, and will endeavor not to repeat that performance. Does this undertaking help to clear your mind, or your bile?

Recently a painter – who I daresay is a friend of yours, as I understand you see a number of people from England in your italian home – came to ask me to contribute something to a show he, Wadsworth, Nash and other people were getting up. I did not wish to exhibit with him or with his friends at all, although the advertisement they would derive from exhibiting with me would be very attractive to them no doubt: for some of them had proved that in the past. I said I did not want to exhibit at the moment which was also true. He said he was sorry, and went away. When the show opened, in the middle of the wall hung a large coloured drawing of mine which Wadsworth had sold to the Gallery, or put into Sothebys,[2] where it could conveniently be bought. . . . I am sorry to have seemed to have afforded the world precedent for such treatment of an artist. I will endeavour to make up for it presently.

You knew that I wished, for the sake of the money, to have a section of my book[3] in any paper that would print a substantial section of it, and pay me properly; you knew that the book was not fiction; yet when it comes to the point, you say that your paper, or your friends paper, "does not want anything but fiction" and gave me the advantage of your opinion that the only sort of writing that should be done is that that is likely to get ones friends out of prison, sell their work, etc.

[1] The London prison.   [2] The Bond Street auctioneers.
[3] *Time and Western Man* or *The Art of Being Ruled.*

I have had a long and unpleasant struggle to get my present work completed. You seem inclined to step in at the last minute and harass the final stages of my work with, I hope sincere, but certainly misplaced, offers of help. Please answer this letter at once.[1]

Yrs.
W. L.

148. *To Robert McAlmon*   Kensington. W.8.
13.7.25.

Dear Macalmon. Thank you for your note. I am at present up in London very little. When I am once more settled here I will arrange to see you. As regards This Quarter I am dealing directly with them, which is more satisfactory. I am sorry you have been troubled with letters and telegrams from them. That is the penalty of being supposed to be in touch with me. There is a penalty on my side, however, as well: for I suppose had it not been for your prompting, in a sense unfavourable to their handling of a considerable section of my work, this matter, which is still hanging fire, would have been settled long ago.[2] – Please note that it would be greatly to my disadvantage if any financial arrangements come to between us were broadcast.

As to the book, you will remember that the last time we met you said you were short of funds owing to some accident, and would be short through the summer: and we agreed that you

---

[1] Pound returned the letter to L. with marginal notes written in. In the first paragraph, beside "Have I said this to you or not?" Pound wrote: "No. You have *not* said this until now." Beside "painter" in the fourth paragraph, he wrote: "Unknown to me. I have very little interest in painters in general." In the penultimate paragraph, beside "your paper," he wrote: "no not my paper"; and beside "sort of writing that should be done": "buncomb." At the end of the letter, he typed a note further disavowing guilt. This concludes: "There are some matters in which you really do behave like, and *some* (some not all) lines in this letter of yours in which you really do write like, a God damn fool.
candidly and
cordially yours
E.P."

[2] *This Quarter* had expressed interest in L.'s writing, and he was hoping to have them print a section of *The Man of the World*.

should have the mss. in the beginning of the autumn. I hope that arrangement still meets with your approval, as I took that as settled, and have planned my work accordingly.

How do you like this hot weather? It must predispose you in favour of London.

Yrs.
W. L.

149. *To Robert McAlmon*   61 Palace Gardens Terrace. W.8.
July 24. 25.

Dear Macalmon. I've been away and your letter followed. Then it is settled that the autumn will be the time for the book. – As regards the other matter: you express the hope that nothing "personal" should be allowed in explanation of anything that has occurred: but I perfectly understand that what is automatic is automatic, and what is personal (not very much) is personal. I do not confuse the doings of the one with the doings of the other. You can therefore absolutely rely on my not, where you are concerned, for example, mixing up what is non-personal or unconscious, with what is "personal": further you can depend on my supposing that what is graceful and amiable is "yourself," and what I think less well-favoured is anonymous. – The fact remains that had you not advised Pound and probably *This Quarter* (since in Paris you informed me that you had considerable influence with them) that my mss. was unsuitable for use in a review (as you told me you had, when we met in Youngs): and that my mss. was scientifically unsound (had I had the advantage of your wide knowledge earlier in that respect how much subsequent trouble should I not have been spared!) I should not have had the difficulties I have had with *This Quarter*. (It may interest you to know that they offered me, oddly enough, the price you advanced me for the other mss. – namely £30: and our correspondence has presumably terminated, my last letter remaining unanswered).

Yours ever
W. L.

150. *To O. R. Drey* Kensington. W.8.
Sept. 4 [1925]

My dear Drey.[1] I believe I am corrupting you: for when I first unmasked you – pulling the rock away and there you were, so to speak – you behaved in a very dignified and suitable way, didn't you? Your mournful indignation left nothing to be desired. But in the blaze of unaccustomed daylight that I have let in I think you are deteriorating. – In the first shock of surprise I am sorry to say you allowed yourself to refer to me as a snake of some sort; my words were "poisonous," "venom" dropped from my pen, I was "malignant." But now I note, with satisfaction, you have entirely withdrawn from that most disobliging position. But I also note with concern that your attitude to yourself has undergone a most regrettable change. You did not even use the expression "many calls on me of late," but were satisfied with the rather off-hand remark that your "reasons were reputable"; you are growing indecent.

You say, let the original arrangement stand: but wheres the *cheque*, old boy? Wheres the esteemed favour that that arrangement arranged for? If the arrangement stands, send the cheque; if you dont I shall know that you have grown shameless, and shall blame myself. If you *cant* evacuate the six pounds, and if you are as constipated about a thing like that as you are about your food, well, tell me so, and there will be an end of the matter. Dont for the love of Mike get ill about it. But unless there is some natural obstruction of that sort, instead of *saying* let the arrangement stand, *do* something; sit down at your desk, draw out your cheque-book, write me a nice polite little note saying you are sorry there has been any trouble, close your eyes, hold your breath, and write *six* – and there you will be straight with me, at all events.

Yours ever
W. L.

[1] This letter was written in the course of an altercation arising from the sale of a drawing. The trouble seems to have started with a confusing plan for payment, the drawing being already in Drey's possession.

151. *To O. R. Drey*　　　　61. Palace Gardens Terrace. W.8.
　　　　　　　　　　　　　　　　Sept. 23/25.

My dear Drey. What a tiresome fellow you are! really. Still, you cant help it, so its no use grumbling to *you*, is it? Your letter in any case does not concern me. If you dont want to pay the other 6 pounds as arranged – well, there is the arrangement, but between friends, of old standing, there is no question of enforcing it: nor for that matter could I probably do so even if I were inclined to make light of those sentimental ties. – As to my dreaming, my dear fellow, that you would try and "get the better of me," as you put it, I am not so fatuous as to suppose that you would exercise your business ability on such an economic cipher as myself. – I am not disposed to take £8 for the drawing: I do not wish to borrow £6. from you, as you suggest – my request was for you to buy a drawing, not lend me money. On the other hand, I do not wish to involve myself in further transactions of the same sort; in that way your other suggestion is answered. Under these circumstances, you had better keep the drawing till I pawn it out. It is in safe, clean, hands, I know, and with people who (you need not have troubled to assure me) will appreciate my little gage. See it is properly dusted and comes to no harm.
　　　　　　　　　　　　　　　　　　　　　　Yrs
　　　　　　　　　　　　　　　　　　　　　　W. L.

152. *To O. R. Drey*　　　　　　　Kensington. W.8.
　　　　　　　　　　　　　　　　　Sept. 26/25.
My dear Drey. . . .
　. . . If my reply did not betray a polite surprise or an effusive welcome, but a perhaps too jocose resignation, that is because I was not at all astonished, and because I make every allowance for the peculiarities of my friends, especially those of old standing. – When you say that *to speak of friendship* under the present painful circumstances would *be the merest hypocrisy*, do not think that I would tempt you into the rôle of a Pecksniff (a "hypocrite" is the last thing a man would desire his friend to be) if I say that I do not at all agree with you. You mean something different by friendship, I suspect; it is evident that your standards are higher than mine. However that may be, I shall continue to employ

that phraseology for ruffians and gentlemen alike: if they are my friends, I shall not examine their actions too closely nor permit other people to do so. (So you see what an exceptionally good friend you've got I hope, one that it would be rather stupid to lose.) My country, right or wrong! – that sort of thing.

Well, god bless you! – if you absolutely insist on being a money-lender, send me the drawing back.[1] But I would much prefer that you should be my pawnbroker at the moment.

Yrs
W. L.

153. *To T. S. Eliot*   [London]
Feb. 19. 26.

Private and confidential.

Dear Eliot. I am sorry to say that I cant do an Art-Note,[2] because I can think of nothing to say for the moment. It may be that as I have not been able for some time to have a studio and practice my delightful calling, that, since I am prevented from doing it, I do not care to *write* about it. – And then the very disobliging things that under any circumstances is all I could ever find to say of the things I see usually, come ill from a person situated as I am. If my writing is a success in any way, no doubt that may make people wish to see me [as] an artist again; in which case I shall be delighted, and, as before, will combine some critical work with my other activities.

Yrs
W. L.

[1] Drey had written that he preferred to return the drawing to L. and have L. owe the six pounds already paid to him until he should be able to redeem the sum.

[2] Eliot wrote to L. on February 12th asking him for the "Criterion notes" which he had agreed to do. Actually L. published only one Art Chronicle in *The Criterion*, that of July 1924.

154. *To Miss I. P. Fassett*   Kensington. W.8.
[March 1926]

Dear Miss Fassett. I wrote Mr. Eliot 2 days ago asking him to give me news of my Mss.[1] or if he were unable to do that to return it for several reasons. If nothing is going to happen with Faber and Gwyers, and I cannot unfortunately wait indefinitely, I must have it back. If I do not get it at once I shall now be in a muddle with my other arrangements. If Mr. Eliot is ill, dead, away on holiday or otherwise inaccessible please arrange for the Mss. to be handed to my messenger tomorrow Friday morning. I am sure that Mr. Eliot were he well, alive or present would instruct you to do so. And it is very urgent that I should have my Mss.

                                        Yours very truly
                                          WYNDHAM LEWIS

155. *To Robert McAlmon*   Kensington. W.8.
March 27. 26.

Dear MacAlmon. Where are you: are you in London or Paris? Some time has passed since our correspondence re. *This Quarter* and I forget how we left the matter of the *Critique of Class*.[2] The mss. has progressed towards its final form: but owing to one thing and another I have been much delayed with all my work. – So let me know now, if you get this, what your publishing arrangements are, if the enormous Stein volume[3] has appeared and the way is clear for publication of a less portentous volume and so forth. The book for you would not be big, and could perhaps be slipped in during this Spring. At any rate, let me hear from you.

                                                      Yrs
                                                     W. LEWIS

[1] Either *Time and Western Man* or *The Lion and the Fox*. Eliot was anxious to place L.'s work with Faber & Gwyer, the firm with which he had recently become associated. On March 26th Miss Fassett replied to L., saying that the manuscript had been returned to him, that Eliot had not been able to get through it all and would like to have it back.

[2] Perhaps another title for *The Art of Being Ruled*.

[3] *The Making of Americans*, published by Contact Editions – Three Mountains Press in 1925.

156. *To Robert McAlmon* [London]
[1926?]

Dear Bob. . . .

Should you get a letter asking if I am respectable, will you say Yes, in spite of anything you may suspect to the contrary? It is a little, cheap flat I am subletting from a woman-artist: for her landlady (to show I am not a burglar or gunman) she has to have two references. I thought of you because I knew you would communicate my address to nobody, if I asked you. Also I dislike applying to pompous "householders", and letting them know my business. . . .

Yrs
W. L.

Of the many editors with whom Lewis was associated during his long and thorny career, C. H. Prentice (d. 1949) of Chatto and Windus was probably the most responsive and most helpful.[1] *Prentice became interested in Lewis's work through* The Art of Being Ruled, *which he brought out in March 1926. During the next six, very significant years of Lewis's writing career, the two worked as an unusually satisfactory editor-author combination in the production of eight books. There were awkwardnesses and conflicts – notably over Prentice's refusal to pay Lewis's price for* The Apes of God *and over the withdrawal of* The Doom of Youth *after a libel threat.*[2] *But throughout this period Prentice read Lewis's work keenly and gave it unstinting support. The letters show the writer's appreciation of his intelligent sympathy.*

[1] At the end of his life, L. found a similarly receptive editor in J. Alan White of Methuen and Company.

[2] It was in large part the failure of Chatto and Windus to support L. against the accusers of *The Doom of Youth* that brought about his break with the firm in 1932. The book had been published in New York earlier the same year by Robert M. McBride.

157. *To C. H. Prentice* 33 Ossington Street
Bayswater. W.2.
April 12/26

Dear Mr. Prentice. Thank you very much for your letter and I am delighted to hear that the part of my book I left with you has made a favourable impression.[1]

As to your believing that you detect a likeness in some of my personnages to people in real life, in that you are mistaken.[2] I have here and there used things, it is true that might suggest some connection. But the cases you choose are not ones I could, I am afraid, remove from my picture. If the bodies I describe fit the morning suits of real people and they thrust [?] them in and lay claim to them, however much the clothes fitted I should not countenance the wearing of such mis-fits by any of my characters, to all of whom I supply suits to measure from *my own* store. As to the point of *collaboration*, that again I could not take out.[3] It marks the Bloomsbury and all similar types of invention. And surely work done in collaboration has in the past often been of a high order, and there is no stigma attached to such a method of production?

I should much prefer you to do the book, and if these obstacles can be overcome, and an agreement as to terms arrived at, I shall be very glad indeed. With my best wishes for your holiday trip,

Yours sincerely
WYNDHAM LEWIS

P.S. I much appreciate your promise to keep strictly to yourself the nature of my mss. I, perhaps naturally, attach great importance to that.

[1] On April 11th Prentice wrote to L., saying of this piece of *The Apes of God*: "It's certainly going to be a remarkable and astonishing book. ... I haven't read anything for months and months that has made such an impression on me." When, eventually, Chatto and Windus refused to give L. what he wanted for the book, he sold it to Nash and Grayson. This firm produced a cheap edition in November 1931, almost eighteen months after L.'s limited edition.

[2] In his letter Prentice singled out the characters of Lionel and Isabel Kein.

[3] Prentice said of the supposed originals: "they might be inclined to take advantage of the suggestion that Isabel wrote Lionel's books for him . . . ."

158. To the Editor of the "Evening Standard," May 6, 1927[1]

Sir, – Mr Arnold Bennett, in a recent reference in your columns to myself, adopted an attitude to a certain word to which I should like to take exception. That word is *enemy*, and its present disuse is a matter of some importance.[2] "Enemy" is a word that is totally banished from the very best social life, and confined entirely to military operations.

Your distinguished critic is a man of the world, and so is, of course, aware that sapping and mining operations take place in drawing rooms as in other places. We cannot all love one another, and there is really no occasion for an armed conflict to establish the fact: indeed, war rather obscures it by its abstract promiscuity: it is too ideal.

Yet, as it is, in the best social life, when a person can no longer be referred to as "my friend So-and-So", he becomes *nothing at all* – there is no term that covers the condition of a man who is not "my friend So-and-So".

"My friend" is not considered a ridiculous figure of speech by any means when used by somebody who is vilifying or – camouflaged in this all-embracing "friendship" of the best social life – conducting some insidious attack upon another: on the contrary. The stage of *nothingness*, when it would be misplaced to say "my friend So-and-So" is seldom reached.

Renaissance men, for instance, would not have understood this attitude. Contemporary man is less naive, and would never admit to partiality or passion. As the outlets for his instincts of competitive violence become more mental and sophisticated, the term "enemy" becomes too vivid and palpable a thing: that is another reason for its disuse. So no one to-day can refer to an "enemy" in the offhand way that would have been natural to Benvenuto Cellini.

What is the remedy for this unhealthy suppression of the word "enemy"? One obvious remedy is the establishment of social

[1] Arnold Bennett reviewed *The Enemy*, *1* (February 1927) in the *Evening Standard* of April 28th. He took the occasion to comment upon L.'s work in general, and to deplore his combativeness.

[2] Bennett wrote: "One of his minor purposes is to disembowel his enemies, who are numerous, for the simple reason that he wants them to be numerous. He would be less tiresome if he were more urbane." He speaks also of "the occasional pettiness" of *The Enemy*.

cliques and camps. But if there is one word that is more taboo, upon which more indignant scorn is heaped, than the word "enemy", it is the word "clique".

Yet what is a "clique" but a group of people rather more sincere than the rest, who do not wish to associate constantly with a mass of individuals with whom they are out of sympathy, whose tastes they do not share, and who are mostly rather active enemies of theirs in consequence.

To licence the "clique" – to withdraw it from the general odium – that is one solution. A more daring and speculative procedure would be simply to reintroduce the word "enemy". If you find a person distasteful to you, be rude to him whenever you meet him as a matter of course; do not refer to him as "my friend So-and-So"; other people would then be compelled to refer to you both as "the enemies So-and-So".

Society would immediately assume much more definite and interesting patterns. There would be a bold arabesque of black and white, in place of the present undescriptive mauve or sickly heliotrope.

WYNDHAM LEWIS

159. *To C. H. Prentice* Hotel Brevoort.
5th Avenue.[1]
Aug. 1. 27.

Dear Mr. Prentice. . . .

I dont know how far you have got with the production of the book.[2] If it means holding up the publication to get the *Complete list* of corrections attended to, then use the *Abbreviated list* only. . . .

. . . It has been very hot. You can here observe "the neo-barbarism" in full flower. The high buildings are very impressive, especially the later ones "hanging-gardens" style. The earlier ones are like particularly long-necked cathedrals or big english parish churches.

Yours sincerely
WYNDHAM LEWIS
P.S. . . .

[1] L. was visiting New York, as he did several times during this period, for the purpose of selling his work.
[2] *Time and Western Man*, which appeared in September 1927.

160. *To T. S. Eliot* 33 Ossington St. W.2.
[September 1927]

Dear Tom. Very many thanks for the lecture you sent me.[1] ...
I will reserve any few remarks I might have to make until we
meet next. It seems to me that your "back to the mirror" move
is wrong, as you can imagine.[2] You are over modest (as usual) in
this case as regards *all* poets, and I do not believe that as a tribe
you are so limp. I think some particular doctrine of beauty must
be involved in your description. Anyhow, the senecan Shakespeare
is "in character", and your lecture full of valuable things. I wish
you would write more.

Yrs W. L.

[Note on side of letter.] I am sending you one of the advance
copies I have been given of *Time & Western Man*.

161. *To John Middleton Murry*†[3]

The Enemy[4] The Arthur Press,[5]
Tel: Park 7986 113a Westbourne Grove,
London, W.
Oct. 18/27

My dear Murry. In making out a list of notices of *The Enemy*
today, for advertisement purposes, I found that your references to

---

[1] T. S. Eliot, *Shakespeare and the Stoicism of Seneca*, published for the Shakespeare Association by the Oxford University Press, 1927. Reprinted in *Selected Essays* (London, 1932), pp. 126–40.

[2] Using L.'s *The Lion and the Fox* as one of his starting-points, Eliot argues that the great poets like Shakespeare are not philosophers but unconscious interpreters of their times.

[3] John Middleton Murry (1889–1957) was at this time editor of *The Adelphi*. He and L. knew one another as compatriots in the literary world. Temperamentally and ideologically they were at opposite poles, as becomes apparent later in these letters.

[4] Having brought out the first number of *The Enemy* in January, L. produced a second number in September 1927 and a third, his final effort as an editor, in January 1929.

[5] The Arthur Press – actually an office and a secretary – was established by L. in 1927 for the purpose of bringing out *The Enemy*. In 1930 he used the imprint for his own edition of *The Apes of God* and for his

it in *The Adelphi* do not figure in the page [?] drawn up some time ago by my lieutenant. As it was a very valuable notice, I want to get hold of it: (they could not trace it at the office from which my paper is published). Can you tell me where old copies of *The Adelphi* can be obtained?

In your letter to me at the time of the publication of The Enemy No. 1. you expressed an interest in the philosophic basis, if any, of my essay, *The Revolutionary Simpleton*.[1] I referred you to the book of which that is a part, namely *Time and Western Man*, which Chatto and Windus have now published. Did they send you a copy? If they have not done so I will see that they do. And I shall be very interested to hear your views with regard to it. – I follow your controversies with Eliot in The Criterion.[2]

Yours sincerely,
WYNDHAM LEWIS

162. *To Herbert Read* Bayswater. W.2.
Nov. 29/27

My dear Read. I have just returned from France, and am writing to thank you for the generous support you gave me in the *Nation* last week.[3] – I am much more alive than you appear to think to the necessity of "organization." I am not exaggerating at all when

pamphlet *Satire and Fiction*. With the publication of the latter in September 1930, The Arthur Press ceased to exist. Its name was chosen because of the proximity of the office to The Arthur Stores. (Geoffrey Wagner attributes it incorrectly in *Wyndham Lewis: A Portrait of the Artist as The Enemy* (New Haven, Conn., 1957).)

[1] Perhaps L.'s best-known attack on romance, "The Revolutionary Simpleton" occupied most of *The Enemy, 1*. Pound, McAlmon, Joyce, *This Quarter*, Gertrude Stein, Charlie Chaplin, and the Russian Ballet are among its targets. Murry wrote L. on February 25th saying that he didn't get "the hang of your underlying (? metaphysical) position" and that he didn't believe in "an absolute opposition between 'the time-mind' and 'the space-mind'."

[2] The controversy, centring on Murry's article "Towards a Synthesis" (June 1927), ran for over a year in *The Monthly Criterion* and involved, as well as Murry and Eliot, Charles Mauron, Ramon Fernandez, Sturge Moore, and M. C. D'Arcy, S.J.

[3] Read's favourable review of *Time and Western Man* appeared in *The Nation and Athenaeum*, November 19th, 1927, pp. 282–4.

I say that in such a book as *Time and Western Man* I am disinterested, and desire only to enlighten and help as far as I am able a world that is in mortal need of any assistance we can give it. Under these circumstances, the last thing I wish for is a self-seeking isolation.

Any organs that we can get on foot (such as *The Enemy*) should be used, it is my opinion, in this common cause; and had I not felt that Eliot might regard it as a weakening of the *Criterion*, I should long ago, for example, have asked you, as formerly, to help me.[1] – That is the point in your criticism that matters most, I think, (though what you say in qualification re. "the eye" and so on I by no means disregard[2] – though I think you attribute to me too *physical* an understanding in my phrase "things of vision"): my present remarks upon that point I hope henceforth you will bear in mind. – I need not add that at any future time should you be able to, and be so inclined, I should very much welcome any contribution from you to *The Enemy*,[3] or any by a writer recommended by you. It is even essential not to give the impression of a single spy, but of a battalion.

Yours
WYNDHAM LEWIS

163. *To Herbert Read*   Bayswater. W.2.
Dec 16/27

Dear Read. The *Criterion* I hear is to continue.[4] Last week after hearing of its suspension, I saw Eliot. He then thought it might

---

[1] Read had for some time been associated with T. S. Eliot in *The Monthly Criterion*.

[2] In his review, Read criticises L.'s doctrine of the supremacy of the eye – "things of vision" – on the ground that it dislodges *reason* in favour of "one particular sense."

[3] In his reply Read said that he would be glad to contribute to *The Enemy* when he had time to turn out something worthy. Nothing by him appeared in the one further number of the review.

[4] On December 5th, Miss Fassett wrote to L., saying that *The Monthly Criterion* was to be discontinued, "owing to differences of opinion between the proprietors on matters of policy." A week later she wrote to say that the review was to continue, "owing to certain concurrences of opinion."

stop. I suggested that he and a few of the more important of his staff of reviewers, should come over into The Enemy lock stock and barrel. I especially had you in mind and Thorpe,[1] who I believe is a friend of yours. I tell you this or otherwise you might not hear about it, and I should like you to know that I did it. I want to show you that on my side I am ready to support your effort, which I consider, in important respects, one with my own. . . .

Yours sincerely
WYNDHAM LEWIS

164. *To the Rev. M. C. D'Arcy, S.J.*[2] Bayswater. W.2.
Dec 16/27

My dear Father D'Arcy. I have only just returned from abroad, and I find your letter and the article from the "Month" which you so kindly sent me.[3] I cannot express my delight that a book I sent you with many misgivings should have met with such a generous and friendly reception. That you speak for the more intelligent portion of the catholic interest [?] in England lends what you say an especially gratifying complexion, but my esteem for what you personally think outweighs even that.

Your strictures I must accept as the account, in an indulgent eye, of blemishes that must, of necessity exist in a book so difficult to write, in such a feverish time. There is only one point on which I should venture to put in a tentative plea, but I am sure that it is owing to my ignorance that I think that such a plea is possible. When you say that you find a contradiction in my statements relative to (1) a non-imminent Deity and (2) experience of the divine on earth, the music of Bach was my example, I cant help feeling that you associate the music of Bach too much with Bach,

---

[1] W. A. Thorpe.

[2] The noted Roman Catholic intellectual leader, Father D'Arcy (b. 1888) was at this time at Oxford, where in 1933 he became master of Campion Hall. Through his interest in L.'s work, he and L. grew to be friends. L. did a portrait drawing of him in 1932. See *Blasting and Bombardiering*.

[3] In the letter, accompanying his review of *Time and Western Man*, Fr. D'Arcy wrote: "I do a certain amount of propaganda for it here in Oxford and find people awake or awakening to your point of view."

the austrian [?] organist, and do not consider it enough as a great perfection existing as it were independently of its human creator. Also I think that I should find it difficult not to believe that the great artist is in possession of an experience the equal, at least, of the mystic. Because it is incarnated for him in an earthly form – which only vulgarly bears his signature – it does not seem to me that it must be relegated to a plane beneath the mystical religious ecstasy.[1]

These few hasty remarks do not perhaps convey very well what I intend to say: but they may perhaps serve to give you a hint of what is for me a chronic difficulty in approaching some other interpretations of this undeniable fact. – I should welcome an opportunity of seeing you when you are in London. I should like very much to have a talk with you on some occasion without the distraction of the presence of several people.... – My deepest thanks again for your gesture with respect to *Time & Western Man*.

Yours sincerely
WYNDHAM LEWIS

P.S. Please note that I am Wyndham Lewis, not P. etc. This is an adjustment that dates from a considerable time back. I find 2 names quite enough for my purposes.

W. L.

165. *To C. H. Prentice* 33. Ossington St.
[December 20th, 1927.]

Dear Prentice. We were so busy the other night considering practical matters that I was unable to take full advantage of your remarks as to the points that had occurred to you about the book of a literary order.[2] (I refer for example to your remark about the

---

[1] On December 20th Fr. D'Arcy wrote in reply to L.: "When reading your book I thought the passage I criticised did not harmonise with your own view of a non-finite God, splendidly defended against James and Alexander etc., with their finite or time God. But now I see from your letter that you had in mind rather a comparison of the artistic and mystical experience."

[2] Having completed in rapid order *The Art of Being Ruled*, *The Lion and the Fox*, *Time and Western Man*, and *The Wild Body*, L. was now

stability of the ghosts before the Bailiff as contrasted with their instability while by themselves). I feel I have neglected perhaps some opportunities in the text as it stands. This was mainly deliberate, as I wished to make the general structure as natural, as *dead natural* as possible, and as little super-natural or miraculous as I could. I feel I may in this first part have been too sparing of marvels. Also I should like to know if you felt that the Bailiff part seemed in any way, in its rather [?] different treatment, to separate itself from the opening? (Of course, I shall now work on it and improve the writing). – Dont please trouble to answer this letter until [?] you have a spare moment when you reach Scotland.

                                    Yours sincerely
                                            W. LEWIS

166. *To C. H. Prentice*   33. Ossington St.
                                                                March 6./28

Dear Prentice. Very many thanks for your letter and I am indeed glad to hear that the new version seems to you a great advance on the old.[1] As to the mountains: the columns of vapour are from the geysers. These are described as rising up to a great height in the characteristic icelandic scenery. In a book I have *Skaptar Jokul* is described as "a volcano" but I will check it in an up to date map.[2] Thank you for pointing out fellaheen – I will attend to it.[3] *Douglas* is a more serious matter; what you tell me is very

well along with the first volume of his philosophical fantasy, *The Childermass*. This was published as *The Childermass: Section I* by Chatto and Windus in June 1928. When L. took up the work again, he changed the title to *The Human Age*. Books 2 and 3 were published by Methuen in one volume in 1955. *The Childermass* was reprinted as Book 1 in 1956.

[1] On March 5th Prentice wrote to L., saying that he had received the revised typescript of *The Childermass* and found a great gain in solidity and clearness.

[2] In his letter Prentice said: "Jokul is properly a glacier; you do not mean the 'vapour' alluded to to be volcanic?" L. was correct, however. He had perhaps been reading T. G. Bonney's *Volcanoes* (London, 1899), in which there is a long account (pp. 35–9) of the Icelandic volcano Skaptár Jökull and its eruption in 1783.

[3] Prentice wrote: "On p. 13 'fellaheen' is plural and should be 'fellah'. . . ."

disappointing as he must wear a kilt and I dislike changing important names.¹ But I will at once get a list of names owning tartans and pick an appropriate one in lieu of Douglas.

I am sorry you think that there are too many *barstards* in the coster part:² but when the proofs come in we can consult about that. A graver matter from my point of view is the question of the nan-men and the kilt,³ but I am glad to see that you do not stress that and I am sure we shall agree entirely on all these minor points. – Thank you very much indeed for having read the mss. so attentively and for your suggestions – in the case of Douglas it is most fortunate that you were able to detect that solecism. . . .

Yours sincerely
WYNDHAM LEWIS

. . .

167. *To C. H. Prentice* [London]
[May 1928]

Dear Prentice. . . .

Thank you very much for the page of suggestions. Most of them had been already detected by Miss W. – *Hanuman* was the ape-god, hanumeta (I think) the monkeys, but *hunaman* was how it was first spelt in English: I have adjusted it in such a way in the dialogue however as to satisfy any faultfinders.⁴ *rachitic* is allowable I think, it is a better sounding word (for some uses) than ricketty.⁵ He "stammers and *steins*" merely means that he

---

¹ Prentice wrote: "Douglas is a Lowland name, not a Highland, and, properly speaking, I doubt if individuals of the name of Douglas should wear a kilt." In the final version L. changed the name of his "beggar clansman" to Macrob. See *The Childermass* (London, 1928), pp. 212 ff.

² Prentice said he was worried about "so much strong language." He suggested omitting some *barstards* and *sods*.

³ *Nanman:* obs. for No Man (NED). Prentice said that "the nan-men appear to be a trifle too brazen at Douglas's expense."

⁴ On May 6th Prentice wrote to L. suggesting certain corrections in the proofs of *The Childermass*. L.'s reply takes up the queries in order, the first being concerned with the spelling of *Hanuman*. In the final version the dialogue reads: "'Hunamans or hanumans they call them: funny name, isn't it, like houyhnhnms! It's hindu I believe, it's an Ape-God.'" *The Childermass*, p. 13.

⁵ See *The Childermass*, p. 11.

expresses himself somewhat in the manner of Miss Stein.[1] archievident is good french (though absurd) and so I think may become for the purposes of absurdity, english.[2]

> I hope the printers are now busy
> Yrs sincerely
> W. LEWIS

168. *To C. H. Prentice* [London]
May 19./28.

Dear Prentice. Thank you very much for your letter and it at least is something that you are so patient with my clumsy attempt to make myself clear in my "business" capacity. In replying to you I want once and for all to have one thing in no doubt: the treatment your firm have given my books, to which you refer, has been, I am not now considering the money side of things, extremely advantageous to me and it has been of an order the general run of publishers however willing they might have been, could not have supplied. Your firm has attributed to me an important place in its lists and obviously taken great trouble in pushing my books and for all that it will not find me, now or at any time, ungrateful. For this I feel that you personally are in the main responsible: and therefore in my mind I am bound to separate you from your firm to some extent. I believe that it is due to your intelligent and sensitive understanding that I owed in the first place this fortunate disposition in your firm and I feel that in the difficult two years and a half during which I have been starting seriously as a writer you constantly have watched over my interests and done all in your power to further them. Without intermittences, I have for a long time now had the fullest sense of the value of the debt that my books owe to your generous mind.

But there remains the question, with which I am forced to close, of what I am going to get for my books: and seventy-five pounds

---

[1] As published the sentence reads: "Satters day-dreams and stares and steins...." There follows an interior monologue written as a parody of the style of Gertrude Stein. See *The Childermass*, pp. 37 ff.

[2] See *The Childermass*, p. 71.

at this time of day for *Tarr* does not sound very rosy or flattering.[1] . . .

I now really have to try and arrange my working life for the immediate future, in this breathing space, in such a way as will enable me to write my books. To sell *Tarr* at all, to anybody, for 75 pounds would be pointless. . . .

If my *Childermass* succeeds your firm will then, I feel, regard me with a more kindly eye, financially, and such matters will be adjusted in the interests of both of us, more favourably as regards me. Meantime I must throw *Tarr* upon the market and wait till it finds a purchaser. . . .

           Yours sincerely
             W. LEWIS

With the publication in America of his post-war books, and his transatlantic selling trips, Lewis's reputation began to climb in the United States in the late 1920's. In the spring of 1928 the New York Herald Tribune *requested an article on him. At Prentice's suggestion, Lewis decided to ask David Garnett (b. 1892), who had Bloomsbury connexions but had already recommended his work to American readers, to do the piece. On April 12th he wrote to Garnett, whom he knew slightly; a little later he sent him the page-proofs for* The Childermass, I. *Garnett unfortunately did not take to the new work.*

169. *To David Garnett*   33 Ossington St. W.2.
                   May 30/28

Dear Garnett. Very many thanks for your letter, just received. As to what you say, I have far too much respect for your judgement not to be disappointed: but that you should like my book at all is very pleasant and flattering for me.[2] The subsequent parts

[1] L. refers to his revision of *Tarr*, which Prentice wanted for Chatto and Windus. Later an agreement was reached and the firm brought out the novel in 1928.

[2] Garnett wrote to L. on May 29th, saying of *The Childermass*: "It has very fine things in it – but I don't like it as a whole. The parody of Joyce is a piece of virtuosity that seems out of place. And altogether there is too much Bailiff. . . . I like the first half best . . . ."

let us hope will turn the scale and make you view it with a more favourable eye.

I should not have ventured to address myself to you if I had not read articles in the american papers of a very generous and encouraging nature, full, as I thought, of the eager assent of a mind in time with my own. But it is evidently quite a different matter now that you have read the *Childermass* and whether from the point of view of the advance-advertisement of that particular book in America (and it will not be appearing there till the autumn)[1] or from that of usefulness to my reputation generally, it would, I am sure you will agree, do me very little good to have an article about a book that no one has seen, and of which no reviews have appeared, saying that it is no doubt this and that, but it is unfortunately also the other, and that it is like the curate's egg and here it stinks though there it is white enough, and that Mr. Lewis is very skilful of course but alas he uses his skill hors d'apropos and misapplies it, and so on. – I very much hope that you have not so far written the article. For if you tell me "I do not like your book" and "I have written an article [about] it you will not like",[2] well that sounds unpromising. If you should have *not* – and this is no slight at all to you, for I should have been very proud and flattered had you found my book to your taste, and it was to you I turned first of all – I suggest that I find somebody else to do the article. If you have already written it or done some of it, I think the matter sufficiently important for it to be worth my while to buy the article from you rather than have it appear. – I am writing you this hurried note to send to your office at Grt. James Street, and I hope you will be free and that we can meet somewhere today as it will be easier to settle about it in conversation than by letter.[3] . . .

Yours sincerely
WYNDHAM LEWIS

[1] The American edition, published by Covici-Friede, appeared in September.

[2] Garnett wrote of his article: "I don't expect you'll like it: as for me, I never like anything I write for newspapers."

[3] Garnett replied to L. on June 4th, enclosing his article and saying that L. was at liberty to suppress it. L. took advantage of the offer.

170. *To H. G. Wells*[1] Bayswater. W.
[ca. August 1928]

Dear Mr. Wells. I have been putting off writing to thank you for your extremely kind letter re. *Childermass* because I have been working incessantly on a book which was due to be sent off a week ago,[2] and I wished to have time to answer your letter properly. That you should like the *Childermass* is a very great satisfaction to me. What you say about the *difficulty* of the book interests me very much.[3] As to how such books can be made known to the great public, so that those for whom they are particularly destined shall get hold of them, that I should say depends on many factors: one of them, the nature of the other books the author may produce – the sort of publicity he, for various reasons, gets, and then the accident of his book reaching the few people who really matter in the whole affair as early as possible.

There are some things in which I am perhaps even obsessedly interested (the questions of art aside) which likewise interest you very deeply: and you have possessed in me for two or three years a reader who has come more and more to respect what you do (I am speaking not of your genius as a storyteller – that would be an impertinence on my part to speak of in that way – but your outlook on our world, of which I take it *Clissold*[4] was a fairly complete expression. Also I refer to articles I have from time to time read, dealing with the questions of war and Peace, which, partly because I was a soldier maybe and have especially reflected on that question, struck me very much.) That is why I sent you a copy of *Childermass*, and I am overjoyed to hear that it met with your approval. When the final part appears (the 2 vols. will

[1] Wells and L. had met casually in Soho. In the 1930's they came to know one another better through their interest in each other's work. But although they had a connexion in Rebecca West, whom L. had known since the war, the two writers did not become friends. They corresponded occasionally up to Wells's death, however.

[2] Probably the revised *Tarr*.

[3] Wells's letter appears in *Satire & Fiction*, p. 28. After announcing his "glowing appreciation" of *The Childermass*, he says: "But when I consider how difficult it was for the book to make me your grateful reader I am really bothered by the problem of publication for such books...."

[4] *The World of William Clissold* (London, 1926).

be published here simultaneously – in America they are to appear as one volume of about the length of the first) I will send them to you.

Yours sincerely
WYNDHAM LEWIS

W. B. Yeats first became interested in Lewis through his friend Olivia Shakespear and her son-in-law, Pound. When Time and Western Man *appeared, the poet found a new enthusiasm. On December 12th, 1927, he wrote to Mrs. Shakespear: "Tell Wyndham Lewis . . . that I am in all essentials his most humble and admiring disciple."*[1] *With* The Childermass, *Yeats's admiration increased, and the two, although they had very likely encountered one another earlier, met at Yeats's request in 1929. According to him, the confrontation was cautious.*[2] *They did though go on seeing one another in London, Yeats's enthusiasm for Lewis's work lasting at least through* The Apes of God, *which he was ready to support when the controversy over it arose.*

171. *To W. B. Yeats*†   Munich.
Sept. 1. 1928.

Dear Yeats. Your letter has just reached me; I have been moving about a great deal during August. What you wrote gave me the greatest pleasure: your remarks on that part of my book that you like best will be an encouragement for me in the writing of the remaining portion, especially as that will mainly be narrative, and not open to the objections that the long dialogues perhaps invite.[3]

[1] *The Letters of W. B. Yeats* (London, 1954), pp. 733–4.
[2] Yeats's account to Mrs. Shakespear of the meeting, which the editor, Allan Wade, places at May 6th, 1929, appears in *The Letters*, p. 763.
[3] Yeats began his letter, "I have read 'Childermass' with excitement," and ended it, "There are moments in the first hundred pages that no writer of romance has surpassed, the entrance upon the fields where all seems stationary for instance." He said that he preferred the first part because it was less dependent on ideas – "as powerful as 'Gulliver' and much more exciting to a modern." The second half "is too much of a pamphlet."

Since I have been away I have met nothing but hunchbacks[1] – they have driven me in cars, blacked my shoes, served me with drinks at cafés, and sold me newspapers – so perhaps I may have disturbed by my activities here such figures as you mention. I may add that all these deformed creatures have been in every instance most willing and polite.

Next week I am returning to London; and I hope that, should you be there at all this winter, we may have an opportunity of meeting. I shall read the book of theory you have revised with very great interest and have already ordered it.

Yours very sincerely,
WYNDHAM LEWIS

172. *To W. B. Yeats*† [London]
[ca. September 1928]

Dear Yeats. Yesterday I showed my publisher here (Chatto) your letter and he thought it would be of great assistance to *Friede Covici* (who are publishing the Childermass in America) if they could quote a few lines from it. Everything to do with the publishing and pushing of a book is disgusting (especially in America) and I hesitate to ask you to let me use something from a letter written to me privately, for such a purpose. Yet, I believe, too, that such a testimony as yours would have a great effect, both in America and here.

The following remarks were selected by my publishers.

"I have read "Childermass" with excitement. ... It is as powerful as "Gulliver" and much more exciting to a modern mind. ... There are moments in the first hundred pages that no writer of romance has surpassed." (from a letter written by W. B. Yeats to the author) So at the risk of disgracing myself by such a request, I suggest you should allow me to use these remarks,

---

[1] In his letter Yeats noted affinities between *The Childermass* and *A Vision*, emphasising the hunchback. He made the point also in a letter to Mrs. Shakespear: "The Baily is of course my Hunch-back – phase 28 – though L. does not know that...." (*The Letters*, p. 745.) He had rewritten *A Vision*, he said, and "I shall put in a couple of foot-notes about you."

anyway for transatlantic use, and if you do not mind, later on here in London.

I would rather be beholden to you in such a matter than to any other celebrated leader: in this as it chances I am most fortunately at one with the present attitude – your opinion is more valued and respected at this moment, than that of any other english writer, both here and in America, and it is also an opinion that is not often given.

I hope you will not mind my asking you this favour: I feel I ought not.[1]

       Yours very sincerely,
          WYNDHAM LEWIS

A. J. A. Symons (1900–41), *now best known for* The Quest for Corvo, *was one of the most active persons in literary London between the wars. A self-cultivated dilettante, he not only wrote and compiled and edited, he was also constantly involving himself in projects connected with books and food and drink. Before he was 22 he organised the First Edition Club; later he was instrumental in launching the Wine and Food Society and a literary dining group called the Sette of Odd Volumes. During these years Symons's nervous vitality broke out in dozens of ventures designed to promote the gentlemanly arts and, of course, himself. But his plans were more ingenious than practicable; usually they ended in ruin. When they met in the late 1920's, Lewis was inevitably attracted to this clever young man full of schemes. Symons, on his part, had found a literary figure exactly to his taste. As the letters indicate, a spirited friendship developed.*[2]

[1] Yeats replied, giving his permission but asking L. to change the second sentence to read: "Those first pages are as powerful as Gulliver." He said: "You must not make me compare this long dialogue to Gulliver which it doesn't resemble at all."

[2] For an account of Symons's life, see his brother Julian's admirable biography, *A. J. A. Symons: His Life and Speculations* (London, 1950).

from AJA Symons
17 Bedford Square
W.C.1

June 27

Dear Wyndham
      The King writes

I have read that part of Mr Lewis's Time & Western Man entitled The Revolutionary Simpleton with so much pleasure that I am particularly sorry to miss this opportunity of meeting him; but alas, on Monday evening I am booked to dine with the Ambassador to the Balearic Islands, and I am never well for a week after dining with him. Please ask me again. And please tell Mr Lewis that *all* revolutionaries are simpletons. —— Yours warmly.

George R I

P.S. Would Mr Lewis care to lecture to the Indians on The Art of Being Ruled? They don't seem quite to understand their advantages at present.

P.P.S. Would Mr. Lewis care to be Viceroy?

Letter from A. J. A. Symons ca. 1928.

173. *To A. J. A. Symons* Bayswater. W.
　　　　　　　　　　　　　　　　　　　　　　Nov 8/28.

Dear Symons. Thank you for your note – very well I shall wear nothing out of the way.¹ – Your volume of the Collected Poems of the Nineties has arrived and I am very indebted to you for the beautiful gift.² I remember some translations of Squire [?] from the french³ one or two of which would have looked very well – but I suppose you wanted as far as possible to confine it to original work. I did not relish very much the examples by "the case of arrested development," Gray,⁴ but I think his longer things must be better.

　　　　　　　　　　　　　　Yours very cordially
　　　　　　　　　　　　　　　　　　　W. LEWIS

174. *To C. H. Prentice* 33. Ossington Street
　　　　　　　　　　　　　　　　　　　　　Nov 27/28

Dear Prentice. Very many thanks for sending me *Essex and Elizabeth*⁵ – much more amusing than the last book you were good enough to send me. It is the *Lion and the Snake*, Essex as the embodiment of simple-hearted chivalry and poor Bacon as the "Machiavel"!⁶ What a villain! One is almost inclined to believe after reading S's book, that he wrote Shakespear's plays and did all the other things he is accused of. Well well well! . . .

　　　　　　　　　　　　　　　　Yrs sincerely
　　　　　　　　　　　　　　　　　　　W. LEWIS

¹ Symons was planning a literary dinner. In his invitation to L. he wrote: "I forgot to say that you may wear any dress, uniform or costume on Wednesday, provided you let me know in advance."
² *An Anthology of 'Nineties' Verse*, compiled and edited by A. J. A. Symons (London, 1928).
³ Perhaps J. C. Squire's translations of Baudelaire.
⁴ John Gray, the catholic poet. Seven poems by him appear in the anthology.
⁵ Lytton Strachey, *Elizabeth and Essex* (London, 1928).
⁶ L. refers to his own *The Lion and the Fox* (London, 1927), in which he sees Othello as the simple-hearted, noble lion and Iago as the wily, vulgar "Machiavel."

175. *To a Tax Inspector*† [London]
[ca. 1928]

Dear Sir I must apologize for the long delay in answering you but the facts re. "The Arthur Press" are as follows. *The Enemy* (of which 2 numbers have appeared so far) is a magazine appearing from time to time, or such is the intention, devoted to art and literature. In order to have some address from which to publish it I obtained the consent of the lady who runs the Typewriting Office at 113-a Westbourne Grove that I should use that address, "The Arthur Press" being of course a fiction, in the sense that there is no *Press* and no other books or papers are published from that address except *The Enemy*.

As to the financial results of the first two ventures. One thousand five hundred copies of *No. 1.* were printed (in Jan. 1927). About 200 copies were accounted for by English and American press. This issue sold out very quickly: but owing to the fact that the printer had broken up the type as we suppose and a run-on was therefore impossible, we lost in rough figures £146 on that issue....

I wrote the whole of no. 1. myself – there are no contributors to pay....

No. 2 has up to date been a failure financially in a much more serious sense than No. 1. I have sold rather more copies, but seeing the number of people who required copies of no. 1. and who were unable to obtain them, and believing I could sell at least 2 or 3 thousand copies in America, I printed 5000. copies.

Had I sold the whole 5000 copies at 3/-6 ... I should have made approximately £550. As it is I have sold under 2000....

I can if you wish give you more detailed figures: but you will see from this general outline of the situation that far from this literary and art venture having made any money that is taxable it has standing against it at present a very heavy loss (which I hope by more careful management in the future to slowly recoup). But at no time can such a venture hope to do much more than just cover expenses....

... There has been to resume what I have said a loss of about £450 on Nos. 1 and 2 of *The Enemy*: and it would have been impossible to run it at all had it not been for the generous support of a friend of mine interested in art and literature.¹

Yours faithfully,
W. LEWIS

176. *To A. J. A. Symons*   33. Ossington St. W.
Feb. 20/29.

Dear AJ. I enclose a letter – I am pursued by the ghost of *Poe* at present. What does this person mean and what is he quoting at me? If you will kindly glance at it you may "remember this." My reply to this Poeist – or is it a Poette? I cant read the name – is that Poe would not have found my writing "difficult."²

Yrs
W. LEWIS

177. *To C. H. Prentice*   33. Ossington St.
W
April 26/29

Dear Prentice. Thank you for your letter: I am glad *Paleface* is to appear on the 9th.³ ...

It is unlikely that *Paleface* will be taken by any American publisher – the Colour question is a very delicate one in the U.S.A. (I have learnt in my visits to N.Y.) and can only be approached with great sentimentality. Anything resembling common sense is greatly disliked. So do not trouble to send a copy over there – no one will pirate it anyhow.⁴

¹ Probably Sir Nicholas or Lady Waterhouse. See p. 216.
² In his reply, Symons explains the argument of L.'s correspondent, then goes on to say that Poe would probably not have liked *The Childermass*; but in the rest of L.'s work "he would have recognised the clarity of perception and expression which was his chief aim." Symons was working on a piece on Poe.
³ *Paleface: The Philosophy of the "Melting Pot,"* L.'s lively attack on romantic primitivism (*e.g.*, D. H. Lawrence), was published by Chatto and Windus in May 1929.
⁴ The book was never published in America.

I will look in soon and have a talk.

                                              Yrs sincerely
                                                    W. LEWIS

178. *To A. J. A. Symons*   London, W. 2.
                                                  Sept. 27 / 1929.

Dear A. J. Many thanks for your letter. I appreciate very much your generous expression of what you think as regards that particular book of mine.[1] – Meantime it is not the "unpunctuated" picture of Ulysses that I had in mind when we discussed it the other evening – that is merely a device (employed by Schnitzler a very long time ago in a story of his)[2] for presenting the disordered spouting of the imbecile low-average mind – it has no other justification (and, I agree, it is a pity Joyce has adopted that gibbering as a vehicle for the expression of *everything*, as at present). It was the newspaper-reporting I meant. . . .

                                                     Yours ever
                                                            W. L.

. . .

179. *To Richard Aldington*†   [London]
                                                  [ca. November 1929]

My dear Aldington. I am glad you thought the article would be useful.[3] If I can do anything else, please let me know.
    Prentice is an excellent man as you say: I like him very much.[4] I am so glad to hear that he liked the article too. The *Walpole*

---

[1] Symons wrote: "Tarr seems to me really to be what Ulysses is given the credit for being – the novel of the last 20 years; and it seems to me to hold more of novelty and instructiveness (technically) than any compound of unpunctuated slang."
[2] Probably "Leutnant Gustl" (1901), a long interior monologue, or "Frau Berta Garlan" (1901), a story with passages of interior monologue.
[3] L. had written approvingly of *The Death of a Hero* in the *Express*. Aldington thanked him in a letter written October 28th.
[4] In his letter Aldington said of C. H. Prentice, his publisher also: "That excellent man in his quiet way has a profound admiration for you." In his autobiography, *Life for Life's Sake* (New York, 1941), Aldington pays tribute to Prentice at length. See pp. 353–8.

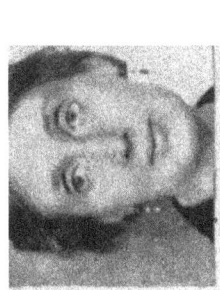

To David Garnett

WITH BEST WISHES FOR NEW YEAR 1930

Jean Wyndham Lewis.

11. New Year's Card to David Garnett

12. Jacket design for *The Apes of God*, 1930

problem does not exist of course, and yet such a person is in a position to inflict a good deal of harm upon books while he is there. You are right never to answer attacks.[1] Bring your criticism however (temporally) down to the 1929 world that suffers Walpoles and Bennetts.[2]

You are no doubt aware of the "Victorian" fashions that for some years have been gaining ground – taste for waxed flowers it began with and has become thorough as a fashion since. Lord Donegal[3] (when he mentioned your book) expressed the aversion to your criticism of "Victorianism" that many people must feel, for you butt head-on into considerable fashion. – Since the War (in which, Mr. D. H. Lawrence writes, we all died in fact, like Jesus upon the Cross) no fresh effort has been anywhere encouraged: the world has slowly been encouraged to return trips to its 19th Century weaknesses and philistinism. (That produced one fair-sized War – who knows, it might produce another one?!) I do not think you have quite succeeded in that part of your book (an opinion merely) but in intention you drive against that return to the antimacassar – the *Back to Victoria*. – I will write again.

Yr W. L.

In June 1930 Lewis published The Apes of God. *The dictionary-sized satire with its striking cover – a limited edition from The Arthur Press – created a furor in literary and artistic London. The models for the characters whom Lewis ridiculed as sham artists and sham bohemians, were in arms, along with their friends and well-wishers. Other writers and artists, judging the book a work of genius, rushed to its defence. Lewis characteristically kept in the thick of the mêlée. By September he had brought out his pamphlet* Satire & Fiction. *This remarkable document first chronicles the case of a favourable review of* The Apes *written by Roy Campbell*

---

[1] Aldington said in his letter: "Nothing I wrote would please Walpole – but does one want to please Walpole? I've decided not to answer any remarks about my novel . . . ." At the time Hugh Walpole was head of the English Book Society and a major force in the book world.

[2] Of the powerful London reviewers, Arnold Bennett was, in fact, the only one to write favourably of *The Death of a Hero*.

[3] The Marquess of Donegall (b. 1903) was at this time writing a weekly column, "Almost in Confidence," for the *Sunday Dispatch*.

and rejected by The New Statesman.¹ *It goes on to print letters and reviews lauding the book, and it ends with a brilliant set of remarks on the subject of its title.*

180. To Richard Aldington† [London]
[July 30th, 1930.]

My dear Aldington. First, let me thank you for the excellent publicity you have given the *Apes of God* in the Referee and for the generous things you have said, and generally for all the help you have given.² When we meet we can go over a few details of arguments to be found in those two notices. Meantime, nothing but thanks for the generous spirit that has animated them.

The *Apes* has caused here in London a good deal of disturbance. My life has been threatened by an airman, even! Then James Joyce has come to see me, to play Odysseus to my Cyclops – quite forgetting that it is *he* not myself who has half-sight. (Joyce is like an over-mellow hot-house pear, with an attractive musical delivery, but he bored me this time). The agony-column of the Times has echoed the rage of people who considered themselves attacked in the Apes – many peculiar things have happened. But in several instances the Press has been got hold of – and the letter I enclose will indicate that now a counter attack is about to begin.³ I am admirably armed – with other makes of gun this time, besides the 'Lewis gun'. I enclose (for your private perusal) a copy of a letter from Roy Campbell,⁴ who wrote an admirable review

---

[1] Campbell had been asked to write the review by Clifford Sharp (1883–1935), editor of *The New Statesman*. By the time the review was sent in, R. Ellis Roberts (1879–1953) had become literary editor of the paper. On July 3rd, Roberts wrote to Campbell rejecting the review as being too laudatory and suggesting that it be revised. Campbell vehemently refused, writing to L. from Martigues that he intended to publish a pamphlet titled *A Rejected Review*. Instead, L. asked him to join forces in *Satire & Fiction*, which included among its subtitles, "The History of a Rejected Review, by Roy Campbell." Roberts himself reviewed *The Apes*, in general favourably, in *The New Statesman* of August 12th, 1930, pp. 597–8.

[2] In *Satire & Fiction*, L. prints a long extract from Aldington's review in *The Referee* and a letter of praise from Aldington. See pp. 23, 32–3.

[3] The Circular Letter that follows.

[4] Campbell's letter appears in *Satire & Fiction*, p. 9.

at Sharps request for the New Statesman, and had it returned *because it was too favourable to my book!* Please *keep these details to yourself* until the Manifesto appears – in a week or so's time. All these transactions are to be printed, and despatched to every corner of the earth. . . .

I was in Marseilles last week – I wish we could have met. I enclose a cutting from todays *Telegraph*. I do not suppose a book has ever been written in which so much attention has been given to the externals – the *shell*, the *pelt* the physical behaviour of people, as the Apes of God. Yet this gentleman sees nothing, but *inside* you will remark.[1] The *Death of a Hero* (a superb book of *action*) also receives its share of the general misunderstanding of what is being attempted today. The Ulyssean "thought-stream" method is only appropriate to the depiction of children, morons, and the extremely infirm (Fredigonde),[2] as I have sufficiently demonstrated I think. Why dont you answer it? I am too busy with my manifesto.

Yrs W. L.

181. *Circular Letter from The Arthur Press*[3]   [London]
[July–August 1930]

Dear Sir,

A copy of Mr. Wyndham Lewis's much discussed book, *The Apes of God*, is being sent you under separate cover. The difficulties that Satire, in every period, has had to contend with – namely, the enraged resistance of the more nimble and active of those influential persons, who regard themselves as attacked – is generally recognised. In the case of *The Apes of God* the effects of such

[1] The article, which appeared in the *Daily Telegraph* of July 30th, was written by Montague Slater and was called "Satire in the Novel." Slater says that *The Apes*, like the first part of *The Death of a Hero*, has no other effect than to make its reader ask angrily, "Who made you a judge over us?" Later on, he finds Joyce, with his "muddied stream of consciousness," representing "a certain tendency in excelsis . . . which makes satiric novels inept. . . . Mr Wyndham Lewis and Mr Aldington lose all their force because of the prevailing convention in which novels are written."

[2] Lady Fredigonde Follet, the "veteran gossip-star" of the Prologue of *The Apes of God*.

[3] As the preceding letter indicates, this "round robin" was sent out to elicit material for *Satire & Fiction*. It appears on p. 22 of the pamphlet.

resentment came too late to affect materially the success of the private edition. It is the welfare of the subsequent popular editions that have to be considered.[1] *The Apes of God* should, in order to reach the general reading public of England and America, not present itself, perhaps, with its detractors unanswered – the rage that it aroused allowed to have the last word.

Under these circumstances, and should you be of our opinion, we hope that you will write to us, expressing your view of Mr. Lewis's book, and allow us to make use of what you say,

Yours, etc.,
For the Arthur Press.

182. *To A. J. A. Symons*   53 – Ossington Street W.2.
[September 1930]

My dear A. J. I am so glad the pamphlet has gone well at no 17. The *page-test* has much in its favour. What things we could do together! *Better than Crosswords!* You see it![2]

Listen A. J – angel! can you pay me for those 9 copies of the *Apes*? I am hard-up. I would not ask you if I were not.

I should be delighted to come next week – let me know the day. – *Satire & Fiction* is almost sold out. I wish you *had* written a letter for it – I didn't want to bother you and thought it might annoy some rich stiffs and big critical magnates you knew, if you did. Only consideration for A. J. prevented me!

Yrs
W. LEWIS

[1] The British cheap edition of *The Apes* was published in London by Nash and Grayson in November 1931. Robert M. McBride brought out the American edition in January 1932.

[2] In *Satire & Fiction* L. proposes that a distinction be made between run-of-the-mill fiction and serious prose narrative. He says that even a taxi-cab driver could discern the difference if presented with a specimen page of each. To illustrate he prints the first page of *Point Counter Point* (which Roberts, in his review, placed above *The Apes* as a novel) and the first page of *The Ivory Tower*. (See pp. 54–63.) Symons wrote to L. that he would like to see a whole volume made up according to this method of criticism. "It could be advertised as 'Better than Crosswords.'"

183. To A. J. A. Symons 53 – Ossington Street. W.2.
[September–October 1930]
Dear A. J. As we were!
You said – "*I* can find *a publisher* all right!" – and oh! would you believe it "the publisher" is "the author," it is *me*!¹ Listen I am no publisher but I passed a very delightful evening on Thursday. Let us forget, perhaps, *Specimen Pages*. As a matter of fact I could under no circumstances – enormously as I should enjoy it – put the necessary time aside just now for collaboration in such a book, unless (1) the publisher (but a real one) was forthcoming, and (2) he agreed to pay us to do it before we put our noses to the grindstone. . . .

Yours ever
W. L.

184. To Augustus John London. W.2.
[September–October 1930]
My dear John.
Many thanks for your letter and I am glad that *Satire & Fiction* pleased you.² It is almost sold out. (I enclose a cutting from *Dispatch*.)
What Yeats meant by 'universal plasticity' was of course the opposite to what is usually described as 'individualism':³ his phrase is very descriptive of the thing in question – a mystical mess. In the general *melting* preparatory to absolute holy fusion (like a world of tallow candles upon a hot afternoon) the members of the world-about-to-melt *would* assume the appearance somewhat of 'homunculi,' – what was meant by 'in bottles' I do not

¹ Symons and L. had met to discuss Symons's idea for a "Better than Crosswords" book. Then Symons wrote to say that he felt The Arthur Press would be the best medium. "We could make it a joint speculation." After L.'s reply, the project was dropped.
² John wrote to L. from Galway, thanking him for the pamphlet and praising him especially for his remarks on satire and fiction. A letter from John appears in *Satire & Fiction*, p. 27.
³ In Yeats's letter in *Satire & Fiction* (p. 29), he said that L., like Pirandello, "portrays the transition from individualism to universal plasticity, though your theme is not, like his, plasticity itself but the attempted substitution for it of ghastly humunculi in bottles." John queried the term "universal plasticity."

know. (If you are in a bottle you cannot *fuse*!) His letter was splendid – except for what he said about Miss Sitwell.¹

Campbell is a very fine fellow *and* a great bull-fighter. He was quite right to make a fuss. What happened in the offices of the *New Statesman* happened (no doubt) in at least half-a-dozen other editorial offices. *The Times, Spectator* & *Nation* all had disgraceful notices. Something had to be done about it and it was a good thing that I had a pugnacious matador (a credit to the Camargue) to take up the banderillo for me! Vive le Roy!²

I wish I could visit Ireland: there is no chance yet. When are you coming back?

I forward a letter sent for you here. A similar looking document reached me and I find it full of letters written by myself to the late Quinn. The most interesting letter – that in which I told him to go to the devil – is not among them. Permission I suppose will have to be given: though letters written to a patron are grim compositions usually.³ In cold print I fear they will make me look rather avaricious, and perhaps also ambitious. Who, anyway, is Lennox Robinson?

Yours ever,
W. LEWIS

185. *Augustus John to Wyndham Lewis*
Kildalton Castle,
Port Ellen,
Isle of Islay, Hebrides.
Oct. 4, 1930

My dear Lewis,

Enclosed a cutting you may or may not have seen. Homunculi means little men not enormous monsters like you make. "Universal

[1] Yeats said that *Gold Coast Customs*, like *The Apes of God*, brought back to literature "passion enobled by intensity, by endurance, by wisdom" – the quality of Swift.

[2] John wrote: "I read Ellis Roberts' review of The Apes in the N.S. Like most of your press, it was almost completely eulogistic and I think Roy Campbell's flurry rather unnecessary. . . . just imagine our cumbersome and overcharged poet in the BULL RING! (at Nimes) farting a volley of epithets as he vaults to safety. Quelle blague!"

[3] There are transcripts of four letters from Lewis to Quinn and many from John to Quinn in the John Quinn Correspondence, which is kept in the Manuscript Room of the New York Public Library. The correspondence has never been published. A sensational attempt was made in 1959 to pirate parts of it.

plasticity" cannot mean the opposite of individualism whatever you may say, because we are all made of dough more or less. Roy is a very fine fellow but not a great bull-fighter as he very frankly confessed. I didn't mean any harm, only his incursion into the Arena struck me – for a moment – as regrettably comic. To prove how he interests me I boiled down one of his best poems in Adamastor and greatly improved it. I have dipped my pen into the red ink-pot inadvertently. *He* was right to make a fuss – but *you*! Its a good job you had *some* disgraceful notices. Unanimity is suspect. These Quinn letters are a dam nuisance. My final letter to him wherein I called him a bloody Irishman is like yours absent. Lennox Robinson is a director of the Abbey Theatre and a playwright. I shall edit my little bunch rather rigourously. Have they any *right* to publish our letters?? You neednt mind looking avaricious and ambitious. My letters make me look – in view of what followed – ridiculously naive and trusting which is worse. I expect to be back in London in a few days and will let you know so that we can meet again.

Yrs. as usual

AUGUSTUS JOHN

186. *To C. H. Prentice* London. W.2.
Oct. 14th 30.

My dear Prentice. If it rested with me I should say no more about *The Apes of God*. Because it is so very distasteful to me to write, in fact, I have delayed for a week or more. Also I will say as little as possible – but to avoid any possibility of misunderstanding, now or in the future, I suppose I must write this. – What your firm offered me for *The Apes of God* seemed to me at the time – so greatly was it out of proportion (1) with your opinion of the book (2) with its dimensions (not its *area* in the private edition, but the quantity of effort that it contained – its quarter of a million of carefully-written and often-corrected words), (3) with the place such a work must occupy in my life, (4) with the six years or more devoted to it, off and on – that at first I thought you were having a joke with me. I still am haunted by the belief that you may have been having a joke with me! At the time – so much, not, I hope, naively, do I believe in your disinterestedness

– I thought the joke might be against your firm not against me.[1] But to put that aside: I have, in the sequel, made more out of the private edition of the book – and that with the miserable resources at my command – than your firm offered me for the whole lot: and I still have a considerable number of copies to sell (although more than you considered it safe to print as a special edition have already been sold and paid for). . . .

I need not repeat here what I have several times written as regards my great appreciation of your attitude towards my work. What I have said above does not alter that: the position as between myself and Chatto's had to be properly defined, that was all.

Now we can turn from these disagreeable business details to a more congenial topic. I have a number of pictures (some of *a tower*, a special set): will you, if in London, come next Sunday, after your dinner; or on the following Monday or Tuesday evening? I should like to show them to you, and see you again.

Yours sincerely,
WYNDHAM LEWIS

187. *Circular Letter from The Arthur Press*

THE ARTHUR PRESS

53 Ossington Street,
London, W.2
[ca. October 1930]

Dear Sirs,

We are shortly publishing a popular edition of Mr. Wyndham Lewis's novel, *The Apes of God*, probably at 7/6d.[2] We are also publishing it *with advertisements*. The adverts. will not be confined to those of publishers and bookshops. We are including adverts. of Steamship Lines, tooth-pastes, and lawn-mowers.

This will be the *first novel* since the age of Dickens to carry advertisements. It will be *a unique event in the publishing world*. It is certain to arouse a great deal of interest and result in a wide

---

[1] Prentice wrote a friendly reply, saying that Chatto's offer had been serious. He made no further offer but said he hoped his firm would have the opportunity of publishing other books by L.

[2] This edition never appeared.

publicity: and at the above price the book is certain to be very widely read.

The charge for a whole page is £5, a half page £2.10.0. We hope you will take this *unusual opportunity* of advertising in *a more permanent* form than the newspaper or the magazine offers – which once read is thrown away. *For one person who reads any given copy of a magazine, a hundred read any given copy of a book.*

As the time is short before the date fixed for our going to press, we hope you will send us your copy at once.

Faithfully yours,
THE ARTHUR PRESS

188. *To Shane Leslie*† [London]
[ca. October 1930]

Dear Leslie. Thank you very much for your letter. What you say about *The Apes of God* gives me very great pleasure.[1] I wish you had not been stopped by the editorial blockade and prevented from expressing your opinion.[2] It would have been a very good thing for the book if you had done an article. – But, if such works are to be made into contraband, to some extent, (of that fiery elixir, truth!) there is the way out I have indicated: in the sort of "speak-easy" edition of *The Apes of God* I am publishing at once (at the very popular price of 7/-6, so it is certain to reach a great many readers) different opinions to those imposed upon critics, as in the case of Roy Campbell, by the literary editors of the London book-pages, can be expressed. If you would write a short article I should be delighted, or a long letter, to The Arthur Press, or to me, would be equally good no doubt. I cant decide which would be the best. What would be best of all would be to print an article of yours as a sort of rejected review, as in fact it would be. With it a note from you mentioning the fact that you experienced difficulty when you turned to the papers for which

---

[1] The Irish Catholic writer Shane Leslie (b. 1885) wrote to L. on October 22nd, saying that he was immensely impressed by *The Apes*. He offered to contribute his opinion for future publication and asked L. what kind of article he would prefer.

[2] Leslie had written to A. J. A. Symons on November 30th, saying that he could not get any periodical to let him review the book.

you were in the habit of writing. This would so tremendously reinforce the evidence already of what happened to Roy Campbell, that The Apes of God had been unjustly treated, for this reason or that. It was evidently, as you said to me on the telephone, "under a boycott". And the support of all people interested in the art of letters would be enlisted against these oppressive manoevres. . . .

Thank you once more for your letter and what you have promised to do. I hope when you return to London we may meet. (A. J. A. Symons had a scheme of an interchange of letters – he to write to you and vice versa. I don't think that would be so good as one of the above arrangements[.] I will ask him to write direct to me.)

Yours sincerely,

189. *To C. H. Prentice* London. W.2.
Feb 2 1931

Dear Prentice.

There was a matter I intended to mention today, but forgot: namely the little book about me you had contemplated. I have turned it over in my mind very carefully and I am quite sure that *Roy Campbell* is the only person.[1] My reasons for this I will give you when we meet on Friday (9:15.). That I believe is somewhat your own feeling too. With a person so grudgingly treated as myself (as you have remarked) it is essential to have no sham 'impartiality' or lukewarmness. I could cooperate with Campbell and supply him with the necessary details regarding my work. (A bibliography, which is overdue in my case, might accompany the book. – Photographs?).

Thank you for the Eliot book. I did not know that you were a friend of the authors. I refrain from comment therefore!

Till Friday.

Yours

W. L.

. . .

[1] Campbell did actually write a monograph on Lewis for Chatto and Windus. It was, however, withdrawn before publication.

By 1930 Lewis's critical investigations had brought him to an interest in contemporary political phenomena. Just as Pound had been moved through concerns originally artistic to support of Mussolini, so Lewis found himself attracted to Hitler. He visited Germany twice at this time and discovered in Nazism a system that favoured not only an "aristocracy of intellect," but peace as well! The racism of Hitler seemed to Lewis only a characteristic German phenomenon, and Der Fuehrer's opposition to Communism – the dread leveller – signified courage and virtue. In January 1931, Lewis began a series of articles on Hitler for Time and Tide, *a paper to which he contributed often during the next five years. These pieces – published in book form as* Hitler *in April 1931 – probably did more harm to their author than all the rest of his controversial writings together.*

190. *To the Editor of "Time and Tide," February 7, 1931*

MR. WYNDHAM LEWIS REPLIES TO HIS CRITICS[1]

Sir, – Of my two critics (in your last week's correspondence columns), Miss Hamilton saw nothing out of the ordinary in Berlin – Berlin after dark is very like Golders Green at the same hour, as far as she is concerned – whereas Mr. Voigt is a great see-er, and a keen hearer, too – the groans of those struck by truncheons and so on – Mr. Voigt has not missed a note.[2] (But always a Communist groans, never a Nazi groans.)

Now if Miss Hamilton – who is a noted authority upon things German – wishes to take away from poor Germany one of its only

[1] The second of the Hitler articles, subtitled "Berlin im Licht," dealt in part with the atmosphere in the German capital. Appearing in the January 24th *Time and Tide*, it provoked correspondence in the issue of the following week.

[2] Cicely Hamilton (1872–1952), playwright and feminist, declared in her letter that she could not "remember anything startling in the way of wickedness and vice." Frederick A. Voigt (1892–1957), a prominent journalist and authority on Germany, began his letter: "It is quite clear that Mr. Wyndham Lewis has simply been stuffed with Nazi propaganda...." He wrote at length of the brutality of the German police to Communist demonstrators. The Nazis, he said, were better armed and suffered less; "the Communists have achieved a good deal in the way of sheer wickedness, but compared with Mr. Wyndham Lewis's 'disinterested' Nazis, they are almost gentlemen."

remaining sources of revenue, namely the tourist traffic, she must, of course, it is her right. (She may not want anyone else to go there!) "Why go to look at the Kurfurstendamm when you have exactly the same thing in your own Tottenham Court Road?" is what her whitewashing of Berlin amounts to – she should be a valuable recruit to the "See your own country first – Cut out Cannes – Come to the Cornish Riviera" Campaign. (After all, is there not a "Lido" in Hyde Park? Miss Hamilton would go to Venice, I am sure, and come sniffing back, saying that as to the Adriatic, well the Serpentine looked much the same to *her*.) I can only reply to Miss Hamilton that (1) the shop-front façades of the Kurfurstendamm look, to my eyes, very different from those of Regent Street, both by day and night: and that (2) if Miss Hamilton insists upon dashing the spirits of the tourist and robbing the night *lokals* of Berlin of foreign custom, I at least will have nothing to do with it. If you rob a beggar of his "wickedness", you leave him naked indeed!

Mr. Voigt is not interested in that side of the matter – Mr. Voigt is the politician pure and simple – too simple. It was like pressing a button, writing my article: up jumped Herr-Mister Voigt, armed to the teeth with Communist argument. I on the other hand am no politician – but having ventured into those fields, I must, I suppose, make some reply, else people might think that there was none, to that flood of conventional denunciation. At the start there is a confusion of some sort in his letter. "Mr. Lewis asserts...that the Prussian police deal more severely with the Communists than with the Nazis. The exact opposite is true." Mr. Voigt has here "told the truth" by accident, I assume; for he proceeds to say that "the police have always dispersed Communist demonstrators with far greater brutality than Nazi demonstrators." Evidently the latter, and not the former is the true Mr. Voigt – he was in a great rage and in his haste to contradict me he put down the reverse of what he intended.

There is no need to point out how very hot a partisan of the Communists we have in Mr. Voigt. And since he is that, it is perfectly clear that Mr. Voigt would not like to see the Nazis sympathetically handled in an influential English paper. I never read the *Manchester Guardian*, which I regard as one of the most insidiously wrong of all great political newspapers in England, but if I did I am sure I should find Mr. Voigt (who is, I understand, an international journalist employed by that paper) supplying the English public with a most unsympathetic account of the Hitler Movement. I have, of course, stressed the purely Nazi standpoint. It was essential to do that if one is to secure for them a fair hearing in England, where there are far too many Mr. Voigts and too few impartial observers. . . .

I hope Mr. Voigt will write again and provide a realistic accompaniment for my article. I hope that he keeps up a drum-fire of Communist recrimination until my fifth article is out, and even then that a parting rumble or two may salute the close of my series. (Miss Hamilton is merely a kill-joy – I am sorry to have to say it: I do not think that she should join us again, and I hope that you will absolutely forget, or discount, at once, her depressing picture.)[1]

I am, etc.

WYNDHAM LEWIS

Despite his rightist sympathies during this period, Lewis always had followers and friends who were liberals. Among the steadiest of these was the writer Naomi Mitchison (b. 1897). Lewis met Mrs. Mitchison, a member of the Haldane family, early in the 1930's when she and her husband, G. R. Mitchison, M.P., were living in Hammersmith. Mrs. Mitchison was first a devotee but soon a warm-hearted friend; likewise Lewis moved from the rôle of master to that of a colleague charmed by the energy and good humour of this younger writer. During the ensuing twenty-five years the two were never out of touch for long, although they saw each other less after the Mitchisons went to live permanently in Scotland. Lewis did drawings for Mrs. Mitchison's Beyond This Limit (1935), *and in the course of their friendship he did portraits of most of her family.*

191. *To Naomi Mitchison* 53, Ossington Street, W. 2.
May 5, 1931.

Dear Naomi,

Your letter and a postcard got underneath the oilcloth and there lay hid until today I saw it at the edge – I am so sorry. . . . I have

[1] Both correspondents wrote again, Miss Hamilton on February 14th and Voigt on the 21st and 28th.

been engaged in a close corps-a-corps business struggle for some weeks, but I am emerging victorious. – *The Diabolical Principle* is a routine pamphlet and printed from *Enemy*.¹ It is of course, all true; but the second ½ of the book is the best, about the *Dithyramb*.² There however I poach a little upon the [?] townships of your favourite land and favourite town – too near perhaps to *Black Sparta*³ for you not to feel I have been too hasty. – I am just about to write the "Liberty" article for Mr. Williamson. After that a little bit of *real* freedom for me, I hope, in the Danube or Ebro! I have often wondered what people meant by setting the *Thames* on fire – or is that shire snobbery? Give me a foreign river. Shades of "The Son of Woman"!⁴ Let me know when you get back.

Yrs.,

WYNDHAM LEWIS

In the late spring of 1931, Lewis and Mrs. Lewis went to North Africa. They travelled extensively in the Atlas Mountains, where the wild landscape and Berber tribesmen supplied Lewis with material to his taste. Instead of working on The Childermass, *as he had intended, he wrote a series of articles about his travels. These appeared in* Everyman *and were published as a book,* Filibusters in Barbary, *in 1932.*⁵

¹ Mrs. Mitchison wrote to L., saying that *Time and Tide* had asked her to review his new book *The Diabolical Principle and the Dithyrambic Spectator*. She said, "So far I don't think I understand it." "The Diabolical Principle" was largely an attack on *transition*; it appeared first in *The Enemy, No. 3*.

² "The Dithyrambic Spectator: An Essay on the Origins and Survivals of Art."

³ Naomi Mitchison, *Black Sparta: Greek Stories* (London, 1928).

⁴ In her letter Mrs. Mitchison said she enjoyed L.'s review (*Time and Tide*, April 18th) of John Middleton Murry's book on D. H. Lawrence. Hence L.'s joke about Lawrence's exoticism, which he had attacked in *Paleface*.

⁵ The London edition, published by Grayson and Grayson, was withdrawn after publication because of libel threats. The New York edition, published by Robert M. McBride and by the National Travel Club, appeared without difficulties.

192. To C. H. Prentice Agadir.
June 25 1931.

Dear Prentice. At last I am settled for a week or so after having moved incessantly about for some time. I have a whitewashed cell here where I can write, and I have started work: in consequence of the propitious scenery and circumstances, at once [*sic*] the *Childermass*. The country is most remarkable and the desert-cities, humped antelopes, Berber brothels etc. abound in suggestions of a sort favourable to the production of the major book. So I have started. Soon I should have a section roughly filled in. Meanwhile money is necessary. . . .

As to the proofs of the *Youth* book,[1] they had better come here. . . . The title of the book I am not quite certain about. What do you think of Youth, as Will and as Idea? – Write me here at the same time that you telegraph.

Yours
WYNDHAM LEWIS

193. To Naomi Mitchison Agadir, Morocco.
July 11, 1931.

Dear Naomi,

Very many thanks for your kind letter – as you see I am here still, upon the edge of the Spanish Sahara, baked by breaths from the Sudan, chilled by winds from the Atlantic luckily, too, and gathering much material for an essay on Barbary – as you know, I expect, *Berberig* is probably just *Barbary*, and I am amazed that Lawrence (D.H. – not the Colonel) did not find it out. I have been to places, and broken bread with people, calculated to lay him out in a foaming ecstasy. At all events, these folks are *the* Barbarians right enough, and they build the most magnificent castles, upon the tops of cyclopean rocks, in the heart of vast mountains. They have to be seen to be believed. And they all poison each other with arsenic whenever they get the chance – even placing arsenic in the babouches (slippers) of their guests, and anywhere else they

[1] *The Doom of Youth* (New York, April 1932). This lively exposé of the cult of youth was appearing in the form of articles in *Time and Tide*. The English edition was brought out by Chatto and Windus in July 1932 and was then withdrawn.

think it may get in to their bodies. Meantime, they are as brave as lions (so the French say) and surely one of the handsomest people in the world. I say "handsome" and it is of course masculine beauty, but there is a great deal of grace too, always among the men. The women are out of it. I am sure you would enjoy being here very much. Next time I come here I shall go on to the Congo. Now I am going back in a day or so to the High Atlas, then I shall probably return to London.

I was so glad to hear that you liked the first article of the series in *Time & Tide*.[1]

The 6 articles *Time & Tide* are using are arguments in chapters from a longish book (which Chatto are publishing in the autumn) and of course a good deal telescoped. I will send you the book. . . .

Yours,
WYNDHAM LEWIS

194. *To A. J. A. Symons* Pall Mall Safe Deposit.
Carlton Street.
Regent Street. W.
Feb. 1. 1932.

My dear A. J. Thank you very much for reading my mss. (first part) of *Snooty Baronet*[2] — putting aside the time to read it and giving me the benefit of your opinion, and I was delighted that you approved of what I had done up-to-date. The Persian scenes will I hope come up to your expectations. — But thank you also very much for reading me the final chapter of your Wilde book which I thought very fine.[3] I should not touch that if I were you — it would I am sure be a mistake to give more detail at that stage (as to Oscar Wilde's dinner-table technique). We will go to Sickert's soon and get him to tell us exactly how the trick was done — I mean the secret of W's conversational magic.

Yrs
W. L.

[1] Mrs. Mitchison said in her letter that she was interested in his new series on "Youth-Politics."
[2] This comic novel was published by Cassell in September 1932.
[3] Symons's life of Wilde was never completed.

Lewis met Roy Campbell (1902–57) when Campbell, still in his teens, first came to London. As he records in his autobiography, the young South African soon became a disciple.[1] *Because Campbell passed most of his life out of England, he and Lewis were never together for long periods; but his work manifests the extent and durability of the master's influence. On his part, Lewis readily appreciated Campbell's personality and talent. He drew his portrait in line, and in words – as "Zulu" Blades in* The Apes of God, *as Rob McPhail in* Snooty Baronet. *The two supported one another publicly until their deaths, which occurred within a month of one another.*

195. *To Roy Campbell*†
London.
April 6th 1932

My dear Campbell.

I enjoyed my visit to Martigues[2] very much. But it was too much overshadowed by SNOOTY. Your appreciation of the book (outside of the personal problem it gave rise to) pleased and encouraged me more than I can say. But there remained a disagreeable feeling that you had misunderstood my intentions. – What in the first instance I wanted to do was to write about something that interested me of course, and, as you can see from the Mackenty passages,[3] the part that would generally be identified, more or less, with you, *as it first stood*, was not a picture that anyone could interpret as unflattering. *That* was all written before "Snooty" came on the scene. The rest resulted from the necessity of altering and dislocating it if [it] was to be used as "fiction," and the forcible fusion of it with the drama of the preposterous "Snooty" resulted in the dramatisation of the things I borrowed from you. And that does certainly give rise to a problem. *Even in play* I feel one should not ask a friend to lie down and pretend to be dead,

---

[1] See *Light on a Dark Horse* (London, 1951), pp. 224–5. See also *Blasting and Bombardiering*, Chapter IV, "The Wedding of Roy Campbell."

[2] Campbell's residence in Camargue, where L. had stopped while on holiday.

[3] In the final version the character became Rob McPhail. Clearly modelled on Campbell, McPhail is, as L. says, sympathetic. But he falls victim to a sham code of honour, being "struck down in a fifth-rate bull-fight."

nor allow an ill-mannered and lunatic puppet to sniff at his corpse – and put upon his actions interpretations that are certainly not (need I say!) in my views true ones – such as proclaiming that you fight bulls because of your *hatred of Man*! (That would indeed be an odd way of regarding the sportive activities of the original (very much *more or less*) of Mackenty – though I do think that *if the world believed* that you harboured those diabolic proclivities they would admire you for it, and if they took that fantastic picture au pied de la lettre it would be no bad advertisement!) But for Heaven's sake do not consider that what my *behaviorist* puppet hints at is a reflection of anything that could ever possibly cross *my* mind. If there is one person I know who is *on the side of Man* more than another it is *you*.

Lastly, always remember this. At a point in my career when many people were combining to defeat me (namely upon the publication of the *Apes of God*) you came forward and with the most disinterested nobleness placed yourself at my side, and defended my book in public in a manner that I believe no other work has ever been defended. And you can accept it as the most hundred per cent true statement that I would consider myself as the last of the ruffians, and the most ungrateful, if I ever by act or word did anything to harm or offend you.

I say all this lest any vestige of doubt should remain in your mind regarding my a little unceremonious juggling with what is but a miserable wraith [words] of the externals of your life. But as soon as I get the complete proofs of the book I shall send these to you, and *anything whatever* in it that you consider (or that your wife considers) liable to be picked up by an enemy of either of us, to be thrown up against us, I will cut out at once.[1] Apart from this problem, and my bloody cold in the head, I had a delightful 3 days with you, and I want you to thank Mary[2] very much for her kindness while I was there. . . . I do rather regard as mismanagement, or a little undesirable the involving of a figure that it would never occur to me to try my hand as a satirist on, with one of the most objectionable puppets it is easy to imagine.

[1] When the book appeared, Campbell wrote to L.: "Snooty was grand." In *Broken Record* (London, 1934) he says that L. conferred on him, in the death of McPhail, "a not unpleasant literary immortality."

[2] Mrs. Campbell, formerly Mary Garman.

196. *To the Editor of "Time and Tide," April* 16, 1932

ARNOLD BENNETT AS CRITIC: MR. WYNDHAM LEWIS
REPLIES[1]

Sir, – Mr. Henry Adler's letter reveals him as a close student of what I have called "the uplift machinery" of contemporary fiction-reviewing – or he is, perhaps, himself a business expert, in the "uplift" business. However this may be, one of the points in his letter deserves an answer.

Mr. Adler writes: "The views he (Mr. Bennett) expressed in the *Evening Standard* did not differ greatly from those that he expressed in the articles which he contributed to the *New Age* from 1908–11." Not only is this statement inexact, but, which is much more to the point, Mr. Arnold Bennett's attitude visibly changed even in the course of his latter-day *Standard* activities. When he first took up that job, Mr. Bennett made an attempt, according to his lights, to provide what he regarded, I suppose, as the sterling stuff of literary criticism (something on the lines of the continental standards in such matters). But he soon discovered, so it seems, the incompatibility of the standards of big-scale book-boosting and those appropriate to the duties he had discharged in the peaceful pages of the *New Age*.

The intelligent principles that governed the management of that review *d'élite* under the editorship of Mr. Orage, were, after all, a very different affair to the requirements of a great newspaper. In the earlier stages of his latter labours Mr. Bennett attempted, somewhat lamely and haltingly, to convert a page of a great booming daily into a not-too-businesslike page of the *New Age*. Letters of protest appear to have flowed in upon him from all sides – to start with he grumbled and swore, he complained bitterly about this bombardment (the opposite of a *fan-mail*). But, protesting the while, he presently accommodated himself to these hostile criticisms. He became so thoroughly cowed by all those pressures and capitulated so thoroughly to those conditions of his

[1] In a review article on the book trade, "A Tip from the Augean Stable" (March 19th and 26th), L. criticised Arnold Bennett for his "Tipster Technique in Literary Criticism" during his reign on the *Evening Standard*. On April 2nd *Time and Tide* printed a letter from Henry Adler defending Bennett against L.'s charge of "reckless optimism."

new Big Business employment, that finally he would praise any book put under his nose, whose author, or whose backers, would be liable to write him a "snooty" letter.

The next stage was a sort of critical dictatorship for the Anglo-Saxon world. It was repeated on all hands that Mr. Arnold Bennett had "made" such and such a book – that a week after he had puffed it, it had sold a million copies. All Mr. Bennett had to do, it was said, was to praise a book, and the public rushed into the shops and bought it. But the power this placed in his hands could only be retained by repeating incessantly these triumphs. The temptation to do the *San Luis Rey* trick again, and yet again, was irresistible.

That Mr. Arnold Bennett was able to write the stuff he did at all was, of course, in the first instance, because he was a "best-seller" himself, when all is said and done – a sort of Vicki Baum, in fact (*Grand Babylon Hotel*, etc.). If he caused *The Bridge of San Luis Rey* to sell ten million copies or whatever it was, it must be remembered that quite genuinely Mr. Bennett would have been extremely proud and happy himself to have written such a book. And if he "saluted", with paeans of pompous puffing, every third-rate German novelist who happened to be translated into English, and told the public that here was another Tolstoy, or a second Dostoevsky – or yet another Gogol – it was because, to some extent, he believed it. It must be recalled, in discussing this question, that Mr. Bennett would not have occupied in Germany the position that he did in England – any more than, for that matter, does Vicki Baum or Feuchtwanger. His mind was not a very interesting one – that is obvious enough – so it was not entirely dishonesty that caused him to produce what he did, namely a travesty of continental criticism (with the intellectual prestige of the *New Age* behind it) for the glorification of the magazine-story and the literature of the station bookstall.

The fact remains, that with the names of the great Russian novelists incessantly on his lips, he betrayed every standard (intellectual or other) of those splendid masters of the mind, in order to boost what was often the completest literary refuse. That he should mention Mr. D. H. Lawrence, Mr. Joyce, or Mrs. Woolf *as well* as all this horde of fictionists, and in terms equally inflated, is natural enough. That particular argument of Mr. Adler's does not, I am afraid, bear examination. *Of course* Mr.

Bennett would pat Mr. T. S. Eliot on the back occasionally, sandwiched in between a broadside of encomium for Vicki and a full-blooded puff for one of our own Baums – our local oaks!

I am, etc.

WYNDHAM LEWIS

His association with Chatto and Windus at an end, Lewis was in 1932 looking round for publishers. He found a sympathetic one in the small firm of Desmond Harmsworth and his partner, Mrs. Winifred Henderson. Harmsworth brought out Lewis's play The Enemy of the Stars (1932); *a portfolio of drawings of celebrities*, Thirty Personalities and a Self-Portrait (1932); *and a political book*, The Old Gang and the New Gang (1933).

197. *To Mrs. Winifred Henderson*†   Percy Street.
May 5th 1932.

My dear old Hen. All I want you to do is to have typed out what you wrote me re. proof-corrections[1] ("I note that you are willing to adhere etc." – all beautifully phrased) but *to cut the cackle* – no "in return for which hand over stuff today" and so on afterwards. See? Meanwhile, keep the printers on the move. I am working night and day. And when you feel convivial, drop round to Percy Street and have a pint.

Yrs etc.
W. LEWIS

I resort to this rather familiar form of address in order to banish that gloomy and formal tone which has so far overclouded your end of this correspondence.

[1] Mrs. Henderson, whom L. had known for many years, wrote him, on May 4th, a formal letter regarding correction clauses in his contracts. She offered certain concessions in exchange for the overdue manuscript of *The Enemy of the Stars*.

198. *To Desmond Harmsworth*[1] 31. Percy Street. W.1.
15 June 1932

My dear Harmsworth Thank you for your letter and I was delighted to hear that you liked *The Enemy of the Stars*. – It is strange that you should ask me at this moment if you could read something in Metre by me, as in fact I have been for some time writing a thing in verse – further stimulated in that direction by the annoyance at having to toe the line marked out for me by this earlier work[2] – and at being forced to operate in a noman's land of my own making between prosody and prose. I will show you my poem when it is finished – it is called *The Song of the Fronts*.[3] (It is nothing to do with war).

The *gros mots* have been removed, without great damage to the text.[4] For "great rolled-up bugger" I have substituted "great rolled-up rotter." (*Rotter* is a good word which has been made to stink by all the rotters who have used it – just as one could say that *cad* is a word that no one but a cad should ever use. But tant pis! – the "great rolled-up rotter" passes muster I think). *Arse-face* becomes *bum-face* – in the american sense of 'silly' and 'knock the spunk out of him' will be less objected to by *the trade* than the more generally used expression.

... I now have about 20 heads out of the 30 done and as soon as I get the remaining 10 ready for the block maker I shall go off somewhere for a change of air. I may go up to Cambridge and draw Eddington: someone is getting Arbuthnot here for me, to represent the Surgeons, and Lady Cholmondeley[5] is sending me a Pilot – a Snider [?] trophy ace.[6] – I am in touch with Carnera.[7]

---

[1] Desmond Harmsworth (b. 1903), himself a painter and writer, succeeded his father as the 2nd Baron Harmsworth in 1948.
[2] The play first appeared in *Blast No. 1*. L. had revised it for publication in book form.
[3] See *One-Way Song* (London, 1933).
[4] In his letter of June 12th praising *The Enemy of the Stars*, Harmsworth said that he doubted if "bugger," "arse-face," and "shit" could get by in an edition that wasn't private.
[5] The Marchioness of Cholmondeley, whom L. had also drawn.
[6] Probably Flight-Commander Orlebar. See *Blasting and Bombardiering*, p. 230.
[7] Primo Carnera (b. 1907), the prize-fighting champion. He does not appear in the portfolio.

Lady Rhondda[1] is half-done. – Is it necessary do you suppose to get "puir blind Jimmie's" permission to reproduce a head of him done in 1920?[2] I will make enquiries about the copyright position – regarding drawings of people.

. . . Have you been doing any more drawing? I was shown the head of Hav. Ellis the other day and thought it excellent. . . .

                                    Yrs
                                    W. LEWIS

199. *To Naomi Mitchison*   31. Percy Street. W.1.
                                                     Oct. 29 1932

My dear Naomi. I have been delaying writing to you because I could not make up my mind whether I ought to come to your party on Guy Fawkes night, because I might frighten ——— – you remember last time he said he was so frightened he wouldn't come into the other room as I was there! But I want to see you, and so all I can say about it is that he'll *have* to have the wind up for once. – I shall dress in a tuxedo. – The other drawing of you sold last week to a musical butcher from Glasgow, who has one of the best small collections of pictures it appears in the country. . . .

                                    Yours
                                    W. L.

200. *To A. J. A. Symons*   [London]
                                                         [1933]

My dear A.J. I shall not attempt to describe the nature of my ailment[3] – I know that you prefer to derive such information from

[1] Margaret Haig Thomas, Viscountess Rhondda (b. 1883), editor and publisher of *Time and Tide*.

[2] Harmsworth wrote from Paris on June 26th saying that Joyce was delighted to be included and that he also suggested that L. include a drawing of Miss Weaver, "which he considers a particularly fine piece of work and will gladly lend for the purpose."

[3] From 1932 to 1936 L. was in and out of nursing homes being operated on and treated for a condition which had arisen perhaps as the result of a much earlier ailment. Symons had written to him on March 8th, asking where and how he was.

persons more capable of large generalisations than the Number One conversant with *all* the facts – but nevertheless I will venture to say that I am *ill* – that I am assured that I run a pretty good chance of recovering – and that if I am lucky enough to do so I believe I shall *then* be in perfect health. But that cannot be for many weeks. – The moment I am convalescent I will let you know and as where I am is not far away hope I may receive a visit from you when I shall have much to talk about. Meanwhile I hope that Food & Wine gains more [?] adherents every day & that you are personally in the pink – & I am bitterly disappointed to have to postpone the portrait I had planned of you. . . .

Yrs ever
W. L.

201. *To Sydney Schiff*†   31 Percy Street,
Tottenham Court Road. W.C.
May 21st 1933.

My dear Schiff.

Thank you very much indeed for the cheque for twenty-five pounds – it is at this moment of the greatest value to me.[1] . . . If I were well – if I had not been for six months unable to work – I should of course not be asking you for financial support. But how miserable it is *never* to be able to have even a month's relief from financial worry, to enable one to do the best work possible you are able to appreciate. Ten years ago I was forced to take a garden-studio (tin shack) built slap on the earth of a London garden (Adam and Eve Mews) because it was cheap. But even that I could not pay for and had to leave. My next and last attempt to rent a studio was in Holland Street. There within a very short time I had an eviction order against me. In despair at these conditions, I retired into rooms: and during the years that I have been writing books I have still produced spasmodically (and as my books achieved notoriety, have sold) pictures and drawings, usually small, (as in a small room it is difficult to paint a large picture). Now I want to have this completely representative show, which I have never had the chance to hold, in the autumn of this

[1] Having helped L. before, notably as a backer of *The Tyro* in 1921, Schiff began to extend aid again during L.'s illness.

year.¹ No one – aside from a handful of people – has seen any work of mine, really, which represents what I am able to do in the matter of painting. The new work I have been completing (and which you expressed yourself as interested to see) I have had to do on a chair, for the simple reason that I have not, since my illness, had the money to spare to buy the necessary easel (price two pounds). . . .

. . . It is quite certain that a large show of all my things would not be unproductive, if properly handled by a dealer who gave himself a little trouble. Is it really out of the question for you, one of the few people who care for pictures in London, to do something to facilitate this? . . .

. . . it is obvious that you have behaved extremely handsomely, and it is no mere form of words when I say that I am very grateful for that help. But alas, that has been swallowed up in the expenses of an illness. That is the difficulty! Here I am, thanks to the help of a few friends, more or less settled with my illness: but unable to go ahead and produce, indeed high and dry, for lack of funds – *because* all the funds have been drawn on for an unreproductive spell of ill-health.

Yours,
W. LEWIS

202. *To Naomi Mitchison* Pall Mall Safe Deposit
December 3, 1933.

Dear Naomi. . . . I am sorry you were unable to persuade the Week-End or Time and Tide:² but the editor of the former told Morley³ he would not have my book reviewed, and Ellis Roberts (of *Satire and Fiction* fame) is the editor of the latter. Your explanation of the cold reception your suggestion received at the hands

---

¹ L.'s next exhibition did not actually come on until December 1937, at the Leicester Galleries. His physical difficulties, continuing through a final operation in 1936, prevented him from getting a sufficient number of pictures ready earlier.

² Mrs. Mitchison wrote to L. saying that she couldn't get a weekly to let her review his book of poems, *One-Way Song*: "I don't think any of them think that women are fit to review poetry."

³ Frank Morley, then with Faber and Faber, publishers of *One-Way Song*.

of the gentlemen credits them with *too* little commonsense: for the fact that there are women – and one not very far away from this piece of paper as you are reading it – who are themselves able to throw a pretty practiced leg over the back of the good nag Pegasus, and *therefore* not the *least* competent to report upon the equestrian feats of others – must be known to even such cattle as Ellis R. or the Week-End editor!

Yours ever, W. L.

203. *To the Editor of "New Britain," December 13, 1933*[1]

"ONE WAY SONG"

Respecting the identity of the "victims" of the Grand Number One of *Engine Fight Talk* in *One Way Song*, and Mr. Herbert Palmer's very interesting speculations regarding the same, I had better state at once, to put an end to a tense situation, that no *personalities* whatever were intended.[2] Minds in general, not certainly any particular group of partisans, were the objects of that puppet's diatribe – though I exonerate Mr. Palmer from any intention of embroiling me with the seventeen poets he mentions, and am quite sure that owing to my evil reputation, he was genuinely misled! Of course I know that the group of writers called *New Signatures* is advertised as making use of the imagery provided by machines: and now and then, I believe I have noticed, they do mention a clutch or a jog-stick. But that is a mere genuflexion in the direction of Moscow, I assume. Stephen Spender – to take one of them, and (to my mind at least) one of the most distinguished of that brilliant coterie – is as innocent of such industrial *bric-a-brac* as was Wordsworth himself, or Chaucer

[1] A review of *One-Way Song* by Herbert Palmer appeared in *New Britain* for November 29th, 1933. The following week, Palmer wrote a letter to the paper expatiating on the victims of L.'s verse attack.

[2] In his review Palmer says that the first part of the book, the part titled "Engine Fight Talk," is "quite clearly a parody and mocking criticism of the team poets of *New Signatures* and *New Country*." In his letter Palmer excluded certain of these "team poets" from L.'s disapproval. "The poets Wyndham Lewis has most prominently parodied and burlesqued," he said, "are Stephen Spender, Day Lewis, and Auden."

for that matter. England has (unlike Russia or Italy) been industrialized for far too long for our people to be able to get any particular kick out of a bolt or a rivet. (We do *not* want, I take it – that is all – daisies and buttercups.) On the other hand, in the second part of Engine Fight Talk I had in mind a concrete somebody – no less a person than my old crony Ezra Pound and those he has influenced: but that was with reference to an *opposite* tendency, namely, an exploitation of the very picturesque local-colour of the *past*, and his notion that this should, with our present, "have a simultaneous existence and compose a simultaneous order". Those snobbish baubles dived for by the scholar, silver-lip shells and those of the Smoky Beard, are pretty enough, but in the end they are as tiresome a *bric-a-brac* as the iron-filings and scrap-iron of the fake factory school – though no one has made a better use of the ocean bed of time (where everything has suffered a sea change into something sumptuous and odd, however commonplace when it came to kick the bucket) than the indefatigable Ezra: and I should be one of his best customers, like my friend Mr. Eliot, were not my tastes a little austerely "classical"!

WYNDHAM LEWIS

204. *To Hugh Gordon Porteus*[1] 21. Chilworth St.
Dec. 20. [1933?]

My dear Portie. Excuse my silence. I was not here on Thursday. After the Christmas season let us arrange for a talk. Murry[2] I hear has a file of letters of yours of a most compromising sort. Why do you correspond with such facility with such crafty gush-bags? – The compliments of the season.

Yrs
W. L.

[1] Author of *Wyndham Lewis: A Discursive Exposition* (London, 1932) and a close friend and ally of L.
[2] John Middleton Murry.

205. *To Naomi Mitchison*   Pall Mall Safe Deposit.
Feb. 11, 1934.

My dear Naomi, . . . your presence will shortly be indispensible.[1] As we are now neighbours, will you drop up one day very soon and get into contact with me? My studio is at   5, Scarsdale Studios, Allen St. High St, Kensington, W.8. but please remember to mention this *to nobody!* You got me a bit wrong the other day – I will straighten that out when we meet.[2] But the seeds of suspicion *must* be sown in the young, I mean the *sheltered* young – because of course the wind is *not* tempered etc. (all these misleading sententious scriptural proverbs ought to be kept out of their way too): de la Rochefoucauld is wiser than Solomon. Lane's *Arabian Nights*, Swift and Samuel Butler ought to be put into their little hands as early as possible. – But you know all this better than I do!

I am glad you saw *New Verse* and approved of the notice of my Song.[3] I am writing a group of small songs – but just at present, as you say, I have to keep my eye fixed on the easel and palette. Love and blessings!

                Yrs,

                W. L.

In the mid-1920's Lewis met Sir Nicholas Waterhouse (b. 1877), partner in the accounting firm of Price, Waterhouse, and his wife Audrey (d. 1945). Not long afterwards Lady Waterhouse, who was especially interested in the arts, enabled Lewis to bring out The Enemy *and* The Apes of God. *Her efforts were continued by her husband, who contributed with increasing regularity to Lewis's support. The amicable relationship between "Professor" (Lewis),*

[1] L. refers to his drawings for Mrs. Mitchison's *Beyond This Limit*.

[2] Mrs. Mitchison wrote to L.: "I did hate what you said about having to be suspicious of people . . . I don't believe it's permanently true. Equally I don't think that one is ever truthful with more than perhaps one or two people . . . ." She went on: "Nor do I think it means that one need teach suspect to the young who aren't yet unfolded and elaborate and can still be truthful to themselves and others."

[3] Mrs. Mitchison commented on the "intelligent review" of *One-Way Song* in *New Verse*.

"*Mov*" (*Lady Waterhouse*), and "*Docker*" (*Sir Nicholas*) *went on until the death of Lady Waterhouse and then of Lewis.*

206. *To Sir Nicholas Waterhouse*† 98 Baker Street,
London. W.1.
Feb 27. 34

Dear Docker. Here I am once more in a nursing home – it is an emergency, as on Sunday I began having a bad bleeding. Now tonight the surgeon (Mr. Millin?) thinks that it *may* be necessary to slit a little hole in my bladder to pull out a dried clot of blood. So just *in case* anything went wrong, I send you this, asking you to settle up immediate medical fees (incurred during last 10 days only) and to look after in any way you are able or it occurs to you, my very much loved wife, Gladys Anne (who, in that unhappy event, would send you this.)

Yrs ever

W. L.

(the A.).

207. *To Richard Aldington*† [London]
April 24. 1934.

My dear Aldington. I feel I ought not impose on your extreme generosity: and yet, the cheque[1] . . . will be so bloody useful and more than useful during the next few weeks, in obtaining for me convalescent *extras* – better and brighter invalid Port! – cream with my asparagus, and *really* new-laid eggs, in addition to settling a debt or two which otherwise would be demanded once a week with menaces – that I, *extremely gratefully*, accept it. . . . I shall not after all remain permanently broke!

The details re. places and hotels in the Dax-Pau district and in Spain will be very useful (also many thanks for the table of vintages!) and for the map.[2] I know Pau and Biarritz – from the

---

[1] Aldington sent L. £25 to help him during his illness.

[2] In his letter Aldington gave information about travelling on the Biscay Coast and in the Pyrenees, where L. was planning to go to recuperate.

former I went to Gavarnie, seven years ago now: and the trouble really might be about that district, Guyaume, that I am so attracted by mountains that I should find it impossible to remain practically at their feet. And the Atlantic would be another powerful magnet. (The only mountains I am proof against are the Alps. Indeed, to be within sight of them spoils the plain for me!) So Spain – with a day or two at some of the french places you name – might be the best.

Anyhow, wherever I go, I will communicate with you as soon as any residence promises some degree of permanence, so that we may perhaps meet, in the course of your tour. Later, I might go to study on the spot a few Central European problems – we might meet then, who knows. . . .

208. *To A. J. A. Symons* [London]
April. 29. [1934?]

My dear A. J. How dare you say "you dont know where to write to me" – what, I ask you, is SAFER than the PALL MALL SAFE DEPOSIT,[1] answer me that! However, expect me at the 1st Ed. Club in about a week, when my calves have filled out a bit more!

Yrs
W. L.

I can scarcely refrain from flying round as it is, but I am holding my muscles in leash [?], it is doctor's orders.

209. *To Sir Nicholas Waterhouse*† Pall Mall Safe Deposit
July 1. 1934.

Dear Docker. . . . As to what you say, obviously I should be *mad* to stop here in London, to work in a backroom in Bayswater, looking out upon a dirty tree, upon which washing is hung, if I could get away. I am afraid you must accept my word for it that I am not entirely up the pole – though I am certainly glued to the

[1] During this period L. often used the Pall Mall Safe Deposit as his address. Some of his friends were amused by this characteristic gesture of secrecy.

spectacle of the sooty Bayswater tree-trunk, festooned with the laundry of the lady in the basement-flat. – As to my health, since my cold it has not been quite so good. I get too little fresh air – I do not like sitting in the Park, and in any case I am working all day usually. But what I have to bear in mind is that I am not merely recovering from a couple of bad operations, but was ill for a year and a half off and on before that, with long spells in bed and much mental anguish. My convalescence has to be measured against that background. I think I am very well, under the circumstances. . . .

                              Yours
                            WYNDHAM LEWIS

210. *To Roy Campbell*†   Pall Mall Safe Deposit
                                              July 3rd. 1934.

Dear Campbell. I bought your book the other day[1] – I have been reading it and to be in touch with you again, as you speak in its pages, has been a great delight. Your father, the surgeon, seems to have been a great guy. Your stuff re. the literary rabble is first rate. As to your references to me, I feel ashamed to be there with that *Snooty* emanation of mine, as one of those bent on consigning you to Nirvana, but otherwise feel a proud man to find myself treated with so much magnificence.[2] – I have seen Greenwood,[3] who showed me a bundle of excellent notices – I hope it will have a correspondingly good sale. Now that I am through with my health troubles, I feel something should be done about a paper. A paper is a waste of time, but I am not sure, if you do not waste time in one way you do not have to waste still more in another. Tell me one thing – if I were on the french-spanish border (between Perpignan and Gerona) would it be possible for us to meet somewhere in Spain? I have to go for a holiday in a week or two (I had intended to get away earlier) and I have made no plans. The South of Spain would be too hot I expect, but I had thought I might go to the Pyrenees. – Are you living on the same

  [1] *Broken Record*, Campbell's first autobiography.
  [2] Campbell refers to L. many times in the book and states his admiration for *The Childermass*.
  [3] C. J. Greenwood, director of Boriswood, Ltd., publisher of *Broken Record*.

lines as at Martigues?¹ Have you rented a house? Is the country round about mountains, plains, or what? I came into Alicante on my way to Oran (in Algiers) but I could see nothing of the city from the steamer. Write me a line soon. Your "Life" is great – I have not read it all yet, but it is written in the way a Life should be. Only you should do more of it, especially the African part.

Yours ever,

211. *To Desmond Flower*²   Pall Mall Safe Deposit.
July 19. 1934.

Dear Desmond Flower. I'm sorry the title cant be changed to *Literary Barrens* too, but if things have gone as far as you say we must have *Men Without Art* after all. So be it. As to the 'rubber shop', I will find a less robustious simile than that certainly³ .... As to the "rich man's crime", it has always been *crime* in the mouth of song-birds I have heard, and 'crime' is I think funnier than 'whim' a little. So let us leave crime.⁴ (Anything else you spot let me know). . . .

Yours sincerely
WYNDHAM LEWIS

¹ Campbell moved to Altea, Alicante, in 1934.
² Desmond Flower (b. 1907) was at this time a director of Cassell Ltd., which began to publish L. in 1932. In addition to L.'s book of literary criticism *Men Without Art* (1934), Cassell brought out *Snooty Baronet* (1932) and *The Revenge for Love* (1937).
³ The simile occurred evidently in a passage in which L. criticises I. A. Richards's ideas of belief and sincerity in literature. The printed sentences read as follows: "Here we see it [sincerity], in Mr. Richards's account, as a sort of *impotence to believe*. These 'means for inducing and promoting it' smack of specifics for more enterprising virility, Pelmanism, or other props for the will or fillips for the senses proper to a shell-shocked society." See *Men Without Art*, p. 88.
⁴ ". . . *all* the moral values of 'honest,' or of 'good,' necessarily came into contempt, as belonging to a vulgar order of servant-girl superstition, as it were.
She was poor, but she was honest,
Victim of a rich man's crime."
Men Without Art, p. 81.

212. *To Denys Kilham Roberts*[1]   Pall Mall Safe Deposit
                                        Oct. 9th 1934.
Dear Mr. Roberts.

Thank you for your very typical lawyerly epistle. You evidently know far more than I do about the clauses in my agreements with my publishers – I am quite unaware of the existence of such a clause in my agreement with Fabers as that brought forward in your letter. But if it is there, I did not put it there, nor was it put there at my request. It certainly was not inserted by me, as you are good enough to imply – *because I have been so much sought after by anthologists* that I simply *had* to protect myself against the nuisance by providing my agreements with such clauses. As I told you (but you are evidently not susceptible to the accents of truth – with you, as with a deaf man, one has to repeat everything twice) I have not only – until you – never been troubled by anthologists: I have never appeared in any anthology, of any sort, nor been asked to do so. – These are matters of business, as you will understand: and that I should be excluded for so long from such collections has no doubt kept money out of my pocket which otherwise would have been in it, and so freed me to do much work I have been prevented from doing.

Your retort, and its implications, are just a usual lawyers lies, to turn the tables (with your "What puzzles me") on the half-witted artist. "If you are not the object of the flattering attentions of anthologists, why have such a clause?" you ask. But that would not go down even in a court of law – for there is the massed evidence of the anthologies, where you will not find my name. This was especially remarked on, even by the distinguished Italian critic, Carlo Linati, in his book about contemporary English and American Literature, published a year or two ago.[2]

But lastly, with regard to this anthology-clause, I have some reason to assume – am I not right in supposing? – that if Messrs Fabers thought of handing out a page of my long poem to some anthologist, that they would, without showing any exaggerated

---

[1] Denys Kilham Roberts (b. 1903), Barrister-at-Law and Secretary-General of the Incorporated Society of Authors, Playwrights and Composers, was co-editor of the series of anthologies titled *The Year's Poetry*, which first appeared in 1934. He wrote to L. asking for permission to include a selection from *One-Way Song*.

[2] *Scrittori anglo americani d'oggi* (Milan, 1932).

consideration for the humble author of same, acquaint him, *in good time*, with what they proposed doing, and in what sort of galère they proposed dropping it. – So much, my dear sir, for your "natural inference" that I did "not want to be bothered with applications from anthologists" etc.

May I finally add, in response to your concluding remarks, that I for my part should hardly address myself to you or your associates, if I wished for information regarding the "best" poems of the year. It is as well, I think, that, "very definitely", you do not promise the public any *qualitative* principle of that order.

Yours very truly
WYNDHAM LEWIS

213. *To Hugh Gordon Porteus* [London]
Oct. 11. 1934.

My dear Portie! I have just seen your review in the *Listener*[1] & I really think you have justified yourself as my official reviewer! Many thanks for the review, and in any case it was a very good piece of work. What is the opinion of the Town – as we are being Dix huitieme siecle[2] – about my Artless Men? Any hard feelings? Where are you? I have been very busy moving house – for seven weeks now.

Yrs sincerely
WYNDHAM LEWIS

214. *To the Editor of "The Spectator," November 2, 1934*

THE CRITICISM OF MR. WYNDHAM LEWIS

Sir, – The reiterated statement in a book-review (namely that of October 19th, by Mr. Stephen Spender) that the literary criticism

---

[1] Porteus reviewed *Men Without Art* for *The Listener* of October 10th, 1934.
[2] There are many references to the eighteenth century in the review. The conclusion reads in part: "Mr. Lewis is simply a man with the best virtues of the bigger eighteenth-century figures, fastidious, penetrating, aloof but unpretentious."

contained in *Men Without Art* is "malicious" – specifically that I "attack" Mrs. Woolf with "a great deal of malice" – compels me to reply, since the phraseology can scarcely be unconsidered or accidental, seeing that "malice" in England does not signify the same thing as *malicieux* in France. So it is the principle of free speech that I am defending as well as myself. Handicapped as we are under a super-individualist legislation – which allows the utmost licence in criticism of the State, in contradistinction to the Individual – it should be a matter of honour, among writers, at least, to refrain from taking advantage of these oppressive laws. I should indeed be "suffocated by Mrs. Woolf" (to quote from a very muddled sally of Mr. Spender's)[1] – though in no other sense that I could imagine – were I to be threatened with the policeman should I happen to mention her *Lighthouse* with disrespect! And others would be "suffocated" by me, if, referring to my *Paleface* with disapproval, the same threat were levelled at them.

Mrs. Woolf appears to be the principal difficulty for Mr. Spender. But in *Men Without Art* I have everywhere stressed that my criticisms are rather a writer's than a reader's. It is the internal creative *machinery* that I expose: not the footlight illusion of the *prima donna*, so much as the latter in process of slimming, voice-production, and make-up. Criticism of this nature is "destructive", of necessity, from the standpoint of pure publicity – especially where a reputation is so flimsy as to be peculiarly susceptible of "destruction".

Of Mr. Hemingway I said, as I was bound to do, that he had lifted intact, for his rather different he-man purposes, the early manner of Miss Stein. But in doing that I was "at my best", it seems:[2] I was behaving with critical decorum (though Mr. Hemingway, I suppose, might hold another opinion, in this respect, to that of Mr. Spender or Mrs. Woolf). But when I refer to the obvious imitation of episodes in *Ulysses* to be met with in *Mrs. Dalloway*, then I am showing "a great deal of malice."[3]

---

[1] Spender takes L. to task for complaining of the "suffocating atmosphere" of Bloomsbury and at the same time objecting to Virginia Woolf's feeling "suffocated by Messrs. Bennett, Wells and Galsworthy." See *The Spectator*, October 19th, 1934, pp. 574–6.

[2] Spender says L. is at his best in his attacks on Hemingway and Faulkner.

[3] "... often the incidents in the local 'masterpieces' are exact and

But this is absurd. Anyone has a right to their opinion of the books of Mrs. Woolf – as also of those of Mr. Roy Campbell: though both these rights are denied me by Mr. Spender. To admire Mr. Campbell's books "does little credit to one's taste," I am told: whereas *not* to admire overmuch those of Mrs. Woolf is simply "malicious".

My reason for assuming that my misdemeanour, in the case of Mrs. Woolf, can only relate to my references to *Mrs. Dalloway*, is that afterwards I am so paradoxically accused of "appropriating" Mr. Eliot's – of all people's – criteria (which is self-evident I could not do if I wished, seeing how greatly I differ from him).[1] But I fail completely to follow the sensitiveness on the score of Mrs. Woolf's "originality" displayed by *all* her supporters. Mr. Ezra Pound – a literary figure as much esteemed as Mrs. Woolf – has, for example, never disguised the fact that he is mainly a translator – an adapter, an arranger, a *pasticheur*, if you like. And Mr. T. S. Eliot has even made a virtue of developing himself into an incarnate Echo, as it were (though an *original* Echo, if one can say that). This imitation method, of the *creator-as-scholar* – which may be traced ultimately to the habits of the American university, spellbound by "culture" – and which academic *un-originality* it was Mr. Ezra Pound's particular originality to import into the adult practice of imaginative literature – does not appeal to me extremely, I confess. But at least no amateurish touchiness on the score of "originality" is involved in it.

Mrs. Woolf is charming, scholarly, intelligent, everything that you will: but here we *have* not a Jane Austen – a Felicia Hemans, rather, as it has been said: for there are some even more "malicious" than I am, I am afraid. Would not anybody, to conclude, in reading Mr. Spender's article, come away with the impression that, as quoted by him, my quip of "taking the cow by the horns"

puerile copies of the scenes in his [Joyce's] Dublin drama (cf. the Viceroy's progress through Dublin in *Ulysses* with the Queen's progress through London in *Mrs. Dalloway* – the latter is a sort of undergraduate imitation of the former, winding up with a smoke-writing in the sky, a pathetic 'crib' of the firework display and the rocket that is the culmination of Mr. Bloom's beach-ecstasy)." *Men Without Art*, p. 168.

[1] Spender writes: "Why when in one chapter he ridicules the criticism of Mr. T. S. Eliot, is he content in later chapters to appropriate his critical conclusions?"

referred to Mrs. Woolf?[1] Yet the same reader, should he turn to p. 170 of my book, where the expression occurs, immediately would discover that this expression refers to the Feminine Principle – specifically stated as equally belonging to those "not technically on the distaff side" – and not to any individual, whether Mrs. Woolf or another.

I am, Sir, etc.

WYNDHAM LEWIS

215. *To the Editor of "The Times Literary Supplement,"*
November 29, 1934

MR. LEWIS AND MR. MURRY

Sir, – In a two-column review in your issue of November 22 it has been my signal honour to be bracketed with Mr. Middleton Murry, as a "leader" of an opposite faction[2] – of an inferior and in every way less satisfactory faction, it would seem: one as confused and irrational as the other is exquisitely lucid and married to sweet reasonableness. Mr. Murry is a Communist – *I am not!* This was the crux of the matter. *Not* to be a Communist is my sin; *to be* a Communist is Mr. Murry's merit: "that is his significance," your reviewer says,[3] and he leaves it in no doubt that *my* significance, or rather insignificance, is to be sought in my non-Communism: for in other ways, as far as a non-Communist may be that, I am "a highly significant figure."

... That your reviewer is a Communist – or perhaps someone so

---

[1] The passage in the review reads in part: "This common-sense point of view is doubtless salubrious, though it provides no real answer to Mrs. Woolf. ... After more hits at Miss Sitwell, Mrs. Woolf, Mr. E. M. Forster and everything he labels Bloomsbury, Mr. Lewis concludes: 'It has been with considerable shaking in my shoes that I have taken the cow by the horns in this chapter.'"

[2] *Men Without Art* was coupled with *Middleton Murry: A Study in Excellent Normality*, by Rayner Heppenstall, in the review titled "Mr. Lewis and Mr. Murry" in the *Times Literary Supplement* of November 22nd, p. 822.

[3] "... Mr. Murry appears as one who has found his way from intellectual bankruptcy to something at least positive (that is his significance), Mr. Lewis as one still bogged in his condition (that, regarded in its consequences, is his)."

highly sympathetic with Communism as to be more Marxist than Marx himself, which is often the way of it – remains in no doubt. This is, in short, a review about a novelist – the author of "Tarr," the "Apes of God," the "Childermass," &c. – by a Marxian sectary. And great as is my respect for the *Literary Supplement* of *The Times* (and for its parent paper, the premier newspaper of Great Britain – standing as it does for the traditional strength and stability of what is still, in spite of everything, the most powerful State in the world), I cannot, with all the humility that is appropriate in a mere "author," refrain from drawing your attention to the very urgent problem that this review admirably serves to illustrate.

That a member of the Society of Jesus would not be an appropriate person to choose to do a review of a reprint of Darwin's Works is obvious – or that any good Catholic, even, would be incompetent to review the novels of a notorious agnostic, that also is plain enough. But surely a Communist or Marxist is disqualified in much the same way, for the purposes of "literary" review. Communism is – as Mr. Murry apparently agrees – a religion: and a particularly bloodthirsty and persecutory one at that.

Now in the past I have perfectly understood that a good deal of hostile criticism that came my way was inspired by political intolerance, but at the time people in general had little understanding of the violence of the political forces at work just beneath their heels. To-day it is otherwise – it is unnecessary for me to mention, even, the strong *Leftish* political colouration of so much of the newest poetry, of the majority of intelligent periodicals.

... in the European world of art in the last half-decade more than one prominent writer or painter has undoubtedly suffered in consequence of his non-adherence to Communism. I need only mention, in the field of painting, the Italian Chirico (as fine a painter as Pirandello is a dramatist), and in the literary field Mr. Aldous Huxley, whose "Brave New World" was an unforgivable offence to Progress and to political uplift of every description.

That this matter is of far-reaching and urgent importance – that the very existence of an art existing upon the same direct, truth-telling, terms as science, an art non-standardized, and reasonably free, is at stake – this alone has prompted me to write this letter, which, I hope, may serve as a first step towards an exposure of this situation, daily growing more intolerable for those who are non-orthodox.

       Yours,

          WYNDHAM LEWIS

216. *To Herbert Read*   Pall Mall Safe Deposit
              Dec. 7th. 1934.

My dear Read. I must apologise for not answering your letter sooner: much business has prevented me. That you had written the review in question was very hard to believe.[1] But one claiming first-hand information assured me that my incredulity was contradicted by facts. However you *did not*, which is the main thing, and I am delighted to hear it: also to know that you have read *Men Without Art*, and like it. That is most excellent news. I was afraid that perhaps my nautical similes might have seemed a little over-fresh to you.

 Some day I will ask you, when you have time, to tell me what you mean by my "negative" attitude. (In the masked "Reviewer's" answer in the *T.L.S.* correspondence columns today I see the word "negative" employed).[2] It is a genuine obtuseness on my part. When, in the review, Murry's "conversion to communism" is mentioned, for instance,[3] I am tempted to ask conversion *from* what? Is all that is not communism "negative" (just as for a catholic not to accept the dogmas of his "universal" church is to be "negative")? Is communism, a shoddily built

[1] L. had queried Read as to his possible authorship of the review of *Men Without Art* in the *Times Literary Supplement*.

[2] Rebuttals from "The Reviewer" and J. Middleton Murry appeared in the *Times Literary Supplement* of December 6th. Both writers disclaimed L.'s attribution to them of "Moscow" Communism. Murry called himself "a democratic Socialist." The Reviewer wrote: "I am neither 'a Marxian sectary' nor 'a Communist....'" He went on to speak, as he did in his review, of "the inadequacies . . . of his [L.'s] negative view of art." Again he accused L. of "refusing to move forward from that negative condition of intellectual bankruptcy."

[3] The review says of Heppenstall's book: "It gives the essence of Mr. Murry's development . . . summarizing . . . his view of the psychological inadequacy of the medieval (that is, the Catholic) synthesis and the necessary conditions of a new: and the relation of this new synthesis . . . to his 'conversion' to Communism."

transitory, or 'transitional', shack (as I see it) – is it so "positive"? Was the typical artist of the anti-religionist Renaissance "negative" (say da Vinci?) Are the Chinese, because they have at all times shown themselves less prone to fanatical emotionality, of a religious order, than have the Semites and the Anglo-saxons – have they been "negative" always, because on the whole laodicean, philosophic, and preoccupied with external beauty? I am all at sea as you perceive! This string of questions is not an *Answer me that!* sort of interrogatory drumfire (as it must a little appear). It is a groping for a something that remains hidden to me. – When you have time drop me a line and enlighten me.[1]

Yours ever
WYNDHAM LEWIS

P.S. *Jesus, Keats, Shakespeare and Marx Ltd* are a great firm, aren't they?[2] (Though Marx comes last on the note paper, it is he that has the *cash*). Though what a german-jewish economist, who is very out-of-date anyway, has to do with the *Ode to the Grecian Urn*, or *Troilus and Cressida*, I am sure I should never be able to fathom – though I suppose it is a case of two minds with but one thought – I. A. Richards, "saving" the world with poetry being the other.[3] (It is that Murryish streak in Richards that made me dislike his utterances from the first. Eliot was – blissfully – oblivious to the resemblance – until today he is going-Murry a little himself, God bless him! though of course he may have been that all along).

[1] Read wrote to L. at length on December 9th. He said that he saw the liberty of the artist "threatened from every side," and that of the threats he preferred communism, because "they are on the side of abstract intellectual ideals as opposed to the instinctive irrational prejudices of the other side." As for aesthetics, Read wrote that he too preferred the external approach. But in thinking of art as "a pure game," L., he said, ran together two incompatibles – the game "directly arising out of our functions of sight, hearing and so forth" and the game arising out of our functions "as trained social animals."

[2] See letter of December 20th.

[3] In his reply Read called "Richards' theory of harmonious impulses" "psychological salvationism!"

217. *To John Grey Murray*†¹   Pall Mall Safe Deposit
[December 1934]

Dear Mr. Murray. . . . Have you seen the enclosed letter in the T.L.S.² What is one to say to a man who asserts that his "religion" is Keats and Marx (with the 'historical Jesus' thrown in);³ or who is a communist when provided with "safeguards", which turn out to be synonymous with *sympathy*, I think: rather as a man might say "you may not call me a *conservative* – you must call me an *independent* – unless you subscribe to the tenets of Disraelian democracy. In the latter case of course you may call me a conservative as much as you like!" I have to answer these letters I suppose – I wish that they were not so stupid it makes one feel a fool, to be dealing with such stuff in the serious manner required of one.

Yours sincerely,

218. *To the Editor of the "New Statesman & Nation,"*
   *December 15th, 1934*⁴

Sir. People who live in glass-houses invariably throw stones, that is the law of nature; all the same, Miss Sitwell has built such a really enormous glass-house for herself in *Aspects of Modern Poetry* that when that big stiff of a brother of hers butted in and

---

¹ Partner in John Murray, publishers. He was interested in a book L. was proposing to do on art and industry.
² Murry's rebuttal of December 6th.
³ See letter of December 20th.
⁴ A controversy over Edith Sitwell's *Aspects of Modern Poetry* had been raging in the *New Statesman* since a review of the book by G. W. Stonier appeared in the paper on November 24th. The main participants were, on one side, Stonier, H. Sydney Pickering, and Geoffrey Grigson – all of whom pointed to Miss Sitwell's borrowings and inaccuracies – and, on the other side, Miss Sitwell and her brother Osbert. In the issue of December 8th Osbert Sitwell wrote, in defending his sister's indebtedness to other critics: "Must every writer be original in his facts; as original, for example, as Mr. Percy Wyndham Lewis, Mr. Stonier's God? In his last book this venerable artist informs us, that Inigo Jones 'had to whistle' for the bill due for the construction of Blenheim Palace: and indeed, why not? . . . Inigo Jones died in 1652; the building of Blenheim began in 1705; but perhaps it was a golden harp and not a whistle, after all?"

discharged a brick at me (a brick from the Palace of the Churchills), I was, for a moment, dumbfounded at his consummate effrontery. I do not know the date of the death of Inigo Jones. But there is one thing about which I am absolutely positive: namely, that it is not 1652 – since a member of the Sitwell family gives it as such! That, I think we can now all agree, is conclusive. The same of course applies to the building of Blenheim. – There is another thing. That Osbert and myself should wag our greybeard-noddles at each other in public defiance is setting a bad example, undoubtedly, to the youthies – to the plump little budding Osberts and just-weaned winsome Wyndhams:[1] but expostulate I must to this extent – Have not I alone, of all critics, refrained from insisting upon misquotations and all that? Did I not quite pass that over in my review of Edith's *Aspects*?[2] And *this* is what I get in return! I cannot suppress a reproachful wag or two! – *Ingrat!* no wonder I exclaim! – Yes, I confined myself – when I came to write of this rococo palace of blunder, this wax-works divided into "giants" before whom you abase yourself, and sots or desperadoes at whose effigies you spit and jeer – to the rather amusing *Circus* aspect of the performance. I tried to bring out the truly disarming picture of these incorrigibly "naughty", delicately shell-shocked, wistfully age-complexed, wartime Peter Pans – dragging out of their old kit-bags for the thousandth time their toy "great men" (about whom they go girlishly lyrical, and cover with a cheap varnish of unreality); their Aunt Sallies; their aviary of love-birds, toucans and tomtits; their droned-out nursery-melodies, accompanying the plunges of the old rocking-horses. A bit sad, a thought dreary, like all circuses that have survived – dominated, this one, by the rusty shriek of the proprietress: all *that* I did my best to bring out and to make people forget the constant and alas! symptomatic lapses of memory occurring in the patter, the placards upside down – letters missing from the gilt blazoning of the announcement, making nonsense as often as not. For this trio *does* "belong to the history of publicity rather than that of poetry" (*cf.* Dr. Leavis): and would you expect Milton to be correctly quoted in an advertisement for Massage or Male-corsets – or

---

[1] L. refers to a long-standing source of dissension: his indictment of the Sitwells at participants in the "youth cult" and Osbert Sitwell's retaliatory jibes at L.'s own seniority – *e.g.*, "venerable artist."

[2] "Sitwell Circus," *Time and Tide*, November 17th, 1934.

Gerard Manley Hopkins to appear without printer's errors in a blurb recommending the tired pirouettes of a Society authoress? It would be unreasonable. It would be asking far too much of everybody concerned.

Yrs etc.
WYNDHAM LEWIS

Hyde Park.[1]

219. *To the Editor of "The Times Literary Supplement,"*
  December 20th, 1934.

MR. LEWIS AND MR. MURRY

Sir, – . . . Mr. Murry falls back upon the good old firm of "Jesus, Blake, Keats and Marx"[2] – Marx comes last on the notepaper, but it is he who has all the cash! (And, of course, the economic factor is pretty important in this connexion, for all non-Communists belong to a "bankrupt" order, it seems: invariably the word "bankrupt" is employed in discussing those without the Marxist fold by these – platonists and Social Democrats!)[3] It is scarcely necessary for me to say what I think of this fantastic hagiolatry, but I suppose I should make some reply. – "Communism is a religion," says Mr. Murry.... But Mr. Murry adapts this religion for the sentimental Anglo-Saxon, that is the idea, by adding to Marx the "historical Jesus" (Christ without God); the author of the "Ode to the Grecian Urn," Johnny Keats; also Sweet Will; also the British Old-Testament prophet, Blake. It is a kindred piece of buffoonery, or such, under correction, it seems to me, to Mr. I. A. Richards' "Salvation of the World by Poetry." There is no God. *Man* is the God; or, to be specific, particularly such men as an extremely out-of-date German-Jewish economist, an English nineteenth-century romantic poet of great "genius," as

[1] Osbert Sitwell wrote from his fashionable Chelsea address.
[2] In his letter to the *Times Literary Supplement* of December 6th, Murry wrote: "I was quite accurately described both by your reviewer and Mr. Heppenstall as the adherent of a Marxism which owes 'as much to Blake and to Jesus, to Shakespeare and to Keats .... as to Marx.'"
[3] See letter to Read of December 7th, note 2. L.'s *platonists* refers also to the reviewer's letter of December 6th, in which he claimed to be "as far from any brand of 'Moscow' Communism as – shall I say? – Plato."

we say – who turned his "gallipot" into a "Grecian Urn"; and, of course, the author of *Troilus and Cressida*. Shakespeare, Keats, Blake, and as many more poets as you happen to admire are susceptible of *religious* treatment, as much as Marx or Mr. Keynes. And this cocktail is none the worse if you throw in the "historical Jesus." It is by no means easy to understand how this strange rubbish gets past anyone liable to read publications of a more elevated order than Sexton Blake;[1] indeed, is it not where William Blake and Sexton Blake appear to kiss (such a monstrous conjugation *is* possible – Mr. Murry has proved it.), in an orgy of fulsome uplift?

WYNDHAM LEWIS

220. *To Naomi Mitchison*   21 Chilworth St, W. 2.
December 28, 1934

Today is the Feast of the
Innocents – Childermass!

My dear Naomi. I am back – a few days disagreeable blank & I am working hard again. Today I took a few of the drawings to Howard to get the work started.[2] ... He says the blocks of the whole 30 will take *one week* to make. So that will be well *inside the limit!* – the limit in this case being your transatlantic *ticket!*[3] – I am certain you will like the stuff when you see it altogether. Tonight I am doing you a little duck of a drawing of the winged maidens in flight. It will be a capital set. ... Next week we shall have to consult. ...

Yours ever
W. L.

...

[1] *The Sexton Blake Library*, twopenny boys' weekly featuring a detective character called Sexton Blake, later taken over by the *Detective Weekly*. See George Orwell, "Boys' Weeklies," *A Collection of Essays* (New York, 1954).

[2] On *Beyond This Limit*, which Jonathan Cape was publishing. G. Wren Howard was Joint Managing Director of the firm.

[3] Mrs. Mitchison was going to the United States.

221. *To Richard Aldington*†   Paddington. W.2.
[Summer 1935]

My dear Aldington. Your Tobago letter[1] hid itself a few hours after I received it and it is still in hiding! But I now hear . . . that you are in New York. As however this letter may never reach you, I will be brief – I am being slowly suffocated – quite literally – here in London. The objectionable damp heat beggars description. But for some weeks yet I must stop on: as I am writing a big book,[2] and must not move till it is finished. Everything has been put aside, for some time now to get this new book (fiction) done.

I have been delightfully immersed in the lives of Etta and Georgina[3] and when I am through with my present work shall write whatever occurs to me about all your books (as part of a new volume of criticism).[4] Recently I have read a good few contemporary English novels, and I have a very high opinion of *The Colonels Daughter* indeed, which I think brings into focus several faculties which are not met with elsewhere. In this short letter I will only say one thing to you – stammer it out on the wing! as I feel it may perhaps be useful if I say it. It is this. The difference in the quality of the writing is so marked between *Women Must Work* and *The Colonels Daughter* (and the reason for that you can account no doubt, whereas I of course cannot) that I think you should put this before yourself as an article of faith: never to write a page of fiction of a less high standard in the *writing*, than you have achieved in the history of the Smithers family. I hope this advice will not seem presumptuous to you. I am not running down the Etta book which contains a great deal of excellent stuff. In some ways the subject is more interesting than the *C.'s Daughter*. – But this is to be a brief message and already I have been led into a couple of pages of perhaps impertinent exhortation I find! The Poems[5] are a revelation to me of what

[1] Aldington wrote to L. March 26th, 1935, from Tobago, where he was staying.
[2] *The Revenge for Love*.
[3] Etta Morison, heroine of Aldington's *Women Must Work* (London, 1934), and Georgina Smithers, heroine of *The Colonel's Daughter* (London, 1931).
[4] This project was abandoned.
[5] *The Poems of Richard Aldington* (London, 1934).

you can do in that line and I shall write you, as soon as I know where you are, about them. What reception have the poems had?...

Yours ever,

222. *To Richard Aldington*†   Paddington. W.2.
[Perhaps not sent.]   Sept. 3. 1935.

My dear Aldington. A brief note only today, to say I have received your letter and am delighted to hear you are having such a satisfactory time in New York. Your american manor-house in Connecticut sounds to me an even more desirable residence than your plantation-quarters in Tobago. – I perfectly understand the nature of your troubles with Eliot.[1] With him, you would find yourself opposing the Virginian, american, values of the grandsons of the Marquis of Esmond, to our Tom's version of the Earl of Castlewood![2] But I am on the side of the Virginians every time! You will not find me unappreciative of the heroic values when I come to write, say, of "Anthony".[3] Though as to style, ah there – to continue the Esmonds – I am as particular as Baroness Bernstein herself;[4] *toisant* a new book, to see if it possesses, in fact, the *bel air*. Nothing is anything without the *manner*. But that you do not require me to tell you. —— Meanwhile, cleave to that Choctaw integrity and simplicity, – pay no attention to that intellectual Macaroni, T.S.E. . . . .

[1] Aldington's essay "The Poetry of T. S. Eliot" appeared in his *Literary Studies and Reviews* (London, 1924). The "troubles with Eliot" to which L. refers were doubtless of a more recent date.
[2] See *Henry Esmond*.
[3] Perhaps L. refers to Aldington's *All Men are Enemies* (London, 1933). The hero of the novel is called Antony Clarendon.
[4] See *The Virginians*.

223. To the Editor of "The Observer," February 2, 1936[1]

London

MR. ERVINE AND THE POETS

Sir, – In Mr. St. John Ervine's articles about the Peevish Pink Poets he has succeeded in conveying the impression (whether inadvertently or because of some confusion in his own mind) that everybody who has rather unconventional tastes in art is a "bolshie" – all except Mr. MacNeice, who somehow succeeds in squaring the circle, and in being at once a law-abiding citizen and a rebel to prosodic law.[2]

Mr. Ervine is very contemptuous about "obscurity", and that is one thing: and he is very contemptuous about Communism, and that is another thing. A difficult author – Mallarmé, Henry James or Hopkins – would be no hero in Russia today. Indeed it should be self-evident that "difficulty" (that is, highly individualised expression) must be regarded not only as anti-popular, but, since useless for purposes of propaganda, a sort of affront like an idle man.

As to "The Arts Today", the book that was responsible for this polemic, it is *not*, as the casual reader of Mr. Ervine's articles

---

[1] This letter is a late entry in a controversy that began in *The Observer* of December 29th, 1935, with a denunciation of the "angry young poets" by St. John Ervine. In his weekly column Ervine chose Auden and MacNeice as his specific targets and charged them both with unintelligibility. The following week Geoffrey Grigson, who was publishing these poets in *New Verse* and had just edited *The Arts To-day*, which included contributions from Auden and MacNeice, retaliated, branding Ervine a reactionary and a philistine. A small battle of the books was on. Ervine stated his case for the old guard in a series of three articles titled "Our Peevish Poets," the first appearing on January 12th. Edith Sitwell, finding an opportunity to vent her animus against Grigson, leaped into the fray on January 19th. In her letter of the following week she announced her discovery that "Mr. Grigson is the perfectly genuine if very small rabbit that, after years of producing nothing but clouds of bats from the belfry, Mr. Percy Wyndham Lewis has at length succeeded in producing from under his hat." It was no doubt this remark – plus his looming large in two sections of *The Arts To-day* – that caused L. to write.

[2] In "Our Peevish Poets" Ervine approved MacNeice's dissociating himself, in *The Arts To-day*, from the communism of Auden, Day Lewis, and Spender; but he criticised MacNeice's poetry along with that of the others.

might infer, a treatise on Marxist art – composed, say, for fireside reading at the Soviet Embassy. Had a "friend of Russia" been doing these articles instead of Mr. Ervine the reader would then most certainly have carried away the impression that Mr. Grigson's book was a piece of hideously "Fascist" special pleading. Where Mr. Ervine saw only a blur of red, the communard would have seen only a dark "reactionary" black – Mr. Wyndham Lewis, in other words, would have blotted out for him the pink songbirds!

Actually, Mr. Grigson is one of the few critics, among the young, who have not been chloroformed by salvationist politics. It is, after all, not his fault, that, except for MacNeice, all his swans are *red*.

Yours, etc.

WYNDHAM LEWIS

224. *To the Rev. M. C. D'Arcy, S.J.*   121 Gloucester Terrace.
Lancaster Gate. W. 2.
April. 14. 1936.

Dear D'Arcy. Gwynn Jones[1] has just been to see me and has been unfolding a scheme in which you, he tells me, are participating. Apart from the fact that I am exceedingly flattered at the part I shall be playing in it, I consider it a very sound plan to show up the "planners," in the manner suggested. Our talk was a very hurried one and I am not quite clear as to the details, but I gathered that the idea is to invite a few people to contribute something. Jones mentioned Porteus and Stonier,[2] for instance. Other names that suggest themselves to me are Roy Campbell, Douglas Jerrold,[3] Muggeridge,[4] Chesterton, Geoffrey Grigson (art critic of Morning Post), and perhaps T. S. Eliot. I will send on these names to Jones, but these are merest suggestions, especially

---

[1] Gwynn H. Jones, later an expert in industrial relations and connected with the Newspaper Society.

[2] G. W. Stonier (b. 1903), author of *Gog Magog and Other Essays* (London, 1933), which contains a critique of L.'s work.

[3] Douglas Jerrold (b. 1893), well-known Roman Catholic author and publisher.

[4] The journalist Malcolm Muggeridge (b. 1905).

as I do not know quite what is intended. At present I have a large (150 thousand word) novel[1] with a publisher with whom I have a "fiction" contract, but they consider some of my expressions too robust and a board of censors is sitting on it. I have just finished a large political book, which I have called *Bourgeois-Bolshevism and World War*.[2] My short novel *The Roaring Queen* is also now finished and Capes are doing it.[3] My political book is rather markedly anti-Leftwing and I do not know what the good old Liberal publisher who is at present examining it will decide.[4]
... Before long I shall be coming to Oxford to give a lecture (or preside at a dinner) and I shall greatly look forward to seeing you again. My health troubles took various grotesque and menacing forms successively, but I am now in good health and apparently none the worse for being knifed, gassed, and poisoned. ...

Yours sincerely
WYNDHAM LEWIS

225. *To Sir Nicholas Waterhouse*† [London]
[Perhaps not sent.] Aug. 10. 1936.

Dear Docker. I am out! And I must write despatch to thank you for the cheque for ten pounds which really did the trick. Only what brought me to my present pass was *the neglect and indifference*, on the part of the surgeon who did my first operation two years ago, *after I had come out of the nursing home*. ... I have suffered in the most awful way for that neglect. A few weeks intensive treatment at the right moment (2 years ago) and I should have required no second operation a fortnight ago – I should not have wasted a year of my life and endured every kind of anxiety and physical misery. – *Now* I appeal to you not to allow the beastly thing to repeat itself. My surgeon will not put

---

[1] *The Revenge for Love.*
[2] Published as *Left Wings over Europe: or, How to Make a War about Nothing* (London, 1936).
[3] Jonathan Cape withdrew the book before publication because of fear of libel actions. There are proof copies in the Houghton Library at Harvard and in the Lewis Collection at Cornell.
[4] Jonathan Cape published the book.

me solidly on the road to health if I do not pay him. . . . I cannot work at once, or only a little every day, for another two weeks. For nearly three months I have not been able to do so and have been helped along by very kind friends up to the present.

. . . As what he has just operated for is what has been (so he says) troubling me ever since those months of neglect 2 years ago, I should now be released for remunerative work (my big exhibition, for instance, which for two years has hung fire).

226. *To Mrs. Roy Campbell*   Lancaster Gate. W.2.
August 1936

Dear Mary Campbell. I should be delighted to come down,[1] but will next week some day be all right? . . . Will you, Roy C. and the family sit for a *family group*? If so I will bring some paper and pencils.[2] I plan a six foot canvas, and should, somewhat in the manner of Goya, put in a conventional rendering of Toledo[3] behind the figure group. Any bullfighting properties would be welcome. Are there any horses at Arundel? I might work in a few of them. Tell me what your reactions are to this proposal.

Yours
W. L.

227. *To Oliver Brown*†[4]   [London]
[Perhaps not sent.]   Oct 16. 1936.

Dear Brown. A bloodvessel will burst in my big toe if economic tension does not terminate. Returning home this afternoon, I found a wolf at the door, his teeth bared; next week is going to be awkward. The four things I have left —— to see are probably, as you suspect, not his cup of tea. Their quality, I know, is neither

---

[1] The Campbells were staying near Arundel in Sussex.

[2] L. did some sketches of Roy and Mary Campbell at this time but did not undertake a painting.

[3] The Campbells had recently come from Toledo, where they had been living.

[4] Partner in the Leicester Galleries, L.'s dealer for many years.

here nor there. I just *must* do nothing now but traditional pictures; beggars cant be choosers (and long illness is bitterly handicapping – I should not have put the last month into work of that sort.)

One relatively well-paid portrait – or two ill-paid ones – would as I said to you today settle all my illness-debts. We must rule out ——— – I feel now that he will not like any of the four pictures brought in today. – To hell with these experimental "difficult" contraptions, which only the Young and impecunious in England, like and which are hard to sell – I will do no more for six months, or until I am solvent. I will really do dreams of beauty, which will sell themselves, as I am bringing them down to the Gallery. This I mean, in sober earnest. Meanwhile do if you *can* help me out of this temporary trouble and find me a sitter, ——— or another as I suggested, (at a very reasonable rate) to free me of health-bills. Excuse this tumultuous communication.

228. *To Roy Campbell* Lancaster Gate.
Oct 25 1936

Dear Campbell. Excuse this delayed reply – I have been trying to get my hack-work finished up so that I could be certain of plenty of time to announce your portrait. . . . I gloried in the title of *Moscardó*.[1] You may rely on me to behave on all occasions in a manner in no way inferior to that of the "Eagle of Castille." Only I have already been beleaguered for at least 10 years! – Pay no more attention to bulletins about my health than you would to the Madrid radio reports of Francoist reverses. My machinery still requires some adjustments – would that it derived not from protoplasm but some straightforward *metal*. But my health is pretty good. . . . – My wife was stupefied with admiration, at your fine appearance. To meet you was a great event for her. She shares my cult for you. – Your collective farm hands must be feeling extremely dejected, as the tide of Marxist world-revolution

[1] In a letter declaring his concern over L.'s health, which had suffered another set-back, Campbell wrote: "Intellectually, you are Moscardó to the whole of Europe; and we cannot afford to lose you." General José Moscardó, of the Franco forces, was celebrated for his heroic defence of the Alcazar at Toledo. Campbell extolls him in his poetry of the period.

recedes, with a sickening hiss![1] How is the Juan March of Red Sussex?

All the best! Yours ever
W. L.

When you come up Mary C. must accompany you – with the dress you spoke of.

229. *To G. Wren Howard*†[2] [London]
[Perhaps not sent.] [November 1936]

Dear Wren Howard. Your letter (of Nov. . . .) has just arrived. I am if anything more astonished and puzzled by this last letter than by the first one. It is now quite evident that there is something in the book of which I myself am totally unaware.[3]

Both with yourself and with your colleague, Mr. Hamish Miles, I discussed, as in the nature of things I had to, the satiric content of the book. With the latter for instance, I discussed the question of the use of *the word* "Bloomsbury", so careful was I not to let myself in for difficulties. But Miles answered that "we do not mind about the *Bloomsburies*" and expressed surprise that I had dealt so gently with the "Bloomsbury" principle. There is, of course, no caricature of any *individual* "Bloomsbury" in the book.

Libels I did not discuss (nor did you, although you are at least as well acquainted as I am with the world I made fun of) because there is no libel there. But in any satire there is always the possibility – indeed almost the probability that someone or other (either with a grudge against the author, or with a keen business sense and desire to turn an honest penny) will come forward and

[1] Campbell had written accounts to L. of his difficulties in "Bolshevik Binstead," the Sussex locale of the farm owned by his Communist in-laws where he and Mrs. Campbell were staying.

[2] As a director of Jonathan Cape, G. Wren Howard had recently published L.'s *Left Wings Over Europe*.

[3] Howard had been writing to L. expressing his concern over possibilities of libel in *The Roaring Queen*, which satirises the contemporary book world and which Cape eventually withdrew before publication.

13. Portrait drawing of the Artist's Wife, 1936

claim financial compensation for an alleged "libel". What happens then? The publisher, in nine cases out of ten, refuses to go to the court with it, however ill-founded the charge. He just hands over money to the claimant, if necessary suppresses the book, and that is not only disagreeable for the publisher, but also for the author.

Under these circumstances, and since I myself have been a conspicuous sufferer in that matter, it is only natural that I should wish to have your *absolute assurance* that there was nothing in my book that you would not be prepared to stand by. . . .

Your letter, I need hardly say, is disingenuous. For to say in this particular case that you carefully read yourself and accept a book satirising the world in the midst of which you live – accept it in all good faith, so to speak – and then all of a sudden discover that it is swarming with atrocious libels, is plain nonsense.

At the very start it was open to you to refuse the book at sight: to say to me: "Look here, I know the business in which I am engaged has its anomalies and absurdities, like all walks of life, but I am after all engaged in it, and I dont propose to publish, satires about it. Besides, I might make myself unpopular with some of my eminent colleagues." That I should have entirely understood. Indeed, I told you that several publishers had refused it; that in the nature of things the *small* publisher would be afraid of publishing it for fear of offending his big colleagues, and that the big publisher would hardly feel very genial about it. You, on the other hand, were one of the 2 or 3 publishers in London who still stuck to a high standard of publishing, and so might do it: such had been my argument. The terms of the agreement I signed with you, on the economic side, were, as I pointed out, in conformity with this line of reasoning. Such a book, going to the "fiction-critic" for review, could not be expected to meet with a very cordial reception: the popular libraries could not be expected to coo over it: so its publisher could not be expected to pay anything to speak of for it.

230. *To Desmond Flower*† [London]
[Perhaps not sent.] [ca. November 1936]

Dear Flower. Now that at last Cassells are, you tell me, proceeding with the publication of my book, *The Revenge for Love*,[1] it is time to address you an appeal, I think. . . . Whatever your motives may have been in that matter, – and I am not so naive as to suppose that was simply an affair of a few outspoken passages, especially as my tale was such a powerfully *moral* one – I am now asking you not to visit your displeasure upon my book. It is appearing under auspices of the most black and disheartening kind. And yet as I was reading my proofs I realised that the book that is thus about to be contemptuously flung upon the market is probably the best complete work of fiction I have written;[2] and you may agree that it will be considered one of the best books in English to appear during the current 12 months. I appeal to you therefore to forget its politics – if you find them displeasing . . . . Surely not so many serious books are written these days that one can afford to spit on and hurry out of sight a 150 thousand word novel, upon such a scale as this . . . . – I have for long been reconciled to working twice as hard, and if I may say so, twice as well, as the generality, and getting less out of it than some pipsqueak journalist. It would be unreasonable to expect that one criticize an orthodoxy, and have that orthodoxy make things easy for me. But here is a book that it is indecent to smother. . . .

231. *To Oliver Brown*† [London]
Feb. 11. 1937.

Dear Brown. . . .

In reviewing my past years activities as a painter I am encouraged to think that the time spent in painting was well spent. Very various paintings – the "Cubist Museum",[3] the "Siege of Barcelona",[4] and a good many more – represent a considerable

[1] L., largely because of his recurring ailments, had been slow in completing the novel. Further time was taken by Cassell's concern over possibilities of censorship on the part of Boots's Lending Library.
[2] L.'s opinion has been confirmed by many of his most perceptive critics.
[3] In the collection of David Cleghorn Thomson.
[4] Now in the Tate Gallery, retitled *The Surrender of Barcelona*.

output. In mere account, I think, it compares very favourably with what most English artists I know of get through in the year. I cannot conjure up enough modesty to feel that, in quality, it ranks below the productions of my ½ dozen most eminent fellow painters.

I dont quite know how best to get at this question. But I will make a start with *public recognition*. In the many institutions for the encouragement of art in this country – such as the Contemporary Art Society, the numerous public galleries, in London and the Provinces – I am unrepresented. The only exception to this rule is the group of drawings left to the Manchester Museum by the late Charles Rutherston, Will Rothenstein's collector-brother.[1] There *was* a large paper-picture of mine in the Tate: but they left it in their cellars, and the Thames in flood destroyed it some years ago. The last that was seen of it, it was floating about on top of the water.

If I may judge from what those best qualified to speak have at one time and another pronounced on the subject (for instance, Walter Sickert, or William Rothenstein) this position is unjustified.

The great influence of Roger Fry in the past militated against my pictures being bought institutionally. On account of his dual rôle of critic and dealer he exercised a great deal of power, and as you know he did not care for me, on personal grounds. But that does not apply to conditions today.

Many little known and relatively undistinguished artists find a lucrative haven for their pictures in public galleries. It is that I am *completely* unrepresented, that is the point I am labouring. It is against that *zero* that I lift up my not unreasonable voice.

If we come to the matter of private patronage; all I can say is that I find that many paintings and pictures are sold weekly in London. . . . Yet, when I experience an urge in my finger tips to make a picture I am compelled immediately to suppress it. . . .

Why cannot I be regarded as a distinguished foreigner? I *am* producing jolly interesting work, about that there is no doubt (else you and other people would not be interested in it). Imagine that I live in Paris, Rome, or Timbuctoo. (Shall we *say* that I do so?)[2] . . .

Yours

[1] The Rutherston Loan Collection, Manchester City Art Galleries.
[2] Brown replied to L. on February 15th, agreeing with his analysis and pointing to the value of a large exhibition. The exhibition of December 1937 at the Leicester Galleries was then arranged.

232. *To Lovat Dickson*†[1] Lancaster Gate. W.2.
[ca. March 1937]

Dear Lovat Dickson. I write with reference to the copy of Mr. ———'s letter of March 19th[2] ... and to a passage to which I take the strongest exception. Here is the passage.

"p. 345. The state[ment] attributed to Lloyd George is presumably another invention or distortion of the author's, but I expect he is used to this."[3]

That is extremely offensive. . . .

You will appreciate how this sort of thing, if allowed to continue with impunity must affect my reputation and livelihood as a writer: . . .

Apart from the question of whether you regard "*another* invention or distortion of the author's" as unexceptionable, if you will refer to the passage in question ... you will see that it is the beginning of a long quotation from an article by Lloyd George; and that my foolish hero, Launcelot,[4] merely expresses disappointment that only the economic side of the British Arms Policy is dealt with by Ll. G. Need I add that Launcelot's foolery had nothing to do with my opinions, and that I consider Ll. G. one of the few statesmen who are consistently right about this "war-in-the-making", and that we all owe him a debt of gratitude in consequence?

Yours sincerely.

The art critic and cultural historian William Gaunt (b. 1900) first met Lewis in the late 1920's. Later he often made one of a congenial little group – others were Constant Lambert, T. W. Earp, and the music critic Cecil Gray – which became a feature of Lewis's social

[1] H. H. Lovat Dickson (b. 1902), at this time Managing Director of Lovat Dickson, Ltd., publisher of L.'s *Count Your Dead: They Are Alive!* or *A New War in the Making* (London, 1937).

[2] L. refers to a letter from the lawyer whom Lovat Dickson had asked to examine the ms. of *Count Your Dead*.

[3] The statement reads: "Then the Jews were awfully good to us, and Lloyd George says we promised them to clear Palestine of the Arabs for them as a reward for their financial accommodation."

[4] "Launcelot Nidwit" is one of L.'s principal personae in this book of political discussion.

life before the war. The Enemy, Gaunt recalls, "acted as 'chairman' and far from monopolising the conversation in a most skilful and civilised fashion kept it going from one to another, inciting Lambert in particular to sparkling brilliance of wit."

233. *To William Gaunt* Lancaster Gate, W.2.
April 10, 1937.

My dear Gaunt. Your book was the most extremely welcome of beautiful presents![1] With your gloomy appetite for the macabre, derelict backside of a factory on Sunday afternoon, of all the disgraceful fungoid oddities of the Machine Age, you are the perfect round peg in the round hole where "Robert des Ruines",[2] etc are concerned. – There are just as many bandits in offices and committee rooms as ever infested Calabria[3] & *you have seen them*. You speak *en connaissance de cause*, from the mokes mouth (with an occasional snort, as from a barbe by Delacroix) & you speak – which is more than most painters do – with suitable eloquence. My best thanks. I hope your book has already had the very great success it deserves. Before long let us meet. I long to hear more about these romantic ancestors of yours – you must have collected a great deal of material.

Yrs

W. L.

234. *To the Editor of "Twentieth Century Verse"*[4]

21st November 1937

Dear Symons,

Thank you for the typed copies of the articles. What a quantity of friends "the Enemy" has nowadays! I am a little abashed. No

[1] Gaunt had sent L. a copy of his *Bandits in a Landscape: A Study of Romantic Painting from Caravaggio to Delacroix* (London, 1937).

[2] Hubert Robert, to whom a chapter of the book is devoted.

[3] In his account of Salvator Rosa, Gaunt emphasises the painter's interest in the bandits of Calabria.

[4] Julian Symons (b. 1912), founder and editor of *Twentieth Century Verse*, asked L. to write a prefatory letter to a special Wyndham Lewis number of the review, No. 6/7, November/December 1937.

company, this, for a public enemy. I am very much afraid that you have compromised me! I have perused these articles rather in the way a notorious bandit would a shower of *many-happy-returns* and other obliging messages, at his birthday breakfast-table in his hide-out, from the local constabulary.

But of course I recognize (and here oddly enough I have the advantage of that fine critic, Mr. Stonier) that I am not *only* an Enemy.[1] So it is with a measure of equanimity I find myself in the thick of these well-wishers. Actually I am of that company catalogued by Stonier, not over against it. He merely sets me thus, I know, for didactic emphasis. But it may be worth while to mention the fact. And, by the way, I am not a "counter-revolutionary." Should this be pointed out, do you think, too?

Almost, by nature, I am the pure revolutionary: like Godwin, say. In me you see *a man of the tabula rasa*, if ever there was one (cf. *The Caliph's Design*).[2] My mind is *ahistoric*, I would welcome the clean sweep. I could build something better, I am sure of that, than has been left us by our fathers that were before us. Only I know this is quite impossible.

This is the heart of what is, apparently, a political mystery – I have learnt my lesson, and, in spite of being the pure revolutionary, I am a bit of a realist too. Hence my extraordinary broadmindedness in politics, for instance. Otherwise I should be a man after Lenin's heart.

Have you ever known a politician, on the Left or on the Right, who did not dislike art? There is a very fundamental reason for this; very fundamental. Art functions in the abstract – like the Cabots it "speaks only with God." That's no use to politics.

Look here, as I am among friends, I will tell you something. I have been much deceived in politicians, and I will never write another line for or against any of them. Your brother shall have his wish![3]

[1] In an article in the special number titled "That Taxi-Driver," G. W. Stonier writes of L.'s importance as a creator as well as a critic. In the latter capacity, L. is, Stonier says, a "counter-revolutionary," as opposed to revolutionaries like Gide, Proust, Joyce, and Eliot.

[2] *The Caliph's Design* was reprinted in the collection of essays *Wyndham Lewis the Artist, from "Blast" to Burlington House* (London, 1939).

[3] A. J. A. Symons's contribution to the special number is titled "The Novelist." It concludes: "It is equally my hope that some lucky turn of fate will absolve him from his political interests, his philosophical tracts,

This must be a short letter. You did not expect it to be written in the periods of Gibbon, did you, or in the style of the Authorised Version? I say this, not because I suppose you did, but for the benefit of the Plain Reader.

Informality lends itself to a misunderstanding, under certain circumstances, which should be cleared up: for if *formality* is the appropriate dish to set before a king *informality* is the salt of life, is it not, and the pepper too?

No American President could outdo me in informality, I flatter myself. As to who can or cannot outdo me in formality, that is a question I can leave to be answered by each man as he thinks fit.

I never write a letter. So I have twice as many books to my credit as anybody else, that is all. Very naturally, a page of a novel, such as *The Revenge for Love*, takes me as long to write as twenty pages of a *Blasting and Bombardiering* – except where the latter demands more formal attention.

Here is perhaps the sort of way in which I can be of help to the reader. My books are of two distinct kinds. I have not written more *formal* books than some other people; there are, besides these, the informal ones. It is, I agree, a somewhat staggering output: for I have already written twenty-four books, I find.

Only an ignorant, or an ill-disposed person (angry, no doubt at observing me write so that "he who runs may read," because an obscure, a "crabbed" Enemy, is greatly to be preferred to one who writes for "he who runs") could confuse them – the familiar style and the formal style. They are as distinct as chalk and cheese. But chalk is well enough in its way, and it is what everybody commits himself to when writing to his friends, just as he goes to the *Excusado*. – As I have no regular friends (being an Enemy) I do it in public; I mean, indulge in the relaxations of the epistolary style. Twenty-four volumes is the result – what a marvellous correspondent I should have made!

But alas that we should in general be so pretentious! And why this strange *pudeur*?

While I'm about it I will clear up another confusion, with which I occasionally meet, and with that bring my letter to an end. As a painter I paint nature as she is (more or less) and nature

his pamphleteering and his restless love of new beginnings, and leave him free to flay, for the pleasure of his readers, the wonderful grotesques of his unmitigated fancy."

as she isn't. These are distinct activities. Both answer a purpose, but the purposes are different. Most painters confine themselves to one or the other: I indulge in both. This should present no difficulties to anyone except the unimaginative and conventional.

WYNDHAM LEWIS

235. To Douglas Jerrold†[1] 29a Kensington Gardens Studios,
Notting Hill Gate. W. 11.[2]
[December 1937]

Dear Jerrold. I am sorry you should have seen no way but to depart from the path of strict veracity. – You envisage your function as a publisher with so disgruntled and sardonic a levity, that no wretched "author" who has been so incautious as to give you a book – ignorant of course of the state of affairs until it is too late – can expect anything but rather grim results. If one adds to that your waspish animosity towards all that is "highbrow" (evidenced, for instance, in your objection to the space devoted in my book to such insignificant people as Joyce, Eliot etc) then the lot of the "author" who is also a "highbrow", once he has placed himself in your hands, is indeed a sorry one.

All this I saw, naturally, too late. A book which I knew any publisher almost could have made a success of was to be published by an embittered "author" turned publisher, who had invented for his own consolation the dogma that "no good book can sell," and had pursued his calling with so much languor that in effect his dogma could be guaranteed to justify itself. There was no drawing back, however. You horrified me when you *insisted* upon my devoting a chapter to what you were so fatuous as to describe as "the English Review period". That I naturally had to refuse to do: but still could not escape from making some reference to yourself

[1] Jerrold was at this time director of Eyre and Spottiswoode, who published L.'s autobiographical book *Blasting and Bombardiering* in October 1937.
[2] The Lewises occupied a flat with a studio above at this address from 1937 to 1939, when they left for America. On their return to London in 1945, they took up residence here again and, except for a short interval, remained in the flat until L.'s death. Thus the address was perhaps the most permanent of L.'s life. Soon after his death the building was pulled down as part of a Notting Hill Gate redevelopment project.

and your friends.¹ Par surcroit de malheur, your autobiography came out just before mine. . . .

. . . *Upon the day of publication* of "Blasting and Bombardiering" I rang you up in the morning, and you gave me an exceedingly depressing picture of the way the book had started. When I expressed my extreme disappointment and surprise, you answered that it was what happened to *your* book.² What my book subscribed, *your* book had subscribed. Here, of course, I was on delicate ground, but as civilly as was possible I pointed out to you that my book was somewhat different from your book (in a way) and that as a matter of fact I was myself not absolutely identical with the late editor of the "English Review", and author of "England".³

That afternoon about four Mrs Millar rang me up of her own accord. She said she thought I would like to know that things were going really exceptionally well.⁴ . . .

You see, all this is far too circumstantial. It cannot be cancelled by a jaunty and impudent disclaimer. And what is more to the point, I do not propose that it shall. . . .

Yours sincerely,

236. *To P. Van der Kruik*†⁵ London W.11.
Dec 27. 1937.

My dear V. der Kruk. For weeks I have had no time to eat or sleep, so you must excuse me for having taken so long to answer you.⁶ . . . I hardly know what to answer, in my role of uncle

---

¹ L.'s drawing of Jerrold is reproduced in *Blasting and Bombardiering*; opposite it (p. 306) is a paragraph of kudos.

² Jerrold had been in correspondence with L. about the problems of selling *Blasting and Bombardiering*. One of his points was the disparity between good reviews and good sales; he spoke also of the small buying public for good books, saying these were particular problems with "your books and mine." L. refers here specifically to Jerrold's autobiography, *Georgian Adventure*, published by Collins in 1937.   ³ *I.e.*, Jerrold.

⁴ In a reply dated December 6th, Jerrold wrote that Mrs. Millar, who worked for Eyre and Spottiswoode, had erred. He apologised for thus misleading L.

⁵ Van der Kruik, a young Dutch intellectual, first came to see L. earlier in 1937. A friendship developed via occasional correspondence and other visits.

⁶ L. had been working on his show at the Leicester Galleries.

"tickler of your mind" and wearer of the stuffiest pants in Europe, except to say "smell on, and welcome!" and that the convulsions that *I* cause are probably not so enervating as those caused by some I could mention.[1] . . . I hope that one of your concluding remarks in your letter is not to be taken *literally* – re "consumptive fingers"? You did not seem very well when I saw you. If I may advise, a visit to the Sally gardens is desirable. You gave me a bloodcurdling picture of a high-pressure life. . . .

Yours

W. LEWIS

Lewis submitted his recently completed portrait of T. S. Eliot (see plate 14) to the annual exhibition of the Royal Academy of Arts in 1938. Late in April the Hanging Committee rejected the painting. Augustus John, R.A., resigned in protest (without seeing the picture)[2] *and Lewis found himself the centre of another public controversy, perhaps the most public of his career. Newspaper placards proclaimed the news on London streets; in a day the "rejected portrait" became a* cause célèbre *in the British press. The larger issue was that of the conservatism and alleged benightedness of the Royal Academy. Thus the battle soon showed itself as one more engagement in the war between old guard and new, between philistine and artist. Its climax came when Winston Churchill, principal speaker at the academy's annual dinner, devoted a large portion of his address to a pronouncement on the controversy and suggestions for its resolution. Firing continued on both sides for several days, but it was clearly on the wane. The academy did not reconsider its decision on Lewis's painting,*[3] *but there was no doubt that he had scored a blow against orthodoxy, and got himself some valuable publicity in the process.*[4]

[1] Van der Kruik had written to L. of the mental upheavals his reading of L.'s books was causing him to undergo.

[2] John was persuaded to take up his membership again two years later.

[3] After Lewis's retrospective exhibition at the Tate Gallery in 1956, a new Secretary of the Royal Academy requested the loan of the portrait. It had, however, already been returned to South Africa and L.'s portrait of John McLeod was shown instead.

[4] For L.'s remarks on the affair see *Wyndham Lewis the Artist*, pp. 373–4, and *Rude Assignment*, p. 17.

237. T. S. Eliot to Wyndham Lewis

THE NEW CRITERION

24 Russell Square,
London, W.C.1.
21 April 1938

Dear Lewis,

I learn from the Telegraph that your portrait of me has been rejected by the Academy. For my own part, I will not disguise my feeling of relief. Had the portrait been accepted, I should have been pleased – that a portrait by you should have been accepted by the Academy would have been a good augury – at least, I should have been gratified by the spectacle of the Royal Academy at Canossa, so to speak. But so far as the sitter is able to judge, it seems to me a very good portrait, and one by which I am quite willing that posterity should know me, if it takes any interest in me at all. And though I may not be the best judge of it as portraiture, I am sure that it is a very fine painting. But I am glad to think that a portrait of myself should *not* appear in the exhibition of the Royal Academy, and I certainly have no desire, now, that my portrait should be painted by any painter whose portrait of me would be accepted by the Royal Academy.

Yours,
T. S. ELIOT

238. To the Editor of the "Daily Telegraph," April 25, 1938[1]

The Leicester Galleries,
Leicester Square.
April 24, 1938.

Sir. I must, with your leave, reply to the remarks of the Royal Academy spokesman, reported in your issue of Saturday, regarding

[1] Having published an interview with L. in its issue of April 22nd, the *Daily Telegraph* the following day devoted a column to the remarks of "a leading member of the Hanging Committee." The Academy, this spokesman declared, "is looking most anxiously for good Modern Art"; it rejected the portrait on the basis of quality, not modernity. He added that the committee could not "give preferential treatment to artists with well-known names."

my portrait of the poet, Mr. T. S. Eliot. – "the picture was rejected," he affirmed, "because it was not as good as others that were passed." But it could hardly be supposed that he would say that it had been rejected because it was *better* than the pictures that were accepted. That would be too much to expect. On the other hand, the rather startling revelation that the Royal Academy "has been criticised for going too far in the direction of modernity" is another matter. The Public (which is really as depressed by platitude as anybody) will be pretty indignant, I venture to think, when it learns the state of affairs: that this fiery institution is held back and condemned to be dull, on account of influential criticisms, which it is unable to ignore. Having come under suspicion for its disquietingly subversive tendencies, its unbridled "modern feeling", great care has to be taken not to seem *too* advanced. There has been no outcry in the Press, as far as I am aware. Not a whisper of this has reached the Public ear. If the Academy was indeed "going gay" until checked by timely criticism, no one not an initiate has detected it. We have, I think, the right to ask for *names*. Who, or what, are these influences, imposing such humiliating standards upon one of our national institutions, standards which we all deplore? – A change of management is indicated, the above admission of the R. A. spokesman proves that to the hilt. Men of a firmer mould are required, it is obvious! But such a revolution can never come as a result of the protests of mere artists. Unless the State can be stimulated into action, the *impasse* will be permanent, generation after generation. And, ultimately, the State is responsible. For it was a Government that established this melancholy institution: and a Government alone can be instrumental in reforming it.

Yrs etc.
WYNDHAM LEWIS

14. T. S. Eliot pointing to the 1938 portrait of himself. (*Photograph taken in Durban in 1954*)

239. *To the Editor of "The Times," May 2,* 1938

THE REJECTED PORTRAIT
POLICY OF THE ROYAL ACADEMY
ART AND NATURE

May 1, 1938

Sir, – Upon page thirteen of your Saturday's issue I would venture to point out that your Art Critic and your leading article are at variance.[1] Your "expert" thinks one thing and the editorial mind another. The former opens his review of this year's Royal Academy in the following words – words which the Royal Academy will not take to heart however often they may be repeated:

"More and more it becomes evident that the Royal Academy is unable or unwilling to accommodate its institutional character to the claims of contemporary art."

Upon the same page, in a leading article, you choose to be facetious at the expense of artists like Mr. Sickert or Mr. John, who retired from the Royal Academy owing precisely to this "inability or unwillingness" on its part to pursue anything but a jealous and a sectarian policy[2] – which, as your Art Critic very acutely points out, is actually a non-traditional (and so a "fashionable") policy.

One of the delusions of the layman is that tradition has its home, or rather shrine, in Burlington House. Nothing could be farther from the truth. At this moment there is no Royal Academician so merely academically accomplished as Mr. Augustus John and Mr. Richard Sickert, both of whom have resigned, not, as is

[1] *The Times* first took note of the controversy on April 26th, when it printed an article telling of the rejection of L.'s portrait and of John's resignation. The article referred to the resignations three years before of Sickert and Stanley Spencer. It was followed by a statement from John. The next three issues of the paper carried letters expressing a variety of opinion. On Saturday the 30th, the first portion of *The Times*' review of the exhibition appeared. The art critic led off by criticising the Royal Academy for sacrificing artistic tradition to a temporary fashion which, he said, was due to the influence of photography. On the same page the paper printed an editorial which commented sardonically on the resignations and reminded readers that the purpose of the exhibition was to make money, "not to stimulate public interest in works of contemporary art."

[2] Sickert had resigned in protest against the censorship of statues by Jacob Epstein destined for public display.

generally supposed, because they are all for rebellion and desire chaos to come again, but because they are for the true tradition as against the false – for the living order against the dead order.

Let me illustrate this from the present Royal Academy Exhibition. The great tradition of English art is best represented there by the painting of Mr. Wilson Steer[1] – who has never sent a picture to the Royal Academy in his life, and has been duly, and to my mind most appropriately, rewarded for this with the Order of Merit, a distinction which, significantly, has not been conferred upon any R.A.

If you turn from this triumph of exquisite scholarship by an outsider (who is only there because the Academy have bought his picture under the terms of the Chantry Bequest) to the photographic frigidity of the official pieces – either portrait or ceremonial set-piece – you are not turning from a rebel to a reactionary but from something human to something inhuman; from something that takes count of all the historic past of the art of painting to something that is ignorant of all but the barbaric present, whose "tradition" dates no farther than the camera obscura. You are in the presence, with such photographic puppetry, not of the noblest tradition of a great human art, but the ignoblest mechanical travesty of nature. For nature is not a photograph – odd as this may sound to a public who thinks of nature at second hand, in terms of movie or Press photography. Nature is only converted into a photograph by the medium of men's machines. And it is because the standards of the Academy are mechanical – not because they are academic – that all artists worth the name detest it. And if in their gallant efforts to loosen the stranglehold of this dead hand (not the "dead hand of tradition" but of the nineteenth-century robot) they are thrown into attitudes reminiscent of Laocoon – more and more "heroic" and "noble," to quote your leading article[2] – it is in spite of themselves: it is merely because the sense of their impotence to effect a change, combined with their ever more outraged sense of the necessity of that change,

[1] Philip Wilson Steer (1860–1942) was represented by "Bird-nesting, Ludlow," which *The Times* critic judged the finest painting in the show "from an artistic point of view."

[2] The editorial mocked the "increasing nobility of the motives" of the recent resignations. Of Spencer's – over the rejection of some of his own pictures – it said: "The least heroic among us can . . . sympathize with this straightforward adult version of the childish 'shan't play!'"

leads them into "something very like direct action."¹ These people are, after all, *painters*. That seems to be forgotten in some quarters.

I am, &c.,
WYNDHAM LEWIS

240. *To the Editor of "The Times," May 4,* 1938

May 3, 1938.

THE REJECTED PORTRAIT

Sir, – The "controversy" regarding the Royal Academy has been decorously interred – that is, the idea – by oratory at a public banquet. But before the echoes of Mr. Winston Churchill's passionate advocacy of platitude have quite died away may I make one or two remarks by way of reply?²

Even the most resounding denunciations poured forth by mere artists, however famous, will just roll like water off the back of the proverbial duck, so long as next minute an eminent ex-Minister of State can be found to turn on the "hydrants" (to use Mr. Churchill's phrase) of romantic Parliamentary rhetoric, to be broadcast by the B.B.C. upon all and sundry who publicly disagree with the potboiling orthodoxy at Burlington House.

If you will allow me, in my turn, to "express my opinion . . . with all that freedom which distinguishes artistic circles,"³ I would like to point out that "authority and respect for authority" is all very well;⁴ but even in the political sphere – in the terms of

¹ The editorial: "A rebuff to one single portrait by a younger painter has roused the great heart of Mr. Augustus John to action, to something very like direct action."

² *The Times* of May 2nd carried a report of the Royal Academy banquet held the previous Saturday at Burlington House. The chief guest was the Prime Minister, Neville Chamberlain, and the principal speaker, Churchill, whose speech had been broadcast. In his address, which the paper described as "eloquent" and printed in full, Churchill placed himself "on the side of the disciplinarians." He said that "the function of such an institution as the Royal Academy is to hold a middle course between tradition and innovation."

³ The report of Churchill's opening remarks concludes: "'I propose to express my opinion . . . with all that freedom which distinguishes artistic circles.' (Laughter.)"

⁴ Churchill said that "no large organisation can long continue without a strong element of authority and respect for authority."

which Mr. Churchill thinks and perorates – a small oligarchy, which is notoriously feeble and superannuated, has never for long succeeded in holding down by force a restless population: and if today a plebiscite were taken of all the artists in Great Britain you would get a 90 per cent majority for the abolition of the Royal Academy of Arts.

"The arts are essential to any complete national life," says Mr. Churchill. Indeed that is the case. You must have art, else you are not "civilized"! Therefore (as Mr. Churchill sees it) let us establish a concentration camp, for this queer but obligatory activity, in the centre of our capital, put the Royal Arms over its gates, and let the fashionable world resort there once a year for a "private view," and, this duty performed, for the rest of the year art can be forgotten about; as for the rest of the week, having gone to church on Sunday, the Sermon on the Mount can be left behind in the pew till next Sabbath comes round.

The Royal Academy is

> an institution of wealth and power for the purpose of encouraging the arts.... It would be disastrous if the control of this machine fell into the hands of any particular school of artistic thought which...would exclude all others.

But it is precisely because it has quite obviously fallen into the hands of just such a "school of artistic thought," which is exclusive in the narrowest commercial sense, that it is regarded by most artists as a "disaster." And in order to continue to prop it up and keep it intact, in the teeth of the opposition of the entire artistic world of England, it is found necessary, whenever a distinguished artist falls foul of it or rushes out of it, to vilify him, or at least to attempt to discredit him by clothing him with the imagery of a passionate horse, bolting from an official procession, or with the empty heroics of the Tale of the Cid.[1] For it cannot be that Burlington House is in the wrong. To admit that would be tantamount to confessing that George III had erred when he conferred

---

[1] Churchill: "Some eminent painters . . . remind me of high mettled palfreys prancing and pawing, sniffing, snorting, foaming, and occasionally kicking, and shying at every puddle they see." "The slightest difference . . . is sufficient to make an eminent artist send in his cap and jacket."

his ill-omened charter. Also the Royal Academy was probably Mr. Churchill's first love, there is always that.

I am, &c.,
WYNDHAM LEWIS

241. *To the Editor of "The Times," May 7,* 1938

May 5, 1938.

THE REJECTED PORTRAIT

Sir, – Sir William Nicholson's solicitude regarding my O.M. does him great credit.[1] But I did what I did with my eyes open, fully aware that it might be held up against me at some future date, and that the stigma attaching to my picture, merely because of its passage (however hurried) through those galleries, would react inevitably upon its author when his O.M. came up for consideration. To the great "nobility" of my character alone this sacrifice must be set down. For somebody had to stop the Academy from eternally protesting that all the good artists were outside because they never sent in! As for Mr. Lamb's letter, most of your readers are probably unaware that the two O.M.s mentioned by him, Watts and Tadema, are dead.[2] It was, of course, the living who were under discussion.

Yours, &c.,
WYNDHAM LEWIS

[1] On May 5th *The Times* printed a letter from the eminent painter Sir William Nicholson (1872–1949). Sir William said he could not understand why L. had "submitted his very fine work for approval to a society of whose policy he himself disapproves and whose work he despises. I should be sorry to think that in this way he may possibly have queered his own pitch for an eventual O.M."

[2] On May 4th, W. R. M. Lamb, Secretary of the Royal Academy, wrote correcting L.'s statement about O.M.s not being conferred on members of the academy. He cited Watts and Alma-Tadema as evidence.

242. *To Naomi Mitchison*† [May?] 30th [1938]

Dear Naomi: The last few weeks has been abominable.[1] The criminal lunatics who bring about the "false values" to which you refer have it all their own way, and other false values, as well, go into currency every day.[2] There is nothing new under the sun, I know. Still *waiting for the bang* (when things have been over inflated for so long) is difficult, when one's personal affairs reflect so accurately the public stress. – "Class" is a bore and I am glad you have found a *terrain* upon which you can exist without that insensate English superstition coming in between you and rational relations with your kind. . . .

Yrs
W. L.

243. *To Sir William Rothenstein*† [London]
July 25. 1938.

My dear Rothenstein. So I have also to thank you for the sale of the Eliot study to Barr.[3] I had supposed that he had dropped out of the blue; but, lo, he after all came out of your hat. Well, I have always thought that Providence was more personal than is generally believed today; and I can imagine no Destiny that I would sooner be indebted to than yourself. – Have you got another Barr or two in your locker, by any chance.

It is very interesting news that you are going to have a Show in the Autumn.[4] I hope (as it is retrospective) that you will include

[1] L. refers presumably to the Royal Academy fracas, and perhaps also to his preparations for an exhibition at the Beaux Arts Gallery which came on in July.

[2] Mrs. Mitchison had gone to live on a farm at Carradale, Scotland. She wrote from there that she had been "talking with people who are apparently almost unhurt by false values and who are prepared to accept me without class barriers."

[3] A study for the rejected portrait. Rothenstein wrote to L. of its purchase at the Beaux Arts Gallery by Alfred Barr, Jr., of the Museum of Modern Art: "I took one Barr, who looks after a gallery of contemporary paintings in the States, to see your paintings – he acquired the Eliot portrait." The picture is now in Eliot House at Harvard.

[4] In his letter, Rothenstein told L. that he was to have a show in October – "Fifty Years of Painting" at the Leicester Galleries. "My

some of those paintings of Jews I first saw of yours. I dimly remember how very fine some of them were, and should like to renew acquaintance with them. What I for my part particularly admire is a thing like that Common Room in the Academy. It is like a page of Proust. It is so dry and so exact and so overwhelmingly and painfully true to the originals. Then lots of portraits! But above all stress what is sober, weighty, and uncompromisingly plain and unadorned: no concessions; in the form of scarlet women, or whorish little landscapes or flowerpieces – if you have any! – You say you have had to hire a garage to house your collection. It is disgraceful that this should be so. But there is this that is good about it – you have been saved, by fortunate economic circumstances, from the temptations that beset so many artists in this country. – so indifferent to art and with so sweet a tooth. . . .

Yours ever.

244. *To R. A. Scott-James*†[1]   Notting Hill Gate. W. 11.
Nov. 17. 1938.

Dear Scott-James. I have your letter.[2] – Your letter is, as you quite well know, a misrepresentation. I cannot allow you to make a fool of me I am afraid, and to give currency to an account of this transaction which is false. You did not offer me "an opportunity

unsuccess," he wrote, "is such that I have to hire a garage to house my great collection of my own works!" In his memoirs Rothenstein quotes from a letter from L. which seems to have been written after this exhibition opened. L. wrote: "I . . . watched with the greatest interest your renderings of the various people that I know. I go primarily for the pattern of the structure of the head and insinuate, rather than stress, the 'psyche'. You, on the contrary, have I think here and there lost yourself a little in your psychology, as witness your T. S. Eliot. I did not even recognize it at first. But how interesting that you should see Tom like that!" *Since Fifty: Men and Memories, 1922–1938* (New York, 1940), p. 73.

[1] R. A. Scott-James (1878–1959), journalist and critic, had known L. for many years. At the time of this letter he was editor of the *London Mercury*.

[2] Scott-James wrote to L. on November 16th, saying he was sorry that a misunderstanding had arisen regarding an art article he had asked L. to do for the *Mercury*.

of some general reflections on the last fifty years of painting".[1] That is nonsense. You mentioned nothing of the sort at the time you commissioned the article. You commissioned me to write an article *upon Sir William Rothenstein's show*, which was called "Fifty Years of Painting" – meaning of *his* painting, not fifty years of other people's painting. There is no doubt as to what you intended – *to start with.* . . .

. . . I met you in High Street Notting Hill Gate. . . . You said that you hoped that my article would not be *all* about Sir William Rothenstein. I replied that *of course* it was all about him, since that was what you had asked me to write about. You were sorry, you answered; but, you said, in a confidential manner, "did not Sir William Rothenstein do *potboilers* – was not that the case? You understood that he did etc." Thereupon I turned back and walked with you to the Tube Station, you will remember, explaining to you your mistake – that you had been misinformed. Whatever could be said about Sir William Rothenstein, that he had deliberately made a practice of doing work to make as much money as possible, or to acquire a vulgar popularity – and that is the definition of "potboiling" – could not be asserted by the most ill-disposed person. I pointed out that, on the contrary, Rothenstein was if anything *too* plain and unvarnished, too uncompromisingly "unattractive" a painter.

There may be many painters that I am, personally, more competent to write about, painters whose work is more akin to my own. Had you asked me to write about Soutine, or Derain, or Paul Klee, I should gladly have welcomed the opportunity of doing so. They are more "in my line". But what sense is there now in saying that what you *really* meant was that I should mix up Sir William Rothenstein with Picasso, Soutine, and Max Ernst, Gauguin and Cézanne, and write a survey of the last fifty years of painting-in-general? That was not the job I was given. And when you said to me on the telephone that you were suppressing my article for my own good – that "it would do me no good" – all

---

[1] In his letter Scott-James said he thought he had made it clear he wanted an article "arising out of" the William Rothenstein show "but not mainly about the show itself. I thought this peg would give you an opportunity for some general reflections on the last fifty years of painting . . . ." He went on to give his reasons for not wanting a specific criticism of this one exhibition.

I can answer to that is that it is the sort of treatment that I am at this moment receiving at your hands that does me *harm* and makes it more difficult for me to make my living – not my celebration of the jubilee-exhibition of a very honest painter, who has been far less of a "potboiler" than many with more pretensions to originality.

Yours sincerely,

P.S. . . .

During the 1930's – through the influence of Desmond Flower and A. J. A. Symons – George Viscount Carlow (1907–44), a young aeroplane pilot and the only son of the Earl of Portarlington, became interested in collecting Lewis's work. In the years preceding the war he purchased a great number of items – manuscripts, corrected proofs, first editions – and had them assembled and beautifully bound and cased. At the same time Carlow got to know Lewis. A friendship developed which was cut short by Carlow's death in an aeroplane crash during the war. His collection is now in the Lockwood Memorial Library at the University of Buffalo.

245. *To Lord Carlow*[1] [London]
Jan. 1939

Dear Carlow. I am glad you have this book, which your friend Humbert Wolfe[2] likes so much. I wish I had Father D'Arcy's brochure to send you, too.[3] – This is the most elaborate and "difficult" for popular reading unfortunately – [word?] of the ideology, or philosophy, implicit in all Western thought or feeling at the present time. This philosophy has now everywhere passed into action. It has received the sanction of the *fait accompli*. The theoretic basis was never very clearly understood, it seems, even by the Gelehrter, and is now quite lost sight of. I have attempted,

---

[1] This letter was written as an inscription in a first edition copy of *Time and Western Man*.

[2] Humbert Wolfe (1885–1940), writer and civil servant.

[3] L. refers either to Father D'Arcy's review in *The Month* or to his discussion of the book in *The Nature of Belief* (London, 1931). See pp. 22–4 in the edition of 1945.

variously, since 1927, to translate this analysis into more popular forms. But you have to go back into the philosophies that went hand-in-hand with Nineteenth Century Science (as, for instance, Nietzsche came out of Darwin and his "survival of the fittest") and into the philosophical glosses [?] of the time-physics, really to master the structure of the contemporary mechanical Juggernaut.

from WYNDHAM LEWIS

246. *To Lord Carlow*[1]   [London] Jan. 1939

Dear Carlow –

"Art is the only thing worth the tragic impulse" (cf. p. xi): yet art cannot be "tragic" in the intense fashion of life, without ceasing to be art. Such is my explanatory paradox. – The "Soldier of Humour" belongs to the same order of thought as this book. – Haven't we in 1939 sort of worked our way round again to this *Preface* of 1915? Nietzsche and Wagner are a potent pair.

W. L.

247. *To P. Van der Kruik*†   [London] June 16. 1939.

Dear Van Kruk. It is grand news that you are cutting adrift from Europe and all its stupid disputes and going to a new country.[2] You will be able to impart, on the other hand, to the colonial Dutch in S. Africa about the only thing Europe has to give any longer – "culture", Kultur, or whatever it is called: some slight *beaux restes* of grace and love of learning which we have inherited and put to such miserable uses! . . . You will dine with us on Tuesday Evening? Wine and – a cigar as big as a torpedo! . . .

Yrs.
WYNDHAM LEWIS

[1] Written as an inscription in a first edition copy of *Tarr*.
[2] Van der Kruik wrote to L. that he was emigrating to South Africa. He was visiting London prior to his departure.

PART IV. 1939-1945

Self Condemned

Lewis spent the six years of World War II in Canada and the United States. Whether or not the move was well-advised, he began to regret it soon after his arrival in America, and he went on regretting it. What had seemed an auspicious transition proved to be nothing of the kind. Life abroad was at best lonely and uncertain, at worst a nightmare. The experience, not as it was but as it felt, is admirably evoked in the novel Self Condemned. *The quality of the book – its revelation of its author's deepened understanding of the human situation – perhaps justifies the unhappiness that produced it. For this period seems to have been as a whole the blackest of Lewis's life.*

Lewis felt that war-time England would be no place for him. He was especially worried as to how he could paint and write profitably in a situation where the arts would be mobilized in service of the state. He knew his chances for official employment were minimal. In America, he assumed, life would be easier. As a well-known painter and writer he should be able to secure commissions and contracts sufficient to support himself and his wife until a time when England would again be possible. The day before Britain declared war, the Lewises, with a small dog, a certain amount of cash and a few prospects of work, sailed for Canada.

They settled first in Buffalo, where Lewis had a commission to do a portrait. This he hoped would lead to more work in the area. When it did not, the couple moved on to New York City. They stayed there from December 1939 till August 1940. Lewis wrote and sold America, I Presume, *but aside from this he was without employment and partially dependent on the benefactions of American well-wishers. One of these provided a summer cottage on Long Island,* which served as a haven till October and a place in which to finish a novel begun in England, The Vulgar Streak. Their one-year visitor's permit (along with a short extension) having by this time expired, the Lewises headed for Canada in November.

If New York seemed cold and competitive, Toronto was to prove completely unsympathetic. Again there was some work – Lewis sold a number of drawings and some articles and gave occasional lectures – but never enough to give any feeling of security. Private life in the pious, provincial city offered almost no satisfaction. As the months drew on, Lewis began to cast about more and more desperately for some kind of sinecure, an official one in Canada or an academic one in the U.S. Occasionally, a prospect would loom tantalizingly in the distance; but except for one sizeable official commission, every promise turned out a mirage.

Finally, after more than two years, the nadir of this black epoch, a break occurred. Assumption College, in Windsor, Ontario, offered a year's lectureship. The pay was low and the work somewhat demanding, but Lewis accepted gratefully. In June 1943 the Lewises moved from Toronto to Windsor, and although they were absent for long stretches, they kept the small city as their base until their return to England. Teaching, though hard work, was amusing, and priests made congenial colleagues.

During much of 1944 they were in St. Louis, where again fortune had intervened in the form of two admirers who set up a programme of work there. After Canada, St. Louis was a kind of relief, but it too was alien territory, and for the cosmopolitan Lewis, a hinterland to boot. With the coming of 1945 and prospects of peace, return to England began to seem both desirable and possible. The Lewises stayed in Windsor till May, then went on to Ottawa, and at last to Montreal, whence they were to sail home. Their ship was the first passenger vessel to leave Canada after VJ day.

In view of his productivity before and after, Lewis's American period was indeed barren. He drew a good deal and he painted a few fine portraits, but he did not advance in artistry or in reputation. As a writer, he was practically fallow, completing only two books and one pamphlet, none of them particularly outstanding. Nor was the social side of the venture very rewarding. Kind and interesting friends cropped up in several cities. But being uprooted, Lewis never during this time experienced the stimulus of belonging to a community, a stimulus which had been the daily bread of his

London life. An Enemy was related, involved – he had cohorts and opponents. A stranger in the land, as all expatriates discover, must needs be at the best of times a stranger.

248. *To T. J. Honeyman*†¹ [Toronto]
Wed. Sept. 13. 1939.

Dear Honeyman. As I had to evacuate London, I thought I might as well get over to New York (where I have 2 books to sell neither of which could now be sold at the London end) and so I joined my young Canadian friend in the boat 20 days ago, and here I am en route for New York. – There appears to be only a half war, or a "limited war", going on at present. But I imagine that that phase will end in a few weeks. Anyhow, the sale of the Eliot portrait to Durban was providential,² as it will afford me time to turn round and make my arrangements on this side. (I shall eventually return on a *neutral* boat; we were 100 miles away from the Athenia when it was torpedoed³ and zig-zagged across with lifebelts on). . . .

I want to get this off quickly so all I will add is the hope that the war will not interfere too much with your official duties in Glasgow. Take care of yourself and of your misses,⁴ to whom my best respects. Yrs.

249. *To T. J. Honeyman*† [Buffalo]
Oct 5. 1939.

My dear Honeyman. Thank you very much for getting the money cabled:⁵ and I am sorry that I had to bother you about it so much.

¹ L. became acquainted with T. J. Honeyman (b. 1891) when he was a director of the Lefevre Gallery. In 1939 Honeyman left this position to become Director of the Glasgow Art Galleries.
² The Lefevre Gallery arranged for the sale of the "rejected portrait" to the Durban Municipal Art Gallery.
³ The British liner *Athenia*, with 1400 passengers aboard, was torpedoed and sunk two hundred miles west of the Hebrides on September 3rd. She was the first passenger ship to go down in the war.
⁴ L. had painted Mrs. Honeyman a few years before. See Charles Handley-Read, *The Art of Wyndham Lewis* (London, 1951), Pl. 36.
⁵ Part of the payment for the portrait of Eliot.

I thought, however, that in the present rather peaceful period of the war it would be easier to carry through such transactions than it would in a moment of great confusion, should the war suddenly come to life. (Let us hope that it will not, and that it goes on being a nice quiet war). Sentiment over here is universally in favour of the Western Powers, and if a few ugly maritime episodes occurred it would not be at all unlikely, I should say, that the U.S.A. joined in. Such an event would shorten the war, which is what we all desire. I have been engaged upon a rather important commission (a portrait)[1] which will be finished about the end of this week or next. After this, New York. When I shall return I am not quite sure. In the crisis-days prior to the war I found the pursuit of my profession none too easy, and in war time I feel that people would be even less ready to have their portraits painted. Over here on the other hand there are distinct openings for that sort of thing. I will let you know how things go and what sort of work I am doing. So far I have been almost entirely occupied with the job in hand – sittings every day from 10 upwards. But soon I hope to get other work under way. – Buffalo is a very handsome city of lawns and trees. The first snow fell today and henceforth we may expect winter temperatures I suppose. I was glad to hear that you and your family were settling in at Glasgow and that you had started seriously directing. You will I know, if you are given a chance, put Glasgow on the map, pictorially.[2]

... What news of London art-circles? Is the Tate closed or is business-as-usual the order of the day? What is all ——'s little Bloomsbury tea-party doing? And the great Sir Kenneth, that illustrious knight?[3]

Yrs

W. L.

[1] L. had received a commission to paint Chancellor Samuel P. Capen (1878–1956) of the University of Buffalo. The portrait now hangs in the Poetry Room of the Lockwood Memorial Library at the university.

[2] Honeyman wrote to L. on October 2nd, saying he was doing what he could in the Glasgow Gallery, which "has been almost dead for some years."

[3] Sir Kenneth Clark (b. 1903), at this time Director of the National Gallery. L. looked on Clark as an emanation of Bloomsbury.

Lewis went to Buffalo because of his acquaintance with Charles D. Abbott (b. 1903), Professor of English and Director of The Lockwood Memorial Library at the University of Buffalo. He had met Abbott when the latter was abroad gathering material for the collection of modern manuscripts which he founded at the university. Hearing of his visit to America, Abbott asked Lewis to come to Buffalo, where he said he would do what he could to obtain some portrait commissions for him. Abbott then arranged for the painting of Chancellor Capen, but he had to leave on a western trip not long after Lewis's arrival.

250. *To Charles D. Abbott*

HOTEL STUYVESANT
BUFFALO
A HOUSE OF HOMES

(Sunday).
Oct. 15. 1939.

Dear Abbott. . . .

No studios were available, or so Mrs. Washburn[1] said, so I rented a room in North Street (2 blocks away). The portrait progresses, & both Chancellor & his wife (who came yesterday to see it) appear pleased with results up-to-date. You may depend upon its being a very good portrait which will do you and myself great credit. Even at the present stage I am able to guarantee that.

Mr. Lockwood[2] was very agreeable & accommodating about [?] business side & paid me 500 bucks after the minimum of parley. Since then I have not seen or heard of Mr. Lockwood, or indeed anybody else. (The cocktail parties you foresaw me frequenting have not materialised). The likelihood therefore of the portrait of Dr. Capen leading to other portraits appears to be slender. That is rather disappointing as I had hoped to make Buffalo my headquarters for a further month or two. Still, we shall see. If by next Thursday nothing happens I shall know that without your magic wand the Buffalo is an animal inaccessible to artistic stimulus. For

[1] Mrs. Gordon Washburn, wife of the Director of the Albright Art Gallery at Buffalo.
[2] Thomas B. Lockwood (1873–1947), a Buffalo lawyer and donor of The Lockwood Memorial Library, had commissioned the portrait.

I am *quite certain* that if you were here it would be eating out of my hand and having itself painted repeatedly!

In 2 weeks & a half, approximately, the portrait of Dr. Capen should be finished. Then various problems of publicity will arise. When photographs of picture are available, they should be broadcast throughout states. How do you think that should be done? ...

... Both I & my wife are immensely grateful to you for your great kindness to us: & for all the trouble you have taken on my behalf, about the Capen portrait & other things, I cannot thank you enough. If the Capen portrait does not lead to other things in Buffalo, it will to something elsewhere, I believe. – I still hope however that something Buffalonian may come along: for I had promised myself to do that painting of your wife on your return. *Some* time we must get that done. – Breathless good wishes for your future safe journey.

Yours ever
WYNDHAM LEWIS

Me pongo a los pies de su señora! Tell her to drench her bowels with the juice of peaches: – that is best specific against excessive goats milk.[1]

251. *To Terence W. L. MacDermot*†[2] [New York]
Dec 15. 1939.

Dear Mr. McDermott. I am stopping here in New York for some weeks anyway. Father Christmas is in full possession of this grim, abstract, metropolis. The Picasso show you should make a point of seeing, by the way.[3] It is beautifully arranged, and really comprehensive. – Have you communicated with your Montreal friend Dr. ——? If I had the certainty of, say, 1 oil-portrait and half-a-dozen chalk or pencil portraits, I should like to come up your way again before long. I have a good deal to do here, but it

---

[1] Abbott wrote to L. from Chicago, where he and his wife had been to call on Carl Sandburg. In his letter he recounted Mrs. Abbott's fear of the after-effects of several glasses of milk from Sandburg's goats.

[2] Terence MacDermot (b. 1896), presently Canadian High Commissioner in Australia, was at this time Master of Upper Canada College in Montreal. He befriended L. when the latter arrived in Canada.

[3] "Picasso: Forty Years of His Art" at the Museum of Modern Art.

should not take more than a month or six weeks. – The American public continue to regard the war as a 'phoney' and particularly uninteresting boxing-match!

            Yours sincerely,

252. *To Mrs. John Rothenstein*†   [Tuscany Hotel]
              [New York]
             [December 1939]

Dear Mrs Rothenstein. I should love to spend Christmas in Kentucky.[1] But it is a long journey and I cant afford to move so far as that without (1) a goodish lecture or (2) a portrait head. I can see what you mean about Kentucky and a slight European dash occasionally to lend variety. I expect it's on the same lines as Buffalo. But I think you are very lucky to be a U.S.A. citizeness. – We (I have my wife and a dog with me) are going just outside N.Y. to Connecticut for the New Year beano. (You say you never know whether people are married or not.[2] My wife and I were most orthodoxly spliced a long time ago. But life has been somewhat of a war for me, and the warriors – the Gauls being an exception – have usually kept the field of battle free of females. Man's domestic nature is stressed here in your American matriarchy and I have found myself rather overshadowed by my wife, as a fact. – She is a very good sort and I am sure you would like her. – We have no children. She is a blonde, she tends to put on fat, her mother was German, her father a good British farmer and as straight as a gun barrel, she has ridden all over the Atlas on a mule and is a great reader of my books: but you can see she is a wife in a thousand). – New York is hideous with Christmas. This hotel is building Christmas trees in the hall full of fairy lights and I should not be surprised if there were a fire before we are through. Your friend Sykes[3] – who I am greatly looking forward to seeing

[1] Mrs. Rothenstein, the Kentucky-born wife of the Director of the Tate Gallery, was visiting her family and wrote asking L. to join them for the holidays. She said she felt the need of her English friends in America now that she was a citizen of both countries.

[2] Speaking of some mutual friends, Mrs. Rothenstein wrote: "I really hardly ever know who married whom or even if they married at all."

[3] The American novelist Gerald Sykes (b. 1903). He had been a reporter on the Kentucky *Post*.

– has not yet turned up. Aren't you coming up at all – though frankly if I lived in Kentucky I should not want to very much to exchange the balmy airs of Lexington for the barren glitter of New York.

Many Christmas wishes, at all events and embrace your husband for me.

Yrs.[1]

Among the first Americans to befriend Lewis after his arrival in New York was Geoffrey Stone (b. 1911), a critic who had long admired his work and had written an essay on his ideas.[2] *Stone invited the Lewises to stay at his farm in Connecticut and helped Lewis financially during these years in America. Their agreeable relationship continued after the war.*

253. *To Geoffrey Stone* Tuscany [Hotel]
March. 7. 1940.

Dear Stone. . . .

– Thank you for the Ezra letters forwarded.[3] (They are full of childish nonsense and interlarded with great he-man oaths). Was glad the Hitler book[4] amused you. It was not intended to be a very serious work – though if properly digested it might be of more use to Great Britain than a new battleship. The adverse analysis of Hit is I believe about as shell-proof and unsinkable as most ships of the line, to put it no higher. . . .

Yrs

W. L.

[1] In *Modern English Painters: Lewis to Moore* (p. 42), Sir John Rothenstein gives an account of a letter similar to this but more elaborate. Either L. revised this draft considerably, or Sir John's memory betrayed him.

[2] "The Ideas of Wyndham Lewis," *The American Review*, October 1933, pp. 578–99, and November 1933, pp. 82–96.

[3] Pound, whom Stone knew, had written to L. at Stone's address.

[4] In a letter to L., Stone praised *The Hitler Cult* (London, 1939), one of the books L. wrote to present his revised opinion of Nazism.

254. *To the Editor of the "New Republic," May 20, 1940*[1]

New York City
[April 24. 1940.]

Sir. The first instalment of angry letters gets us nowhere. In your April Fool number I announce the "death of Abstract Art." A group of people retort, "Yah! – dead yourself!" How very intelligent! I must begin by congratulating your correspondents upon their vituperative prowess – *and* their learned excursions into literary criticism. Great readers obviously – better bookworms than they are painters, I can but surmise. "Abstract Art," the first asserts, "is still to have its day": implying that still more glorious Picassos, Braques, and Brancusis will yet arise. I am sorry to differ from Mr. Reinhardt[2] – who may himself, for all I know, be the man who is to eclipse the performances of those famous abstractors (some of whose work no one admires more than I do). The fact remains that the young generation in Europe is not an abstract generation. Nature, apprehended newly, and an often perfervid romanticism are the order of the day. Many young Americans, and not the least talented, have followed the same path – which is *not* "academicism" at all.[3] If it were that, there would not be this profound disturbance in the pages of such an organ of ideas as the *New Republic*. As to being "more like a businessman than an artist"[4] thank god for that! Art is a trade – not a gentlemanly pastime, nor a week-end amusement for dud draughtsmen or ineffectual painters, whose starved vanities find a ready outlet in this way, behind a barrage of pretentious mumbo-jumbo, which any journalist in his spare-time, or art-expert, can supply. In England the young communist-inspired "Social Realists" are

[1] L. wrote for *The New Republic* of April 1st, 1940, an aggressive article titled "The End of Abstract Art" (pp. 438–9). He declared unequivocally that abstract art was dead, that it had no longer any value or meaning. In its issue of May 20th, the magazine printed a sampling of the "mad letters" it had been receiving in response to the article. These, and presumably the letters not printed, had been previously submitted to L.; thus his rebuttal appeared along with them.
[2] The American abstract painter Ad Reinhardt (b. 1913).
[3] L. J. Salter suggested that L. might be "at heart 'the Academician' who has the misfortune of a balky brain."
[4] An accusation in a letter from Cecil Allen.

far more dogmatically "back to nature" than I am. And they are locked in a death-struggle with the rear-guard of abstractists led by Mr. Read. In spite of the fearful handicap of the "nine stuffy centuries" upon their backs, they are doing quite well. (And, by the way, is art international or is it a parish pump affair? What have the Star Spangled Banner or the Union Jack got to do with Abstract Art?). – To conclude. That great function in the state represented by the arts of painting, sculpture and design, Mr. Roosevelt was the first statesman in the world to recognise. But something very radical will have to be done today if it is to continue to exist in anything but name. The artist must, if he is to survive, come to terms with the people at large, and no longer accept the role of a purveyor of sensation, or of a highbrow clown, to a handful of socialites: for in no great capital are there more than a few dozen people, with the means necessary to set up as private patrons, who even pretend to care for pictures. – Such is the plain truth of the matter. If I am unacceptable, as the instrument for administering these important truths, let some one else come forward and say it in America. For it has to be said: and whatever ganging up may occur to stifle it, it will be said.

WYNDHAM LEWIS

255. *To Charles D. Abbott* Main Street. Sag Harbor.
Long Island, N Y
Aug. 14, 1940.

Dear Abbott. Your letter after repeated journeys up & down N. Y. state – has reached me at last. Thank you for the information about Washington State Dept. I am doing what I can about that.[1] – Daily accounts of the Blitzing of England is not pleasant reading. I suppose what will happen in the end is that Germany will discover that North Sea & English Channel, *plus* the British fleet is too much altogether, and then a stalemate will ensue. But heaven knows what destruction will have to be recorded, in more and more grim daily bulletins, before that point is reached. I wish the stupid word *Blitz* had never been added to my vocabulary.

[1] The Lewises' one-year visitors' permits were soon to expire; L. was hoping to get an extension to enable them to stay longer in the U.S.

We are down here for the summer. A large house has been put at our disposal and we have been leading a fairly idyllic life for some time, with thank goodness no rent to pay. – I am quite sure that some day New York will say that it has been very kind to me. But the fact is that the means of livelihood have not been put in my way there during the last nine months. So I am extremely glad to find myself in this haven & account myself very lucky. – I hope you & your family are having a pleasant holiday & will return refreshed to Buffalo.Send me a line here where I shall be for at least another 2 weeks.

My best regards & also Froanna's[1] to your wife,

Yrs ever
W. L.

256. *To Leonard Amster*†[2]   [Sag Harbor]
[ca. August 1940]

Dear Mr. Amster. Difficulties have prevented me from getting this to you before. *The Childermass* when it is finished will be my principal work in fiction I suppose (if you can call it "fiction"). (1) *Tarr*, (2) *Snooty Baronet*, and (3) *The Revenge for Love*, are all straight novels (in the most important sense [?].) *The Apes of God* is hardly a novel, though people remember the name of that best. It is a very long book (actually longer than *Ulysses*) and was portentously large in its original format. It is in its third edition. In England it was even financially a successful book. – I have written so many books (26 I think) that it is difficult to enumerate them. The novels (as above) is all you need mention in connection with *America I Presume*.

In 1914 I produced a huge review called *Blast*, which for the most part I wrote myself. That was my first public appearance. Immediately the War broke out and put an end to all that. I was

---

[1] Mrs. Lewis. The nickname began as a humorous corruption of "Frau Anna." A German woman friend in London had so addressed Mrs. Lewis, and L., amused, had followed suit.

[2] Leonard Amster was at this time with the New York publisher Howell, Soskin, who brought out L.'s *America, I Presume* in August 1940. L. was writing to Amster with regard to publicity for the burlesque travel book.

as you know a soldier and wasted four years of my life. (I regard anything as *waste* that is not spent in giving the fullest play possible to a person's aptitudes, and mine are very marked in all the arts except music. At present I am a *painter without a workshop*, and a writer who is capable of such productions as the *Childermass* forced to write – well, very jolly stuff, but not providing such a scope as nature clearly intended. – However, we all waste our lives. I reckon I waste 99 per cent of mine, without ever getting reconciled to it. Society is not organised properly. The money-value everywhere usurps the place that belongs to the values of greater importance.)

I started life as what is called a "revolutionary" (in art and letters): a man of the *tabula rasa*. I thought everything could be wiped out in a day, and rebuilt nearer to the hearts desire. I designed an entirely new London, for instance.[1] I was not then acquainted with "ancient lights". It took me a long time to discover that men never change (cf. "Creatures of Habit and Creatures of Change").[2] I am often today called a *reactionary*. I am not that at all. But I at times have accepted the conservative viewpoint, for conservative action seemed to me all that people were capable of, and that more could be got out of them by indulging their conservatism than by whipping them up into novel efforts.

(I have never varied in what I have considered *desirable*. But I have varied a good deal in what I regarded as feasible. I still believe that nations, – Russian, French, English, for instance – are very rigid, and grow slowly like trees. The theoretician has his chance in moments of shake-up like the present, when they become not molten but disorganised. They soon sink alas back however into the national pattern).

The career of Mr. Lewis is often divided according to Mr. Lewis's change of approach to this problem of change. The fact that when Mr. Lewis attempted to force his way into the Royal Academy (2 years ago) he caused a greater disturbance than ever he did by planting [?] "bombs" aloofly outside is perhaps typical. (The way really to agitate people in New York City at this moment is to say that Nature is fine and Abstraction extinct. This does not mean, of course, that one should say it. I only cite it as an instance of the dynamics of opinion).

[1] See *The Caliph's Design*.
[2] See *The Calendar of Modern Letters*, April 1926, pp. 17–44.

I find it extremely difficult to know what to tell you, because I am uncertain as to what is good publicity here. You can really make me into anything for the occasion – whatever you think would please or interest readers best. At seventeen years old I was at the Heimann Academy in Munich, but I learnt about painting principally in Holland, Paris and Madrid (there is nothing to learn about painting, as you are aware, in Germany.) My trade is painting. Many of my books are merely a protest against Anglo-saxon civilisation, which puts so many obstacles in the way of the artist. – I really do believe in music, pictures, and books: that is a completely authentic obsession of mine. The politician and the religionist mean very little to me, except in relation to those activities – which are the instruments of men, to make life bearable, and independent of systems just as much as science.

You can say my father was an American, but I leave that to you. I have been painter, sculptor, novelist, poet, philosopher, editor (cf. *Blast, Tyro, Enemy*), soldier, war-artist, traveller, lecturer, journalist. As to my "age-class" and my companions, they have been T. S. Eliot, Joyce, Ez Pound, T. E. Hulme.

257. To Geoffrey Stone　　　　　　　　The Jermain House,
　　　　　　　　　　　　　　　　　　　　　　Sag Harbour
　　　　　　　　　　　　　　　　　　　　　Oct. 3rd. 1940

Dear Stone. For a month I have not known where I should be the following day. In order to get permission to remain in this delectable spot I have had to have my fingers and toes inked and impressed upon printed forms and a lot of other clownishness. However, I believe that now I shall be in the States for a month or so longer: though whether I shall be here in L. Island I cannot say. That will depend upon cosmic forces over which none of us has any control. – The war settles down it seems into what is called a "test of endurance." That marvellous "conqueror", Herr Hitler (our rotarian latter-day Napoleon) has been stopped for good. But heaven knows how much blood must be shed – and torture of all sorts endured, everywhere, by all kinds of people – before this pipe-dream of Corporal No. 2 comes to an end. . . .

　　　　　　　　　　　　　　　　　　　　　　Yrs,
　　　　　　　　　　　　　　　　　　　　W. LEWIS

In December 1939 Lewis met James Johnson Sweeney (b. 1900), the well-known authority on modern art. The two men quickly became friends. They saw one another frequently during the Lewises' stay in the New York area; they corresponded and continued to meet after the Lewises left the city. Sweeney, at this time associated with the Museum of Modern Art and later (1952–60) Director of The Solomon R. Guggenheim Museum, extended a helping hand when the going was rough. He also did what he could to find a position for Lewis in the States, but to no avail. As the letters show, the friendship endured after the war.

258. *To James Johnson Sweeney*† [New York]
Sunday. Oct 27. 1940.

Dear Sweeney. You asked me I believe to let you know how I got on with my book.[1] I am sorry to say I have wasted the week here in New York and the publisher who asked me to hold things in suspense has decided after all not to publish the book. – Whether anyone else will publish it, heaven knows! For I have reached the conclusion that there is *nothing* that I can do here that can possibly be acceptable. This was not one of the publishers, either, whose lists are overweighted with refugee books: it is just that I can do nothing right. Even when (as I was told – and that was why I waited) I have done a "magnificent job" – the "best book in my opinion you have written": still it is no good. – That I am driven into the position of being a suppliant to you or anybody else is not because I have been idle or not have not tried absolutely *every* door – only to find every door shut. Many many people are asked to lecture at Columbia, for instance. I was taken to see ⎯⎯ some six months ago, who introduced me at lunch to the most influential member of his committee. But no lecture resulted. My efforts to obtain journalistic work have been equally unsuccessful. During twelve months spent in or near New York, it has been impossible to make any arrangement with a gallery, or to sell a scratch or a smudge of any kind. – These facts are indisputable. If you should ask me why I did not foresee all this and spare myself and my wife these fearful risks and worries, I can only

[1] *The Vulgar Streak*. The novel, which came out in England in 1941, was never published in America.

answer that that was impossible to foresee, without having actually experienced it. – But now having got as far as N. York, I have to scuttle out into Canada,¹ and a short time will have to elapse before I can get money from England. . . . – When you read me that letter the other night I found myself envying James Joyce at Vichy – so much nearer the centre of his world and of mine: with so many more friends than I have too, within some sort of reach. I feel as if I were in some stony desert, full of shadows, in human form. I have never imagined the likes of it, in my worst nightmares.

Yrs.

259. *To Terence W. L. MacDermot*†   [Toronto]
Nov. 19. 1940.

Dear Mac Dermot. . . . – I greatly enjoyed my talk with your wife (and also the interesting young refugee). – The more I think of that Hart House burlesque, the more I feel that if the Master (whom I rather highhandedly borrowed to have a little fun with) realised how *impressed* I was – for I can say with my hand on my heart that I do not believe another such educational, or recreative, wonder is to be found anywhere on this earth, and that it is a tremendous feat to have built up that *hive* of collegiate activity – he would not mind the burlesque form my admiration took.² – Anyone reading it misses the point you could tell him – who does not see that the emphasis is upon the last scene of all, where the wife of the stupid Englishman, having listened spell-bound to his story, cries:

"But how *tremendous* ... It is like the Arabian Nights, what you have told me. It is what is so wonderful in America and could be found in no other country. ... It is staggering! It is like the Pyramids. It is more than the skyscrapers and the waterfalls. It is

¹ The Lewises had received their two-month extension, but this was now at an end.
² See "I Dine With the Warden," *America, I Presume*. In this long, humorous account of a visit to a social and athletic centre in Toronto, L. calls the building "Brunswick Hall." Its original, Hart House, is a part of the University of Toronto. MacDermot had expressed his fear lest the real warden, satirised as "Brandeleboyes" in the book, should be offended.

a cataract of young bodies. ... You *stupid Englishman*! How I wish I were a man!"¹

Really my piece was a hymn of praise, couched in burlesque form, using the "Rugger Blue" motif to produce the slapstick. — No great harm seems to have been done, fortunately, but above is the appropriate (and true) answer, should it be brought up at any time.

I think I will try and avail myself of your extremely kind offer to use the walls of your house for an afternoon to show pictures. I must try and get hold of the pictures (or drawings, rather). Meanwhile should one or two suitable sitters for chalk portraits (50 to 80 dollars) occur to you, please send them to me.

Yours etc.
WYNDHAM LEWIS

260. *To Geoffrey Stone* c/o Thomas Cook & Son.
68. King Street (West)
Toronto.
Nov. 20. 1940.

My dear Stone. We have moved to an interim dwelling — an apartment-hotel² which is cheap at least. ...

... This seems a "land of opportunity": though of course one's problem is to keep calm while this or that opportunity is pruned down and secured to one.

While travelling up and down I have often thought over the *lost intellectual* of Bethlehem: and as I know you have a great deal more in you than politics, you should not really be lost because (happily) removed from their baleful proximity. — I feel that you could write some very powerful short stories, or rather I know you could. With your savage and pessimistic humor you could beat out some short tales which would be far better worth doing than political essays. Why don't you try your hand?

For instance. 1. Hoffmann³ was *not* killed by the bear – or

¹ *America, I Presume*, p. 262.

² The Tudor Hotel, which became the Lewises' permanent residence in Toronto and the memorable setting of *Self Condemned*.

³ William F. Hoffman, a friend of Stone's. Stone had told L. of a moose-hunting trip he had made with Hoffman, on which they had encountered a furious she-bear.

drowned in the lake. But he might have been. It might not have been that very charming young catholic (no need whatever to use *him*). It might have been Philip Johnson[1] – whom you had never seen before. – The *first person*, I think. "I took the plane at the La Guardia field inwardly saluting the name of that great and good mayor etc. etc." – 2. Phil[2] is obviously the hero of a short story. The dark and graceful (though possibly exotic) rider who vanquished Phil in the re-run race: the grocer with wide hips who walks his horse about as if it were a dog on a leash. 3. Calder[3] and his "mobiles" is a promising clay for the fingers of a Tchekov. 4. Fitzgerald[4] ... but I need go no further. Your immediate experience swarms with material for the art of the fictionist. And you have the irony – the knowledge of the social mechanism that is necessary – the eye for the mordant detail. If you followed my advice, you would attend to this at once – without of course *neglecting* the cows and pigs – who, in conjunction with Stanley,[5] might supply you with something very valuable. (Four pages say, carefully written. Write and rewrite, as carefully as you write a poem). . . .

Yrs

W. L.

. . .

261. *To John Slocum*†[6]   Toronto.
Nov. 21. 1940.

Dear Slocum. I really dont know what to say about all this.[7] It would be an extremely serious matter for me if I did not sell my

---

[1] L. had met Stone through the architect Philip Johnson (b. 1906).

[2] The hired farmer of a friend of Stone's. Phil had defeated Stone in a horse-race.

[3] The sculptor Alexander Calder (b. 1898) was a neighbour of Stone's.

[4] William Fitzgerald, poet and a friend of Stone's.

[5] Stone's hired farmer.

[6] John Slocum (b. 1914), an expert on Joyce now serving with the United States State Department, met L. in New York in 1940. He saw a good deal of him during the year, helped him financially, and lent him the house in Sag Harbor. Working at the time as a literary agent with the firm of Russell & Volkening, Slocum took on *The Vulgar Streak* and attempted to sell it in the U.S.

[7] Slocum wrote to L. on November 16th, saying that the novel was

novel in New York: quite apart from the fact that the humiliation and unpleasantness I had to endure in order to be able to write it would have been endured in vain. The best thing would be for us to adhere to our contractual arrangement, and for me to give my individual attention to the marketing of it. I reserved that right to myself in my contract because the matter of such a book as this is immeasurably more important than the sale of a story or an article. – I believe that if I took certain steps about it I could secure its publication, accompanied by an adequate advance. When —— return it to you (for I feel sure that will happen as I told you) I want you immediately to mail it to me here in Toronto. I will show it to a person who can use some influence in securing its respectful reception and just treatment.

By the way, may I correct you upon a point which may be only a verbal carelessness on your part, but which if repeated might have unfortunate results? There is of course no "criticism of England" involved in this book – not of *England*, but of something that handicaps England intellectually. In so far as the theme may be detached from the pure storytelling, the educational system of the English Middle Class as organised by Dr. Arnold in the last century comes under fire.

Most educated men are agreed that the Arnold system is inferior to that obtaining in Scotland, where social snobbery (the bane of the Arnold system) scarcely exists at all, and it is within the reach of the poorest crofter's child to acquire a speech and behaviour that fit him for any position in the state, however high. – To dramatize that situation (in so far as that has been done in my book) is not to "criticize England" therefore, but to deplore Dr. Arnold. Moreover it is very much to the interest of England that attention should be directed (however inadequately, and in the course of a mere story) to the problems of coarseness and illiteracy. . . .

The weather here is mild and sunny. On the whole I prefer Montreal as a city – if only because there one does not have to sign so many slips of paper in order to buy a bottle of Scotch.

Yours sincerely
WYNDHAM LEWIS

being returned to him by a publisher who, like the publisher previously applied to, thought "that it was too critical of England to be accepted by the American people at this time."

262. *To Geoffrey Stone* [Toronto]
Dec. 5. 1940.

Dear Stone I have been up in Ottawa among the civil servants and statesmen, and found your letter on my return. Better address us now *Hotel Tudor* .... We shall be here for a little anyway. (It is an apartment hotel – 14 bucks a week. One big room, kitchen and bathroom).

... – I was glad that my advice is to be followed and that you will try the short story (or the "poem in prose"). Eight hundred words to five thousand. You are perfectly equipped for it: it is only a matter of getting into the way. Don't be afraid of using the hog-pen, the cows, Stanley, Rastas,[1] Deucey (?)[2] with the chicken round her neck: and (if Miss Ford did not think you were taking a leaf out of the reporter's notebook)[3] one of those beautiful little pictures – the Virgin in the Sky, or the Virgin of Leon Bloy. – Leon Bloy and Deucey with the chicken-necklace and the Western saddle – the thunder of the competing farmers in the lane[4] and the Lithuanian publicum:[5] that is a lively backcloth for a little tale. – You ought to be able to do a better childhood or schoolboy piece than Saroyan. Don't forget "doin' me penmanship" and "who wants to know!"[6] There must be a lot more where that came from –. As to politics, you realize that there are politics in everything: in Western saddles, hogpens, and Wop-penmanship! Much more *real* politics than one usually gets in a formal essay. – *And* you have an admirable ear for dialogue. ...

Yrs
W. L.

[1] Stanley's Labrador retriever.

[2] A mongrel terrier belonging to the Stones. To cure him of killing chickens, they tried hanging one of his victims around his neck.

[3] Mrs. Stone's foster-mother was Lauren Ford (b. 1891), a wealthy painter and illustrator of books for children. Miss Ford's work had been featured several times in *Life*, and she had suffered from publicity as a result. "The Virgin in the Sky" was a picture of hers that L. had seen.

[4] The horse-race referred to in L.'s letter of November 20th.

[5] Many farmers in the Stones' neighbourhood were of Lithuanian descent.

[6] Phrases from a story Stone had told L. of an early experience with some ill-bred schoolmates.

263. *To Geoffrey Stone*
Tudor Hotel,
559 Sherbourne Street,
Toronto.
Dec. 7. 1940.

Dear Stone. For the first time since our arrival I now have a chance of establishing myself. – Next Thursday I give the first of three talks on the radio. Up at Ottawa again I arrived at a moment when "war-records" were uppermost in the mind of the director of the museum.[1] He has asked me to give a lecture there . . . and he proposed that I do five portrait-drawings of prominent army and navy personalities. . . . Also he is confident he can obtain portrait-commissions for me in Ottawa. Further, I met many personages in Ottawa who showed benevolence. . . . – Here in Toronto there is likewise business to be done. I am preparing a pamphlet (50 pages)[2] . . . . Also we go to dinner with one of Toronto's bigwigs on Sunday . . . .

In New York it was a blank wall, and a particularly malignant blank at that. In my worst dreams I have never imagined such a situation. Some day I will tell you all the details of it – they are terrifying, but enlightening. Here of course, people are more in touch with England, and so, aside from anything else, I do benefit by that. . . .

. . . – After the winter of my discontent in the long and chilly shadow of that statue of Liberty, I feel as if I had come up out of a coalmine or a dungeon into the fresh air again. All I need is one more heave, and, to change to equestrian metaphor, I shall be in the saddle. . . .

Yours,
W. L.

[1] Any interest in war-records would, L. assumes, redound to his benefit, since he had participated in the Beaverbrook scheme in the first war, and his painting *A Canadian Gunpit*, a fruit of the scheme, was in the National Gallery of Canada.

[2] *Anglo-Saxony: A League that Works* (Toronto, 1941).

264. *To Geoffrey Stone* Toronto.
Monday.
[December 1940]

Dear Stone. . . .

This city is said to be the most American of Canadian cities; but it is a mournful Scottish version of America (union with which it yearns for dismally). However outside the business classes there are a number of pleasant people here: and anywhere I can find work is a good place to me. The Romain Building is a blackmail pile, plastered with statues, dated 1852 – erected by my grt-uncle Charles Romain,[1] which gives me a certain sentimental footing. Surely he must have been one of the earliest Torontonians, before the Scotch swamped the original French and English and with their asphyxiating godliness set up a reign of terror for the toper and the whoremaster, which makes life curiously difficult for the person who likes a couple of mild cocktails a day. – Do not let this rather sombre picture deter you however from paying the place a visit. Where there's a will there's a way and closetted in my little studio we could satisfy our craving for alcohol. Not far away are places of terrific beauty: and Hart House is a place that has to be seen to be believed. I also listened to a Czech refugee playing Johann Sebastian Bach the other day as well as I have ever heard it done.

I have been wondering what results you have got up to date in the story line. . . . – Have you made any expeditions to Boston or New York? – Canadians by the way are now finger-printed before entering the U.S.A.: and one who visited Buffalo for the day had five dollars removed from him at the frontier, and was left with 35 cents to go into Buffalo with. But Americans coming here are not subjected to such annoyances. . . .

Yrs

W. L.

. . .

[1] A relative on his father's side.

265. *To Henry T. Volkening*†¹ [Toronto]
[January 1941]

Dear Mr. Volkening. Is *How Green was My Valley* or *The Corn is Green* anti-anything but a system that requires overhauling – and which, Mr. Churchill has assured Englishmen, the war will see put right?² – In the U.S.A. I suffered quite enough on account of the fact that I was prominent in England as a writer (and so it was good fun to aim kicks at me) and I struggled for long enough with a childish anti-Englishness, to find your remarks strongly irritating (as well as defamatory) as doubtless you intend them to be. – What however is true is that this book was written for England, and that in the U.S.A. just at present, anything that has a bearing upon the internal social structure of England and the problems that will demand attention in the future, would not be regarded as apropos, for *first* and quite rightly it is necessary to awaken the American people to their peril, and to show them only the magnificent endurance of a people at war. – You, as a German-American, can feel little sympathy for poor old England, I know and I do not blame you. But speaking as one who has travelled a good deal about this world – and whose mother was as Irish as your partner Mr. Russell³ – I venture to assert that for humanity, *modesty*, and a desire for justice the inhabitants of England far excel any other people I have so far met. And an Irish chieftain (the O'Gorman) once said the same thing to me, and affirmed that his own people were in every way inferior to the much-abused "Sassenach" (to use Mr. Woodburn's word).⁴

Yours sincerely

¹ Partner in the firm of Russell & Volkening, literary agents.
² Volkening wrote to L. on January 6th, saying that *The Vulgar Streak* had been again returned by a publisher. He explained that editors were afraid of the novel because "the attitude is mildly anti-British."
³ Diarmuid Russell, son of the poet A.E.
⁴ John Woodburn, of Doubleday Doran.

266. *To Geoffrey Stone* [Toronto]
Jan 15. 1941

Dear Stone. I was glad to know that work had started in the stone-study,[1] and that you had plunged back to your sources (unsaroyan-like, gott sie dank!) Do not forget "I'm doin' me penmanship", and "Who wants to know!" – When you go to Philadelphia to learn all about how to coat the Connecticut rock with a film of dung,[2] take your notebook, and return from that fortnight with at least *one* short story. – The journey there, and the one back, should supply two more, or at least material.

I work like a helot and march up and down to my studio in blizzards. If you can come up here I can promise you a little company – not the local magnates, but odds and ends of people who entertain. A little French Canadian cousin of mine (Pierette) is good value, and relates how her grandfather at Christmas would stand in the doorway of the farm to welcome his thirty or forty children and grandchildren, who would kneel and receive his blessing. – Almost a scene from the notebook of [1 or 2 words]. . . .

Yrs. W. L.

267. *To Augustus John*† Toronto, Canada.
April 3rd 1941.

Dear John. How are you getting on? For eighteen months I have been in the land of the Yankees. That has not been a pleasure – I was obliged to go there to see what could be done, as the war would have prevented me from making even a precarious living in England. Even with Peace in full flower, in the States things were difficult. Here in Canada I am doing better.

I have often greatly desired to get back to England, but never had money enough. From very garbled versions I have followed in the American press the course of events. Thank goodness the English have succeeded in keeping Germany out, from all accounts there seems very little chance of a successful invasion now.

Last summer in New York everybody was convinced that

---

[1] Stone's study was in a stone wing of a mainly wooden house.
[2] Stone was going to take a short course in "bio-dynamic farming."

England was about to be invaded. I pointed out that twenty miles of water controlled by the most powerful fleet in the world was a problem for which the German Staff had no solution. At the time that was regarded as pathetic patriotism. Now they are betting in New York 80 to one against invasion. Meanwhile I know that England is suffering in the most terrible way. I was greatly relieved to see photographs of you and Dorelia[1] (in *Picture Post*) which seemed to indicate that you were profitably employed in painting instead of wasting time in some official capacity for which other people are better suited. Please remember me very kindly to Dorelia: and may the time come soon when this nightmare past we can meet again.

If that evil genius of these latter days, Herr Hitler, would only dispatch himself and allow the world to return to peaceful occupations! I have lost everything – thousands of books, pictures and belongings. But that is nothing to what many people have lost and will lose. – In these sheltered countries (even Canada) they have not the least shadow of a notion what war signifies. The only consolation is that the people who provoked it – the stupid vulgar and violent gang in Berlin – will lose the gamble. That at least is certain now. – What pictures have you painted? And an *autobiography*![2] Marshalling the past is a fantastically difficult operation, I have discovered. I shall buy *Horizon* and get a whiff of the old air we breathed together once, on those incredibly peaceful horizons of pre-war No. 1.

Yours ever,
WYNDHAM LEWIS

268. *To Robert Hale*†[3]   [Toronto]
April 16. 1941.

Dear Hale. At last we are in touch – your letter of March 27 is just to hand. When I arrived here in Canada five months ago I

[1] Mrs. John.

[2] John had written to L. saying that he was at work on a series of recollections, some of which were appearing in *Horizon*. These were not assembled in book form until 1953, when John published *Chiaroscuro: Fragments of Autobiography: First Series*.

[3] Robert Hale, Ltd. had contracted to publish L.'s next novel, *The Vulgar Streak*.

made enquiries about the safest route for the dispatch of the MSS and found that by the Clipper a packet of that weight would cost in the neighbourhood of fifty dollars. All other means of transport are unsafe, and they do not grow more safe as time goes on. – I wrote you: . . . I cabled you. Your letter received today is the first response I have had.

Now in 10 days time a lady of my acquaintance is leaving on the Clipper for England, and she has offered to take the Mss. and see that you get it the moment she reaches London. She will cable me as soon as it has been delivered into your hands. This is the best bet, it seems to me, and I am entrusting it to her. She is a very rich woman, and probably she will not be delayed at Lisbon or anything of that kind. . . .

The novel is extremely carefully written and I feel pretty sure that you will be pleased with it. It is a tragedy. I do not know how at a time like this, when people ask for light reading and "escape" literature, it will fare. If there *is* any place for the tragic, it will at least be at home in a Blitzed society.

From another point of view it should be apposite, for it deals, incidentally, with the oppressive and withering effects of class discrimination: how many of the strongest and most potentially useful intellects in England have been held back, occulted, and denied expansion on account of the obsession of the "Top Drawer", or the Old School Tie. I have named it "The Vulgar Streak". – If things are not too utterly disorganized – if a bomb doesn't hit the printing works just as the sheets have been stacked up to go to the Binders – it should be helpful to the firm of Hale. . . .

I am glad to be out of the States. Who was it, by the way, who told you I was an American?[1] That is so little true that in order to get a two months extension of my visitors permit I had to be fingerprinted and had such a dose of American officialdom that – although we have to be polite to the States in the hope that at long last they may agree to come in and help us – I am thoroughly sick of the Stars and Stripes and all they stand for. Needless to say, this is not for publication. In New York I ran into a great deal of anti-English sentiment – a hangover from Fenian days: but the mentality of the sturdily-rebellious colony, the inferiority-complex

---

[1] Hale said in his letter that he was surprised to learn of L.'s American citizenship. He said he thought L. must find his "native land" more pleasant than Europe.

of a "new" society, is everywhere present, even at this late date. – I think they have a better president than they deserve in Mr. Roosevelt, who will help England in *every* way, if they will let him.

My presence on the North American continent is a question of force majeure. I can earn a living here whereas I doubt if I could in England. When the war started I wanted to go back, but at the time I was going through a minor economic Blitz of my own, and had not the necessary jack.

269. *To Lorne Pierce*†[1] [Toronto?]
 [May 1941]

Dear Dr. Pierce. . . .

I was very very interested in *The Armoury in our Halls*,[2] and have been wondering a lot about the whole issue you raise there – of nationhood for a small English-speaking state, isolated in a New World, in close proximity to a state so great as the U.S.A. The lassitude you speak of I too have noticed. But between England and the States – England distant, aloof, and snooty; the States near, dynamic, and a bit snooty too – poor Canada has not had much chance to find itself. It is trebly divided – between a West and an East, and a French and an English, in addition to the New World and the Old World division of loyalty. Yet it has produced one thing that is as good in its field as anything else on the North American continent, namely the Canadian school of painting. – Of particular interest to me were pages 16–19. I should like to see you write an entire pamphlet on *that* theme.[3] . . . The "*practical politicians*" and . . . their stable-mates the "hardboiled businessmen" have somehow or other to be tamed, if not civilised, in any

---

[1] Lorne Pierce (b. 1890) was at this time Editor-in-Chief of the Ryerson Press in Toronto. L. went to him first with the idea of drawing him. Pierce was pleased with the resulting portrait; he liked also L.'s outline for a small propaganda book on the British Commonwealth. At his urging, L. completed the work, and the Ryerson Press published it as *Anglosaxony: A League That Works* in July 1941.

[2] A brochure by Pierce (privately printed at the Ryerson Press in 1941) on the theme of Canadian nationalism and closer Commonwealth relations.

[3] Under the title "Literature and Life," Pierce argues the importance to a nation of its writers and artists and warns of the dangers of poor education in the arts.

country: and brain-trusts should be established immune from their interference. . . .

Yours sincerely.

270. *To Lorne Pierce*† [Montreal]
Friday, May 31, 1941.

My dear Dr. Pierce. . . .

Now as to *the title*.¹ – . . . Like a man's name, the title of a book is important: but I want this book to go into the shops and news-stands with a name that will help you to sell it, and I shall let you have the last word.

The world we live in is tame and trite: but too tame or trite a title might defeat its own ends. As you said, "Democracy" for instance is a word in a title that makes people shy away. – Of the titles suggested by you I like best

Anglosaxon Commonwealth.
*A League that will Work.*²

As to the other 3 you mention, "breed" – like in other contexts "breeding" – is a word that cannot be used. (The "Bulldog Breed" has done that in for good, as a "woman of breeding" haughtily purred by some soap manufacturers wife tends to disqualify the other).

"Not by Guns Alone" is next best to "Anglosaxon Commonwealth"; but, as you point out, it might suggest some mental reservation about the use of guns that one does not wish to convey. It is only behind our guns that we can build up the *other* things that interest us more.

What I consider one of the most important features of my pamphlet is the stuff about the "universalism" of so-called "Anglosaxon" Man. Miss Dor. Thompson³ a week ago referred to the "Cosmic virtues" of the American people: and it seems to me that the English, owing to their seafaring habits, possess, in their different way, those cosmic virtues too. That of course is why they are so tolerant, and suffer so little (comparatively) from xenophobia.

¹ Of L.'s forthcoming book.
² Pierce wrote to L. on May 28th, saying that he had picked this main title and subtitle out of half a dozen choices.
³ The American columnist and broadcaster.

More and more it becomes apparent that we the island-nations, with our sea-power, will be the *outsiders,* in the coming years: I mean that of the big power-groups that are in process of formation, we are the inhabitants or controllers of the great ocean wastes, *outside* the old continental nucleus. I agree with Miss Dor. Thompson, that we shall probably be driven out [of] the Mediterranean (the new Air power techniques having caught us napping). I cannot see the war ending neatly in two years, say, in a routine peace-treaty. I think we should be prepared to take our stand as a vast peripheral force, as in effect we have always been. We shall subdue the land-citadel in the end.

Whether such a pattern proves to be correct or not, unquestionably both English and American power and security rests upon the use of the great oceans, and until seaplanes can be built of the dimensions of the Queen Mary that must remain so. Hence my insistence upon the cosmic destiny – and the certain *abstractness* of mind that goes with it, like the Beduin – of the so-called Anglosaxons.

It is in *that* direction that I should look for my title. . . .

Yours sincerely,

271. *To Lorne Pierce*†   [Montreal]
June 12, 1941.

My dear Dr. Pierce. First: "A League that Works"!¹ It is rather like forcing Augustus John to wear a top-hat – or dressing President Roosevelt up in one of Goering's uniforms.

That, and nothing but that, is *so* flat and colourless – it is so inexact as a title descriptive of the contents – that I have to *insister* a little about its use.

You can print "Anglosaxony – A League that *Works*",² in type of equal size, if you like. . . . But as I wrote the book, you must allow me *one letter* of my own in the title: namely a Y. . . .

Yrs sincerely

¹ Pierce telegraphed to L. on June 11th: "Everyone here votes for 'A League that Works.'"
² For another week Pierce and his colleagues resisted the inclusion of "Anglo-Saxon" in the title; then they gave in.

272. *To Lorne Pierce*† [Montreal]
June 17. 1941.

Dear Dr. Pierce. As the publication date for the pamphlet is now not far off, a few things have to be considered. . . .

Do not entrust a blurb to a local intelligentsia (or to the individual who "read" the mss. and held us up at the start). . . .

At this juncture it may be as well to tell you that I did not exactly hit it off with the intellectuals of Toronto. Toronto is probably not a good place to be an intellectual in, and I suppose that it is too much to expect that intellectuals from more clement regions (more clement towards the Intelligence) should be welcomed. . . .

All I want to obviate where possible, is the thing falling into the hands of some ex-fellow-traveller who remembers me as a critic of Communism; or some University professor who thinks I am too big for my boots. . . .

. . . – The matter of the destination of advance or publicity copies also has to be considered. . . . A copy to my friend Mrs. Alice Roosevelt Longworth in Washington – it will make her very angry, because she loathes Democracy and all its works! One to my friend Chancellor Capen, of Buffalo University, who *likes* Democracy. And one to Edmund Wilson who is so fond of Marx he cant see the point of anything else, but who would review it. . . .

Yours sincerely

273. *To T. Sturge Moore*† [Toronto]
July 15. [1941]

Dear Moore. Here is an attempt to reach you with a note; but since I do not know if you still live at Well Walk, and seeing that my note has to run the gauntlet of torpedo and bomb, not to mention the mail and the censor, heaven knows if you will ever get it! – I am in this odd corner of the world by accident, not by design. Where you came to see me in London in '39 was the nicest place I've ever had: things had started to look up – another year or so and I should no longer have been poor! But the shadow of approaching war chilled the business-world: during the year preceding the outbreak of war debts began piling up, so I went to

New York, intending to collect enough good American dollars to pay my debts at least, and get back in 6 to 9 months. Alas, New York was crowded with people on the same errand as myself – and they were smarter than I was, apparently. I spent what I'd taken with me and then things became grim. They have remained grim ever since. I have not been able to make enough money to pay my fare back – owing to currency controls I cannot get a penny from England and here I am. However, I have been miraculously fed and sheltered. (I have what the American's call an "angel"). But I long some day to be delivered out of the land of the "new" nations, back into the "old" world. – So much for *my* news. What are you doing? Nothing unpleasant has happened to any friend of mine in England, so far as I have heard. So it has never occurred to me that any mischance could have befallen you in Hampstead, especially as the Germans do not appear to have visited it much. You put in safety your belongings I expect: but send me a line to tell me you are well.

When the war-drums began beating, and that dreadful war-dance commenced again, I was – as you may have heard – very greatly exercised about it. Our tribe had suffered so fearfully the last time. It seemed to me to be my duty to provide such feeble discouragements as I could. In retrospect this seems unrealistic of me, and a great waste of energy. I feel pretty certain that this particular convulsion has some purpose, and promises some concrete settlement of outstanding injustice and follies. It seems almost mathematically demonstrable that in the end, we shall defeat the Axis. The world which will emerge from that defeat will be purged: there is an uncommonly good chance, since the peace will be global and the victors absolute master of the world, that the peace will endure. Whereas the very scale and intensity of the misery that will threaten every nation afterwards will assure heroic measures of public control, which automatically should end the selfish chaos into which our western society had drifted. – I hope I am not too sanguine. But I have been very impressed by the intelligence and humanity of Mr. Roosevelt, as observed at fairly close hand. His "new-deal" might extend – though not of course directed from or imposed from any centre – to all corners of the earth. A "new-deal" in some form or other is sorely needed, in almost every nation, where industrial technique has outstripped social organisation, and made a nonsense of government on the old lines. Well, we shall see. When you answer this – if you ever get it – give me any news you can, of things in general (books that have appeared?) and more especially tell me how you have got on yourself in the midst of this military hurricane. How calm those days were before the epoch of wars and social revolution, when you used to sit on one side of your work-table and I on the other, and we would talk – with trees and creepers of the placid Hampstead domesticity beyond the windows, and you used to grunt with a philosophic despondence I greatly enjoyed. It was the last days of the Victorian world of artificial peacefulness – of the R.S.P.C.A. and London Bobbies, of 'slumming' and Buzzards cakes. As at that time I had never heard of anything else, it seemed to my young mind in the order of nature. You – I suppose – knew it was all like the stunt of an illusionist. You taught me many things. But you never taught me *that*. I first discovered about it in 1914 – with growing surprise and disgust. – With all good wishes.

274. *To Lorne Pierce*† [Toronto]
July 16. 1941.

My dear Dr. Pierce. . . . To begin with your last item first: it is no surprise to *me* that the local sheets do not tumble over each other to review my pamphlet. First, and I daresay most important – it was not published in New York or London, but in Queen St. Toronto. A prominent bookseller, unsolicited, took me aside the other day and said: If he might venture to give me a little advice, another time if I thought of publishing, it would be much better to have it published in New York or London. – This was entirely unsolicited, had no connection with anything I had been saying to him (except that I asked how the book had been selling).[1]

I am sure you are better acquainted than I am with your compatriots peculiarities: but perhaps you have not fathomed the depth of their distrust for anything Canadian (that is one of the things that made success so difficult for the Canadian School of

[1] Pierce wrote to L. on July 18th, declaring his disappointment in the sales of L.'s book and adding: "There's some truth in what the Toronto bookseller says."

Painters). And this distrust extends to anything appearing here, or to any stranger stopping here – for more than 2 or 3 days!

It is a very important fact: for if you cannot break their attitude you will never have any more artists or writers here. Or so it seems to me.

As [for?] a visitor like myself, from another planet – bringing with him a great reputation – they sniff at him suspiciously. They ask each other – "What the heck is he doing *here*. For just as there is something degrading about a book having itself brought out here, so there is presumably something degrading about *being* here. . . .

For the rest my discouraging remarks about political uplift, and the need for cutting our garment according to our cloth (our cloth being mere human nature) is quite enough to shoo off the "idealist" of which species you have a fair share in Toronto.

Thus the lady who does your advertising asked me to give an interview to the trade paper the "Nomad". A Miss —— duly turned up, interviewed me for an hour and a quarter: said she would write at once, both for the Nomad and the other trade paper, sending me the mss. next day for my okay. Of course she didn't. I learn she has now left on vacation. So if she ever does write anything, it will appear in October, when it is too late to be of any help to the book.[1]

Why is this thus? I can easily explain that. Miss —— is an "Idealist" – she identifies the term "Democracy" with all the injustices that the Marxist would forever abolish. And she asked me whether I thought these injustices should be tolerated just because a war was on. – I answered that I was just as alive as she was to these injustices: but while the bombs were showering down (not it is true in Toronto) we should think only of winning the war: that Democracy was an asset that we could not afford to neglect while the war lasted anyway and that we could not hope *to have at the same time* a great war and a great social revolution. I fear Miss —— was not satisfied. . . .

Yours sincerely,

[1] Pierce wrote in his letter that the interview would appear in August.

275. *To Robert Hale*†   Toronto.
Aug. 10. 1941.

Dear Hale. I forget what I said to you in my last letter. But as far as I can recall it was not much – mainly to do with book.[1] . . . The trouble about getting it published in the States seems to be (1) that any English writer writing about the English scene, is required at present to show a martial England, and not to impinge upon social problems. (Even in the States social problems are a bit shelved.) Now my book is a straight novelist's novel, if ever there was one: but the character selected for depiction – the key-pin of the story – is so deeply stained with the deposits on the obscure bed of the life-stream, which have nothing to do with England-at-war (though they may have a lot to do with England-at-peace) that there is a snag as seen in N.Y. where England is news-value just now. *England* just means *propaganda* today, and thank goodness it does! – There is a point (2): the English writer (qua *writer*) is not popular in the U.S.A. as you probably know. Then beyond that is the fact that the book-business, in America has been annexed to politics and reduced to a level of ephemeralness, news-value, and mere fact-finding past belief. A dramatised record of fact-finding, worked up as political instrument, like *The Grapes of Wrath* – that is the standard requirement. Had those rules of literary production obtained at the time of Dickens, we should have had a book called *Do The Boys Hall*, which would have been all about that particular abuse: and another called *Chops and Tomato Sauce*, which would have been all about the iniquities of the Sergeant Buzzfuzzes of this life: a book aiming at the reform of the Breach of Promise laws. As Dickens would have done them they would have been admirable – though it is doubtful if he would have been allowed to do them in *his* way. We should however have lost four-fifths of the things we are all agreed in admiring in his packed canvasses.

You may think that I have kept pretty closely to a theme in *The Vulgar Streak*: even the title rather implying that: which is true enough. But the book has not that didactive bareness that always distinguishes a propaganda book, or a purely political book: or even a play of strict social import, such as the *Médecin Malgré Lui*. . . .

[1] *The Vulgar Streak*.

I find it difficult to make a guess as to the condition of the booktrade. It is down fifty per cent, I suppose, in sales. Many things being equal, which they're not! – I imagine the lending libraries should function as usual. But how can people read books with warplanes incessantly bumbling away over their heads. As a soldier I found it wellnigh impossible to read. – Yet I hear there is a good bit of reading done. Perhaps you can supply me with the facts: for it has some bearing upon how I should occupy my time.

The obvious book for me to write just now is a "fact-finding" – factual – book. And the facts within reach are facts about America. – But it would be utterly impossible for me to do that. Any English writer temporarily resident here is debarred not only from uttering a word of criticism, but any word at all, relative to the U.S.A. or to Canada. For there is nothing you can say that is not interpreted as *criticism*. The reason for this excessive, pathological, sensitiveness is complex. *They* say it is the fault of the Britisher: and I think England has some responsibility. But that accounts for only a fraction of this far from robust reaction to detached observation.

(There is a book entitled *Thanks Twice!* written by 2 children aged 12 and 13.[1] This precocious pair are "war-guests" and they do criticize their hosts – American and Canadian. The book has aroused a storm of controversy here. People refuse to buy it in Canada, because, they say, they refuse to put any money in the childrens pockets! It may be that this little book is too "outspoken" I don't know, for the present period of nervous stress.)

. . . – Do I like America? I am so sick of answering that question here that I no longer know what the correct answer is. But I think probably I should say that if you have lots of money America is very nice. The landscape (Vermont, Western New York etc.) is marvellous. Half the population have diabetes, and their cooking is far too sweet: but it has points. Their youth is the best-looking in the world – to that I am prepared to swear anywhere. But you know all that: you've been here. I so infinitely prefer Europe to America that I find it difficult to answer the stock question about how do you like the latter. But I suppose I like it all right. . . .

Yours,

[1] Caroline and Eddie Bell, *Thank You Twice: or How We Like America*, ed. by Alden Hatch (New York, 1941).

276. *To Geoffrey Stone* Toronto
Sept. 3. 1941.

Dear Stone. . . . Things have come to an awful pass here: if I don't do something to break out of the net, I shall end my days in a Toronto flophouse. . . . Anything is worth trying. – A war causes fearful misery – I am only one of the multitude of victims of this one: but the misery of having no money in a strange land is not the least unpleasant of the many varieties of blight. – My novel is published this month in London ("The Vulgar Streak", it is called). If I could only get money *into* this blasted country I could start writing another book and should be given a good advance on signing my contract. . . . – Well, now I must return to *contriving*. I am determined to free myself somehow. – My best blessings on all the Stones.

Yr. W. L.

277. *To Geoffrey Stone*† Toronto.
Sept. 23. 1941

Dear Stone. . . . I am back as you see in this godforsaken city and have been rushing up and down this tedious land; on "business" errands. I have just returned from the Maritime Provinces, where I went to paint a magnate. Back now, making ready to portray another big shot. For all of which I make less money than the least I should get elsewhere. But times being what they are! – As to visiting you in Connecticut, which both of us would dearly love to do, there are apparently great difficulties about moving from one country to the other . . . . Furthermore, the problem of merely keeping alive – of dovetailing one little financial return into the next – has kept me pretty well screwed down to one place. There have been moments when it looked as if things were going to shape up into something less oppressively *tout juste.* But there is great opposition here to any outsider, especially an Englishman (and even more – the last offence! – a well-known one). As one naturalised Canadian explained to me "No one would be *here* who could be anywhere else." He admitted he would much rather be in Europe, or the U.S.A. but said he was very stupid, and bad at his job so he couldn't help himself! – However my next portrait is of a *very* big shot. If I am not assasinated by the local portrait-painters it should put me on the map with so offensive a prominence that perhaps the wife of the local Provision Merchant (the Macy of Ontario) would vamp herself up and come round to sit. Then I should move into a higher income bracket at one bound. I might even decorate her chapel (though a methodist, she has candles and genuflexions).

Meanwhile the war, I fear is all set for a ten-year run. In Russia Herr Hitler has a gloomy mixture of success and unsuccess which promises to continue interminably: we do not seem able to develop enough strength to settle the matter once and for all; and the U.S.A. seems to look forward to 1944 as a propitious time to declare itself. Everything conspires to prolong the agony.

What news from Connecticut? Has there been any alteration? Nothing should ever change in so beautiful a place. . . .

Yrs W. L.

278. *To Naomi Mitchison*† [Toronto]
Sept. 24. 1941.

Dear Naomi. . . .

It is impossible in a letter to describe conditions here (in the States or Canada). In theory a picture dealer in 57th Street should be as serviceable for myself – or Moore, or Epstein or Grant – as a Bond Street dealer. In practice such is not the case. – Certainly I have done a lot of work here, in one way and another. It has mostly been portraits. But because I am a stranger they give me less than they would give a native: they are tough babies and often very silly babies too. . . .

. . . As to how I like it here, the answer is not at all. It is difficult to get permission to stop in the States for more than a year or so. But however much money I were offered I would not *live* in the States: and as to this place, all I need say is I like it no better. I feel that someone is sitting on my chest – having to start with gagged me – and singing Moody and Sankey all day long.

You will see that, suffering from such sensations as these I shall before long be moving on. But even if I had not these sensations, I should return to England soon, because, if the war is going on indefinitely, I should not wish to exile myself beyond a limited period: and the end of the war seems farther off every day.

I have, while in America, engaged in as much unofficial British propaganda as possible: and at first that was very unpopular for the English cause was very little understood. I had an article commissioned in New York and returned to me on the grounds that it was "British propaganda," and that they could not publish it unless I removed a passage referring to Nietzsche's dislike of German nationalism. I quoted from Nietzsche, where he said he could not advocate "nationalism and race-hatred ... on account of which the nations of Europe are at present bounded off and secluded from one another as if by quarantine ... a system of politics that makes the German nation barren by making it vain, and which is a *petty* system besides." – The editor seemed intensely surprised to hear that Nietzsche had written in this strain, and seemed to half-believe I had made it up! ...

I wonder how things are shaping in England? The artificial and temporary socialisation which a great war always imposes will I imagine in this instance remain in force after it is over, to a large extent. How will that affect all of us? ... – England will have to be rebuilt and that ought to stimulate everybody terrifically: are steps already being taken? The new Houses of Parliament – or whatever the building that houses the deliberative assembly may be called – will have to be pretty superlative, and would be none the worse for a lot of big semi-abstract panels. Anything doing in that direction do you suppose? Or would Sir —— still be there – the "master of paralysis" – standing in my way? ...

Yours ever

279. *To Frank Morley*†[1] [Toronto]
Oct. 17. 1941.

Dear Morley. The other day I had a very unpleasant surprise. For twenty years I had worn the same glasses, and I went to an eye-specialist to get new ones. He informed me that one of my eyes (which had always been weak, as the result of a youthful injury) was practically extinct. My other eye he said would be the same

---

[1] Morley had returned to America in 1939 to become a Director of Harcourt Brace and Company.

in six months time – if I had what he thought I had: namely glaucoma.

For a final diagnosis he required to make a test for *pressure* which consists of standing an instrument up on the eyeball. That I was unable to have done at the moment, as it might quite well I thought upset my eyes, and I had work to do the next day.

I cabled at once to ——— – who is also Eliot's doctor – in Harley Street. ——— cabled back that about two years ago when he examined my eyes there was no sign of glaucoma, but it might have developed in the meanwhile.

Next I visited a second eye-doctor to secure a second opinion. *He* was quite sure I had *not* got glaucoma. The first doctor, on the other hand, is one of the most highly esteemed specialists here: the second is much less well-known.

No. 1. doctor said that if the pressure-test gave a negative result, that then another cause must be looked for, and that *teeth* stood first on the list. – When I tell you that I have not been to a dentist since the last war, you will see that my teeth are not unlikely to rank as a septic centre of the first order.

Now as you know my year in New York and its neighbourhood was a hideous disaster – I could neither sell pictures, nor articles, nor stories, nor get lectures, nor do anything else that would produce a blue cent. I had a fair amount of money when I got there. When that was spent things became nightmarish to an unspeakable degree.[1] – No wonder *something* went wrong with me: alas that it should have been my eyes!

Here in Canada I have been able to make a living of sorts by

[1] In an earlier draft of this letter, L. expanded on his experience in New York: "I never thought I should hate a *street*: but I know and abominate every building in Fifth Avenue. I must have gone up and down it, in omnibus or on foot (according to whether I had the dime or not for the bus) – seeing the top of the wretched little Arc de Triomphe at the bottom appear over the edge of the hill at 34th St. – slowly increase in size as I marched or rumbled towards it – at least a thousand times. – For the people (the hard vulgarity, the silly 'toughness' of the Irish immigrant mass, shellacked into a sly, bluff, servility) I like no better than their city. (And this although in the abstract I have always liked the idea of America, and the American workman has a beautiful friendliness all his own.) The element that is so often regarded as the least attractive I found the best: namely the Jewish. My best friend in New York is a Russian Jewish young woman who writes – physically a Virginia Wolf of the Bronx, shrinking, and by turns mildly bold."

painting. But Canada is a small and very backward country . . . and I have done about all there is to do in these parts.[1] . . .

As for the *eyes*, I do not believe that I have glaucoma (which has of course the sound of wishful thinking). Something is the matter, and I believe it is the teeth. . . . if my eyes go I go too. Loathsome as the world is, I do like to *see* it. *That* sort of blackout I could not live in.

To return to England is impossible, because the journey requires at least seven hundred dollars. An eye-operation, if that were necessary, would cost five hundred dollars, no doubt: the hospitals here charge even for the cotton-wool. Where one's health, or life, is at stake, naturally extortion runs riot. – *Teeth* is the only expense I *could* aspire to. . . .

With this letter I am sending you the mss. of a short book, for which I should be able to get *something*. – It is the case for Democracy: the sympathetic approach, and the commonsense of that. I like the old drab: I have done my best by her in *The Ideas with Which We Fight*.[2] . . .

                    Yrs

Lewis met Archibald MacLeish (b. 1892) in Paris in the 1920's, possibly through their mutual acquaintance, Ernest Hemingway. They never became close friends but continued to see one another and to correspond occasionally in the ensuing years. When Lewis was casting about for employment in the United States, he turned to MacLeish, who was then Librarian of Congress, for assistance. MacLeish and members of his staff made efforts to find a suitable opening, but these all proved fruitless.

[1] Here the earlier draft reads: "Things have come to such a pass here in my private affairs – I thought I had two final portraits, but the subject of one of them has heart-trouble and does not get better as fast as he expected, and the other job hangs fire – that I actually now want money to pay my rent next Tuesday, it is as bad as that."

[2] A revised and lengthened version of *Anglosaxony*. It was never published.

280. *To Archibald MacLeish*† [Toronto]
Oct 21. 1941.

Dear MacLeish. I have an ambition, and you might be able to help me realise it. I dearly long to be a "resident artist" at a university. . . .

Although I have succeeded in making a living of sorts here in Canada – mostly by portrait-painting – it is very gruesome work struggling with people about the shapes of their noses and the size of their feet: and Canada being so small and backward a country does not make it any easier. The "Royal Academy" seems to them a quasi-divine institution: and although I give them something worthy of the Uffizi or Prado the fact is that if Bellini or Goya came to Toronto they would probably be regarded as "reds" or "bums". I feel that until the war's end something taking with it a regular salary however small, and some time on the side to do my own work is what I should try and get. . . .

. . . I know more about painting than most people – I mean modern painting – and removed from the necessity of painting portraits I should be able to do non-pot-boiling work, which should be of great interest to the students. I should really be an asset to a College.

There was no harm I thought in explaining these simple requirements to you; placed as you are in the centre of things you may be able to help me. – I expect you are passably busy. The war has reached a hideous stage. The military mind has come up against the stone wall of popular resistance, and is dashing its head – or the heads of its cannon-fodder – against it. If Hitler takes Moscow, he will have still a hundred battles before him. And how many Germans I wonder will he have left at the end of it? – I am sure that *Germans* – not rubber, or oil – is the raw material that Herr Hitler will be most desperately in want of, before he has done.

Yours sincerely

281. *To John Crowe Ransom*†[1] [Toronto]
Oct 22 1941.

My dear Mr. Ransom. Since last corresponding with you I have been, first, living in Long Island (where I wrote a novel, "The Vulgar Streak", which is published this month in London); and after that, my twelve-month's, my visitor's permission for the U.S. having expired, I have been painting portraits of opulent methodists up in this ice-box. I dont want to go on doing this too long, and the climate does not suit me. I should like to go south again. And I can do so, I find, *if* I can discover some college in the U.S. that would like a "resident artist". Do you know of such a college? . . .

The large and famous universities, like Harvard and Yale, have a considerable personnel covering the field of art-instruction, and it is no use applying to them. It is the smaller, and more remote, colleges that are the best bet.

Perhaps you know of one: or perhaps you could sound out some place of which you have knowledge. Of course I should not want the fact that I am looking out in this way broadcast at all (alas I have enemies): but I know you will regard this letter as confidential.

As to the type of teaching I would do, or influence I would exert: I have really no bee in my bonnet *for* or *against* the most experimental types of painting. I have committed every enormity myself, in the painting line – and still do so. What I said about Picasso and the rest in New York got me into great hot water. All I meant by these articles, as a matter of fact, was that the artist must make enough money to support himself – must not live on the charity of a few rich people: that an art to be healthy must be independent of fashion and advertisement. – All artists, good and bad, understand this: only they are usually voiceless and get pushed around. But as to *teaching*, no one is better equipped than I am to explain every phase of modern art. . . .

I hope your very interesting paper is going along well, in spite of present conditions. There are few enough good reviews left on

[1] John Crowe Ransom (b. 1888) was at this time Carnegie Professor of Poetry at Kenyon College in Ohio and Editor of the *Kenyon Review*. He had been in correspondence with L. about possible articles for the review.

this tormented earth: and few enough people with the spirit left to run them. It will take at least another 2 years I should say to lay Hitler by the heels. Stalin, however, is not likely I feel to try another experiment in appeasement: and every day that raw material that is more essential even than oil or rubber – namely *Germans* – is diminishing, in battles after battle. – Well, please let me know if you can help me to find that College I seek!

Yours sincerely,

282. *To Lorne Pierce*† [Toronto?]
[October? 1941]

Dear Dr. Pierce. . . .
Young Le Pan told me that the University people "seem afraid of you." . . . You see what it means is this: should an artist (a figure-painter) arise in Canada who was of that small number who will not and cannot commercialize their work, he would starve.[1] He could not locate here. Even in the States, as you know, it is none too easy. Of the herds turned out annually by the schools, 99.9 per cent become commercial artists. – All this is, I believe, very well worth while excogitating. For the visual arts have been a very great factor in all civilised life. If we squeeze them out of existence – and there is a great deal more than a risk of that happening – we shall be like an animal that has lost a vital organ. I doubt if there can be any very fine culture without visual arts of a high order. – But I wrote a book once, *Men Without Art*, which is all about that. – The prestige of the visual arts is such that it still serves to maintain a great number of highly-salaried parasites, as the custodians of pictures and statuary mostly of dead artists. A *live* artist terrifies that gentry nearly out of their wits, where they browse comatosely in their offices! But I have strayed far afield, into abstract considerations. – Consider the reception your drawing received from the dozen or so people who have seen it. Had I done a similar thing of them, what would they have

[1] Dr. Pierce was making an effort to get L. some portrait commissions. He wrote to him on October 14th saying, "Too many, I fear, want something like a tinted photograph." Douglas LePan, now Professor of English at Queen's University, Kingston, Ontario, was the son of the Superintendent of the University of Toronto.

said? – Yet it is an admirable drawing, a "likeness", too. It is merely *not* like a photograph.

Yours sincerely

. . .

283. *To Robert Hale*†   Toronto
Nov. 9. 1941

Dear Hale. I should have written you before but have been much occupied and have waited for a relatively quiet spell. First, there are one or two things from your last letter to answer. There is *no* living, original or any sort for *any* of the characters, major or minor, in *The Vulgar Streak*. This is so absolutely the case that I forgot to answer your question in an earlier letter; but now, with the utmost emphasis, do so. For God knows *who* may turn up and say "That's me!" – In the past I have, as you know, had very great trouble in that connection. But it is some time since that I vowed that I would never introduce into any book of criticism, as evidence of something I disliked, quotes from the writing, or even the name, of any living "author" or journalist. The same *verbot* applies to fiction.

In *The Vulgar Streak* Mr. Vincent Penhale is not a pseudonym that covers some well-known (or little known) figure. If such a person exists anywhere he is not known to me. He was intended to be a sort of Julien Sorel (the hero of *Le Rouge et le Noir* of Stendhal.) Julien, you may recall, was the projection, in fictional literature, of the "ruthlessness" of Napoleon. Dostoievsky's Raskolnikoff (in *Crime and Punishment*) was suggested by Julien Sorel: and Raskolnikoff is always asking himself "What would Napoleon do if he were in my situation?" That accounts for the *crime*: and the *punishment* was what mostly overtakes such arrogance, or *hubris* as the Greeks called it.

My poor hero was another hero of that line. But Mr. Penhale was not an admirer of Hitler as Raskolnikoff. On the contrary: but he slowly comes to realize that the same *mal de siècle* which afflicts Herr Hitler – the worship of *force* and *action* – afflicts him too. His "heart-to-heart with Mr. Perl" (the title of one of the chapters) is where this enlightenment first comes to him. And in the last chapter but one – that in which his friend Martin sees him for the last time – he explains to his friend what his *fault* – if not his *crime* – has been. – In short, Vincent Penhale, though not himself a Fascist, nor yet a Communist, is a child of his time and infected with the disease that as a by-product gives us Fascism.

You will see from this account of my hero – and I give it you in such detail, not out of "author's vanity" but so that there should be *no possible mistake* – you will see that it would be a little difficult, even if one wanted to, to take some friend or acquaintance and turn him into a symbolical figure of this kind. It would be highly inartistic, of course, as well. But it would be very difficult. – It is not the way that the satirist goes about the pillorying of some character in real life. It is altogether too serious a writing project to be that. – It is not a social satire: it is a piece of tragic fiction.

As to Penhale's Horatio, Martin Penny-Smyth. I know no such person. He is described as a "pocket-Belloc." That (only 30 years younger) is what he is supposed to be. Belloc is the only person who might object. Only, as it obviously is *not* intended to be Mr. Belloc, he could not either. – Mrs and Miss Mallow, are, I hope, lifelike. But they are not portraits of anyone I know, or have known. So on all through the minor characters.

I am sick and tired of being victimised by people who attack my books via the law of libel. If such a thing happened again, and it became a habit to try and suppress my books on such pretexts, I would spend the last penny I could scrape together to defend myself and my livelihood. – Because most people are unable to imagine anything, and are only able to copy and caricature something under their noses, that does not apply to *me*.

So much for that: and I hope I have provided you with a full answer to any blackmailer or indignant coastguard or country doctor called Vincent Penhale.

... Canada is a small and backward country: the tongue of half of it is French. The English half is probably the dumbest English-speaking population anywhere. It reads less per capita than any other known civilised population.

As to whether I am an American: no, I am not. I should not be *here* if I were, in the first place. The U.S.A. only grants 12 months visit-permits for foreigners, and my 12 months is up. But if I had been an American I couldn't have held a commission in the English Army. – Now its up to you to say [in] what paper you saw it.¹ It's not important, except that such things usually have a purpose. – If you only knew how my wife and myself *enjoy* being over here! As I wrote you before I think, had I had the dough – the round sum necessary, clear and intact – I should have come back long ago. An idea for a new novel is kicking about in my mind. I dont know how things are shaping over there, but I just announce that I am, as it were, *enceint*. I do not feel I can go about very much longer without something happening. I just tell you this in case you are able to take on any new books, and that a novel is what you want.

Please send copies of *The Vulgar Streak* to the following people:

(1) Naomi Mitchison . . .

(2) to Mr. Orwell (I dont know his first name) author of "Lion and Unicorn", published by Gollanz² (cant spell *his* name!)

(3) H. G. Wells (address?) . . .

Well, good luck: and may Hitler go slower and slower until he stops altogether, and may that be *soon*.

Yours,

284. *To Mrs. Thomas W. Lamont*†³ [Toronto]
Nov. 11. 1941.

Dear Mrs. Lamont. . . .

I was greatly diverted by your account of the Aid to Russia reception. What, I wonder, would M. Stalin have thought, could he have seen the Patriarch grooming himself in the corner?⁴

With regard to the war, up here in Canada a strange apathy

¹ Hale wrote that he saw the item in the *Evening Standard*.

² *The Lion and the Unicorn: Socialism and the English Genius* (London, 1941). Actually this book was published by Secker and Warburg, although Gollancz was publishing Orwell at this time.

³ Mrs. Lamont (d. 1952) was a noted patron of the arts and friend of writers. L. met her in New York in the 1920's and saw her on his later visits. He was in correspondence with her regarding the Artist-in-Residence programme of the Carnegie Corporation, of which her husband was a director. L. hoped to secure a position in an American college under the auspices of the programme.

⁴ Writing to L. on November 8th, Mrs. Lamont gave an account of a reception she had given for the Committee for Russian War Relief. Among the guests was a prominent Metropolitan of the Russian Orthodox Church who "sat in a corner and combed his long white hair and longer white beard with a little pocket comb."

prevails. I have been here twelve months today, and I have never heard anyone, man or woman, in shop, hotel, or street-car, even mention the war. The subject is not taboo. It just does not interest. As there are many soldiers about, a sensation of unreality results. This effect of unreality attained its maximum the other day I think, when a tank moved down the street and as it was abreast a group of people, myself among them, waiting to cross the road, it let fly at a range of fifteen feet with a quite sizeable little cannon it had hidden in its flank. Its red flash darted at us, there was a deafening roar, the tank stopped and rocked. – I saw the first tank-attack at the battle of Messines: but in Bloor St. I was more deeply astonished. The monster rumbled on, firing as it went at shoppers. No one took the slightest notice. That was what was so queer. I got the feeling that something unreal was happening: and it was the people who gave it me.

Yrs sincerely

285. *To Leonard W. Brockington*†[1]   Toronto.
Nov. 15. 1941.

Dear Mr. Brockington. Thank you very much for so kindly returning me the cuttings from *Picture Post*. – I can imagine that, as you say, the Ottawa officials "charged with the task of creation," loathe their task.[2] Myself, I have always been well aware of the attitude of *l'homme moyen sensuel* to all inventive or creative things and persons – though in the older societies he is restrained somewhat, by fear, from indulging his dislike where the *persons* are concerned. It is a great pity, if I may say so, that you are so occupied with purely political matters, and that you do not, rather, fill some role in which you could influence the creative development of this comparatively small community, rather unfortunately dissipated in space. I am afraid nothing could be done

[1] Leonard W. Brockington, C.M.G. (b. 1888), was at this time serving as Special War-time Assistant to the Prime Minister of Canada. L. met him when he first went to Montreal and asked him for assistance in obtaining some kind of position connected with the arts in the Canadian government.
[2] In a letter written on November 11th, Brockington said that he was making no progress in his efforts for L. He complained of the anti-creative nature of those "charged with the task of creation."

with Toronto: but Montreal or Ottawa might be worked up into a cultural center.

Yours sincerely,

286. *To Edmund Wilson*[1] [Toronto]
Nov 15. 1941.

Dear Wilson. Since seeing you in New York I have been living up in this sanctimonious ice-box – my visitors permit having expired – painting portraits of the opulent methodists of Toronto. Often I have desired to take ship to England but have never had the money (I have my wife here, and today the combined fares amount to a considerable item). – You were so good as to suggest that I send you an occasional article. Enclosed is one that probably will not be suitable for the *New Republic* – but one never knows.[2] It is an accurate generalisation, I think, of something I have not seen stated anywhere.

The war drags on and sluggishly expands. The militarist is never in any hurry to end a war – especially as in the present case he cannot hope to win it. If Russians were more methodical people the Germans would stand no chance in a war with them. As it is, they have won the war for the Western nations, it seems to me – I mean have put Germany in such a position that, when England and America attack, the result is a foregone conclusion. I dont think Hitler is much more than a soapboxers mask for the Junker machine. Should the machine *remove* its mask, what do we do then? Not, I hope, raise our hats and say: "Oh, I didn't know it was *you*!"

Someone told me you were coming up here but there was some obstruction. There is no likelihood I suppose of your coming now?

Sincerely,
WYNDHAM LEWIS

P.S. Are you connected with any other papers, editorially or as adviser?

[1] L. met Edmund Wilson during a visit to New York in the 1920's. They saw one another several times after that, and when L. was in New York in 1940, he called on Wilson at the *New Republic*.

[2] Wilson replied that he no longer had any connexion with the *New Republic* and suggested some other magazines for L. to try.

287. To J. M. Dent & Son, Ltd.†¹ Toronto
Nov. 22. 1941.

Dear Sirs. Enclosed is the mss of a book, the title of which ("The Ideas with Which we Fight") describes its purpose. *The commonsense about Democracy* – in contradistinction to the lyrical approach – is the groundwork of the argument. Next, the true innards of Fascism are uncovered: its rise traced back to the cafe-philosopher, Marinetti, with his epileptic outpourings in praise of *speed* and *force*: (the "father of Fascism", as he was described in Rome when he was fêted some years ago as such). My own relations with this earliest Fascist are briefly described. – Then the "universalism of the Anglosaxon" is discussed: the open-mindedness and tolerance of the man who has a footing in every land, and whose "homeland" is really the ocean – in stark opposition to the *Blut und Boden* approach of the Nazis, and the stuffy conservatism of the land-locked peasant-mind. Finally, comes a series of papers (under the heading "Studies in Contemporary Democratic Technique") 2 or 3 of which have been used as articles, though rewritten here, developing the earlier arguments.

The *first* part of this book – now revised – was published in Toronto a few months ago as a pamphlet, entitled "Anglosaxony". . . .

As for my personal count: I am here in Canada because my visitors permit for the U.S.A. expired. I am dreadfully homesick and so is my wife. Everyone writing from England advises us not to return, because artists and writers they say are all washed up, busted and sunk. All the same, I shall get back as soon as I can. I would rather live as a shoeblack in London than be a Bank President in these parts (no disrespect meant, naturally, for the citizens of these transatlantic lands: just a feeling I have!)

Last summer, in Long Island, I wrote a novel called *The Vulgar Streak*, which I had started in England (for Hale). That should be out by now. Here I have been painting portraits of the opulent methodists of Toronto, and writing a certain number of political articles in the local Press (principally for the *Star* here in Toronto, the paper for which Hemingway worked).² – If Hitler cracks in

[1] Publishers of *The Hitler Cult*, L.'s last book to appear in England before his departure.
[2] The Toronto *Star* has no record of L.'s articles. Ernest Hemingway wrote for the *Star Weekly* from 1920 to 1923.

twelve months, I shall be back in London to see him crack from there. If, on the other hand, he catches a fatal chill on the Russian Front during the next few months, I shall probably still be here – trying to keep warm in this blasted ice-box, still limning the rugged features of its sons. (These latter remarks not for publication).

Faithfully yours,
WYNDHAM LEWIS

288. *To Geoffrey Stone* Hotel Tudor.
Jan 5th 1942

Dear Stone. . . . – We have as you see stuck apparently in the Tudor period. For so progressive a man as myself to get away from the *spacious days* and oh so intolerably overheated nights (*why* when they invented hot water pipes did they not arrange for some gadget to make you turn them off – or when they provided such a gadget, why did they so fix them that they *never* work?) – I was just about to get an appointment in the States when, the very week in which it was all being settled, bang – bang – bang! went the filthy little descendants of the Hokusai: and my appointment went up in smoke.[1] So I am still marooned here . . . . Must mail this with some other letters and get out before the blizzard starts, which I see coming over the rooftops. . . .

Yrs.
W. LEWIS

. . .

[1] L. was hoping to be appointed Resident Artist, under the Carnegie Foundation scheme, at Reed College in Oregon. In the midst of negotiations, Dexter M. Keezer (b. 1896), the President of Reed, was called to a war-time position in Washington.

289. *To R. D. Jameson*†¹ Toronto.
Jan 10. 1942.

Dear Mr. Jameson. Enclosed is a letter from Olivet. So Brewer² had a "resident artist" already! I am sure that you will be as surprised to hear this as I was. In British textbooks on surgery there is, usually, I understand, a caveat standing at the opening of the Kidney section. Before removing a kidney, it warns, do not omit to enquire whether the patient has had a kidney removed already. It has occasionally happened, it seems, that a hospital doctor has removed the only remaining kidney of an unfortunate patient without making this all important enquiry. – I wonder if college presidents ought on the same principle be asked whether they *already* have etc! After all a poor girl always tries to find out if the gentleman she is proposing to wed already has a wife. – Ah well.

Yours sincerely,

290. *To Sir Nicholas Waterhouse*† Toronto
Jan 27. 1942.

My dear Docker. Your letter – like all I receive from England, for that matter – saddened me.³ I must be a "creature of habit" – I hate to hear of the destruction of a little personal world, consisting of a beautiful old house like that at Swan Walk, and of those Squash Courts of yours, the scene of so many perspiring exploits of he who was, and thank god still is, "Caspar": and the bashing in of the antidiluvian Rolls – and that historic Rolls in which, as Mauve was crossing Putney Bridge with her old cook, she heard the latters inimitable retort "Oh are yer!" when Mauve informed her, "We are now crossing Putney Bridge": the smashing of the

¹ R. D. Jameson (b. 1895) was from 1938 to 1942 Administrator of Consultant Service at the Library of Congress. He was helping L., who had been referred to him by MacLeish, in his effort to secure a position as a resident artist.
² Joseph Brewer (b. 1898), an acquaintance of L., was at this time President of Olivet College in Michigan. L. had been in correspondence with him regarding a position.
³ Sir Nicholas wrote to L. on December 8th, giving an account of the destruction of his property in Swan Walk, Chelsea.

old Rolls is I think the worst of the lot! And Jebbitt[1] clanging his way round blacked out London in an ambulance is right and proper – it commands my dutiful respect, but it gives me no pleasure. – Still what has *pleasure* got to do with life: life is a "vale of tears", is it not, of sweat and blood. I have no *right* to these feelings: but at least I can – figuratively – add *my* tear to the sweat and blood, so to speak. In that way I, in a certain sort, become part of the melancholy picture. . . .

There is no one I wrote to who has not had their house or office hit. Thus the collotypes of my drawings, for a book that was to appear, have been destroyed: that was at an office. Naomi M.'s nice old house in the Mall, Hammersmith was blitzed. *All* my friends dwellings seem to have been picked out for destruction, though I am happy to say that so far I have not received news of any human demise among them, at least in my small circle of intimates (except for poor Joyce, but that was in Switzerland).[2] – Your staff-member who has ended up a prisoner in Athens had an interesting journey – you should have his diary published, if it displays any powers of observation.[3] Russia, though heaven knows it must be a grim and savage place, has gone up in my estimation. I think Joseph Stalin looks as if he might be the hero of this war. The Germans certainly caught a Tartar when they poked their stupid noses into Russia. They must have been strangely ill-informed regarding the efficiency of the new revolutionary army of the Soviets. – It is unbelievable how ignorant every government has seemed to be regarding the intentions and resources of *other* governments. Pearl Harbour was an example on our side: but Hitler's ideas about the Moscow push-over, and the pic-nic in the Caucasus, is the most glaring of all and has no doubt decided the war.

How does the betting in the City go regarding the war's duration? I saw somewhere that "well-informed quarters in London" reckoned on another four or five years of war. I cant see the Germans standing up against Stalin for another four years – with England on the other side of them. And I certainly *hope* it will terminate quicker than that, as I expect you do.

[1] The Waterhouses' chauffeur.
[2] Joyce died in Zürich on January 13th, 1941.
[3] Sir Nicholas spoke of having a diary, written by a member of his staff, describing a war-time journey through Finland and Russia to Turkey.

I was awfully sorry to hear about Mov's illness¹. . . .

As to myself, I have an attack of influenza – a mere 'flu but very annoying. I am awaiting news from the States about an appointment I believe I am getting. This place bores me in the most fearful way and I shall be glad when I find myself among Americans again. At least they drink highballs and cocktails openly . . . these people here . . . out-dour the Scotch. All the time I wish I were in England. But I don't know what I should do there – for the publishers have no paper and the dealers have no exhibitions any more. So my occupation, such as it was, would be gone.

Well I am very glad to think of you both at Effingham² – not huddled up among a lot of other houses, but safer, I suppose, because of your isolation. . . . Rationing is beginning here. There are no ration cards: people are "put on their honour", of all unpleasant things, not to purchase more than a pound of sugar a week. It is very embarrassing in shops being asked, on your honour, whether you have extended your quota of lump sugar. To go about looking noble and like a citizen in whose mouth sugar wouldn't melt, is peculiarly beastly. I would much rather have a ration card. – With all the best wishes, then.

Your,
Professor. (W. LEWIS)

P.S. Write me again!

291. *To Lady Waterhouse*†   Toronto
Jan. 27. 1942.

Dear Mov. It was splendid to see your fair fist again, and to know, from the spirit that petillated from beneath your pencillings, that all was well with you, in spite of what Docker had told me about your illness. If however *your* heart is involved, then I fear you must rest, as Docker says: for practically everybody here has heart attacks, and they always lie flat on their backs for at least three

---

¹ Sir Nicholas told of the serious illness of Lady Waterhouse.
² The Waterhouses' country place in Surrey.

months. When they *dont* they rue it. – I wish I had heard your Cockney Concert.[1] You might have become the Bairnsfather of the Blitz,[2] had it not been for that bomb on Broadcasting House. Why not do it again? Spend your enforced idleness in writing *more* Blitz Ballads, and when you arise, parade your evacuee team from the Old Kent Road, and start rehearsals straight away. ("Knocked 'em in the Old Kent Road", new style: then Flo wot ad er bloomers bombed orf er, *and* "the golden 'air was 'angin darn 'er back:" All the janitors in Toronto are Cockneys. One janitor, at a building in the ravine, whenever he sees me exclaims: "Ere I say sir! Ar abart Rotten Row! – Ere sir. Did yew know the Burlinton Arcade. I see it on the pitchers yestday. They didn't arf give it a Blitzin." He hasn't been in England for thirty-seven years. His cockney is pure Albert Chevalier,[3] and he is so fastidious that he doesn't even say okay or okeydoke. The cockney is practically a pariah here: even the Glasgow Irish immigrant wont be seen talking to them. One janitor where I had a studio came out as an inspector for the R.S.P.C.A. but he interfered with people who were illtreating animals and lost his job. He is practically insane now (they call him "dopey") and I used to go down and sit with him beside the furnace and yarn about the Harrow Road and Portobello Road. I gave him a dollar bill. He looked at it in surprise and said, "Wots this for?" Then he handed it back. He hadn't seen a "tip" for seventeen years and though he got starvation wages it made him feel *too* déclassé. I finally had a struggle with him in the hall one day and forced a dollar bill into his pocket. (He had saved my life: he had saved me from roasting alive). These exiles from the New Cut are like phantoms of the Nineties. No one can understand them. They go about talking to themselves – in the purest idiom of the Pearly King. . . .

Robert Hale published a book of mine the other day – exactly when I dont know. It is a novel, called "The Vulgar Streak."

[1] In a letter to L., Lady Waterhouse told of her adventure with evacuee children from London. She wrote cockney songs for them, which led to a variety show and a tour of canteens and hospitals: "We used to go down like Nervo and Knox on Saturday night at the Palladium." The B.B.C. recorded the numbers, she said, but the records disappeared in the Blitz.

[2] The artist and journalist Captain Bruce Bairnsfather (b. 1888) is best known for his colloquial war humour.

[3] A celebrated music-hall entertainer (1861–1923).

I wish you would get it and tell me what you think of it. My idea was a *sort* of *Le Rouge et le Noir*. My hero, like Sorel, takes his own life: he is a careerist of a somewhat similar type: he is a child of the era of Mussolini and Hitler as much as Sorel was of that of Napoleon: his tragedy being that he has *too much will* (like most Europeans) and is fooled by the idea of *force* – of the blow on the jaw or the charge of the Stuka. . . .

You ask me what my feelings are as regards the war. I now believe that a great explosion of some kind was unavoidable. It was our duty to attempt to avert it. But I doubt if anything could have done so. It *can* turn out to be a blessing in disguise. Whether it does or not will depend on the amount of intelligence we collectively possess. The cruder sorts of patriotism scarcely come into it. I can quite understand how you might find some manifestation of jingoism displeasing. But one cannot help feeling *solidaire* with the nation to which one belongs. Patriotism is like love – if a man manifests his love too publicly and blatantly he offends. But as I said, I do not believe that nationalism comes into this earthquake very much.

I had not heard that Tommy Earp[1] was over here. Where is he? MacNeice I met: and Auden was over in Brooklyn, where he is preparing himself for citizenship. Richard Aldington is also signing on as an American.[2] Unwise in both cases I should say. Auden seems so very specially English a flower. It is far easier (experience seems to show) to bring an American to England, than to transplant an Englishman to America. But this is a time of great upheaval. – Have you any gossip of the town or other news? I had lost touch with Earp and was glad to hear where he was. John Collier[3] is growing flowers – or vegetables – in Kentucky. "Grey Eminence" by Huxley has been a wow over here. Churchill was a popular success:[4] his great skill and facility as a speaker seemed to impress everybody – though there was an embarrassed hush in the parliament in Ottawa when he quoted Harry Lauder. Mixing up the sublime and the ridiculous in that way took a bit of

---

[1] The art critic Thomas W. Earp (1892–1958). He and L. had known one another for many years.

[2] Later Aldington left America and went to live in France.

[3] John Collier (b. 1901), the English novelist and short-story writer.

[4] Churchill addressed the Canadian Parliament on December 31st, 1941.

swallowing, on the part of these solemn yokels. – Write me another letter Mov, acushla: and get yourself well quick.

Your,

292. *To R. D. Jameson*†   Toronto.
Feb. 14. 1942.

Dear Jameson.

I am reduced to writing articles to fill in the time – and my pocket – on "Will there be a Canadian Renaissance?"[1] The bigger I picture the "renaissance" (whatever they mean by that) the more money I get. So I make it a quite spectacular explosion of intellectual energy. The only intelligent people here – like the painter, Jackson,[2] – regard a marriage with the States as their best bet, and I think the same. Meanwhile I cudgel my brains to imagine Toronto as a sort of Florence or Padua in a great cultural birththroe. By the time I cross that frontier of yours again I shall be a semi-idiot.

Yrs sincerely,

293. *To Mrs. Thomas W. Lamont*†   Toronto.
March 17. 1942.

Dear Mrs Lamont. Thank you for your letter – which I delayed answering until I had news about the last triumphant phase – as I hoped – of the Keezer-Carnegie arrangement. . . . Should anything go wrong with *this* college president,[3] I shall begin to think I am bewitched. And there is always the possibility that the Carnegie may be turning to Mars, and away from the Muses – Heaven avert the omen!

I cannot help being extremely disturbed by all that is happening in Asia – by all this confusion about India, for instance.[4] Public

[1] L. was contributing occasional articles to *Saturday Night: The Canadian Weekly*, and other Canadian papers.
[2] A. Y. Jackson, C.M.G. (b. 1882).
[3] A new prospect for a position as Resident Artist.
[4] India had assumed new importance in the war, because of Japanese advances, and agitation for independence was nearing a crisis.

opinion is so emotional and ill-informed, on this continent as elsewhere and tends to brand all Englishmen as oppressors of Hindustan. The fact is that Englishmen are very gentle and agreeable persons and I would far rather be "oppressed" myself by Englishmen – if I were a "native" – than by anybody else. We are all agreed that it was clumsy and silly not to grant India some semblance of political autonomy long ago – before the Japanese were muscling around within military reach of Calcutta. Within three months however or sooner they will be in India, if they want to go there. No time in which to train and equip more Indians, as soldiers, unfortunately. If we are not careful we shall have the Moslems on our backs, as well as the Bose-ites (the fascist Bengalees). It looks like a bad muddle. But let us hope the Japs have other fish to fry – and burn their fingers in the frying: that a powerful American airfleet assembles, to help defend the British Raj – on the understanding that that Raj will reform itself, upon more democratic lines, later on. The "open door" in India, resulting from these events (on the model of the open door in China) would be a relief to all intelligent Englishmen.

As to India defending *itself*: an Indian friend of mine informed me that his ancestors had not taken life for three thousand years. I asked him how he knew that. He replied at once: "I know it because if they had I shôuld not belong to the Caste I do." – Not a promising subject for universal Hindu conscription!

My own hope is that the German army will be so weakened by next autumn – in its titanic struggle with the Russians – that the war in Europe will be as good as over, and the German people tire of the unprofitable role of world-conqueror. The Japanese cannot stand out alone, even if they have overrun the whole of Asia, once Germany has thrown in its hand. Litvinov, I think, is right about a "second front", perhaps up in Norway. But I know absolutely nothing about it. At all cost the route to Russia has to be kept open, it would seem: why not demolish the Finns? Because they once were great payers of their debts, that is no good reason to allow them to obstruct in a life and death issue. So it seems to a necessarily half-informed observer – sitting in an ice-box and listening to a babel of voices coming out of a radio cabinet.

You mention Cripps[1] and say you were unfavourably impressed.

[1] Sir Stafford Cripps had just been named General Representative of the Government in the House of Commons and Lord Privy Seal.

I once had the job of doing a portrait-head of him for the *London Mercury*: one of Stafford Cripps and one of Oswald Mosely. ("Fuhrers of the Future?" or some such journalistic nonsense as that). Whether it was by *contrast*, or whether for relativist reasons, Cripps struck me as strangely sincere for a politician. He has a Fabian mind, I should say. How effective he is I have no idea – nor of course what he really wants. Hitler, I take it, is a plebeian mask worn for a while by the Junker caste. In looking at a politician I always have to ask myself, as an artist, what the mask means. And often I am extremely puzzled, and quite often wrong. But I felt strongly that Cripps believed in *something*.

I was interested to hear that Julian Huxley was staying with you. Our last meeting was in his Zoo office, beneath the portrait of his admirable grandfather. What an agreable destiny – to inherit, as it were, the animal kingdom. Please remember me to him!

Yours sincerely

294. *To Leonard W. Brockington*†   Toronto.
March 25. 1942.

Dear Brockington. It would probably be an illusion to suppose you are less busy at present than a few months ago: but probably you are importuned less by ambitious persons, excited by your nearness to the Prime Minister.[1] As you know *I* am not an *ambitieux*, I have no appetite for the splendors and miseries of bureaucratic life – I want to climb nowhere, except onto some modest perch out of the storm. And I still want to do that. I have become a sort of involuntary squatter. But the new law requiring men under 45 to transfer themselves to essential industries might, it has occurred to me, provide me with a chance. So much in the center of things still and having access to so many people, you might, if you could spare the time, be instrumental in rescuing me from a rather humiliating situation – of impotence and wasted hours. I have no idea in what direction it would be best to look. Some ill-paid, half-time, job would be the ideal, in which I was left half my time free for my usual work, of writing and painting – though a 48 hour

[1] Brockington had left his position as Special War-time Assistant to the Prime Minister.

week would be okay with me. Such places as the Ministry of Information or the Press Department are, I think, closed to an Englishman – unless he is very insignificant. – I once wrote

> '*I think this is a time to be small in,*'
> Said an intelligent Flea. . . .

Since we last met many unpleasant events have crowded into the history book, being so noisily written under our eyes – and *you* have ranged far afield, and I hope enjoyed your changes of scene.[1] Now America is in, there is at least no doubt of the issue of the war, thank goodness. It is very much less pleasant being a rather useless civilian in a war, I find, than being a soldier.

Yours sincerely,

295. *To Theodore Spencer*†[2]   Toronto
April 30. 1942.

My dear Spencer. Since we last met the world has not grown a quieter place.[3] How has the war affected your activities? By Oct 1st next we shall all know I think whether we have a Thirty Years War on our hands or just a further year or so before the Germans ask for an armistice. Russia holds the answer. Meanwhile we are heading for an economic freeze-up of so total a kind that life upon this continent – or this planet, rather – will become impossible for any person not ensconced in some occupational, salaried, niche. Already I am shivering a little: six months hence I shall be frozen to death. – You do not have to tell me that Harvard is out of the

[1] Brockington had been to England.

[2] L. first met the poet and teacher Theodore Spencer (1902–49) in England. He saw him again in 1932, when he visited Harvard at the behest of Joseph W. Alsop (b. 1910). The well-known journalist was then a senior at Harvard and had been writing a long paper on L.'s work. L. renewed his acquaintance with Spencer when he went to speak at Harvard in 1940.

[3] An earlier draft of this opening reads: "Since seeing you I have been up here all the time, in this sanctimonious ice-box – mostly in Toronto. . . . However, some portraits came my way: and I have been monotonously plying my brush, and supplicating whatever is left of God for other people when Mr. Eliot and the Cabots have finished with him, that I might one day be restored to civilised life."

question for me, of course. As far as I am concerned, you are the only bright spot in Harvard; though I have spent some very pleasant hours there – thanks to you! Then I know that all American universities are faced with all the difficulties inseparable from the drafting of young men of college age. Yet I must try to get in *somewhere*, however poorly paid the post and insignificant the place of learning I go to. For even in normal times – and I have been slow in acquiring this knowledge – into the American universities are gathered all those people who in Europe would be artists, journalists, or what not. Ever since the old Alsop days you have put yourself out a great deal to show me a friendly welcome – . . . so I know that you will do all you can to find me some cubby-hole now, into which I can crawl out of the economic blizzard; where I honestly believe I may perish just as literally as one would in a monstrous storm in the arctic.

It is because I know that all people are not (1) so good natured, and (2) so friendly disposed as you are towards myself that I enjoin you not to leave this letter upon your desk where it can be glimpsed by the prowling eye of the evil visitor; and not oh *not* to discuss it with colleagues . . . . For people will go to very little trouble to help anybody, but my god they will give themselves no end of trouble to obstruct. Probably you will bear me out that that is human nature. . . . – I am determined not to be frozen to death; you can help me avoid that fate – but do not ask advice of colleagues; if you know some old colleague or pupil who is now President of a Girls College (an inferior Vassar) or of some obscure Western or Southern university, write him and tell him about me. Tell him that I am one of those animals who only is *méchant* when attacked. Tell him I do beautiful pictures: that I had the Slade Scholarship and learned the artists trade in every art-centre in Europe: that I will teach drawing or painting, lecture or whatever is required (throwing in English instruction) and that all I want is a living wage.[1] Before everything shrivels up and no one

---

[1] In another draft, L. wrote at this point: "Sometimes I find that the more sophisticated flowers of humanity are less useful (at all events to me) than the more direct and normal type. It might be that a College President whose livre de chevet was Auden or the Marquis de Sade would be less good than a fellow who read mystery stories and smoked a pipe. By saying this I merely mean not to be afraid of suggesting a practical, administrative type of man, even if a bit dull. I wish Mr. Roosevelt were a college President, rather than what he is."

has a spare cent left I just *have* to get in somewhere: already up here "Fortress-economics" have set in – and this is an unbelievably backward and poor country, where university professors can only afford one bottle of beer a week and a pipe of shag on Sundays, both they and their wives being fearfully undernourished. (And Mitch Hepburn believe it or not threatens periodically to close the universities if they persist in teaching *communism*!)

What is your news of England? Lord Carlow came through Canada on his way to Rio last week and told me that the author of *South Wind* and many other unusual visitors are in London. My novel, *The Vulgar Streak* (it came out 6 months ago) was as successful as could be expected at such a time. Give me your news when you write – about what happened to your book of poems,[1] and if you still have your office in that sort of High Street.

Yrs.

296. *To Theodore Spencer*†   Toronto.
May 8. 1942.

My dear Spencer. Thank you very much indeed for lending me a hand so promptly in my search for an academic retreat.[2] – The Baptist place sounds good. I am no Baptist myself; but my grandfather was a Baptist (Welsh). He married a catholic; as a result his wife eventually stopped going to Mass; but he stopped going to Church, too. Rome and the baptismal bathing-pool cancelled each other out! And then to complicate matters still further my mother was catholic, also. (Marrying Rome was becoming a habit). – Which is too bad, otherwise I could take to Colgate as a duck takes to water (no blemish of holy water in my backgrounds to mar the picture). However, Mr. Thomas Eliot has about boxed the compass of the Christian sects, so I see no reason why I shouldn't agree to be a Baptist for a year or two. In the last war I tried, when we paraded on Sunday, to go to the Catholic Church

---

[1] *The Paradox in the Circle* (Norfolk, Conn., 1941), Spencer's first book of poems.

[2] Spencer wrote to L. on May 5th, suggesting Colgate University in Hamilton, New York, as a possibility in his search for a position. He described it as "a smallish college, pre-eminently Baptist" and went on to say, "Of course, for all I know, you may be a Baptist yourself."

but they wouldn't let me. In this war I cant see why I shouldn't go and watch people splashing about, in emulation of 'The Great Fish', Jesus of Nazareth.

You remind me that your office walls have never received the little group of pictures I said I would send you – which is a kind thought, for I knew you would show them to the right people and something might result.[1] A quantity of things done by me up here you would personally like I know (for my red horse[2] pleased you enough, so your wife told me, for you to stable it in your summer villa – what is the American word? Farm. Camp?) . . .

I was glad to hear that your book of poems went so well:[3] when next I pass through Harvard I shall have a look at your copy. I liked very much the things you had when I was there. – You may have seen just after Christmas that my novel was the Times book of the week. You no doubt still get the *Times Lit. Sup.* I do think that the English have set an example of imperturbability, though half of them are soldiers or the next thing to it.

Well, god bless you (in true Baptist style) and let me know at once if ought transpires.

Yours

297. *To Eric Kennington*†[4] Toronto.
June [?] 26. 1942.

Dear Kennington. . . .

As to what you say about my patriotism, I do not understand what you mean.[5] It is rather important I think that I should. In

[1] Spencer had offered to hang some of L.'s pictures in the hope of stirring up some trade for him.   [2] A drawing L. did for Spencer.

[3] Spencer said in his letter that he thought his new volume had been very successful.

[4] L. had known the sculptor Eric Kennington (d. 1960) before the war. In April 1942 he learned that Kennington was connected with the War Artists' Advisory Committee in London. He wrote to him then, soliciting his help in obtaining a commission from the committee. A commission for a large painting was eventually promised, but payment was delayed over a period of many months. L. chose an industrial subject and had done a version by the time he received the second half of the promised sum. He was dissatisfied with the painting, however, and went on working on it, leaving it unfinished at his death.

[5] In his letter to L., Kennington mentioned a young artist, a mutual acquaintance, and spoke of his "detachment" in regard to the war. L. took the remark as an allusion to his own absence from England.

the last war like yourself I joined the army, instead of wangling myself into some safe job in London, as I could quite well have done. About young ——'s patriotism or "detachment" I know nothing – except that he is at present a seaman on Atlantic convoy duty, which is considerably more dangerous and I daresay more useful than what many I could name are doing.

It may have occurred to you . . . that my desire as expressed formerly in books and articles not to see England plunged into a second European war, although it might imply a self-sacrificing devotion to the welfare of England (self-sacrificing because so extremely unpopular) was evidence of an unmartial spirit. And it is true that I was for some years almost frantically concerned at the sound of the angry rolling of the war drums again. I thought it boded ill for our tribe – which the *last* war had left pretty battered. I now see that I thought if anything too much about our tribe if not *too little*, as you are so good as to tell me): not enough about "le genre humain" of the revolutionary song, which it is now my sincere belief will benefit from the present social convulsion. Ultimately and in the large view England will benefit too.

Long ago however it became apparent to me that I had been wrong, like so many other people, in opposing war. Before the Munich Conference enlightened us all upon that subject, I saw too clearly, with anger and dismay, that Hitler was that most detestable of things a chronic and unteachable little militarist, who just would have his good old second war, because it is for such hideous childishness that such men live. Nor can they understand how anybody else can do otherwise than love violence too. If the latter advertise a distaste for it and show that they regard it as screwy and unattractive, why then they must be "decadent". Just as the artist is labelled "decadent" who departs from the Salon norm, or that of the Royal Academy, by the Hitlerite pundit of "sanity."

We, I take it, in England, and over here it is the same, are *citizen soldiers*. We are not and do not desire to be professionals of the sport of (armament) kings. That is to say we take up arms – *with indignation* – because we are forced to do so, by the brutal lunatics exploiting the romantic weaknesses of a great neighboring state. Any virtues we have as soldiers rest upon that feeling –that indignant feeling – that what we are compelled to do is an outrage upon our intelligence, the fundamentals of our religious traditions, and our status, such as it is, as civilised men. Threatened with attack by those who *refuse* to grow up – for it amounts to a curiously beastly case of boyscoutism, of arrested development or cretinism – we issue from these bloody debauches degraded and ashamed. But we have had no alternative. – The present war like the last is about that situation: it is *about war*. That is why it would be so great a tragedy if the Axis won it: the most cockey and materialist of Asiatics, the most philistine, vulgar and shallow of Europeans.

No, I do not share ———'s "detachment". . . . Nor do I approve of the behaviour of many people who are young and vigorous and who are keeping themselves out of harms way very successfully in this war. They owe, some of them, just as much to England as I do or as you do: some materially owe more. I think they ought to fight, or be London firemen, unless they can do something really valuable in other directions. Not *many* people are too big intellectual assets to be firemen.

Over here, miserably exiled, I have taken every opportunity that presented itself, in articles and lectures, to promote an understanding of England, in a milieu where there is far too little understanding. Every defeat of ours has released the "tired old nation" stuff. One has to keep on hammering at them. They have the "young nation" complex. It is hard work. . . .

. . . it may of course simply be that I am over here, and not in Oxfordshire, armed and alert to meet the invader. – If you mean *that* let me answer it at once, for it is only too easy. You have money and I have none. My presence on this continent is purely economic. I dont mean I am here to get rich, I mean I am here to try to make my bread and butter and a bit over to pay my debts. I came here as a result of an economic miscalculation. I remain here under an economic compulsion. I mean I can't get away.

. . . – It did not take long for me to discover that art labelled *British* is not very highly considered in the States: *French* is the correct label. (It isn't *very* highly considered in Bond Street or St. James' where the correct label also is *French*: so this is not so surprising). I spent a year in New York and its neighborhood, much of that time so poor that it was as much as I could do to pay the car-fare up and down that not very attractive city. It was the worst year of my life – years of illness excepted. No hard feelings:

a penniless American in London no doubt would have a pretty tough time. . . .

. . . Here in Canada I had a break for a few months. Today however I am screwed down as firmly as it is possible to be. I owe two months rent in this hotel – which in a foreign city is no joke. What is going to happen to us in the end I do not know. Taxes have just been announced in the newspapers (yesterday) which will cause the few people who so far have spent a little money on "luxuries" to stop doing so. . . .

Is there something else I should say? – Although scarcely of subaltern age, why do I not apply for some military job? Here is the answer. From 1932–37 I was very seriously ill, as you may have heard, as a result of a gland infection contracted in the last war. Between '32 and '37 I had half a dozen operations, and was in half the hospitals and nursing homes in London. – That thank god did not remove from me the ability to paint, to read and to write (although to add to the general cheerfulness of life, an eye-specialist here eight months ago announced that I should be *blind* within six months unless I allowed him to operate on me. – But he it turned out was a crooked doctor and one of my eyes at least is still 100 per cent strong). My long illness all the same left behind it certain physical handicaps. I could not even masquerade as a soldier. . . .

Yours sincerely

298. *To Sir Nicholas Waterhouse*† Toronto
June 27. 1942.

Dear Docker. I wonder if my two letters ever reached you? I sent one to you and one to Mov, at the time you both wrote me – at the time you remember when poor Mov had had a bout of illness. From her letter however I judged her to be in her usual form. I conclude therefore that she got comfortably over that. – A good few letters I think are suffering seachange into something rich and strange – down at the bottom of the herring-pond, in less professorial or extremely learned language. If mine are there the fishes, as they swim in and out of my sentences, must experience the warm glow that radiates from them, and must be enjoying in their chilly organisms some of the cordial effects intended for my poor sick Mov and your own dockerish self. – Last night I dreamed I heard on the radio the announcer book "Lady Waterhouse and her Cockney Choir!" and then I heard Mov's voice, speaking in cockney, but embellished with splashes of Spanish. "Yalo creo big boy – not 'arf I did Syd!" That sort of thing. Well, I shall be glad when I can hear that voice again. That may not be so very long. – I hope to be able to be getting started for England by Sept 1st. When I see you I will tell you all my misadventures: better than writing them. I have no Guildhall in ruins a hundred yards away or anything grandiose of that kind in my squalid saga. A few little touches here and there, which amuse while they distress. "Methodism and Money" in this city has produced a sort of hell of dullness. . . .

The war seemed to be going better. A couple of months ago I really thought we were nearer the point where the beginnings of German collapse would be visible. The Libyan business is very disappointing. As I write a battle has started at Mersa Matruh in Egypt. Let us hope we shall turn the tables on Rommel. By the time this reaches you we may be in Tripoli. My feeling is that the overthrow of the Axis cannot be expected until '44. May it be sooner. – for all that out of the way, a really new world can begin to be built up. We have to try anyhow to make it more intelligent, and I truly believe we shall have a better chance than ever before. . . . Do you still gather mushrooms in the field? Or is the field used as a camping sight for Mov's Cockney Choir? I will conclude my letter with that beautiful thought – Docker gathering mushrooms for the evening meal. There can be no such thing as a field with mushrooms in it in Ontario, and if there were you couldn't pick them. The Black Fly would put a stop to all that. Good luck – send me a line when you get this.

Your Professor.
(WYNDHAM LEWIS)

299. *To Naomi Mitchison*†   Toronto.
July 8th 1942.

Dear Naomi. This is going to be air-mailed, and a carbon of it will go by ship. One or the other ought to reach you. – Since part of

America has moved over to the North of Ireland, from which you are separated by so short a strip of water, I have felt nearer to you.

Often I wonder what Kintyre is like and how being with the simple folk all the time, year after year, suits you: or have you been down in London sometimes, since I imagine the Blitz is a thing of the past? I wonder whether there are farms where you can get an occasional extra egg: whether you have your own chickens, onions, and potatoes, and perhaps a pig or two: whether there is an illicit still in the neighbourhood where one can get a little bootleg whiskey. . . . Wars have never yet been fought without whiskey, rum, vodka or schnappes, and this time the non-combatants being warriors too there must be a big bootleg business. If I didn't know your aversion to tobacco I would send you a box of cigarettes!

I have never told you anything about my existence over here. As a matter of fact it has been almost indescribable. – After my interminable illness – (six operations, the inmate in turn of half the nursing homes and hospitals in London) – I crawled back into life full of pep. It is extraordinary. (I dont understand myself). Things began to look up, economically I mean. A little while, perhaps two years, and I should no longer have been poor. Then the war began to cast its shadow before.

My attitude to war was not dictated by self-interest. Indeed had I consulted my own personal interest I should have joined in the war-dance. I know what actions are popular and what are not. – The War drums had begun rolling again, people were working themselves up into a fever. As you know I was against war. To my mind war is a very great crime, which men should at all cost shun and abominate. In the insignificant way that lies within the power of a mere member of the public I did what I could to discourage the bellicose. Our tribe had suffered terribly the last time it went to war: when I heard the war-drums rolling again I was almost madly concerned. I turned upon the leftwing you remember, because it seemed to be from that quarter that the war-psychosis came. – It is now very apparent to me that I thought too much of our tribe: too little of the "genre humain". . . . The benefits that may – or we must say *shall* – ensue for the "genre humain" as a result of this war are incalculable. For life on this continent, unpleasant as it has been, has given me a close-up of Roosevelt. All the hostility I felt for the *centralizer* I no longer feel. If you

15. Draft of a letter to Sir William Rothenstein

are a really *global* centralizer, as Roosevelt is, then it is a different matter. And perhaps you have to get outside of Europe to see *the earth*. I feel as if I were on the moon. Decentralization, upon so small a planet, is an absurdity. This global war must produce a global peace: at the worst a kind of universalism – which is much better than internationalism – will have been imported into the thinking of every national. – It will be like a political circumnavigation of the globe? Dont you agree? Some of these truths were evident to me by the time the Munich conference had rubbed all our noses in the fact that the little proletarian mask with its Chaplin moustache assumed by the Junker was as much a war-mask as any Japanese grimace, such as we see in the colourprints portraying famous actors. It was Bismarck disguised as a boyscout. No diplomacy could have saved England from war, except on terms that would have been ignominious (that is of course from the purely nationalist standpoint). So much became absurdly plain when Mr. Chamberlain began flying about with his umbrella. – But the rolling of the war-drums did not only agitate me. They had an exceedingly depressing effect upon the business world of England, and that caused my modest personal economy to shake and sag again. In the nine months preceding the outbreak of war our debts were steadily piling up. . . . It was under these circumstances that I collected what I could, and made a bee line for New York. With lectures, a few portraits and so forth I should return before very long to London with enough good American dollars to settle my debts, at least: and then I would see. Such was the plan.

I was very simple. That really awful city, New York, was packed with people from every country on earth, upon the same errand as myself. There were many factors however. As a result at the end of six months I was penniless, and with slight fluctuations of fortune, have remained pretty much the same ever since. . . .

. . . – Both I and my wife loathe this place and the States so heartily that nothing would ever persuade either of us to set foot on American soil again. Do not however misunderstand me: I dont mean we dislike individual Americans, some of whom are very kind and intelligent people. There are no hard feelings. It is just that however nice the turnkeys were in a prison you would not be reconciled to the place. And we have been obliged to stop where we were, against our will, longing to return to England but never able to buy a ticket, or even begin to do such a thing. – I owe two months rent at this hotel so you will see I can hardly pay the six hundred dollars necessary for 2 tickets!

My divulging of these ugly facts has seemed adviseable, as otherwise, it has occurred to me, you might misconstrue my absence. Not that you would think I ought to be at home braving German bombs or anything heroic of that kind: nor would you suppose that I was indifferent to what was happening, or had been happening to England, and my friends who are there. You might form a picture of me over on this side *enjoying* myself. I should hate to think that anyone should so egregiously misdraw the picture of myself in what I call my "Tudor period". The supernatural, in the form of *luck* as we say, has been present: we have been miraculously fed and sheltered. And I was delivered out of New York by supernatural intervention likewise – for I scarcely know how I got here. But even so, it is very cheerless and fearful. And I have had nearly 3 years of it!

This is a special effort, of clarification. For of course, when I write a letter in the ordinary way to someone in England – even to someone I know so well as I do you – I leave out all mention of the background from which I am writing. It would depress and bore the reader as it does me. And the person to whom one is addressing the letter may quite well have a great deal to worry them, and to alarm them. Having said it, we can forget about it – for I have explained matters in the present instance for various reasons. But we need not dwell upon it, for this room where I write is quite comfortable: I am looking out of the windows into the branches of a maple tree, which is full of fat Canadian sparrows and a few jays probably and a cat bird. We have, as I said, had *de la chance*. We are not "in the dough" but we *live* after a fashion. . . .

Yours ever.

300. *To Louis MacNeice*†¹ [Toronto]
July 13. 1942.

Dear MacNeice. . . . It seems a tremendously long time ago that we sat upon the terrace of the Brevoort, wrangling with the Cuban waiters, although – or *because* – absolutely nothing has happened to me since then: except that I made my way up here, exchanging the effete glamours of New York for the "Methodism and Money" of this bush-metropolis of the Orange Lodges. Economically that move was merely out of the frying pan into the fire. In New York I latterly worked on a margin of two bucks, here as a rule I am a buck and a half off the gutter or flophouse. . . .

The more I ponder the speeches of Vice-president Wallace and others who speak for the Washington administration, the more I feel convinced that this war may achieve what the last pretended to be doing. It may "end war": it may even make a world slightly less unfit for artists to live in. – The outcome of the whole business must depend a great deal upon the intelligence and tact and of course honesty of the rulers of America: and upon President Roosevelt or somebody who will carry on his policies, being there when the last shot is fired. But as to the *blueprint*, the model as adumbrated in speeches like that of Henry Wallace, it looks to me the most promising thing since I have interested myself in politics – because it is *global*. Here at last are people thinking about *the earth*. . . . What is most the matter with Adolf Hitler is that his is a Balkanic mind. What can be seen from the Alps on a fine day is *his* earth. Mr. Roosevelt surveys mankind from China to Peru and beyond. Why we are better than the German is because our backgrounds are Plassey, Ticonderoga – Vancouver and Port Elizabeth. (Not meaning as little imperialists: just that we've looked all round the ball).

Such are the kind of reflections which course through my mind as I grovel in Toronto before the ugly teetotal Baal set up in these parts by the most parochial nationette on earth – although there are a few enlightened persons who help me to beguile the endless hours of waiting. . . . I *hope* to wrench myself out of this quicksand by the early autumn.

Yrs

[1] L. had known MacNeice (b. 1907) in England. In 1940 MacNeice showed himself a generous friend during one of L.'s financial crises in New York.

301. *To H. G. Wells*† [Toronto]
[July 15th, 1942.]

My dear Wells. Your letter – which you have long ago forgotten you wrote probably! – has been on my trail for many a month.¹ It has run me to earth after all this time and it has given me great pleasure. I will not at this late date return to the subject of its very interesting critical reactions. . . . I will tell you rather how glad I was to be reminded of your robust and generous personality: and your encouraging and friendly words gave me great help and comfort – in this drab wilderness.² . . .

¹ After the appearance of *The Vulgar Streak*, Wells wrote to L., in care of his London publisher, congratulating him on the novel.

² In an earlier draft of this letter, L. did discuss the novel. He wrote: "My novel, *The Vulgar Streak*, which I wrote two summers ago in Long Island, was not intended to be a 'shocker.' But I was very interested to hear that it struck you as that – as also apparently some not good judges. I will tell you, in as few words as possible, what I *thought* I was doing. The time in which we live appears to me, qua period, to be a 'shocker'. A 'thriller' is too mild a term for it. Well, the rather shocking nature of my book was to my mind a faithful interpretation of an epoch where violence is everywhere.

"The hero in *Le Rouge et la Noir* lived his tragic life according to the Napoleonic canon of conduct. The 'ruthless' way. (What a poisonous word 'ruthless' is – what thrills it administers to a horde of small sensationalists.) In *Crime and Punishment* the hero follows in the footsteps of Julien Sorel (and of Napoleon). It seemed to me that the time had come to add another book to this line: that the doctrine extracted by Mussolini from *Les Reflections sur la Violence* and from Nietzsche (who got his stuff fundamentally from Darwin) – it seemed to me that this doctrine taken over by Hitler, and influencing so many minds in Europe, might be made to do its fell work in the soul of a character in fiction, once again. On very different lines, it was time to project another Sorel or Raskolnikoff; whose bug could not be the Napoleonic bug this time, but rather the selfconsciousness 'power', 'force', and 'action' that has infected so many people today.

"You, if I may say so, could do this wonderfully well: so could Joseph Conrad. However I myself, am highly qualified to do it, also: and if I have not, it must be because I took too much for granted that everybody would see what I was after. – For the rest, there was another pattern woven into my book: at the same time I would strike a blow against the class-nonsense, that weakens us in England so much. A fearful superstition, that condemns ninety per cent of Englishmen to bring their contribution to our common life under an absurd handicap. There is scarcely any country where this situation exists as it does in England.

New York you know – it is no place to go to when you really have to make money, though quite agreeable otherwise. I like the poor American very much. For me Americans are divided into two classes: poor and nice, and rich and nasty. Why a dollar currency should affect the disposition differently from a sterling currency I cannot say.

New York I found packed with people of every nationality, upon the same errand as myself: after American dollars. – The American country is sometimes meltingly beautiful, and the "small town" far more rustic and backward than ours, and very soothing to live in – like a chapter of Hawthorne, or a page of Mark Twain. But the cities are not proper human habitations.

Since I have been over on this side I have been able to understand Roosevelt better. He seems to have the right answer for the kind of cattle he has to deal with – which have none of the deceptive charm that makes our lot tolerable if one doesn't look too closely. Roosevelt I believe is an unusually good politician – or he and Wallace combined, Wallace giving voice to what it is inexpedient for the President himself to utter. . . .

Like the last, this war is *about war*. But it has a much better chance of *ending war* than the Wilson and Lloyd George set-up

The Scotch with their more masculine good sense, have nothing of that kind. It is no disgrace in France to be a peasant. As I cant see why our social problems cannot be approached from that standpoint of commonsense – instead of from the sham-religious angle of so much modern theory of revolution – (and the commonsense approach is the traditional one, too) I am inclined to attempt to put into fictional form – not as tracts but as living vernacular stories – matter that would help people to realize what snobbish boobies they are, and what a fearful tragedy it is, in the sequel for the hospital patient, say, who is poor and old, as much as it is for the young man who has a brain to work with, but no raw material available to put the brain to work on, because he is excluded from such benefits on account of his unsatisfactory origins. – That the capitalist system as worked at present is an iniquity any fool can see: but what we want as well is a more concrete sense of others sufferings, which we are losing every day at an alarming rate.

"You will see how appropriate it is, as against *power* and *force* – against this *too much will* from which Europeans suffer and of which Hitler's armies, like those of Napoleon, are an obvious example – to bring forward and reinvigorate this other thing Europeans are so rapidly losing (all ways of that thought and feeling which leads to forbearance, to acts of mercy, to modesty and the advertisement of gentleness rather than of bluster, Bigstickism etc.)."

had. Or am I too sanguine? Anyhow all of us have to see that it does not fizzle out in an orgy of mass-selfishness. *You* can do much to promote and enforce a new-deal for everybody in England. Eighty per cent of all the initiative and intelligence there goes to waste, owing to the Popular Education fraud, and that complex English people have about the way they speak.[1]

When I first heard the war-drums rolling again I was immensely depressed. Our tribe had been so fearfully battered last time: and there it was, dancing that fearful dance again, and working itself up into a fever. The least I could do I felt was to discourage and obstruct, in such small way as I could: provide ridicule and sedative. – But I see now that I thought too much about our tribe, too little about the "genre humain" of the revolutionary song. – Well, my best wishes, and thank you very much for your kind and interesting letter.

Yours ever,
WYNDHAM LEWIS

Early in 1942 Lewis had a letter from a young British Columbian named David Kahma. Kahma (b. 1919), the son of a Scotch-Irish father and a Finnish mother, had it in mind to establish a kind of intellectual centre in Vancouver; Lewis, whose books he admired, was to be its first star. Funds were lacking, but they would be

[1] This subject too was interestingly expanded in the earlier draft. L. wrote: "What sort of society we shall evolve I have not the slightest idea. That does not seem anything like so clear as the certainty that, by our victory, we shall be able to build anything that seems good to us. Collectively, we still seem uncommonly stupid about everything. Here in Canada the French and English are cat and dog, and the Liberals and Conservative fill the Press with their factious cries. Labor scarcely is heard. In the fifteen months I have never once heard the war mentioned in public – in street or shop. – It is difficult therefore to imagine quite what will occur, the war ended. But I do think there will be an opportunity to be intelligent, such as may never recur: and there are omens of promise – in much that Mr. Roosevelt has done, or in the splendid massive jujitsu of the Russians, and the consistent dignity displayed by Stalin. How admirable is a politician who keeps his mouth shut, like that. – *We* are the people whose medium is words – though everyone *thinks* they can use them. Chacun à son métier! Stalin certainly has understood his."

supplied in plenty by an inheritance the young enthusiast was about to receive. Sceptical but fascinated, Lewis found himself drawn into a prolonged, sometimes hectic correspondence which continued till the end of the year, when it became apparent that Kahma's dream was not to be realised. In the course of this, Kahma revealed his own ideas and plans about writing, and Lewis offered advice and encouragement. Then after a lapse of more than four years, Kahma revived the association. He had vast manuscripts to show – projects in drama, fiction, poetry, criticism. He wanted to send food parcels. Lewis, still interested in his unseen disciple, accepted the gambit, and the two corresponded from 1947 to 1955. Kahma despatched manuscripts and parcels; the master returned advice and fulsome thanks. (See letter of August 17th, 1947, ff.) Though Kahma's volubility was unbeatable, Lewis more than held up his side. Out of a possible escape in the dark days of Toronto had emerged one of the most curious and touching relationships of Lewis's later life.

302. *To David Kahma*   Toronto.
August 6. 1942.

Thank you for your communication, with the interesting notes regarding the principles upon which you founded the formal problems of your play. The *serious-parody* notion is an excellent one I believe. Even "Arabia Deserta" I regard as a parody – though "in the still blossoming gardens of the Lord" I found myself transported a far greater distance than the few paltry centuries that separated its author from his archaic original. Which has some bearing upon the *time* problem! "The Ancient Mariner" is a parody, too – and the "Ballad of Reading Gaol" is a parody of a parody. – Details I must discuss with you when we meet: and I will give you a pamphlet if I can find it called "Satire Fiction." – It is good news that you believe now you will be able to unfreeze your inheritance: I suppose however that "the law's delays" may drag things out a good while yet. I am frantically busy or I would have answered your letter earlier. There is an article I have to get off to the States, and all the snags attendant upon (1) the conditions of the time, and (2) the extreme susceptibility of all Americans where a European writer is concerned, make it a long and wearisome task: but I shall be in the dough when their cheque comes along. So!

Yours sincerely,
WYNDHAM LEWIS

303. *To Sir Nicholas Waterhouse*†   Toronto
Sept. 10. 1942.

My dear Docker. Your news of Mov is very dispiriting.[1] It is I suppose the excitement and strain of the last 3 years. Why doesn't she lie low until the storm has passed – just potter about at Effingham, write her memoirs, write a letter to me, one to "Norman," another to somebody else, study astrology, and work in her victory-garden? She is not strong enough to follow in Jebbitt's footsteps and drive an ambulance. She was a nurse in the last war, and would make a fearfully bad nurse anyway. – How does she get to the Dorchester – in a bus? That is tiring. Tell her to write a book entitled "From Mauve Decade to Blitz". On the cover there can be a mixed photograph – one Move in black silk slacks playing on a saw, and one Move towering over her Cockney Choir in a sunbonnet.

– My diagnosis is this. She is deprived all of a sudden of all the social stimulus she received from her group of friends, who are all dispersed. The best way to recover that is by the Proustian method. *A la recherche du temps perdu.* – War, for us who cannot this time be soldiers, or nurses, or anything very physically active, is a sort of blindness. So we have to see with the mind's-eye, until its conclusion, which cannot be so far off since we are now in the fourth year. . . .

. . . Soon I ought to be getting a little jack. Before *very* long I shall be back. The war gets a kind of set look as if it were there for some time and I have had more than enough of foreign parts. – Tell Mov not to be a fool about her ticker. I prescribe quiet. All the best.

Yrs.
WYNDHAM LEWIS

[1] Sir Nicholas wrote to L. on July 18th, telling him of the continued ill-health of Lady Waterhouse.

304. *To James Johnson Sweeney*† Toronto
Sept. 15th 1942.

Dear Sweeney. Thank you for your letter. ——— I am afraid is not going to be of any use:¹ making all allowance for the fact that Americans, as correspondents, have decreed for themselves a latitude of extended silence that is unknown elsewhere, I think ——— would, since you told him how urgent it was, have answered by now. However, let me know about your talk with him when you next go to Chicago, as it will be useful to know what he says. – I am not quite so desperately situated as before, although that does not mean that I have resolved my difficulties . . . .

. . . It will interest you to hear that I am talking to the catholics here, who have within a radius of a thousand miles most flourishing institutions and number among them some intelligent men. Are you a fan of Rouault's? I am trying to make them take a little art. I do not see why the religious mind should be so hostile or indifferent to art. But I suppose the vicar of the church where Bach first was played would have looked askance at a parishioner who began to develop a veneration for that great music. Or is it such a fight for Rome to keep alive in the modern world that it has no time for play? Or is it just racial – that in Anglosaxon countries the Catholics like everybody else are a little anti-art? What do you think about this? Well all the best to both of you, my Froanna wishing to be especially remembered.
Yrs

305. *To John Burgess*†² Toronto.
Sunday. Oct 25. 1942.

Dear Mr. Burgess. I should have answered your letter earlier, but concentration upon the affairs of the mucous membrane prevented

¹ Sweeney was writing to various people in an effort to help L. find work in the U.S. In the letter to which this is a reply, he asked if L. had heard from a Chicago museum official to whom he (Sweeney) had recommended him.

² Not long after his arrival in Toronto, L. became friendly with John Burgess, a chemist with strong philosophical and religious interests. They saw one another often during the Lewises' residence, Burgess offering some financial assistance as well as the pleasure of civilised conversation.

me. The arrival of your letter, gave me great pleasure – it was not vanity of authorship but real satisfaction that I had said something that you felt was worth saying and which might do some good.¹

The civilised values have to be defended against barbarians at home as much as against Prussian materialism: and with us – Europeans and Americans – the civilised values are the Christian values. So, however much we are obliged to play our part in the blood-and-iron game, there is, after all, the Sermon on the Mount. If the soldier has momentarily to stop his ears against it, we need not. No soldier wants to return either, to a savagery, of which he has usually had enough by the time he is through: he would be disgusted and amazed to find us all foaming at the mouth, our eyes full of bloodlust. The other matters we will talk about before long. I should be about again tomorrow.

Yours sincerely,

306. *To Augustus John*† Toronto.
Nov. 5th 1942.

My dear John. It was a great pleasure to get your letter, and therein to catch a glimpse of you in some smoky den in Soho (for if Nina was there, it must have been a den) exchanging iron fisted he-man salutations with our Vaquero – to whom please give, should you encounter him again, my best wishes.² It is really capital news that he has got out of Spain, where he was liable, because of his over-fervent papist nature to get involved in all kinds of abominable nonsense. – As to your poem, I understand D. Thomas wanting you to go and join the poets.³ I think that all the literary must feel that you belong among them, though I hope that all this flattery wont stop you painting altogether. . . . – I

---

¹ In the letter referred to, Burgess praised a piece by Lewis in the Toronto paper *Saturday Night*.

² John wrote in his letter of October 5th: "I came upon Roy Campbell some time ago in a Soho speak-easy in the company of Nina Hamnett, who it appeared was affording Roy her boundless hospitality while he awaited the return of his family from Lisbon." The artist and writer Nina Hamnett was a well-known Soho personage.

³ John wrote: "I met Dylan Thomas the other day. He had just read some verse I had sent to Tommy Earp and advised me to give up painting! Here they are."

dont know how conditions affected you, in the year or two prior to war, but I was nearly flattened out.¹ Debts grew – thirty pounds to a dentist, twenty pounds to Sielle for frames – tailors and even butchers. I have never been able to pay a penny of these debts. War itself would plainly mean bankruptcy, and my only chance of collecting enough money to pay debts and get a reserve for the war years was the States it seemed to me. How good a chance it was I did not know, but it was the only one. So I headed for New York, taking my wife with me. . . .

But I am determined to discover some means of getting us back, as it would be quite impossible to convey the sensations of acute boredom I experience in this sanctimonious bush-babylon. . . .

P.S. Thank you for telling me about Horizon. I shall try and get something done for them. It will be great fun reading your account of the old days in Haddon Street and the "Cave of the Golden Calf."²

307. *To John Rothenstein*†   Toronto.
                                                                                            Nov. 17. 1942.

My dear Rothenstein. A bad attack of influenza lasting about a month has confused things. I have here a rough draft of a letter but I cannot remember whether it was mailed. So I may be repeating myself if I thank you for your excellent letter and the enclosures about Tate exhibitions. You certainly seem to have been uncommonly active, and what you tell regarding the demand for good pictures in England is highly encouraging. On the other hand I was distressed to hear about your father's health. I very much hope that spell of illness is now at an end.³ . . .

¹ John wrote: "I can't think what you can be doing in Canada. I should have thought it was hardly your element."
² John wrote: "I keep writing bits of reminiscences for Horizon. Cyril Connolly I know would love to have something from you for Horizon. I have dug up a mass of M^{de} Strindberg's out-pourings – also some by her menials, Anushka and Andrea etc. What a scabrous business!" See *Horizon*, August 1942, pp, 128–40, and *Chiaroscuro*.
³ In the rough draft, written September 17th, L. digressed here: "You must urge him to lie low for a little and not to expose himself to

Now regarding my return to England. Were anyone to make me a present of two tickets this evening at 6 o'clock, tomorrow at 10 o'clock I should be telephoning whatever office it is handles the request for Atlantic bookings. It takes about 6 weeks I understand for them to fit you in. The more you pay the better – and safer – accommodations you get naturally. I say if someone made me a present, for I have not enough money myself to transport myself across Lake Ontario, much less to England. – Such has been my state of mind ever since the time we met in New York. But neither you nor anybody else will or can send me two such tickets. So it remains a wish only. My mind is constantly focussed upon means of getting back however. I shall make it before long.

But I wish you could tell me how I shall keep alive once I am back! The reason I am here, after all, is because conditions in my trade became so awful that I had to see whether I couldn't make a little money in the country where traditionally there is supposed to be a good deal of capital. One of my last experiences let us recall was the sale of a large portrait for one hundred pounds! That was no fault of yours: for if they wont supply you with funds to buy pictures ... But to come down to realities – how shall I find the means to buy food, pay my rent and so forth? It worries me a lot. Will they make me director of art education: could I secure the editorship of the "Listener" or something like that? Could I get some post like that occupied by Arthur Bliss at the B.B.C.?[1] Would the King appoint me Keeper of his ceramics? Or shall I just be there, trying to sell a picture to a non-existent rentier, or an article to a paper whose space has been cut by half?

It is a very serious problem. I do not ask to be allowed to *create*: of course not – it has been my experience that creative persons are obliged to waste ninety per cent of their life in futile tasks: and I certainly am tired of being rewarded for such creative activities as one may manage to cheat fate and perform, one-tenth

fatigue. I received a very sad letter from Sturge Moore yesterday, who sounded extremely mournful – in the bright sun of Torquay – the rays of which he described as 'acceptable', which is not quite the way to speak about the sun. It has a sound like that classic 'I dont mind if I do' with which those charladies you say I am versed in received the offer of a second cup of tea."

[1] Sir Arthur Bliss (b. 1891) was at this time Director of Music at the B.B.C. He and L. had seen a good deal of one another just after World War I.

what some wise guy received for doing nothing. – But there *may* be some kind of a second or third-rate job which nobody else wants, that will keep the wolf away from the door. – I am approaching the age when society usually says to itself: "We might as well recognise the existence of that unpleasant person. He'll be dead soon." So there may be some sort of chance? What do you think?

To be serious – for of course the above is merely my way of trying to be funny. Since life for a free-lance painter-novelist-journalist would be impossible at such a time as this, is there any post you know of that I could occupy? Is there such a thing as art-professor at Oxford or Cambridge? . . . South Kensington? You smile: but (for a short-while) why not? – Or is there some old, much-bombed Lighthouse that needs a keeper! Have they been asking for someone, on nights of Blitz, to accouch the Zebras at the Zoo?

Ponder these problems – study the landscape carefully – sound anybody who has fat livings, or lean ones in his giving, and let me know the result. I will get back somehow, before long. If an appointment awaited me at the other end, this translation might be facilitated. – Meanwhile all the best to you and great solicitude about your father, to whom I hope you will take my affectionate greetings.

Yours ever.

308. *To James Johnson Sweeney*†   Toronto.
Dec 30. 1942.

Dear Sweeney. It was very nice to have your Christmas message, and my wife joins me in wishing you and Laura a satisfactory New Year – a *happy* one I suppose none of us can aspire to. My situation here continues to be easier. . . .

As to Rouault; I do not know any French artists personally. The Dublin incident does not surprise me.[1] That the average priest should not understand his religion – or what is good for it – is only

---

[1] In Sweeney's Christmas letter, he spoke of his admiration for Rouault as a person and asked L. if he knew him. Sweeney said he had just learned that an important Rouault had been turned down by the municipal gallery of Dublin "primarily due to Catholic hostility towards its treatment of the subject matter."

to be expected; and when Cromwell and his ghastly puritans disported themselves in Ireland I feel they must have left behind some moral infection. I know that when I was in Spain as a student some priests in my pension discussed very learnedly about the local brothels and, unsolicited, strongly recommended one as being the cleanest. That seems the healthy attitude. But the objections to the Rouault picture in Dublin may have been on other grounds.

"New Directions", I have been told, has an article by Ezra about me.¹ I wonder what it is about. Have you seen it? Being here is much the same as if one were in Baffin Land. A compilation called "Twentieth Century Authors"² in which there is apparently an account of me was noticed in a local paper. But the bookshops dont stock it, as their clients are practically Eskimos.

With more good wishes to both of you, for 1943.

Yrs W. L.

309. *To Henry Moore*†³   Toronto
                               (Jan. 26.) 43.

My dear Moore. Thank you for your letter dated Jan 5 which reached me yesterday afternoon, and for your having so expeditiously attended to the matter about which I wrote you. It is welcome news that an advance is being telegraphed (by the Ministry I suppose). . . .

Thank you too for the details about your own commissions. You appear to have received for a number of drawings about what I got in the last war for a large painting! A sculptor of course cannot exactly be commissioned to do marbles of shelter-life: though I

¹ An article by Pound, "Augment of the Novel," dealing mainly with *The Apes of God* appeared in *New Directions in Prose and Poetry: 1941* (Norfolk, Conn., 1941). Or L. may refer to Pound's contribution to a symposium, "Homage to Ford Madox Ford," which appeared in *New Directions Number 7* (Norfolk, Conn., 1942). Pound mentions L. in this piece, although only in passing.

² Stanley J. Kunitz and Howard Haycraft, eds., *Twentieth Century Authors* (New York, 1942).

³ L. had met Henry Moore before the war. He wrote to him in November 1942, asking him to do what he could to speed up payment of his commission from the War Artists Advisory Committee. Moore replied that he had looked into the matter and that L. could expect some money by cable.

suppose if you were Jagger[1] you would be doing gigantic bronzes of sternly noble miners or if a Rodin amorphous groups of huddled humanity, and be rewarded in accordance with the status of the sculptor's art rather than that of the mere draughtsman. I hope before the war-chapter is closed you will do something big in wood or stone. . . .

I did not know you had been a miner. D. H. Lawrence used that romantic fact to better purpose than you have. This place is chock full of mines: radium, nickel, cobalt, and gold, but no coal apparently. The little bush-cities where the mines are located are very bright and lively centres of fashion I understand. A polack tailor in one of them was fined heavily the other day for making a zoot-suit; very extreme male fashion as you probably know, requiring a lot of cloth – and sumptuary laws are in force in Canada. – This is after Africa the second largest gold-producing centre on the planet. Are they I wonder going to go on digging up that stuff after this war, which surely, if anything could, should have demonstrated that "the metal" as the City boys call it is anything but indispensable. Many a good man and true has been blown to bits by "air-blasts" in the process of getting it out of the earth; and how many billions of men have not met an equally violent end as a result of its malefic power once it is above ground? Not that *paper* cant do just as much harm! Ah well.

The announcement of the Beveridge Report a little time ago made cheerful reading.[2] That seems the minimum requirement, and it is an excellent thing that it should have been stated in black and white. I hope the "progressive" parties will stand on that: really make their stand on that and not allow the smallest fraction of it to be whittled away. Not allow it to be treated, as a maximum, but as an absolute *minimum*.

I was glad to learn that from various sources you had learned of my continued existence. I hope that the reports were true. If so they will have told you of great difficulties . . . . – Before the present convulsion, indeed ever since I first made my (rather violent) bow, in 1913, I have got less materially out of the society to which I belong – in proportion to my effort – than anyone else I can

---

[1] The sculptor Charles Sargeant Jagger (1885–1934) was noted for his war monuments, such as the Artillery Memorial at Hyde Park Corner.

[2] The Beveridge report was published in December 1942 and was being widely discussed at this time.

think of. I have been too busy I suppose doing things to have had time to attend to the practical side of life. For the rest of my days I have much to do but I propose to *make* time to attend to the dirty business of life: though I am much exercised at the thought that poverty having driven me to this worked-out gold mine of a continent, poverty having kept me here, if I succeed in getting *back*, what is there but starvation there for me? A baffling problem!

Well, all the best, and thanks again very much for your kind offices.

Yours sincerely,
WYNDHAM LEWIS

310. *To Naomi Mitchison*†   Toronto.
Jan. 26. 43.

My dear Naomi. Thank you for your beautiful long circumstantial letter. You lucky cow-herd and grandmother! your head full of kiddies and cattle. How you shall get a cow out of one field into the next field, without breaking a rule: how you shall get your brood out of places of education into military units, hospitals, and ships-of-war, smoothly and efficiently. – And you suppose I "want you to speak of books and pictures"!¹ I wish on the contrary you would tell me *more* about milk and cheese, buckwheat and beets, babies and battles. It is great stuff, sister! and if you say you are writing poetry, I am not sure that you have a right to do that. Will you leave nothing to the poor childless and cowless poets? – Àpropos. —— about whom you enquire I have heard nothing of him for a long while. If he was swallowed up before the war by the vast America, he is even more engulfed just now. Somebody told me that he would be drafted, as he is now an American. – I know what service he will choose too. *The Navy*. He will plump for the boys-in-blue every time and be divinely happy in a cosy little corvette bobbing about on the great rough ocean. – I may add in confidence that I think —— was ill advised to go to the

¹ In her letter of December 15th, Mrs. Mitchison, having told of her life as a farmer in Argyll and given the news of her children, apologised: "You won't want to know about potatoes though! And I feel myself incapable of writing about art and literature!"

U.S.A. No one was ever less *for export* than ——, and though his *moeurs* may help, his Englishness is a great handicap. In New York Louis MacNeice who had been staying with —— in Brooklyn asked me to go over: I would have done so but keeping my head above water, day by day, was so exacting a task, I never made it.
– At a house where I passed some weeks in the country in Western New York, they recounted how, when —— stopped there, he never made use of the towels provided for him. They set a watch on his ablutions. The servant would rush down and shake her head, indicating that the towels were still untouched though he had spent some time in the bath room. He was a guest there for a week. But for a little splashing of his face, he remained austerely dirty. Blond and dirty. What does that mean? – *Wrinkles* is my guess. But it heightened his prestige with the natives. MacNeice went down nothing like so well. He washed his face and blew his nose just like anybody else.

Your friends who found Canada not very "sympathetic" to her "war-guests" reported correctly I am afraid. They tend to divide "old-country" people into two sorts: poor white trash, and people who have cars and servants and play golf. The former they deeply despise – for after all they were once that themselves. About the servant-keeping monied highhatters they have mixed feelings: they are inclined to ask *how many* servants they have where they come from – how *large* their house is. They are suspicious: one woman who was here told them she had a "nice little house in Westminster." They were scandalised: "She says she lives in a *little* house!" they whispered to each other. Remarking how badly this was received, the woman in question thereafter was careful to mention her butler and her cook, and her very *large* Palladian residence in the country, and even that she enlarged for the occasion, giving it an extra wing or two, so as not to lose face. – But since it is quite impossible to have so much as a penny-piece transferred from England to Canada, some of the women who have come here with their children – like McEvoys pretty daughter – are "poverty-struck." That is bad. And the R.F. turned up here and they said she "grabbed" their men. After that they queried the soundness of her social backgrounds. They came to the conclusion that she was only *partly* a lady. They could not decide – for apparently there was no information accessible at the moment – whether it was her mother, or her father, that was not out of the top drawer. But they knew there must be *something* wrong with her "background", for no 100 per cent lady would "grab" men.

Apropos. – Are we going to have a 100 per cent new deal in England after the war: will the brand of inferiority be lifted from those whose family has not been smart enough to amass money and become what we laughingly call ladies and gentlemen? Ninety per cent of the genius of the country is locked up and battened down. It can only be released by a 100 per cent debunk of the class-nonsense and a great reversal of tradition. – Is the Beveridge Report going to be accepted 100 per cent? Will the "progressive" parties stand on that as a *minimum*: or will it be regarded as a maximum? Is your husband still aiming at a parliamentary seat: who is he allied with now?[1] What on earth has Cripps been doing?

President Roosevelt told the new congress that all this global misery and heartbreak would be a "sacrilege" unless something came of it, more than just an empty military victory. That is a mild way of putting it.

From what I gather from listening to the radio and scrutinizing the Press, the war in Europe should end next year. For my own part I have made many efforts to return to England, and am trying to collect the money: it was my poverty that caused me to come to this dud-goldmine of a continent: the same has kept me here. What sort of living I can make when I get *back* heaven knows.... If the new diplomatic revolution announced here this morning is not a mere pretence I might be appointed minister to Venezuela, as I speak Spanish so well. They might appoint me head of the Royal College of Art, but I dont think so. – Or have you seen a Keeper advertised for, for some tumbledown old much-bombed lighthouse? Keep an eye open – I authorize you to apply on my behalf. Say I could, with luck, present myself for duty three months from the time of my appointment. Explain I am marooned on a lakeshore in Upper Canada, but am an awfully good man and you know I would love the work.

Yrs ever,
WYNDHAM LEWIS

[1] G. R. Mitchison was elected to Parliament in 1945 as Labour member from the Kettering Division of Northamptonshire.

P.S. This city is mainly Scotch – I dont see how you can feel as you do about Scotland.¹ Are you Presbyterian or Methodist?

311. *To Lord Carlow*†   Toronto.
Jan. 28. 1943.

Dear Carlow. Our letters crossed – and did not yours perhaps provide a clue to how my present problem, which is a fairly limited one, might be solved?² For there is no book I can imagine myself more fitted to illustrate than the Ancient Mariner, no designs I should be better pleased to find myself engaged on, than those you propose I might do for it. The Wedding Guest who beat his breast, for he heard the loud bassoon, steps out of the first few lines, and presents himself for portrayal. I would read again "The Road to Xanadu," which is full of quotations of the sources, in books of travel, from which Coleridge got his exotic material. – And the Albatross, we would have him, with his *ailes de géant*, which *empêche de marcher*: it is a poem that is more full of imagery and romantic allusion than any I can think of. So you chose well.

That is fine that you will be coming back to Toronto probably. We can talk *Ancient Mariner* then. A bientôt and thank you for having thought of me to do that lovely job.

                             Yrs
                             W. L.
                       (WYNDHAM LEWIS)

312. *To Theodore Spencer*†   Toronto.
[Perhaps not finished.]   Jan 30. 1943.

Dear Spencer. In the current Nation I see that a book of yours has been published,³ which brought to my mind the fact that I

¹ Mrs. Mitchison wrote that as a resident of Scotland she was "becoming increasingly nationalist in feeling."
² Lord Carlow wrote to L. suggesting a plan for printing at his private press an edition of "The Ancient Mariner" with illustrations by L. The continuation of the war and Carlow's sudden death caused the project to be abandoned.
³ *Shakespeare and the Nature of Man* (Toronto, 1942).

had not answered your last letter. In that missive you explained that it was not out of the question for me to go to Harvard because I had not a degree. . . . – Why it is extremely unlikely that I could teach art at Harvard (or could have, for by this time I imagine all art-teaching in American universities is at an end) is because my views upon that subject would be out of tune with the so-called "Fogg-factory",[1] which has dominated that institution. I believe that if art, as a serious craft, is to survive, the artist has to be taught to be a workman again: whereas the "Fog" would tend to encourage a training that would lead to a pretentious dilettantism, wholly divorced from the existence of the common man. –

In January 1943 Lewis – having been visited in Toronto by Father J. Stanley Murphy, then Registrar of Assumption College of Windsor, Ontario[2] – lectured at Windsor. While there he met several of the Basilian priests on the faculty of the small Roman Catholic institution. There was talk of his returning to the college as a visiting lecturer. On his return to Toronto, Lewis had a letter from Father Murphy offering him a position for the academic year 1943–4.

313. *To the Rev. J. Stanley Murphy*†   Toronto.
                                                                        Feb 12. 1943.

Dear Father Murphy. Your letter has just reached me, and I am delighted to learn that I am to come to Assumption College, and am personally enormously obliged to you, for bringing to so happy and expeditious a conclusion this plan you spoke to me about while I was in Windsor. I cannot imagine for myself more congenial surroundings: and I greatly appreciate the favourable periods of work you outline, though you must not hesitate to ask me to do more, if and when that is desireable. – I hope you will express to Fathers Lee and Garvey, and to Father Young, my

[1] The Fogg Art Museum, headquarters of the Harvard Department of Fine Arts.
[2] At this time Assumption College was affiliated with the University of Western Ontario. It later broke the affiliation and in 1956 changed its name to Assumption University of Windsor.

thanks for the ready welcome they accorded your proposal. I know I shall work alongside of them harmoniously.

As to the nature of that work. It will I suppose consist of daily lectures, of an informal type. That is what teaching amounts to, isn't it? In that I have some experience. – For the *subject*: history would be the simplest, provided it were a period of which I had sufficient knowledge.

For some time I have been assembling material for a book about American notions of Liberty. It was in the course of that reading that I came across, for instance, Hollis's book, *The American Heresy*,[1] which we discussed the other day. It is his position, of course, – and it must be the position of anybody I should say, if they give it a moment's thought – that in the matter of the famous "Rights of Man", all "rights" must and only can derive from God, there being no other discoverable sense in the expression. And all this business of "rights" is very fundamental to the political doctrine of Democracy.

I shall be pretty familiar with the minds and lives of Alexander Hamilton, Gouverneur Morris, Jefferson and Madison, Washington and Marshall. I have thought a good deal about Woodrow Wilson and the 2 Roosevelts; Abe Lincoln I am getting to know. – That, at all events, is what I have been occupying myself with.[2] I give you this information not with a view to prompting you to start me in teaching the early days of the American Republic and the origins of those *idées fixes* which every Amer. citizen inherits, but only by way of enabling you to find out which frame to pop me into . . . .

I ought I suppose, on my side, to "put it in writing", as they say, that: I W.L. gladly agree to come to Assumption College for the period specified in your letter, namely beginning June 28 1943 for a period of ten months: and that I am agreable as to the fees you mention, namely 200 dollars a month. (It is very generous of you, by the way, to have these fees still payable during the vacation months, when I shall not be teaching.)

As we shall be in Windsor for practically a year, I think that my wife and I might as well rent an apartment for that period (though a furnished apartment may not be easy to find?) Two

---

[1] Christopher Hollis, *The American Heresy* (New York, 1930).
[2] This work, and L.'s lectures on the subject at Assumption College, became the basis of *America and Cosmic Man* (1948).

rooms, a kitchen and bathroom – a front door of our own – is all that is necessary: and of course as near as possible to the College. If you were successful in locating one or two, I could come down for the day and okay it. – In spite of what I was saying the other night about my complacence re. the physically repellent, I am affected by what I look at out of a window, and a brick wall 4 feet away induces in me an unwholesome melancholy. Otherwise, am fairly easy to please.

Thank you for the cutting[1] – quite a good write-up. Mistakes, of course, occur: as where he makes me speak of a "fascinating theological problem." The word was "philosophical" not "theological": it was when I was referring to the *philosopher's* approach (say W. James). Then where the reporter writes "evil is too inventive and evasive", he evidently misheard me. What I said was *inveterate* and *pervasive*. But these are small matters in a press report. I am sending you a typed copy of the original lecture.

Again, really very great thanks: and I am looking forward in every way to coming among you again, to teach alongside of you and your colleagues.

Yours sincerely,

314. *To Eric Kennington*† Toronto.
March 31. 1943.

My dear Kennington. . . .

Since I have been given the choice, I paint a picture in oils.[2] I believe I can put my hands on the money to buy the canvas: and I can get free transport to the factory. Wish me luck! – it is a lulu as they say here: a most rugged subject, full of the apparatus of industry, which by screeching and roaring stages becomes in due course the apparatus of war.

I have received several letters recently seeking in the most flattering way to persuade me to return. Of course at present physically I *cannot* – the three hundred pounds[3] . . . will go, all but 200 dollars, in debts contracted while I waited and waited. But when I ask my correspondents if anyone can use some influence

---

[1] A newspaper article on L.'s lecture.
[2] For the War Artists Advisory Committee.
[3] The amount of L.'s commission from the War Artists Advisory Committee.

to obtain me a suitable post . . . they say – *why get a job*. That is to talk as if the war had changed nothing economically.

After the war, it seems pretty clear to me, the *rentier* will have disappeared: the painter or other artist will have to depend upon state patronage. But in this violent interim, when such poor little half-hearted "patrons" as are left are hiding from bombs and not feeling much like highly speculative investments: when the publishers have no paper (complain that conditions are "awful") how could I *begin* to live, in Notting Hill Gate, or Chalfont St. Peters, or Lands End?

These questions worry me a lot – for I *want* to get back. I do not think that anyone realized how I *just* managed to live before. I lived under a tremendous strain: I spurned an easy bankruptcy which might have eased things, and really believe that before very long I should have come through. But that sort of life I propose to live no more. It is a bad joke I have had enough of – to watch every smooth little clown occupying a fat job, well-paid by state or city, and I wasting 90 per cent of my time trying to scrape a dangerous living (and often having to go and ask favours of the smooth little clown).

I suppose it is just impossible to live as a so-called "creative artist" in our society: *then* I prefer to be an official rather than any longer make the vain attempt: an official naturally in some field where a lifetime of experience accumulated for purposes of creation can be put to some public use. Perhaps, the war over, things may take a turn for the better. – I have given as much to England as England has given to me: I believe I can say: I have, for an artist, worked like a nigger. (Better than a nigger, because a nigger it seems works none too well). I have written just on 30 books, most not easy books to write. One of the best of them, the *Childermass*, is only half-finished, because I have never been able to raise the money to finish it. – I believe at this stage of the proceedings I deserve the salary of a second-rate bank-manager, and (desert apart) think I could help in the cultural life of England. . . .

You may wonder why I write you like this. But I haven't spoken for nearly four years: so when I sit down and write a letter I relieve my feelings, if I can do nothing more. – These *total* wars of our age are so different from the napoleonic wars say: all our lives are held up and conditioned by them upon a total pattern.

Anything in the form of normal adjustment is impossible. In any case there was not *any* margin for an economic readjustment.

We are freezing out here slowly, in this icebox of a country. This hotel burned down six weeks ago, all but the annexe. I am living in the ruins. It was 30 degrees below zero at the time of the fire. The cold was so great it made the firemen's noses bleed, icicles hung from their eyelashes – their moustaches froze. While the fire was raging over the front furnace, I and another man went for warmth into the rear furnace room, which was full of smoke but *warm*.[1]

Carlow seemed frightfully unreal – I dont know if I seemed so to him. His way of appearing and disappearing partakes of the world of Maskelyne and Devant![2] These airmen, these cloud-men.

I bought the last box of white conté in the "Art Metropole" here the other day. I am turning over in my mind methods of making paints, when the last brush and last tubes of Burnt Sienna and Venetian Red are sold and I and the few others here are back where Cimabue was – lassoing hogs and cutting their hair off for brushes. – There is a lot of hoarding going on, of artists materials I believe.

There is some good news I am thankful to say. We have the Mareth Line and I cant see how the Germans can live for long in the upper right-hand corner of Tunisia. – Many sincere thanks for having helped me over the commission. . . .

Yrs

315. *To the Rev. J. Stanley Murphy*†   Toronto.
March 31. 1943.

Dear Father Murphy. Thank you very much for your letter. I have waited a few days before answering it, as I had hoped by the weekend to be able to fix a day for coming to Windsor. . . . your

---

[1] The fire was to become a high point of *Self Condemned*.
[2] John Nevill Maskelyne (1839–1917) was a celebrated conjurer and entrepreneur of the Egyptian Hall ("England's Home of Mystery") and later of St. George's Hall. David Devant, his one-time partner and a popular prestidigitator, left Maskelyne for the music halls.

idea that I should come down is just what I should have suggested myself. I shall then be able to play my part in home-finding, and we can go over together the question of my Summer School talks, and also my subsequent line of work. – *Modern art and Literature* would, as you say, suit me very well. The philosophical backgrounds of art (painting, the drama and so on) are of great importance to everybody, and, as you say, interest a wide audience – a far wider audience than the actual arts in question do.

The Lion and the Fox, which Mort. Adler mentioned, is about the political and philosophic backgrounds of Shakespeare's mind: Machiavelli appeared to me a prime influence (T. S. Eliot answered by writing a pamphlet, in which he substituted Seneca for Machiavelli).[1]

... – Meanwhile here I am working all the time in the factories – the job I told you about for the British Government. Everybody has been extremely helpful and it is a very pleasant and interesting experience. I am painting a line of furnaces serviced by an infernal personnel (mainly Central European and Russian). Then in another place I am working on a monster having a solitary claw and which goes up to a furnace, thrusts its claw inside, and draws out a huge jar full of molten glass. Such are my occupations for the moment. Still I pile up notes about the ideologic foundations of the U.S.A. ...

Till we meet then, as soon as ever I can make it.

Cordially yours.

316. *To Naomi Mitchison*†   Toronto.
May 31. 1943.

Dear Naomi. How are you? I can tell you nothing about myself, because the same blanket of war that envelops you envelops me, only with me there are 2 or 3 other blankets as well. In your last letter I remember you said something about a report that I was not very comfortable here. I think it implied that they had not offered me a high official post, or commissioned me to paint the Prime Ministers portrait. It is of course quite true that nothing pleasant has happened to me here. But I dont think that *anybody*

[1] *Shakespeare and the Stoicism of Seneca.*

coming in from the outside – from Europe – would have a very nice time in this place. This is a province: but with a provincialism that has no equal for exclusiveness and jealousy. It is impossible for instance to obtain a post in a university here, because they tell you that only Canadians can occupy such posts: and there are no "extension" lectures, because the colleges have no money: rich men when they die never have bequeathed money to them, and professors are so poorly paid that they are barely able to offer you a glass of beer (none can afford whiskey) if you go to see them. – When I first arrived I had the sensation of being a dog who had strayed into a farm-yard, and had there discovered a dozen indigenous dogs standing fiery-eyed and softly growling around one very lean bone indeed. . . .

. . . Having no human society is no inconvenience to me. Sometimes for six months on end we have seen nobody – we might have been on the sub-arctic continent. . . .

. . . we are able to make short trips to the States, and it is a blessed relief to breathe that more intelligent air for a while: though oh for a half-hour of Europe! – for relatively agreeable as the States are (after this sanctimonious icebox) the North American continent is not a place I like stopping in for more than a month or two. – So there you are: many people have had a lovely time during this war, and some have made more money than they ever dreamed of making before – in London I suppose as much as over here. "P.M." calls it a positive Klondike. But I have none of those arts. All I can say is that had I been in England I should be bankrupt. I often write to old buddies of mine in England, asking them if they can secure me a fitting job there (for if I got some proper appointment, I could get me passage paid). They treat this as a joke. I find it impossible to explain to them that, if I had the chance, I would not take up again the existence you saw me living in Kensington, loaded with debts. When one thinks of all the parasites art carries on its back – K.C.B.s like —— and dozens of other costly and superfluous officers – it occurs to one, or it does to me, that if we are to have some kind of stale socialism after the war, where everyone turns into a bureaucrat, why shouldn't I do so – usurp the place of one of those peacocks, as they have usurped mine? – If that is not too rational, why if MacLeish gets appointed head of the Library of Congress, couldn't I be made director of the British Museum? Most people respect me more than they do

MacLeish, so why shouldn't that happen. Or the London Library would suit me just as well. . . .

. . . Or does Wormwood Scrubs want a janitor do you suppose?

I wonder if you could tell me what sort of things are likely to happen to G.B. when the war ends? This is a serious question: I cannot gather very much from reading the reviews or papers. No country in Europe, I imagine, will escape civil war, or at least a grandscale purge. The vacuum left in Europe by the passing of Germany as a major power will provoke a sudden readjustment all over. (In these parts many people seem to be thinking about that in very old-fashioned terms). Having destroyed – at a cost of three hundred billion dollars for the U.S.A. alone – the arch exponent of Nationalism, Germany, are we all going to practice it ourselves, from the Scot in his Tam O'Shanter to the Greek in his white cotton kilts? I hope not: I am all for what Mrs. Luce[1] calls "Globaloney". I hope you are one of the globaloney girls still.

> ... et demain
> ça sera le genre humain.

Or is all that after all baloney? – I am as you will see trying to provoke some response. If you answer this letter in Gaelic, I shall know then acushla, that its no use asking you about such things in future. But I hope this will not happen. Give me some straight news of what is on foot, if there are any promising leaders, besides Cripps and those I know: whether *all* capital is going down the drain and what effect socially will that leave: Will Thomas Beecham, Lady Astor, Edward Wadsworth, have any money left? You know the kind of thing. And what you and your family have been doing: if you have spent much time this winter in London: if you are still pleased with your home at Campbelltown. My best wishes to your husband.

Yrs ever.

[1] Clare Boothe Luce (b. 1903).

317. To Malcolm MacDonald†[1]
Windsor.
July 17. 1943.

Dear Malcolm Macdonald. Yesterday I duly received the cheque for 664 dollars and enclosed is the receipt slip for your office. Without your personal intervention I feel sure I should never have got this money, or got it so late that it would have caused me endless difficulties, so again I have to thank you for all the trouble you have taken.

It may interest you to know that I am teaching here (at the College of the Assumption) the philosophic principles implicit in various works of fiction – from *War and Peace* to *Of Mice and Men*. Only 50 minutes each day (5 days a week) is required of me but it keeps me pretty busy reading and preparing my stuff. In the autumn I am to deliver a lecture once or twice a week on the origins of American democracy: about the two political poles, you know, of Hamilton and Jefferson, and the respective influences that produced these two opposing groups, which contended under the shades of Washington. What I think has happened to this dual political heritage today is that everybody *practices* Hamiltonian politics, and *professes* Jeffersonian. These lectures and much other material I have collected on the subject of America, will appear as a book. I find many things to like and admire in things American, but am well aware what a very unstable mass the U.S.A. is, and how little it in reality has to do today, with those original English 'founding fathers'.

It has been *malgré moi* that I have spent all this time over here – and am still spending it: so I might as well turn this circumstance to some account. . . .

Yours sincerely,

[1] The Rt. Hon. Malcolm MacDonald (b. 1901), son of Ramsay MacDonald and since 1955 High Commissioner for the United Kingdom in India, was between 1941 and 1946 United Kingdom High Commissioner in Canada. L. asked him to intercede in his behalf with regard to payment of the remainder of his £300 commission. He had so far received half of the money.

318. *To John Burgess*† Windsor.
July 17. 1943.

Dear Mr. Burgess. Well at last I sit down to write a few letters: except for my note to you and a couple of postcards I have written nothing since we have been here. Literally I have not had time: I work for an hour or so every morning before going to deliver my lecture, and then, on my return, work solidly until midnight on the next days talk with breaks only for meals. A great deal of reading is entailed: hence this incessant application.

My class, as you supposed, consists mainly of teachers. What they have to write their essay on is the "intellectual virtues." I am teaching them the intellectual virtues! If you would like to join my class I suggest you read "Art and Scholasticism" by Maritain,[1] and "Art and Prudence" by Mortimer Adler[2] (a follower, to some extent, of Maritain's). Aristotle's Ethics would come in handy too. – Of course, I have to adapt my pedagogy to their requirements, and Maritain, as you know, is their supreme contemporary authority. But I am given a perfectly free hand. "Art and Prudence" was suggested by the people here: but the purpose of that is merely to instruct my class not to allow prudence to hamper them, which is a healthy teaching. Long ago Adler wrote very nice things about my early books, and, though a little self-conscious, his big bland volume contains good things. – My priestly colleagues are pleasant fellows. How good the religious disciplines are for people! By the way, in the course of my work on Hegel, I came upon a magnificent fragment of Soren Kierkegaard – Barth's philosophical inspiration, you remember. He said all that is necessary to say about Hegel and other "existential systems". But I now learn that several of Kierkegaard's books have recently been translated into English. I am getting one at least of them and I think you should agitate for copies in the university library at Toronto. . . .

Windsor is a very agreeable little city, and quite charmingly arranged. This place is about 3 blocks up Ouillette from the shopping area (at Ouillette and Ellis) and Ouillette is a handsome

[1] Jacques Maritain, *Art and Scholasticism, with Other Essays* (New York, 1930).
[2] Mortimer Adler, *Art and Prudence, a Study in Practical Philosophy* (New York, 1937).

street, with the Detroit skyscrapers at the end of it. We possess a spare bed: and *if* by any chance you would be persuaded to come here for a week-end, we should be able to put you up. I wish you could manage it! – Will write you soon again.

Yours sincerely,

319. *To Malcolm MacDonald*† Apt. 2. Royal Apartments.
30 Ellis, East.
Windsor. Ontario.
July 27. 1943.

Dear Macdonald. Thank you very much for your letter. I was most encouraged by your remarks regarding my plan for a book about America.¹ – There is less straight nationalism in England than in any country I know, thank goodness: and nationalist feeling is the greatest obstacle to understanding. At least in addressing an English audience one does not have to grapple with inflated nationalism: so my task should be relatively easy. Who is going to do this job at the other end – or how – I do not know.

To achieve a true "union" of so vast a nation as the States, nationalist uplift could not be dispensed with, no doubt. The English have been put under contribution, alas, in the concocting of this jingo-pep of theirs: perhaps we provide indeed the main ingredient. I am sure that the present U.S. Administration would like to modify that recipe. But the old emotional habit is there. Yet what frank, goodhearted, amusing people lots of Americans are – especially the plain simple people – the butchers and railway men, electricians, ice men, tree-surgeons and fishermen. I can still feel the hand of the bus-conductor on my shoulder going up Fifth Avenue, recounting a joke about one of the Presidential candidates at the last Election. (One should read the *Leaves of Grass* while living in the States). But those are not quite the people one has to deal with. – The intellectual is awful. What T. S. Eliot said about the New York intellectuals, that they are "like a lot of mischievous children" is exact. But even in *them* that great native warm-heartedness sometimes peeps out, in unexpected places.

¹ MacDonald wrote to L. on July 22nd expressing his interest in the prospect of L.'s book about America and stressing the importance of Anglo-American understanding.

Enclosed is the article.¹ I have not done anything about it, because (1) I am not well-acquainted with the American art periodicals; and (2) dont know what is happening about the Studio, Burlington etc. in England. It is longish (4,000 words) – I read it this morning to my class. They seemed to get very excited and pleased, so it is all right as far as Canadians go. But it is written of course for a non-Canadian public. . . .

Yours sincerely,

320. *To Malcolm MacDonald*† Windsor.
Aug. 8th 1943.

Dear Macdonald. Thank you for your very interesting letter.² . . .
As you no doubt realised, the main object of my article was to do a personal service to Jackson.³ I made myself his advocate, and

¹ MacDonald asked L. to send him a copy of his article on Canadian painting. A version of the article appeared as "Canadian Nature and Its Painters" in *The Listener* for August 29th, 1946.
² MacDonald wrote to L. on August 5th, praising his article, "Nature's Place in Canadian Culture," and giving his own views on Canadian painting. He hopes that "'regionalism' will continue to mark the work of all sorts of artists in Canada."
³ In an earlier draft of this letter, L. explained himself as follows: "My subject was only incidentally 'Canadian Painting': I wanted to defend Jackson against the sort of criticism that treats the nature-painters as out-of-date 'romantics'. It is rather like defending Augustus John against the aspersions of the Bloomsburies (as in fact I did). When Clive Bell described the things in the John show at Tooth's as 'practically worthless' – on the ground, of course, that they depended on *subject matter*, and were in the bad old naturalist tradition – it was necessary to register disapproval. Like the Bloomsburies, I myself much prefer other types of painting. But the facts remain that if the Negro heads by John were 'worthless' then a very similarly painted (and no more ably painted) head by Rubens is worthless too. And the bumptious intellectualism of Clive Bell would hardly convince anybody that *Rubens* was worthless.
"The gifts of John were so great that he, quite literally, had he lived in the seventeenth Century, could have stood beside Rubens as an equal. With Jackson it is simply a case of a French Impressionist (of a period when Impressionism was moving over into what Fry called Postimpressionism) going out into the Canadian Bush and struggling with a much harsher nature than Monet or Sisley ever had to meet. Fundamentally, the problem is *Nature*, rather than *Jackson*."

was glad to stress the publicity value to Canadians of their zeroland. (Why mind being treated as snowbound "hicks"?)[1] – But life along the St. Lawrence is going to match the civilised swarming on the Hudson River: the small bush-airlines will turn into giant concerns: the Laurier tradition is about to expire (if the Ontario elections mean anything): of the mood of Schiller, or Ossian, of Leatherstocking, there will be tomorrow, in Canada, hardly a trace – there will be much less pioneer-nostalgia than in the States: the English connection has held them back from participation in the vulgarly red-blood American attitude (the lady and gentlemen complex).

So, by all the signs, there will be a very long interval before they think about Nature again. . . .

The summer-school ended here this week-end. All the nuns have departed. The local Press photographed Father Donovan (brother of "wild Bill Donovan") and myself. Now I start preparing the "Heywood Broun Lectures" – and do my best to cope with the sub-tropical heat!

Yours sincerely,

In July 1943, hearing that Lewis was teaching at Windsor, Marshall McLuhan[2] and Felix Giovanelli,[3] both instructors at Saint Louis University (R.C.), went north to meet and talk with him. The visit was a success. McLuhan and Giovanelli returned to St. Louis full of plans to make it possible for Lewis to come there. The idea was to arrange for lectures and portrait commissions, and the two young men threw themselves into the effort with the zeal of enthusiasts.

[1] Again the earlier draft is more explicit here: "My argument was merely that *Nature* is still there. Furthermore it is a damned good advertisement for the Canadians: and if they consulted their own interests – and were not so afraid of being treated as 'hicks' – they would pretend they were much nearer to the Pole than in fact they are."

[2] Canadian by birth, H. Marshall McLuhan (b. 1911) is now Professor of English at St. Michael's College in the University of Toronto. He is known for his writing on social aspects of culture. An article by him, "Wyndham Lewis: His Theory of Art and Communication," appeared in the special Lewis number of *Shenandoah* (Summer-Autumn 1953).

[3] Felix Giovanelli now teaches Romance Languages at New York University.

321. *To Felix Giovanelli*   Windsor.
Aug. 11. 1943.

Dear Giovanelli. Your letter just arrived, and it sounds to me as if you were doing wonders in St. Louis. Your youthful élan seems to have softened up the over-cautious ———.[1] And now I have to weigh in with such poor persuasiveness as I can muster. — I spend my life disarming and reassuring people (who expect the "Enemy" to explode in their face). But I gather with ——— that he wants a soupçon of dynamite in an otherwise fairly mild composition.

You know what my feeling about "abstract art" is. To reduce the material of the visual world to the abstractness of a musical composition is quite impossible. What you get if you attempt to do so, is inescapably concrete. It has been tried out, and the results are unsatisfactory. The visual has not the emotional appeal of the aural: another difficulty. Very nice effects can be obtained in the course of such attempts heroically to *abstract*, but, *in the mass* the effect is very empty. There is no sensuous language at the end of it: there is geometry or nothing. — But I will, as you suggest, write a page or so on this subject and mail it, with a note, to Mr. (or is it Dr?) ———. . . .

. . . A thousand thanks, and please thank McLuhan for all his activity on my behalf, for you tell me that he is plotting my good in other directions.

Cordially
LEWIS

322. *To Naomi Mitchison*†   Windsor.
Aug. 15. 43.

My dear Naomi. . . .

Please give me news of yourself, your family and friends. I see you in my mind's eye in a kilt, somewhat thinner (though about to have another child) sallying forth with your kilted gamekeeper to secure more hares and blackbirds for the family table: or sitting on an empty keg on a little jetty, awaiting your private fishing-fleet, speculating on the catch: *or* repairing, spade in hand, to your victory garden. — All very wide of the mark I expect. You

[1] One of the people in St. Louis with whom they were hoping to arrange a lecture engagement.

are back in London, having tea in the garden with Mrs. Cole[1] and a couple of handsome Doughboys. Yes that is probably it.

I was sitting in a garden here myself the other day watching the blue jays (very pretty) having a shower-bath in a lawn-sprayer, and my young French Canadian hostess was saying to me after an appreciable moment of hesitation, "Did you see what they said about you in the *Star* a few days ago?" (The *Star* is the local paper) "No" I answered her, "I didn't – what was that?" and racked my brains to think what it could be. Recalling the way their minds are apt to work, I thought they might have hinted I was an emissary of the British Government – my assignment being most probably to undermine or block Canadian emancipation and arrange for the assassination of the local M.P., who favours union with the States.

So I shook my head, as my hostess remained silent, and asked her again what it was that "Star" had said. She seemed to regret having referred to the matter; but pressed by me, she spoke as follows. "Well," she said, "they described you as Mr. W. L. the celebrated English *wit*. I thought you would have seen it, and wondered what you thought about it. It wasn't very *nice* ...". It took me some time to understand that she regarded the term *wit* as offensive and damaging. An hour before that I had been going over a "collegiate school" with her and had seen 3 books of mine in the students library. Probably they would not have been there, had it been realised that their author was a "wit"!

This is what they are like. The same all over Canada. In the States on the other hand, they know what "wit" means, having a number themselves.

Across the river in Michigan they are even prepared for worse things than "wits". Mr. —— was engaged to teach at a school or little college. He made it a condition that he should bring with him a swarthy young Bronx violinist. When he got there he went on something terrible however; the moeurs of the *Phaedrus* became a commonplace of the campus. The staff at last rebelled against these hellenic aberrations. Ensuing upon a campus storm, —— departed, a short while ago.

I thought you would like to hear this piece of scandal as you know —— so well, but of course it is for your private ear.

---

[1] Mrs. G. D. H. Cole (Margaret Isabel Postgate).

Quite literally I work from morning till night. As you know I am here malgré moi: but I attempt to put to some serious use my prolonged immersion in this N. American civilisation.

Economically, I am able to live not too uncomfortably, but with no margin whatever. Without that margin I cannot move far – and certainly am unable to purchase clipper tickets for 2 people back to G.B.

But lately I have reached a great decision: never, under any circumstances, to return to my hand-to-mouth existence in London. . . . I am tired of seeing the parasitic bureaucrats which the Fine Arts attract, in a dozen lucrative assignments, who naturally despise me for being poor – for living like a bum because, I have wanted to try to write good books and paint good pictures. In London I have always wasted 80 per cent of my time pestering myself about money. In my new post I shall have *more* time, not less, to write or paint (perhaps 35 per cent instead of only 20!) *And* I shall be in the running for Minister of Fine Arts if a socialist state comes into being. My aim is the *bureaucracy*. Meanwhile I remain buried alive here until Somebody says to Somebody else, "I suppose we had better give Mr. Lewis a job of some sort."

The Detroit Radio and the "Detroit Free Press" inform me that the end of the war is not far off. I imagine we shall be in Rome in a week or two and the Germans are moving back in Russia. So we *may* be seeing each other at not too distant a date. Keep a warm spot in your heart for me. In a year or two I may be very adequately rewarded by the State for doing very little in some bureaucratic capacity, and be a highly respected citizen.

Yours ever,
WYNDHAM LEWIS

323. *To John Rothenstein*†   Windsor.
Aug. 17. 1943.

Dear Rothenstein. Well, the picture representing Canadas War Effort is finished. The "advance" even arrived at last . . . .

. . . It is still as much as I can do to keep alive. But there is something else, namely: Where would be the use of that fare [to England] to me if I had it? I dont want a fare back without some guarantee that at the other end I shall not be plunged into economic miseries worse even than before. I have told you all this before, once or twice! but as I know you would like to know how I am getting on, I will say it over again. I will not ever return to my hand-to-mouth existence in London. I have a great horror of it. I have a natural dislike of being patronised by sleek gentlemen for whom the fine arts is a fine lucrative official assignment, and a road up to the social summits for the clever climber. I dont like that, in fact it makes me feel a little sick . . . .

There is something to be said I know for keeping the place a land fit for mediocrity to live in: but I can't help hoping that *some* day my disturbing influence will once more be felt in the British Isles: but I just have to wait I suppose until Somebody says to Somebody else that *some* paltry job had better be offered to the importunate Mr. Lewis – just so that we can have him back here dont you know where we can do him a bad turn now and then. – Britannia has received more at my hands than I have at Britannia's: I should not mind a spell of fifty-fifty. What chances do you see of such a ratio?

Meanwhile I exist here (for "the Royal Apartments – Windsor" is a somewhat deceptive address: I have no Clark to "keep" my Rowlandsons).[1] Being here, immersed in transatlantic civilization malgré moi, I attempt to turn my experience to some profit. We shall see.

Remember me to your father if you see him.

Yrs.

324. *To John Burgess*†　　　　　　　　　　　　　　　　Windsor
　　　　　　　　　　　　　　　　　　　　　　　　August. 17. 1943.

Dear Mr. Burgess. . . .

Since my stay here I have learnt much that would be of interest to you. The priests are very pleasant and do not mind at all my not being a catholic. They accept me as a well-wisher: they respect the principles of others I find: for much as I like them, I possess some beliefs that are not theirs. They are however, I understand, a particularly liberal order. They have treated me with great kindness, as also the nuns.

[1] Sir Kenneth Clark was Surveyor of the King's Pictures from 1934 to 1944.

A great deal of sentiment against the English is noticeable here, and oddly enough, a good deal against Americans. A curious situation. (These sensations are not shared of course by my catholic hosts). Then there is the black versus white problem, that broods over this neighbourhood. They are very saddening, all these categories. What a quarrelsome family the Anglosaxon is! The inter-group and inter-racial quarrels seem to grow in number and in virulence, rather than diminish. It was supposed that as the world grew small or, as a result of enormously magnified communicability, travel facilities and so on, people would live more harmoniously together. It is the exact opposite, it seems to me.

This place is actually *south* of Detroit, and one participates much more in the life of the States than in Toronto. I have been hearing a lot of talk about what appears to me a most promising movement in American education: namely the socalled "essentialist", as opposed to the "progressive" principle. Adler and Buchanan[1] are originally responsible for it. It is practiced at Annapolis and elsewhere. (Stringfellow Barr is the presiding genius at Annapolis). It is popularly called the "Hundred Books" experiment. Have you heard anything about it? They make their students thoroughly master a single book at a time – like *War and Peace*, Homer's *Odyssey* or what not – instead of flitting over a too extended field. Other items too, which seem good. It is being tried out in California and elsewhere....

Yours sincerely

325. *To Charles Nagel*†[2]   Windsor.
Friday. Aug. 20. 1943.

Dear Mr. Nagel. Thank you for your letter and I should like very much to come to St. Louis and deliver the lecture for the opening of your February exhibition. The fee you mention, one hundred and fifty dollars, will be all right. Since that exhibition will

[1] Scott Buchanan (b. 1895) was Dean of St. John's College, Annapolis, during the presidency of F. Stringfellow Barr (b. 1897), which lasted from 1937 to 1947.
[2] Charles Nagel (b. 1899) was Acting Director of the City Art Museum of St. Louis from 1942 to 1946. After a period as Director of the Brooklyn Museum, he returned to St. Louis as Director in 1955. Giovanelli put L. in touch with Nagel in the course of his campaign on L.'s behalf.

represent all the phases of modern American art, I shall much prefer probably the non-abstract to the abstract pictures (most of the latter are not very good I am afraid). But I am quite ready to explain, in the simplest vocabulary, the *principle* of all such attempts at abstraction (which *can* be – however seldom in fact they are that – very serious experiments).

It might also be a good thing to point out how those principles are to be found in all good pictures: in a Burchfield of a few wayside houses (I am thinking of one in particular) all that is valuable in those principles can be shown to exist. Even a still life by Varnum Poor is *good* because that austere skeleton of the abstractist presided at its composition. I can see how it must be a problem for you, enlightening the average citizen. – I have my problems too! I should like to do a few portraits in St. Louis, while I am down there, and I am wondering if my appearance as an authority on the maddest of mad art will not compromise me with my prospective sitters. However I must risk that. . . .

Yours sincerely,

326. *To Marshall McLuhan*†   Windsor.
Aug. 21. [1943]

Dear Mc Luhan. Giovanelli writes me that you have obtained a copy of *The Vulgar Streak*. I am sorry about that as I have one here I was about to send you.

Perhaps I should warn regarding this book (referred to by the Times as "Mr. W.L.'s *Evan Harrington*") that there is no "autobiographical key" to be looked for in it. It is really *fiction*. I mean, I did not myself appear on the stage from nowhere, like Mr. Penhale: I really am like Cunninghame Graham, descended from the kings of Scotland (maternally) and did not have to contend, personally, with those particular handicaps. I genuinely hate to see a man thus handicapped because his father was not (probably) some rascally solicitor or (probably) equally rascally physician, who with his ill-gotten jack sends his little offspring to a Public School. (My father never made a cent in his life: the jack with which he paid my fees at an English Public School came from a silver spoon he found at birth stuck in his mouth by a good fairy: and if he *hadn't* been provided for in this fortunate manner I am positive he could never have made enough money to feed me let alone provide me with one of the most expensive and prolonged educations I have ever heard of). But to clear up these points or my American readers would be looking for vulgar streaks in *me*. There are none. The old-school-tie's the genuine McCoy.

Knowing England as you do, you are aware how half the people live in a superstitious social eclipse, scarcely venturing to open their poor dumb mouths lest they "drop one aitch". There will be released an immense volume of energy the moment we can uncork in Britain the magic bottle – labelled class. There will be a bad smell at first – how could it be otherwise, after a confinement of a thousand years? Then we shall get results. (Dynamism is nothing, I know. – I have had many opportunities of observing that. But it's necessary. I hate to think how much inter-state competition there is going to be after this war). . . .
[Rest of copy missing.]

327. *To Edgar Preston Richardson*†[1]   Windsor.
Oct. 15. 1943.

Dear Richardson. I have been reading your book and like it very much.[2] An ambitious design, but it seems to me you have handled it admirably. – On the very first page – or is it the second?–I came upon a passage which I consider a perfect subject for a lecture and particularly timely. But I will quote your words and you will see what I mean.

"There is a common, though I believe entirely falacious notion that a connection between our culture and that of other countries is a sign of weakness or provincialism. On the contrary, we would in my opinion most certainly be provincial if we had no connection with the rest of the Western world, as an individual is provincial, if, being deprived of education, he is cut off from the intellectual heritage of his race and the development of his time.

---

[1] Edgar Preston Richardson (b. 1902) was Assistant Director of the Detroit Institute of Arts from 1934 to 1945 and has been its Director since 1945. L. met him on one of his frequent visits to Detroit and had been invited to lecture at the Institute.
[2] *The Way of Western Art 1776–1914* (Cambridge, Mass., 1939).

It is impossible for me to conceive of civilisation except as a cumulative thing, to which each generation adds a little, while receiving infinitely more from the past; nor can I conceive that any man or people is benefitted by being cut off from the accumulated best that the human race has produced, which is the spiritual inheritance of us all. The notion that a nation or an individual is harmed by that inheritance and must refashion the world of civilisation for itself is romantic nonsense."[1]

These things must be said over and over again – and how well you have said them in what I have just quoted! And in no period, so much as the present, is it necessary to insist upon these principles. As the world shrinks to the size of a pea, and as every day it becomes more absurd for people to square up to each other and treat each other as creatures of a strange and hostile species – as all this becomes glaringly evident, people tend artificially to entrench themselves *more*, rather than less, in a stupid nationalism and growling isolation: as if we were Neanderthal Man rather than Twentieth Century Man. Schopenhauer said somewhere that a man who was proud of being a Frenchman, or a Spaniard, or an Englishman or what not could have very little else to be proud of. (He meant of course that there were more important things about an individual – or should be – than his national label.) – We will *all* be "globalonists" tomorrow.

Provincialism is just as bad for art, as it is for mankind in general. And how well you bring out the relation of exclusiveness as between nations to that other exclusion of the past. I remember that clown Marinetti (the "father of fascism") and his bellowings about "passéisme" and his proposal to destroy all the pictures and buildings reminding people of the Past in Italy.

Anyway, a lecture voicing and elaborating the point of view expressed in the passage from your book I have quoted, under such title as "Isolation in Art," or "What are Art's Frontiers?" or "Native Art and Universal Art", is my first choice of a subject. – There are others. . . .

Yours sincerely,

[1] *Ibid.*, p. viii.

328. *To Marshall McLuhan*† Windsor.
Nov. 9. 1943.

Dear Mc Luhan. First let me thank you for your extreme kindness in sending me H. Ford.[1] I will return him soon and let you know what I think. – I gobble gladly down by the way *anything* having reference to principles of American politics. Especially am I short of Letters and Memoirs (of period 1760–1815).

... – Why I have not acknowledged your letter before is that owing to my moving into new apartments all the time – struggling with landlords who supply their tenants with the minimum of heat until the tenant's kicks become so fierce they release (with howls of rage) another sack of coal for the furnace. – because of all this my lectures were on before I could say knife. (The first one was yesterday evening). So for a week or so now I have done *nothing* but write away at that. ...

I must again take up the question of marketing *The Vulgar Streak* in America. The almost dogmatic commercialism of the N.Y. publishers has reached such a pitch that any book that seems "queer" or "sordid" is looked at askance: and the kind of nationalist-fascism that is in preparation here (or so most intelligent young Americans predict) tends to the exclusion of English authors – except of course Cronin or somebody of that sort. Three years ago in New York they were saying that no intelligent book *could* get accepted by a N.Y. publisher, except perhaps a little publisher, who would give you a maximum of a thousand berries and no one would review it. All the reviewing space is naturally reserved for the books on which the big firms have spent money in publicity. I dont think you realise how "anti-intellectual" the set-up is. As to the Moving Picture business I know nothing whatever about that, except that I suppose it is all done in Hollywood and that no book that had not passed into big circulation ... would stand much chance. – Intelligent books will eventually be circulated in the way that pornographic literature used to be under Queen Victoria – bootlegged round the country. – The Public live in a more and more unreal world, necessarily. ...

If you think the picture I have sketched above is over-black,

[1] Henry Jones Ford, *The Rise and Growth of American Politics* (New York, 1898).

please tell me. Well, till next time, and I will shoot this off special delivery, with all my excuses for the unavoidable delay.

Yours sincerely,

329. *To John Burgess*†   Windsor
Nov. 24. 1943.

Dear Mr. Burgess. Please forgive me for my silence. Our movement into new quarters was accompanied by difficulties with the other tenants, wasting a great deal of time; and the 'flu of last spring apparently knocked my wife's teeth about. So "teeth" ate up time. But most of all I have had to give 3 or 4 lectures a week (the 2 lecture-series overlapping) and this has often kept me at it till well into night. In 2 or 3 weeks the big effort – the Heywood Broun Lectures – will be over.

Prof. —— wrote me and I am answering his letter at same time as this. As I was in Toronto for nearly 3 years and the University studiously ignored my existence, I should answer him differently if he were not a friend of yours. As it is, I enclose a copy of the reply I have made. . . .

It is my plan to paint one of the priests here. He is a whole-hogging Thomist; and I should call it "The Thomist". – Lately I have been reading up the Stoics and was surprised to learn how much St. Thomas got from them. (I am quite convinced, by the way, that Seneca was what could be called a crypto-Christian. I am attempting to obtain his correspondence with St. Paul – probably not so apocryphal as it is now said to be).

Some weeks ago I had a talk with Maritain – and was photographed with him afterwards.[1] I must say I like him. It appears however that —— (I think his name is, a Belgian professor at Laval University) is conducting successful attacks against Maritain. You will hear much more of this. There are (as you are aware I expect) many Canadian priests who are *not* followers of Maritain, especially those who were trained at Louvain. They think he is inclined to import too much mysticism into the teaching of philosophy. . . .

---

[1] The meeting took place when Jacques Maritain visited Assumption College. The photograph is reproduced in *Rude Assignment*, p. 160.

... I wish fate would waft you this way, upon some business journey.

Yrs sincerely
WYNDHAM LEWIS

P.S. Thank you very much for the Sheen cuttings. The Monsignor is greatly criticised in some quarters for his hostility to the Soviet. I have always disliked communism but in this case dont know what to think about it. Think we should "cooperate", at the present stage of the proceedings. – Sheen is a very able man: I daresay however that he is not the man to negotiate a truce between the Churches. Compromise is not anywhere in his nature. He is a pugnacious Irish soul.

330. *To Felix Giovanelli* Windsor.
Dec. 5. 1943.

My dear Giovanelli. Thank you for your letter....

... As you surmise, I may be able to sell some of the things I do in my spare time in neighboring American cities. Even have a little show. But I understand believe me the mechanical and conventional nature of the provincial American mind. It is impossible to overstate the rigidity and mechanical coldness of that mind – I mean of the rich and dutifully-cultured bourgeoisie. – Fate picked for me the two *best* agents: it is not at all as you say....

... I am an even worse man of business than you claim to be (or confess to being). But because of much experience even I possess a little business knowledge. And one of my business axioms is "never compete in vulgarity with experts in same; you will fail. In approaching MORON, do not disguise yourself. Go as yourself. – Showers of gold will *not* gush out of the MORON. There is a routine fee which is better than nothing. Take the cash and let the credit go, nor heed the rumble of a distant drum." It almost sounds like the wisdom of Platon Karataev![1]

Both I and my wife are greatly looking forward to our visit to St. Louis – to seeing you both again, and meeting your families. My wife was greatly impressed by the number of your "fillings".

---

[1] See *War and Peace*.

We were surprised to hear you knew what a dentist was! Well, saluts! –

Yrs.
WYNDHAM LEWIS

. . .

331. *To Marshall McLuhan*†   Windsor.
Dec 5. 1943.

My dear Mc Luhan. Thank you for all the great trouble you have taken: and it was indeed good news that you are successfully on the track of a couple of clubs. . . .

Last week I delivered a lecture in the Detroit Art Institute. I got slightly tight beforehand in the only good restaurant I have set foot in since I left New York, and it really was *delivered*. It was I was informed on all hands a success. I really dont lecture at all badly: and seeing the gas-shortage whittles down all lecture-audiences, I had quite a lot of people.

As a matter of fact at my first Hey. Broun lecture here in Windsor, the largest lecture room they have at the College (to their great astonishment) completely filled – with people who had come over from Detroit. (Father Murphy who is always very kind, seemed delighted. The success of my lectures pleases him I think as much as me.) People never know what to expect, as you are aware. I must say I think I have given them their money's worth here and I am very glad to have done so, for this little college is probably not rich and has more enterprise than some more pretentious institutions. The problem of "holding down a job" does not come into it where priests are concerned and that makes a difference. I get on well with the priests and like Father Murphy very much.

A Professor —— of Toronto University (head of —— department) wrote me the other day asking me to speak to his students. Can you beat it? We were nearly 3 years in that disgusting spot. The moment I come down here, they learn that I am in Canada.

But it is just wasting time talking about them. Let us both be silent about that episode in my career. (I will break that silence some day, I promise you).[1] . . .

Cordially and with renewed thanks.

[1] In a sense, L. kept this promise in writing *Self Condemned*.

332. *To Marshall McLuhan*† Windsor.
Dec. 11. 1943.

My dear McLuhan. . . .

The remark of the St. Louis clubwoman, about my *platform appearance*, has made me think I will order a suit! It takes well-nigh 2 months – so will it be in time? Its a dark blue, with a submerged stripe and I think it will be a lulu.

Deliberately I have held back Ford a few days, in order to extract some more quotes and ponder a passage or two. He is a valuable chap. – My book progresses. I think their collectivist training has weakened the Americans' personal responses, and the "profit-motive" and epic of "opportunity" of so low an order has stunted their minds: but I persist in my optimism about the great jelly-like chaos. I also do like very much many Americans, educated and not. – Do you suppose "our boys" when they come home are going New Deal or Old Deal? Are we (or you) going to have a second Grant as President? – My class keeps asking me whether Washington was the first President. A Paramount (Nesbitt) picture informed them there were seven Presidents before Washington. What the hell does Paramount mean by sowing doubt in my class; for I stick to the old story that Washington was the first. . . .

Very sincerely

P.S. I hope that [as in] Fords concluding lyrical hope the Republic *will* "issue in perfect power and beauty."[1] But in 1898 he had to do his prophesying in ignorance of so many factors. There has been a revolution in Russia, and other things. – Again, he seems to think of his ideal Chief Executive too much as an *individual* (like George III or Charles II). It is not certain that personal power is a way of escaping from those "interests", plutocratic and oligarchical, which Ford would at all cost shake off. – However he says *many* interesting things . . . .

[1] ". . . amid the baleful confusion of our politics patriotism may cherish the hope that a purified and ennobled republic will emerge –

'*Product of deathly fire and turbulent chaos,
Forth from its spasms of fury and its poisons,
Issuing at last in perfect power and beauty.*'"
The Rise and Growth of American Politics, p. 382.

333. *To Mrs. Roy Campbell*†   Windsor
Jan 5. 1944.

My dear Mary C. Your letter was a welcome reminder of friends I have not seen for far too long. However, c'est la guerre. My lectures here possess very little edification – I fear.¹ They are about America. I am by way of composing a book . . . to explain a few things about Americans to the public in England: how America came to exist, why it is so big, noisy, and prosperous; what to expect of it and what not to expect of it. . . . The lectures have been the rough draught of the book.

. . . I am here with my wife (in a border-city) strictly speaking because I am marooned here – upon a vast, densely populated, island. . . .

As to the war, it is my belief that some good will come of this convulsion: once the bloody thing *started*, well there it was, and I have steadily hoped that what my Leftwing friends foresaw – social justice and the destruction of much nonsense – would ensue. In spite of some dark portents, I still hope that. My politics before the war were in the main a fierce attempt to avert wholesale violence of all sorts. A vain gesture.

How long has R.C. been in Africa? Is he stopping there? Please give me his address. I was glad to learn from Augustus that he had exchanged his requeté uniform² for that of the Home Guard. The best Catholic opinion now – and I speak from very near the horses mouth – is that the requetés were on the wrong side in the land of the flowering rifle.³ – I wish I had more news of London. Please tell me all about anyone of interest to me. I gather from Augustus that the pub-life of London is functioning as of yore: you dwell yourself in Hampstead, I observe. You go to Soho and so on doubtless; what kind of people do you see? Your brother Garman⁴ and others? There have been no casualties, I imagine,

---

¹ Mary Campbell wrote to L. on December 12th saying that she had heard he was lecturing in Canada and asking him about his topics.

² The requetés, with whom Campbell had been allied, were the Carlists of Navarre. Militant Catholics and Royalists, they allied themselves with Franco at the beginning of the Civil War.

³ See Roy Campbell, *Flowering Rifle, a Poem from the Battlefield of Spain* (London, 1939).

⁴ Douglas Garman, a left-wing intellectual and one of the founding editors of *The Calendar of Modern Letters*.

among the intelligentsia – I hope I stimulate you to purvey some faits divers.

I am constantly desirous of returning to England, but, as I said, unless I were to occupy some post I do not see how I could live. ... Give me your personal news, and tell me whether R.C. has managed to get any work done. All the best for the New Year.

Yr

334. *To Felix Giovanelli*†   Windsor
Jan. 13. 1944.

Dear Giovanelli. The temptation to accept your incredibly generous offer to occupy your apartment while in St. Louis is very great . ... I dont know what to say about it. I feel we shouldn't, or rather I know we shouldn't. Then I know I shouldn't eat a mutton chop, since it involves the murder of a helpless and rather charming, if foolish, animal, and as to pheasants and partridges! I do all these things, never making up my mind to take the great step, and confine my depredations to the vegetable kingdom. So now I cannot make up my mind. My wife who is far more brutal than I am (though sharing my compunctions regarding "livestock" and game) is delighted at the idea of turning you out. – I dont know what to do. . . .

We both are tickled to death at the idea of all the curious and entertaining things in store for us in the birthplace of T.S.E. But most of all we are looking forward to seeing you. . . .

Yrs most cordially

335. *To Felix Giovanelli*   Windsor
Jan 28th 1944.

My dear Giovanelli. . . . – We are on the grim side just now. The death of our hirsute gremlin[1] has left an ugly gap. You will understand that people never forgive you for possessing more of anything than themselves – more reputation is a sore offence: and if you put yourself in their power they can make you tolerably

---

[1] The Lewises' dog.

uncomfortable. By coming to Canada – in the middle of a world-war – I did that. And my wife has had to pay as well as myself. So this small creature, which stood for all that was benevolent in the universe, sweetened the bitter medicine for her. Like the spirit of a simpler and saner time, this fragment of primitive life confided his destiny to her, and went through all the black days beside us. She feels she has been wanting in some care – for why should this growth in his side, almost as big as his head, have gone undetected? – Such are the reflections that beset her. Whereas I am just another human being – by no means a well of primitive joie-de-vivre: so not much comfort!

McL. tells me you are busy preparing publicity material. I don't know if it will be of any use but I am sending you a book about myself you may not have seen, out of which several things might be picked. But as it is the only copy I have, do not lend it to anyone. Take great care of it. – I see at the beginning a quote from Carlo Linati, the (non-fascist) Milan critic, who, with Mario Praz, seemed to know most about other literatures and had great standing as a critic there – though like Praz he had his style cramped by the Fascists. He wrote:

> "Wyndham Lewis non è scrittore popolare, è piuttosto un *outcast*, una specie di poeta maledetto che fa parte a se e che pochi buoni [?] stimano, appunto anche per questo."[1]

Such stuff would be bad publicity indeed – but there are other things that would serve their turn. . . .

Yrs.

Weekend. Your letter has arrived before I could get this off. As regards your apartment, I ought to have spoken to you about the rental, for we certainly couldn't let you go on paying for it while we occupied it. But when we arrive we can settle that. Please dont worry about writing if you are in the midst of redtape trouble – but do not deprive us of the great pleasure of receiving your letters when that is past and you have the time.

W. L.

[1] Quoted from *Scrittori anglo americani d'oggi*, in Hugh Gordon Porteus, *Wyndham Lewis: A Discursive Exposition*, p. [2].

336. *To T. S. Eliot*†　　　　　　　　　　　　St. Louis.
　　　　　　　　　　　　　　　　　　　　April 11. 1944.

My dear Eliot. Thank you for your letter.¹ . . .

. . . What you told me of your activities suggested a day packed with official duties. You may I hope have found some time for writing poetry. – Your family is remembered here (that grandfather who crossed the Mississippi on a raft to found a university)² but all memory of you seems to have faded. With that depressed class, the teaching profession, it is of course otherwise: and you will be interested to hear that your play "Murder in the Cathedral" was performed last Christmas at Assumption College – though I was not there to see it, as it was feared that some of the passages would offend my English susceptibilities. Well may we soon be discussing another bottle of Mr. Lyons good wine at his Palace in Kensington.³

　　　　　　　　　　　　　　　　　　　　Yrs. ever.

337. *To Pauline Bondy*†⁴　　　　　　　　Fairmont Hotel,
　　　　　　　　　　　　　　　　　　　　4907 Maryland,
　　　　　　　　　　　　　　　　　　　　St. Louis. – Missouri.
　　　　　　　　　　　　　　　　　　　　April 20. 1944.

My dear Pauline. Was sorry not to see you. . . . – After an interlude of tornados the Spring has burst forth, with magnolia and wild plum and a full cast of subtropical birds. The local Zoo, a very good one, is scratching, bellowing, growling and whistling to mark the advent of the exciting season. – We prowl about in our thick Canadian overcoats like a pair of exotics. Only the bears understand us!

　　　　　　　　　　　　　　　　　　　　Yrs
　　　　　　　　　　　　　　　　　WYNDHAM LEWIS

¹ Eliot wrote to L. on February 20th, telling him of his war-time life in London.
² Rev. William Greenleaf Eliot (1811–87), founder of Washington University.
³ The Kensington Palace Hotel.
⁴ Pauline Bondy, a teacher, became a friend of the Lewises during their residence in Toronto. The letter refers to a quick trip to Canada made during L.'s stay in St. Louis.

338. *To Gerty T. Cori*†[1] Windsor.
Aug 20. 1944.

My dear Mrs Cori. Thank you for your letter. . . . All that you, Dr. Erlanger[2] and other non-natives of St. Louis warned us was but too true: and if July was the coolest they have had there for some time, well we were there until the 17th and aggravated by the studio – under the roof and with two large sun-smitten windows. – We *may* make it a bit before the 7th but not much.

The war seems to me practically over; but one animal named Cedric Foster[3] has just bellowed at me on the radio that I am a sucker to believe that. – He will be without an occupation once the war's over, it's probably that. *We* already have decided upon a villa or farm near Oxford, the Peace permitting (for it may be a bitch of a Peace).

The article you mention by Koestler I have recently perused. Where he remarks "the distance between the library and the bedroom is astronomical,"[4] I as usual dissent. You see I do not believe in an intelligent bedroom, first of all: but more important the library – or the laboratory – belongs to the same system of circumscribed existence as does the bedroom. We are animals who read. We procreate, we think about procreation and other things, and we embody our reflections in books. A divine Observer, overlooking our researches, in the library or laboratory, knows all the answers. The answer is there all the time: we "discover" it. So if the bright new world were only bright enough, it would abolish *us* to start with. Ubermensch religious dreaming, at bottom, and an awful lot of phoney ethics. – All revolutions produce a new system (after a bit of heavy going) like Stalins. I respect much in the Trotskyite and like several personally. But Stalin has a working state-system, with the air purged of humbug. I cannot

---

[1] Dr. Gerty Cori (b. 1896) has been since 1947 Professor of Biological Chemistry at Washington University. She and her husband, joint winners of the Nobel Prize in Medicine and Physiology (1947), befriended L. in St. Louis.

[2] Dr. Joseph Erlanger (b. 1874), another Nobel winner (1944), was at this time head of the Department of Physiology at Washington University. L. painted his portrait when he was in St. Louis.

[3] American news analyst (b. 1900).

[4] Arthur Koestler, "The Intelligentsia," *Partisan Review*, Summer 1944, p. 269.

share the horror and discouragement felt by the "Partisan" at the sight of Uncle Joe.

This place continues a model of what a place should be in August. At six o'clock on Friday evening last the thermometer registered 60, which is fine and dandy. The —— are in Wisconsin, on Lake Michigan, and there it is cool too, though I expect dull. You have to go up to Lake Superior for it to get interesting. My Basilian blessings upon you and your family and cordial greetings from my wife.

Yours sincerely,

339. *To Dwight Macdonald*†[1]   St. Louis.
Oct 9. 1944.

Dear Mr. Macdonald. Thank you for your letter and I am very obliged to you for putting me on your free list. . . .

It is most kind of you to suggest my writing for you: I should like to – will think over *what*. One trouble is that I am a foreigner. The American ego is a big raw brash healthy one and reacts against "criticism" with ferocity. – You may steal a horse, I may not look over a hedge! But I think something can be done. . . .

Well, soon I will send along some little contribution for your perusal. Congratulations anent your paper.

Cordially yours.

340. *To James Johnson Sweeney*†   St. Louis.
Nov. 10. 1944.

Dear Sweeney. I was pleased to hear that you were in the same place, even if other people are not in the same place. As to my continued stay in the middle of America, it is I assure you no choice of mine. The East is far more to my taste. Eastwards, could I see a way, I would come. On 26th of this month, however, far from travelling eastward, I go north to that really unspeakable

---

[1] Dwight Macdonald was at this time editor of *Politics*. L. had written to him praising the review. The correspondence so struck up continued spasmodically for several years, but the two never met.

national zero, Canada. . . . The winter of my discontent has been a terribly long and hard one.

All these big cities hereabouts are overgrown villages. Chicago they tell one is the same as the rest. And a huge city that is a village, without the charm and humanity of the village, is a monstrosity. Up in Detroit all the socialites commute to New York so much that the city has never grown to have any life of its own, except a business life. Whereas here New York is a little too far for that – yet people still live on the memory of their last visit to New York, even if it was five years ago: and there is no *public* life at all. They all live in their clubs and "residences". I get to feel, frankly, like an animal. – How can I lift myself to an evolutionary status superior to that of an animal? I do not know. . . .

It often crosses my mind how you may be passing your time. Do you still teach, and lecture?

Yrs sincerely.

341. *To T. S. Eliot*†
Windsor.
March 13. 1945.

My dear Eliot. . . .

As you see, I have left the birth-place of Josephine Baker and Gerald Swope. To tell you what I am doing, I paint people of all shapes and sizes in this neighbourhood, lecturing [*sic*]. Ann Arbor and Lansing[1] my last 2 places of call. There is not much to say about these places. A group of old hacks teaching English, though they have some difficulty in speaking it, supported by a deferential group of young hacks, entertain one to liquorless and beerless six o'clock suppers (I always carry a flask of alcohol, snorts of which I consume in the privacy of my rooms prior to submitting to these routine hospitalities). What the devil they or their students think they're doing I dont know. As a subject, agriculture gains ground daily however. "Efficient living" is another very popular course. That mostly treats of marriage. The fraternities and the sororities flock to it. My sitters make a very different impression – those in America of course. What I find in all these cities is that the people with money commute: as much of their time as possible is spent in New York, even Chicagoans.

[1] The homes of the University of Michigan and Michigan State University.

As formerly, I await the end of the war – the end I mean of German resistance. There still is no alternative: a cattle-boat – probably the slowest in the convoy – or stop here. Long ago I have given up suggesting to people in England that some kind of job should be found for me, that I have been here long enough. I suppose that except among officials, existence is very abnormal. Before too long I trust we may again however find ourselves at a table of that convenient Kensington hotel where we met the last time before I sailed. If destroyed, Demario's perhaps.

Give me your news. No bombs I hope unduly near, and publishing going strong most of it with American paper and printers I suppose. Good Wishes.

Yrs

P.S. Between writing and typing the war has got much nearer its end. We learn here that the "Hell-on-wheels" outfit has reached the Elbe. Hooray!

342. *To Allen Tate*†[1] Windsor.
May 14. 1945.

Dear Mr. Tate. Thank you for your letter and cheque. It gave me great pleasure to learn that you liked my article. It is true, as you say, that during my unconscionably long visit to this continent I have contributed to no reviews or weeklies, except for the New Republic (in 1940). This is of course because there are practically no literary reviews; and the big popular monthlies – Harpers, Scribners, Atlantic – do not publish anything of the kind I write. The article I sent you is part of the material of a projected book.

I am quite sure, from the internal evidence of your Virginia Quart. article,[2] that our viewpoint on many things is not so dissimilar. I do not feel incredulous, I assure you, at anyone at this moment – whatever his antecedents may have been – believing

---

[1] Allen Tate (b. 1899) was from 1944 to 1947 editor of the *Sewanee Review*. L. sent him "The Cosmic Uniform of Peace," a chapter from *America and Cosmic Man*. This appeared in the Autumn 1945 number of the review, pp. 507–31.

[2] "The New Provincialism," *Virginia Quarterly Review*, Spring 1945, pp. 262–72.

that the sun has set upon exclusive models. The cosmic uniform is actually to my taste; but it will prove to be de riguer.

I wish I could have seen the deep South. Virginia, 50 miles south of Washington – I found so frightfully like England, lanes, oaks, and all, that I could scarcely believe my eyes, entirely different from New England. Missouri again was pleasantly familiar. It is fascinating to disentangle the various cultures – Southern, MidWest, German, French – in the birthplace of Josephine Baker and Gerald Swope, where I spent upwards of a year. But I regret my failure to push down to Mississippi and Tennessee. Next time I must do that.

As regards the publication date for my article. Publish it by all means in the same issue as Eliots[1] – the place of honor doesn't matter. Or perhaps October would suit you better? . . .

Yours sincerely,

343. To Allen Tate[†]   Ottawa
June 13. 1945.

Dear Tate. At Customs today they informed me I had to pay just on two dollars for Democracy in America:[2] One-third of the price of the book. Part of the 1.93 (slip enclosed) is a *war-tax*. They knock nothing off for the end of the European war. I just left it there as a gesture, though I shall go back some time and bail it out. I wish somebody would send me a copy of the Bible, to see if they war-tax that Book they are so fond of quoting from.

They have retained their censors office here so I am debarred from telling you what I think of this place: but if you turn to the Book of Genesis you will see that towards the end of the week God became awfully tired. It was in the last few minutes (He was not feeling at all good) that He produced a country beginning with C. It might have been Canaan; or perhaps it was a place over which a King reigns who is however only a commoner. A pretty tough one that!

Sincerely,

[1] "The Man of Letters and the Future of Europe," *Sewanee Review*, Summer 1945, pp. 335–42.
[2] Tate had sent L. a copy of Tocqueville.

344. *To Augustus John*†   c/o The Dominion Bank,
214 Sparks,
Ottawa, Ontario,
Canada.
June 19. 1945.

My dear John. Your letter cheered me up – it is excellent to be reminded that there is, somewhere, however inaccessible, a more civilised and intelligent world. You ask me in your letter (forwarded me from Windsor) why on earth I remain over here, and in Canada of all places. The answer is terribly simple. Although the war is over there is still no means of having money sent from England and *here* it is impossible, for me at least, to make anything over and above that needed to pay hotel bill (for 2 people) and satisfy hunger and very moderate thirst.

Painting, or pastelling, portraits of people in moderation is fine. I do nothing else: that is how I exist: in some localities I have made thousands of dollars; in St. Louis Missouri for instance, where we spent about a year. But all these cities, because of the war, are jampacked with people. In some it is quite impossible to find accommodation except in a hotel. Here in Ottawa one even is legally debarred from renting an apartment (flat) or house: only officials and the military and naval office staffs are allowed to do that. . . .

The peculiar state of mind of these people cannot be conveyed in a letter. In Toronto, where I started painting portraits as soon as I arrived . . . I was reminded of stories in Vasari of the jealous guildsmen on guard against intruders in every italian city. And yet when these folks come to London with their pictures they are well-received. – But these reflections will not help me to get back: and that somehow or other I must do without delay.

I am like a travelling circus. A long baggage train, of crates and boxes, accompanies me. To get from Ottawa to London (2 people and baggage) will cost approximately 725 dollars or 182 pounds sterling. There is no means, that I can see, at this end, of getting such a sum. . . .

What you can do is this. You can communicate these sickening and idiotic facts and figures to anybody who might be interested . . . there are plenty of people whose duty it is to see that I should not be stuck eternally upon this not over-hospitable continent.

Whose business it is to get me back to England not (as you have suggested) to defend the ancient freedoms of the English, but to take up my position as full-back, before the cultural goal. . . .

          Yours ever,
          WYNDHAM LEWIS

345. *To Allen Tate*†   Ottawa.
               June 29. 1945.

Dear Tate. What fun it would be if I were in Sewanee! I was delighted at your suggestion that at some future time I should go there, and almost could see myself for a moment in that pleasant Southern land, a mint-julep (made the right way!) just arrived upon the table, and you at my side, in some delapidated hotel – not like the vulgar palaces further north. And then I woke up.

For six years on this continent I have bummed it from city to city – . . . no man can live in the United States, except on ample monies brought from elsewhere. Everywhere else except within the walls of . . . learned institutions is a howling commercial wilderness. The thing that never ceases to surprise me is how the common or garden American has succeeded in preserving intact his nice disposition, his friendly heart. For everything round about him is this great tough clamorous abyss of Dollar madness. I shall never lose my terror of New York. I should not mind being cut off from my country – by a shutting down of the exchanges – in Paris. I should go and sleep in the corner of someone's studio for a while. But in the shadows of those architectural monsters in Manhattan there is no economic quarter. Or its a kind of huge Adding-machine one has affronted by not passing in the requisite number of dollars. The odd thing is how attractive it is under most other circumstances. – Once its skyscrapers have shown you their ugly side, though, you would feel a certain reserve thenceforth I think, however well-padded with dollar-bills you might be. – The problem of course is that New York is America (the universities apart) from a writers standpoint, or for that matter an artists. All the publishers, the big book-trade bosses and experts are there: all the machinery, that makes, or unmakes, a reputation, say, like that of Faulkner or Hemingway: gives them money and freedom or witholds it. And it has become for books what Hollywood is for the theatre.) Is it possible to say anything worse than that.

These reflections may be traceable to the fact that soon quite likely I shall be finding myself in New York again, for a few days on the way to England. . . .

Yrs.

. . .

PART V. 1945-1956

The Writer and the Absolute

The final eleven years of Lewis's life marked a fulfilment in many ways, some of them ironic. In 1949 Lewis the painter had a successful show in London which included a second, publicised portrait of T. S. Eliot. In 1956 he received the accolade of a full-scale retrospective exhibition at the Tate Gallery. As a writer his achievement rivalled that of the late 1920's and his public recognition was greater than ever before.

Between 1948 and 1956 Lewis produced eight new volumes. None of these is wholly negligible; at least two – Self Condemned and The Human Age: Books 2 and 3 – will doubtless belong to the body of work on which his reputation rests. In addition, he was for the first time in his life regularly associated with a paper. Lewis began to contribute art reviews to The Listener *in 1946 and continued as its art critic till 1951. Thanks to an enterprising producer, he found the new outlet of radio, where several adaptations of his work were given. It was, in fact, the broadcast success of* The Childermass, *Part I that made possible the continuation of the opus (retitled* The Human Age) *in both radio and book form.*

The Enemy was almost respectable. The academic world and even the state joined the Tate Gallery and the B.B.C. in honouring him. In 1951 he was granted a small Civil List pension by the Labour Government, the sum being increased after the Conservatives returned to power. In 1952 he was awarded a D.Litt. by the University of Leeds.

The irony of official recognition was obvious and in a way humorous. A deeper and more moving irony lay in another kind of culmination. By 1949 it was clear that Lewis, who had based his aesthetic (even in a sense his metaphysic) on "the EYE,*" was losing* his sight. The trouble of which he had complained in Canada had been only a prelude. Now, however, it was too late for help – if it had ever not been. A growth that could not be removed was pressing on the optic nerve. Despite a number of costly efforts to find a way of avoiding the calamity, Lewis's vision had by 1951 deteriorated to the ability to distinguish hazily between dark and light. A couple of years later he was totally blind. By 1956 the growth in his skull had reached lethal proportions. After months of illness, he died of it in March 1957.

The bleak aspect of these later years was considerably brightened by the fact that he was at least on home ground. Although he could not afford his illness, Lewis was never in these years completely cut off from financial resources, as he had been so often during the war. And he was much richer in friends and helpers. Mrs. Lewis, combining the roles of housekeeper, secretary, nurse, and companion, was a prop of great strength. Old friends, like Agnes Bedford, T. S. Eliot, and Sir Nicholas Waterhouse, offered editorial or financial assistance as well as company. New, younger friends, such as Michael Ayrton and Geoffrey Bridson, appeared and were drawn close into the family circle. A number of valued associations with Americans continued via correspondence. And Lewis had the good fortune of finding a sympathetic publisher in J. Alan White of Methuen and two zealous commentators in Charles Handley-Read and Hugh Kenner.

Whether all this human support was a cause or effect, there is no mistaking the fact that the Enemy had become himself a more benevolent human being. The gentleness and sympathy that had appeared before in glints now declared themselves more easily. Lewis returned kindness with kindness. A number of times, moved solely by his belief in their talent, he used his new respectability in efforts to advance young artists. In his relationship with the young Canadian David Kahma, he undertook the whole education of a writer, as the remarkable series of letters to Kahma illustrates. In his dealings with Ezra Pound he proved himself a paragon of loyalty. The letters testify to his adherence to the cause of Pound's freedom, no matter how much his old friend might irritate him.

Irritation remained till the end a ready response. The veteran "Frontkämpfer" flourished side by side with the new humanitarian. On their return from Canada the Lewises found the studio and flat at Notting Hill Gate a shambles. Hardly had they made the place livable when dry rot was discovered. *The England which Lewis had so missed throughout the war seemed also a rotting shambles – with its annoying shortages and taxes, its inefficient "welfare" government. Within two years of leaving North America, he was contemplating a trip back. Nor had "the post-war" brought any improvement in the plight of the arts, not to mention the general benightedness. The old controversialist felt compelled more than once to take to the press in the cause of enlightenment. Again, it seems fitting that one of his last letters was in the nature of a public vindication of himself. This time, however, Lewis was too ill to pursue the fight.*

346. *To Lady Waterhouse*† Flat A. 29 Notting Hill Gate.
London. W.11.
Sept 19. 1945.

Dear Moove. Since my visit much has happened but finally I'm back where I was before, where you came to see the portrait I did of Don Norman.[1] The countless flights of stairs, I have doggedly mounted in this city-of-many-stairs since coming to Effingham of which mine are the storiest if not the highest. Why no comforts modernes? The Telephone Co – this is the latest – claim thirty-six pounds for the "rental" of their instrument, which has been sitting quietly, half buried in dust, upon my window sill for 6 years. – The number of times I have given shop assistants half a crown and got change for a two shilling piece: they seem to know I'm green, but my God they might be Canadians! . . . What is your news? What books? Love to Docker. À bientôt.

Yrs
W. L.

347. *To Sir Nicholas Waterhouse*† London, W.2.
[September 1945]

My dear Docker. I cant say much to you, you know that. Suddenly to learn of Mov's death[2] was a shock to me, what it must be to

[1] The Waterhouses' name for their friend John McLeod. See p. 336.
[2] Lady Waterhouse died at Effingham a few days after L. had written the preceding letter to her.

you I can see only too well. But you must keep your end up, as you put it, and not allow yourself to mope, for your friend's sake. – I had no idea there was any immediate danger of this sort. Having got my affairs a little in order I wrote to Mov – thought some day soon I might drop down again. It must I suppose have been some further complication. What a hell of a silly life it is that Mov with all her intelligence and charm should be snatched away from us, instead of, well lots of others. – Be a good stout-hearted fellow anyway, and you're not on your own, because you have many people, I among them, who have a great liking for Docker. – Till one of these days soon I hope.

Yrs
W. L.
("the Professor")

348. *To Allan Gwynne-Jones*†[1]   29 Notting Hill Gate, W.11.
Oct 23. 1945.

Dear Gwynne-Jones. Thank you for your letter. As to the portrait of Ezra Pound, for the C.E.M.A. show, I can see how attractive this might prove, from the macabre point of view: a kind of Madame Tussaud exhibit. It is not mine, but as far as I am concerned, I should not choose this particular moment to show it.[2] I have a few things here, two very good (not exhibited before). Drop up when you are next in London – mailing me a post-card day beforehand.

What is the "C.E.M.A."? I was awfully glad to hear you liked the Miss Sitwell portrait. By all means bring along your Note for the projected exhibition – not that I am a very good person to

---

[1] The painter and etcher Allan Gwynne-Jones (b. 1892) knew L. before the war. He wrote to him with regard to an exhibition he was arranging for the Council for the Encouragement of Music and the Arts. Gwynne-Jones wanted to include the 1938 portrait of Ezra Pound, which the Tate Gallery had purchased in 1939.

[2] In a second letter, written October 26th, L. explained his feelings: "If you want any reason for that decision, it is because Pound will at any moment now be tried for his life. Far be it from me to suppose that a man who broadcasts from an enemy capital in time of war can expect anything else. But I have known Pound a very long time, and I do not like the idea of helping to put him on show."

consult as to how much offence it is safe to give. If you want a quiet life you will give *no* offence. But it is difficult to see how you can talk about Nineteenth Century portraits without being a little insulting.

Sincerely,

349. *To Naomi Mitchison*†   London, W.11.
Oct. 27. 1945.

Dear Naomi. It was very pleasant to hear of your multifarious activities and feel oneself not too far away: though it would seem from what you say that we shall not be meeting just yet, which is a pity. You should leave the crops to the yokel, and bring your strenuous person down here and rout what you call the "*gangs*" with your epic. – I have seen no one, except dealers and publishers. Everybody seems to have been out of London and to find it impossible to get back owing to the jampacked condition. Our things, unknown to me, did not go into storage but remained where I left them. Removing six years of dust etc, was rather like excavating at Pompeii, say, and finding underneath Mr. Lewis's books and pictures, and furniture just as he left them in '39 – a great many centuries ago. – So here I am, now, alone in London. As it happens, I am not sorry, for I have taken on the writing of a book,[1] and for all my application have only reached the eleventh chapter, at the end of six or seven weeks work. – As we live suspended between two worlds, and have been for a long time now, it is not easy to paint. Writing has fewer economic complications. Furthermore, for a solid six years in America I have been plying my brush morning noon and night and do not mind putting it down for a while.

Very glad to hear that your husband has got his wish.[2] I was devoutly thankful to learn the Tories had not got in. In orderly progression let us hope all necessary measures of nationalisation will be carried through, and exploitation of the people (us and the rest) be made impossible. Capitalism is rampant as never before:

[1] Presumably *America and Cosmic Man*, which was completed some time before it appeared in 1948.
[2] In her letter of October 19th, Mrs. Mitchison told of her husband's victory in the General Election.

a scarcity after its own heart. Some goods have nearly trebled in price, but others cost ten or twenty times what they did. And my landlord – or his agent – is the ugliest capitalist of the lot. It is difficult to see why the Government does not go for my landlord, and why it is so tolerant. They know that since people are unable to buy soap they have to buy shaving-sticks. And has the price soared – oh boy! Why not step in and see that we should not ruin ourselves to have clean faces? You know all the answers. – Hope to get hold of the Life of Mrs Webb,[1] which from reviews seems interesting. I was very shocked to learn that she did not like people who had no money – that is, "the poor". My head spins at times. Am I a better socialist than Beatrice Webb? or was she a rotten socialist. I like the proletariat just as well as the Middle Class. Or is the male Webb better? or has your friend Mrs Cole given a misleading account? I shall try and get a Life of Sidney Webb at the same time. I must get at the heart of this mystery. – Tell me when you write which people you approve of in the Government. Aneurin Bevan has (or had) an excellent head.

The batch of drawings of the children I will get a gallery to pack up for me and mail you at Carradale. They are very slight, but one or two good likenesses.[2]

Yrs.

350. *To Augustus John*† [London]
29 Nov. 1945.

My dear John. It is good to hear that you are up here at last and within reach. But so far I have not succeeded in reaching you by telephone. Tried again this morning at 12.40, but no luck. To telephone is not easy. The Post Office refuse to instal a new telephone here: that means I must queue up for a call. Once inside the box, one has an angry and impatient mob of women at one's back. *C'est la guerre* I know – ou bien c'est la Paix. But it feels like a vast plot to waste one's time. – But after this very long interval I am most anxious to see you again .... You asked me in your note from Fordingbridge what I thought of London.

---

[1] Margaret Cole, *Beatrice Webb* (London, 1945).
[2] A portrait drawing of Mrs. Mitchison's son Avrion is reproduced in Handley-Read, Pl. 44.

Well, above I have begun to answer that. People like wars so much that, once the popping and banging has stopped, they seek in every way to prolong them: there has even been a Black-out in this borough for the past week because the bloody gas company refuse to increase the men's wages, although everything costs twice as much as it did when last the matter of their wages was discussed. – And, by the way, do you receive twice as much for your pictures as in 1939? I hope you are not so spiritless as not to have adjusted your prices according to the cost of living index. Well, all the best, and if you are still up here dont omit to write me a line.

Yrs ever.

351. *To Allen Tate*† [London]
March 7. 1946.

My dear Tate. For five months I have been struggling to get a book finished in time, so that it should get published before the next war starts or we blow ourselves all up in some other way. . . . No visits to France, as I should normally be making. From all accounts it is only possible to visit it if you have a friend who will put you up. A friend of mine had a simple lunch in Paris six weeks ago – he was lunching two people – and it cost him 18 pounds. Today it would cost double that. The days of Paris as cultural centre are no doubt at an end – Mexico City, I believe, is where the writers and artists will go in the future. Instead of George Moore's "great moonlights of the Place Pigalle" it will be a café beneath an Aztec moon, nine thousand feet up. . . .

Cordially

After Lewis left England in 1939, *he and Pound were seldom in communication. They were completely out of touch by the time of Pound's arrest in Italy and his deportation to the U.S. for trial. Lewis attempted to resume contact after the war, but nothing happened until April* 1946, *when he received a letter from T. S. Eliot, enclosing one from Pound (to Eliot). Writing from St. Elizabeth's*

Hospital, Pound spoke warmly of Lewis and sent him greetings.[1]
Eliot wrote: "I don't think I can do better than to pass it on to you."

352. *To T. S. Eliot*† [London]
April 29. 1946.

My dear Tom. Thank you for your note and the enclosed epistle from Ezra. I will of course write to him at once. I am not very good at deciphering his impulsive and temperamental script but I believe I detected a note of humility in one place. A bad sign I am afraid: although otherwise he seems much as usual. There is one thing – probably he feeds better than we do, and it will be part of the duties of the attendant psychiatrists to read all his Cantos and to encourage him to discuss them.

Let me see you before you go to America.

Yrs ever
WYNDHAM LEWIS

353. *To Ezra Pound*† [London]
June 30. 1946.

My dear old Ezra. How are you, and what are you doing with yourself. T. S. Eliot sent along your letter and I was rejoiced to see your handwriting again, and receive your messages. I am told that you believe yourself to be Napoleon – or is it Mussolini? What a pity you did not choose Buddha while you were about it, instead of a politician. – To turn to more serious matters, I was in several bookshops in the Charing Cross Road not long ago, and saw in each piles of your books. I was informed they were selling well. Eliot told me you were projecting a volume on Confucius,[2]

---

[1] "Now as to ole Wyndham whose address I have not, to thee and him these presents. While I yet cohere, he once sd/a facefull. & apart from 3 dead and one aged [word?] who gave me 3 useful hints. ole W is my only critic – you have eulogized and some minors have analysis'd or dissected –

all of which please tell the old ruffian if you can unearth him."

[2] Ezra Pound, trans., *Confucius: The Unwobbling Pivot and The Great Digest* (Norfolk, Conn., [1951]). (First published by New Directions as *Pharos* IV, Winter 1947.)

which seems an excellent idea. It is a good time to sell books over here, for everything is in very short supply. If your publisher can, or will, find the necessary paper (which alas is in short supply too) you can be sure of every copy selling. Fifteen thousand copies should assure to you a royalty of 2,000 pounds sterling, minus of course taxes. – I heard with the greatest concern about your money difficulties: this might be a way to solve them. The buying of books has simply become a disease of the English: I went into a bookshop the other day, but it was so full of people I could not get near the shelves I wanted. It doesn't seem to matter what the book *is*. . . . The North American continent is an amazingly beautiful place. I still prefer the American people in some ways to any other: but I think it is going to be tough organising life there in such a way that the artistic man will have a chance. There is an immensity of talent, which is frittered away in the most trivial tasks. But the future lies there, if anywhere. What a pity it is that the lure of history kept you locked up in the dusty old Mediterranean. The Hudson River Valley would have been a better place. – Are you writing anything? Please drop me a line; and if I can get you any books or anything of that sort be sure I will do so.

With my best wishes.

P.S. My wife sends you her best wishes, and hopes we shall all see you again before too long.

354. *To Allen Tate*† London. W.11.
 24 Sept. 1946.

My dear Tate. Your letter reached me last night. Its contents pleased me very much: for that Holt would like to publish a book of mine is the main thing.[1] Our views regarding the desireability of publishing such a book about America just now (or perhaps at any time) entirely coincide. The more I thought about it – and the more I read the August and September newspapers – the more

[1] Tate was editor of poetry and belles-lettres for Henry Holt and Company from 1946 to 1948. L. had sent him the manuscript of *America and Cosmic Man*. Tate wrote back saying that Holt wanted to do the book but not as things stood. The book was finally brought out in America by Doubleday in June 1949.

uneasy I became. *America and Cosmic Man* would have given the enemies of England, and, even more, my personal enemies a golden opportunity of shooting at me. – I certainly should offer the book to no other publishers: so please do as you say – hold it for the present and we shall see about later on.

Reading your letter made me realize how this particular mss. must have presented itself to *you* – rather as if you sent *me* a mss dealing with French art from David to Van Gogh, say full of the most confident assertions about the place in the history of art of all the Nineteenth Century masters. (Here I am perhaps unjustifiably assuming that you are much less familiar with those matters than I am). Your remark about the Woodrow Wilson section for instance, is very just. However much I documented myself, I am sure I should feel just the same about the Presbyterian Priest: but to discuss a President venerated by many people, in what might. appear too casual and slapdash a vein would be a palpable mistake – I am afraid however that that would apply to *any* President. Nothing but the most exhaustive documentation would sanction judgements, arrived at by an outsider, judgements contradictory, as well, to a great deal of American opinion. – I know more about America than any but a few Englishmen: and the book was for the English Public primarily. It was never intended to be a solid and sober study, but an *aperçu*. You will remember that when Lord Acton was asked by somebody whether a book he was writing (and never completed) would soon be ready, he replied, "When I have read another five hundred books." Only professors of American History probably should choose such a subject as *America and Cosmic Man*: On the other hand they would leave out Cosmic Man! Then busily showing off their historiographical methodology to their watchful rivals they would forget that the best history is fiction. – "L'honnête homme n'a pas besoin d'avoir lu tous les livres." There's much to be said for Descarte's "honnête homme."

The weak spot in the book was exposition of the Party game. You have watched that at close quarters all your life, and know a thousand illuminating items to my one. If there *were* any questions, at a later date, of doing the book, I should have especially to give that my attention. . . .

I am sure we see with not too dissimilar eyes what goes on forward in the world. The State has taken the place of the Church, and is doing the sort of things the Church did at its worst. People here are both lethargic and ill tempered. It is rather distressing.

American luxury liners, I note with satisfaction, are muscling in and advertising cross-Atlantic passages at pre-war rates. I feel that about the time – say eight months hence – I shall be free to float over to N. York for a breather, the trip will be reasonably cheap.

Yrs ever,
WYNDHAM LEWIS

355. *To Ezra Pound*†   London, W.11.
Sept. 24. 1946.

Dear Pound. Unless I answer letters quickly, I am apt to lose them, and I have lost Dorothy's. What is her address? – As to your note, I have not seen Eliot for many months, though I believe he is back from America. If I come across him I will suggest he publish something of yours . . . . – The book-boom maintains itself, though people are now able to go tripping about and that will take some money away from books. – Why does not Laughlin[1] publish something in New York? He now has an office I see in Fifth Avenue. But I am not, as you say, au courant, and perhaps he has already done so. – I am sorry my views about America provoke your mirth.[2] I enjoy a great many things, you must remember, that have not the same appeal to you: the wonderful landscapes

---

[1] James Laughlin (b. 1914), founder and president of New Directions, which became Pound's American publisher in 1947.

[2] Pound wrote, presumably in response to L.'s letter of June 30th:
"W.L.
Incurable Borrovian. Le Chateaubriand de nos jours – still enamoured of the primeval forrest. Waal you aint vury au courant (factual) re Ez."

In a letter dated November 28th, he seems to be replying to L.'s rejoinder:

"Buttt
my deerly beeloved
   Wyndham:
         Aapart from the
  botany and geology?
the most uninteresting country on
earth because it takes the
  least interest in truth."

met with everywhere in America: and simple pleasant people (butchers, bakers and candlestick makers) whom you would despise. But believe me I am not blind to the horrors of Hollywood or the universal ballyhoo. Then what appeals to you very much – the *his-torical* – leaves me cold. It even makes me uncomfortable to be in a place where something happened four hundred years ago, but that has fallen into decay. I prefer Willow Run to that. You should chuck all politics, get out of that place, and become an American. Boogie Woogie is better than Sole Mio. – But perhaps again I am not au courant!

Yrs ever,

356. *To Augustus John*†   London. W.11.
Oct 11. 1946.

My dear John. . . .

I will explain again my plan.[1] I take it we are agreed that your reputation has entered a bad patch of reaction. That usually happens: but I should like to see if I could correct this a little. All I want is to be serviceable: but our ideas may differ as to the method.

Anything in the nature of crude "puffing" as you will realise would do more harm than good.[2] It was my idea to select photographs of 6 of the very best things you have ever done: and if adhering to the original plan, 6 of your sister's. A "family of genius" has an immediate appeal to the public. Otherwise I could have to illustrate my ten thousand word book 12 things of yours.

The nature of things chosen is of great importance. It must be the best six as *I see it* – for I come into it of course: and I am sure you will find that that will be the most satisfactory, as most people today see roughly as I see. So far I have in mind the "Eve Balfour," and the "Marchese Casati:"[3] also a first-rate drawing the Mayor Gallery has on show at present. . . .

[1] L. was planning to do a short illustrated book on John and his sister Gwen.

[2] John, who had gone to stay in France, wrote back: "I, of course, would never expect anything from you except your own personal expression which I know how to value – par exemple! I would rather be attacked than 'puffed' any day. I am not in the least concerned about my bad patch of reaction."

[3] This portrait, dated 1919, is reproduced in John Rothenstein, *Augustus John* (Oxford and London, 1945), Pl. 57.

Better than most I am aware of your powers. But people today want things done in a way that is not always your way.¹ Show them that you have done things in the way they want them done, better than their favourites, and it should undermine a lot of loose criticism. – I am not saying that the way of doing things that is popular today is the best (in many respects I have a contempt for it): but you will remember that I have certain predilections myself. And it is very much to your interest that the support I give you in this book be a homage from, as it were, the other camp. Merely an old friend saying what an awfully good artist you are would not change things very much, you see. – My only idea, as I have already said, is to be serviceable.

I am sure your powers are as great today as they ever were: and I shall certainly go when Poppette returns and see the things at Tite Street.² . . .

Meanwhile, smuggle me back a bottle of Armagnac, enjoy yourself, sois sage, do a little portrait of the ugliest old crone in Arks (you neglect the ill-favoured: *they would bring you luck!*)³ and all the best to Dorelia.

Yrs ever.

357. *To Augustus John*†   London. W.11.
Oct 29. 1946.

My dear John. Your card, announcing your move into the Mas, just arrived. "Le Robinson"⁴ has an inviting look, in spite of its anglo-saxon name. *There* is where I could get an omelette au Rhum and some good wine – a thing that I find I miss. . . .

I was delighted with your letter – to hear that the plan for an illustrated book, as outlined by me, met with your approval: also that you seemed so content with your stay in Provence – and were fishing for hags, as I had been so fresh as to suggest. The proximity

¹ John replied: "As to what people want I have never considered the question seriously. I would prefer to impose what I want myself on them – which would probably be what in fact they do want."

² John's daughter was to show L. the pictures he had stored in London.

³ John replied: "I won't forget the Armagnac or the ugliest woman – il y a une choix."

⁴ An inn at St.-Remy-de-Provence (B.-du-R.). John wrote on the card: "Le Café Robinson represents the Frenchman's idea of Robinson Crusoe's habitat."

of "Le Robinson" will not, I trust, distract you too much (though I cannot see how it *wont*) and that some work will get done.

... (I never use an agent – like lawyers, they usually seem more concerned to get a bargain for the other party, than for their ostensible client.[)] There will, I think, be little difficulty in arranging for the publication of the Gwen John book, as it is a very good bet from the publisher's standpoint. ——

On your way back you should collect a few of the highbrow magazines in Paris, "Nef" etc. When are you returning? And will Popette be back in Tite Street soon?

Yours ever,
WYNDHAM LEWIS

P.S. Your information re. the Flemish settlement in Pembroke is not only interesting on account of Gwen, but yourself also.[1] Were they all in one locality? The Flemish have certainly shown themselves more disposed to paint pictures than the Welsh. Such a brother and sister require some accounting for! A good deal of the blood of Taliesin must have got mixed in with the blood of the Vermeers however.[2]

WL.

PPS. The King is showing all his pictures at the R.A. It appears however that all the best of the royal collection was sold by Cromwell. What a ruffian! We also are told that Charles I was royal collector no. 1. It is typical he should have been beheaded. Oh, and the Duke of Windsor popped over to England the other day and lost almost immediately half a million pounds worth of jewels.[3] That is the sort of thing he collects.

WL.

---

[1] L. had sent to John his article "The Art of Gwen John" (*The Listener*, October 10th, 1946, p. 484), in which he referred to Mabuse and Vermeer. Thanking him, John wrote: "Your reference to Flemish masters is interesting. Haverfordwest was the centre of the considerable Flemish settlement (12th cent.) in Pembrokeshire and the element combining with the Welsh has chiefly formed the present population."

[2] John replied: "Yes, all the 'Flemings', out-of-work mercenaries, were settled in S. Pembrokeshire by Henry 1 and 2 to keep the unruly Welsh in order. Perhaps this accounts for the conflicting nature of one or two of the results. I'd rather have a touch of Breughel, Roger van der Weyden or Memling than Vermeer."

[3] The theft of the Duchess of Windsor's jewel case from the couple's temporary residence at Sunningdale was reported in the press on October 18th.

358. *To Augustus John*† [London]
[November 3rd? 1946.]

Dear John. Very many thanks for the photographs. Edwin[1] and Dylan Thomas make excellent pair. – The menu of the "Robinson", as reported in your letter, has ruined my appetite for the rest of the week.[2] .... – Have you in your neighbourhood intellectually brilliant or socially attractive London figures, for I hear that St. Remy is quite a central locality. – I am glad to hear you are ——ing the landscape:[3] but dont neglect the picturesque hags I made bold to recommend. ("Cult of ugliness" and all that). – Was down with Influenza and am rising rather unsteadily to my feet. All the best.

W. L.

359. *To Geoffrey Grigson*† [London]
Dec. 5th 1946.

Dear Grigson. Thank you for your note. .... I wonder by the way if like *Contact* you pay upon acceptance of Mss?[4] It is an excellent principle, as all serious people are starving half the time, and there seems no way of altering that.

For nine days I had 'flu': my first day out I was sprung at by a motor bike, moving en marge at a speed greatly exceeding the rest of the traffic. I knocked it out (now I am speaking like Campbell) but I have a hole in my right leg, which rests upon two chairs. The healing process is wearisome, but I believe will not take very much longer.

A gang-warfare seems to have started in the correspondence of

---

[1] John's son.
[2] John wrote: "Besides an omelette and wine you could get tripes, andouilles, boudins noir, chitterlings & other good things."
[3] John wrote: "This landscape, like some women I have heard of, takes a deal of getting into."
[4] Grigson had taken L.'s article "DeTocqueville's 'Democracy in America'" for his miscellany, *The Mint* (see No. 2, 1948). L.'s article "American Melting Pot" appeared in *Britain Between East and West* (London, 1946), a Contact book.

the Listener. This morning I find myself attacked.¹ I do not know who Sylvester is, but apparently I "wrecked" myself for him by not agreeing with his friends. Rouse is an unspeakable idiot. What a pity it is there are so few people who do not eat out of the hand of the Golden Woman² or are not clients of the Horizon-New Writing crowd.

                                                                              Yrs.

360. *To Dwight Macdonald*†   London W.11
                                                                                      Jan 26. 1947.

Dear Mr. Macdonald. It is extremely kind of you to send me copies of Politics.³ A thing of Agees was terribly good I thought – about the incontinence of a sweet little girl, at the climax of a solemn ceremony of dedication.⁴ (I thought at first it was something that had really happened: it was the dear little girl that opened my eyes to the deception). I follow with rapt attention your controversy with *The Partisan Review*: in which I become a partisan I find – for you.⁵

That Review, by the way – which Eliot describes as 'the Horizon of New York' – is going to be published over here. Why? The Londoner, for his sins, has his own *Horizon* – edited by one of the smaller and squarer of the saurians (to further the identification, let me add that their method of apprising the world of their feelings is a *croak* – not a *hiss*). Ours is not so fine a specimen of his kind, as your Mr. Wilson, for whom *Horizon* advertises a

---

¹ A. D. B. Sylvester wrote criticising A. L. Rowse, who had written the preceding week, for his defence of Roy Campbell. Sylvester accused Rowse of being bemused by the quality of hysteria in Campbell; he went on to say: "Just this hysteria – 'I am the Enemy' – is wrecking Campbell's work as it wrecked that of Wyndham Lewis." See "Poetry Reviewing," *The Listener*, December 5th, 1946, p. 799.
² Edith Sitwell?
³ Having founded *Politics* in February 1944, Macdonald edited it until its demise with the winter number, 1949.
⁴ James Agee, "Dedication Day: Rough Sketch for a Moving Picture," *Politics*, April 1946, pp. 121–5. L. knew Agee in London.
⁵ In *Politics* for December 1946, Macdonald makes a rebuttal to an attack on him in the current number of the *Partisan Review*. See "'Partisan Review' and 'Politics,'" pp. 400–3.

boundless admiration, and vice versa. A fraternal croak across the Herring Pond!

But this is an indiscreet aside. My guess is that noticing the *Horizon* of London is in extremis, the Horizon of New York thought it could not allow a horizontal vacuum to come into existence, following the demise of its London opposite number.[1]

Anarchy is going strong over here: the Godwin book by Woodcock has attracted much attention.[2] I lunched with Herbert Read a few days ago, who wrote the preface for it, and he spoke much of Anarchy. – I like policemen, I am afraid=*but not too many*.

Woodcock appears to have a serious mind – which is more than can be said for Mr. Orwell, who is a silly billy.[3] He's full of political tittletattle – but he gets it all wrong. He thinks people are always falling in love with political Stars. I am so glad that emotional publicschoolboy has transferred his excitable loyalties to the Partisans – if I am interpreting the signs correctly. – Congratulations.

Sincerely
WYNDHAM LEWIS

361. *To Ezra Pound*† [London]
April 1947.

Dear Ezra. I often think about you: and I have been writing about you too. At least a year must elapse however before the book in which that occurs sees the light.[4] Shortages of paper etc etc. makes it very long. I never know what to say to you when I sit down to write you as I am doing now. Do you find time to write anything or rather – for you have time enough no doubt – are you able to? In what way you had served our not very endearing kind was the subject I referred to in passing. How would you answer that – I mean *poetry apart*, for that is obvious? It seemed to me that you were responsible not for Joyce of course but for Joyce getting heard

[1] Despite its difficulties, *Horizon* continued to appear until 1950. *Partisan Review* was never published in England.

[2] George Woodcock, *William Godwin, a Biographical Study* (London, 1946).

[3] An article on Orwell by Woodcock, "George Orwell, 19th Century Liberal," appeared in *Politics* for December 1946, pp. 384–8.

[4] See *Rude Assignment*, pp. 122–3.

about in the way that he did – seeing that you sold the idea of Joyce to Miss Weaver, and she was the nearest approach to supernatural experience Jimmie J ever knew.[1] – and the intervention of the supernatural world in his personal affairs was the theme of quite a lot of his conversation. – Then there was 'Cathay'. That Hueffer described as 'the most beautiful book in the world' I remember. But other people (who were Chinese experts) thought that too apparently: and you started a translation racket, with which the name of Waley (or Whaley?) is conspicuously associated. Correct?[2] Any information of that sort I should welcome. – Have you been visited in your retreat by any literary lights? Cummings for instance? I saw him when I was in N.Y. But he was such a jumpy and peppery little creature it was impossible to talk to him much. He has succeeded in writing some very excellent verses. As Washington is so near to N.Y. I suppose you may have seen him. – My wife sends her kindest regards. If there is anything I can do – !

Yrs.

The painter and writer Michael Ayrton (b. 1921) first met Lewis in 1946 after having praised him as a draughtsman in his book British Drawings.[3] *A pleasant acquaintance ensued. Lewis reviewed Ayrton's next show favourably (see below) and later did a short article on him;*[4] *Ayrton, in turn, wrote the foreword to the catalogue of Lewis's 1949 exhibition at the Redfern Gallery. The two were brought together again in 1953, with the result that they became*

---

[1] In a letter dated April 17th, Pound replied: "Yass – that iz, I tried to sell idea of keepin' up lit. but, to qt. you, he (J.) threw himself on it like starved dog; and swallowed enough to have publish'd the necessary of the 4 footmen. / the drive for bro Possum backfired an Valleryed. – 'Arriet swallow'd the 'ook line an sinker and that ended the fishin.'' On May 24th, Mrs. Pound wrote: "Ezra says while you are on his merits ... not only got Joyce into print in Eng. and U.S. but was the first to publish criticism of Ulysses in France. His article in Mercure de France preceding Valery Larbug's in 'La Nouvelle Purée Françoise' by 15 days."

[2] Pound replied: "Yes, I cert did show the —— that chink cd/ be made into english but *that* dilutation aint the ultima parola – cert. the - - - was paralized before the gate wuz op'd:"

[3] Ayrton has written vividly of his relationship with L. in "Tarr and Flying Feathers," *Golden Sections* (London, 1957), pp. 146–55.

[4] "A Note on Michael Ayrton," *Nine* (August 1950), pp. 184–5.

close allies and remained such until Lewis's death. The senior artist's esteem for this young friend was evidenced in his choosing Ayrton to design the jackets for his last books and to make the illustrations for The Human Age. *In the course of this work Ayrton did several drawings and a painting of the blinded Lewis.*

362. *To Michael Ayrton*† [London]
April. 1947.

Dear Ayrton. I should have sent you this note sooner but for the demoralisation which with me always accompanies 'flu. I just got to your show at the Redfern in time before I was laid low. My congratulations: I felt I was at a cross-roads. Down one road I saw a great marine-painter making his way; down another moved a great slumscape painter, with his bullseye flashing into dark corners to locate wharf-rats: and down a third, less distinct, the figure of a figure-painter, perhaps a combiner of figures with something else. There were two or three other vistas too. The picture I regarded as the most original was the one with the recumbent pig in the foreground. With that (somewhat less complete) a seascape. – One general observation: I was very impressed with the absence of pictures that one identifies with one or other of a dozen fashionable masters. I find it tiresome in the end to have to say "Ah Rouault!" – or "Oh Delvaux! Not bad. Well, and a bit of Miro there in the corner. That's very cute now." You must excuse me if this sounds patronizing and remember I have seen nothing of yours before. Apart from the beauty and vigour of many of the things shown, this strong-mindedness astonished me. I see of course that the vitalism – in contrast to the aestheticism of the painter showing in the gallery at the back – accounts for this to some extent. – I must wait for your next show to see which of these roads you take: advising however that you bring figures and animals into the landscapes.

Sincerely,

363. *To James Thrall Soby*†¹ [London]
April 9th 1947.

Dear Mr. Soby. Geoffrey Grigson sent me along your letter of Feb 24. I should have acted sooner but have been moving about. I was much gratified by what you wrote. Without immodesty I can agree with you that I substituted for what Roger Fry proposed that England should have (a diluted and sentimentalised 'post-impressionism') something so much more severe as to be as a matter of fact out of its element in England. This action of mine naturally displeased Fry and his "Bloomsbury" friends. (It still displeases the knightly Sir ——, who . . . has inherited the guardianship of Fry's pets).

Here are a few facts of the kind you will *probably* want to know. Mostly I found in the States that I was asked about very abstract things I did to start with. There were not great numbers of those things, they were not done for very long, and they have all disappeared. They were as 'abstract' as Mondrian, say: not originating in a still-life or a portrait, as was always the case with the cubists. I remember one canvas in golden yellows and mustards, looking like the cross-section of a bee-hive, which it is a pity I was not able to preserve. The date of this type of work was roughly 1912 to August 1914. It was only in 1914 that suddenly I became well-known. I had had no time to form the habit of photographing my work as I did it, before the war blotted everything out. You have to think of a little narrow segment of time, on the far side of world war i. That first war, you have to regard, as far as I am concerned, as a black solid mass, cutting off all that went before it. The dirty trough between the two wars was another time. The being a soldier and all the futilities related to that divides my life into compartments, world war ii being another walling off of the same kind. (I am afraid I am allergic to wars).

In the compartment no. 2. (the trough between the wars) you will find nothing that you are looking for, I imagine. What with the war and the epidemic that followed it, my convalescence, demobilisation etc. etc. etc. life restarted in 1920. From 1920 to

¹ The American art critic James Thrall Soby (b. 1906) wrote to L. in the process of preparing an article on his work. This historical and critical study, titled "Wyndham Lewis' Vorticism," became a chapter (pp. 115–21) in Soby's *Contemporary Painters* (New York, 1948).

'25 I did many designs or little pictures which were very far from naturalist canons: but not more so than I am liable to do now, or than those I got ready for my Leicester Galleries exhibit in the late 'thirties (such as "Stage scene" 1 and 2,[1] "Stations of the Dead,"[2] "Creation Myth"[3] and so forth). Mrs Ernest Stix,[4] ... has one of the best designs I did while in America (in 1944 I think). I shall send you 'Pavilion' with a big colour print of "The Surrender of Barcelona".[5] But that was in the N.Y. world fair and it is probably not what you want. Polynesian influences (to which you refer in your letter) occur all along. We have here in the British Museum some very fine collections of New Ireland masks, Easter Island monoliths, and other varieties of Pacific and S. America stuff. Even when at the Slade School I was directed to go to the Print Room at the Museum and study the drawings of Raphael and Michaelangelo I had always to pass between cases full of more savage symbols on my way to the shrines of the cinquecento. In an early sketchbook the other day full of Leonardo's old man with the swollen underlip and Michaelangelo's writhing heavyweights I came across Pacific Island masks.

In a few days I will send you what I can scrape together by way of photographs. Meanwhile I shall be very happy to help you in any way I can.

Sincerely,

364. *To Naomi Mitchison*† [London]
April. 1947.

Dear Naomi. An influenza visitation leaves me a little jaded – before that I was to the exclusion of all else finishing a book, which is why I have been so long in answering your letter. . . .

[1] One of these, "Players on the Stage," is reproduced in Handley-Read, Pl. 20.
[2] Reproduced in Handley-Read, Pl. 19.
[3] Reproduced in the catalogue of the exhibition "Wyndham Lewis and Vorticism" at the Tate Gallery, July 6th to August 19th, 1956, Pl. 9. [4] Of St. Louis.
[5] The picture was reproduced in conjunction with L.'s article "Towards an Earth Culture or the Electric Culture of the Transition" in *The Pavilion*, edited by Myfanwy Evans (London, [1946]). See Handley-Read, Pl. 16.

The Highlands – and still more the Islands – have a damp and bleak sound to me. But Notting Hill Gate it is true is not much better. I dont understand your reference to my quarreling. Certainly I have been obliged to defend myself on a number of occasions during the past thirty or forty years: but I have never gone out of my way to quarrel with people; nor do I enjoy brawling. If Macdiarmid[1] is so quarrelsome as you say it may be just to keep warm up in Scotland: or is it not possibly a part of his publicity? – There are at least a dozen people trying to quarrel with me at present. I may be obliged to take some notice of one of them before long: he will then go clattering around everywhere denouncing me as an aggressor. *He* will be all injured innocence. They tell me Macdiarmid's dialect verse is splendid stuff. If that is so, it would cause a lot of people to quarrel with him; and you may get the impression that it is he who is doing it all. It has made me feel quite tired thinking of all the "quarrelling" that I am supposed to have done and that Macdiarmid does, so I will put down my pen and go and have two teaspoonfuls of Metatone. I suppose you would say I am engaged in a quarrel with these bacilli which have forced their way into my bloodstream? – A final word: you have a very good young scottish artist named Colquhoun.[2]

Yrs ever.

365. *To Felix Giovanelli*†   [London]
[April? 1947]

Dear Gio. Your letter with its magnificent proposal[3] has just arrived. This most kind and generous impulse of yours will certainly help us to combat "austerity": The only way to live in this country at present is to have a small estate, cattle, poultry, pigs and so forth. Or if you are very rich, you can live in a suite at a big hotel, having your meals sent up: or there are a certain number of night-clubs. Practically all our friends live out of London: and in the country there is much more food. But *we* get on our ration what is really inadequate, and has to be supplemented in any way we can devise. The theory is, of course, that no one should be

---

[1] Hugh McDiarmid (Christopher Murray Grieve) (b. 1892).
[2] Robert Colquhoun (b. 1914).   [3] An offer to send food parcels.

living my kind of life – writing books and all that kind of nonsense. Meanwhile, as you may have heard, keeping warm is a big problem here. I bought myself a beautiful great big *Essa* stove, and then one ton of anthracite (my ration). Alas, the anthracite was 50% inferior coal. The stove eats up the coal at a terrible rate, so that very soon my ration will be exhausted. I rush to my telephone that the unethical coal company should not remain a moment longer in ignorance of my opinion of them. At the instrument I stop: I move away despondently, for the Government is now the owner of the mines. Not however that anyone has a monopoly of dishonesty. The Gas and Coke Co. whether they give you a miserable flicker of gas (as they always do if it is a peculiarly cold day) or a blaze of heat, charge just the same. – England at present is like a tale by some early xix century romantic. The 47 million people here *cannot* be fed, under present conditions, anymore than the 70 million in Germany could be – except by wars of conquest. Among other things, the climate has completely changed. There is no rain, the sun shines all the time. Today it is abominably cold, snow is announced as "on the way", but the sun still shines. . . .

I have told you a bit about how things are here: now *you* must give me a glimpse of yourself – issuing from 13th St. in the morning, debouching into Fifth Avenue, turning towards my old hotel (since 1927) the Brevoort, *or* more ambitiously pointing your nose up-town. . . . What is the town-talk? Is the Partisan Rev still the only regular lit. rev.? Is "Politics" continuing? I must say I thought Macdonald did a very excellent job on Wallace – he scarcely left an eyelash intact.[1] In fine, any bits of news that you think might amuse. And let me hear of your doings.

Saluts à toi et à Margot

[1] See Dwight Macdonald, "Henry Wallace," *Politics*, March–April 1946, pp. 33–44.

366. *To Mrs. K. H. Webb*†[1]   London. W.11.
May 29th 1947.

Dear Mrs. Webb. . . . The novel I am proposing to write is not a satire.[2] – like 'The Apes of God.' It will be a straight novel, a normal narrative, as much as 'Tarr' for instance: or – oh, Mr. Morgan's 'Fountain'. As now planned it will be dominated by the 'everything or nothing' principle. This means a character who is what today colloquially is known as a perfectionist. Woman has been called 'the eternal enemy of the absolute': so our perfectionist must encounter immediate difficulties when he comes in contact with woman.

No such man as this, I should add, is known to me, so no one could say (as in the case of Merediths 'Egoist' for instance) that I had founded the character on him. In any case, the character is not displeasing.

Yours sincerely,

367. *To Allen Tate*†   [London]
17 August 1947.

Dear Tate. The manner you have found of communicating to me the news of the refusal of my book[3] by your firm suggests of course such rejoinders as these: (1) I have no recollection of being a centre back in any team of which you were a member. (2) I do not remember any occasion on which I followed automatically 'the direction' taken by people around me – nor, I believe I am right in saying, has it been your habit to do so in the past, whatever

[1] Mrs. Webb was a director of Hutchinson's, for whom L. was writing *Rude Assignment*.
[2] The novel, L.'s first since *The Vulgar Streak*, became *Self Condemned*. It was published by Methuen in 1954.
[3] "The Politics of the Intellect," which became *Rude Assignment*. Tate wrote to L. on July 31st, saying he was unhappy that Holt would not publish the book, which L. had sent him. He recalled that he "was personally very close to all the controversies of which you were the center back in the 20's and 30's" and said he thought that since the war "the younger generation are looking in other directions." In conclusion, he asked if there was anything he could "do about the manuscript here in New York."

may be your procedure now. − But why provoke such rejoinders? If a New York firm does not wish to publish a book of mine, there is nothing new in that. Would it not have been possible to convey that information without involving yourself in that refusal? Surely you do not believe that I imagine *you* are H. Holt and Co.? . . .

                                                              Yrs.

. . .

368. *To David Kahma*†   [London]
                                                                     25. Aug. 1947.

Dear Mr. Kahma. . . .

The situation in this country is distressing: for there is no possible end to it. As a result of two great wars for the position of cock of the walk in Europe both England and Germany are finally ruined, and naturally the rest of Europe with them. Whether the type of state socialism which will take the place of the mercantile prosperity of Europe at the beginning of the century will be a good or a bad thing for the "Greatest Number" I cannot tell you. But the art of writing and the other arts will gradually be extinguished. Much more life is to be found in Paris than here. There always was. But it is very doubtful if it could survive another blow − such as a war or revolution. Even as it is the world of Sartre and Camus is a very sick one indeed. . . .

    Mr. Orwell (as they call him here "bore-well") is an excitable idiot, who spends his time affixing political labels to people.[1] There is no foundation whatever for the rumour you mention that I become a politician. I impartially dislike all factions: and I am not susceptible as is silly Mr. Orwell, to the fascination of political Stars (nor ever have been). I have always been inclined to keep a stupid old bitch known as Brittania out of dog-fights, that is all.

    [1] In the letter L. is answering, Kahma had called his attention to some remarks in Orwell's "London Letter" in the *Partisan Review* for Summer 1946. Orwell wrote: "Wyndham Lewis, I am credibly informed, has become a Communist or at least a strong sympathiser, and is writing a book in praise of Stalin to balance his previous books in favor of Hitler" (p. 323). L. replied publicly in *Rude Assignment*, which includes a three-page counter-attack against Orwell. (See Ch. XV, "Libel and the Game of Labelling," p. 78.) He wrote about Orwell again in *The Writer and the Absolute* (London, 1952).

She is still my only political attachment (pace the London correspondent of the Partisan Rev.). – This letter has been all about myself . . . . My next communication will be about yourself.

With my sincerest thanks,

369. *To James Thrall Soby*†   London. W.11.
20 Sept. 1947.

Dear Mr. Soby. Thank you for your letter – which I did not receive at once as I have been moving about. . . .

As to your question: Why has modern English painting not been treated with some perspective. The answer is complex and somewhat squalid. (1) Pundits such as my friend Read like to suggest that life is always just beginning and they are in at the birth if not the actual midwife. (2) More important, *promotion* here has always been in the hands of rich impresarios, like Roger Fry, or (at present) Sir ——. The interests of such people are naturally not scholarly or historical, but personal and of the moment.

You have nothing of that kind in the United States: so it is something you have especially to bear in mind. – The wealthy promoter collects together a few favourites and creates a little nuclear society of his own. Roger Fry for instance invented Duncan Grant – a little fairylike individual who could have received no attention in any country except England. He and Vanessa Bell (sister to Virginia Woolf) were two of his closest friends. No artist possessed of much talent makes a very good protégé: the result is that support of this kind goes invariably to the second-rate. Mr. Grant was handed on by Fry to —— . . . . So in the Penguin Books of English Painters,[1] for instance, the world is offered a very imperfect survey of British painting.

You mention Colquhoun and MacBryde.[2] Let me explain how you happened to see them in Buffalo.[3] They are both very young men of excellent promise. (They live a few streets away from me, here in Kensington). —— would have nothing to do with them.

[1] *The Penguin Modern Painters*, edited by Sir Kenneth Clark.
[2] Robert MacBryde (b. 1914).
[3] In the exhibition "British Contemporary Painters" at the Albright Art Gallery. There is no mention of MacBryde in the catalogue.

They were too good. Also MacBryde is the son of a scottish-tanner and wears a rather dirty little kilt. —— when he met them asked them why they did not go back to Glasgow. How *they* have managed to survive is because a Scottish dealer here supports them. Otherwise you would never have heard of them. All of which has the sound of gossip: it is what a London Vasari would be writing if he was here, and it is the kind of information the foreign observer has to be in possession of. Why Henry Moore is acceptable to the Patron-impresario is because he has done the simple workman's stuff to such good effect that they have the feeling they are back in the cinquecento visiting the workshop of a master-mason. – I hope these few hints will be useful to you. They tell you nothing regarding the quality of such and such, but explain their emergence or occultation. There is much talent here just now. There is a good man you did not mention called Vaughan.[1] I must get hold of a catalogue of travelling exhibitions in the U.S.A. and see what they are sending round.

Sincerely,

370. *To Mrs. Ezra Pound*† [London]
20 Sept. 1947.

My dear Dorothy. Mr. Moore[2] the lawyer came to see me on Tuesday of this week and we had a long talk. I am now in possession of the facts relating to the situation of E.P., and a beastly situation it is. However, as they say it is always the unexpected that happens. – I was very happy to learn that our Ezra was in better shape than heretofore, able to walk freely in the grounds of the establishment, able to receive visitors, plenty of books, etc. Not such a bad life – except for the freedom! – The lawyer sent me a lot of papers dealing with the case. The outrageous treatment at Pisa was what American newspapers call an 'all-time low'. What brutes. And this gives me a picture too of what *you* must have suffered – from the moment E left the house to escape the Partisans – to wherever was the next time you got news of him.

[1] (John) Keith Vaughan (b. 1912).
[2] A. V. Moore, a solicitor with Shakespear and Parkyn, the firm in which Mrs. Pound's father was a partner. He visited L. to discuss the legal aspects of Pound's situation and possibilities of securing his freedom.

And I hear, with very great concern, that you are none too well now.

You may think this rather fresh but there is something that has occurred to me. The pound sterling is sliding down hill. It now fetches two dollars on the Black Market: and it is still losing ground. Ought you not to try to transfer money to Canada, or the Bahamas? Lord —— (a Douglasite? – Orage had something to do with him) has emigrated to S. Africa and taken his money with him. He is able to do this because it is a 'sterling area'. But once there he can I suppose do what he likes with it. – Property is the only safe thing however, as I feel a financial blizzard will be smiting us shortly.

Just heard from Paige again.[1] He seems a straightforward young man, which is satisfactory. I wanted to make sure that Weiss[2] did not censor anything I wrote about E.P. but Paige is apparently in charge. He wants me to write a general estimate of Ezra's work, which I shall start work on very soon. – Messages from E.P. enjoin me to 'say what you want.' All I *want* to say is: 'Let Ez out quick Uncle Sam!' – I do hope this special number does a lot of good. I am sure however that it will. I was very disgusted with Carlos Williams performance in the records sent me by Mr. Moore.

It is extremely kind of you and E to send a food parcel. If you can imagine for anybody of my particular economic status – a sensitive plant at the best of times – a bankrupt country inopportunely blessed with an ambitious socialist government presents many knotty problems. I should like to have sat out these storms in an American university – with a sinecure. But even Eliot cant get that. It may be that a little later on I can get enough lectures to justify the trip. But do not worry yourself about food parcels please: you have quite enough to think about where you are. – A book of new stuff of Ezra's ought to be published at once. Anyway in this country. With best wishes and salute E.P. for me.

Yrs.

[1] D. D. Paige, later editor of *The Letters of Ezra Pound*, had invited L. to contribute to the special Pound number of the *Quarterly Review of Literature*. Paige was guest editor of the number, which did not actually appear until late in 1949 (Vol. V, No. 2).

[2] Professor Theodore Weiss (b. 1916) of Bard College, publisher and editor of the *Quarterly Review of Literature*.

371. *To the Editor of "The Times Literary Supplement,"*
    September 27th, 1947

Sir, – In an article entitled "Satire in the Twenties,"[1] in your issue of September 13, I find the following, where the reviewer is about to speak of my novel *Tarr*: "described by its author as 'the first book of its epoch in England'". This is no doubt a reference to a review of *Tarr* which appeared at the time in *New Witness*. In that review *Tarr* was described as "a book of great importance ... because it will become a date in literature ... because here we have the forerunner of the prose and probably of the manner that is to come." It must be to that notice that your reviewer refers. It was not therefore a boast of mine, but something written in a contemporary notice of my book.[2]

One other point. The principal character in the novel in question is the German Kreisler – not a very Petrouchka-like figure.[3] And, although I am aware how difficult it is to define Satire, I should myself have described *Tarr* simply as a novel: a quite different type of work from *South Wind* and *Antic Hay* or the books of Ronald Firbank[4] – a very 'ninetyish company.

The *Apes of God* on the other hand I should not classify as a novel, but as satire, for as satire it was written, and not as a realistic narrative, as was *Tarr*, though I think it would make a volume of Firbank's somewhat uncomfortable, if it were jammed up against it on a bookshelf, as a result of a misunderstanding regarding their consanguinity.

WYNDHAM LEWIS

[1] A review of three republished novels by William Gerhardi, p. 464.

[2] In a note printed beneath L.'s letter, the reviewer replies by quoting the cited phrase from L.'s preface to the 1928 edition of *Tarr*. In the preface L. was quoting indirectly from a review of the 1918 edition.

[3] The review speaks of *Tarr* as blowing "an early variant of what was to become the familiar Petrouschkan air, with a hero also Nietzschean, though – unlike Clovis or Bassington – no tame cat."

[4] All mentioned in the review.

372. *To Mrs. Ezra Pound*† [London]
9 Oct 1947.

Dear Dorothy. Thank you for your kind letter and enclosure. They should I think, create a post for me, of general cultural expert! – It is too bad that Fabers will not publish the "Confucius". Surely a Chinese sage is harmless enough.[1] – A long time ago I talked with – or was talked to by – Major Douglas[2] until it became completely dark and I could scarcely see him. He explained to me not only his economic theory, but his view of how this wicked world was governed. Also I have read a good deal of his literature. Eliot interested himself in this a good deal some fifteen years ago I remember. You must think me very immoral, but I do not consider ours a very rational or ethical world: if I am told that some one is darkly plotting it seems as natural to me as that somebody else is (or was) trying to split the atom. I confine myself to devoutly hoping they will blow themselves up and not me. In any case, I believe the world is heading at topspeed for a physical calamity. So desperate that all, good and bad together, will go tumbling into it. Our pious hope must be that our extraordinarily intelligent kind will be somewhat sobered by the experience. – In this country at present one is like a patient, who, so long as he does not move about, goes along well enough: but let him attempt to undertake a journey, and up goes his temperature by leaps and bounds. However, I am not referring of course to a fever-chart but to expenditure. The other day I went up north for a few days and it cost me fifty pounds. One struggles with an inflation which sends me mad. – A little theatre called the 'Lindsay'[3] has opened at this end of Palace Gardens terrace. They are playing 'Tobacco Road'. The censor will not allow it to be played in the West End, but thinks apparently that Kensington, is all right. Two plays of Sartre at Hammersmith. You should tell Ezra by the way to read *La Peste* by Camus and inform you what

[1] In her letter, written September 29th, Mrs. Pound asked why everyone was afraid to publish Pound's Confucius book. Faber had rejected it, she said, possibly on the ground that "it might interfere with certain ideas due to Christianity."

[2] The Social Credit authority, C. H. Douglas (1879–1952). Mrs. Pound mentioned him in her letter.

[3] The New Lindsay Theatre, since demolished.

he thinks of it. . . . – Is not this under the circs. a very good way of communicating with E.P.?

Yrs

. . .

373. *To David Kahma*† [London]
19 Oct. 1947.

Dear Kahma. . . . Far too much time has slipped by – I should have written you a week or so ago. And even now I cannot write as fully as I should like. Things will be much easier next month.

Now as to the play.[1] There is practically no chance, at the best of times, for a play: and this is not the best of times. The war-time boom in books is over – the paper shortage continues: worst of all, printers and binders are understaffed. That is why I spoke of something relatively easy to read. I have perhaps acted with too much precipitation. You tell me you have never contemplated publication. Do not let me urge you to publish – Joubert (contemp. of Chateaubriand) who is being written up a good deal now never published in his life time. Placed as you are secluded in an agreeable business city – really much more remote than it probably *feels* – a certain procedure is imposed on you. If you had 20 poems of 12 lines each about, say like Dylan Thomas (as good as that) one would approach a publisher with hope – one who liked publishing poetry. But from what I gather Satirogenitus[2] is another cup of tea: it would take a hundred times more paper *and it* has something to do with *Satire*. You must reflect. The author of "Finnigans Wake" living in the center of things, began with "Dubliners" and so on. It is a good policy if you *wish* to publish to lead off with something written with great simplicity – even if later on you give them the most gothic piece of machinery you ever saw. – Your novel may be the very thing the enterprising publisher is praying for (minus the lexicon!). If you would send me the first ten pages and no more I might be able to form an opinion.

You realize that everything is drying up here – I mean culturally? The publishers lists speak for themselves. Nothing new is being done. And as to the political scene, a period of great

[1] Kahma had sent to L. in July a five-act play in blank verse.
[2] A long prose work which Kahma had also sent.

additional 'austerity' is setting in. It is like a moral tale, is it not? What would you say was the cardinal sin of which the 47 million inhabitants of this island have been guilty? Last winter I sat at lunch in one of the best restaurants in the City, full of well-to-do business men. It was about 28 above zero. We sat in our hats and overcoats – there was no heat. I looked round at these extraordinary men. Their breath came from each of their mouths, a pale blue plume. They betrayed no sign of noticing that anything out of the ordinary was happening. But meanwhile *I* was very very cold! What I always fear in this country is that I shall be asked to dispense with glass at my windows – everybody else likewise of course but I shall never be able to say there is a draught because no one else will notice it. If the rations get any smaller there will be nothing. But I shall never be able to say I am hungry!

... But you see the denudation goes through everything. When there are no new books published anymore (except mine and a small devotional volume of Eliots every two years) no one will *notice* it. – It is a time when everything is withered and rotted. ... Meanwhile, why not try a plain tale?

Good wishes and more thanks.

374. *To David Khama*†   [London]
Nov. 15. 1947.

Dear Kahma. First, your long and most interesting letter. It was not my idea that you should try to do anything that goes against the grain. You would do it badly. So long as you understand that (1) these wars, and the conditions that they produce, and (2) the abyss of commercialism into which publishing has sunk in New York, are in neither case favourable for a young writer, you at least know where you stand. The —— publisher told me just before the war that the policy of the N.Y. publishers was to have one good book "to sweeten their list". I dont think they worry about that now. But *here* the set-up is quite different. What is the matter with them is not so much *kitsch* as stuffiness. Also they fear the bookshops – consequently if a 'difficult' book is offered them their feeling naturally is that they will not be able to sell it. (Naturally if they have a name to sell they do not worry so much).

But that is no reason why you should sit down and write the kind of book you dont want to. – A way out of this difficulty I have thought of is a small critical book, to start with: comparing perhaps contemporary European with American literature: or if you like just about American. This may not be an idea that recommends itself to you. You could write about Finns. I just think you should make a start, and that is one way. – As we do not know each other, except by correspondence, I may be being clumsy. It might amuse you to write about a philosophic *voyageur*: it must have been rather wonderful coming upon Niagara (or Great Bear Lake sounds a horrible spot) – or anyway since the present inhabitants of Vancouver would murder you if you wrote a line of contemporary life which they did not like, why not go to the past if not in one way in another? Je cherche! . . .

Once more to the other matter. This letter is getting to look like an American radio program. If my letters have been spasmodic and irregular, please do not put that down to carelessness. I have been very much driven. This place where I write is infested with workmen: as they get here early I have to go to bed earlier, when I usually attend to letters. . . . – With your Finnish-Irish ancestry and American birth you can take no conceivable interest in this country except as a cultural relic. Do you regard the North American continent as more important than a "boarding-house" (to use Theodore Roosevelt's expression)? I dont see why you should – or shouldn't. The only part of my letter this question could relate to is that dealing with projects for work. But I should like the information apart from that. – Can you read French?

Well from beneath they have made a hole in the floor of this room and are wafting as much of the blow-pipe fumes as possible up through the hole. I open the windows. But it is cold, so I compromise. I shall leave and go to the National Gallery where the old masters are in imminent danger of being destroyed by the most radical kind of cleaning. Those that survive look perfectly wonderful however, as if painted yesterday. This as you can see is a problem. With my best wishes to yourself and your wife.

375. *To Mrs. Ezra Pound*† [London]
Nov 15. 1947.

Dear Dorothy. . . . What of course dismays one about the entire situation here is the realisation that it is a matter of policy, the "standard of life has to go down." How is it in the States? Since you have been there have you found that food has increased greatly in price? They say in the English papers it is 50% up, over the pre-war level. Half ones time is wasted in taking action about food supplies and suchlike. But Princess Elizabeth's Wedding Cake, nine foot high, is on view in John Barkers: Sir Alfred Munnings, the President of the Royal Academy, is holding an exhibition at the Leicester Galleries, where sixteen thousand pounds worth of pictures have already sold: pictures of horse-races, the jockeys riding out to the starting line, of hunting and portraits of horses. Yesterday I found the galleries full of people – owners of racing stables identifying Winners in the Oaks etc. – in their excitement inclined to mistake Brown and Philips[1] for bookies! Meanwhile young writers and I suppose painters are being conscripted for labour. . . .

Will you say: Dear Ezz. Why doan yew warble about Washington, same as Osky did bout Reading and ole Verlaine tew when same cause took him to same place. Yew could bring it out nonymous-like.

Yrs ever.

376. *To William Gaunt*† [London]
29 Nov. 1947.

Dear Gaunt. Long ago I should have written you about your show,[2] but we are having the most dreadful disturbance here. Dry rot starting in the Christian Science Shop underneath, is spreading rapidly all over the building, pursued by a mad carpenter. Our lavatory is a shambles and the roof of the lobby is gone. This has been going on for at least a month, and it accounts a little for my

---

[1] Proprietors of the Leicester Galleries.
[2] A show of drawings at the Walker Gallery.

remissness.¹ It was a pity your show came too late for me to be able to give it a puff in my Listener article; but I was glad to notice that such adventitious aids were unnecessary, since at least half had a red spot. If it is possible to say that without seeming to patronize, the present collection marks a great advance. I like the cool, the simple, the direct, and in many of these street scenes I got it. I like the interior looking from one room into the other with a green curtain between, and many more. Congratulations on the distinguished show – most terribly hung in that extraordinary gallery. When my present miseries are over we must meet.

Yrs.

377. *To James Thrall Soby*† [London]
Nov. 29. 1947.

Dear Mr. Soby. Excuse this seemingly dilatory answer but such energy as is left when I have finished with breadwinning for the day has been absorbed in writing letters of thanks to the various people who send me parcels from America – discussing the respective merits of Crisco and Sunflower seed Oil, delicately hinting that Wieners (which I loathe) are a bad buy etc. etc. Then the climate has changed here. It was 10 above the other night which is cold for England, and the sun never stops shining – the moon too – instead of the perpetual rain which is the rule. I have a new miniature furnace in my studio which wastes about $2\frac{1}{2}$ hours out of the twenty four. It radiates heat for about 2 yards: 4 yards from it you are as cold as you are in the street. – Why these lunatics dont have central heating passes my understanding. I think it is to harden themselves for their ultimate resting place....

As to Chirico. The first time I met Chirico was in 1932, at the Lefevre Gallery, when the Gal. Director introduced us: nor did I ever hold any communication with him. I do not think that pictures of mine were exhibited in Paris before 1914, the time was so short. It is quite possible on the other hand that Chirico

¹ This calamity (see also letter to Kahma above) provided the theme for *Rotting Hill* (London, 1951), a collection of stories and sketches illustrating the social and cultural decay of post-war England. The title is Pound's corruption of Notting Hill.

saw "Blast", which was sold in Paris and I suppose in Italy and made use of the "Plan of War" for the three pictures you mention.[1] Or it may have been an accidental similarity. You tell me he is a difficult customer. That comes I think in part out of ideological differences – not that I suppose for a moment that Chirico was a fascist. By the time I met him in '32 he had deteriorated in the most surprising way, however. Sugary nymphs in foam actually, for the British market. – Sorry to hear a Briton called Gibbings is giving trouble. Surely no one will join in his witch-hunt, addicted as we all are to that sport.[2]

I do hope this little point about Chirico will have reached you in time. With my best wishes for your new book!

378. *To David Kahma*†   [London]
                                                                                13 Dec. 1947.

Dear Kahma. Thank you for your long letter and now this further one about the baths in Finland. It is not a good moment for me to reply at all fully. To come immediately to the point however regarding which of the two books I recommend you to occupy yourself with, (1) the critical, or (2) the autobiographical, I should say certainly the latter (not as the experiences of Kahma, of course, but of a fictional character.) The typical English couple taking England with them literally – so that a miniature Dovedale, Cotswolds, Windermere is with them there in their hearts: and in that they continue in truth to live: installed at the foot of those very high unfriendly mountains, and the excellent position of Vancouver for the observation of the omens regarding white empire in Asia and (if that might be said and the author still live) how with great suddenness white empire has ended, England become an absurdly overpopulated island-slum (48 millions) and I suppose the English colony at Vancouver (or is it Victoria?) hard hit – extinguished. Or do those noble exiles pull in their belts and stick out their chins – or *what*? It is an interesting spot in the

---

[1] In *Contemporary Painters*, Soby cites Chirico's *The War* and *The Revolt of the Sage* as being related to L.'s picture. (See p. 119.) He asked L. if there was any possibility of direct influence.

[2] See T. H. Robsjohn-Gibbings, *Mona Lisa's Mustache, a Dissection of Modern Art* (New York, 1947).

English speaking world, your city. And do not forget in the event of a war it is the first city of any size that *could* be occupied by the Russians if they were successful – which is highly improbable unless they have some very secret weapon which is even more deadly than "Gilda". (When above I say "I recommend" you write such and such a book, you must use your own judgement, mine is just an opinion). . . .

W. L.

P.S. . . . By the way, the postal service here is quite unlike that in Spain or Italy – or even France – it is extremely reliable. Unless your letter is a very important one, or in the case of a very long letter, it is quite safe not to register it and perhaps better. The postman gets us out of bed and looks at us reproachfully.

My best wishes for Christmas.

379. *To Felix Giovanelli*† [London]
21. Dec. 1947.

Dear Giovanelli. . . .

I have not got your letter here and am answering it from memory. The little criminal in Camus's novel who approved of the Plague – like the Blackmarketeer who thrives on Famine – and whom you find the only sympathetic figure in the book, is from the world of 'L'Etranger'.

I think I like 'La Peste'. The present is an economic plague – you, although not rich, send us provisions. You do not care for Camus' anti-peste tract and yet there you are acting against a peste: not a bubonic plague, it is true, but a nasty little squalid plague that deprives one of fats, drains one's marrow, causes lumps of chalk to emerge on one's face (the bread being full of chalk and bran) etc. etc. etc. – I was sorry to hear of your end-of-the-year feeling of nervous exhaustion. New York is a tiring place to live in constantly. Later on perhaps you will be able to arrange for breaks of a few weeks at Cape Cod or Montauk or somewhere.

────── as you know is a smart man and a great linguist so it can be no surprise to you his becoming a great authority on contemporary German literature. One of the prides of the English faculty in Toronto University is a full professor who teaches nothing but Goethe. Year in and year out he teaches Faust, Wilhelm Meister,

Hermann und Dorothea, and so on. But when Germans have visited Toronto and have addressed him in German, to the surprise of his colleagues, he remains silent. So great is their respect for him that they have put a benevolent interpretation upon this. . . . Our combined good wishes for the New Year for yourself and Margaret.

Your

380. *To Ezra Pound*† [London]
[January 1948]

Dear Ezra. Good luck in the new year, is my tardy salute. Christmas holiday etc., is with me a lump of knots in the otherwise reasonably level stretch of day to day. Good luck I hope may take the form of a relenting on the part of Uncle Sam.

. . . You sent me a cutting announcing the decease of John Bull (are we still interested in such events, such entities?)[1] and it will not surprise you to learn therefore that one of John Bulls houses – the one in which I dwell – is dropping to pieces, afflicted with a disease known as "dry rot." We found one of our windows wobbling about in its socket: we informed the landlord. It was a case of *dry rot*! Workmen were already engaged upon dry rot cases in other parts of the building. As a consequence for many weeks we have lived upstairs (where you sat for your portrait). Yesterday we came *downstairs*: the workmen now go upstairs, where dry rot abounds. The beam on which the glass roof rests is full of it: they will, I think, remove the roof. . . .

There is completely nothing to talk about regarding books and

[1] The clipping, sent with Christmas greetings on December 19th, read:
"John Bull, Dies at 85
St. Helier, Jersey, Channel Islands,
Dec. 18 (AP) – John Bull, 85, retired
circusman who once trained animals for
P. T. Barnum, died at his Jersey home
yesterday."

On the side Pound wrote: "note usual time lag." In a letter of February 2nd, Mrs. Pound explained: "Re John Bull – The only point of interest was the 'time-lag,' of the obit in getting over here. Time-lag here increased – used to be 20 years according to EP, and now is apparently 40 – Picasso just begun to 'go' in N.Y. . . ."

things here. Most people live in the country – they have not come into London again to live, only to work, and go back to country. This greatly diminishes sociability. But the cost of a bottle of whisky does not help matters either. The great expense in a good restaurant, and very poor return for your money, is another discouraging factor. – I spend most of my time, when not working, with my lawyer, trying to keep my publishers in order. England, like yours, is a lock-up, its size unimportant really. However, I have certain privileges you do not have. – When are you having published that Confucius book? Keep well!

Yr.

381. *To David Kahma*†   [London]
13 Jan. 1948.

Dear Karma. A second outrider. – Thanks for the cuttings. The uses to which you propose to put Brilliant could not fail to secure my approval but except for Henry Miller who remains?[1] There are few dark unconscious druidesses left in these parts. I cant help feeling that Henry Wallace belongs somehow in Brilliant. – Your Major Robinson[2] looks like Blum (ex. P.M. France) only much more dignified.

If you want to do a narrative book – and if it's not a thing you wish to do, probably just as well not to start – you should waste no time but make a serious beginning. I do not have to tell you that you do not just begin *living* a book. Your descriptions of the Canutes with their tight suits, of the intriguing professors, the old English colonels (retired) and Maj. Robinson in the cafeteria is vivacious: you should probably have Fieldings "Tom Jones" on your desk and let Squire Western shout *pox* at you a little and fart his sister out of the room: a good model when dealing with Canutes. – I should have said that my remarks about writing

[1] Brilliant was the capital in British Columbia of the sect of Russian emigrés called Doukhobors. Kahma had become interested in the Doukhobors through meeting one of them at the University of British Columbia. He wrote to Lewis telling of his plan for a fictional work set in Brilliant, suggesting evidently that Henry Miller might feel at home there.

[2] A Vancouver personage and friend of Kahma, who had sent L. his photograph.

P*

satire in Vancouver and living did not refer to the rough rage of such as the Canutes but to a more serious form of retaliation about which I would hear wherever I went in Canada. To illustrate: a young man I knew had a brother who worked for the Toronto "Star" – a good job, but he had a wife and children and after a time he thought he ought to get a rise. He was refused. He allowed a certain interval to elapse and asked again. Exasperated, he said he would find work elsewhere: but he was informed that he would not be able to, that no one would employ him.

This kind of thing is not confined to the newspaper world – for what they said to him was the truth, of course. So it seemed to me not unreasonable to conclude that, in Canada, unless you were acting on behalf of some powerful interest, you could not publish satire. – It may interest you to know that during the war the Ryerson Press published a propaganda pamphlet of mine called "Anglosaxony". Their literary editor wrote personally to all the principal newspaper editors in Canada, asking them to give it special attention. The only review that appeared was in a Hamilton paper. – Now who do you suppose engineered that boycott? – In a quite superficial book written to make money in 1940 for a New York publisher I recorded, in comic terms, a visit to Hart House which caused great offence. That act of satiric aggression would no doubt have been invoked in justification of the boycott, though by the time of the appearance of the pamphlet great hostility had been generated, on all sides about nothing.

It is, you see, my knowledge of these conditions that makes me wonder what sort of book can be written about Vancouver, by a person living in Vancouver. Economically, in such a small place, they have you by the throat as much as they had me by the throat in Toronto. You *could* write a Doukhobor book, with the whole world seen from Brilliant. Not Steinbeck-factual stuff but the Prince of Peace worshipped from the belly of a cow. Is your hero going to be a Finnish fisherman married to a Doukhobor? Could it be said in your publicity that *you* were half Doukhobor? In any case, the Doukhobors are a terrific asset for Vancouver. – Let me know when you begin to get a plan. . . .

Yrs.

382. *To Geoffrey Stone*† London. W.11
Jan. 15. 1948

My dear Stone. . . .

As to conditions in these islands. We now get no eggs at all, or at most one a piece every month. (But we prefer *no* eggs to *powdered* eggs). The ingredients of the bread is said by medical men to be actually injurious to health and is so dry and gritty as to be disagreable to eat. We eat no bread. We buy baps; but they contain no yeast, which it seems is a serious deficiency. In general, absence of fats of all kinds from the diet is the worst feature . . . . The water is now so heavily chlorinated it is almost undrinkable. When the taste of the chlorine wears off, you taste the sewage, which is worse. The reason for this is that it has not been possible to renew the filters at the waterworks. We have found that sometimes for a short while the water tastes quite normal again and we fill our jugs (I suppose garbage has ceased momentarily to flow into it, or they have run out of chlorine). These are just a few details. The most horrible thing of all is that everything gets worse monthly and is certain never to stop getting worse. Consider. This is the capital of a dying empire – not crashing down in flames and smoke but expiring in a peculiar muffled way. The 47 million people on these islands can by no means be fed because they have to be nourished by means of imported food which a great rich empire could buy but not the present dwindling polity in this greatly altered world. Also, why it is certain to become worser and worser for us is that we are in the midst of a socialist experiment (on the Swedish pattern) and we shall be squeezed more and more. . . . At this point (Jan 15) a series of upheavals occurred: we had been living in the upstairs part of our apartment, the workmen entrenched on the floor beneath. But at last they announced their desire to come *up*. Everything had thereupon to be moved *down*. Everything got lost: for days and nights I was living in a whirlpool of furniture and food and blow lamps and typewriters. At last things are relatively quiet: and it is *Jan. 25*! In the meantime your admirable essay 'American Life and Catholic Culture'[1] has turned up, and I have perused it with the greatest interest. You do not say *quite* enough about American Life, I think. Why not boldly imagine a Catholic America? Where did you get your idea

[1] Geoffrey Stone, "American Life and Catholic Culture," *Thought*, December 1947, pp. 679–87.

of a catholic ghetto from – observation of the social ostracism of the irish catholics in Boston? – I enjoyed the *writing* of your article throughout. What I felt to be a mistake was the introduction in so short a piece of a special definition of the terms "culture" and "civilisation". But that would be my only criticism. Are you, may I ask, a Maritain devotee: or do you consider what he writes dangerous doctrine, as many do? Are you on the side of the Louvain teaching – in brief do you consider that the existence of God can be mathematically proved, and that the missionary should go to work on those lines? Or are you more of a mystic than that?

. . . We both hate the "purchase tax" more than we have ever hated anything. Next to that we loathe an expression which our conquerors never cease to employ.

It is this: "Too much money chasing too few goods". – But farewell, and best wishes from Froanna and myself,

Yours

W. L.

383. *To Herbert Read*† London. W. 11.
Jan 29th 1948

My dear Read.

I have not I fear your excuse of many absences abroad for a long silence – I have been here but emulating the hermit.

As to the exhibition, and pictures done by me before world war i (of which none remain, as far as I know).[1] – What you do yourself in the literary art is so perfectly dissimilar from what you so pertinaciously push in the visual art that the secret of this duality would be for me quite impenetrable had I not known you in the days when Hulme was lecturing on "Abstract Art".

But in this particular phase of your showmanship I must depart from my normally indolent rule: and say I do not look upon it with favour. . . . To speak frankly, I have come to object a great deal at seeing myself consistently mis-represented in mixed exhibitions, by people who affect not to know what I have done for the past thirty years or so – or where anything of mine could be found, etc. etc. And this etcetera covers a lot, for busybodies

---

[1] Read was arranging an exhibition of modern art for the launching of the Institute of Contemporary Arts in February. He had written to L. to ask him where he might find examples of his early work.

abound. – As soon as this cold spell has ended and we can sit in a restaurant without danger of frostbite I will see if I can arrange a lunch.

Yrs,

384. *To David Kahma*†   London. W. 11.
Jan 30th. 1948.

Dear Kahma. . . .

. . . The prose (style, rhythm etc.) as exemplified in the descriptive part of your letter is admirable. You need have no anxiety on that score. In writing narrative – unless it is stilted like Meredith, or formal of course – you keep close all the time to everyday speech, you will of course remember that: in dialogue you reproduce it (if you follow my advice) as if you were writing for the stage. – I was very glad to find as you began writing about familiar things that your style became familiar too. You are so deeply grounded in the theory and practice of the formal in language, there is no fear of the familiar passing over into the vulgar (even if it employed coarseness, which as you know, is not synonymous with vulgarity).

As to the case ending,[1] I am quite incompetent myself to decide a matter of that kind, but am positive it must be right as the proofs of T. and W.M. were combed for mistakes by a double-first, a gimlet-eyed rat steeped in classical learning. – Ezra Pound was the originator of the pomp of bogus scholarship – he had a touch of Captain Cook (the one who "reached the Pole"). In a kind of way, doubtless, he knew quite a lot of latin. But when in his translation of Propertius[2] he made the sort of comic mistake schoolboys are laughed at for making, and everybody *laughed*, he became extremely angry. Naturally he *should* have said: "I am a poet, not a scholar. I *have* produced poetry. Let us alter the slips, due to my imperfect latinity." But no. He was theatrical. He wished to be "the scholar". He wanted to impress. It gave his enemies in England a wonderful opportunity.

---

[1] A professor at the University of British Columbia had questioned the accuracy of a Latin quotation in *Time and Western Man*; Kahma passed the query on to L.

[2] "Homage to Sextus Propertius" first appeared in *Quia Pauper Amavi* (London, 1919).

This is a story – not a lecture: but I do think you can afford in your narrative just to sink yourself in the story-telling: and the technical problems are not slight. – All this I am afraid sounds rather impertinent.

Lastly, the length of the book.¹ Have I told you, it *must* be 75 to 90 thousand words? From 75 to 90 thousand is the average length – and 75 is on the short side here. These are standards fixed by popular fiction. There is no help for it. . . .

Yrs in some haste,
W. L.

. . .

385. *To Alan Pryce-Jones*†²   [London]
                                             [February 1948]

Dear Pryce-Jones. . . .

I had no "warning", as you call it, of what was in store for my typescript or needless to say I should never have sent it in. . . . But when I say I should not have sent in my typescript, what should I have done with it? The subject is extremely unattractive. The trouble is that I pay my rent and so on from what money I can make, writing is my trade. . . .

In your last letter I see that your defence is that articles have to be not merely unsigned but endowed with anonymity, so their authorship could not be detected. But in the case of my own text, far from anonymity – or something characterless and neutral – supervening, a quite distinct, and *different*, personality to mine was there! I could never have written the words "emphatically an archipelago", on the second galley. I should have laughed at

¹ The fictional work on the Doukhobors on which Kahma was now embarking.
² Late in 1947 the *Times Literary Supplement* asked L. to review *No Voice is Wholly Lost: Writers and Thinkers in War and Peace*, by Harry Slochower (London, 1946). Upon receiving the review, Alan Pryce-Jones (b. 1908), then editor of *TLS*, wrote to L. thanking him for "the most lively article." On February 3rd, proofs were dispatched to L. along with a note from Pryce-Jones saying, "I hope you will not be too much shocked by the changes I have made here and there," and explaining that these were intended "to make your article fit easily into our normal scheme of anonymity. . . ." Thus began the dispute of which L.'s letter forms part. The review under discussion never appeared.

them. Again, "on the *very* title page" (last line of first galley) I could not have written. But there is *somebody* – you or another – who expresses himself in just that way.

It would be impossible to publish the article in that form because it is not my article. I write suggesting that (1) I change the first person into the third person wherever it occurs: or (2) the article should not appear. . . .

. . . I would be glad to know what there is so crassly incompetent about my article that (except for the question of the first person singular here and there) makes it impossible to publish it without your intervention on every line? You will appreciate that for the author of so many books, and a veteran journalist, like myself, it is a charge that I cannot ignore.

Sincerely

386. *To Felix Giovanelli* London. W. 11
Feb 17th 1948.

My dear Gio. According to *our* standards it is long ago since we last were in contact. However, let your last letter be my point of departure. One little matter I am able to clear up for you. – ——. If —— says he has "paid his way"[1] (oh ghastly British bourgeois) apart from being a stupid thing to say, it is funny. He was married to a rich . . . lady called ——. She kept him in some style. On one occasion I visited them in a small – very famous – hotel in the most fashionable —— Street, run by an ex-mistress of Lord Ribblesdale, known as ——. Her bar was the resort of "Champagne Charlies". —— was discovered in a flowered dressing gown of a thick, rich 'Nineties variety. I do not think his books produced that flowery aura of leisured dilettantism, nor the Tyrol etc. – Two penniless American wives ("——" and another) seemed to him I assume *enough poor wives* – with whom certainly he was obliged to pay his way. But —— paid it for him for a good stretch, until I grew to think of him as one of those wise literary men who had married money. – Then one fine day ——'s son (by an earlier husband) married a Jewish young lady (why I do not know, for she was ill-favoured and without cash). Alas, one day, shortly after

[1] The phrase was quoted by Giovanelli from an autobiographical work by the English writer in question, a contemporary of L.

this, ——'s new daughter-in-law made eyes at him, one is to assume. The next we heard was that the susceptible —— (——) had done a bunk – fouté le camp – with his son-in-law's wife, or his wife's daughter-in-law. He turned his back upon Great Britain and took his prize to New York. There in 1940 I came across him: —— was where he dwelt, under such very much less attractive conditions than with . . . as to be a little shocking. – So I suppose he *did* begin "paying his way" again. Of that necessity he typically makes a virtue. – He used to be like a nice dog – a handsome, a little fierce looking blue-eyed German dog. Curse him though for saying that about publisher's advances. What a silly babbling rat. . . .

With the two articles I sent you you are temporarily bogged down I suppose.[1] You see it is not (though people might say that) the penetrating quality of my psychological discernment. The matter is very simple as far as the U.S. goes. All the *good* literary papers are first-and-foremost political organs – organs of propaganda for intellectuals, financed in order to colour the young educated mind. And I have steadily refused to be first-and-foremost political. I am not interested in people or in situations because of their party bearing first-and-foremost (though very often in their political bearing). Not toeing any line, I am, in the eyes of a fanatical politician, in a political vacuum. (To this I perhaps should add that I have too good an understanding of politics to care for party – since adherence to a party means the end of political thinking, and I enjoy thinking politically and believe it is good for me).

For a writer like myself the horrible situation is this. The papers to which one is artistically attracted are all – like "The Partisan Review" – too partisan. Those not party-papers are apt to exist in a sort of dull, pietistic, discretely Tory limbo.

Lastly, there remains to be mentioned what an American catholic friend of mine refers to as "the Catholic Ghetto". You can go and live in that, of course, if a conversion obliges you to do so. Not many intelligent people read your books. Then the

[1] Giovanelli had offered to act as a kind of promoter-agent for L. in New York. The articles were "Is There an Intellectual?" and "The Rot." The latter, a part of *Rotting Hill*, appeared in the *Sewanee Review* for October–November 1949. The former was incorporated in Part I, Section A ("The Intellectual") of *Rude Assignment*.

catholics, like the communists (stalinist or trotskyite), have a great big dogmatic axe to grind. And what have I – anymore than Montaigne – to do with a great big dogmatic axe?

It was a blessed situation, when Joyce, Eliot, Hemingway, and myself began. The reference was in altogether different directions – towards scientific, or artistic, truth. There is no return to that: it was a utopian accident. – With wonderful good will and all your energy, you will find it less easy than you thought to place two unobjectionable articles. For the self-styled "partisan", *one* is "reactionary," not because from the standpoint of Rahv and Phillips[1] there is anything *wrong* with it, but because as it were there is not anything *right* with it: nothing *party*. My contention of course is this. Upon exactly the same footing as the scientist, the writer should be permitted to investigate and to aim at any objective (not a subjective) truth.* In that way, the best results, obviously, are obtained. Even I go further: that is the *only* method. Such a position, however, is unpopular. Even if I modified this, substituting: "That is the kind of truth that *interests me*", it would be no good either. Yet should you impose upon the scientist the kind of truth he *must* find, he would decline so to make the facts fit a preordained solution: that would not be research but concealment. – The *kind* of truth. Such is the issue. One is an adulterated truth, and is not worth having. That is the truth of the *partisan.* Yet the latter gent says *your* truth is *against* him, because it is not *for* him. Truth as I see it lies outside the *for* and the *against.*

For the "Sewanee" my "Is there an Intellectual" article was "too much on one side". What side is that? (There we have another sort of partisan). . . .

Oh – E.P. and you. From long experience I assure you that the above-mentioned great American poet and translator is one of the most tiresome idiots that ever stepped in some ways . . . . But his remarks re. ––––– I can explain. Formerly E.P. possessed a healthy disgust for the –––––'s. There is a smelly little fellow called ––––– however (. . .). E.P. wrote me to say "If you want to please your old Uncle Ezz" (such it is his habit to style himself) write something me deah Windhum for '–––––'". That is his . . . magazine, of which he sends me copies regularly. Never do I pick up a number without encountering the name of –––––. *Often* –––––

[1] Philip Rahv and William Phillips, editors of the *Partisan Review.*

is writing, with intent to advertise . . . the ——'s. So the ——'s are protegés of ——: —— is a highly valued supporter of E.P. That is the story.

More later. Blessings.

Yrs

W. L.

. . .

* Rahv has written that there is no "objectivity" – it is impossible – in politics. Meaning party politics – it goes without saying.

387. *To David Kahma*†   London. W. 11.
Feb. 27. 1948.

Dear Kahma. . . .

To come at once to the point re the typescript of your novel – batch one – just arrived. . . . I must without delay make a few remarks . . . which a publisher's reader would certainly make, or if the book ever got published in this form, the critics you would find would make with *brio*. . . .

Listen carefully. There is a new publisher (or a new partner) and I have friendly access to this firm. If you sent me anything like a saleable book I could get them to take it I think. It is an opportunity. – With this in mind, I feel justified in being frank.

To begin with, I read with satisfacton and pleasant anticipation the account of a naked brass-limbed Superman of the Comics who springs up trampling upon the faces of his wives, and then, after savage incantations and terrifying roars, plunges into a mountain lake. Eight other, less important, wives are preparing his breakfast. Delightful – as also his gazebo.

We then leave this exotic creature in his gazebo: and, oh! an essay begins, very boring by comparison, about Canadian culture, "Maria Chapdelaine" etc. Intense disillusion! Was I to believe that he of the double jack-knife dive and the he-man harem – who found it very difficult to speak or write English – was composing this tame essay on the cultural situation of Canada? – The book should begin p. 6. The "Chapdelaine" and other material (if retained) up to 6 become an "Advertisement to the Reader." I do not know enough of your plan to decide where best place for scene in the "palace" in the mountains, with Superman Doukobor.

P.3 I have 3 notes. *One* is "tiny minority *that* would transform U.K. etc." My note: No politics! – *Two* Better not say "writing for English public." – *Three*. Here (and throughout) refrain from coyness with reader. "I must still speak of books, if you will be patient for just a little longer." – There would be no need, of course, to keep apologising for not coming to the point, of giving them "a bit of action," if you separated this from the narrative.

I am one of those who believe that the less the author of a novel obtrudes himself into his narrative the better. The incessant garrulity and cosiness with "the Reader," of the XVIIIth and earlier XIXth century English novelists, is absent in the more intellectual French novelists (Stendhal or Flaubert). But heaven preserve me from getting between a man and his Public if he wants to be matey! Dont be *too* confidential, that is all!

P. 6. I have a note: "where I learned what little English I have etc." – This will be impossible to sustain. It would only irritate people. You must arrange that the "I" who tells the story has learned English perfectly somewhere.

Now you may, or may not, remember, what I said in an earlier letter about dialogue. But anyway, whatever you thought of that, you must *have* dialogue in a novel. (There is almost no dialogue in a late Henry James: but they are books of great elaboration and subtlety – you are not attempting that, and if you were, no agent would take on the job of selling it for you). As I survey the long solid paragraphs of prose, page after page – only broken on p. 24. for a few lines by dialogue, mostly the word *Da* – I feel considerable misgivings as to what will happen if I do not speak. Hundreds of solid pages of long paragraphs of unrelieved description, it is my belief, might quite well arrive, with only 10 lines of dialogue to every 50 pages, which would be insufficient to do what the earthworms do to the soil. . . .

You should invent a language for your Doukobor. Buy an English-Russian Conversation. Concoct a sort of Thieves slang of Russian and of American slang, Indian, and indeed anything you can think of. As to more orthodox Canadians, make them speak exactly as they do speak – do not *improve* or you ruin. – But shake up the stately massed battalions of your prose: get the fat off its bones. On the eighth page from where your narrative starts, *some* dialogue is a good thing, if its only "Please pass me the salt." For heavens sake describe a battle between Douks and those who dislike Douks, or between fishwives, or Chinese: or a Douk miscarriage in a street car. . . .

Having said all this, let me say how much I admired the swing and swagger of the opening scene in the palace, and how excellent the use of language is in detail throughout the narrative – about the mother and the earl for instance. (I expect noblemen did literally swarm out to Western Canada?) You do not have to be assailed with doubt on the score of your narrative ability, only, if I might say so, of the use to which you may put it, and the extent to which you are prepared to organise it. . . .

I shall be much freer now and I will answer a few of your many letters and cope with a few of the many problems they pose. . . . Much more then in a further epistle, which you may expect fairly soon.

Yrs

388. *To Ezra Pound*†   London. W. 11.
Feb. 28. 1948.

Dear Ezra. Your letter and enclosure gave me great pleasure. At the moment I was unable to answer properly as lawyers and publishers were on my chest, in my ears and navel and *surtout* in my hair. Having profitably dispersed of them I blow my nose and turn to you.[1] —— I will write for that production you sent me:[2] I like Williams's little article about Milton.[3] I think that our old friend T.S.E.'s business about Milton was merely a feature in his long build-up . . . . Like all these manoeuvres of our honoured colleague, this one was quite misunderstood – and *he*, forseeing that it would be taken as a serious literary contribution playfully miltonised all over the globe. It would be better of course if people took no notice of him. (alas Williams got quite worked up about

[1] L. had been in controversy over the publication of *America and Cosmic Man*.

[2] *Four Pages*, a new periodical pamphlet produced in Galveston, Texas, by Dallam Simpson, a disciple of Pound. Nothing by L. appeared in the subsequent numbers.

[3] William Carlos Williams, "With Forced Fingers Rude," *Four Pages*, February 1948. The article, taking up most of the number, is largely an attack on Eliot's new pronouncement on Milton, which he had just delivered in New York. See T. S. Eliot, *Milton* (London, [1948]).

Milton however!) – I will see if I can get worked up about something which I should like to make an exhibition of myself getting worked up about in public. I'm sure I can.

Why do all Americans without exception pretend that everything they do and have ever done and will ever do is for the *young*?¹ I am not worked up about this believe me, but somebody ought to be. Both Eliot and Carlos Williams writing about Milton speak as if art were a department of education.² Also il ya de l'idée du progres ladedans.

Looking out from that funny old place you've got yourself into you may notice that the world is in an extremely unsettled state. Will write you soon again.

Your

389. *To Mrs. Ezra Pound*†   London. W. 11.
29 Feb 1948

Dear Dorothy. Thank you for your nice letter. Recent weeks have been passed by me in a nightmare of desperate activity. I have for instance succeeded in extracting £50 costs from a publisher and other advantages: my American book³ should be at last appearing in about 3½ months time. My big volume bursts forth in the autumn⁴ – I struggle with proofs at this present moment. There is a shorter 60 thousand word critical book (literary)⁵ which should appear in 5 months. In June I have agreed to paint a portrait of

---

¹ Williams accuses Eliot of betraying our young poets by allowing them to read Milton. He argues that Milton would be a bad influence on the style of a young poet of today. In a letter of March 4th, Pound replied to L.'s jibe: "They wd/ de facto have to 'fr. the young' as the adult *pop*ulation is practically non-existent. As a Yourupeean you hv/ got the o. f° 'abit of pre-supposing an adult pubk or @ least an adult element in the goulash."
² Pound replied: "I hv/ ever held that a academic cock-shy has its uses. =but it shd/ of course cast back the cocoanuts – *re arising* in a long-since and monumented past you sd they wd/n't – and I that they wd/. & to carry on."
³ *America and Cosmic Man.*
⁴ Presumably *Rude Assignment*, which did not actually appear till November 1950.
⁵ Probably *The Writer and the Absolute*, which appeared in June 1952.

the musician Schnabel (is that the spelling?)[1] A busy year. Further, I restart (no. 4.) the "Enemy".[2] All this is well enough but there is a very great danger of war, it appears to me. Events have started to speed up again. I am not very easy in my mind about it. If anyone blows up a U.S. warship in the Mediterranean I shall be in the soup, for I thought we had say a couple of years without having to make plans. Because of my trade, or no-trade, war is hopeless for me, I have to withdraw if possible from the scene of its grimmest visitation. So much for me. —— That E.P. should plump up round the centre is natural:[3] though perhaps a little unbecoming, it is at least evidence that Uncle Sam is feeding him well. It is easily removed. When he is released, he can play a few dozen games of fives and he will be himself again. —— It pleased me to learn that you liked my "Barcelona". It belongs to the Tate, where it now hangs, in a very favourable position indeed, having the place of honour in one of the two small octagonal rooms. Ezra I did not see: perhaps he is travelling. They send the pictures on tour and all the galleries – indeed most of them – are not open. A large Chagall show is proceeding in 3 of the galleries – not at all my favourite artist. The great big childs colour-box pictures are coarse, repetitive, and often silly. I thought before I went that he was a barbaric slave analogue of Gauguin. I apologize to Gauguin. Best Wishes.

Your,
WYNDHAM LEWIS

390. *To David Kahma*†   London. W. 11.
March 14th 1948.

Dear Kahma. . . .

With regard to the text sent me so far: having liquidated that terrible first six pages about Canadian intellectuals etc. I would pass solid archai-homespun narrative* for 20 pages or so, if I knew that at last I should reach a spot where human speech would be heard again. The point was (hence my alarm) that a feeling crept over me, as page succeeded page, that you would be so

---

[1] The picture was never painted.
[2] This project was dropped.
[3] In her letter of February 2nd, Mrs. Pound reported that Pound was putting on weight because of lack of exercise.

enamoured of the rhythmic roll of the vocables that bore you easily along to the million-word mark and beyond, that there would be never more than a possible well-bred exchange of the compliments of the season between a Carrier Indian and (say) a Moldavian immigrant in search of a strayed cow. I see that my fears are groundless: I await your further progress with great interest.

As to *politics*. I referred only to the *politics* of these islands at the present moment. A savage Doukobor who tramples upon a carpet of naked wives as he springs to life in the morning, and the rest of it, is *not in character*, surely when he is giving one the benefit of his opinion (an exceedingly low one) regarding Mr. Atlee and Sir Stafford Cripps. Not only is it inartistic, it would excite hatred in the critic – in several cases, of those who eventually would review the book. If you feel strongly enough – therefore – by all means give expression. Otherwise............

No other politics barred, I think. It is quite all right now to say that Russia is less democratically governed than Switzerland.

As to Freud, use him or abuse him to your hearts content. Some not uninfluential people identify Freud in some ways with Marx. Except that both were Jewish, I cannot see how they can be pulled together. But not being a great fan of either, I am no judge of that.

Since the receipt of your last letter I have had no time at all to sit down and turn my attention to your critical stuff. Shall do so at the first opportunity that offers. It was a really horrible idea of yours to introduce a critical essay into the middle of your novel: you are assailed at times by the most terrible ideas. There should be some one on the spot to nip them in the bud. The reader would be asked to believe into the bargain that it was written by a wild Doukobor, seven feet high, how could scarcely speak English, and was as mad as a hatter. I was aghast. Reflect. If midway in 'The Sun Also Rises,' 'Sanctuary', 'Madame Bovary', or 'Pride and Prejudice', to take a few good novels, a big non-narrative lump had suddenly loomed up before the mystified but disgusted reader: a work of literary criticism, which he would have to wade through or clamber over before the narrative started up again! This is a *novel* that you have set out to write. . . .

All this must sound a little rough, reminiscent of your professors. But I take more interest in you than I expect those gentlemen did: I want you *to be strict with yourself*. You have I am sure, the goods. The Problem – to get the goods into the shop window. You seem disposed to crowd them all in at once.

Several times you have mentioned Kenneth Burke. 18 or 19 years ago I saw a little of him in New York[1] – had dinner, went to night spots and so on. He is a little, pinched, partly Jewish, fellow, whose books I have never seen, but have glanced at the odd article. I should never be interested in anything Burke wrote. – Do you make use of what he has written at all? If so, what line does he follow?

Please do not allow yourself to be in any way discouraged by my disciplinary exhortations. We shall I am sure have a fine book in the end. But you must avoid mere verbal inflation (which covers paper but nothing else). – I shall keep on like this, until we have our book! Best wishes.

W. L.

P.S. . . .

P.P.S. This letter held up (for air-mail envelopes). Mr. Truman just addressed the U.S. Congress.[2] That time-factor seems to be cropping up in my life again. My America book comes out in six weeks, for Whitsun: two other books – one a big one – this year. I am dogged by the dogs of War.

* Result of too literal a study of Defoe or xviii century writers.

391. *To Ezra Pound*†   London W. 11.
March 30. 1948.

Dear Ezz. Since all my time has been fully occupied writing 3.000 words for your memorial number none remained for correspondence. Probably the stuff arrived too late. I hope if you ever see it you wont disapprove of it too much. – No news this end – unless a sort of centenary volume that I have promised to write something for, celebrating Eliot's sixtieth birthday, is news. A book has appeared called "The Last of the Pre-Raphaelites," by a certain

---

[1] Probably during the time when Burke (b. 1897) was music critic for *The Dial*.

[2] President Truman's special message on the international crisis was delivered to the Joint Session of March 17th.

Douglas Goldring.¹ He was Hueffer's secretary in the English Review days. Of course Goldring has arranged Ford upon a suitable biographical pedestal: or so it appears for I have not read the book. This has turned the critical columns of the press, I am afraid, into a coconut-shy with Ford as the Aunt Sally. Goldring was obliged to confess for instance that his hero was an inveterate liar. It was impossible to disguise the fact that he was a social snob (more than half his departures from the truth involved with this fact). But seeing what England is in the matter of social snobbery, it is difficult to see how *one* snob more would make any difference. And I thought some reviewers need not have devoted all their space to his untruthfulness – his fabulous baronial estates in Prussia and his imaginary schooling at Eton – but have spoken of his doings as a critic. *That* they dismissed, however, with the statement that he attached too much importance to the young. Hueffer was never a favourite of mine: but several times in the past few weeks I have felt like providing an answer to their attacks.²
– In my article re. yourself I mentioned Hueffer....

A little hasty good wishes,

Yours
W. L.

P.S. In 4 or 5 weeks my book about the U.S.A. will be published. As it is something you know all about I shall not of course send you a copy.³ It is a fact, merely, of camaradish interest. I forgot to say that I will certainly do something for the outfit copy of which was sent me. I will just draw breath, do the bit about Eliot, for his centenary volume, then take up the 3 pages of "little mag" prose.

[1] Douglas Goldring, *The Last Pre-Raphaelite; a Record of the Life and Writings of Ford Madox Ford* (London, 1948). Issued in the U.S. as *Trained for Genius*.

[2] In his reply of April 6th, Pound wrote: "the old walrus hd/ his pts. and ∴ they kuss him."

[3] Pound replied: "as you hv seen *much* more of it in the past 40, than I hv. & as I njoyed 'I presume' so much – you send it on ... all you can tell is welcom. my iggurunce is VAST. & the no/ of writ^rs whom I *can* rd/ wthout nausea
 SO
 FEW
 ! !"

392. *To David Kahma*† London W. 11.
April 1st. 1948.

Dear Kahma. . . .

Keep in the back of your mind, of course, that the Doukobor represents a human maximum of revolt against social make believe and insincerity, and how, à l'état pûr, it is obvious he would provide a great *subject* for a work of art – such as the fathers-and-sons subject of the Karamazov. The clowning of the Douks about whom you write, and their disgusting habits, is a tragedy: it is how the epic of purity (of the Doukobor à l'état pûr) ends.

Lenin, for instance, was so it seems – a little man who believed in a society that was not *a State* – that had no government, or body of professional administrators, any more than a Swiss valley community. People would take it in turn to administer the Posts and Telegraphs, for instance. (All of which was good marxism). I am not expressing any opinion regarding Lenin's early theory: all I mean is that the violent military imperialism we all observe today is strangely unlike what we are told Lenin had originally in mind.

Returning once more to the subject of making the novel, you project a kind of Noah's Ark into which all your literary belongings will be crowded. I am glad that you have decided to leave some of them behind. It would be so remarkable if a Canadian wrote a good novel that I really think the world would be impressed: but this is the moment – tarry not, or people may have other things to think about. The publisher I have in mind might grow tired of publishing, etc. etc. etc.

. . . Good wishes.

393. *To David Kahma*† London W.11.
3 June. 1948.

Dear Kahma. The first piece of the novel has come: so let us get down to business. The story is like this, according to your letter. Superman, and his dazzling consort, are after a while assailed by the 'nameless' Many (in Parts ii and iii): mined, bombed, and we hope at length blown up. – Well and good. On the practical side – as a novel – you start with an enormous handicap, which is implicit in the nature of book. Human sympathy is not its strong suit (nor do you mean it to be): it is forbiddingly chilly. If the reader feels no sympathy for the characters, or interest in them, then the *narrative* factor obviously is immaterial. The wives are a herd of dummies, Constanzia gleams and glitters but is robotic, Stirk does not arouse sympathy or pity. To this you must add the handicap of comedy. All pleasant anticipation of that most inescapable result of *hubris* and such unutterable self-complacency is quite lost by the method Superman uses to cope with the bomb. (I refer to the fire-hose).

I am not saying you are wrong, in doing things that way. That is how you get most satisfaction out of it. Also it will relate your novel to the other things you have written. . . . And congratulations on the several scenes (where the Douk takes Stirk on his knee – where he lies in the lake smiling up at the Palace etc).

Are you trying to fool the Brit Public into believing there is a kind of Rider Haggard Superman up in the Kootenay Mountains? The Brits are terrible suckers but very rapidly some woman at the Canadian High Commissioner's Office in Whitehall who came from those parts would enlighten an inquisitive journalist. – Do not make your emperor and empress contemporary, is my first (and will probably be my last) reaction. Dont make Douk chat with his Harvard secretary about the Cominform and "Finnigan's Wake." Couldn't the time be in the 'Nineties? – This reaction was of course overwhelming until, as I read on, I concluded that you were saying to people: "The Kootenays are no more real (as they appear here) than Lilliput." That of course will not be as well received in Vancouver or New York as in Mayfair.

Now for technical details. Refering to your letter: you certainly must cut the *Vault scene*. You must make him talk to himself or *something*: people will not support the verbosity entailed by the locomotion of that hundred ton robot . . . .

Dialogue is apt to be wooden. This is very serious indeed. But it is easily remedied – for you are aiming at familiar naturalistic dialogue and any fool can write fairish dialogue as the ordinary mystery story proves. You suffer from being a little too grand and stiff – you must get a copy of "The Postman always Knocks Twice" or "The Sun Also Rises" and analyse the dialogue. – Good dialogue is always brief, like stage dialogue: *but* as the reader cannot see the speaker, you have continually to conjure up for him, by a "said Jack, thoughtfully picking his nose;" or answered Jill, slowly rubbing her button nose", the persons speaking. Or you bring your dialogue to life by writing: "They both looked and smiled, as 3 revolver shots crashed out in quick succession at the back of the apartment in the Lindsay Theatre. "'Nine-thirty' she said."*

. . . Then there is the use of words. You often write "The Doukobor boomed." Since the word "boomed" is in such vulgar use it is best to avoid it. And so on.

This is very outspoken: it is of much more use for me to follow that course than to wrap up my meaning. After all this is a trade, a metier, and you are trying your hand for the first time with these particular tools.

A little satire is a dangerous thing – if it is that. I do not like p. 62: "The muscles of her incomparable throat rippled divinely as she swallowed the coffee." The *incomparable throat* sounds like advertisement language. Muscles always "ripple." Can no other word be found for what they do, just to make a change? As to *divinely*, is not that needlessly enthusiastic on the part of the author? (No objection otherwise). . . .

Yrs.

W. L.

* Bit of factual stuff. Happens every evening in our apartment, when we are at home.

W. L.

Supplement No. 1.
I have given much thought and attention to what you sent me. These four pages are an insignificant outcome, certainly. I have more to say. – You are not writing a novel. You are adding a dramatic prose work to your stock (not, I hope, to your gallery of unpublished works). It was my idea that by means of a semi-autobiographical novel – if you could bring yourself to that – that you had, now, while you are still young, a chance of breaking into the publishing world. But it would have had to have been as easy to read as 'A Journey to a War' – or at least as 'The Portrait of the Artist': and you must remember that Joyce was favoured somewhat by the political situation of the time: he was Irish – he wrote of Ireland: and even so, in spite of his great gift, it was touch and go.

When I had read half of the typescript you sent me, however, it became clear that that was not how you would, or perhaps could, go about it: you would not meet the public three-quarters of the way, but preferred to summon the public *to you*. You may be taking exactly the course that is most likely to secure your acceptance by a publisher and recognition. This I say seriously, being defective in the business sense. Above all, I do not wish, if you are unsuccessful, to be held responsible. You seem to have a great inclination for the type of thing you are doing: better to let nature take its course, and for me to confine myself to making severely critical (but very useful) observations about details of the stuff you send me as you go along. . . .

W. L.

394. *To Geoffrey Stone*†   London. W. 11.
12 June. 1948.

Dear Stone. . . .

. . . – Have you changed your allegiance in the election preliminaries? Everybody here thinks you are going to have Vandenberg as President. My publisher has commissioned a life of V. so sure is he.

As regards Taft, your choice, he is the most isolationist politician of any prominence in the U.S. As a European my reactions to that should naturally be *that* having eagerly encouraged England to go to war, having subsequently laid in rubble the cities of Europe with fortresses: then – at Yalta etc – arranged for an iron-curtain to hang right across the centre of it (and the other things that go with that, such as servitude of the states on the wrong side of the curtain) it is incomprehensible then to withdraw, and act as if this were 1898, or even 1939. That is what I should say as a European: but I do not think there is any Europe any longer. So I should have a twinge, a deep twinge and say something quite different. Taft however would not appeal to me. I should vote for Harry Truman – described as "Rotarian Caesar" in my book.[1] His false teeth always on view are *truer* than anyone elses I can espy. I prefer that rotarian smile to more complicated grimaces.

I am not in the best of moods: I backed a horse in the Derby and it was not even placed. I am still sore about it. I did not know what now I have learned: namely (1) that only French horses can

[1] *America and Cosmic Man.*

win in such a race, because English horses (like us) get scant and inferior food: (2) that the Aga Khan, the Maharaja of Baroda, and a French man called Volterra . . . juggle the order of arrivals at the winning post to suit themselves. Thus *My Love* at 100 to 8, came in first.[1] My horse was English: like me, the poor beast was underfed (and all the newspapers admit that is why our poor old nags pant along at the tale of the Parlayvoos) and I lost my money. A whole battalion of French horses is being flown over for Ascot.

. . . – When is your book appearing?[2] I shall no doubt be able to get it out of the library here, if it is Sheed and Ward. You know what my limitations are when it comes to matters mystical. – You are no longer by language, but are you by faith cut off from André Gide. If not, a glance at his Journals might be worth while. But there is a book – a novel – that you would not be likely to hear of: "Cefalu".[3] It was published here in the autumn (*Poetry London* – publishers). It is the best book I have seen for a long time. Tells of the Minotaur – Cefalu is in Crete. A tourist ship – the tourists visit the Labyrinth and lose themselves in it. They hear a roar – it is the M –! . . . The author's name, I forgot to say, is Durrell. He is young – was in Greece for some time, and at present is British Consul (or vice-consul?) somewhere in Mexico.[4]

Our best remembrances and wishes to the family circle.

Yours ever

P.S. Here is a cutting about Ascot – factual stuff you know, and testimony showing I am no romancer. Ascot, I should perhaps say, is – or was – the climax of the racing season. "Royal Ascot" – the "Derby" at Epsom an institution for the multitude. But you may be well versed in matters Britannic. I have learnt to take nothing for granted, however.

[1] My Love, who won the Derby on June 5th, was owned by the Aga Khan and Leon Volterra, a French movie magnate. The second horse was also owned by Volterra and the third by the Aga Khan.

[2] *Melville*, a study of the novelist, was published in New York by Sheed and Ward in 1949.

[3] Lawrence Durrell, *Cefalû* (London, 1948).

[4] L. seems to be under a misapprehension; there is no record of Durrell's having been with the foreign service in Mexico.

Perhaps the liveliest controversy arising from Lewis's activities as art critic for The Listener *began with his review of the Courtauld Memorial Exhibition at the Tate Gallery. (See* The Listener, *June 10th, 1948, p. 944.) Among the pictures on display was Seurat's* Une Baignade, *which Lewis condemned as a "dull, monotonous expanse." In a letter printed the following week, Ralph Edwards (b. 1894), then Keeper in the Department of Woodwork at the Victoria and Albert Museum, averred that Herbert Read had in a recent* Listener *proclaimed* Une Baignade *a masterpiece. Edwards deplored the lack of common standards among critics. Lewis's reply to Edwards appeared in the issue of the 24th, along with new entries in the controversy. In his letter Lewis pointed to the increasing complexity of the situation in the fine arts "ever since the clear-cut battle of the romantics and classicists." His chief new attacker, A. C. Sewter, currently Senior Lecturer in the History of Art at the University of Manchester, accused Edwards of taking too seriously the reactions of "an average art critic of the daily and weekly papers." Art criticism, he said, had become completely separated from art history and from the philosophy of aesthetics.*

395. *To the Editor of "The Listener," July 1, 1948*

London. W.11.

STANDARDS IN ART CRITICISM

Sir, – Mr. Sewter begins and ends upon a personally offensive note. I will inspect such argument as is to be discovered in between. No *sincere* expression of other than the deepest admiration for 'Une Baignade' is possible – all that is settled once and for all. Such is Mr. Sewter's position. But Seurat died in 1891 at the age of thirty-one: 'Une Baignade' was exhibited in 1884 – not 1684. Every art movement, for a century or so, as it has rapidly given place to the next, has furnished its quota of 'masters' and 'masterpieces' for great 'art-historians' and 'aesthetic philosophers' like Mr. Sewter, Neo-impressionism with the rest. Nothing could be less selective. There is no experiment that is not, after the lapse of a few decades – or sooner – canonised. For these philosophies of Mr. Sewter's are, in fact, of the creative-evolutionary type, with a cult of something-in-the-making. Today the nineteenth-century notion of progress has been generally repudiated. In the arts, however, the glorification of *means* is still operative – if in the main retrospectively.

That such values as those Mr. Sewter would reserve for Seurat are so eternally fixed, is untrue, even as that regards the estimates and mental habits – bad as they are – of the contemporary mind. Values have shifted a great deal with regard to Gauguin, and now Van Gogh is in process of revaluation. Seurat is surely not under a glass case. He perpetuated all that Impressionism absorbed from the photograph, especially in his earliest work: and in his 'divisionism' he consummated in the most absolute fashion the typically nineteenth-century *mésalliance* of art and science.

For the rest, there is the not especially edifying spectacle of Mr. Sewter, in a vulgar jeering way, exulting over the press 'expert', so inferior in knowledge to himself (Assistant Director at the Barber Institute[1]). The grotesque insufficiency of the press 'Art Critic', it may be as well to remind this strangely boastful official, is something that the artist, too often its victim, with better right than a mere rampant bookworm, has denounced. Yet were the Barber Institute (to take that as a compliment to Mr. Sewter) and the famous 'Fogg Factory' in Boston to train and supply all Art Critics, here and in the United States, the result would be terrible. Subsequently, no doubt, schools and museums would ask for one of these Barber's blocks (so to speak) or Fogg robots. Indeed already in the United States many provincial museums and institutes have Fogg curators. In conclusion. As to Mr. Sewter's personal offensiveness, it has, in my ears, a familiar ring. In origin, like most personal offensiveness, it is personal, and irrelevant.

Yours, etc.

WYNDHAM LEWIS

396. *To David Kahma*† London. W. 11.
July 3rd. 1948.

Dear Kharma. . . .

Again, as you see, you are shoving the responsibility for this book upon my shoulders. I will not for a moment take the responsibility for what you are doing. You may write a very successful book indeed upon the lines you have selected – but *you* must write

[1] In Manchester.

it. I cannot hold your hand. No good book was ever written that way. You are not a student writing a thesis. You are a great big hairy man: you must sit down at your typewriter and wrestle with your big book. – To speak earnestly and dont ask me to say it too often, I can help you no more *at this stage*. In your letters to me you may discuss points (not in too great detail). I shall read no more text till you have finished.

Finally, your disingenuous account of how you believed you were beginning a novel like *Barchester Towers* or *Farewell to Arms* has for me the charm of the unfamiliar: as also when you declare yourself unable to understand the term "novel" etc. etc.[1] – The fact is, of course, that *my* plan did not appeal to you.... It is of not the faintest importance: you may have the better idea of how to launch Kharma upon the world. My offer is still there to hand it personally to a publisher (unless you take so long that this chap has spent all his money!)....

Then you must not have a great deal of jaw (which leads nowhere, except to what can be read in any account of the Douks). And there is *no action*. No love – no homicide – no death – no suicide – no earthquake – no dénouement of any sort. All you have in that way is birth, which occurs in the first few pages. Nobody loves anyone, or hates anyone, no one wants to make a fortune, or sleep with a woman. It is because it is *about* nothing, that one gets the feeling of a lot of people walking about (or posing for the spectator) and engaging in polite conversation. If you could read "La Condition Humaine" by Malraux, or some pure action book, it would perhaps help. – I must get this into the letter-box.

Yrs.
W. L.

[1] In another version of this letter, L. challenged a third aspect of Kahma's defence of his novel: "There is a thing called an argumentum ad hominem: this does not quite apply but in discussing the novel to drag in *my* novels – however flatteringly – and as a kind of walloping trump in the way you did, is a breach of the rules! However, I agree that the atmosphere of predestination in 'Tarr' – the obvious purpose of the Schicksaal – precludes suspense."

397. To the Editor of "The Listener," July 8, 1948

London. W.11.

STANDARDS IN ART CRITICISM

Sir, – Reading this correspondence, Miss Porter's mind has strayed to other levelments than those that would supervene were Mr. Read, myself, and everybody else to reach on all occasions identical judgment about pictures.[1] I made use of the term 'standardisation': in imagination it led her off imperiously to the food-queue and to where 'utility' garments are displayed. 'Standardisation, as we ... are rapidly coming to know ... reduces all life to the lowest level, and results in the abandonment of standards.' So you see, the decay of genteel standards, which Miss Porter attributes to standardisation, she confuses with the relationship of the cultural standardisation necessarily ensuing upon the establishment of a fixed rule, or canon. She is mixing up, so to speak, the Parthenon Frieze with her clothes coupons.

Where Miss Porter speaks of changeless and fundamental qualities, persisting, and providing the obvious nucleus of a universal criterion, she is correct. But where she goes on to use the words 'without in any way affecting the development of ideas ... of successive generations', she forgets how the twentieth-century art-scene has been one of extreme revolution – not one of people quietly 'developing their ideas', watched over by the Eternal Verities. Finally: standardisation is desirable or the reverse according to the quality of the standard. Of course there are standards. I was astonished by Miss Porter's assumption that I had denied this. What is more, personally I should much prefer on principle a generally recognized rule; but not today.

Yours, etc.,

WYNDHAM LEWIS

[1] In a letter printed the preceding week, Margery Porter, writing from Edinburgh, accused L. of regarding standards in art as being synonymous with standardisation. She insisted on certain fundamental qualities – such as construction, rhythm, and balance – "which persist throughout the centuries."

398. *To Geoffrey Stone*†   London. W. 11.
14 July. 1948.

Dear Stone. Well I'm damned! You have circled round me and made your appearance where I least should have expected to find you, cheek by jowl with Tito.¹ However, there you are and I hope you enjoy the Siberian winds in the Austrian valleys more than I enjoy them on this misbegotten damp old island. For we freeze: and it never stops blowing. Get as far south as you can, it is going to be a ghastly summer.

The romantic hill country in the extreme south of Italy, Calabria, a profusion of ruins and bits of old Greek cities, would be attractive and might be warm. Friends have given me alluring accounts of the Abruzzi: but that is not a place to visit with a family. I should pass the time in Rome. But Berlin is one of the most *comfortable* places in Europe, apparently, for an American, with wonderful restaurants, yacht-clubs, swimming pools etc. . . .

Next the Roll Mix. The Parcel you sent before leaving arrived in good time. The bread it enables us to make spares in certain measure what everyone suffers from most in England: aggravated forms of constipation. I find if I eat your bread 4 days running I function as smoothly as possible for I am not of the constipated kind; but two days of British bread and I am back again where I was before. One has to take Glauber Salts or something to expel the bran. – These filthy conditions make it impossible to write a letter without touching on the clinical. Europe as you see is dying, it has committed suicide, and we the cells of which it is composed have all this thrust upon us.

Whether it be the constant cold and rain, or a little two-tooth dental plate, a thundering toothache fills my head with pain. This may mean a revolution: I trust it will depart, for it is the tooth to which my plate is anchored. For some days I have been working with this ache. I had a letter to answer yesterday for instance in the "Listener", a man who had called me a savage cat. My ache made me feel so like that wild cat I was described as being. The "Listener" articles, by the way, are about pictures, not books, and I only do them occasionally.

---

¹ Stone and his family had left the U.S. He wrote from Austria, where they were temporarily settled.

... – Poor Harry Truman, to the accompaniment of half-hearted shrieks of tepid joy, will I assume become democratic nominee. The subsequent November election will be dull since a foregone conclusion. Quite apart from Dewey's face, what he *does* when he mounts the throne may be interesting. The U.S. has not of late had so physically energetic and alert a President as Dewey will be. – But my tooth is beginning to ache at the thought of the strenuousness. I hope this letter reaches you safely.

Yrs como sempre

W. L.

399. *To the Editor of "The Listener," July* 15, 1948

London. W.11.

STANDARDS IN ART CRITICISM

Sir, – Mr. Sewter takes eighteen lines to protest that he is quite untouched by what he describes as a vicious attack by a wild cat (namely my last letter – a very savage piece of work you will, I am sure, agree!).[1] I occupy, unfortunately, so much more of Mr. Sewter's field of vision than does Seurat. Again, he states, although he knows this to be inaccurate, that my view of Seurat is 'merely personal'. He is the kind of person who soon would bring any argument to the Tweedledum and Tweedledee stage. So he has growled (with a grimace of heavy insouciance reaching for my imaginary tail) – 'Nohow!' Instead of making the appropriate answer, I signify that as far as I am concerned the correspondence ends.

But Seurat is a subject of far more interest than Sewter; let me add a few remarks for the reading public. If 'Une Baignade' or 'La Grande Jatte' appear 'architectural', or seem to introduce design once more into painting, it is largely because Seurat built up his pictures as it were with a lot of little bricks (namely the

[1] L. is replying to a letter by Sewter (answering his of the 1st) which appeared in *The Listener* on July 8th. Sewter declared himself not terrified by L.'s behaviour, which he compared to that of a "bad-tempered cat," with "savagely arched back and quivering tail." He went on to explain his position as not advocating "eternally fixed" values, but as respecting "the historical view" of art over L.'s "merely personal subjective reaction."

dots of the *pointilliste* technique). Everything came to look more rigorous and less haphazard: he had frozen impressionism into his formula, imprisoned its untidy freedom in a net of dots. Yet 'Une Baignade', as a picture-postcard, uncoloured, would pass for a photograph. There is no new factor of 'architecture' or 'composition' there – less so than is to be found in Degas. The fact that in this early work Seurat still in the main used the old earthen palette contributes to its dullness. But a big, bald, unbeautiful picture is a big, bald, unbeautiful picture, whatever part it may play in the professional life of the art-history pundit: in this case a picture so unprepossessing that even Miss Porter and Mr. Sewter admit to feeling, in spite of History, small attraction for it.[1]

WYNDHAM LEWIS

400. *To Ezra Pound*† London. W. 11.
July 20th 1948.

My dear Ezz. The writing (and reading) you would have me do is impossible.[2] It takes me all my time to keep alive. I have none on my hands at all. Eliot however – who is over in the States, someone told me, but no matter – has more time than I have by far. . . .

Meanwhile my American book is announced for publication July 26. Other books will drift out I expect this year – if there is not another war. In the latter case you are in a much better position than I am. Indeed a so much better position that there is no comparison. I should be locked up in this island, with hardly any means of earning a living, with practically no food I could eat, with a variety of disgusting missiles raining down (if the place was not actually invaded) and this would last indefinitely. However, if war holds off another 12 months, a few books will be published.

In speaking of your situation in this unceremonious way, understand that mine is quite respectably unpleasant, because of the

[1] Sewter wrote of *Une Baignade*: ". . . masterpiece though it is, I don't like it either."

[2] In Pound's most recent letter, he recommended a number of readings on economics: "Dizzy on Bentinck," Brooks Adams, Kitson. He also wanted L. to read Frobenius and to write about him.

awful state this country is in. But I never take your incarceration for granted. A petition ought to be started up at the proper moment: say next April.

Yours,
W. L.

401. *To David Kahma*†　　　　　　　　　　London. W. 11.
　　　　　　　　　　　　　　　　　　　　　　　26 July 1948.
Dear Khama. . . .

I was glad you had resolved to pound out the rest of the volume and to work hard at it. "For Whom the Bells Toll" was not mentioned by me, was it? It is Hemingway's first *bad* book. I am sure I should not suggest your reading that when "Farewell to Arms" is equally easy to obtain. But you know without my telling you why people read a fiction book: it is the story, the writer interests them in the destiny of an individual, or several, and there is what is called an *action*: the will, the desires, of this individual, or this group, are exposed to a variety of obstructions, which they duly overcome. If it is a very sad book, they do *not*. But the reader must personally care what happens to them and mimetically identify himself with one or other.

What you say about *action alone* – if such a thing were possible, action by robots – is perfectly true. It would interest no one. I said as much regarding the empty gymnastics of your Superman. (It was my duty to tell you that). Malraux's books are full of violence, in France he has had an immense public. *activism* does not appeal to me: I was indicating one of the factors that make for success. Also, Malraux tells a story, which progresses to a climax. But I mentioned Hemingway as a master of realistic dialogue. After the publication of "The Sun Also Rises" he asked me if he had got the dialogue all right where the English lady-of-fashion was concerned (I forget the name – was it Brett?) he did not feel quite confident about it. But there was no occasion for anxiety. He has a wonderful memory and ear. To study his handling of dialogue is especially useful to you because he like yourself is an American.

At this stage you perhaps should ask yourself, however, what you consider most deserving of labouring upon. Hemingway, of whom we have been speaking, while still extremely young got into an immense war, in shock-troops, was wounded, and turned all that into a novel, rather on folk art lines. Tolstoy as a young man was at Sebastopol: probably if he had not been in the Russian bastions facing Disraeli's expeditionary force no inky canonballs at an imaginary Borodino would ever have been discharged in "War and Peace". What is the subject-matter of Flaubert? The *bourgeois*. It ate him up – it was his dragon. Of James Joyce? Ireland, of course, his love – like Dante's Beatrice. I do not say that all writers are obsessed – do not make me say that. But you appear to be peculiarly in a void. Yet I am positive that staring you in the face – or gnawing at your vitals – there is something or other which ought in fact to be the subject of any book you write.

. . . – Let me know how you progress, and when we may expect the whole work.
              Best wishes.
                W. L.

402. *To Augustus John*[†]   London. W. 11.
               17 Aug. 1948.

Dear John. By all means make use of both the letter and the poem. I should be very pleased and flattered to find them in your autobiography.[1] The poem is not really so disgustingly bad as I feared it might be. As to the letter, it can be used intact, except I should like you to do this. When you arrive at the word "familiar", 5 lines from bottom of page 1, you will be obliged to put several dots, my illegible hand at that time making this necessary. Will you *go on* and omit the words that follow, namely "what world, however ideal, what world would be, indeed, poetic, without the rooster and his dunghill – planked in the midst of the story of Christ." When we are all dead they will stick the words back again no doubt. The omission removes a blemish from the text. The trouble is that I never looked at the "story of Christ" after I was 7 years old. It remained the snow-white spiritual clinic of the kindergarten.

 No wonder you cannot decipher my letters. I cannot begin to do

[1] Neither of the items which John asked permission to use appeared in *Chiaroscuro*. The letter, dated "1914?," appears on p. 64 of this book. L. reproduced the poem, written when he was still at the Slade, in *Rude Assignment*, p. 116.

so myself. When my mother died a good many came into my possession. They were not only badly written but some of an unbelievable immaturity. Ah well. You mention my American book. I should have sent it you but somehow felt the western hemisphere was not your glass of coca-cola. . . . – I may add that the book is going to be very scurvily treated – because the press has shrunk to a few sheets, and every prominent position is controlled or occupied by an enemy. . . .

Before world war ii I could manage to live. At Whiteley's I would buy excellent French wine for 2/9 or 3/- a bottle, quite drinkable for less. Once I had a superb brandy for far less than the cost of a *half a bottle* of gin today. A good shirt could be had for 10/- or 12/-: but I need not recall in detail all the advantages of that wonderful period. I could live like a prince without great expense – all but the spangles, gilt, the etiquette, in which I am not at all interested. I could go to mountains if I wanted to, to America, China: I had the same freedom of displacement as a present-day socialist M.P. It was time for a man who had no need to prostitute his mind, or become a crook, and to get rich. . . . – But *now*! what a different story. I can make no more money I find – if as much – as in 1939. But 100 pounds is in fact only 30 or 40 pounds. . . . What I do is to eliminate every expenditure outside of food and cigarettes and the odd bottle of gin, and I shall wear the clothes I have until they drop off my back. – What an awful letter to have to write! But there it is. – What are you doing with yourself outside of literary labours? . . .

Yours ever,
WYNDHAM LEWIS

403. *To Kenneth Allott*†[1] [London]
18 Aug. 1948

Dear Mr. Allott. Thank you for your letter. It pleased me so much where you said you were puzzled I did not write any more verse.

[1] Kenneth Allott, currently Senior Lecturer in English at the University of Liverpool, was in correspondence with L. regarding selections from *One-Way Song* which were to be included in Allott's *Penguin Book of Contemporary Verse* (Harmondsworth, 1950). L.'s reply of August 18th was actually redrafted and sent on August 25th, but the first version is the more interesting.

I wish you could print that remark somewhere (and let me know the place): it would displease someone so much, who was snooty about my Song. – I should have worked on it a great deal. As it is it carries too much easy rhetoric, and the passages such as those you picked – which were all right – are compromised. That any fool could see; and as soon as I have a week or two to spare at least I shall be able to chop away, if I cannot do much new building. . . .[1]

Yours sincerely,

404. *To Geoffrey Stone*†   London. W. 11.
Sept. 21. 1948.

My Dear Stone. So that is where you are![2] It is tantalising to think of your relative nearness, for it would please me greatly to see you again. When this letter arrives you should be just about back from Rome. When you write next I hope you will tell me about that city. – which I should like to see before it is banged about in the next idiot war: to be shown where the Senate stood, the Forum, the slums between the hills, and have traced out for me by some guide-book the limits of the antique city while still a republic. What you say you feel about Florence I think I should feel too, as a place of residence: that it was a little cold and colourless. I would rather live in Venice, stinks and all.

It is a pity you lost the copies of the "Listener", the finale was superb. Having called me a wild cat Prof. Sewter withdrew, but Edwards became so enraged at my last letter in which I unmasked him, that he lost his head completely . . . .[3]

Tomorrow I will send you a copy of my American book. . . . The Presidents I discuss you would see with a very different eye – I will not say tory, for you are not that, but traditional. (The man who can support Taft . . . ! But perhaps that was just a *cranerie*, or a contrariness). And my "cosmic man" will probably give you a pain in the neck. You must remind yourself that what I recommend is a matter of expediency only – of necessity, I think – not

[1] L. never achieved this proposed revision.
[2] Stone wrote from Fiesole.
[3] L. refers to his letter of July 22nd (not included here) in the "Standards in Art" controversy and to Ralph Edwards's reply the following week.

what I should myself enjoy. The choice to my mind is a black one, between (1) cosmic or universal man: or (2) no man at all. The earth is too small to sustain all the old romantic tribal and national identities.

In the same way my liberalism is, in the XXth century a question of *force majeure*. Social justice must be practised very actively, if the world is not to be gobbled up by communism. – My historical chapters – very superficial of course, but I believe the correct approach – may interest you a little. About the religions of the U.S. I am silent. That would be a separate and independent study.

It is a wonderfully tempting suggestion that Froanna and I should spend a short holiday in your Fiesole flat a little later on. ... Are your surroundings, I wonder, making an impression on you of obsessive kind, as so often has been the case, especially with British and American: or do you find that your dogmatic, religious, preoccupations insulate? The Renaissance is the most pagan thing that ever happened – a re-birth of *paganism*, destroying or secularising the mysticism from which it was a "liberation". How does it feel to be surrounded by masterworks of great power of that most anti-dogmatic era? A puzzling situation, regarded from outside. ...

Yrs.
WYNDHAM LEWIS

405. *To Geoffrey Stone*†[1]   [ca. Oct. 1948]

Very dear Geoffrey Stone. Forgive the time this copy has taken to make its way to you. It has been for weeks on top of my desk ready to entrain: but it is with undiminished apprehension I finally dispatch it. For it is about your Mother. – I should prefer you not to read it. Just put it aside, and read instead the "Federalist" & the "Leaves of Grass".

[1] This message was written to accompany a copy of *America and Cosmic Man*.

406. *To David Low*†¹ London. W. 11.
1st Oct. 1948.

My dear Low. It is very kind of you to allow me to use the drawings, and those you selected were precisely what I wanted.² – Dryden described the satirist as flying over his victims and dropping "molten iron" upon them. I do not know what the correct image would be for your satire, but it would be far more insidious and equally destructive. It is more destructive, I think, by far than the fantastic variety – like Will Dyson³ – which would do very little damage. The subject, at all events – which I discuss in my book – is full of interest. Every politician worth his salt should possess a discriminating knowledge of the potency of the cartoon. – Well, really thank you tremendously.

Yrs,
WYNDHAM LEWIS

407. *To Keidrych Rhys*†⁴ London W. 11.
9th Oct. 1948.

My dear Rhys. It was good news indeed that you like my massive vignette well enough to take it off right away to the printers. . . .

An exhibition at the Redfern Gallery, Cork Str., which opened Oct. 5, is *unusually* good. The artist is Ceri Richards, whose work you know. These pictures, I am told, are a great advance: but it seems the better he gets the more difficult his pictures are to sell. The woman at the Gallery was wringing her hands over "poor

---

¹ L. had written to David Low (b. 1891) asking him to select some of his cartoons for reproduction in *Rude Assignment*. The subjects suggested in this letter are treated at length in the book.

² Of these L. chose one depicting Neville Chamberlain. It appears opposite p. 64 of *Rude Assignment*.

³ Will Dyson (1880–1938), the celebrated Australian-born cartoonist of the *Daily Herald*, worked first in London for *The New Age*.

⁴ Keidrych Rhys (b. 1915), the founder and editor of *Wales*, and his wife, the poet Lynette Roberts, were among the people in and around London with whom L. became friendly after the war. When Rhys asked him to write for *Wales*, L. submitted "The Rot," which appeared in the November 1948 number of the review.

Ceri". I have provided him with a big puff in the "Listener".[1] This I will send you when it appears. I tell you of this because I thought you might like to ask him for some photographs. He is far and away the best of the younger painters – with, perhaps Colquhoun. But that Scottish piece of stiff solemnity, when he is not imitating Picasso does often pictures of Scottish peasant women of which Richards would be artistically incapable. He is too fine an artist.

Yrs.
WYNDHAM LEWIS

408. *To David Kahma*†   London. W. 11.
Oct 9th 1948.

Dear Kharma. This again is no lengthy epistle. It is most kind of your wife and you to be concerned about my health. Happily for the present I am all right, the trouble having been surmounted. The Frenchman who said "La santé, c'est un état précaire, qui ne presage rien de bon," was a sensible man. . . .

When next I hear from you I hope your letter will be full of Doukobor lore and that you will tell me how the Douks have palaces, hangars full of private planes, a port packed with steam yachts, a private railway system with a stable-full of locomotives. I hope also you will report the early completion of your book. . . .

I am sending you a copy of my American book, not because it can be of much interest to you, since it is about things with which you are familiar, and a good deal of it is merely information, easily digestible for the English public – not for that, but because if I do not send it, you may be seeing notices, your curiosity be aroused, and it might seem unfriendly of me *not* to have mailed you a copy. This week, for example, there is a three and a half column notice in the "Times Literary Supplement",[2] which is all attack. It was written by Raymond Mortimer – an old Bloomsbury

---

[1] L. praises Ceri Richards (b. 1903) highly in "Round the London Art Exhibitions" in *The Listener* for October 14th.

[2] This review of *America and Cosmic Man* appeared in *The Times Literary Supplement* for October 2nd. L. wrote an angry rejoinder, which was printed in *TLS* for October 16th; three weeks later the reviewer replied to L. in the same columns.

... who is responsible for many of the big reviews in that paper....

It is the anonymity that is particularly troublesome. They appear as portentously learned little pundits – after a visit to the London Library or Brit. Museum. Whereas, if such an article were signed Raymond Mortimer, everyone knowing that his acquaintance with American history is probably no more than you could put in a thimble, would smile. He could be answered as he should be.

Were I to give you a list of all the things to which I am obliged to attend, such as this review – and one or two are far more serious than this – you would understand why I am at this particular moment a bad correspondent. But I follow with the interest of a serial-reader the fate of the poor lady who has just lost her job. Will she get another one? Or will she cut the cats throat and gas herself? I am jocular. But of course I am really awfully sorry for her, after what you have told me....

Yrs.
W. L.

. . .

409. *To D. D. Paige*†   London. W. 11.
                                                      Oct. 14. 1948.

Dear Paige. Enclosed are copies of 12 E.P. letters.[1] About as many again will follow some time soon....

Are you staying in Italy for the winter? I supposed you would be back in the U.S. by now. Advise me please a week or so beforehand when you *do* return to America, otherwise I might send off a packet of letters. They are not the originals, it is true, but it would be a minor disaster were even copies to be lost, since E.P.'s text requires a great deal of attention on part of typist. When he writes (facetiously) "Muster", say for "Mister", or "Musterd" for Mustard", the eye is very apt to neglect so small a departure

[1] Paige was now embarked on his edition of *The Letters of Ezra Pound: 1907–1941*. He had written to L. asking for copies of any letters from Pound he had kept. Of the transcripts L. sent, Paige included ten letters in the book.

from the norm: or time is wasted deciding whether it is a typing error or a *Witz*. . . .

Sincerely,
WYNDHAM LEWIS

. . .

[Excerpts from L.'s NOTES which accompanied the Pound letters.]

. . . – You will remark in these very early letters the germ of his subsequent extravagant jerkiness. It grows on him rapidly towards 1919 and 1920. (same paragraph). "(sent to sure to Miss E. Pound."[1] is how it is in text. – I am going carefully through these letters, checking line by line. In future I will not comment on such anomalies. You may take it is found in E.P.'s text. . . .

The letter F (in my typing) you will sometimes find levitating above the line, at other times attempting to escape in a downward plunge, only its top curl visible. Apologies. . . .

(p. 16.) As you will perceive he is rereading *Blast* (review – magenta coloured – I did in 1914–1915). Attempts – periodically would do so – to stimulate me to restart "Blast". "Robert" is Bob Macalmon (!) and "Gawge" is George Antheil.[2] . . .

E.P.'s attitude always that of responsibility for the intellectual brood – "scolding old hen" etc. He once wrote that certain people (meaning Eliot and myself) looked upon him as a "bon vieux papa bourgeois": This was absurd, for it was he who insisted on looking upon himself in this way: p. 21. A few months ago (1948) E.P. wrote a very similar letter to this.[3] Had I read Marx etc. – a few more. – The article in *Time and Tide* to which he refers he ought to have realized was policy: for of course I understand Social Credit as well as he does. I do not believe it can *do* anything and is in fact a little silly. Have no wish to read more economics – have something better to do. However many times I say this he returns to the charge. All this of interest to you and I believe to literary posterity. Reveals character of this great poet. . . . He is a pig-headed dominy, but a benevolent one. – Forgive me for these criticial observations: but letters demand some comments. . . .

[1] See *The Letters*, p. 118. [2] See *The Letters*, p. 190.
[3] The letter L. is commenting on was presumably omitted by Paige.

410. *To Felix Giovanelli*† [London]
Monday. Oct 18 1948.

Dear Gio. . . .

Let us deal with points one by one.[1] . . .

(3) *Photo.* – Quite right – one on book-jacket hideous and silly. . . . – The pipe, as you know, I acquired in order to suggest Englishness. Otherwise I turn out *Americano del norte* – of the educational "doctor" class. So I am told.

(4) *Postscript to book*: – Of course should be altered. If Dewey is there, would push him in. He is a stiff little guy but he will keep down crime of the simple kind, homicide and petty theft – and *no man* can keep down the other sort.

(5) *Preface.* – A "delicate matter", as you say. It is I suppose desireable not to give the impression (to a Doubleday-shop-public) that this is a *left* book: a kind of Henry Wallace view of things. Yet I am afraid no rightist writer (Pegler por ejemplo!) would be available. – Burnham is no use: my dear friend Rebecca Citkovitch sent a very generous and flattering review of "The Revenge for Love" to the "Partisan Rev." in Burnham's reign.[2] 3 times he returned it – the 3rd time with the remark that "if Percy Hardcaster was *her* idea of a communist it was not *his*." The author of the "Managerial Rev" has changed his ideas about communism, but not, I should guess, about me. – Also I speak disrespectfully of the "Managerial Rev" in my soon-to-appear book, "Rude Assignment."

. . . As my great-grandfather was born and married in Boston: as my father fought in the Civil War (in Sheridan's Cavalry) – always wore a Grand Army button – wrote books about it – I did at least have pumped into me a lot of *that*. My infant mind was filled with the hubbub of battles. A part of the garden was converted into the field of the "Wilderness". It should also be remembered that at 6 years old I frisked and frollicked with other little American boys on the New England coast – *not* with little Britons on the English coast. The American beginnings are irrelevant, except that I could not help imbibing from my very American father much Stimmung, a certain sentiment, and a lot

---

[1] Points concerned with the publication of *America and Cosmic Man* in the U.S. by Doubleday.
[2] James Burnham (b. 1905) began to contribute to the *Partisan Review* in 1938. He was on its Advisory Board from 1948 to 1953.

about the Civil War. And my mother was more American than Irish, and her memories are mine. I have masses of my uncle's letters, who was an American coal magnate. It adds up to nothing very solid, but must be reckoned in.

... At the time of "Blast" publication – or few years later I remember telling Pound of my American origin. He laughed a great deal. – "Oh if the *deah* British public only knew that *three* Americans – he, Eliot, and self – were responsible for all this disturbance, *Blasting, Imagism, Vorticism!* etc." said he – *very* amused....

Thanks for "Tigers Eye"[1] arrived Saturday. Like a duller and thinner "Partisan Rev" – but vaguely stalinist instead of mildly trotskyist.

In Haste
Yrs.
W. L.

...

411. *To Felix Giovanelli*† [London]
Oct. 18. 1948.

Dear Gio. I have had a respite of a few hours and have been going through odds and ends of publicity material. ...

When is book liable to appear?[2] – Within 48 hours I shall send you two important prospective contributions for magazines. Not *Tigers Eye*. It has the look of being a very private little puddle, in which old baby-boys and baby-girls float their intellectual cockleshells. No capitals in titles of articles – different coloured papers – impossible to find *Contents* at first and no names accompanying contributions: and routine commonplace modernity in art: *and* Spender expanding himself nostalgically regarding the earlier Russian films – pointing to them, as the ideal *new*, which when he was young superceded "modernism" (for instance "The Waste Land," which bit of modernismus appeared a few years

---

[1] *The Tiger's Eye*, a magazine of the arts, first appeared in New York in October 1947. Nine numbers were published, the last in October 1949.

[2] *America and Cosmic Man* was published in New York in June 1949.

before). All very mournful, pointless, and muddled. – Who did you say financed this paper? . . .
Best wishes.

W. L.

. . .

412. *To the Rev. Willis Feast*†¹ London. W. 11.
Oct. 21. 1948.

Dear Father Feast. . . . As to the Press-notice situation:² I am unable to agree with you that I have not much to complain about. When two months and a half after publication my book has not been reviewed in any Sunday paper, "Sunday Times," "Observer" etc. – in any weekly paper, "New Statesman," "Time and Tide," "Spectator," "John of London" etc. – nor in the "Daily Telegraph" (Harold Nicolson), "D. Mail" (Quennell), "News Chronicle" (Stephen Potter), "Manchester Guardian," "Liverpool Post," "Yorkshire Post," "Western Mail," "Scotsman" *etc. etc.*, I feel that it has not been awfully well treated . . . except for the supplement of "The Times" (and how!) But it is a very personal reaction. I would not dispute the point that it is all a question in such cases of what value you attach to the book, how important you consider the author. – If the argument that space is limited were advanced, then I should be inclined discreetly to wonder how it came about that Mr. Gorers book on America,³ appearing at the same time as my own, received in many instances reviews upon the day of publication. Of course, it is probably a much more important book. From the reviews I gathered that the Oedipus Complex was the highly original principle upon which his destructive thesis rested. I should no doubt be very satisfied with

---

[1] Willis Feast, an Anglican minister in Norfolk, wrote to L. after the publication of *America and Cosmic Man*. They began to correspond, then met when Feast asked L. to do a drawing of himself. L. did two sketches, and in the course of sittings the men became friends. Feast sat for L. as well in the story "The Bishop's Fool" in *Rotting Hill*.
[2] Re *America and Cosmic Man*.
[3] Geoffrey Gorer, *The Americans: A Study in National Character* (London, 1948). Published in the U.S. as *The American People*.

3½ columns of detraction in the "Times Lit. Sup.", which is carefully studied by the Trade every week. . . .

Yrs.
W. L.

. . .

413. *To D. D. Paige*†   London. W. 11.
Oct. 25. 1948.

My dear Mr. Paige. Thank you for your letter. I am glad the packet of E.P. letters seemed to you worth copying out. The originals I rather prize, and should not care to entrust them to the European mail in our untidy epoch. On the other hand, so as to check their bonafides, I should have no objection to the eventual publisher doing this. . . . I should hate people to say that *I* had myself introduced some of the less obliging remarks *à l'égard de tel et tel*, or indeed other matters. . . .

My view – and I must ask your indulgence if I express it forcibly – is categoric. E.P.'s letters tidied up would no longer be E.P.'s letters. The "old hickory" flavour is essential. The more "Waal me deah Wyndamm" you have the better. Change this to "Well my dear Wyndham", and it is somebody else speaking – writing. It is not a Yankee-exoticism (its desirability, or otherwise) that is at issue. I prefer E.P. as he *is* – it is a question of portraiture and of accuracy. One cannot afford to jettison a single misplaced letter. E.P.'s correspondence is worth troubling about. If you gave them the whole works, without trimming – in every sense – you would have a great literary curiosity, and something which would soften the heart of the world towards this so-very-human prisoner.

Finally: the letters will in all likelihood, never be reprinted. The publisher *who dulls these letters down* and deguts them will not only be doing a great disservice to Ezra but to the public of today and also tomorrow.

. . . If I might venture to advise you, cling on all you can to the letter of the text. Ezra's fondness for the pen, for tumbling words about, and giving them capitals that dont belong to them etc. etc. is of the same order as Joyce's – and, as I have stressed already, it preceded it. It is as necessary to retain these distortions in presenting E.P.'s letters as not to tidy up a text of Joyce's, from "Ulysses" onwards. . . .

I have been a little *emporté*, I fear. But for hours I have, just the other day, pored over these old epistles. My extremism – for *the letter of the text* – represents a very sincere conviction. – I would go so far as to say that, if I found that ―― was proposing to ruin them I would keep mine back – unless this disturbed your plans. . . .

―――――

The petition.[1]

The timing is v. important. Dewey it seems will be the next President. It would be a fallacy to suppose that, in the first few months of his incumbency at the White House, Dewey would indulge in acts of clemency calculated to arouse a storm of protest among a powerful group. The key-petitioners would represent no powerful group. The *protesters* would.

It is all very difficult. A year hence is the obvious time: but it might turn out no better, when Oct. Nov. 1949 came round – external politics might be blotting everything else out. – The present is I suppose as good as any other. Mr. and Mrs. Pound may have been ill-advised to stop their lawyer from acting. . . .

. . . I'm always in trouble with [Pound] about [the Jewish question.] (I am not philosemite. It merely seems to me silly to blame a slick business man when it is one's own failings (moral and intellectual) which ought to be denounced – and corrected. It is like accusing a tree one has run into in a daydream).

Here lies the fundamental difficulty. Once released E.P. would embark upon a violent crusade. – In St. Elizabeth Hospital his reputation as a poet increases by leaps and bounds and will continue to do so. In a letter this week a N.Y. friend, for instance, refers to him as "le grand prisonnier." . . . [Certainly,] "Gerontion" or "Hollow Men," where Eliot is at his best, would never have been written had it not been for his contacts with Pound and imbibing of Pound's teachings. . . . – A Pound vogue will I suppose almost necessarily (though it would be more satisfactory if it didn't) take this form – involve . . . comparisons and with

[1] Paige sent to L. the draft of a petition which he planned to circulate and then present to the President of the United States in the cause of Pound's release.

them a reaction against Eliot. But however that may be, it will be a strong movement of homage to – or re-discovery, or discovery of – Ezra Pound.

This will be almost automatic: one can see it happening, and remark its growth. – But if E.P. should then, say in a year, obtaining a parole or a pardon, go crusading, in a few months all the ground gained would be lost. It might be another 50 years before he was brought forward again.

It may be because of some such considerations that —— believes – as he expressed it to me when we discussed this matter – that "for his own sake" it would be better for him to remain where he is, in St. Elizabeth Hospital. Even —— – somewhat to my surprise – expressed the same view. He argues that if E.P. were allowed to leave St. Elizabeth and go to a private nursing institution, within a short time Ezra would walk off, turn up in New York, and express himself in characteristic fashion. A great scandal would ensue. – It, however, is too cold-blooded a view for me to adopt, that he should forever remain under restraint. If I were in E.P.'s position I should feel rather strongly about the view that for my own good I had better stop in an asylum. So I under all circumstances will do what lies in my power to secure his release.

I return you the draft of the petition and cannot suggest any improvement. I am not sure that it is the artist's function to have anything to do with morals. What I should be inclined to emphasize is the superlative quality of E.P.'s art – not the moral attributes. But you are probably right, it is the latter that weigh most with those to whom the petition will be addressed. It is very good, I think. You may rely upon my discretion, and I certainly shall not mention it in a letter to Ezra.

... It is my dream to get a "resident artist" assignment to some U.S. university for 6 months or longer if possible. A chance to do one's own work, receive daily a group of students to talk about pictures one was painting, to emit an aura of "creative" enlightenment – not of course be "art-master". – At the back of that dream is a super-dream: namely that I might become a "cultural expert resident". I could then finish a book of mine called "Childermass", and vary that occupation by producing paintings and talking art and literature to youths and maidens.

I confide to you this super-dream, but it is I imagine too vague-looking to be practical, or too marvellous to materialise. . . .

            Yrs.
           WYNDHAM LEWIS

P.S. If you get the petition ready soon, please send me several copies. I feel sure I can find a number of people to sign it. Define the standard of celebrity required. Would my little friend —— pass muster? He . . . is fairly well known as a very high-brow journalist – but no celebrity. Is it to be *all artists*, or only writers?

414. *To Edgar Preston Richardson*†   London. W. 11.
                  Oct 27. 1948.

My dear Richardson. It was a very pleasant surprise to see *Detroit* and the rest of the address on the envelope, and upon opening it to be with you again. . . .

Let me speak of the first year of *the Peace*, upon our return. That first twelvemonth I could do nothing but struggle with the environment. England has become a very different place. National bankruptcy *plus* socialism is no joke. Let me say at once that I am not anti-socialist. It would be stupid to be that: at this stage in human history some form of it seems indicated – though of course it is a necessary but disagreeable phase imposed by humanity's natural backwardness and wickedness, not a splendid culmination of human genius and endeavour. But there is one piece of political information I have most painfully and unwillingly acquired. *State-socialism* (in contrast to some other types of socialism) is not a theory of the state. It is a very grave complaint to which human society is apt to fall victim. – National bankruptcy is – well, let us say very bad for the patient – for a nation suffering from state-socialism. – I read this morning that, as well as medicine, *law* is going to be nationalised. Nationalisation, of course, and state-socialism are inseparable.

Conditions here are not the straightforward disaster of a country the currency of which has become worthless – as in Germany after world war 1. Disaster is disguised as "austerity". As a result to an outsider the mere registering of actual conditions must have a sound of unwarranted complaint. – And very little complaint – alas – is heard here: dunning rulers in the past have carefully trained this people to "keep a stiff upper lip", to "keep smiling", to be fine fellows who can "take it"....

You cannot defeat the English. You can publicly rob them and fool them; ruin them, and eventually enslave them. But you cannot *defeat* them. They do not (as has so often been said) know when they're beaten!

... It all *looks* the same you see – but it isn't quite the same! It is the most hypocritical and insidious type of inflation. Most writers have crowded into safe official jobs – B.B.C., Brit. Council, or a Ministry. Literature does not benefit.... Then, as a limit of 5 shillings per meal per person is now statutory, (plus a "cover charge") it is impossible to nourish oneself in a restaurant. A lunch at the Café Royal for instance is just the negation of sustenance. A couple of months ago we lunched with James Sweeney and his wife at a hotel in Half Moon Street, off Piccadilly. The restaurant is well-known, smallish and expensive. (The most reckless of my dealers always takes me there for lunch). The dish that was one of the two pièces de resistance I could not eat, because it was putrid....

But enough of these miseries....

Yrs
WYNDHAM LEWIS

415. *To David Kahma*†   London. W. 11.
Nov. 1, 1948.

My dear Kahma. There has been a week's blank. A violent head cold.... (I should perhaps observe that I have always made a fuss about a cold. Lock myself in – sneeze and sweat and sleep. Sobre todo – SLEEP). I must apologise for breaking into a foreign tongue, but I have just been reading a lot of Pound's lucubrations, and oh boy, oh là là, que la tête me tourne! – *Waal!*

Let me however wrench myself out of that bog of polyglot verbosity. Your stuff about the Doukobors was very interesting....

Relations appear to be becoming increasingly embittered between Western Nations and Russia. What I have felt is that unless some temporary truce re. Berlin took form at Paris, things must get worse. Now on one side and the other, they are using the word *liar* a lot. Looks bad. But in a few weeks a new and tough U.S. President will be functioning. Might have a salutary effect. (Mukden has fallen. Very aggressive of muscovites and Dewey very hot regarding China.) . . .

. . . Best wishes for just now, and so to speak hasta luego – si Dios quiere y la gran Puta.

Waal. – oh boy waal! Why oh why does uncle Ezz as he likes to call himself play the hayseed! Do you know?

Yrs.

W. L.

416. *To D. D. Paige*†   London. W. 11.
Nov. 6. 1948.

Dear Mr. Paige. . . .

To return to the petition. . . . – How *I* should argue would be as follows: Nations at war traditionally execute (the block, the yardarm, or blindfolded against a wall) any of their citizens who consort with and side with the enemy. But as war is today rather an affair of ideology than of national interest, more like a Civil War, the issue is not so stark as that. In the States for instance Italian and other large racial groups were in fact against the war. So the conditions, for an American, paralleled the American Civil War rather than a European national war.

On the other hand there exists another powerful opinion in the U.S. fanatically hostile to fascism. What I should say to myself would be that were I to put down in my petition anything that could be interpreted as: "This man is a great poet, great moralist. His *collaboration* must be excused because of this," then that group would at once roar – "*What!* Because a man is a versifier etc. is he allowed to commit every crime! May he commit murder or treason with impunity?!" Afterwards these objectors would ask whether it is just for Best[1] because he does not write verses to languish in prison, while E.P. goes free to versify.

[1] The Nazi collaborator R. H. Best was found guilty of treason on April 17th, 1948. On July 1st he was sentenced to life imprisonment. He died in prison on December 21st, 1952.

The above is the point of view of the average uneducated man, for whom *our* values mean nothing. We are in fact claiming *privilege* for E.P. For me personally it is a scandal that so valuable a man should be shut away and prevented from functioning. In what I have just said I have tried to realize the opposite (and majority) standpoint, and how that can be inflamed by partisans.

I lay *too much* stress I am sure upon this: I exaggerate the allowance one ought to make on account of such obstacles. I should be disposed to advance no plea of *justification* (although obviously there is no monopoly of truth or justice for those who spurred the United States to intervention in the European war, and it would not be a crime to oppose that intervention, and to denounce the interventionists *in the judgement of the angels*, but only of men, and of men committed to one of these two policies – namely the interventionist). I should rather concentrate as a petitioner upon the enormous cultural importance of Pound. This would be purely a question of diplomacy (and would be I expect over-diplomatic). I might enquire what would have happened had Dante's fellow-countrymen been able to seize him and burn him alive. I should speak of Pound's failing health (if there are *any* symptoms upon which to base that plea), of his age etc.

You must have excellent reasons for choosing a more positive approach. And I am no advocate at all for what would be my line of action. I state it not in order to influence you, but merely to explain the kind of answers you would be likely to receive from me upon this very important matter. . . .

. . . Also —— has lent me a copy of a brochure, which Miss Rudge has had printed of broadcasts.[1] Was much amused by E.P.'s remarks about myself, and how we never agreed about anything! . . .

Best wishes, very sincerely
WYNDHAM LEWIS

. . .

[1] "*If This Be Treason . . .*" (Siena, printed for Olga Rudge by Tip. Nuova, 1948).

417. *To T. S. Eliot* London. W. 11.
Nov. 9. 1948.

Dear Eliot. Your book, *Notes towards the Definition of Culture*, which you were so kind as to direct Fabers to send me, has just arrived. I have only had time to read a little at the beginning: that is Chapter i. Even already there is much that I like; and to some things of course I demur. Whether one agrees or not, however, when anyone like yourself, with such care as there is evidence of here, defines and clarifies the frontiers of his mind, the contemporary scene is the gainer. Vagueness is what is bad. Even if we are going to have nonsense, it is important that it should be clear nonsense. I shall follow you as you develop those definitions, and I may pass on a few observations, if they seem of any value.

I learned that you were in America. Shall try and get your address there, otherwise sending this to Fabers.

Yrs,
WYNDHAM LEWIS

P.S. *Nov. 15*. Mailing this today to U.S. – You are wrong, to my mind, about England, Ireland, Wales, and Scotland.[1]

W. L.

418. *To D. D. Paige*† London. W. 11.
Nov. 12. 1948.

My dear Mr. Paige. Thank you for your letter and the specimen E.P. letter enclosed. Regarding the letter, *that* amount of tidying-up would not matter. If I were you I should never cease to press for the minimum of alterations throughout and the maximum of photostats and of letters given verbatim. The *exuberance* would both amuse and endear. I agree with what you say 100 per cent that the publication of these letters would work in Pound's favour more than anything else. . . . – Are the exuberantly spellt and expressed letters all later ones? It is a point that interests me. At what date did the letters begin to be eccentric? . . .

. . . Once, a considerable time ago, I suggested to Dorothy

[1] See Chapter III, "Unity and Diversity: The Region," *Notes towards the Definition of Culture* (London, 1948).

Pound that *exile* might be a possible penalty, one that both would welcome. She . . . is longing to get back to Italy: and I suppose Ezra would prefer to return to what has become his home. But he would not I expect invite the loss of U.S. citizenship. Otherwise *that* might be a way out. Personally I like being in the U.S., and very greatly admire the *scene* – the structure of the hills on the upper Hudson and near those strangely named cities – Syracuse, Utica etc – the physical beauty is extraordinary. Aldington I remember wrote me once that Connecticut was more beautiful than anywhere in England. With that I heartily agree. But when (cautiously confining it to this merely geological and topographical plane) I have talked like that to Ezra he has been indulgent but amused. "You dont *know* the place, Windamm!" is all I ever got. So why could not he say: "I am an Italian resident and wish to be exiled there forever. Banish me! I will gladly guarantee never to come back. Take away my rights as an American." – In a few years he could secure a pardon, and return to Washington – to the Mayflower Hotel, not the Saint Elizabeth – in triumph! His banishment would bring home to people that a great American was forbidden access to his native land, of which he was one of the principal ornaments.

He of course never would bring himself to take that course. I wonder if U.S. law provides for banishment with deprivation of rights etc? – This is however little more than idle musing. One is driven to it because of the formidable difficulties inherent in less fanciful approaches. E.P.'s obstreperous intractableness is, all the time, the main difficulty. It is like Doughty, in "the fanatic Arabia", pig-headedly refusing to say "Allah is great". . . .

Sincerely,
WYNDHAM LEWIS

. . .

419. *To Geoffrey Stone* London. W. 11.
Nov. 15. 1948.

Dear Stone. . . . The young chap in the New York publishing office who introduced *America and Cosmic Man* to his firm – which in its turn, accepted it unanimously I was informed – showed great enthusiasm. This obviously was not simply commercial – he was too young. It is far more than I had hoped that you and other nephews and nieces of Uncle Sam should be sympathetic.

The book was intended primarily for English people: to supply some potted history, and at the same time indulge in what I hope may be useful speculation regarding the future development of human society. It seemed to me most urgent for the public to digest unromantic truths. The present archaic division into "nations", which are really competing businesses, each armed with increasingly devastating weapons, is the central political fact of our miserable existence as social beings in this most disagreable century. It is of course bad business for these great businesses to perpetuate mass homicide (not to mention the fact that a new religion has joined in.) For look where we all are. In England 50 million bankrupts live on an American dole: meanwhile our political aim is gradually to transform England into something like Russia – the most backward state in Europe. Fabian state-socialism will in many respects be drabber, more unfree, more unintelligent than Stalinism. Germany – one of the 3 greatest businesses in the world 30 years ago has almost ceased to exist. – How can a European think of France today without despairing? – Those are the backgrounds, as you are especially trained to understand, of my idea of "cosmic man".

... – Well, the Taft-Hartley Bill brought back Harry Truman! Plus no doubt the high cost of living, and Dewey's puppet-like appearance. – I wonder who is Marshall's mentor? And what is it in the State Department that paralyses U.S. policy in the matter of China?

Yrs
W. L.

420. *To Felix Giovanelli* London. W. 11.
19 Nov. 1948.

Dear Giovanelli. . . .

... For the cuttings many thanks, especially the one with the photos.[1] – She has changed since the days when I painted her portrait. She now has become a Van Eyck. . . .

[1] Newspaper photographs of the Sitwells, who were on tour in the U.S.

What you say of E.P. is indeed worrying. He sends me tit-bits from American papers – Pegler on Franklin Roosevelt, for instance. Far from *laying off* that type of subject he persists in regarding himself as a saviour of the human race. . . . I hope Thomas Eliot will pray for him, for *I* dont know what to do and thats a fact.

More shortly,

Yr,
W. L.

421. *To David Kahma*†   London. W.
6 Dec. 1948.

Dear Kharma. . . .

What you said about my American book pleased and encouraged me a great deal. – The progress of communism in China is most depressing: and it is Secretary Marshall after all who is responsible for the policy of allowing Chiang Kai-shek to stew in his own juice. The whole of Asia, I fear, will be communist before the light-hearted Harry stops playing with the presidential yacht and becomes conscious of the danger. – Dewey would have been more active. On the other hand, unless the U.S. armed – and built up a large modern Panzer host – and signed an unbreakable military pact with England and West Europe – and insisted upon this country and France arming too – without that what is the use of being tough? There is nothing to stop the U.S.S.R. from going to Gibraltar and beyond that to the Cape of Good Hope *at present*.

There is great danger, in the U.S., in the G.O.P. being in the White House and dominating the Congress. It would, by its stupid arrogance, short-sightedness, harsh and egotist action, bring to birth an authentic radical opposition. Communism would expand and frightfully flourish. – As it is, gradually every other part of the earth except N. America, will become Communist or practically communist. But it will take some years.

An American friend of mine is very depressed and apprehensive about Harry Truman. He says we are all going to Hell in a hand-basket. That of course is so. How long shall we take to get there? It is *the meanwhile* that is important.* At all events, that is what

I feel like this afternoon! – Not that I am *comfortable* in the hand-basket.

Best wishes,
WL.

* In a few years the Russ. communist régime might dissolve.

422. *To Archibald MacLeish*† London. W. 11.
18 Dec. 1948.

Dear MacLeish. Thank you for your letter, and as to the subjects I propose to discourse on, that will depend (as your question implies) on the nature of the audience.[1]

At the Arts Club in Chicago, for instance, and elsewhere, I lectured on "Rouault and Original Sin." Such a subject would bewilder and enrage many audiences.

If I were addressing relatively intelligent audiences I would like this time (as an example) to talk about the American and Irish literary flowerings of the first three decades of this century – comparable to the sudden creative vitality in Russia in mid xixth century.

It is obvious that the American and the Irish outburst is over. I mean there are no *new* writers: the series appears to have closed. Merely to catalogue the names of the Irish group – Synge, Yeats, Russell, Joyce, Stephens, O'Flaherty, O'Faolain etc. – or some of their works, "The Playboy of the Western World," "Finnigans Wake", "Ulysses", "The Informer", "The Countess Kathleen" – bears out the analogy with mid-xixth century Russia. And the U.S., in the same way, Henry James belonging to the same grouping as T. S. Eliot, Ezra Pound, Cummings and yourself (poetry, or prose-poetry? very important in the American, and only less in the Irish, whereas in the Russian group, it hardly appears), then Hemingway and his school, Faulkner etc.: – this American group is just as impressive. The above is of course a very crude statement. But when one considers the historic reasons

[1] L. had written to MacLeish on November 15th telling him that he proposed to make a lecture tour in the U.S. in 1949 and expressing the hope that they might meet. MacLeish, in his reply, asked for more details. The proposed tour never came about, although L. went on making plans for several months.

for these collective flowerings – what causes and what favours them, and what does not, one has, I think, plenty to talk about.

If it were a question of an audience so wide as to be utterly uninterested in books, then there is only one subject: the fact that I speak with an English accent and they with an American. There are many ways of approaching this. A book of mine is named "The Mysterious Mr. Bull". I could discourse about John Bull, as fireeater, as fabian, etc. – One can of course escape from the banalities of that subject very easily, once the common ground is established – of national incompatibility. . . .

As to my motive in desiring to lecture in the U.S.: to live in a bankrupt country in the throes of violent economic transformation, presided over by the dry genius of fabian state-socialism, is an experience that may have its *moral* satisfactions but is a stern ordeal. I am bored, only mildly uplifted, and it is about time, I feel, that I had a spell in other parts of the earth.

To conclude: I was glad to read that you had returned to writing.

Yours sincerely,
WYNDHAM LEWIS

423. *To D. D. Paige*†   London. W. 11.
24 Jan. 1949.

Dear Paige. . . .

To teach Eng. literature for a short while would be all right.[1] (The fact that I have no university degree would not matter at Bard, I assume?) . . . .

What does teaching English entail? (1) What would the hours be – 2 or 6 weekly lectures etc? (2) Is it confined to one period (say 18th Century). If so one could mug that up. I asked Louis MacNeice, who taught at Cornell in 1940, what happened if one of the sweet little brats asked one something one did not know. MacNeice answered that his method was to say "Ah, a *very* interesting question that" and to talk around it for a minute or two while he looked up the name or date or whatever in a book. – I should say what an Irish doctor once said to me: "Wait till I look in me book."

[1] Paige, who had connexions at Bard College, wrote to L. suggesting that he might teach there as a visiting professor. The matter was pursued for some time before L. decided against it.

I should not contemplate teaching for any longer than possible. – What, with the cost of living as it stands now, do two people require per annum, to live in Cape Cod or Connecticut, modestly as regards living-quarters, but with plenty of eggs, bread, cauliflowers, bits of meat and Cuban Honey – cigarettes (2 packs a day) and a bottle of gin a week? Gin was 3.50 when we were there. What would you say was needed per week? We did it in Sag Harbour for 30 dollars – that was without counting rent. There is money to be picked up in various ways. I like painting, and have a reputation. I like writing books. . . .

. . . With a great many sincere thanks for your active help.

Yrs,

424. *To Julian Symons*† [London]
Feb. 11. 1949.

Dear Symons. . . . – Your offer is most generous; unexpected and unnecessary. But I cannot recall a single instance of anyone offering me money and my not accepting it. I cant help saying yes. So, if you can spare it ... ! . . .

. . . – Re. Dickens.[1] Do not forget to say that it was his habit to roar with laughter all the time when he was writing comedy and he would give his thigh resounding slaps at an especially happy sally. . . .

Yours,

425. *To Felix Giovanelli* London, W. 11.
March 3. 1949.

My dear Gio. Your letter, like all your letters full of sunshine and the authentic sparkle of the grape-growing races, abounded in news – abounded in bad news! How little it pleased you to be its bearer was revealed by the piecemeal discretion with which you fed it out. But at length I saw that *everything* had gone badly. As to loyalty, of which you speak, it would never occur to me for a single moment – in *anything* – to suppose you capable of being

[1] Symons mentioned that he was writing on Dickens. See Julian Symons, *Charles Dickens* (London, 1951).

wanting in that respect. I know you are incapable of double-dealing. You have set yourself a difficult task, that is all. I am sorry I am the more or less innocent cause of so much fruitless activity. . . .

It was too bad about "The ———."[1] Your explanation – respectability, pietism – is the answer. . . . But there you are: between communist action and "reaction" there is nowhere for an honest mind to be accommodated.

> – And what wind
> serves to advance an honest mind?

It is the same wind today as in Donne's day. . . .

Sorry you have a bugger-book on your back.[2] Homoism died down in the 'thirties, but is so prevalent now as to be the [word] among the student or intellectual young. Of course it is all one as far as I am concerned, except that people always make a religion out of anything they do against the rules. . . .

. . . There are a lot of people who like my books. But these mags are a ring – or two rings. What a bore it is that we have to talk about all this stuff. Well, blessings.

Your

WYNDHAM LEWIS

P.S. Never be afraid of hurting my feelings. Have none. "England has no friends or enemies – only interests." I don't mean that type of thing – nothing pretentiously hard-boiled. – If Mr. W. L. were a hospital patient he would not be so stupid as to feel the pain if it would lead to *la guérison*. – Always inform me Gio of anything unpleasant crudely. Ne me ménage pas – c'est pas la peine. . . .

What is your view of books of Miss Elizabeth Bowen?

426. *To Augustus John*†
London.
7 March. 1949.

My dear John. . . .

The next time you come up let us have a little drink – at the Burlington in Cork Street or somewhere else. My telephone

[1] Giovanelli had approached a New York review with the idea of their doing a Lewis number.

[2] Giovanelli was translating *Special Friendships* by Roger Peyrefitte (New York, 1950).

number is Bayswater 2089. *Private.* There are many good reasons for having it private. Please observe discretion regarding it.

It interested me to learn that you were working on a large composition – though I was shocked at what you said about chopping it in two.[1] Why do you not do some small compositions as well. It would interest everyone very much, and profit you. (1) An Interior: Dodo[2] and a neighbour or two engaged in conversation – each figure not above 12 or 15 inches high. (2) The local Pub – the landlord playing darts with Caspar or David[3] or a group of Hants yokels. (3) You have never painted animals – you will be the only great artist who has never painted an animal – certainly the only one in G.B. Think of Hogarth and his dog. Repair this omission at once. If there are any animals in the house, make a composition with them. Or a self portrait. How about a cat on your shoulder? Or self-and-cow? (4) Paint the house, somebody at every window. (5) Close your eyes and conjure up the scene of a cliff-face in Normandy and you forcing a couple of Scotch lassies up the cliff side. That would be à la Rowlandson. (6) Close your eyes again, and you will see yourself (and yours truly) sitting at a table in the square of a Norman town (forget the name) entertaining a band of gypsies.[4] Paint these things naively – a lot of little sunburnt bonhommes and a big bearded fellow, and yours truly probably drinking a Source Badois, swarthy, a lot of hair. Figures 8 or 9 inches. (7) Open your eyes, but while open turn them inward, and begin painting whatever comes into your head – man or monster, witch on a broomstick, or any shapes it amuses you to paint. I mean what is disrespectfully called doodling. It would not be that if you did it. (8) For luck [word?] a composition of 10 nude girls bathing in – oh a forest stream. All 12 to 15 inches high. It would only take you a week, and you'd sell it for a thousand pounds. You could soon get together a show (with no portraits – or very few): just a number of small and smallish compositions. It would be a great novelty – it would delight us all – and

[1] In a letter of February 3rd, John wrote: "I've been involved for long in a vast composition which has changed and changed. Now I think I'll cut it into two (or three)."

[2] Mrs. John.

[3] John's sons. Sir Caspar John (b. 1903) is now First Lord of the Admiralty.

[4] John recalls this episode, which took place at Bayeux, in *Chiaroscuro*, p. 86.

once you decided to go on a holiday, as it were, and paint whatever blooming well blew into your head, all would be well.

What you said about my piece in "Wales" delighted me.[1] I do not know your Pole, or I daresay I might have tried my hand.[2] Didn't see Matthew Smith.[3] De costumbre es demasiado *lush* para mi. No me *gusta*, sabe. A question of *taste*, only: for I know he is a serious artist, and the best judges have particularly admired his work. When you see him, by the way, please ask him what kind of a man an Englishman called —— is, teaching English at Arles or Aix.

Yrs ever

427. *To Gene Nash*†[4]   London. W. 11.
March 7. 1949.

My dear Nash. . . . The reason for my deep silence has been that I have undertaken far more than I can perform. The exhibition of my pictures I have been obliged to push off until May 1.[5] This likewise pushes on the date of our departure for the U.S. It is a problem of extricating oneself from things that cling around one like lianas. Half of them are essentially unimportant. But it is difficult to distinguish the unimportant from the important – breathlessly splashing about in the middle of them, one gets in a flat spin.

For the second time (the last 1938) I am doing a large portrait of Eliot (T.S.) The Nobel Prize and Sweden has freshened him up. But he still becomes drowsy when immobilised in one position and his bottom "goes to sleep". I have only just begun. I believe however that I shall make a good picture out of it. – You ask me what I think of the present government. Mine will not be a political answer, but a human one. To be taxed more than any

[1] John praised "The Rot" in his letter.
[2] John wrote: "You're always so good at *Poles*, I wish you would polish off one I know – too well."
[3] John said that he found Matthew Smith's show (at the Mayor Gallery) "quite stunning."
[4] Gene Nash was among the young people of intellectual interests whom L. got to know in St. Louis. After L.'s return to England, Nash went into the paper business in Louisiana and then moved to California. He and L. corresponded sporadically for several years.
[5] The Redfern Exhibition opened May 5th.

society has ever been taxed before is not, obviously, *agreable*. The indirect taxes are the most idiotically burdensome of all.

A pack of cigarettes for instance is $3\frac{1}{2}$ times as much as 10 years ago: a lot of that is what is called "purchase tax": namely, a government rake-off. In this way *everything* is taxed (up to 100 per cent) from a lead-pencil to an automobile, from a thumb-tack to a tractor. If I wish to go to Europe, I am allowed to take 35 pounds in my pocket – and prices everywhere are terribly inflated. Our government refused to buy meat from Ireland, as an example, so Ireland sells its meat to Holland for half as much again as we were asked to pay. Holland cans this meat, and the next thing is that it is being sold in English shops for an extravagant price – and people buy this canned meat, because now the weekly fresh meat ration is fantastically small. – This is of course a direct criticism of the government's poor business sense. The fundamental fact is that England, after two terrific and ruinous wars, is bankrupt – one cannot escape from that. And on top of that a government with its mind full of revolutionary domestic alterations does not improve the situation as far as *comfort* is concerned. Again, a concentration on the welfare of the coalheaver and the dustman means that what once was the middleclass is discriminated against and of course impoverished and must soon disappear. But no doubt you understand all that. What you *cannot* understand (politics aside, and barring discussion of the rights and wrongs of social revolution) is how amazingly disagreeable and irritating controls and inflation are. If I could emigrate I would: for I am not interested in politics, and would go wherever I should be left alone to work – to write and to paint. . . . – This has become a whopping letter again. My next will be more restrained – like yours. But remember, we are all overstrained over here.

Cordiallest regards,
WYNDHAM LEWIS

428. *To David Kahma*† London. W. 11.
[March?] 8, 1949.

My dear Khama. . . .

It seems to me very wise of you to plan a straight novel, on the completion of the Douk book. You are very able to write it. When you describe things to me you do so with exceptional clearness and vivacity – I mean the things of common everyday life. That naturally does not make a novel even if you string them all together. But once you have the ability in question, it should not be too difficult to decide *what* myth you wish to project. Since you have a clear and coherent philosophy, differing a good deal from that of your neighbours, your story should be original – without any forced or affected originality – merely because you think differently. And this would be apparent without your holding forth or obtruding any mental machinery which spoils a novel.

As soon as you send me the Douk book I will take it where I think it has the best chance: or see that it gets there. It might be that the likeliest publisher would have someone of their executive staff ill-disposed where I am concerned, and that would not be propitious....

Next, let me refer to earlier parcels. Here is an outline ... of the splendid and useful foods etc. you have sent, and a note or two by the way.

brilliantine (stuff we get here stinks, clots and clogs)

soaps (if you knew the difference of Yardley here and Yardley where you are)....

chinese paper (amuse visitors)

envelopes (as strong as leather).

folders (bring order out of chaos)....

... – When you come to write your book, its scene our day to day life, I should put in the sods. Sartre has shown what a superb figure of comedy a homo can be. (Daniel Sereno).[1] Just now I have a picture dealer who is that way inclined. There is a cardboard *profile* that follows him around, alert, impassible, bright-eyed, like a discreet male-nurse. Over one of his shoulders one always sees this profile of a handsome lackey, – expressionless, punctilious; posing first on the ball of the right foot and looking brightly but indifferently to the left, then resting on the ball of the left foot and looking to the right. *Always* a Profile: I have never seen his front face....

        Yours, gratefullest of all
        the host of those parcel-
        fed, kept-clean, pommaded
        and otherwise maintained
        in a civilised condition,

             WYNDHAM LEWIS

[1] See *Les chemins de la liberté* (Paris, 1945–9).

429. *To James Thrall Soby*† London.
10 March 1949.

My dear Mr. Soby. . . .

The personality of artists interests me, and I thought it might be that you shared this interest. Therefore I send you a few pages out of the current number of "Picture Post."

But more important, I send you a number of photographs of pictures by a young artist who has just had his first show (Leicester Gallery) – incidentally a surprisingly successful one, considering. As an illustration of this his show was running at the same time as a very big one-man-show of Mintons[1] paintings and drawings (filling all 3 rooms in the Lefevre) and Evans, at the Leicester Gallery, sold 3 times as much work as Minton at the Lefevre. This is odd, because Evans work is very intellectual, and pretty abstract, whereas Mintons is work from nature, and sometimes most seductively coloured.

Merlyn Evans, as his name suggests, was born in Wales, and he is very much the celtic temperament (if you are familiar with the racial difference of temperament in these islands). His exhibition had a startlingly good press (which doubtless helped the selling which was also promoted by the enthusiasm of the Gallery executive): and no show I have seen for a long time has shown so much (1) promise and (2) actual achievement. The pictures are mostly large, some even very large: and I cannot imagine photographs less calculated to give an idea of the pictures. I hesitated even to send them, they seemed so inadequate. Evans is getting some better photos, and when they are ready I will send you some.

It is unnecessary to describe the character of these pictures, as, wretched as are the photos, they will enable you to divine the general character at least. I know how especially your interests lie in the direction of the abstract: and whereas in the works of Minton and Vaughan we have a stylised and austerely ordered naturalism, and often a considerable degree of naturalism in Colquhoun and MacBryde, in Evans we are always moving in the abstract. He seems disinclined to call in nature to help at all. I am sure you would like him very much.

My purpose in sending these things to you – apart from the fact that I should like you to be acquainted with them – is that I hoped you might show them to some Gallery director, or directors, who

[1] John Minton (b. 1917).

would perhaps consider having a show of Evans work. If, for whatever reason, you are debarred from doing this, can you advise a Gallery, and tell me what steps Evans can take towards proposing a show. I shall be personally obliged if you will be so kind as to give this your attention, if you can, or otherwise to give me the benefit of your counsel. Abstract art is *not* on the *increase*, as you know, and here is a young man risking his life – for that is what it means – in practicing it. So we must all lend him a hand.

Cordially,

430. *To J. E. Palmer*†[1] London. W. 11.
March 18. 1949.

Dear Mr. Palmer. Thank you very much for extracting the relevant passage from the correspondence concerning my article, "The Intellectual."[2] Your correspondent is most fierce and contentious – I am glad his "ten-foot pole" is not a *lance*, and I a knight (however thick my armour) against whom this fiery paladin is driving in the Lists. – However, his only valid weapon, ultimately is the human reason (oh how subjectively wielded): and in this merely dialectical field, although I brandish no "Ten-foot pole," I feel I shall prevail because his reasoning is as fallacious as it is noisy.

We will dispose, anyhow, of this business first, before I turn to the most agreeable news your letter otherwise contained.

It seems that Gilson felt that my remarks re. Bloy and Berth[3] merited a bit of catholic thunder and a flash or two of scornful lightning – though needless to say he does not attempt to refute what I said: namely, that as members of a *universal* church

[1] J. E. Palmer (b. 1914), currently editor of the *Yale Review*, was from 1946 to 1952 editor of the *Sewanee Review*.

[2] With the idea presumably of stimulating a controversy, Palmer had sent L.'s article – in part an attack on French catholic actionist thinkers – to Etienne Gilson (b. 1884). For whatever reason, the *Sewanee* did not print any of this material.

[3] L.'s particular targets are Léon Bloy (*L'âme de Napoléon*) and especially Edouard Berth (*Les mésfaits des intellectuels*). Against them he opposes Julien Benda's defence of detachment in *Le trahison des clercs*. See *Rude Assignment*, pp. 29–42.

catholics should seek to pacify the nations, instead of violently taking sides, and inciting brother (and christian) to destroy brother and christian. It was upon this point alone and some of the action it involves, that I offered criticism of the catholics: and it was not as a catholic, you may have noticed, that Gilson contradicted me, but as a *clerc*.

The defense of Benda was, however, disingenuous. I made it plain enough, surely, how greatly I respected Benda's "Trahison des Clercs" – indeed, it was Benda I was defending against Berth, was it not? *Therefore* (how typical, alas, Monsieur Gilson!) Benda is defended against *me*, in a sort of inverted tit-for-tat!

At the end of my "Intellectual" article – it is only there that I observe how, quite recently, Benda has abandoned his detachment from politics and so damaged his unique reputation of one *en dessus de la melée* – or *en dehors*, rather.

But to conclude my comments on the Gilson passage you quote in your letter: *of course* Benda is speaking first, last, and all the time of the corrupt, partisan, propagandist *clerc* or clerk – of the *bad* clerk – is upholding the ideal of the *good* clerk. (These remarks of Gilson's are merely devices of the skilled controversialist). *Of course* "clerc" or clerk (an archaic word standing for something that does not exactly exist today) is not identical with "intellectual". On the other hand undoubtedly today any *clerc* who strayed into our age would be classified as an "intellectual". St. Thomas Aquinas would unquestionably, in such a case, find himself described as an "intellectual" or a "highbrow".

It was necessary to reply to Gilson: but please do not think that I am hostile to catholics or to Gilson. Nothing could be farther from the truth. Please do not, in your mind, cast me for a rôle in which I represent one side, the catholics the opposite side. No: were I a Catholic I should speak in precisely the same way. I should invoke Tertullian, the early Fathers of the Church, and denounce Catholic toleration of man's inhumanity to man, and wasteful violences.

Now I come to the other matter: I was delighted to learn that "The Rot" pleased you,[1] and that you proposed to use it. As regards the book – in which I included it purely as an *illustration*

[1] "The Rot" was recommended to Palmer by Cleanth Brooks (b. 1906), whose attention had been called to it by Hugh Kenner, then at Yale.

of something I was saying – the small publishing firm which were going to publish that small book, are, it seems, going out of business. In that case, another publisher has to be found, and there is not one chance in ten thousand that it will appear for at least 12 months. English publishers, and booksellers, have an almost neurotic objection to small books – which is really a great bore.

It was with much pleasure that I heard of the good word put in for my "Rotting Hill" sketch by Cleanth Brooks. Indeed I am particularly glad to think that I have his good will. . . .

. . . *What* a long letter: mostly Gilson's fault!

Cordially yours,

431. *To Theodore Weiss*†[1]   London. W. 11.
April 19. 1949.

Dear Weiss. . . .

Enclosed is a photo, taken six weeks ago. My friends (Eliot among them, who says it is like the anaesthetist when he was having an operation) disapprove: generally describe it as so characterless as to be a photo of Mr. X – not certainly of myself. But London is a terrible place to have a simple photo taken. I send it *faute de mieux*. As soon as possible it will be followed by a copy of a press photograph taken in America a few years ago. At least in *that* I look frightfully determined! . . .

As to the two further items, I have done my best to produce a vita: very difficult not to appear to be "blowing" all the time. As to my qualifications to instruct in philosophy, they reside mainly in my books. But since it is one of my books that I shall be teaching – namely *Time and Western Man* – that perhaps will not matter so much. – I was at Rugby School – where they invented the game of football which everyone plays over here. In spite of the demands made upon me by football, and other athletics, I began to read philosophy there. I did not go from Public School to University: Paris, where I went soon after Rugby, was my University. There I followed Bergson's lectures at the Collège de France, and shared the philosophical studies of friends of mine then at the Ecole Normale. (But I am not a *normalien*.)

[1] Professor Weiss wrote from Bard College saying that perhaps it could be arranged for L. to teach Philosophy there, rather than English, as was originally suggested.

What I should aim to impart at Bard would be more especially the projection *downwards*, as it were, upon the social plane, of certain modern philosophies: what in practice they stood for. And I should show, by way of classical analogy, how Plato's teaching would work out on the social plane, what his teaching was calculated to do to those who came beneath his sway, upon the social and political plane: what type of life was adumbrated in his philosophy.

This was, of course, the kind of problem which occupied me in *Time and Western Man*. Treating metaphysics as arbitrary myths, almost as much as does Professor Ayer[1] – as doctrinal propaganda for an individual, or a group, personality and its way of life (cf. Hegel and the god-State, as example of *group* expression, Vico as example of *personal*), I set out to analyse, from this standpoint, the contemporary systems in which the concept Time played so revealing and monopolistic a part.

Some of the above, however, belongs to my vita, to which I now will turn.

The Vita.

Was born in America, leaving when I was six or seven years old. Thenceforth my home was in England, except for some student-years in Europe, and (all told) seven or eight years in America.

The usual "private schools", then Rugby. Possessed school-French of course, but acquired colloquial French during six months residence in Holland, where I lived with a Belgian family. Then came my long Paris residence as student: several years: and it was then that I first seriously gave myself up to the study of philosophy. – Bergson was an excellent lecturer, dry and impersonal. I began by embracing his evolutionary system. From that I passed to Renouvier and thus to Kant. When one is young *on fait des bêtises, quoi!*

In world war i I was a soldier, artillery officer, Frontkampfer. My first book was a novel, *Tarr* – which has frequently been compared, of late, to *L'Age de Raison*, of Sartre. *Tarr* appeared during, and just after the war.

Of my big group of books, the first appeared in 1926, as is

[1] The logical positivist A. J. Ayer (b. 1910) was at this time Grote Professor of the Philosophy of Mind and Logic in the University of London.

shown in the bibliography with which this concludes. It is called *The Art of Being Ruled*. Machiavelli's *Prince* gave instruction in the art of *ruling*: my book deals with the far more complex and difficult art of *being ruled*.

This book was followed by *The Lion and the Fox*. Machiavelli had said that the *Prince*, or Ruler, must be brave as the lion, but at the same time cunning as the fox. In *The Lion and the Fox* I conduct an enquiry into the personal politics discoverable by a careful reading of Shakespeare's plays, and those of other Tudor dramatists.

Next came *Time and Western Man* .... A group of books, critical and creative – the offspring as it were of this key philosophical volume – followed immediately.

My life has positively seethed with and abounded in controversy of course, a consequence of the unorthodox character of these books, and also of my writing of a 250 thousand word book of satire.[1] These would constitute a good proportion of the *events* of a *Life*, but they have no place in a *vita*.

A vita is an institution which is new to me . . . I do hope I have succeeded in producing the kind of thing that is required.

Yours very sincerely,
WYNDHAM LEWIS

432. *To the Rev. Willis Feast*†   [London]
April. 1949.

Dear Mr. Feast. . . . The show opens May 1. Had to push it on one month. I met two nuns yesterday and asked them to pray for me! . . . – Why are you buying my books, nom d'un nom d'un nom! You should be psychoanalysed. . . .

Yrs in abominable haste

[1] *The Apes of God*.

433. *To the Editor of "Partisan Review"*†[1]

[London]
[ca. April 1949]

Sir. Excuse me for breaking in upon your as it were private, and partisan, history-making. In your April issue, which I have just been sent, I learn that Mr. Ezra Pound founded *Blast*, and that very obligingly Gaudier-Brzeska and myself turned up to lend him a hand – to give *Blast*, I suppose an arty flavour. But let me quote from Mr. Berryman's article. "Pound ... edited *Des Imagistes* which appeared in March of 1914. By the time Miss Lowell arrived with her retinue that summer, Pound, joined now with Wyndham Lewis and the sculptor Gaudier-Brzeska, had launched Vorticism, in the opening *Blast*."[2]

Why put "joined now with Wyndham Lewis etc"? Why not just say "Pound had launched Vorticism and *Blast*?" The statement would gain by this simplification. There is one thing, anyhow, that is quite plain to me. I am *de trop*. I ought never to have been there at all.

Why I barged in at all and edited *Blast* I cannot imagine. And, believe me, sir, I should not now be writing to you, were it not for the fact that I have a genuine pity for that much over-worked technician, the Historian (whether of Art, Religion, or Politics) who wastes all the best years of his life sifting out what is factual from what is fictional.

No credence need be given to this – just let me say it, and then forget it once and for all. I, Wyndham Lewis, had the not very original idea of founding an art paper, to advertise and popularise a movement in the visual arts which I had initiated. As I am of a somewhat literary turn, I decided to have writing in it too. My only trouble was that nothing was being written just then that seemed within a million leagues of the stark radicalism of the *visuals*. It was with regret I included the poems of my friend Ezra Pound: they "let down", I felt, the radical purism of the visual contents, or the propaganda of same. I must confess that even Gaudier seemed a little too naturalistic and not starkly

[1] This letter, written in response to an article by John Berryman, "The Poetry of Ezra Pound," in the *Partisan Review* for April 1949, was never printed. It may be that L. decided against sending it.
[2] See "The Poetry of Ezra Pound," p. 379.

XX century enough. Pound, however, cheered things up a little by a couple of "fresh" lines: namely "The twitching of two abdominal muscles. Cannot be a lasting Nirvana." John Lane, the publisher of Blast, asked me to come and see him, and I was obliged to allow him to black out these two lines. Happily the black bars laid across them by the printer were transparent. This helped the sales.[1]

That *Blast* was my idea, that I was the editor, that in short the whole show was mine, finally, that *vorticism* was purely a painters affair (as *imagism* was a purely literary movement, having no relation whatever to *vorticism*, nor anything in common with it) need not worry you. I should be a very fussy person if I expected people to bother about details of this order. Indeed I was rather gratified to see my name at all. – I apologise for my intrusion.

Dissatisfied with prospects at Bard and still hoping to get to the U.S., Lewis wrote in April to Hugh Kenner, asking if he knew of any openings. The two had had no prior contact. Kenner (b. 1923) had taught at Assumption College after Lewis and was acquainted with McLuhan and Giovanelli. Hence Lewis was aware of him, of his being a graduate student at Yale and interested in Lewis's books. Kenner recommended "The Rot" to Cleanth Brooks but was not placed to do more at the time. The correspondence then lapsed until October 1953, when Lewis was shown (by Methuen) the typescript of Kenner's Wyndham Lewis *and cabled congratulations. From then until Lewis's death, they remained in communication, meeting when Kenner visited London in November 1956.[2] In addition to his book-length study, Kenner, now Chairman of the Department of English at Santa Barbara College (University of California), has written several articles and reviews concerning Lewis's work.*

[1] The poem, in *Blast No. 1*, was "Fratres Minores." As originally printed the lines read:

> *They complain in delicate and exhausted metres*
> *That the twitching of three abdominal nerves*
> *Is incapable of producing a lasting Nirvana.*

In some copies the black bars of which L. speaks do not appear.

[2] Kenner gives an affecting account of their first meeting in his memorial tribute to L. See "Stele for Hephaestus," *Poetry*, August 1957, pp. 306–10.

434. *To Hugh Kenner*†　　　　　　　　　　　London. W. 11.
　　　　　　　　　　　　　　　　　　　　　May 9th. 1949.

Dear Mr. Kenner. Am just back from a flying-visit to Paris, which accounts for the lateness of this answering note. I am extremely grateful for the prompt action you have taken: and please tell Cleanth Brooks how greatly I appreciate what he has done and has so kindly consented to do. . . .

If you are interested in Joyce,[1] I have somewhere a print of a drawing I did of him. . . . A line profile. When we meet, as I hope we may, I shall be glad to discuss the points you mention. Freud, Vico, Flaubert, Stevenson and Pound are the five names it is *indispensible* to remember in any kind of study of Joyce, as you will perhaps agree, except that it is not generally recognised the part Pound, with his encyclopoedic pretentions and polyglot propensities – *and* his epistolary style! – played. . . . – May something be unearthed that will provide my wife and self with a living and enable me to write and paint *as well*.

　　　　　　　　　　　　　　　　　Most cordially,
　　　　　　　　　　　　　　　　　WYNDHAM LEWIS

435. *To T. W. Earp*†　　　　　　　　　　　　　[London]
　　　　　　　　　　　　　　　　　　　　　11 May 1949.

My dear Earp. I cannot tell you how pleased I was with your notice in the Telegraph:[2] and its use will be boundless. As a droll instance of this, today my Viennese dentist, who was being urged by me to construct a new plate over two stumps rather than extract them, said "Mr Lewis! Were it just anybody, I should not worry at all. Why should I? If they preferred to injure their health by refusing to part with their bad teeth, that would be all the same to me! But in you I am interested. I know you are a great artist ... oh yes I have seen. That is why I tell you. Those two teeth ought to come out." – Before leaving he informed me he had read your notice in the Daily Telegraph. – It is true, he is a Viennese. But your article will get me a great artist's dental plate instead of the average man's.

[1] Kenner was working on a doctoral dissertation on Joyce which became *Dublin's Joyce* (Bloomington, Ind., 1956).　　　[2] Of the Redfern show.

Do not forget that some time before long you and May (à laquelle mes devoirs n'est-ce pas) are coming to dinner.

Yours ever,
WYNDHAM LEWIS

436. *To David Kahma*†   London. W. 11.
May 19th. 1949.

Dear Khama. . . .

. . . I have thrown up the philosophy-professorship in the States. If I *must* continue to waste my time (cursing that two-legged tragedy, Man – a phrase of the editor of Horizon purloined from the French[1] – which with compunction I employ), I would prefer to waste it with my brush and palette rather than in jawing away to a lot of sodden brats about Plato and Plotinus. – The show has become unexpectedly successful. They have already sold ten thousand dollars worth of stuff. Alas, only a small proportion of the exhibits are my property. . . .

. . . By the way, I ought not to have suggested a Pansy Book to you. It would be far less of a fairy-tale (although actually about fairies) than the Douk Book. But oh dear. Who would publish that? You must fix your mind on average humanity like Shakespeare – more or less. Throw in a fairy or two of course – that is *natural*. I still think in Vancouver you have a goldmine if you could only discover how to work it. – I do not praise your dexterity in providing a fake-canto[2] because it is mere monkey-work and unless you wish to forge something for profit it is suggestive of life-wasting. You might get to know the ballet-dancers, and do a Degas-story of them. Oh hell oh hail – one keeps her old mother – she falls for a plump-faced university instructor and has twins. No room in her life, economically, for both twins and mother. Big stuff. Honour thy mother *versus* maternal instinct. Very modern – to hell with the old girl! Any plot even this well-handled is very good – just to set your mind working I give you the poor girl torn between her twins and her old ma. – Best wishes.

Yr
W. L.

[1] See "Comment," *Horizon*, May 1949, p. 306.
[2] Part of a longer poem titled "The Portrait of Ezra Pound."

437. *To T. S. Eliot*† London. W. 11.
21 May. 1949.

Dear Eliot. Thank you for the copy of your note for "Time", and for certain handsome passages of same.¹ If that graveyard scene of yours – you snugly boxed away under the daisies thinking of your Redfern portrait without experiencing a postmortem tantrum – if that does not sell the picture I shall be astonished.

Yrs ever,
W. L.

438. *To David Kahma*† London. W. 11.
June 18. 1949.

My dear Khama. . . . – My book was published (I suppose) on 9 June in the U.S.² Heaven knows what they are going to say about it. My New York friend is away in Cuba, most unfortunately, though in the end I shall get some cuttings from him. Am writing Doubledays to see if they can do anything about it. – Typically, no clipping agency over here does any clipping from the Press of dollar countries. These remarks you must not interpret as meaning that I expect to read anything pleasant. Critics in the U.S. are of three kinds. There are (1) the men-of-letters who teach in universities. They are the heavyweights who quote Aristotle, and *they* show how smart they are, how much more they know than you do, and generally treat your book as if it were the thesis of a particularly muddle-headed, lazy, slovenly, and a little cocky student who they have it in for and wish publicly to shame. To show what fair-minded men they are they concede that if you had only known how to write the book (as they would) you *might* have written quite a good book. (2) There are the paid hacks who kick

¹ *Time* reviewed L.'s Redfern show in its May 30th issue (p. 60). The review focuses on the new portrait of Eliot and carries illustrations of it and the 1938 portrait. There are quotations from L. and from Eliot, but the sentence referred to in this letter is not included. In Eliot's note it reads: "I shall not turn in my grave if, after I am settled in the cemetery, this portrait is the image that will come into people's minds when my name is mentioned."
² *America and Cosmic Man.*

you around with great relish if you are not one of the heavily-advertised, "best-selling", type of author; or fawn on you if you *are*. (I have been both, so I know). And there are the few stray people, quite uninfluential, from whom one may get a civil word.

. . . Will write very soon.

439. *To John Rothenstein*† [London]
[Perhaps not sent.] 24. June. 1949.

Dear Rothenstein: I have just learned from someone at the Tate that my portrait of T.S. Eliot was not bought.[1] When I saw you three days ago and you observed (prefacing your remarks by saying "I know you will not like this") that the piece of paper at the side of the picture was the best thing in it, I should of course have taken it away. . . . This has become almost a technique of yours, has it not? I recall that when I sent you my portrait of Dr. Erlanger you wrote back to say how good the *hands* were. . . .

440. *To Felix Giovanelli*† [London]
[ca. July 1949]
Thursday.

My dear Gio. . . . Please do not offer to send me money for a European holiday. Your friends here must have misinformed you . . . regarding my situation. It is not economically brilliant of course. But shortness of money is not the trouble here – it is other shortages. Besides if I wanted to I could go and live in France for some months cheaper than I could live in England. They are accommodating to artists – the restrictions are relaxed for certain classes of people. – Admire E.P.'s poetry as much as you can, but for Mike's sake do not listen to him . . . in any matter concerning myself. . . . Finally, as a warning against what you hear: I am astonished what *facts* people will invent concerning me – people I have never seen in my life. Every variety of lie or distortion. Achtung! therefore, darling Gio. – I am sorry to hear that Mr.

[1] At the close of the Redfern show, L. submitted the new portrait to the Tate Gallery. It was later purchased and presented to Magdalene College, Cambridge.

This and Mr. That are "timid": but I do not blame them at all.
... [there] is no very good reason why people should sacrifice themselves to [a] crank. Considering all the shits there are in the world how any one can be so pathetically silly as to talk about the Jews (who are neither better nor worse than anybody else) or any other particular race passes my understanding. –

... Terrific blessings.

W. L.

P.S. Very sorry to hear about poor old Born.[1] Mans life is but a vibration in an eyelash of God. We are Born, we Die. In life we are in the midst of death. . . .

W. L.

441. *To David Kahma*†   London. W. 11.
                                                                        July 9 1949.

My dear Khama. . . .

I have before me your letter of 28 May. That is to go a long way back. But it is a most interesting letter which I regretted at the time it was impossible to answer owing to pressure of petty but relentless affairs. I wish I were a *rentier* like Samuel Butler. What a lot of work I should be able to do! For most of the "pressure" is not caused by *work*.

What you said about the New York "Intellectual" struck me as very excellent sense. What is so deadly in American life is the ferocious and aggressive pride in the possession of money, and the stultifying effect of this upon the "Intellectuals", necessarily in "low income brackets" either writers or in universities. The American appears to me to experience a sensation of even *physical diminutiveness* in contact with a bigger "income bracket" than himself – with a man possessed of ten times – or twice – as much money. The value placed upon money (not what it procures for you, but *it*) is pathologic. It is the great American malady. It is in every way as strong as the abasement and sensation of physical *smallness* and insignificance felt by an English peasant girl in the presence of a noble lady, in the Victorian age. – The possession of learning, of genius in the arts or sciences – *nothing* seems to weigh

[1] At the time of his death, Wolfgang Born (1894–1949) was Assistant Professor of Art at the City College of New York. He was teaching in St. Louis when L. went there to stay.

in the U.S. in comparison with money. It may weigh when money is not anywhere around, but the moment Money makes its appearance, all other values dwindle. Nothing compensates for the absence of wealth – not in the eyes of the "Intellectual" any more than in the eyes of the rich man. Surely it is this (from our standpoint) in which America differs from England, France, Germany etc., or from Greece, or Rome: where there has always been a *value*, there is a *blank*. It is something raw, novel, and astounding. For with American poets, professors, writers, the impression I *always* get is how humble and unimportant-feeling they are underneath, even if they really have some reason to look down on mere riches. Still they *look up*. There is no one to give them encouragement except their own kind: and like a currency valid for the family circle only, that is not much use.

In the end this terrible superstition will be overcome: the emotion at once craven and silly, will be exorcised. But *until* such time, it must remain incredibly difficult, unless one is rich, to write a first-rate book in the United States. Not because the *time* cannot be found. Fundamentally, it is a problem of *freedom*.

I know an Irish Canadian priest (in Ontario) who is a very independent man. He smoked long cigars: wore a long handsome sweeping black cape (non-clerical): I suspect that he drank gin *to excess* – and he taught the *Summa*. Age about 37: He told me that he had been a seminarian, but had not wished to enter the priesthood, so had obtained a job. But he said that the *cringing* subservience that was demanded of him, as of all members of an office staff, was more than he could stomach. He did not wish to cringe his way up to some modest eminence. Consequently he quit and entered the priesthood after all – a teaching order – specialising in philosophy.

Now this cringing in offices – and of the most abject kind – I have witnessed myself in Toronto offices. (Have I spoken of this before I wonder). Even in art-circles I have listened with disgust throughout a party to the *whining* of an artist paying court to the President of the local Academy. "Oh *Fred!*" (a whining Fr-a-iid – almost a wail) "Do you think, Fred, I should do this, Fred" (or that Fred). Fred was always being respectfully consulted (though here power rather than money was involved). – But I am telling you what you know better than I do. You could give *me* a thousand instances for every one I have been able to note.

Money is not the whole thing, but what a big factor it is. If one wrote something for public consumption on these lines people would sneer, genuinely bored. "Oh yes. The 'almighty dollar' you mean!" – Of course it *is* what I should mean. But it is one of those things which, if only they can survive *identification* and *denunciation*, can go on forever and brazenly endure. Yawns greet its mention: everything has been said about it that can be said. It is then in the same category as *war*. Yet I feel perfectly certain that this well-worn topic must always remain bitterly topical for us, who are interested in the expressive arts. Until that superstition is exorcised; until that missing value is reinstated (for it was once there in the U.S.), American writers will be tempted to retire to England or Cuba. . . .

. . . – Where you discuss Eliot's audience, with a view to deciding whether they were all in the "Cactus Land" already when he came along, or whether Eliot led them in like a Pied Piper, you must bear in mind one thing; namely, what an enormous herd of poets and 'tesses there are today – and were in the 'twenties. I do not think any of them were in the Cactus Land: they were mostly in bed together, trying to escape from blistering *Weltschmerzen* in one another's backsides. But it was very easy to get them into the Cactus Land, since they were feeling a little cactussy just then, with Heartbreak House and all that.

If you have never been "in a dark country" – to change the subject – (except for the arctic circle) you should come here. It is a dark country.

As to "Cosmic Man". All reviews I have seen so far – except one – have been favourable, and some very favourable. The exception was a professorial wigging I got, dismissing me as a lazy, untidy, and strangely ignorant pupil.[1] The critic flung himself about like a district attorney mouthing "irrelevant, immaterial" – what are the other words in an Erle Stanley Gardner lawcourt? . . .

Yrs.
WYNDHAM LEWIS

[1] See Allan Nevins, "Citizens of the World, Unite," *Saturday Review of Literature*, June 25th, 1949, p. 14.

442. *To Alfred Barr Jr.*†¹   London. W. 11.
                                    10 July. 1949.

Dear Mr. Barr. A young Negro artist named Denis Williams² (of British Guiana) is passing through New York, on his way home. A *British Council* scholarship to study art brought him to London: he has been working latterly in the Colonial Ministry.

I am writing you this letter because (1) I regard him as a young man of *very unusual talent*: and (2) it is obvious that that talent will be wasted unless he can somehow, at this juncture, arrange his life in such a way as to enable him to paint. – On his return to British Guiana he will take up again civil service work – just as he has been wasting two years out of three here as a clerk in a Ministry.

Caribbean people, technically "British", are in fact culturally Americans. Mexico City, New York, are for him the centers of his world – not London. May he visit you and will you give him any encouragement or advice you are able to? . . .

                                    Sincerely yours,

443. *To Felix Giovanelli*†   London. W. 11.
                                    July 10. 1949

My dear Gio. . . .

You and Mack³ seem to have toured around. Good old Mack *n'est-ce pas!* Did you visit the Washington Shrine again? I hear that most of the inmates in the part of St. Eliz. where E.P. is housed think that they are dead. If you converse with them they ask you when you died. . . .

I do some art-criticism as you no doubt have heard. A few days ago I discovered a young Negro of great talent as a painter. He was exhibiting with the son of a paramount chief of the Gold Coast,⁴ who is as dull as he is bright. His name is Denis Williams. British Guiana is his home (S. America). The "British Council"

---

[1] L. met Alfred Barr, Jr. (b. 1902), Director of Museum Collections at the Museum of Modern Art, when he was in New York in 1940. This letter was sent also to James Thrall Soby.

[2] L. reviewed Williams's exhibition at the Berkeley Gallery most favourably in *The Listener* for July 14th, p. 68.

[3] Marshall McLuhan.   [4] Kofi Antubam.

(a cultural organisation subsidised by the Government to the tune of 25 million dollars annually) gave Williams a year's scholarship to study art in London: after which he worked for two years in the Colonial Ministry – I asked him to visit me and he did so last night; when the above facts were communicated to me. Also that he sails next Tuesday (or flies) to New York.

What the position as regards Negroes is in N.Y. I do not know: but I have taken the great liberty of giving him your address. There is no responsibility whatever attached to this contact. . . . He will not cost you a cent.

(This I say because Negroes are in such a weak position that, like other people in weak positions, they must often be very hard-up).

Denis Williams is an extremely *intelligent* young man – he cannot be more than 24 or 25. He will not be a disagreeable contact (though I hope he will not be a socially embarrassing one). What you can do is to give him a few necessary bits of information. . . . – Then you may by chance know a Negro artist? – you might assist him re any charitable organisation to help visiting Negroes of the student type. That sort of thing.

Finally: it seems to me abominable for the British Council to give him *one years* lift, and then drop him. Guiana is no place in which to be a painter. It would be wonderful if he could stay in New York. Otherwise he fancies Mexico City and Havana. . . . – The main fact in all this is that he is a *very unusually promising artist*. I hope I have not done the wrong thing in giving this young chap your address. . . .

Yours, a little anxiously,
W. L.

444. *To David Kahma†*   London. W. 11.
                                                               6 Aug. 1949.

Dear Khama. Thank you for your long and very interesting letter. . . .

Your proposal to shape your response to my remarks about American intellectuals into an article seems to me a very good one. I will see what I can do with it. Do not take too long finishing it! . . .

... When your letter is found, I will make a few observations. The U.S. factory-owning class is very raw, arrogant, and ignorant. Their women *rape* "culture" (clubs, "circles" for weekly absorption of potted literature etc). And that tough and cocky selfishness of the U.S. rich does not *improve*. The refugee and other European elements are of great value.

P.S. Have just found letter. Here are a few notes on what interests me most. (Your later notes on what might be called the *psychology of God* would need great care. Where you say that God is afraid (or would be) of making a fool of Himself – those kinds of things you would have to think about a lot.)

---

1. America and its cultural future. "The pathological obsession with money in the abstract" (I use your words) – the "abstraction" is an impoverishment: a searing up of life. What by? – The answer to this, which you on the spot must be able to analyse back to, is highly important.

2. A good point you make about the *extension* of the sensation of smallness. "having been made to feel small in the Money-context" (cf. the sight of the Joneses newer and larger refrigerator, or, of course, car) "their *sensation of smallness* has become a habit" etc. etc.

3. "the impersonal forces of nature" (as a source of *small-feeling*) must be insisted on always. The other day Lynette Roberts, a Welsh-Argentinian poetess (quite good sometimes, when not parodying Dylan Thomas) told us that it was her belief that there could not possibly be a God because of the vast size, remoteness, and number of stars.

Yrs
WYNDHAM LEWIS

445. *To a London Photographer*†   London. W. 11.
6 Aug. 1949.

Dear Mr. ———. I am afraid that although *one* of the shots you took of me seemed fairly good *to me* (the one with the fist pressed up against the cheek) no one I knew shared that view: and the majority regard it as a bad photograph of myself. As for the others, and I hope you will forgive me for speaking plainly: several are unspeakable, and none are otherwise than highly displeasing to me and to everybody else. One or two are what might be described as photographic insults. Needless to say, I can make no commercial use of them, which was my purpose in having them taken. – I recall that in the preliminary talk we had you pointed out that it was altogether incorrect to say that "the camera cannot lie". I suppose that it is also correct to say that the results can be infinitely manipulated. Of course I am sure you produced these photos with the best of highbrow intentions. But there it is. I have not exaggerated the displeasing impression, and in some cases the horror induced. . . .

Sincerely,
WYNDHAM LEWIS

P.S. . . . Probably you ought to have a bigger camera – but I know nothing about it. There is *something* the matter: what it is I am not competent to say.

W. L.

446. *To Charles Handley-Read*†¹   London. W. 11.
12 August. 1949.

Dear Handley Read. . . .

My work is very simply divisible into four productive periods. (1) 1912–14. The paintings of that period are all lost, only a few small things are left. (2) The 'twenties – mainly 1920–26. (3) The 'thirties, 1933–39. (4) The present day. – I certainly was producing more or less throughout the blanks separating these periods of constant work at painting, but things of a minor kind. The Miss Sitwell was begun in the 'twenties and repainted and completed in the 'thirties. 1931–33 I was seriously ill. The "Siege of Barcelona" was painted in Gloucester Terrace and completed here (Notting Hill Gate); 1934 to 1937 therefore is the date. . . .

Yours sincerely,

¹ Early in 1949 Charles Handley-Read, then an art master at Bryanston School, proposed to Faber & Faber that he should do an illustrated book on L. After consultation with L., Faber's agreed to publish the work, which became *The Art of Wyndham Lewis*. Handley-Read communicated frequently with L., by letter and in person, while preparing his manuscript.

447. *To Charles Handley-Read* London, W. 11
Sept 2nd. 1949.

My dear Mr. Handley-Read. . . .

I suggest that, in your preliminary note, you define Mr. W.L.'s complete divorce from the external sensuous reality in 1913–14, exemplified (not very adequately I fear) by "The Portrait of an Englishwoman." (You are at liberty to use these exact words if you so wish, and this applies more or less throughout). With this 1914 specimen compare Mr. W.L.'s return to nature after World War I – in say 3 degrees (*étapes*) – et des fois je les ai brulés! of naturalist-abstract composition. I suppose the nearest to the 1914 absolute of abstraction would be "The Geographer"[1] – minus the Geographer. For the latter's vertical mental projection – like smoke going up from a chimney – takes cartographic form. The figure itself is naturalistic, so perhaps some other work would be better. – The next compartment or region of form, on the road back to nature, would perhaps be "What the Sea looks like at Night"[2] (Redfern exhibition 1949) – or perhaps "Players on a Stage" (Oil) would be a better example. Perhaps the "Mud Clinic"[3] might be instanced as the last compartment before one reaches nature *au grand complet* (John MacLeod or one of the drawings of people).[4]

(I would draw your attention to the fact that "The Planners"[5] is *a title* merely found for this drawing for the purposes of exhibition – by Nan Kivell,[6] I think. The way those things were done – are done, by whoever uses this method of expression – is that a mental-emotive* impulse is let loose upon a lot of blocks and lines of various dimensions, and encouraged to push them around and to arrange them as it will. It is of course not an accidental, isolated, mood: but it is recurrent groups of emotions and coagulations of thinking, as it were, that is involved).

You may of course use this letter intact: or, better, boil it in to your own text. Either will do. But dont bother if you dont want

---

[1] Abstraction dating from 1949.
[2] Dates from 1949, illustrated in Handley-Read, Pl. 25.
[3] Dates from 1937, illustrated in Handley-Read, Pl. 21.
[4] *Portrait of John MacLeod* (1938), illustrated in Handley-Read, Pl. 48.
[5] Non-objective drawing of 1913, illustrated in Handley-Read, Pl. 4.
[6] Rex Nan Kivell, Director of the Redfern Gallery.

to do either. All this just to speed-up – to make more interesting to public. Just to help.

Then you should, I think, on your own, *describe* (briefly) the various kinds of abstractions, or the mixed idiom of pure-abstraction-and-stylized-nature. I mean by this, take "What the Sea looks like at Night" (I use these only because I at once recall them – you could take other examples.) point out that in greatly stylized image of the ocean, semi-human animals plunge and obtrude themselves, as if they had found their way into this from another dimension etc.

Next, show how, whereas on the musical-abstract (symbols) of 1914 the emotive intellect is let loose (though under some control) upon a multitude of blocks and lines, and composes its fugue: *quite otherwise* in 1935 (or whenever it was) in "The Mud Clinic", *the literary imagination* is invited to compose – in a highly selective, but far more complex, world of forms – usually dominated by one colour – say saffron, or blue.

Excuse these hasty notes. I trust they will be of use.

W. L.

* By this is meant subjective intellection, like magic or religion.

[Note on side of page] Describe creatures in "mud clinic" – made of mud, characterised by apathy, of x race etc. *What* is their complaint? Ask likewise *who* are monsters in ocean, so affrighting the pink lady?

448. *To David Kahma*†　　　　　　　　　　London. W. 11.
　　　　　　　　　　　　　　　　　　　　Sept 3rd. 1949.

Dear Khama. I am interested in your *autobiography* and I am interested in your dissertations: but do allow me to say that they mix awfully badly. You ought to cut out *cleanly* and implacably the *vita* material from this typescript you have sent me. Amplify it in every way – add all the bits (about Sutton[1] etc) in former letters. *Then* send it me. But let us have a pact together. When I start reading the moment I see an extraneous opinion obtruding,

[1] Major-General F. A. Sutton (1884–1944). Much of his life was spent as an advisor to Chinese generals. He lived in Vancouver from 1927 to 1931.

or a dissertation beginning, or didactics lifting its ugly head, I tear it up without more ado.

This does not mean that I have not found much that you say about "The Future", or the superior good sense of the Indian fishers over the Cominform (though Indians are a part of the local colour) or about Einstein or Eliot, intelligent and worth reading. It is just that *in your best interest* I have to pin you down to something, if that is possible, and to get something out of you which one day it will be too late to extract. The relevant sections in this rambling discourse (about your childhood and boyhood) are excellent. You write a thousand times better than you did 2 years ago. You are not stilted now: you no longer use 50 words where 3 is all that is needed. However, you must work seriously, and not let your mind wander all over the place. Remember, you cannot reasonably despise *all* the people who do something, if you do not do something yourself, since it is obvious that you do not, and have not for a considerable time, wished to remain an amused spectator of mens follies, and efforts: you have desired to *perform* yourself. It is most necessary now to think of publishing.

Your Douk book you should have consulted me about before putting pen to paper. You are not a "planner", are you? You just rush in, improvise, and hope for the best. I am outspoken because you consult me. But it is no use consulting me if you do not consult me *at the beginning* – and before the beginning. It is no use handing me a book already started on a wrong track and asking me to drag you step by step across an unpromising terrain.

I am *quite sure* you could write a book about your life which would put you on the map, as they say. Why not let me help you to achieve geographical identity? The preliminary task would be perfectly simple now. Piece together *every* scrap you have ever written to me about *your life of experiences* (factual). Include all that you have written about your adopted parents at Gibsons.[1] (Do not call it Gibsons – call it Paulton's or Garricks, or Garrison's or Williamsons.) Describe their appearance – tastes – clothes – their *smell*: their speech (urbane or rough etc.), beliefs, weaknesses, talents, say whether they drank, quarrelled (if so, what about). Describe their home in England (Downs, Fen Country).

Describe *the scene*. The mountain at the back is high? Is it

---

[1] Gibsons, B.C., a small coastal community where Kahma lived as a boy.

covered with firs? Is it rock? Is Gibsons inland? How far? What is the coast like? Is it cold in winter? Much snow? Put in about loggers who visited (or lived in) Gibsons. How do people live – how many are there? What do they eat – fish? How many miles from Vancouver? —— Next. Your father came to Gibsons as a young man, as principal of the local school. Obviously that is how you came to get there. Was your mother there?

... For p. 23 I have a note full of optimism, however. Here it is.
"Land at last!" – This is the solution. Your *Father*. Charles Dickens father (Mr. Micawber) was the making of Dickens. And certainly Osbert's Father supplied all that is tolerable in *his* book – if it is permissable to use so ignoble an illustration. Fathers are often the making of their sons. – Here is *another* Father perhaps. He is a schoolmaster. Excellent. He teaches his child algebra so that some of the labour may be taken off his back of marking papers. He was an Irishman. Cannot you cook up this Father – since it is not really *you*, it need not be him – not altogether your Father – cannot you dress him up into a great Paternal success?

Actually he is a father you admire. This need not complicate matters. Change him! He rides a horse in a fine way. Also he has his *humours*. Cannot you build up a figure to anchor your story to – or *two* figures. (1) Your finnish mother, and her most picturesque relatives in Finland (which alone of all countries pays its debts): and (2) your mathematical Irish father.

This of course is delicate ground. – He was born in Ireland? Or his father was? In Donegal or Tyrone? Very few Canadian Irish come from Eire? Was *his* mother Irish? Coming from the North of Ireland he had no potato famine backgrounds. – He was protestant? – I do not say he need be the principal figure. James Joyce portrayed some of his improvident, impecunious, father in Bloom. The identification need not be easy. – Fathers have always been popular in fiction. But if the Father in question just wont fit in, tant pis. Then he *is* I think alive. . . .

There are unwise notes – failures of tact (e.g. pp 55. 56.) *ME lifted above the corruption of the world* sounds priggish. pp. 13. 14. You should say simply "I was an infant prodigy." People will remark, as it is, "At 2 he could not speak – though he has made up for it since. At 6 he knew as much astral physics as we do." – Were you to say your father was a math teacher and pumped you full of the weight of stars, distances in light-years, and de Sitters[1] sophistries, that would be quite different.

Votre enfance pascalienne je trouve effroyable (pour m'en servir de votre mot). Or so I found *at first* (as witness page of typescript I extract and mail). Afterwards I reconsidered this. You have something there, with your babyhood among the canadian stars. Only a bit less of "Pascal and I": it sounds like *blowing*. I know it is not of course. It's just the sound.

In the early stages of my reading I made this note: "All didactic stuff should be relentlessly cut out. . . . – Of course I soon saw that you did not really intend to restrain your didactic impulses, and so shifted my position towards what I was reading.

p. 11. Note. "Well, you know all about Heaven!" This note of mine is typical of what I wrote in one or two places. And one of the things you *must* be careful about is not to give the impression of "blowing" or of pretentiousness, or of a jejune intimacy with the divine. This does not matter with me: but we must begin thinking of *the printed page* from now on. You must get something published. The next thing you send must not be a letter to me, but a piece of writing I can show to somebody and which *could* be published. – Excuse the notes I scribbled on the text, in the pages excised. These douches of cold water have stiffened you up a great deal. There were lots of pages about which I had no observation to make. You have given an excellent idea of [General] Sutton and his woman, the child-gangs. There must I feel be lots more. Avoid always giving yourself the *beau rôle*. And dont be afraid of writing of Vancouver itself. BUT PLAN AT ONCE (with me) WHAT TO MAKE YOUR HERO. *Your* experience up to 18 years. Then what?

Yours
WL.

P.S. I hope I have not given the impression that I was disappointed about your performance. On the contrary! There are certain faults, inseparable from isolated situation, which require drastic correction. But disquisitions aside (which would have their use later on) it was a most promising batch of stuff.

W. L.

[1] Willem de Sitter (1872–1934), Dutch astronomer.

449. *To W. K. Rose*[1]　　　　　　　　　　London. W. 11.
　　　　　　　　　　　　　　　　　　　　　　4 Sept. 1949.

Dear Mr. Rose. Thank you for your letter. The reason I asked you for enlightenment was because, had you been an undergraduate at Harvard, your tutor or someone might have been known to me. I hope you become Dr. Rose without hitch. – The answer to your questions about Margot is that Communism has something to do with everyone.[2] Even when it seems a long way off. All types of person – unfortunately – are in the same world. There is no especial type who alone may be used in a book in which the main figure is a communist. – If your question is political, that should be an adequate answer too. – Give me more news of your activities.

　　　　　　　　　　　　　　　　　Yrs sincerely,
　　　　　　　　　　　　　　　　　WYNDHAM LEWIS

450. *To the Rev. Henry Swabey*†[3]　　　　　　　　[London]
　　　　　　　　　　　　　　　　　　　　　　21 Oct. 1949.

Dear Swabey. No man is my equal as a bad correspondent. However. Thank you for the very interesting material and also news of impending events. The Thaxted gentleman is active I see. He urges his parish to support the Peace Conference.[4] Three artists, two of whom I greatly admire, wrote me the other day, seeking

[1] The editor (b. 1924) was at this time teaching English at Williams College in Massachusetts and completing a doctoral dissertation (for Cornell) on Lewis's work. In the course of this project he exchanged letters with L. and became acquainted with him in London in 1953.
[2] The questions concerned a seeming incongruity in *The Revenge for Love* – the involvement of the sympathetic heroine, Margot Stamp, with the unsympathetic Communists. Previously the editor had queried Margot's marriage to Stamp, so much her inferior in "stature." L. had replied that "the objects of men's love, or of women's, [are] not related to 'their stature.' Goethe married his cook."
[3] Henry Swabey, a long-time friend and follower of Pound, became acquainted with L. in 1949. Swabey was then at Lindsell Vicarage, Dunmow. His situation there – as an advocate of decentralised schools (in the cause of family unity) and a fellow-diocesan of the communistic vicar of Thaxted, Jack Putterill – became the basis of "Parents and Horses," one of the pieces in *Rotting Hill*.
[4] Presumably the World Congress of Partisans of Peace held in 1950.

to obtain my adherence to this Peace movement. To me it seems criminal lunacy to engage in what is euphemistically called "war": but is not this peace organisation rather a spurious one – just a move in a most aggressive cold-war-game? I suppose I have to answer. In a letter from Peter Russell I learn that "Red Jack" (I think he called him) of Thaxted, preaches a very fine sermon. I wish I had heard him. Is he a soap-boxer?

... There is one thing you can help with. In the writings of St. Augustine, a most unpleasant saint, "The Family" has no standing, to put it mildly. He tells people to purge their hearts of all affection for home, parents, children, and friends. Now *how*, at what date, and *in what* terms did the Family Unit become the especial care of the Church? And do the Anglican and Roman communion derive *from the same source* their policy regarding the sacred nature of the Family? – From the Christian standpoint I believe you are right in defending the integrity of the Family? But I really dont know why I do.

Yrs.

451. *To David Kahma*†   London. W. 11.
21 Oct. 1949.

My dear Khama. ... Everything is so desperate today, as you know, over here. Everyone hysterical – but suppressing it which produces an unhealthy calm. One has literally to work one's head off, and then there is a conspiracy to waste one's time. For instance, one buys a shirt. Nice blue checks. Swiss import. In first weeks wash it shrinks $2\frac{1}{2}$ inches. You go to the store: endless arguments, threats – you get the shirt replaced. But there is *a hole* in the new shirt. Back to the store – "high words" – threats. Another shirt. One opens the packet when one gets home: it stinks. However, see what it comes out like in wash. Etc. Etc. Etc.

Do not listen to what I say about Douk book if you want to have a try with it. ...

W. L.

...

P.S. .... – *As to punctuation*. I agree with those who regard the semi-colon (;) as redundant. The full stop, the comma, and the colon are quite enough. ...

Your mss. & proposals.

After a success (of any kind) with autobiographical book you could return to Douk book and offer it to a publisher. It is my advice that you do not dream of offering it now. Cut out all the biographical bits – the low life in Vancouver part – and incorporate them in the *new* book. You have copies of the material you send to me? Take out all these bits, place them before you on a table, and fit them together like a jigsaw puzzle. (Your wife perhaps helping.) You will soon discover that they will become organic if you fill in the gaps a little with other reminiscences. When you reach the stage at which it is all joining up and bulking out, become an organism, you must think what you are going to call all these people. Harry Smith, Katie Jones, Johnny Robinson and what *theme* you are going to impose on this mass. – It is not quite the way to write even a very autobiographical novel, but with luck and a little persistence it should work, and the circumstances seem to make it difficult to do it in any other manner.

As to papa, if I may be frank, he seems a most typical Canadian. The animal which is house-trained, chained up, domesticated, in Europe, on emigration to the New World celebrates its freedom. In a hotel in which we spent some time there was a certain couple, the woman enceinte. A week before the child arrived the man vanished. The woman entered a clinic, bore the child. The husband was untraceable. The child grew to be quite a big boy – she was still in the clinic: the clinic people would not let her out until she paid, and she of course had relied upon her husband to pay. *She* had no money. Eventually the prisoner was liberated by her mother. – This is highly typical of what we encountered everywhere. In the same hotel a man and woman lived underneath us. The man beat his wife every night, and at last strangled her. Her life was saved and she did not return. He then used to beat his friends or they beat him. In the next apartment but one was living an Indian married to a very teutonic-looking young woman from Kitchener: he unmercifully beat the little german every night and sometimes in the middle of the day. She bellowed at the top of her voice and I gathered derived much pleasure from it. On one occasion I heard the landlord, an Englishman, address the Indian in these terms: "A gentleman does not call a lady a bitch." The Indian was stupefied by this. The apartments not occupied by intoxicated men maltreating their intoxicated wives were full of intoxicated men engaged in incessant brawls. The only apartment that was quiet was that in the occupation of a drug-addict, who, to a moderate extent, lesbianized as well. Every hotel we were in, beginning with the —— and ending with the ——, rocked all night with hysterical whoopee at least once a week – when bedrooms were rented for the night by the hairdressers, or plumbers whatnot of the city, in which bedrooms after a banquet downstairs, they rioted all night long. Of course this was the mere exterior of life: I should not surprise, but I should revolt, you I hope if I retailed what I got to hear of the private lives of people. It was not until we moved to the Lord Elgin in Ottawa that we enjoyed normally peaceful occupation, and the scandals were of a more decorous and diplomatic kind. . . . In the States things are much quieter. It is these *Canadian* conditions that are interesting to outsiders. You should exploit them.

Please do not regard this as an "indictment". The conditions are almost "frontier" conditions – oddly disguised in urban refinements (which you would find equally at Timmins or at Churchill[1] or at the North Pole) and with the millionaire, in great luxury. – You *have* to have your father or someone like him in your book. He explains everything, after all . . . .

Your uncle is good, too. He must be a major figure, but not *the* figure. – Finally, I can only speak for myself, but I at once become bored in a story when I feel that situations and events are being doctored, trimmed up, falsified and cooked. In a thing of this kind, you depart from the factual truth at your peril. Were you for instance to make your father a large bearded man, or a German, or a very abstemious person, then it would be some *other* story. . . .

One more word. You must shun as you would death all suggestion of (1) self-righteousness: (2) all suggestion that butter would not melt in your mouth: (3) any hint of inordinate scholarly pretentions. The more modest, candid, unaffected you are, the more *disarming*, the more likely you are to succeed. The material is rich: you have the literary talent. . . . But for heavens sake no *essays* in the middle of narrative, conceal your learning, think of yourself as a miserable sinner.

W. L.

[1] Timmins is in north-western Ontario; Churchill is on Hudson Bay in Saskatchewan.

452. *To David Kahma*† London. W. 11.
Dec. 9. 1949.

My dear Khama. . . . We cannot possibly express our gratitude to you and your wife for all these good things! and so many of them necessary things, such as butter. Our life would be a very different one without this help. I even notice some *jam*. And the Vancouver jam is whole fruit and much of it as good as the Australian which is the best in the world. The jam here gets worse and worse. More turnip in it every day.

The Mix parcel mercifully arrived to time. Of the 12 Mixes in question we have used 4. We have now eight left. We bake two at a time and that lasts about five days. We have therefore enough for 20 days. Of course to eat a certain amount of the stuff they sell here does not matter. It is *a solid consumption*, day in day out, of animal feed from the Black Sea that is harmful. Many doctors have said it is harmful: but they can always find some crooked doctor to certify that it is "better than white bread" and that the more bran and chalk in it the better. . . . We have a busy period ahead of us this Christmas: several friends coming up from the country – one to get a divorce. It is a divorce case in which I shall play a part, for one of the main contentions of the woman's husband (countering her charges of cruelty) is that she purchased works by Mr. Wyndham Lewis (one an oil painting) during a period of hard-upness! . . .

Our blessings on your combined heads!
W. L.

. . .

453. *To Augustus John*† [London]
12 Dec. 1949.

My dear John. Thank you for your note and for The Delphic Review.[1] I was glad to hear I had given proof of second sight, and to learn that you had definitely called Mantegna in as partner in

[1] The *Delphic Review*, edited in John's village of Fordingbridge, appeared twice: Winter 1949 and Spring 1950.

your new enterprise.¹ I shall be most interested to see the results. I greatly admired your "Old Gypsy". I suggested it for the "Listener" cover and thought it made a very good appearance there. – the drawing actually survived the mass-production.

Your "Frontiers"² was full of good things. As you say, people of all nations can live perfectly comfortably together: witness the Poles, Wops, Germans, etc. in American cities. They would be killing each other over here (because of national sovereignty) – over there they go about their business peaceably. It does not matter in the least what they *call* themselves, all modern Governments are an unspeakable curse. They are far worse than any kings, or emperors, or czars. In the Wars of the Roses here, for instance, it was the king and nobility that were concerned: it appears that people in general were hardly touched by this civil brawl which so preoccupies the historian and trade flourished. The people were no more troubled than Chicagoans are by gang-wars. But *today*! The "total", the "collective", principle changes everything.

Where you write re. "Good Europeans ... not thinking in terms of black and white," how excellent that is. – Then what you say about the "abolition of frontiers." Not forgetting what you and Mantegna are cooperating on you should write more upon such subjects. Let us meet as you say: send me a line some hours in advance, if you will be coming up and are free.

Yours ever,
W. L.

[1] In his "Round the London Art Galleries" in *The Listener* for November 17th, L. praised John's drawings at the Lefevre Gallery. He emphasised John's olympian detachment from time – "for John I am sure Mantegna is as contemporary as Matisse" – and said that "The Head of an Old Gypsy" (which is reproduced on the paper's cover) "would do credit to any of the greatest masters of the Renaissance" (p. 860). Thanking him in a letter of November 30th, John wrote: "... you mentioned Mantegna's spiritual proximity as much closer to my mind than that of Matisse. Have you second-sight? In a composition I am doing, I have lifted a figure bodily from the former master so as to set the tone to the rest of the company."

[2] See *Delphic Review*, Vol. I, No. 1, pp. 6–11. In this brief article John advocates the abolition of frontiers and the eventual disappearance of states.

454. *To David Kahma*† London. W. 11.
27 Dec. 1949.

My dear Khama. In this pause, during a long holiday, let me get the promised letter written. . . .

My wife put the icing on the cake you sent. I look at it with fear! We have over-eaten and over-drunk. Your Christmas Pudding was not made any less rich by the brandy-butter we eat with it and the rest of the traditional Christmas foodstuffs. Christmas is a loathsome holiday. All there is to be said for it is that it enables one to write a few letters.

Tomorrow life begins again, and with it *eyes* have the spotlight.[1] My myopia is relatively slight: there is nothing visibly wrong with the eyes, but it is said that the optic nerve is being injured by some toxin. So *remove the poison* is the cry. I tremble to think what steps may be taken to expel the toxin. But no operation is contemplated, thank heaven. Almost certainly the teeth under the eyes will go. I shall be unpleasantly occupied after Christmas.

If you can get a New Year's day copy of Die Tat (Zurich) you will read me on "The next 50 years for Western society." Also Prof Toynbee. – Tell you these unimportant items as I know you like to be kept posted. – The brawl still rages over the Pound poetry award. In the editorial of "Hudson Review" strong language is used (Nov. or Dec.) – against that lousiest of all U.S. publications, the "Sat. Rev. of Literature."[2] . . .

. . . – Thank you for the admirable photos of yourself. – the one with wife is my favourite now. There you look *very* grave. It is, I feel, the author of "Satirogenitus". Shall have it enlarged. Your wife with her head back, as if she were dancing, is caught at a good moment too.[3] . . .

All good wishes for you both for the new year from my wife and myself.

W. L.

[1] L.'s first mention of his eyes since his return to England.
[2] See "Comment," *Hudson Review*, Autumn 1949, pp. 325–6. The *Hudson Review* supported Pound strongly in the controversy that arose when he received the Bollingen Award.
[3] Speaking of Kahma's photographs in an earlier letter, L. remarked: "What strange people get into street-photographs, in the background always looking as if they were tailing the main character!"

P.S. A buff form has arrived this morning from H.M. Excise & Customs, who affect to believe that your parcel of stationery is merchandise which you ship me for sale in England – presumably I run a stationery business. Curse them.

W. L.

455. *To J. E. Palmer*† [London]
8 Jan 1950.

My dear Mr. Palmer. . . . it would be a most agreeable task to discuss the four books you mention.[1]

Malraux (whose philosophy of art book I have not read) tends always to identify art and life. My own views are opposed to this as black is to white. When the Romans crucified living men upon their stages they were guilty (as I see it) of a crime against art. When the Athenian dramatists decreed that the consummation of the physical tragedy should not occur on the stage – the audience only *hearing of it*, not seeing it, they showed an understanding of the nature of art. (And Sartre, of course, with his philosophy of action, is Malraux's true disciple).[2] I hope you will not mind my offering criticism of this type? It takes all sorts to make a *civilised* world. When there is only *one* sort we may know civilisation has ended. There are plenty of Frenchmen, too, living and dead, who would agree with me. ("Je hai le mouvement qui deplace les lignes" Baudelaire's interpretation) ... ...

If after this demonstration of how critically (though respectfully bien entendu) I should approach the Malraux book, you still want me to review these books, how many words have you in mind?

I wish I knew Louisiana, where you Christmassed. I never got farther south than the Hillcroft[3] School in Virginia, near the Blue Mountains. That was not at all "southern." In fact, with its

[1] This projected review did not appear, L. having to abandon work on it in order to attend to his eyes. The book L. refers to here is André Malraux's *Museum Without Walls* (New York, 1949).

[2] This subject is discussed at length in Part III of *The Writer and the Absolute*.

[3] Probably the Foxcroft School in Middleburg, Virginia.

hedges, oaks, haystacks etc. it was so exactly like an English county that I could scarcely believe my eyes – unlike New England, which is not like England. – Next time I must press on South and to the Pacific.

Cordially yours,

456. *To Sir Nicholas Waterhouse*†   Notting Hill Gate. W. 11.
13. Jan 1950.

Dear Docker. The doctors are urgent: if some toxin is not removed I lose my sight. Monday they start pumping in penicillin. Two days later starts the pulling out of lots of teeth. For two weeks or more I shall be invisible. . . . Pray for me.

Yr
W. L.

457. *To Ezra Pound*†   [London]
[ca. January 1950.]

Dear E.P. I perceive I have offended – though what in my article provoked retaliatory biographical ... I cannot guess.[1] (1). Were I to become an active addict or partisan in the economic crusade which still engrosses you, I might soon find myself like yourself in a place of detention: but I have not a wealthy wife to do me the services yours does for you. Nor, I will be bound, would people be writing nice long flattering articles about me, trying to assist my case. No: you should not be cross on that account. (2) But something or everything in the social-biographical part caused an unpleasant reaction? The article was wholly benevolent. I wish I

---

[1] The article in question is presumably "Ezra: The Portrait of a Personality," L.'s contribution to the Pound number of the *Quarterly Review of Literature*, which appeared in December 1949. (Revised and reprinted as "Ezra Pound" in Peter Russell's *An Examination of Ezra Pound* [Norfolk, Conn., 1950].) L.'s reminiscence *cum* estimate is affectionate but characteristically sharp. He extols Pound the poet and entrepreneur of letters but declares his impatience with regard to the "credit crank." It was perhaps this last reservation that upset Pound and led to this contretemps.

had not written it. At least I shall not make the mistake of consenting to write other things of this nature.

W. L.

458. *To T. S. Eliot* [London]
12 March. 1950.

My dear Eliot. It was very kind of you to send me a copy of "The Cocktail Party."¹ I have now read it with great care and with unusual interest. I have seen it objected that your use of so popular a figure as the Mental Doctor was bad form, but for my part I was rejoiced to meet you disguised as a psychopathic quack. About half way through I decided that it was in the nature of a large naval gun mounted on a Thames houseboat of shallow draught. This of course might strike one as inartistic. But later on I learned that the big gun was part of the fixtures of the houseboat: and my last glimpse of this heavy ordnance was its festive departure in the company of Julia (of Mrs Porter's family I surmise)² to *other* cocktail parties. – That it is a success as a play (and I wouldn't know about that) is demonstrated by its tremendous reception in New York. You will I expect be responsible for the death of a number of libidinous Yankee damsels, for surely U.S. Psychologists will not be slow to take the hint and will dispatch the more dewy-eyed of their patients where they may be swallowed by alligators or pecked to death by vicious tropical birds. – As I went along, I felt that quite apart from the question involved in the blood-sacrifice, there was much highly interesting material being used in connection with the adulterous couple, who were inadequate vessels but it could with advantage be drawn on for another play; not exactly a comedy. – I congratulate you on your work and its great success in the U.S. This success will, I hope, be repeated here in London.

Yours ever,
W. L.

¹ *The Cocktail Party* was published in London on March 9th, 1950.
² See "The Waste Land" (III. The Fire Sermon):

> O the moon shone bright on Mrs. Porter
> And on her daughter
> They wash their feet in soda water . . . . (ll. 199–201.)

459. *T. S. Eliot to Wyndham Lewis*
Faber and Faber Limited
24 Russell Square London W.C.1.
13 March 1950.

My dear WyndhaM,

You are quite right – no one else has yet remarked that Julia is a niece of Mrs. Porter, and that Reilly's mother was a Sweeney (but no doubt James J. Sweeney will be looking into the matter). Possibly the houseboat is a Mississippi houseboat –

Down the Mississippi, Baby, we will float along;
In our little houseboat, maybe, life's one grand sweet song.

I await statistics of the self-immolation of young women from the Long Island suburbs.

Yours ever
T. S. E.

460. *To Meyrick Booth*†[1] [London]
22nd March. 1950.

My dear Meyrick. We were both delighted to get your letter, which took, by the way, 12 days to reach this address. (All mail from Ireland is I suppose examined by thousands of well-paid clerks, who elaborately note the destination, name and address of sender, indications of political orientation of same. These stimulating data are filed and repose in the archives of Scotland Yard). The past week I have been too busy with a matter connected with my eyesight to touch any correspondence.

... – The rest of my news is that if the U.S. is not much of a place for a visiting writer and artist, this place is scarcely better

---

[1] Meyrick Booth (b. 1883), a writer on social and political subjects, became acquainted with L. in the 1920's. They saw something of one another in the early 1930's when they shared many interests: Booth's *Youth and Sex* appeared the same year as *The Doom of Youth*; both men travelled in Germany and wrote of what they found there; Booth contributed a letter to *Satire and Fiction*. With the war the friends lost contact, staying out of touch until Booth wrote to L. early in 1950. With L.'s reply the friendship was re-established. Correspondence continued and later on L. visited Booth at his farm in County Cork.

for a resident same and does not improve. Socialism does a lot of things good and bad, but a socialist politician is apt to identify philistinism and socialism. The political scene is more violent and chaotic than ever: or for us it is the calm spot at the centre of the tornado. How you can manage to cling to your romantic feelings in the matter of Jews I cannot understand. That is such a simplification of what is very complex. I gather from your letter that if some murderous tyrant decided to kill all Jews he could lay his hand on you would be prepared to regard him as rather a sound man. Yesterday I had a young Swiss here who believes that Germany ought to associate itself with Russia. He asserts that all the most vigorous minds in Germany are of that opinion. I do not see how that historical racial emotion can survive the *next* war. The earth is only the size of a football, I learned in America. One thing: there is no close association of Germany with Russia *today* that would not be a bondage. Germany would become a slum like the Soviet.

All of which does not mean that should we be able to come and visit you in *Kark* in the Emerald Isle, I should fail to relish the Irishness of my surroundings. It is said that when the Irish see a Briton coming they put on the *tark* and put up their prices. I should not mind that. I should expect to have to pay for a little freedom, and a nice beef-steak. Then, as there is no Purchase Tax in Ireland living on the whole must be much cheaper. The greatest news of all is that you have taken to the brush and palette! Are you a *Douanier*, or a *pompier*? Do you dab in your "impressions" or do you paint more solidly? Send a show over here and I will puff you as the Welsh Wizard of County Cork, drunk with the beauty of the bogs and the Killarneys! But, "to be serious" as once men, said, what sort of pics do you paint? (The censor's office will regard this about *pics* and Douaniers as a code). The farm is frightfully exciting too. Hedwig ploughs the land and churns the milk while you paint her! – Have you a big or little farm? What kind of land is it: rock, sand, or loam 50 feet down? Have you a Combined Harvester, or do you go out with a sickle and hack away at the corn? More particulars! Are you in the north of county Cork, or near the sea? Are you in the midst of a colony of artists – are you near Elizabeth Bowen:[1] who are

---

[1] Elizabeth Bowen's family seat, Bowen's Court, is in County Cork.

your nearest friends? Are you catholics? If so, have you a pleasant priest? etc. etc. etc. etc. etc. etc. etc. etc. etc. etc. etc.
                    Affectionately from both to dear Heidi
            and yourself.
                                                Yrs.
                                                W. L.

461. *To David Kahma*†   London. W. 11
                                                8 April. 1950.

My dear Kahma. First, let me say that I am for some reason glad to learn that you are not black.[1] Can it be that I secrete a colour-bar? I should not like to think that. It must simply be that having built up an image of you as Finnish and Irish, to have to destroy that, give you blue lips and purple fingernails, would communicate a sense of instability about the whole waxworks. Nevertheless I still feel a little uneasy on the colour-bar score! – I write this in the depths of the paschal oasis of peace and quiet. More than a week ago your letter reached me in which you anticipate the Archangel's arrival in Vancouver.[2] You were to meet him and fly with him to his hotel. I shall soon I hope receive the next instalment of this story of fanaticism and crime, of bombs and beatitudes, of Rolls-Royces and religiosity. . . .
                                                Yrs.
                                                W. L.

[1] Stimulated by the publicity given the arrival in London of the Bechuanaland chief, Seretse Khama, L. had quite good-naturedly broached the colour question to his Canadian protégé. Kahma wrote back that *his* name was indeed Finnish, being the family name of his mother before she married his Irish father.

[2] In pursuing his interest in the Doukhobors, Kahma had grown friendly with the "divine ruler" of the British Columbian members of the sect, Michael Archangel Verigin. In 1950 Verigin became implicated in the misdeeds of the Sons of Freedom, a fanatical Doukhobor group. He was accused by the British Columbian government of "seditious conspiracy" and convicted on that charge in June. Less than a year later the conviction was annulled; the Archangel died in July 1951.

462. *To Roy Campbell*†   London. W. 11.
28 June 1950

Dear Campbell. It is evident from your note that you are passing a far pleasanter summer than I am. My eyes have been giving me a great deal of trouble. A few days ago I returned from a visit to Switzerland where I was examined by the star Swiss eye-doctor at the Augenklinik in Zurich. Now I have to see another variety of doctor. In spite of my present mode of life which does not dispose me to sharing joy, I am delighted to learn that the inhabitants of Toulouse have honoured you in the way you describe, in recognition of a life-long devotion to bullbaiting.[1] It has been with great pleasure by the way that I have noted, for some time now, that if you have suffered neglect, until recently, as a sportsman, your reputation as a poet has been anything but in eclipse. I do not speak of the tremendous reception given your poems a few years ago, led by Desmond MacCarthy, but of a continued tendency on the part of the young to escape from the spell of smart-alecry in verse and to find themselves able again to tolerate and even to enjoy the grand style and an epic mood, which puts you and Homer on the bill again.

Aldington seems to be arranging to live in the right place.[2] There is no substitute for France. Let me know when you are back.

Yours ever
W. L.

. . .

463. *To Helen Saunders*†   [London]
Aug 4. 1950

Dear Miss Saunders. The facts, extremely briefly, are these.[3] (1) My absence from England during the war was a matter of

---

[1] Campbell wrote from his home in Var that he had been given the freedom of the city of Toulon and that a corrida had been held in his honour at Arles.

[2] In his letter Campbell said that he had been seeing Richard Aldington, who was living six miles away.

[3] L.'s friend and colleague of *Blast* days had been out of touch with him for many years. She wrote to ask after his health, having heard that he was having trouble with his eyes.

force majeure. . . . (2) Upon my return I saw my eye-doctor. He advised an immediate operation, told me that something was pressing on my optic nerves – I thought I would wait and see: and until seven months ago I got along fairly well. Then I went to another eye-doctor. He informed me, after x-ray had been taken, that a tumour or cist – inside the skull – was pressing up against the optic nerves: that an operation would be far too dangerous to contemplate, and that I must rely on x-ray therapy to reduce the pressure and prevent a worsening of my condition. In this way I have a good chance of surviving: but the condition of my eyes will no longer permit me to work as a painter. . . .

Yours sincerely

464. *To T. S. Eliot*†   London. W. 11.
12 Sept. 1950.

Dear Eliot. What I propose, briefly, is a seventy or seventy-five thousand word book (it had better be a full-length book) on the visual arts at the present time.[1] This might be entitled "Bread and Ballyhoo." An article of mine in "The Listener" had this title:[2] It dealt with the enormous disparity between the public funds devoted to "culture" ballyhoo, and to England-the-cultured-nation advertisement, to visual education-of-the-million activities, to the staging of expensive exhibitions of old masters and foreign artists, and the maintenance of an army of officials, not only in museums and galleries but in "Councils" far more costly than a Ministry of Fine Arts – the disparity between this immense political and educational outlay and the public money expended for the encouragement of *creative* work in contemporary art, which is insignificant. It is almost as if it were tacitly accepted that

---

[1] L. had suggested that he do a book on the arts for Faber & Faber. Eliot, writing for Faber's, asked him to present them with some sort of prospectus. The proposal, as outlined in this letter, was rejected. Eliot wrote on September 18th, saying that it sounded as if the book would incorporate too much material already published. Faber's, he said, would be interested in a new and coherent work by L. *The Demon of Progress in the Arts*, published by Methuen in 1954, develops some of the themes indicated here.

[2] See *The Listener*, September 8th, 1949, p. 407.

creation is at an end. At a time when taxation is making private patronage impossible, the artist in England watches the State spending its millions in advertising its "interest in the arts" with feelings of profound frustration. – Much factual material would be supplied: such as the effects of the propaganda against the easel picture, the effects of Child Art snobisme and sentiment etc. etc. etc.

Next I would describe and analyse the situation in Paris today in the visual arts – if they can still be called visual (with pictures?). After that, a half-dozen of the best younger artists in England will be discussed . . . .

Next in order, probably, would come an account of the visual arts in England during the last 40 years (with pictures?). I would have a chapter on the Royal Academy (an expansion of my article in "Contact" 1950).[1] A chapter too on England's palladian palaces and other borrowed art-forms. Several articles I have written for "The Listener" during the last two years, somewhat expanded, might be included.

Naturally this is not a complete list of the subjects to be treated. . . . I could start on this book right away and finish it in four months say. . . .

Yrs,

W. L.

465. *To Sir Nicholas Waterhouse*† [London]
[September 1950]

Dear Docker. In case we do not meet on Friday next, although I hope we shall: the X-ray treatment appears to have set me back – not to have advanced me. My G.P. informs me that in a textbook on the subject it is said that sometimes X-ray treatment produces a liquid (discharge?) which temporarily impairs the sight. On the other hand my eye-doctor assures me that in all his experience he has never known X-ray to be responsible for such a reaction. *But* there is no question that between 28 Aug. and 11 Sept my sight worsened: i.e. the period during which I was treated. – Naturally I am alarmed: although of course it may be only a temporary decline. My confidence in my eye-doctor is a

[1] See *Contact*, May–June 1950.

little shaken and I think I should at least consult two other specialists, to check on what my eye-doctor is advising. Also on 28 Aug. he prescribed me slightly stronger glasses which will be arriving at any moment now. All this obliges me to ask you if you could send me say twenty-five pounds, all of which I now shall need, and alas, have not got. – This note, as I have said, in case our Friday meeting, does not occur. I can explain to you much better what has happened of course if Friday turns out to be all right.

Yr
PROFESSOR

466. *To Meyrick Booth*† London. W. 11.
7 Oct. 1950

My dear Booth. Your details about the farm surprised me in one respect. I am most ignorant of farming but 43 acres sounded too large for a farm the purpose of which is to feed two or three people but too small if the sale of the produce were the object, when very expensive machines like the "combined harvester" would have to be bought. What you told me about the necessity perhaps to introduce guests into your farm house saddened me. I wish to goodness I could help, as I should. But what my position is, can be told in a few words. It is not primarily my *eyes* that is the trouble, but two optic nerves (which are inside the skull). It is now practically certain that I must have an operation, involving opening the skull. You can imagine what this is going to cost, though happily the money can be raised. Artists seldom have any money – not as is popularly supposed because of the artistic temperament, but because *art* is not something a sufficient number of people are interested in to justify the existence of *artists*. The world has a bad conscience about its philistinism and so hides up the *degree* of its indifference. All it says is that artists are usually rather deliciously hard-up. That "ART" today is not a possible way of making a living is what ought to be made clear and art-schools closed, to clinch the matter. Artists do live economically disorderly lives but this is not, as a rule, dishonesty, but the blundering progress of a sleeper gradually awaking. As to serious books, that is what a university professor writes during vacations, or a diplomat in idle moments. – So it is not surprising that things are as they are with me. Meanwhile I am informed by eye-doctors that death, total blindness, paralysis, or insanity probably await me as a result of that operation. This is in confidence – in great confidence. I may survive.[1]

I will terminate this rather abruptly. I fear I allowed myself to be carried away. Will write and tell you what is going to happen to me. All this sounds beastly dramatic. It is only just an operation such as thousands are having every day. When I next write I shall not fill my letter with MYSELF.

15 October

Since writing this have consulted neuro-surgeon. He says *death* only – not the other things. – What has been arranged is that we wait until after Christmas. It is assumed that by then I shall be much worse and can be killed without reproach to surgeon. – Let me however add that the surgeon I visited was quite a decent human being. He did his best to persuade me to scrape along as best I could, in view of my age. My reply to that was that I should not make a very good blind man or even a hopelessly myopic one. But the surgeon insists that I must be worse before he will take a hand. There is a further difficulty. There can be no surgery until I have gone into hospital and had coloured liquid squirted into the carotid artery, an X-ray being simultaneously taken. This is called an arteriogram. The coloured liquid suffuses the interior of the skull, and the X-ray establishes whether a so-called aneurism (spelling?) is present. The latter is the term used for a sort of large bubble developing upon a bloodvessel. – You can see from all this that I am in for a fairly hot time. But it is after all the kind of thing one has to expect if one allows oneself to be born. Had I been a suitably obstreperous foetus all this could have been avoided.

[1] The operation was never performed, L.'s condition having been judged too far advanced.

467. *To Herbert Read*†   29 Notting Hill Gate. W. 11.
17 Nov 1950

Dear Read. Thank you for your letter. You tell me that you always endeavour to please me, but alas without success. A pretty little self-portrait, I must say, of a blameless and self-effacing man. Turning however (not rudely) from your dream-self to Child Art, I share your enthusiasm for what children do. I am sorry, though, that you are less disposed to give the teachers their due than is your friend Phillip James. I was very impressed by the work of the teachers in the last Child Art show.[1] Incidentally, can you tell me where I should apply, to obtain photographs of the exhibits?

Regarding your Penguin book, the plates for that will of course be illustrations of your view of contemporary British art.[2] Choose anything of mine that fits in with your account. Lastly, as you did not mention Denis Williams, I assume you have not seen his paintings. Committeeman! the British Council has been helpful with regard to this young Negro, but if he is to survive he must be found a job.[3] Because of colour this presents great difficulties. It is a pity that all this talent should be lost for no better reason than that its possessors skin is controversial. I understand, for instance, that it is going to be exceedingly difficult to find a school prepared to engage a Negro teacher. As his dealer says, Williams

[1] L. reviewed the exhibition "Children's Art 1950" in *The Listener* for September 21st. He called it "by far the most interesting of current exhibitions," but questioned the degree of influence exerted on the exhibitors: "Those chosen are sent in by a school possessing a teacher inspired by Mr. Herbert Read .... The Innocent Eye has been disciplined, the virgin vision harnessed. Mr. Read is to be complimented on what is largely the result of his teaching." In support of his thesis, L. quoted from the show's catalogue where Philip James (b. 1901), then Director of Art for the Arts Council, states: "This exhibition is more a tribute to teachers ... than a showing-off ground for children ...." (See "Round the London Art Galleries," p. 388.) In Read's letter to L. he took exception to L.'s emphasis on the teachers' influence. The story "My Disciple," in *Rotting Hill*, contains an amusing spoof on the subject.
[2] See Herbert Read, *Contemporary British Art* (Harmondsworth, 1951).
[3] Williams had returned to England. L. later succeeded in finding him a position at the Central School of Art in London.

could not live on his work as an artist. At this juncture, Committeeman Read, your vigorous action might be decisive.

Yrs.
WYNDHAM LEWIS

It has already been said that J. Alan White of Methuen & Co. was, along with C. H. Prentice, the most interested and sympathetic of Lewis's many publishers. Long a reader of Lewis's books, White took him on as a writer in 1950 and began by reissuing Tarr *in 1951. From then until Lewis's death, Methuen continued to publish his work, while his professional association with White deepened to friendship.*

468. *To J. Alan White* 29 Notting Hill Gate W. 11.
26 Nov. 1950.

My dear Mr. White. It gave me the greatest pleasure to hear that "Rude Assignment" interested you. In Harold Nicolson's *Observer* review this morning no mention was made of the fact (a not unfriendly omission) that really some acquaintance with my books is necessary, otherwise the reader of "Rude Assignment" would half the time be at sea, and in a rough sea at that. . . .

Apropos of what you said regarding my supposed inaccessibility, the original (a long way off) of "The Bishop's Fool" was up in town a few days ago. He read my "Rude Assignment". . . . He remarked how "violent" my writing was, how "gentle" I was myself. Of course I protested about the *violence*, and he explained that all *truth* was *violent*. So that was all right. But I do recognise a discrepancy between Mr. W. L. the writer and my own easy-going, anything but contentious, self. So I *can* see what kind of person a reader must deduce, responsible for (at times) so fiery a text. . . .

Yours sincerely,
WYNDHAM LEWIS

A second passionate controversy began in The Listener *when Lewis, in his article of November 9th, 1950, praised a statue by Henry*

Moore titled "Head of a Child." The emphasis of the critic's remarks on the figure – which appeared in an accompanying photograph (see p. 508) – was that Moore had succeeded in overcoming "the limitations of the round." Lewis stressed "how important it is to know how to circumvent the natural platitude of the dimensions of life." The theme, which he had been promulgating for almost forty years, was still volatile enough to launch a discussion that ran in the paper for the next two months. The first opposing voice was that of Lord Brand (b. 1878), whose letter in The Listener *for November 23rd complained of the "queerness" of modern sculpture and of the critics' explanations. Lord Brand stated his preference for Greece and the Italian Renaissance, and asked Lewis to explain what he meant by "the natural platitude of the dimension of life."*

469. To the Editor of "The Listener," November 30, 1950

London. W. 11.

HENRY MOORE'S "HEAD OF A CHILD"

Sir . . . .

It is easy to understand Lord Brand's feelings at finding himself in an age when a sculptor flattens a female face as if some titan had sat on it and is applauded for doing so. Where is the lovely naturalistic profile of Hellenic art?

But many people today, myself among them, consider that the Greeks of antiquity were, with their naturalism, fastening upon Europe for 2000 years a theory of art which is radically mistaken. The third dimension is dangerous for the European artist: there lies in wait for him the naturalistic canon of tradition as nowhere else. The second dimension is, by reason of its limitation, less prone to perpetrate this ancestral vitalist mistake. By platitude, I mean, in this connection, the platitude inherent in the natural. To identify nature with art is in an artist a deadly sin. . . .

Yours, etc.,
WYNDHAM LEWIS

470. *To Meyrick Booth*† London. W. 11.
24 Dec. 1950.

Dear Booth. The address of the Paris doctor has been found . . . so, if it seems worthwhile, I can present myself in the Boulevard Malsherbes.[1] It is much too late, though, I fear. One year ago would have been the time to know of a *treatment*. But one can never hear of these things until too late, because the general practitioners are not interested in them economically. They prefer visiting you at a pound a time, and then getting their rake-off on a £250 – or a £1000 – operation. My sight does not improve. The influenza I have just recovered from affected it. Please thank your *french* friend for his great kindness. . . . He has no doubt explained to you the nature of the treatment. If it has anything to do with x-ray therapy, I am afraid that would not do. However I suppose I shall soon hear.

Thank you for your remarks about my book.[2] There is not anything you think about politicians that could exceed my own thoughts about them, in disgust and anger. I see the *two* corridors in place of the *one* pre-war corridor (Poland): I see and I understand what is happening in Korea, in Western Europe as regards defence. It does not bear talking about. But what one thinks cannot be written in a book. I fear you do not understand quite how desperate a situation has supervened, for *everybody*. The world is plunging headfirst into slavery, and the old licence as regards "free speech" is obsolete.

Of course, if I said exactly what I think it would not be identical with what you think. You tend to over-simplify to my mind: to consider that all the dirty dogs in the world are of one colour, whereas I believe they are of every colour and kind.

Then I think more of human kind, you more of nations. However, while I am still able to see, I must try and get over to Ireland, and we shall then be able to discuss those sorts of things better than in a letter. . . .

London has been a dirty brown this Christmas. One has been uncertain most of the time if it were night or day. Whether I find there any help for my eyesight or not, it will be pleasant to be in

[1] Booth had sent to L. the name of a French eye specialist who, according to a Parisian friend, offered a treatment which might be of use.
[2] *Rude Assignment*.

Paris again for a bit. I cannot thank you enough for the kind thoughts and effort to help.

Yours ever,

. . .

471. *To the Editor of "The Listener," December 28, 1950*

London. W. 11.

NATURE AND ART

Sir, – The Slade School somewhat tardily joins Lord Brand's protest.[1] . . .

Identification with nature, and the use of nature, are quite distinct. The Greeks of antiquity were the pioneers in a mistake on which centres the main controversy today. It was the mistake of confusing scientific values with aesthetic values and so giving western art its naturalist canon.

The view that it does not matter whether you are showing the third dimension upon a flat surface (a wall, or board, or canvas) or have gone over into the third dimension itself and are carving in a solid material seems to me to be disproved by the work of Michelangelo. How Michelangelo's titanic dreams are betrayed, when they emerge in marble! What a sadly different thing the Sistine 'Adam' would be in white marble. The Greek naturalism, in some way, was neutralised in the flat. To affect to prefer Michelangelo's sculpture to his other forms of expression, including poetry, is the result of the literary approach. The 'classic' naturalism comes out better on a flat surface than in the round. The last statement will not, I hope, raise the whole City of London against me.

Yours, etc.

WYNDHAM LEWIS

[1] A letter signed by J. Evleigh and H. M. Robson, who gave their address as "Slade School of Fine Arts," appeared in *The Listener* for December 21st. The writers attacked L.'s letter of November 30th, arguing that Moore's statue *is* three-dimensional. They asked L. if the Egyptian, Greek, Gothic, and Renaissance sculptors and the great European painters, such as Giotto and Rembrandt, were "labouring under the deadly sin of identifying nature with art."

472. *To James Laughlin*† London. W. 11.
Dec. 31. 1950.

Dear Laughlin¹. . . . Has it ever occurred to you that New Directions is an alibi, or a kind of alibi, for the New York publishers? Why do you not stop publishing? The true situation would then be even more obvious. It was with the best motives you started publishing. You could stop doing so, with even more clear-sighted purpose.

Sincerely,

473. *To the Editor of "The Listener," January* 4, 1951

London. W. 11.

NATURE AND ART

Sir, – Mr. A. K. Lawrence, R.A., proposes a debate on what is "beautiful".² There would be little sense in debating that with a Royal Academician. If the white marble Lady Godiva which dominated the sculpture gallery at the last Royal Academy exhibition is beautiful, then I do not like beauty. I prefer the ugly, such as we find in Henry Moore's head, reproduced in THE LISTENER last November, or let us say Epstein's head of Einstein.

I will not discuss beauty: but it was a happy thought of Mr. Lawrence to mention the contemporary theatre. His definition of *art* is the trouble taken by an actor or an actress to make us believe that we are looking at a scene in real life. That is not how I would define it. It does not seem to occur to Mr. Lawrence that the type of play in which an actor is obliged to do this is not the only type of play. The so-called "realistic" theatre of Ibsen, Shaw and Priestley, useful as it is in providing moral instruction, or comedy of no artistic pretensions, is anything but an example of a high art form. However much, as ardent feminists, we may

¹ Laughlin wrote to L. in November suggesting the republication by New Direction of some of his novels.
² In a letter printed the preceding week, A. K. Lawrence, R.A. (b. 1893), argued against L.'s criticism of the Greeks. The Greeks did not copy nature, he stated; they "loved beauty, and their art is an expression of that love."

approve of "The Doll's House", as artists we should prefer a play by Racine. The theatre of Ibsen identified itself with nature in the way intended by me when I made use of those words.[1] And in deploring the triumph of that type of theatre, I should not be advocating the banishing from the stage of everything remotely resembling what is human. I am not particularly pro-abstract.

Yours, etc.,

WYNDHAM LEWIS

474. *To the Editor of "The Listener," January* 18, 1951

London. W. 11.

NATURE AND ART

Sir, – *Another* noisy Academician! What a peppery body: Mr. A. K. Lawrence's letter was like the banging of doors by an angry man, but it is, of course, mostly bluff.[2]

Now, I am not going to expound commonplaces of contemporary thinking for a Royal Academician. And this flying to arms in defence of Hellas by the likes of Mr. Lawrence is remarkably burlesque. I must confess to a scandalised amazement (as well as amusement) when in his first letter I saw this slick portraitist indicating as his alibi the figures of the Parthenon. The Greeks were wonderful artists even if one may criticise their direction. The gentlemen who carry on business in Piccadilly, for whom Mr. Lawrence is the spokesman, are the children of the camera, not of the idealised archetypes, of Phideas' images of physical perfection, nor do they think like Plato, but like the businessmen they are. I should not have spoken so plainly of course had Mr. Lawrence not talked tough.

... He pounces upon Epstein's head of Einstein as I meant him to do. Ah, so he likes naturalism! He was triumphant. But of course such naturalism as *that* no one can fail to admire. I was speaking of the principles shaping our culture. Because in general

---

[1] Lawrence quarrelled with L.'s phrase (in a letter to *The Listener* for December 14th) "identify nature with art" as L. applied it to the Greeks. "The word 'identify' means," Lawrence said, "'to make to be the same.'"

[2] Lawrence replied to L.'s letter of the 4th, accusing him of evasion, distortion, and muddled thinking. See *The Listener*, January 11th, 1951, p. 64.

their naturalism, when we compare it with the Chinese, must be condemned, Hogarth's "Shrimp Girl" is nevertheless one of my favorite pictures.

Mr. Lawrence correctly describes the function of this paper as in part educational. But it would be anything but edifying were the local fishmonger to burst into a lectureroom and denounce the lecturer because, through the window, he had thought he had heard him saying "stinking fish". There are few people in England today who regard the Royal Academy as a factor in education. It is wasting people's time to take this heckler seriously. And this is the last occasion on which I shall do so. We know what his Party is: it is the Party of Mammon.

Yours, etc.

WYNDHAM LEWIS

475. *To David Kahma*†   London. W. 11.
[ca. Feb. 1st, 1951]

Dear Kahma. The letter you received a week or so ago was posted a week or more after it was written. Here is the reason for my erratic behaviour. My wife is suffering a breakdown in health.... My sight meanwhile does not improve. I go to Paris however as I told you in an earlier letter to consult a doctor. Intended to go earlier, but was prevented.

I must say what I can see and hear of the war business is hardly encouraging. You who live much nearer Korea than we do must be more emotionally affected at the moment, but it will be our turn tomorrow. For the Rhine is nearer to us than Korea is to Vancouver....

Yours.

P.s. ...

But tell me more about Madame ———,[1] who would have copulation-centres all over the city, like comfort-stations, where the male and female of the species could repair, for a nickel, and squirt their trop plein at any hour of the day. Such promiscuity is likely to supervene, as our society develops. There would be big baby-farms, to which women would surrender the fruit of their bellies,

[1] A Vancouver acquaintance of Kahma.

when they pupped. One can see them saying, when the little brat appears, saying: "Ah! it was that cute commissionaire, with the black moustaches, that did it, that sultry Wednesday afternoon, just before my periods stopped. It has got his eyes."

Madame —— sounds a distinct acquisition to any society. Give me the economic low-down. Where and how does she get the money to eat, dress etc. I have a passion for basic economic facts. She seems to be a very lively woman. Her gossipy low-down on Einstein the usual chit-chat on the great. I found that the refugees brightened up the United States a lot. Canada needs them too.

P.P.S. Sunday Feb. 4th. Have just returned from Paris. Doctor I am afraid not much use. Had most delicious ice flavoured with rum coming back on the Golden Arrow. Also, at the Ecu de France had a Moet which I still dream about. Paris for the belly. The Frenchmen say when one asks them about the war which impends, "Oh hang it all! A war's just over. Don't begin talking about another one." . . .

476. *To I. A. Richards*†[1] [London]
[Perhaps not sent.] February 26. 1951.

My dear Richards. . . .

Your few lines regarding the state of affairs in China confirmed what I had surmised. Obviously American policy has been mistaken. Things look extremely unpleasant everywhere, and I suppose we must anticipate another of these insane world-wars. Meanwhile, I was glad to hear that poor Ted Spencer was the subject of an oratorical tribute by our eminent friend.[2]

The Childermass has another chance (if it is a chance) of getting

---

[1] L. had known I. A. Richards (b. 1893) slightly for many years when, in 1949, they came into closer contact over the placing of L.'s portrait of Eliot at Magdalene College, of which Richards was a fellow. From then until L.'s death they corresponded occasionally and saw one another when Richards came to London on holiday from his University Professorship at Harvard.

[2] Richards wrote to L. of Eliot's delivery of the first Theopore Spencer Memorial Lecture at Harvard on November 21st, 1950. The lecture, *Poetry and Drama*, was published by the Harvard University Press in 1951.

finished.¹ The fact that it has remained unfinished all this time has grieved me a great deal, and my feelings of frustration do not diminish as the time draws near when such a work will be beyond my powers. The difficulty has been, and remains, economic. . . . There is a further complication, namely the condition of my eyes. I have what is known as an Optic Atrophy. It appears that I have suffered from this for a very considerable time, although it has only been during the past fifteen months that I have known the facts. My eyesight at present is so bad that I am obliged to dictate this letter. Of course, this handicap is not quite what it would have been fifty years ago: a friend is procuring for me an up-to-date dictaphone, but even so it involves a heavy typing bill. The position is that I can move about, and shall, in all probability never be totally blind. But my sight must progressively deteriorate, and at present the so-called 'central vision' is as I have described. . . .

Yrs.

477. *To Naomi Mitchison*† London. W. 11.
April 9th 1951.

Dear Naomi. I was very pleased to receive such a nice long letter from Pakistan. In it you said you would probably be back at the beginning of April, and I hope this may catch you before you fly off again to some distant part of the earth. . . . – You will be sorry (I hope, in spite of the fact that I have never yet known anyone to be sorry for another's misfortunes) but I am going blind. Very few writers that I have ever heard of have gone blind, and I am reduced to gazing at Milton with his three troublesome daughters across the intervening centuries. It is far more common for a writer to go mad: if I had done that I could wave a salute to Swift, to begin with. But there it is. It is the optic nerves which are being squeezed by a beastly little cist, with a beautiful name of pharyngioma. At present the position is that I have lost my "central vision," cannot see to read or write and hardly to eat, but can see things around me in an impressionistic way—— But

¹ Arrangements were under way for the broadcasting of *The Childermass* by the B.B.C. and for the grant that would enable L. to complete the work.

enough of my beastly eyesight. The Festival should attract you to this misbegotten city, and one of these days I hope we may meet.

> With affectionate greetings,
> Your

478. *To J. R. Ackerley*†¹ [London]
[ca. April 1951]

My dear Ackerley. I am afraid I depressed you by my account of the dark room into which I am going to be locked. But there is an *interval*. May it be long! And we are all going into some even darker room after all: we none of us ever give a thought to that, so why should I anticipate my more limited black-out? – Meanwhile there is the question of my inability to do more articles making such demands upon my eyesight. The editor is perfectly right. In fact the statement which I suppose must ultimately be framed must be very carefully worded, for a reason I will not now divulge.² – Thank you, whatever I may say, for your great kindness. But I know how to value, in spite of these remarks, such extraordinary kindness as inspired your letter. Speaking for the Listener too, what you said made me feel that my work for that has been worth doing and I must repeat how grieved I am to have to finally give it up.

> Yrs.

479. *To Cynthia Thompson*†³ [London]
June 8th 1951.

Dear Cynthia Thompson. I have been away in Ireland, with no mail forwarded and did not receive your kind and charming letter until my return. My article in the Listener has brought me a quantity of letters, though of course my object was only (1) to

¹ J. R. Ackerley (b. 1896) was at this time Literary Editor of *The Listener*.
² See the witty and moving valedictory titled "The Sea-Mists of Winter," which appeared in *The Listener* for May 10th.
³ Cynthia Thompson was one of the many readers of *The Listener* who wrote to L. after reading "The Sea-Mists of Winter."

explain to Listener readers why I was no longer writing Art Articles and (2) to inform all those here and elsewhere of the *exact* nature of my calamity – otherwise rumour builds up strange images. I am so glad I succeed in making you laugh in unison with me. For it is of course idiotically funny suddenly to be deprived of one's main prop, the EYE. My blessing.

480. *To Miss Vanner*†[1]   [London]
June 9th 1951.

Dear Miss Vanner. Your interesting letter arrived while I was away in Ireland. I now hasten to acknowledge it. You enquire whether my trouble is the same as yours. Well, mine is an Optic Atrophy. Your problem is operation or no operation. The decisive factors, as I understand it, are these: (1) Age (2) duration of the trouble. They are more willing to operate on you at thirty-three than at sixty-three, for you have to be under an anaesthetic for four or five hours if the operation involves opening the skull. As to the time question it is apparently very much easier to operate on *anything* which has only been there a few months than if it has been there, as in my case, for the best part of twenty years. This latter factor is of extreme importance. Whether you choose to be operated on or not must depend on (1) how long you expect to live, (2) if you have any means, (3) how long the surgeon thinks your good eye will keep good (and this we must qualify by whether you regard your surgeon as honest, competent, and sensible). Of course there are a hundred other things to be considered. If the mischief is inside your skull as with me I can give you the names of the three best neuro-surgeons in England. If it is the eyes themselves I can supply you with the name of a good eye-man. Anyway, good luck.

                                                Sincerely,

481. *To Julian Symons*†   [London]
June 9th 1951.

Dear Symons. Thank you for your note and for the various activities on my behalf you announce.... I am full of eager

[1] Miss Vanner wrote as a result of "The Sea-Mists of Winter."

anticipation with respect to your study of Carlyle.¹ There is no writer who belongs so narrowly to the century of Victoria as he. I am sure you will score a goal with this football – this windbag. . . .

All the best.

482. *To Stephen Spender*†²   [London]
[June 1951]

Dear Mr. Spender. Your letter gave me the greatest pleasure: coming from a one-time sitter and a poet I have always admired, from the day when I was first shown specimens of his work in the 'twenties, I value particularly this letter of yours. I could not of course think of allowing you to waste your time in the drudgery of reading which you so generously offer to do. But what I should very much enjoy would be if you would visit me when you are next in London. – – – Until a day or two ago I was in Ireland, which is why this answer has been a little slow in coming. I was staying in an enormous practically unfurnished house; I was surrounded by violently coughing heads; for my hosts appeared unable to buy fuel. But I consoled myself by sitting in a conservatory beside an Indian tulip tree, and found that the Irish Sun through glass is quite respectably hot. But you are in Verona and do not have to sit beneath glass to feel a little warm!

With my cordialest good wishes.
Yours sincerely,

It was the imagination of the poet and B.B.C. producer D. G. Bridson that conceived the possibility of a radio version of The Childermass. *Bridson, long an admirer of Pound and Lewis, presented the idea to Lewis early in* 1951. *Lewis was enthusiastic.*

¹ See Julian Symons, *Thomas Carlyle: The Life and Ideas of a Prophet* (London, 1952.)
² Stephen Spender (b. 1909) first met L. when he was an undergraduate at Oxford. They were occasionally in touch after that, but never became friends. L. painted the young poet in 1938. (The portrait is now in the Public Museum and Art Gallery, Hanley.) On learning of L.'s blindness, Spender wrote from Italy offering to come and read to him after his return to London.

A script and score (by Walter Goehr) were prepared; the production, featuring Donald Wolfit, went into rehearsal and was ultimately broadcast on the Third Programme on June 18th. The success of this undertaking enabled Lewis to embark, under B.B.C. sponsorship, on the completion of the trilogy, of which there was yet only Part I, dating from 1928. Radio versions of Parts II and III, now retitled The Human Age, *were given under Bridson's direction on May 26th and 28th, 1955.*

483. *To D. G. Bridson* 18 Ashley Mansions,
254 Vauxhall Bridge Road,
London, S.W. 1.
[June 1951]

Dear Bridson (Mister I must no longer say). It is easy to thank an actor for giving a magnificent performance, but it is a very different matter to thank you. The Childermass is the book I set most store by, and it is for me an almost miraculous event for it suddenly to spring into concrete life, with live actors bestowing upon it an almost startling physical reality, and a very able and ingenious living composer playing the bailiff's barge across the mournful river and jazzing the appellants into a bacchic dance. Sitting at your rehearsals I could hardly believe my ears. *You* are the magician who has called into life this extraordinary apparition. Just to thank you would be absurd. All I can do is to salute you as one would some benignant spirit who had suddenly materialised and transformed one's existence.

WYNDHAM LEWIS

484. *To Augustus John*† London. S.W. 1.
June 27th, 1951.

My dear John. As you will see from the enclosed slip I have changed my residence. This place is at the Victoria Station end of the Vauxhall Bridge Road. Your second letter about the broadcast of The Childermass gave me tremendous pleasure.[1] You asked me

[1] John wrote that he "listened to *The Childermass* with immense excitement."

what I thought of the production: it seemed to me that Wolfit did a really splendid job as the Bailiff, and all the rest of the cast were astonishingly well-chosen. I was at the rehearsals and I know how much intelligence the producer must put into it before so finished an article emerges. – I am glad to hear that you are to be in London again now and then. I should of course be delighted to see Romilly.[1] The condition of my eyes circumscribes my movements, but I hope you will pay me a visit at the above address. Drop me a line or telephone.

Yours ever,

485. *To David Kahma*† London. S.W. 1.
July 5th 1951.

Dear Khama. The enclosed new address slip will partly explain my delay in answering your extremely kind and interesting letter. Also the two pages from "The Radio Times," counted for a good deal, for Froanna and I were at the Rehearsals of the Radio Version of The Childermass, at a party to listen in, and since then have been a good deal occupied with matters relating to this. We did not get to bed till after four last night, returning thoroughly exhausted from the Turkish Embassy – where we were both greatly disappointed to see no trace of a harem. But what overshadows everything else is that I have been commissioned by the British Broadcasting Co. to complete The Childermass.

As regards my eyes, in order to obtain a really serious advice from a doctor at the other end of the world, one would have to put him in possession of every relevant fact.[2] From what you tell me I feel sure that Dr. —— is a very sound man. But my case, for the purposes of such a letter as this, is complicated by the fact that I do not know whether the pressure from the optic nerve is caused by a pharyngioma or an aneurism. The only means of deciding this would be to inject a coloured fluid into the carotid artery; this suffuses the brain with a colouration of some kind, and the skull is then X-rayed. Another complication: for years I have been practically blind in the left eye, first noticing that something was the matter about two years before the war. So this

[1] John's son.
[2] Kahma had offered to consult a Vancouver specialist about L.'s case.

has been going for a long time. One of the two best known neurosurgeons in this country said, 'You have been going blind for a long time.' But during the past two years the deterioration of the right eye has certainly speeded up, the final loss of the "central vision" occurring six months ago—and much too quickly it seems to me for it to be a pharyngioma. To explain this last statement, the thing was first supposed to be a pituitary tumour, until X-ray revealed that it was something *above* the pituitary. An eye-doctor I was seeing expressed himself as 'rather glad' that it was a pharyngioma, since the latter proceeded much more slowly than a pituitary trouble.

With doctors, one does of course exist in a maze of contradictions. I just have catalogued a few facts: but for a proper diagnosis, Dr. ——, or any other specialist, would require a great deal more than that. What struck me in your letter was the expression about getting air to the pharyngioma. What on earth does that mean. Boring a little hole in the skull? Any facts that you can obtain for me re. pharyngiomas or any recent publication relating to these cysts, would be welcome. In any case, tell me what *airing* means.

The sympathy expressed by you and your dear wife is very affecting. It of course means a great deal more to me than that of the majority of people, as you have come to stand in a particular relationship to myself, during recent years. In consulting a Vancouver doctor on my behalf, bear in mind how misleading these things are apt to be at a distance. But you *might* hit on something important. . . . Best wishes to both.

Yrs.

486. *To Roy Campbell*   Studio A. Kensington Garden Studios
29 Notting Hill Gate,
London, W. 11.
July 14. 1951.

Dear Campbell. Your article in Time and Tide about Tarr etc.[1] has just reached me. It should be a tremendous lot of good and

[1] See "Wyndham Lewis," *Time and Tide*, July 7th, 1951, p. 650. Ostensibly a review of the just republished *Tarr*, the piece is actually a general paean to L.

I am deeply grateful. To find you still at my side is a matter of the greatest satisfaction to me: and I hope we shall always remain comrades-in-arms against the forces of philistia. As I learn from you that twenty years ago I was described as an 'old volcano'[1] let me say I shall always be prepared to erupt and pour out a stream of lava upon our foes.

With the sincerest thanks and all
good wishes,
Yours Ever,
WYNDHAM LEWIS

487. *To Sir Louis Fergusson*†[2] [London]
[August 18th, 1951.]

My dear Fergusson. Your letter brings back in a rush many images of great remoteness. I see cafés in Paris before the motor-age, before the Deluge: I see a bear dancing, with lots of pretty little girls at parties in a London dancing Academy: I see the beautiful features of a famous dancer, M.M.: there is a scene on the crest of Church Street at a dinner-table, and I remember how the Welsh miners shouted to a scottish lecturer, 'But what has that got to do with the Social Revolution?' But the scene has shifted to Glasgow but what you are doing *there* I cannot imagine. Anyhow, let all your activities be attended with good luck.

Yrs

. . .

[1] Campbell recalls W. H. Auden's referring to L. in the 1930's as "that lonely old volcano of the Right."

[2] Sir Louis Fergusson (b. 1878), Clerk of the Council and Keeper of the Records of the Duchy of Lancaster from 1927 to 1945, had been out of touch with L. for many years when he wrote to express his sympathy on hearing of L.'s blindness. The two had been friends before World War I and had produced together, in 1919, the memorial volume *Harold Gilman*.

488. *To David Kahma*† London. W. 11.
August 26. 1951.

Dear Kahma. As you will see from the address at the top of this letter we have fled from Ashley Mansions back to our old place. And a beastly fuss it has been, involving wild attempts to sublet Ashley, the packing and moving of a thousand books, the finding of a workroom (actually I now have one opposite the Mercury Theatre where Murder in the Cathedral was first performed) and many other outrageous calls upon my time and patience. . . .

The news of the Archangel's death saddens even me. For of course I am a long way from British Columbia. I have an eighteenth century repugnance for 'enthusiasm', and Russians are the classical enthusiasts, just as the French are so superbly the reverse, at their best. Michael appears to have been notably anti-enthusiasm. . . . I was distressed to hear that you had once more contrived to injure yourself in the surf. . . . I have been suffering this week myself from a very bad pain in the neck, caused by the six volumes of an individual named Professor Toynbee, which for one reason and another I have been obliged to read. . . .

Yours,

489. *To Mrs. Ezra Pound*† [London]
August 26th 1951.

Dear Dorothy. . . . First let me say how extremely depressed I was by my interview, a few weeks ago, with your young friend Simpson.[1] His account of Ezra's condition made me feel that something should be done at once to rescue him. Is there any likelihood of a concerted action, in the near future, to get him out of that place? What an existence for you too! How you must long to be back in England or in Italy! If there is anything I can do you have only to tell me the sort of action which would be useful.

Recently I have been seeing much of the sprightly Omar.[2] He escorted me over to Cork a short time ago. He came into

[1] Dallam Simpson, editor of *Four Pages*.
[2] The Pounds' son, Omar, was visiting in England. A student of eastern languages, he now teaches at the Roxbury Latin School in Boston, Massachusetts.

16. Wyndham Lewis at 29 Notting Hill Gate in 1951

conflict with an ancient Church leader, who was our carriage companion as we lumbered through South Wales, – though they seemed to come together in connection with Islam and Omar declaimed in Persian some passages from the Koran. He attracted the interests in Cork of Kitty ——, daughter of Col. ——: but alas Kitty betrayed the stigma of superstition; in fact, she told him that there was a giant who lived underneath her house, whose beard grew into a table. This was too much for Omar, and he saw Kitty —— no more. Meanwhile, he now, as you know, is the possessor of two or three fine drawings,[1] and we are awaiting photographs of these, from the photographic offices of the National Gallery. Omar is a live wire, but he needs fixing down to something.

490. *To D. G. Bridson*†   London W. 11.
Oct 19th 1951.

Dear Bridson. Let me explain to begin with why I have not written earlier. My desire to get *everything* out of the way in order to begin the full-scale work on Childermass II. has caused me to live a hermit's life. Two days ago, I had not been out for ten days. My beard reaching an ambitious length; but of a disgusting dirty colour – or no-colour. Why do the chin and cheek hairs lose their pigment sooner than the scalp. My nails had grown so long they kept catching in things. And I had ceased to write letters. I am completing the long novel about which I spoke to you.[2] Both my wife and I have been extremely hard at it. Prior to that there were a series of migrations, which ate up a lot of time. . . . I was much entertained by the photograph of Jane Russell and yourself.[3] (I only write the names in this order in the interest of euphony, not from gallantry). I await the lowdown on Hollywood, when you return. The English colony especially attracts my curiosity. . . . I have hired a radio to listen to Election news. *All* socialist star-speeches stress christian nature of socialism. (Stokes, Griffiths[4] etc.)

[1] By L.   [2] *Self Condemned.*   [3] Bridson was visiting the U.S.
[4] W. H. Stokes (b. 1894), Member of the Iron and Steel Corporation of Great Britain; Rt. Hon. James Griffiths (b. 1890), Secretary of State for the Colonies and Member of the National Executive of the Labour Party.

I am delighted to learn that Richards is recording in New York a broadcast about *Childermass*.¹ I can remember hardly any other publicity relating to my work which gives me so much pleasure. I.A.R. read with a beautiful intelligence the other night (Third Programme) Marvell's *Garden*.

Finally, needless to say planning for the Childermass has been constantly going on. It bristles with difficulties. God is a big problem. The sorting out of the dialogue is another. As a theologian I am inferior to what Eliot is supposed to be. That must be remedied! . . . Will write you again very shortly.

Yours ever.
W. L.

491. *To I. A. Richards*†   London. W. 11.
Dec. 17. 1951.

Dear Richards. . . . What you say about the B.B.C.'s "Childermass", is of course true.² But if they had not done it, what then? Their use of announcers is unfortunate: then ―― has a thin cold expressionless voice (as you say, not the "voice of God" as he is said to have). But Wolfit is another matter: to find a strong voice, a great vitality, the quick-witted resourcefulness, is so rare a combination that I think I must be very thankful to have secured Wolfit. High intellectual understanding is not to be found among actors. As to the man who played ――, he is an old B.B.C. hack who, although I exhorted him to realise that ―― was arrogant and "superior," that there must be no didactic emphasis, he would insist on sawing away tum tum *tum*, tum tum *tum*, in approved B.B.C. "talks" style. But the accompanying music appeared to my untutored ear, extremely good.

To come back to what I began by saying: the B.B.C. are not

¹ Richards's "Talk" was broadcast over the Third Programme on March 10th, 1952.
² In a letter written from Harvard and dated "Guy Fawkes Day," Richards said that he had finally heard a transcription of the BBC version of *The Childermass*. He was pleased, he said, with Bridson's work, and he could praise Wolfit's Bailiff. The performance of another well-known actor he declared a "real failure." He also deplored the "BBC Standard Announcer's meaningless voice in the early descriptions."

organised to produce very finished performances, but what else is here of this kind, here or in America? (Is it not time something were started? It is not costly, like celluloid.)

Your broadcast will be the most important critical event of what I laughingly call my career. I await it naturally with impatience. The hint you give that not only Athens and Florence, but also the Isle of Wight, are invoked makes me naturally very curious to learn what you have said.[1]. . .

Yours,

492. *To I. A. Richards*†   [London]
April 3rd. 1952.

Dear Richards. . . .

. . . Your talk was beautifully and ingeniously written; I hope it may be preserved in some way. In a week or two I begin work on The Childermass; that it has your support is a great thing. . . .

Your broadcast drew my attention to Fielding's "A Journey from this World to the Next".[2] I have just got it out of The London Library but have not started to read it yet. I hope it may help me to get Pulley across the river and safely within the Gates of the Magnetic City.[3] . . .

Yrs.

493. *To Sir Nicholas Waterhouse*†   London. W. 11.
June 19th 1952

My dear Docker. After reading your reminiscences, I have a feeling of having been severely rationed.[4] Each phase of your lief, *one anecdote*. That is much too restricted a diet. You write with skill and grace; one reads of your enchanting contacts with

---

[1] Richards reported that he had "written my bit for the BBC" and that he had "put the book in very good company," mentioning Plato, Dante, and Fielding.

[2] In Fielding's *Miscellanies* (3 vols.; 1743).

[3] See "Monstre Gai," *The Human Age: Books 2 and 3*.

[4] Sir Nicholas, not a literary man, had sent a short ms. to L. and asked for his opinion.

Spooner.¹ This whets one's appetite for *more* stories about "The Spoo", and about other whimsical dons . . . .

Again, without running any risk you might be a little risqué sometimes. You have a perfect style for that, so correct and unimpassioned, you could get away with murder – with bedroom scenes, with stumer cheques, with nepotism, bigamy and sodomy.

. . . With little trouble you could compose a very rich volume of Memoirs. What is your excuse for not bringing it into being?

Your affectionate but reproachful
WYNDHAM LEWIS

494. *To Ezra Pound*† [London]
Sept. 10. 1952.

My dear Ezz. Thank you for your communication re *Writer and Absolute*. It is no use protesting about your *absolute* nationalism, of course.² But I know you are not such a fool as to think that it makes any difference whether you live beside the Thames or beside the Potomac. What *does* matter is *how* you live and the sooner you get out of that Asylum the better. Do you think Oozenstink as you call him might be inclined to forget your insults to Mr. Roosevelt?

It wearies me your remaining where you are. To take up a strategic position in a lunatic asylum is idiotic. If I dont see you make an effort to get out *soon*, I shall conclude, either that your present residence has a snobbish appeal for you, or that you are timid with regard to Fate. – Ask your wife to give the signal to your horde of friends to go into battle for you. Anyhow, my love to you and Dorothy.

Yours,

¹ William Archibald Spooner (1844–1930), of the celebrated impediment, was a Fellow of New College, Oxford, when Sir Nicholas was an undergraduate there. Spooner became Warden of New College in 1903.

² Having read L.'s new book (out in June) on the writer's lack of freedom, Pound wrote to him about it, taking exception to an allusion to his own "incomprehensible intervention" on the side of Mussolini. (See p. 41.) In his letter Pound insisted that he was not an Italian nationalist: "naturally my Doug/ and Gesellism had NO italian origins/ and was NOT part of govt/ program."

495. *To David Kahma*† London. W. 11.
[October] 26th 1952.

My dear Kahma. It is, I am ashamed to say, some months since I wrote you. Not long after our last exchange of letters, T. S. Eliot was dining here and I talked to him about you. The Douks is not a subject that interests him, I regret to say. He gave his opinion of all Russians. I told him that the Archangel would have agreed with him entirely on the subject of Russians. . . .

. . . Last night I was listening to a Radio celebration of Flaherty,[1] author of Nanook of the North. His tremendous advantage was to have lived near Eskimos. Now, Vancouver is not exotic, like Coronation Gulf: but it is worth your while to remember that there are practically no Canadian writers who have familiarized other nations with the Canadian scene. And I continue to feel that the enormous mountains, the Indians and yes the Doukobors, and other things known to you but not to me, are something definite, an identity not without interest. You must not be discouraged about your Douk proposals failing. If only you work away, I am sure you will succeed. . . .

Yours sincerely,

496. *To Henry Regnery*†[2] [London]
June 17. 1953.

Dear Mr. Regnery. Thank you for your letter. I thought England's advertisement of Monarchy might have attracted you.[3] Now I shall look forward to seeing you in the Autumn.

Personally, I approve of Monarchy (or, in the U.S., Republicanism). My eyes are less starry than anybody's. The "Liberalism" in this unhappy land which encourages the Mau-Mau in Kenya to

---

[1] "Portrait of Robert Flaherty," broadcast on the Third Programme on October 22nd.

[2] Henry Regnery (b. 1912) founded the publishing firm of Henry Regnery Co. in Chicago in 1947. He became L.'s American publisher with the appearance of *Rotting Hill* in April 1952.

[3] Regnery had written earlier that he was planning a visit to London. L. assumed that he would arrive in time for the coronation on June 2nd; when he failed to appear, L. wrote asking for news of his plans.

kill all the White Settlers, displeases me. I would have Pritt[1] and all his friends shot. Feeling like this about our famous English "Liberalism", I feel there is something to be said for Monarchy. The drums and trumpets of the Footguards warm my heart. I hate disorder; I call this "The Politics of Genius."[2] Those who indulge in baby-talk about feeling brotherly towards highly-organised terrorist armies in Malaya, or Kenya, or elsewhere, make me weak with accumulated exasperation. Such "reactionary" outbursts as this must fall harshly upon Uncle Sam's ear.

Sincerely,

497. *To Stuart Gilbert*†[3]   [London]
24th July 1953.

My dear Stuart Gilbert. . . .

We correspond but never meet, which I must regret. Returning from Zurich, where I had gone to consult the Star of the Augenklinik, I passed a couple of weeks in Paris, was there about three years ago again about eyes. Now I am blind. Blindness is not for me what it is for ninety-nine per cent of men. This does not mean that I like it, however, nor that I have not my share of problems. I am not a hundred per cent blind: and so long as the visible world is there, if indistinct, one has not that lonely feeling which total blindness must impose. –

And you? The other day I read a translation[4] of Malraux's "Museum Without Walls". A perfect translation, however, as good as having the French text. . . .

. . . Oh dear, editing the letters of a friend who is dead must be a sad task – especially such a friend as Joyce.

Yours,

. . .

[1] D. N. Pritt (b. 1887), a prominent left-wing K.C., defended Jomo Kenyatta and five other African terrorists in their trial which ended in conviction on April 8th.

[2] See "The Politics of the Intellect," *The Art of Being Ruled* (New York, 1926), pp. 447–50.

[3] Stuart Gilbert and L. first came in contact in the 1920's through their mutual friend Joyce. Although they saw one another infrequently and corresponded rarely, they continued to know one another till L.'s death. The immediate cause for writing in 1953 was Gilbert's edition of the *Letters of James Joyce* (London, 1957), for which he was collecting material. Having in his possession only two or three brief notes from Joyce, L. was unable to contribute to the volume.   [4] By Gilbert.

498. *To T. S. Eliot*†   29 Notting Hill Gate. W. 11.
                                   23rd November 1953

Dear Eliot,

I was shown a letter today of Ezra's, to Miss Agnes Bedford, with whom he often corresponds. In it he expressed himself as follows (I translate): "It is time that a little more intelligence was used to get Grandpa out of the bughouse."

If Ezra seems to wish that a major effort should be made to secure his release from prison, then a few of his friends should draw up a programme, and go into action. In that case perhaps an appeal might be printed, and mailed to a considerable number of people, in all parts of the world. A space should be left somewhere for them to write their names quite legibly, endorsing the appeal. When these names have been collected, this appeal would be printed on a large and imposing sheet, with all the signatures massed underneath. The first step then would be, I suppose, to send it to the President of the United States. The Times (London), and the New York Times might be asked to publish this appeal with signatures.

I daresay this is not the best way to do it, but I feel that something should be done, and here, for the start, is my suggestion. As to the friends of Ezra of whom I spoke above, you and I are his two oldest friends in England, and we could start the ball rolling.[1]

                                   Yours ever,

[1] Eliot replied on December 4th. He told L. that he gathered from American opinion that public agitation outside of the U.S. for Pound's release was not advisable. He noted that Pound didn't want "anything in the nature of a pardon" – since that would constitute an admission of guilt – and that Pound didn't feel he could stand a trial. Eliot enclosed an account of the situation by Pound's lawyer in Washington, in which the latter questioned any immediate attempt to "force any change in his status." When it became clear that any action to free Pound must originate in the U.S., L. dropped his campaign. He did, however, pursue it for some time after this letter. See his letter of December 19th.

499. To Hugh Kenner† [London]
23rd November 1953.

Dear Kenner,

This is merely a few small things which I noticed in reading your typescript:[1] See page enclosed. At the same time, while they are still fresh in my memory, I will make some observations, about one thing and another. I am not suggesting any modification in your text. Of course, at this late date, I have nothing of that kind in mind, but merely a private communication.

(1) Where you quote a passage from *Tarr*, of intense imagery, and compare it with the writing in *The Revenge for Love*,[2] you do not seem to realize what I had in mind in writing my later novels (post *Apes of God*). First let me say that were you to compare any of the highly-energised imagery which can be found in *Tarr* with the text of *Madame Bovary*, or *War and Peace*, or *The Possessed* or *Le Rouge et le Noir*, you would find nothing in them anywhere resembling the above-mentioned descriptions. This does not make the novels in question inferior to *Tarr*, for a quite different form of expression is involved. In *Tarr* I had in view a publique d'élite who could be addressed in blank verse, and the style of the poème en prose might suddenly be used, or be employed for half a page. Down to Fielding or Thackeray in England, and in all the great Russian novelists it was an aristocratic audience which was being addressed. The narrator in a book which sets out to tell a story is restricted to a manner of recital avoiding eccentricity – not acting *oneself*, but tacitly impersonating someone altogether less extraordinary than a poet, a painter, a philosopher, etc. etc.

In *Tarr* (1914–15) I was an extremist. In editing *Blast* I regarded the contributions of Ezra as compromisingly passéiste, and wished I could find two or three literary extremists. In writing *Tarr* I wanted at the same time for it to be a novel, and to do a piece of writing worthy of the hand of the abstractist innovator (which was an impossible combination). Anyhow it was my object to eliminate anything less essential than a noun or a verb.

---

[1] L. had already written thanking and congratulating Kenner on his study when he first read the typescript a month before.

[2] This specific juxtaposition does not appear in Kenner's book; the writing of *The Revenge for Love* is, however, discussed in relation to L.'s earlier style. See *Wyndham Lewis*, pp. 14, 123–6, 136.

Prepositions, pronouns, articles – the small fry – as far as might be, I would abolish. Of course I was unable to do this, but for the purposes of the *novel*, I produced a somewhat jagged prose.

This is becoming an article. I apologise. However I will send it off. Let me thank you once more for your grand *Hudson* article.[1]...

Most cordially,

500. *To T. S. Eliot*†   29 Notting Hill Gate. W. 11.
Dec 19th 1953

Dear Eliot. Thank you for your letter, and the copy of the lawyer's letter.[2] Your departure for South Africa disposes for the time being of my projected action. On your return I would be glad if you would let me know, and we can perhaps consider this again.

It would be in Ezra's best interest (perhaps) to stand his trial, and I cannot believe the lawyer is right about his frailty. But I do not see him taking this step. He will choose the alternative – to be rescued, namely. It is most unlikely that the rescue initiative will come from America. Consequently (most inappropriately) an appeal for his release seems destined to originate in these islands.

I should say myself that the almost daily revelations in the U.S. regarding President Delano Roosevelt's Administration, are a golden opportunity, either for Ezra to stand his trial, or for an appeal for his release. At the least, they are a factor favouring any action of that kind.

But should the Democrats win the next election and an Administration of Roosevelt-Truman type come roaring back, the atmosphere would at once become adverse for an appeal-for-release of a man whose main crime was first of all personal abuse of Roosevelt, and a tendency to compare Mussolini to Jefferson, with the object of emphasising what an American President ought really to be like. – I hardly think that Republicanism will have such luck as it had in Chicago 1952: if that assumption proves correct then there is really no time to be lost.

If I were placed as you are, and *you* were writing to *me* upon

[1] "The Revenge of the Void," *Hudson Review*, Autumn 1953, pp. 382–97. Much of the article, which deals mainly with *The Revenge for Love*, is incorporated in Kenner's book.

[2] See note to L.'s letter of November 23rd.

this subject, I understand how irritated I should feel. I should know how this undertaking must interfere with my work; and I expect that in the past a great deal of time would have been lost in connection with the problem of Ezra's release, as I am sure it must have been in your case.

All the same, I have always said that I would do whatever I could whenever Ezra gave me the word. He has now done so, and since I regard your cooperation as a paramount necessity, I shall renew my effort to secure it upon your return from the long holiday which your health imposes on you.[1]

Yours ever,

501. *To Marshall McLuhan*† [London]
[Incomplete draft.] Jan 17. 1954.

My dear McLuhan. . . .

On several occasions you have expressed annoyance at being so far from N.Y. North America should be one unit, instead of three. But as Government and business men in Canada insist on things remaining as they are, writing (and *reading*) in Canada should be stimulated. This is one of those tiresome *oughts*. . . .

There is a quite indecent interest in Ford Madox Hueffer. This is the doing of Ezra;[2] but there ought to (ought again) be a collective critical intelligence in U.S. forbidding the establishment of such a wrong value as *that* just as an exclusion should be made impossible (a literary exclusion for political reasons). What is the matter with the U.S. in this lit-intellectual department? A question like that of the mechanical bride.[3]

---

[1] Before his departure for South Africa, Eliot took up the subject in two further letters to L. He again declared his concern over Pound's situation and said he would ask the Washington lawyer to write directly to L. He said that after so many years in which nothing had been attempted, he saw less objection to starting something outside the U.S. Finally, in his letter of December 24th, he wrote: "Possibly it would be a good thing to get him out even if the way he was got out didn't please him."

[2] Since 1940 Pound had published pieces on Ford in *Furioso*, *New Directions in Prose and Poetry*, and *Western Review*.

[3] See H. Marshall McLuhan, *The Mechanical Bride: Folklore of Industrial Man* (New York, 1951).

According to T. S. Eliot's modest account, when Lewis completed Part II of The Human Age, *Eliot offered to read through the typescript catching any inconsistencies that might have occurred as a result of Lewis's inability to see his own copy. As the letters indicate, however, Eliot's interest in the book went beyond that of a proofreader; and Lewis, it is clear, thought of him as more than that. Eliot went on to write "A Note for* Monstre Gai*" to accompany the first publication of a part of the work, in the Winter* 1955 Hudson Review. *He also read Part III, "Malign Fiesta," in proof, and introduced the radio adaptation of "Monstre Gai" and "Malign Fiesta."*

502. *To T. S. Eliot*   London. W. 11.
AL/WL   Aug 5. 1954.

Dear Eliot. The Monstre Gai is, of course, the Bailiff.[1] He is the key figure in this book; in the next Lucifer, Son of the Morning, supercedes him.

To help you with the reading. You will have to read up to page 29, say, for a start. Points in book in which meaning is concentrated are –

(1) Pullman's talk with Mannock, bottom page 185, down to page 198.[2]

(2) Another part in which the meaning of this book, or, perhaps I should say, the argument, is condensed, is the last paragraph of page 298, down to page 311.[3]

A personal question. I should be glad and proud to learn that your house-mate[4] had looked at my manuscript: but I should prefer that you would not show it to anyone else – you will understand my reasons. I am sure I could have spared myself the

---

[1] Eliot wrote to L. raising the question of identity.

[2] Pp. 160–70 in the printed edition.

[3] Presumably either pp. 261–7 or pp. 290–8 in the printed edition. Eliot wrote to L. on August 21st, saying that the cited passages had improved his understanding of the book. He declared himself still mystified as to the ultimate denouement, the fact that people should die in the "Third City," and various details. But two readings assured him, he said, that this was a first-rate work.

[4] John Hayward (b. 1905).

trouble of writing this, that it is supremely unlikely that you wish to do anything of the sort. But we authors . . . !

Yours ever,
WYNDHAM LEWIS

503. *To Hugh Kenner*†   [London]
Sept 21 1954.

Dear Kenner: What I call a "holiday" is ended and I am once more in harness. When I arrived here the other day I found your magnificent book,[1] for which I cannot thank you enough. I think I have been most fortunate, or think my books have, in finding someone with so much intelligence, literary artistry, curious discernment, and goodwill, and I am sure that their future in the world will greatly benefit from this splendid study. I cannot thank you enough, or sufficiently often. At the same time as the book, I received a cutting from the New York Times, which seems to show that your book is having a success. I was glad to read in this cutting that the writer gave it as his opinion that your book was the best of the series in which it is appearing.[2] . . .

You must, I imagine, have received some personal communications, for and against, regarding your book. I should be greatly interested to peruse them, if you would care to let me see them – even if they are most disagreeable. My hide is thick. . . .

Yrs.

504. *To T. S. Eliot*   London. W. 11.
Oct 11th 1954.

Dear Eliot. Have you a copy of your note of Oct 9? What you say is quite accurate as regards what I wish to be understood – destinations of men, various survivals, and other possibilities.[3] Third

---

[1] The American edition of Kenner's *Wyndham Lewis* appeared on July 7th. The English edition followed in November.

[2] New Directions. The Makers of Modern Literature Series.

[3] Eliot wrote: "I get the impression that you want to distinguish between Death on Earth – the process by which people get from Earth

City, I suppose, had been designed otherwise than the place we see. I cannot believe in the impossibility of an existence superior to this, just as no man, is so stupid that he cannot imagine a variety of far worse lives than this one. I reserve for my Third City characters a Heaven and a Hell, as the alternative, when they leave that place. – As to the men who have left the earth being assured that immortality is not necessarily for them, if, on speeding away from their mortal habitat they had the pleasing illusion that immortality, at least, is assured, the Bailiff puts them right on that point.[1] . . . – Cigarettes are not allowed, but there is a large bootleg supply. Bailiff's vast income is in part derived from tobacco.[2] – Normal end of Mannock etc.[3] If Lucifer occupied Third City, he would be smuggled off to Heaven.

Thank you extremely for helping me in this way. I am sure the book will be a better one as a result of your scrutiny.

Yours ever,
W. L.

P.S. When Pullman says to his fag "you'll have to die some day" that is just a jeer.

to the Camp and the City, and a second form of Death which is complete Extinction. I gather that in the City-Existence, for which the nearest analogy is some form of Purgatory, people can either proceed to something more admirable, or . . . decamp to Hell, or be completely wiped out. I do not take it that anybody stays forever in the Magnetic City . . . ."

[1] Eliot said that it should be made clear "that transit from this world to the Magnetic City is not to be taken as a guarantee of immortality."

[2] Eliot asked: "I gather that smoking is allowed in the City?" On hearing from L., he replied on October 14th that he had at first assumed that – since after lunch neither Mannock nor his guests smoked – tobacco, like alcohol, was prohibited. But then Sentoryen, he said, is mentioned lighting a cigarette in public, which would be imprudent if cigarettes were bootlegged. To this stricture, L. replied, in his next letter, that he would attend to what Eliot said about Sentoryen. "You may have remarked that cigarettes," he went on, "as well as drinks, were offered to guests by negroes, at the Bailiff's party. Then Sentoryen was a 'Hell Boy', who would be capable of doing anything in public. But if I caught him doing anything illegal publicly I certainly would stop him, and shall do so."

[3] Eliot wrote: "What I want to know is the normal end of people like Mannock and his friends. & what would happen to the entire population if Lucifer brought his bombardment to a triumphant conclusion. P. 101 Pully says to Satters: 'You have to die some day.'" See p. 88 of the printed edition.

505. *To Mrs. Amor Liber*†¹ [London]
Dec 3rd 1954.

Dear Rebecca. . . .

Self Condemned has, I believe, found a provincial U.S. publisher who will accept it.² No New York publisher could be found. In your letter you said that your husband was like René.³ That, I hope is incorrect: for to be like René is very dangerous. . . .

Now that I have given you my news, how about yours. Do you like the part of New York where you are living? . . . I told you, I believe, that Partisan refused a story of mine, saying it was too reactionary . . . . Are there any new well-financed magazines, I wonder? Here, in England, there is a chronic absence of outlet of that kind. A short-story, when written, remains in my drawer – except for Encounter,⁴ which is half American. . . . Unless he is stimulated by politics (Left or Right) the man with money is rarely willing to risk a little capital in a magazine. But I gossip . . . .

Yours,

506. *To Ezra Pound*† [London]
Dec 31. 1954.

Dear Ezz. I greatly value your good opinion, so what you say about Self Condemned gives great pleasure.⁵ About June a very big book is appearing:⁶ I will send a copy to Dorothy: if I sent it to Saint Eliz the Management might not consider it suitable

¹ L. had known and admired Mrs. Liber as a young woman, then Rebecca Citkowitz, in New York in 1940. They had fallen out of touch after L.'s return to England. Then Mrs. Liber wrote to him on reading *Self Condemned*.
² Henry Regnery brought out *Self Condemned* in March 1955.
³ René Harding, the uncompromising, semi-autobiographical hero of *Self Condemned*.
⁴ L. published two stories in *Encounter*: "Doppelgänger" (January 1954) and "Pish-Tush" (February 1956).
⁵ Having received *Self Condemned* and read most of it, Pound wrote to L. on November 19th. His letter began: "Yuss. my beamish buckO! this IZ some book." A second letter, dated December 6th, begins: "to confirm HIGH opinion of 'Self-Cndd'/ it and Rot-Hill all, past 2nd hell lit/ yet discovered among ruins of Albion. Shd/ git yu the Nobble."
⁶ Presumably *The Human Age: Books 2 and 3*. It appeared in November 1955.

reading for you. I hear rumours which are promising regarding your probable freedom. Hemingway was helpful, I believe. . . .

I have just been reading a Babylonish cosmogony by an admirer of yours. Many echoes of your private lingo.

Best wishes for freedom in New Year.

Yrs.

. . .

507. *To J. Alan White*† London. W. 11.
January 26th 1955.

Dear White. I have at last settled upon a title; "The Human Age." You remember that Sammael's[1] idea was to combine the best of the Human spirit with his Angel's nature: and in the last book of the series there is to be a final volume in which this is debated.[2]

Yrs.

P.S. Another title would be "The Human Dream." But I think people would say that I meant that the Christian religion was only a dream.

508. *To J. Alan White*† London. W. 11.
Feb 15th 1955.

Dear White. . . .

There are two points only that I need discuss.[3] First, it may be said that I have no Greek; but there are, I believe, two forms of the signs, one only recurring at the end of a word. . . .

The second matter is the problem associated with the question of obscenity. I have modified the offensive passages in a number of cases, removed objectionable words. The words used in the dispute, in Fifth Piazza . . . I would rather like to leave untouched – I mean the abusive exchanges of the two giants.[4] The

[1] Fallen angel in "Malign Fiesta."

[2] This volume, tentatively titled *The Trial of Man*, was never completed, L. having written only notes for it before his final illness.

[3] White wrote to L. raising a number of points about the ms. of *The Human Age: Books 2 and 3*.

[4] As printed the exchanges are quite innocuous. See "Monstre Gai," pp. 109–10.

descriptive passages, connected with the bestial goat-men,¹ I think do not need to be watered down; but I will be guided by you regarding this. . . .

Finally, when the Bailiff is spoken about as the "The old Bailey" I think *Bailey* is the best way of spelling that particular word. Do you agree with this?

Yours sincerely,

509. *To Sir Nicholas Waterhouse*† [London]
March 31. 1955.

Dear Docker. . . . As Agnes has no doubt told you, I have been busy preparing for the publication of my two books in June, and for the Broadcast of three plays in May. . . .

After the very severe winter I find the persistently cold March unusually tiresome. Scientists seem to me to be lying when they say that the filthy weather is in no way connected with the filthy bombs. I wish that it was not considered necessary to pay a lot of men of science to fool one dont you? I would much rather that they treated one as of so little importance that it was not worth while to do that. . . .

Much love,
Yrs,

510. *To Ruthven Todd*†² [London]
April 2nd. 1955.

Dear Todd. . . .

Thank you for interesting yourself in *Self Condemned*.³ Some of its features are of interest to those not familiar with the No. American continent. In [sic] shipping one's hero across the Atlantic involves explanations – as you can see had I placed him

¹ See "Monstre Gai," pp. 105 ff.
² L. got to know the British writer Ruthven Todd in London in the 1930's. Because of L.'s long absence from Britain during the war and Todd's expatriation to the U.S. in 1947, they saw little of one another after that but remained in casual contact.
³ Todd had obtained a copy of the novel for review in the New York Times. See *New York Times Book Review*, May 8th, 1955, p. 5.

in Martha's Vineyard. . . . in certain writing of Wagner I remarked errors regarding my works which seem to me deliberate.¹ He is, you know, a nephew of Fanny Wadsworth. He is a nice fellow but he may inherit family feuds.

Enough of self at present. Your settlement in America interests me. An Englishman, I suppose, develops into an expert on Great Britain. [unreadable sentences]

The last time I saw him was on the platform of the station at Babylon, hurrying along beneath a load of flowers. He was saluting a woman friend who was going to summer in Long Island. But he did not confine himself to saying it in flowers. When we went to a party at his studio he invariably took my wife in his arms. He prolonged this greeting on one occasion. His wife burst into tears, and they retired into their private apartment, amid distant howls. T. S. Eliot knew him. But he thinks he is dead, since he no longer sees him upon his visits to New York. He is, or was, the Scot who bodily reminded me of Boswell, just as Wales appears to gush forth [from?] Augustus John.

Yours very cordially,

511. *To Frederick Morgan*†²   [London]
May 6th 1955.

Dear Mr. Morgan. Here is the Col. Lawrence article.³ I do not know if you ever use photographs, but if you should then I suggest one of Col. Lawrence in Arab dress, looking very coy. . . . I secured a gift copy from Jonathan Cape's office of the unexpurgated edition of *The Mint*⁴ – a bawdy song or two, and thousands of soldiers oaths, nothing more. . . .

Yours very sincerely,

¹ See Geoffrey Wagner, *Wyndham Lewis: A Portrait of the Artist as the Enemy*. L. saw some pieces of the book before it was completed.

² Founder and editor of the *Hudson Review*.

³ "Perspectives on Lawrence," *Hudson Review*, Winter 1956, pp. 596–608. Morgan had asked L. to review *en bloc* a number of recent books pertaining to T. E. Lawrence. L. gives a vivid account of his acquaintance with Lawrence in *Blasting and Bombardiering*.

⁴ T. E. Lawrence, *The Mint* (London, 1955).

512. *To Hugh Kenner*† [London]
August 29th 1955.

My dear Kenner. . . .

"The Human Age" is the title at present of what I have done,[1] but I am proposing to write a further book which will necessitate an alteration of the overall title. You will notice that Malign Fiesta significantly ends by two White Angels carrying off Pullman. He finds himself, in the final book, in the Celestial Camp. This is very much to his satisfaction. 'Monstre Gai' shows him entrapped by the Bailiff, in whose power he reluctantly remains. There is a passage in that book in which he analyses his dilemma (it occurs in the covered walk along the side of Tenth Piazza).[2] The Bailiff is, of course, not Divine. Then the same situation is repeated in Malign Fiesta, only even more tragically, and the figure in that case is Divine, though Diabolic. In the last book of all the hero, Pullman, is at last in Divine Society. He favours the Divine. I favour the Divine. There is a gigantic debate, in which Sammael's purpose to combine the Human and the Angelic, is discussed, the Celestial spokesman naturally attacking Sammael's big idea. In the discussions (in Malign Fiesta) between Pullman and his master, the Devil, all of the latter's plan is revealed – in order to save his life Pullman gives it his support. But Pullman is, of course, an adherent of the Divine, not of the Diabolic. Under these circumstances, a new overall title will be required. . . .

Yours ever,

[1] Kenner wrote to L. of his intention to do an article on *The Human Age*. He incorporated a large section of this letter into the piece, which appeared as "The Devil and Wyndham Lewis" in *Shenandoah* for Autumn 1955. (Reprinted in *Gnomon* [New York, 1958], pp. 215–41.) Thanks to his conversations with L. in 1956, Kenner was able to learn more about plans for Book 4. This additional information is included in the essay in *Gnomon*.

[2] See *The Human Age: Books 2 and 3*, pp. 262 ff.

513. *To Russell Kirk*†[1] London. W. 11.
Aug. 29th 1955.

My dear Kirk. First of all, let me thank you very much for your interesting article in Yale Review.[2] I was delighted (though what the hell you meant by what I lacked for perfection was ... !), and secondly, let me say how much I enjoyed your three books, sent me by Regnery.[3] You are the latest, and by no means the least, of that brilliant group of Americans advocating that of all unamerican things, the Traditional Spirit. Your praise of Edmund Burke is very much to my taste. Your witty prophecy of the immediate future should be enlarged. . . .

Yrs,

514. *To T. S. Eliot* 28 Notting Hill Gate. W. 11.
Oct 19th 1955.

Dear Eliot. The news of your return – your safe return – reached me some time ago, but I was completing a novel, and all my time was taken up by that. Now I am free I hasten to write to you and to suggest a meeting. Will you be free soon for a dinner at this flat . . . .

I heard, with alarm that you were in a nursing home. It was your feet, I understand, and hoped that it was nothing worse.[4] . . .

I am anxious to believe that when you go into a nursing home you are escaping from a horde of ——, or even closer friends. If I had the money, and acted as a magnet to many people as you do, I believe I should often flee into a nursing home, and I should sometimes say that it was because of my feet, sometimes my knee, and sometimes higher up. –

[1] Russell Kirk (b. 1918) is Professor of Political Science at Post College, Long Island University, and is best known for his writing on and advocacy of American conservatism. He met L. in London in 1955 and visited him after that.

[2] Russell Kirk, "Wyndham Lewis's First Principles," *Yale Review*, Summer 1955, pp. 520–34. (Reprinted in *Beyond the Dreams of Avarice* [Chicago, 1956].) Kirk had sent the article to L.

[3] Presumably *The Conservative Mind* (1953), *A Program for Conservatives* (1954), and *Academic Freedom* (1955).

[4] Eliot replied on October 24th, saying that his ailment was athlete's foot.

I have no designs but merely should be very glad to see you. So – perhaps I shall see you.

Many blessings

Yours ever,
W. L.

515. *To Ezra Pound*† [London]
[ca. January 1956]

Dear Ezz. Your last letter undecipherable, just cannot imagine what lies beneath the words. Have you anything really to say? . . .

How did you and Dorothy get through the Christmas and New Year? Did the Warders and Doctors sing you Carols, as the Nurses and Doctors did in hospitals here? Best wishes, anyway, best wishes to both of you. I expect you heard that He, you call Possum lies in the London Clinic. It is not, I understand, in any way alarming.

Yrs,

516. *To Hugh Kenner*† London. W. 11.
[ca. March 1956]

Dear Kenner. To begin with many thanks for what you wrote in the Poetry Magazine.[1] It will, as you said, acquaint many Americans with One Way Song. Those with dictatorial power over all verse writing in this country . . . remained unblushedly silent about One Way Song. It is certainly an imperfect work, but I come [on] pieces of it at times with pleasure and surprise.

My Red Priest, a novel, is getting printed here.[2] I am following this with a novel about an artist[3] – not about a man who did anything very much, except sleep with his models, and squeeze pigment out of fat tubes. I like his smell, but would not marry him

[1] "A Tongue that Naked Goes" (review of *One-Way Song, Demon of Progress in the Arts, The Human Age,* Vol. II), *Poetry,* January 1956, pp. 247–52.
[2] Methuen published *The Red Priest* in August 1956.
[3] Kenner says a few words about this projected book, tentatively titled *Twentieth Century Palette,* in "The Devil and Wyndham Lewis." (See *Gnomon,* p. 240.) A draft of the novel is in the Lewis collection at Cornell.

to my favourite girl. I married him to what Miss Mitford calls "the Hons".

I have had a letter from Ez recently which is friendly again. Are they going to let him out? He ought to wear a pale grey tophat and a tail coat in prison perhaps. I am sure Mr. Franklin Delano would have done that, if he had met Ezra's fate. – Another Canadian (from Vancouver) has just sent me a literary work of about five thousand lines. Why should a man think that if he writes something too long for anyone to be able to read that it is meritorious? It is a Canadian idea as I have received three. When are you coming to London? I want to keep a place open for you and your wife.

My best blessings.

517. *To Ezra Pound*† [London]
July 29th 1956.

Dear Ezra. . . .

I spent one evening with I. A. Richards the other night. He gave me a very promising account of efforts to be of use to you – indeed, to get you out – going on at Harvard. Do be a little diplomatic with this fellow at Harvard offering to help you. It would be such fun to have you at large again! And this can only be done by an American, and one not hated by the Authorities.

Have had a big Retrospective Show Picture Exhibition at the Tate, with your portrait prominent, and greatly admired. . . .

Blessings.

The Tate Gallery Exhibition "Wyndham Lewis and Vorticism" (July 6th to August 19th) marked the apogee of Lewis's reputation as an artist. Coming less than a year before his death, the large retrospective was also his last *public recognition. It is fittingly ironic that this final triumph should have occasioned a final tempest. Ignoring the fact that the show was intended primarily as a Lewis retrospective, William Roberts wrote several angry letters to the press, protesting the Tate's treatment of the other "Vorticists" who were represented. (Roberts himself had seven works in the show.) When the letters were not printed, Roberts, who had had his baptism in invective fighting at Lewis's side in the* Blast *days, published them privately as a pamphlet titled* The Resurrection of Vorticism and the Apotheosis of Wyndham Lewis. *This was followed by three more publications, the last of them an attack on John Rothenstein's* Modern English Painters: Lewis to Moore. *When the pamphlets were brought to his attention, Lewis was of course exercised. He consulted a lawyer and wrote the facts out for him. He draughted a letter to the press. By this time, however, his health had deteriorated too far to make any action feasible and he did not pursue the matter. Thus, although the press made some note of the affair, it did not become a full-fledged controversy till months after Lewis's death. On November 22nd, 1957, the* Times Literary Supplement *published a review of the four Roberts pamphlets (p. 200). Written from the old Bell-Fry point of view – harking back (another irony) to the Omega troubles of* 1913 *– the notice took Roberts's part, accused Lewis of being "self-contradictory" and "not over scrupulous." It described him as "a virulent hater" and "not a great painter or anything like one." With Sir John Rothenstein and Michael Ayrton lining up on one side and Roberts and "Your Reviewer" on the other, the correspondence columns of* TLS *boiled for the next six weeks. One feels the Enemy's spirit was still abroad.*

518. *To Michael Ayrton* London, W. 11.
August 28th 1956.

Dear Michael. . . .

Have you seen the booklet written by Roberts entitled Vorticism? I cannot understand how he got it printed. In the main it is abuse of me. He believes that the Tate Show was organised by me, that I am very proud of Vorticism, wish to make use of him, chose the pictures, insisting on his own being very few, etc. etc. etc. He regards you as a bad-man too. This poor little creature apparently did not read my bit in the catalogue,[1] otherwise he would have seen that he attaches more importance by Vorticism than I do. If you have seen this wretched little squib give me your views.

Hope you will be up some time – soon. Not about above matter but just dont see you often enough.

Yours ever,
WYNDHAM LEWIS

[1] L.'s "Introduction," pp. 3–4.

519. *To a London Editor*† [London]
[Not sent.] [ca. September 1956]

Dear Sir. A lot of venomous misunderstandings have been scattered abroad. . . . I would be greatly obliged if I [might] make use of your columns to publish a few facts which it is necessary for people to know to disinfect this booklet, called 'Vorticism', written about me by a little Mister X.

I found myself given a huge exhibition of my pictures at the Tate. This was the work of Sir John Rothenstein and his youthful assistants, and no one else. Anyone resenting this outburst of my work should blame them, not me. I did not use my malign influence to inspire this miscarriage of justice, and certainly I was not responsible for Mr. X. being insufficiently represented at the Tate. I cannot see to read a book or write a letter, and was quite unable to see my own pictures, and certainly am not interested enough to vote for or against Mr. X's canvases. Lastly, Vorticism. This name is an invention of Ezra Pound. When he writes me from his prison in Washington he addresses me as 'Old Vort'. What does this word mean? I do not know. How anyone can get angry about it, I cannot imagine, but let me say I did not ask for this meaningless word to be revived at the Tate. We live in a world of Art Historians: they do funny things. I wish that Mr. X would not misunderstand and [words] their disgruntledness against me. I sold one small drawing to a lady at Blackheath: and practically none of the pictures were for sale. So Mr. X has not the "proceeds" to envy.

Yrs
WYNDHAM LEWIS

Index

Numbers in *italics* indicate letters. SMALL CAPITALS indicate pictures.

Abbott, Charles D., *267–8, 272–3*
Ackerley, J. R., *537*
Adelphi, The, 170–1
Adler, Henry, 207–9
Adler, Mortimer, 353, 357, 365
Agee, James, 402
Aldington, Richard: 62, 316, 522; *188–91, 217–18, 233–4*
Allott, Kenneth, *456–7*
Alsop, Joseph W., 320(n)
America and Cosmic Man, 349(n), 358, 381, 391, 437, 441, 445, 457–8, 463, 465–6, 474–5, 495, 499
America, I Presume, 263, 273, 277–8, 426
"American Melting Pot," 401(n)
Amster, Leonard, *273–5*
Anderson, Margaret, 87(n)
Anglosaxony, 282, 288–91, 293–4, 301(n), 310, 426
Antheil, George, 462
Apes of God, The, 121, 123, 133, 134–41, 143(n), 149, 166–7, 170(n), 181, 189–92, 194(n), 195–8, 205–6, 216, 226, 273, 410, 415, 490, 552
Arabian Nights, 216
Archipenko, Alexander, 112, 128
Aristotle, 357, 495
ARMADA, THE, 121
Arnold, Dr., 280
Art and Letters, 101–3, 112
Art of Being Ruled, The, 121, 137(n), 147(n), 155–6, 159(n), 165(n), 166, 174(n), 490, 550(n)
"Art of Gwen John, The," 400

Arthur Press, The: 170, 186, 189, 193(n); Circular Letters from, *191–2, 196–7*
Arts To-day, The, 235–6
Assumption College, 264, 348–50, 352–3, 356–8, 360, 364–5, 370–371, 372–5, 377, 492
Athenaeum, The, 116–19
Atkinson, Lawrence, 62
Auden, W. H., 214(n), 235(n), 316, 321(n), 444, 543
Augustine, St., 510
Austen, Jane, 224, 439
Ayer, A. J., 489
Ayrton, Michael, 388, 404; *405, 566*

Bach, 35, 173–4, 283, 337
Baker, Capt. Guy, 96; *74–5*
Baker, Josephine, 380, 382
Balla, 60
Barbusse, Henri, 90–1
Bard College, 478, 488–9, 492
Barr, Alfred, Jr., 258; *500*
Barr, F. Stringfellow, 365
BATTERY SHELLED, A, 111
Baudelaire, 45, 516
Baum, Vicki, 208–9
Beach, Sylvia, 126, 131
Beaumont, Cyril, 101
Bedford, Agnes, 388, 551; *124, 130, 157–8*
Beecham, Sir Thomas, 157–8, 355
Bell, Caroline and Eddie, *Thank You Twice*, 296
Bell, Clive, 52, 79(n), 136, 152(n), 359(n); *50–1, 53*

568

Bell, Vanessa, 412
Benda, Julien, 486–7
Bennett, Arnold, 112, 168–9, 189, 207–9, 223(n)
Bergson, 488–9
Berryman, John, 491–2
Berth, Edouard, 486–7
Best, R. H., 471
Bevan, Aneurin, 392
Binyon, Laurence, 2, 16–17, 35, 84
Blake, William, 86, 117, 231–2
Blast, 42, 60–1, 69, 137, 145(n), 273, 422, 462, 464, 491–2, 522(n), 552, 566; *Blast, I*, 210(n), 492; *Blast No. 2*, 66–8, 134
Blasting and Bombardiering, 42, 53(n), 62(n), 65(n), 67(n), 74, 85(n), 88, 94(n), 96, 114(n), 127(n), 130(n), 133(n), 134(n), 143(n), 173(n), 205(n), 210(n), 247, 248–9, 561(n)
Bliss, Sir Arthur, 340
Bloomsbury, 141, 167, 223(n), 225(n), 240, 266, 359(n), 406, 460–1
Bloy, Léon, 281, 486–7
Bomberg, David, 57, 60, 62–3, 68, 73
Bondy, Pauline, *377*
Bonham-Carter, Lady Violet, 81
Booth, Meyrick, *519–21*, *525–6*, *530–1*
Borden, Mary (Mrs. Turner, Lady Spears), 42, 67, 84; *73–4*
Bowen, Elizabeth, 480, 520
Brancusi, 129(n), 271
Brand, Lord, 529, 531
"Bread and Ballyhoo," 523
Brewer, Joseph, 312
Bridson, Geoffrey, 388, 539; *540*, *545–6*
Brighton Exhibition, 10(n), 57–9
B.B.C., 340, 387, 470, 539–41, 546
British Council, 470, 500–1, 527
British Museum, 2, 40, 354, 407, 461

Brockington, Leonard W., *308–9*, *319–20*
Brooks, Cleanth, 487(n), 488, 492–3
Brown, Oliver, 114, 420; *238–9*, *242–3*
Bruce, Kathleen (Kathleen Scott), 9–10, 16, 19–20
Bryher, Winifred, 127
Buchanan, Scott, 365
Burchfield, Charles, 366
Burgess, John, *337–8*, *357–8*, *364–5*, *370–1*
Burke, Edmund, 563
Burke, Kenneth, 440
Burnham, James, 463
Butler, Samuel, 16, 216, 497

Cabaret Theatre Club (Cave of the Golden Calf), 45–6, 48, 53–4, 339
Cain, James, 443
Calder, Alexander, 279
Caldwell, Erskine, 416
Calendar of Modern Letters, The, 149(n), 153–4, 274(n), 374(n)
Caliph's Design, The, 105(n), 110, 246, 274
Camden Town Group, 41–2, 56–7, 115(n)
Campbell, Roy, 122, 189, 190, 194–5, 197–8, 224, 236, 238, 338(n), 374, 401, 402(n); *205–206*, *219–20*, *239–40*, *522*, *542–543*
Campbell, Mrs. Roy, 206, 240; *238*, *374–5*
Camus, 411, 416, 423
Canada, L.'s residence in, 263–385
CANADIAN GUN PIT, A, 102(n), 104, 113, 282(n)
"Canadian Nature and its Painters," 359(n)
Canadian War Memorials scheme, 97, 113, 282
"Cantleman's Spring-Mate," 82
Jonathan Cape, 237, 240–1

Capen, S. P., 291
Carlow, Lord, 322, 352; *261–2, 347*
Carlyle, 539
Chagall, 438
Chamberlain, Neville, 255(n), 329, 459
Chaplin, Charlie, 171(n)
Charles I, 400
Chatto and Windus, 155(n), 166–9, 171, 177–8, 196, 203, 209
Chesterton, G. K., 236
Chevalier, Albert, 315
Childermass, The (Part I), 121, 137(n), 174–83, 187(n), 203, 226, 273–4, 351, 468, 535–6, 539–41, 546–7; *see also The Human Age*
Chirico, 226, 421–2
Cholmondeley, Lady, 210
Christ, 64, 228–9, 231–2, 455
Churchill, Sir Winston, 250, 255–257, 284, 316
Cimabue, 352
Clark, Sir Kenneth, 266, 364, 412
Cobden-Sanderson, R., *138*
Coburn, Alvin Langdon, 66
Cole, Mrs. G. D. H., 362, 392
Coleridge, 335, 347
Collier, John, 316
Colquhoun, Robert, 408, 412–13, 460, 485
Connolly, Cyril, 339(n)
Conrad, Joseph, 332(n)
Contact Publishing Company and Three Mountains Press, 155–6, 165
Cori, Gerty, *378–9*
Count Your Dead; They Are Alive!, 244
CREATION, 10, 57, 59
CREATION MYTH, 407
"Creatures of Habit and Creatures of Change," 274
Cripps, Sir Stafford, 318–19, 346, 355, 439

Criterion, The, 134–41, 147–54, 164
Cromwell, 342, 400
Cronin, A. J., 369
CUBIST MUSEUM, 242
Cummings, E. E., 404, 477
Cunard, Lady, 42, 129(n), 132, 157–8
Cunard, Nancy, 129

Daily Telegraph, *251–2*
Dante, 455, 472, 547(n)
D'Arcy, Rev. M. C., 171(n), 261; *173–4, 236–7*
Day Lewis, C., 214(n), 235(n)
Degas, 453, 494
Demon of Progress in the Arts, The, 523, 564(n)
J. M. Dent & Sons, *310–11*
Derain, 60, 117–18, 260
Derby, the, 445–6
"De Tocqueville's 'Democracy in America,'" 382, 401(n)
Dewey, Thomas E., 452, 463, 467, 471, 475, 476
Diabolical Principle and the Dithyrambic Spectator, The, 147–154
Dial, The, 120, 440(n)
Dickens, 15, 196, 295, 479, 507
Dickson, H. H. Lovat, *244*
Die Tat (Zürich), 515
Dismorr, Jessie, 73, 111, 115
Dobson, Frank, 111
Donegal, Lord, 189
Donne, 480
Doom of Youth, The, 121, 166, 203, 519(n)
"Doppelgänger," 558(n)
Doré Gallery, 49, 51, 53(n), 54, 73
Dostoevsky, 208, 305, 332(n), 442, 552
Doughty, Charles M., 335, 474
Douglas, Major C. H., 416, 548(n)
Douglas, Norman, 322, 415

570

Doukhobors, 425(n), 426, 434–6, 439, 442–4, 448–9, 460, 470, 483–4, 494, 521, 544, 549
Drey, O. R., 141–3; *162–4*
Drey, Mrs. O. R. (Anne Estelle Rice), 141–3; *145–6*
Drogheda, Lady, 42
Dryden, 459
Durrell, Lawrence, 446
Dyson, Will, 459

Earp, T. W., 244, 316, 338(n); *493*
Editor, a London, *567*
Edwards, Ralph, 447, 457
Egoist, The, 62(n), 66, 76–7, 95
The Egoist, Ltd., 75(n), 105(n), 126(n), 131
Eliot, T. S.: 41, 66, 68, 111–12, 123, 130, 165, 171, 172, 198, 209, 224, 228, 234, 236, 248, 259(n), 275, 300, 320(n), 322, 353, 358, 375, 382, 388, 393, 397, 414, 416, 418, 433, 436–7, 440, 462, 464–5, 467–8, 476, 477, 499, 506, 535, 544, 561; the rejected portrait, 123, 250; *134–8, 139–41, 147–9, 152–4, 164, 170, 377, 380–1, 394, 473, 495, 518, 523–4, 551, 553–4, 555–6, 556–7, 563–4*; letters from, *150–1, 251, 519*
Ellerman, Sir John, 127, 129(n)
Encounter, 558
"End of Abstract Art, The," 271
Enemy, The, 121, 170–3, 186, 216, 275, 438; I, 168, 171; No. 3, 202
Enemy of the Stars, The, 209–10
English Review, The, 39, 41, 112, 248, 441
Epstein, Sir Jacob, 53(n), 54–9, 63, 66, 253(n), 298, 532–3
Ervine, St. John, 235–6
"Essay on the Objective of Plastic Art," 131–2
Etchells, Frederick, 47–50, 57, 59, 62, 73, 85, 111; *60*

Evans, Merlyn, 485–6
Evans, Myfanwy (*The Pavilion*), 407(n)
Evening Standard, 207; *168–9*
Everett, Henry, 32, 35

Fassett, Miss I. P., 149, 154, 172(n); *165*
Faulkner, William, 223(n), 385, 439, 477
Feast, Rev. Willis, *465–6, 490*
Fergusson, Sir Louis, 56(n); *543*
Fielding, Henry, 425, 547, 552
Fifteen Drawings, 105(n), 111
Filibusters in Barbary, 202
Firbank, Ronald, 415
Flaherty, Robert, 549
Flaubert, 435, 439, 455, *493*, 552
Flower, Desmond, 261; *220, 242*
Ford, Ford Madox, *see* Hueffer
Ford, H. J., 369, 373
Ford, Lauren, 281
Forster, E. M., 225(n)
Four Pages, 436, 441, 554(n)
France, Anatole, 17
Freud, 439, *493*
Frobenius, 453
Fry, Roger, 42, 47–55, 79, 115, 116, 243, 359(n), 406, 412; *46–7*
Futurism: 41–2, 61–3; *see also* Marinetti

Garman, Douglas, 153(n), 374
Garnett, David, *178–9*
Gatty, D. I. V., 9, 19
Gaudier-Brzeska, 57, 59, 62, 73, 105, 491
Gauguin, 260, 438, 448
Gaunt, William, *244–5, 420–1*
Gide, André, 446
Gilbert, Stuart, 130(n); *550*
Gilman, Harold, 56, 91
Gilson, Etienne, 486–7
Ginner, Charles, 115
Giovanelli, Felix, 365(n), 366, 492; *360–1, 371–2, 375–6, 408–409, 423–4, 431–4, 463–5, 475–6, 479–80, 496–7, 500–1*

571

Godwin, William, 246, 403
Goehr, Walter, 540
Goethe, 423–4, 509(n)
Goldring, Douglas, 440–1
Gore, Spencer, 6, 32, 47–53, 56–7
Gorer, Geoffrey, 465
Gorky, 17
Goya, 7, 238, 302
Gozzoli, 129
Grafton Gallery, 17(n), 46
Grant, Duncan, 52, 117–18, 298, 412
Granville-Barker, H., 44
Gray, Cecil, 244
Gray, John, 185
Grigson, Geoffrey, 229(n), 235–6, 406; *401–2*
"Guns" exhibition, 102, 110
Gwynne-Jones, Allan, *390–1*

Hale, Robert, *286–8, 295–6, 305–7*
Hals, 13
Hamilton, Alexander, 349, 356, 458
Hamilton, Cicely, 199–201
Hamilton, Cuthbert, 45, 47–50, 62, 115; *46*
Hamnett, Nina, 338
Handley-Read, Charles, 43(n), 265(n), 388, 407(n); *503–5*
Harmsworth, Lord (Desmond Harmsworth), 209; *210–11*
Harold Gilman, 56(n), 543(n)
Harris, Mrs. Percy, *53–4*
Harrison, Jane, 147
Hart-Davis, Rupert, *101*
Hart-Davis, Sybil, 101
Harvard, 303, 320–1, 348, 443, 509, 565
Hastings, Beatrice, *63*
Hayward, John, 555
Hegel, 357, 489
Hemingway, Ernest, 223, 301, 310, 385, 433, 439, 443, 449, 454–5, 477, 559
Henderson, Mrs. Winifred, 209
Hepburn, Mitchell, 322

Heppenstall, Rayner, 225(n), 231(n)
Hitler, 43, 123, 199–201, 275, 286, 298, 302, 305, 307, 309, 310, 313, 316, 319, 324, 329, 331, 332–3(n), 411(n)
Hitler, 199
Hitler Cult, The, 270, 310(n)
Hogarth, William, 117, 481, 534
Holland, L.'s visit to, 13–15, 21–4
Hollis, Christopher, 349
Henry Holt and Company, 395, 410–11
Honeyman, T. J., *265–6*
Horizon, 286, 339, 402–3, 494
Horne, H. P., 19
Howard, G. Wren, 232; *240–1*
Hudson, W. H., 17
Hudson Review, 515, 553, 555
Hueffer, Ford Madox, 39, 41, 67(n), 68, 84, 137, 156(n), 440–441, 554
Hulme, T. E., 42, 54, 59, 63, 132, 275, 428
Human Age, The, 134, 175(n), 405; Books 2 and 3, 387, 540–1, 545–7, 555–60, 562, 564(n)
Hunt, Violet, 41–2, 45(n), 59(n), 67(n); *84–5*
Huxley, Aldous, 153, 192(n), 226, 316, 415
Huxley, Sir Julian, 319

Ibsen, 26, 532–3
Ida (friend in Paris), 2–3, 18, 21–4, 26–7, 29, 31–9
Ideal Home Exhibition (1913), 47–53
"Ideas with Which we Fight, The," 301, 310
"Imaginary Letters," 90, 93, 96
Imperial War Pictures, 111(n), 116
"Inferior Religions," 96, 112

Jackson, A. Y., 317, 359–60
Jagger, C. S., 343

James, Henry, 192(n), 235, 435, 477
James, Philip, 527
Jameson, R. D., *312, 317*
Jealoux, Edmond, 132
Jefferson, Thomas, 349, 356, 458, 553
Jerrold, Douglas, 236; *248–9*
John, Augustus, 3, 11–13, 17, 29, 31, 35–9, 41, 61, 66, 79, 122, 250, 253, 255(n), 290, 359(n), 374, 561; *44–5, 64–5, 70–3, 193–4, 285–6, 338–9, 383–4, 392–3, 398–401, 455–6, 480–2, 513–14, 540–1*; letter from, *194–5*
John, Mrs. Augustus (Dorelia), 286
John, Mrs. Augustus (Ida), 31, 33, 35–6
John, Sir Caspar, 481
John, Gwen, 12, 398, 400
Johnson, Jack, 56
Johnson, Philip, 279
"Joint," 148(n)
Jones, Gwynn H., 236
Jones, Inigo, 229(n), 230
Joubert, 417
Joyce, James, 41, 122–3, 126, 130, 134, 154, 156(n), 157, 171(n), 178(n), 188, 190–1, 208, 223–4, 248, 273, 275, 277, 279(n), 313, 403–4, 417, 433, 443–4, 455, 466–7, 477, 493, 507; Letters, 130(n), 550; *131*

Kahma, David, 334, 388; *335–6, 411–12, 417–19, 422–3, 425–6, 429–30, 434–6, 438–40, 442–5, 448–9, 454–5, 460–1, 470–1, 476–7, 483–4, 494, 495–6, 497–9, 501–2, 505–8, 510–13, 515–16, 521, 534–5, 541–2, 544, 549*
Kant, 139–40, 489
Kauffer, E. McKnight, 111–12, 114; *115*
Keats, 228–9, 231–2

Keezer, Dexter, 311(n), 317
Kenner, Hugh, 388, 487(n), 492; *493, 552–3, 556, 562, 564–5*
Kennington, Eric, *323–6, 350–2*
KERMESSE, 79–80
"Khan and Company," 44
Kierkegaard, 357
Kirk, Russell, *563*
Kisling, 112
Kivell, Rex Nan, 504
Koestler, Arthur, 378
Konody, P. G., 51, 102; *52*
Kruik, P. Van der, *249–50, 262*

Lamb, Henry, 45, 60, 72
Lamb, W. R. M., 257
Lambert, Constant, 244
Lamont, Mrs. T. W., *307–8, 317–319*
Lane, Sir Hugh, 64
Lane, John, 74, 492
Laughlin, James (New Directions), 397; *532*
Lawrence, A. K., 532–4
Lawrence, D. H., 123, 153, 187, 189, 202, 203, 208, 343
Lawrence, T. E., 561
Lechmere, Kate, 42, 59; *69*
Left Wings over Europe, 237, 240(n)
Leicester Galleries, 112(n), 124(n), 213(n), 238–9, 242–3, 251, 258(n), 407, 420, 485
Lenbach, F. von, 28
Lenin, 442
Leonardo, 116–17, 228
Le Pan, Douglas, 304
Leslie, Sir Shane, *197–8*
Lewis, Anne Stuart (mother), 1–3, 119; *4–39, 78, 81–3, 85–6, 88–9*
Lewis, C. E. (father), 1–2, 5, 6, 9, 25, 33, 38, 366–7, 463
Lewis, D. B. Wyndham, 158(n)
Lewis, Mrs. Wyndham, 122, 202, 217, 269, 273(n), 376, 388
Liber, Mrs. Amor (Rebecca Citkovitch), 300(n), 463; *558*

Linati, Carlo, 221, 376
Lion and the Fox, The, 121, 165(n), 170(n), 174(n), 185, 353, 490
Listener, The, 340, 387, 400(n), 421, 451, 457, 460, 514, 523, 524, 527, 528, 537–8; *447–8, 450, 452–3, 529, 531, 532–4*
Little Review, The, 42, 66, 82, 87, 90, 93, 96, 129
Lloyd George, 81, 244, 333
Lockwood, Thomas B., 267
London Group, 42, 57, 59, 115
London, L.'s residence in, 40–262, 387–567
Longworth, Alice, 291
Louvain, University of, 370, 428
Low, David, *459*
Loy, Mina, 128
Luce, Clare Boothe, 355
Ludovici, Anthony M., 54–6

MacBryde, Robert, 412–13, 485
MacCarthy, Desmond, 522
MacDermot, T. W. L., *268–9, 277–8*
Macdonald, Dwight, 409; *Politics* (ed.), 379, 402, 409; *379, 402–403*
MacDonald, Malcolm, *356, 358–360*
Machiavelli, 353, 490
MacLeish, Archibald, 312(n), 354; *301–2, 477–8*
MacNeice, Louis, 235–6, 316, 345, 478; *331*
Madrid, L. studies in, 2, 6–7
Malraux, André, 449, 454
Manchester Guardian, 200
Manners, Lady Diana (Cooper), 96, 132(n)
"Man of the World, The," 136–139, 146, 147(n), 155(n), 160(n)
Mantegna, 513–14
Marchant, William, 110, 119
Marinetti, F. T., 42, 53–4, 60, 61–3, 159, 310, 368
Maritain, Jacques, 357, 370, 428

Marsden, Dora, 77
Marshall, George C., 476
Marx, 226–9, 231–2, 439, 462
Masefield, John, 44
Maskelyne and Devant, 352
Masterman, C. F. G., 80, 84
Matisse, 112, 117–19, 514(n)
McAlmon, Robert, 159, 171(n), 462; *127–9, 132–3, 155–7, 160–1, 165–6*
McDiarmid, Hugh, 408
McEvoy, Ambrose, 36, 96
McEvoy, Charles, 65
McLuhan, H. Marshall, 360–1, 376, 492, 500; *366–7, 369–70, 372–3, 554–5*
Men Without Art, 121, 134(n), 220, 222–32, 304
Meredith, George, 366, 410, 429
Methuen and Company, 166(n), 388, 492, 523(n), 528
Michelangelo, 407, 531
Miller, Henry, 425
Milton, 230, 436–7, 536
Minton, John, 485
Mitchison, G. R., 346, 391
Mitchison, Naomi, 122, 307, 313; *201–2, 203–4, 211, 213–14, 216, 232, 258, 298–9, 327–30, 344–7, 353–5, 361–3, 391–2, 407–8, 536–7*
Modigliani, 112
Molière, 295
Mondrian, 406
Monro, Harold, 153
Montaigne, 98, 433
Monthly Criterion, The, 171–3
Moore, A. V., 413–14
Moore, Henry, 298, 413, 529, 531(n), 532; *342–4*
Moore, T. Sturge, 2, 16–17, 35, 41, 68, 170(n), 340(n); *39–40, 75–6, 87–8, 98–9, 100, 291–3*; letter from, *99–100*
Morgan, Hon. Evan, 82
Morgan, Frederick, *561*
Morley, Frank, 213; *299–301*

Mortimer, Raymond, 460–1
Mosley, Oswald, 319
MUD CLINIC, THE, 504–5
Muggeridge, Malcolm, 236
Munich, L.'s visit to, 2, 24–9
Munnings, Sir Alfred, 420
Murphy, Rev. J. Stanley, 372; *348–50, 352–3*
Murray, John Grey, *229*
Murry, John Middleton, 202, 215, 225–9, 231–2; *170–1*
Mussolini, 199, 316, 332(n), 394, 553
Mysterious Mr. Bull, The, 478

Nansen, F., 5, 28(n)
Napoleon, 275, 305, 316, 332–3(n), 394
Nash, Gene, *482–3*
Nash, Paul, 159; *106–8, 109, 113–114*; letter from, *108–9*
Nation and Athenaeum, The, 79, 136, 194
National Gallery, 261(n), 419, 545
"Nature's Place in Canadian Culture," 359–60
Nevins, Allan, 499
Nevinson, C. R. W., 57, 59, 61–3, 73, 89, 102–3, 159
New Age, The, 62(n), 63(n), 64, 207–8, 459(n); *54–9*
New Britain, *214–15*
New Criterion, The, 138(n)
New English Art Club, 13, 21, 58(n)
New Republic, The, 309, 381; *271–2*
New Signatures, 214
New Statesman and Nation, The, 190, 194, 465; *229–31*
New Verse, 216, 235(n)
New Weekly, 61(n)
New Writing, 402
New York Herald Tribune, 178
Nicholson, Sir William, 257
Nicolson, Sir Harold, 528
Nietzsche, 37, 54–5, 262, 299, 332(n)

Nine, 404(n)
North Africa, L's. visit to, 202–4
"Note on Michael Ayrton, A," 404

Observer, The, 528; *62–3, 235–6*
Old Gang and the New Gang, The, 209
Omega Workshops, 42, 46–53, 106
One-Way Song, 210, 213–16, 221, 456–7, 564
Orage, A. R., 63(n), 207
Orpen, Sir William, 96

Paige, D. D., 414; *The Letters of Ezra Pound* (ed.), 66(n), 84(n), 129(n), 461; *461–2, 466–9, 471–2, 473–4, 478–9*
Paleface, 121, 187, 202(n), 223
Palmer, Herbert, 214
Palmer, J. E., *486–8, 516–17*
Paris, L.'s residence in, 2–3, 8–40
"Paris Versus the World," 120(n)
Partisan Review, 402–3, 409, 432–3, 463–4, 558; *491–2*
Paul, St., 370
Pegler, Westbrook, 463, 476
"Perspectives on Lawrence," 561
Peto, Ruby, 132
Philippe, Charles-Louis, 60
Phillips, William, 433
Photographer, a London, *502–3*
Picasso, 60, 87, 112, 118(n), 119, 123, 260, 268, 271, 303, 424(n), 460
Pierce, Lorne, *288–91, 293–4, 304–5*
Pinker, J. B., *43–4*
"Pish-Tush," 558(n)
PLANNERS, 504
PLAN OF WAR, 422
Plato, 362, 489, 494, 533, 547(n)
PLAYERS ON THE STAGE, 407
Poe, 187
"Pole, The," 39(n)
Poor, Henry Varnum, 366
Porter, Margery, 450, 453

Porteus, Hugh Gordon, 236, 376(n); *215, 222*
Portraits: S. P. Capen, 266–8
  Marchioness of Cholmondeley, 210(n)
  Nancy Cunard in Venice, 132
  M. C. D'Arcy, S.J., 173(n)
  T. S. Eliot, (I) 121, 134, 265, 495(n) (*see also* Eliot, rejected portrait); (II) 134, 387, 482, 495–6, 535(n)
  An Englishwoman, 504
  Dr. Joseph Erlanger, 378(n), 496
  Mrs. T. J. Honeyman, 265
  James Joyce, 211
  John McLeod, 250(n), 389, 504
  Avrion Mitchison, 392
  Flight-Commander Orlebar, 210
  Ezra Pound, 121, 390, 438
  Viscountess Rhondda, 211
  Edith Sitwell, 121, 390, 503
  Stephen Spender, 539(n)
  Harriet Shaw Weaver, 211(n)
Post-Impressionist Exhibition (Rutter's), 48–9, 53, 79(n)
Pound, Ezra, 41–2, 59, 62, 65, 81–2, 87(n), 88, 99, 103–4, 111, 121–4, 129–31, 134, 136, 156(n), 161, 171(n), 181, 199, 215, 224, 270, 275, 342, 388, 393–4, 413–17, 421(n), 429, 433, 438, 461–2, 464, 466–9, 471–4, 476, 477, 491–2, 496, 500, 509(n), 515, 539, 551–4, 567; L.'s "Ezra: The Portrait of a Personality," 517–18; *66–8, 79–80, 83–4, 85, 90, 92–5, 96–8, 158–60, 394–5, 397–8, 403–4, 424–5, 436–7, 440–1, 453–4, 517–18, 548, 558–9, 564, 565*
Pound, Mrs. Ezra, 67–8, 473–4; *413–14, 416–17, 420, 437–8, 544–5*
Pound, Omar, 544–5
Poynter, Sir Edward, 66
PRAXITELLA, 126

Praz, Mario, 376
Prentice, C. H., 122, 528; *167, 169, 174–8, 185, 187–8, 195–6, 198, 203*
Priestley, J. B., 532
Pritt, D. N., 550
Proust, 259, 336
Pryce-Jones, Alan, *430–1*

Quarterly Review of Literature (Pound number), 414, 517–18
Quinn, John, 42, 66, 68, 73, 79–81, 83, 85, 194–5; *86–7, 103–4, 109–13, 119–20*

Racine, 533
Rahv, Philip, 433–4
Ransom, John Crowe (*Kenyon Review*), *303–4*
Raphael, 407
Read, Sir Herbert, 272, 412, 447, 450; *101–3, 131–2, 171–3, 227–8, 428–9, 527–8*
Rebel Art Centre, 42, 49(n), 59–63
Redfern exhibition, 404, 482, 493, 495–6, 504
Red Priest, The, 564
Regnery, Henry, 558(n); *549–50*
Reinhardt, Ad, 271
Renouvier, 489
Revenge for Love, The, 121, 220(n), 233, 237, 242, 247, 273, 463, 509(n), 552, 553(n)
Reynolds, Victor, 18
Rhondda, Lady, 211(n)
Rhys, Keidrych, *459–60*
Richards, Ceri, 459–60
Richards, I. A.: 220(n), 228, 231, 565; *535–6, 546–7*
Richardson, E. P., 367–8, 469–70
Ricketts, Charles, 44
Rivers, W. H. R., 149(n)
Roaring Queen, The, 237, 240–1
Robert, Hubert, 245
Roberts, Denys Kilham, *221–2*
Roberts, Lynette, 459(n), 502
Roberts, R. Ellis, 190(n), 192(n), 194(n), 213–14

Roberts, William, 62, 73, 85, 96–7, 111, 115, 565–7
Robinson, Lennox, 194–5
Robsjohn-Gibbings, T. H., 422
Rochefoucauld, 216
Rodin, 343
Rodker, John, 111, 129, 132; *105–106, 124–6*
Roosevelt, Franklin D., 272, 288, 290, 292, 321(n), 328–9, 331, 333, 334(n), 346, 349, 476, 553, 565
Rose, Arthur, 55–6
Rose, W. K., *509*
Rossetti, D. G., 86
"Rot, The," 432, 459(n), 482, 487–8, 492
Rothenstein, Sir John, 47(n), 57(n), 61(n), 106(n), 270, 566–7; *339–41, 363–4, 496*
Rothenstein, Lady, *269–70*
Rothenstein, Sir William, 2, 14, 36(n), 243, 260–1; *258–9*
Rotting Hill, 421(n), 432(n), 465(n), 509(n), 527(n), 549(n), 558(n)
Rouault, 337, 341–2, 405
"Round Robin," *47–50*
"Round the London Art Galleries," 514(n), 527
Rowlandson, Thomas, 111, 364, 481
Rowse, A. L., 402
Royal Academy (Burlington House), 57(n), 66(n), 116, 123, 250–8, 274(n), 302, 324, 400, 420, 524, 532–4
Rubens, 359(n)
Rude Assignment, 45(n), 47(n), 130(n), 250(n), 370(n), 403, 410(n), 411(n), 432(n), 437, 455(n), 459, 463, 528, 530
Rudge, Olga, 472
Rugby School, 5–6, 20, 488–9
Russell, Diarmuid, 284
Russell, Jane, 545
Russell, Peter, 65(n), 510, 517(n)
Rutherston, Albert, 89

Rutherston, Charles, 243
Rutter, Frank, 48–9, 51, 53, 101–103

Salter, L. J., 271
Saroyan, William, 281, 285
Sartre, Jean-Paul, 411, 416, 484, 489, 516
Satire & Fiction, 171(n), 180(n), 189–95, 213, 335
Saturday Night, 317, 338(n)
Saturday Review of Literature, 515
Saunders, Helen, 73, 90, 97; *91, 522–3*
Schepeler, Alick, 61, 68–9, 89–90, *91–2*
Schiff, Sydney (Stephen Hudson), 126(n), 153; *212–13*
Schnabel, Arthur, 437–8
Schnitzler, 188
Schopenhauer, 368
Scott-James, R.A., *259–61*
"Sea-Mists of Winter, The," 537–8
Self Condemned, 263, 278(n), 372(n), 387, 410, 545, 560
Seneca, 170(n), 353, 370
Seurat, 447–8, 452–3
Sewanee Review, 381–2, 432(n), 433, 486, 516
Sewter, A. C., 447–8, 452–3, 457
Sexton Blake Library, 232
Shakespear, Olivia, 42, 67(n), 181, 182(n)
Shakespeare, William, 170(n), 185, 228, 231–2, 353, 490, 494
Sharp, Clifford, 190(n), 191
Shaw, G. B., 44, 532
Sheen, Rev. Fulton, 371
Shenandoah (Lewis number), 360(n)
Sickert, Walter, 57–9, 204, 243, 253
Simpson, Dallam, 436(n), 544
Sinclair, May, 139
Sitwell, Dame Edith, 133, 156(n), 194, 225(n), 229–31, 235(n), 402(n), 475

577

Sitwell, Sir Osbert, 45(n), 103, 229–31; *133–4*
Sitwells, the, 111–12, 123, 133
Sketch, The, 129
Slade School of Art, 2, 321, 407, 455(n), 531
Slater, Montague, 191
Slocum, John, *279–80*
Smith, G. Elliot, 147, 149(n)
Smith, Sir Matthew, 482
Snooty Baronet, 204–6, 219, 220(n), 273
Soby, James Thrall, 500; *406–7, 412–13, 421–2, 485–6*
Somerset, Lord Henry, 18
Sorel, Georges, 332(n)
Soutine, 260
Spectator, The, 194; *222–5*
Spencer, Sir Stanley, 253(n), 254(n)
Spencer, Theodore, 535; *320–3, 347–8*
Spender, Stephen, 214, 222–5, 235(n), 464; *539*
Spooner, W. A., 548
Stalin, 307, 313, 334(n), 378, 411(n)
STATIONS OF THE DEAD, 407
Steer, Wilson, 2, 254
Stein, Gertrude, 123, 156(n), 165, 171(n), 177, 223
Steinbeck, John, 295, 356, 426
Stendahl, 305, 316, 332(n), 435, 552
Stone, Geoffrey, *270, 275, 278–9, 281–3, 285, 297–8, 311, 427–8, 445–6, 451–2, 457–8, 474–5*
Stonier, G. W., 229, 236, 246
Strachey, Lytton, 185
Streatfield, R. A., 2, 17
Strindberg, Mme, 42, 45–6, 339(n)
Stuart, Mrs. (grandmother), 1; *3–4*
Stulik, 85
SURRENDER OF BARCELONA, THE, 121, 242, 407, 438, 503
Survage, 112
Swabey, Rev. Henry, *509–10*

Sweeney, James Johnson, 470, 519; *276–7, 337, 341–2, 379–80*
Swift, 181(n), 182–3, 216, 536
Swope, Gerald, 380, 382
Sykes, Gerald, 269
Sylvester, A. D. B., 402
Symons, A. J. A., 122, 183, 197(n), 198, 246, 261; *185, 187, 188, 192–3, 204, 211–12, 218*; facsimile letter, *184*
Symons, Arthur, 58
Symons, Julian, 183(n); *479, 538–9*; see also *Twentieth Century Verse*

Taft, Robert, 445, 457
Tarr, 2, 41–3, 45, 65, 74–6, 87, 95, 98–100, 120, 178, 180, 188, 226, 262, 273, 410, 415, 489, 528, 552–3
Tate, Allen, *381–2, 384–5, 393, 395–7, 410–11*
Tate Gallery, 133(n), 242(n), 243, 339, 387, 407(n), 438, 447, 496, 565–7
Tax Inspector, *186–7*
Tertullian, 487
Thackeray, 234, 552
Thirty Personalities, 209–11
This Quarter, 158, 160–1, 165, 171(n)
Thomas, Dylan, 338, 401, 417, 502
Thomas Aquinas, St., 370, 487
Thompson, Cynthia, *537–8*
Thompson, Dorothy, 289–90
Thorpe, W. A., 173
Tiger's Eye, The, 464–5
Time, 495
Time and Tide, 203(n), 204, 211(n), 213, 462, 465; *199–201, 207–9*
Time and Western Man, 121, 127, 130, 137(n), 139–40, 155, 159(n), 165(n), 169–74, 181, 261, 429, 488–90
Times, The, 194, 226, 551; *253–7*

Times Literary Supplement, The, 99, 227–9, 430–1, 460–1, 465–6, 566; *225–7, 231–2, 415*
Timon of Athens folio, 68, 90
"Tip from the Augean Stable, A," 207(n)
Tito, Marshal, 451
Todd, Ruthven, *560–1*
Tolstoy, 208, 356, 365, 371, 455, 552
Tomkins (servant in L.'s youth), 1, 10, 15, 21–2, 25, 30
Tonks, Henry, 2, 96
Toronto Star, 310, 362, 426
"Towards an Earth Culture or the Electric Culture of the Transition," 407(n)
Transatlantic Review, The, 137
transition, 123, 202(n)
Trollope, 449
Truman, Harry S., 440, 445, 452, 475–6, 553
Turnbull, John, 111, 115
"Twentieth Century Palette," 564–5
Twentieth Century Verse, 245–8
Tyro, The, 121, 126, 131–2, 134, 137, 212(n), 275; No. 1, 105(n), 124–7; No. 2, 124(n), 126, 129(n), 131–2
"Tyros and Portraits" exhibition, 112(n), 124

United States, L.'s visits to, 169, 263–4, 268–77, 377–80

Vanner, Miss, *538*
Vasari, 413
Vaughan, Keith, 413, 485
Verlaine, 65, 68, 70, 420
Vermeer, 400
Vico, 489, 493
Vlaminck, 112, 117
Voigt, Frederick A., 199–201
Volkening, Henry T., *284*
Vorticism, 42, 49(n), 59–63, 65, 67, 73, 85, 114, 491–2, 565–7

Vulgar Streak, The, 264, 276, 279–80, 284, 286–8, 295–7, 303, 305–7, 310, 315–16, 322–3, 332–4, 369, 410(n)

Wadsworth, Edward, 47–50, 57, 59, 62, 67, 73, 84, 85, 93, 105, 111, 126(n), 141–3, 159, 355
Wadsworth, Mrs. Edward, 141–3, 561; *142*
Wagner, Geoffrey, 171(n), 561
Wagner, Richard, 262
Walden, Herwarth, 128
Wales, 459(n), 482
Waley, Arthur, 404
Wallace, Henry, 331, 333, 409, 463
Walpole, Sir Hugh, 188–9
"War Baby, The," 101–2
Washington, George, 349, 356, 373
Waterhouse, Sir Nicholas, 122, 187(n), 216, 388; *217, 218–19, 237–8, 312–14, 326–7, 336, 389–90, 517, 524–5, 547–8, 560*
Waterhouse, Lady, 187(n), 216–217, 312, 314, 326–7, 336, 389–90; *314–17, 389*
Weaver, Harriet Shaw, 42, 130(n), 404; *76–7, 95, 126–7*
Webb, Beatrice and Sydney, 392
Webb, Mrs. K. H., *410*
Week-End, The, 213–14
Weiss, Theodore, 414; *488–90*
Wells, H. G., 126, 223(n), 307; *180–1, 332–4*
West, Rebecca, 180(n)
WHAT THE SEA LOOKS LIKE AT NIGHT, 504–5
Whibley, Charles, *154–5*
Whistler, 17, 19–20, 108
White, J. Alan, 166(n), 388; *528, 559–60*
Whitman, Walt, 358, 458
Wilcox, Mrs., The Worlds and I, 116–17

Wild Body, The, 96(n), 112, 174(n)
Wilde, Oscar, 58, 204, 335, 420
Wilder, Thornton, 208
Wilenski, R. H., 95, 116–17
Williams, Dennis, 500–1, 527–8
Williams, William Carlos, 414, 436–7
Wilson, Edmund, 291, 402–3; *309*
Wilson, Woodrow, 349, 396
Windsor, Duke of, 400
Wolfe, Humbert, 261
Wolfit, Donald, 540–1, 546
Woodcock, George, 403
Woolf, Virginia, 47(n), 208, 223–5, 300(n), 412

Writer and the Absolute, The, 411(n), 437, 548
Wyndham Lewis: The Artist, 121, 132(n), 250(n)
"Wyndham Lewis and Vorticism" (catalogue), 407(n), 566; (exhibition), 250(n), 387, 565–7
Wyndham, Richard, 122, 132(n), 141; *142–5, 146–7*

X Group, 42, 111–12, 114–15

Yale, 303, 492
Yalta, 445
Yeats, W. B., 67, 75, 193–5, 477; *181–3*
Yellow Book, The, 58–9

For Product Safety Concerns and Information please contact our EU representative GPSR@taylorandfrancis.com
Taylor & Francis Verlag GmbH, Kaufingerstraße 24, 80331 München, Germany